Conflict & Bargaining in the Middle East

Also by the Author

The Beginning of the Gestapo System
  (Jerusalem, 1969)

Reinhard Heydrich und die Frühgeschichte von Gestapo und SD
  (Stuttgart, 1972)

CONFLICT & BARGAINING IN THE MIDDLE EAST
An Israeli Perspective

Shlomo Aronson

The Johns Hopkins University Press
Baltimore and London

Manufactured in the United States of America

The Johns Hopkins University Press, Baltimore, Maryland 21218
The Johns Hopkins Press Ltd., London

Library of Congress Catalog Card Number 77–10967
ISBN 0-8018-2046-4

Library of Congress Cataloging in Publication data will be found on the last printed page of this book.

Contents

Preface

The aim of this book is threefold: (1) to give a historical analysis of Israel's domestic structures, elite behavior, and public opinion role, with regard to foreign and defense policies since 1960; (2) to offer a description and an analysis of Israeli foreign policy and defense decisions within the context of Israeli perceptions of developments in the Arab world, Israeli-American relations, and the role of the Soviet Union in the Middle East; and (3) to suggest a more comprehensive analysis of current events in the Middle East, based on my own research into American, Arab, and Soviet behavior in the area. In light of this analysis, other theoretical, yet empirical, generalizations may be drawn concerning (a) different types of modern nationalism; (b) elite and mass behavior in complex conflicts; (c) strategies of conflict and bargaining in complex conflicts; (d) linkages between domestic situations and foreign policy decisions; (e) characteristics of leaderships in new-old nations like Israel; (f) the role of superpowers, mainly the United States, in complex regional conflicts; (g) the role of intermediaries in complex conflicts; and (h) the role of conventional weapon systems and a "nuclear option" in a particular conflict area. The same analysis may also provide the reader with background information for the future of Israeli-Arab relations.

The periodization of this book is based upon Israel's domestic and foreign policy developments, related to the ups and downs of the Middle East conflict itself. In order to understand current issues and to offer some kind of forecasting, I chose a crucial moment of change in Israeli domestic politics that was the beginning of a gradual departure from its traditional behavior in the conflict: the decline of Ben-Gurion's regime in 1960. I went back to 1948 and even ventured to the 1930s to explain Israeli elite behavior until that moment of change. But I have refrained from repeating the story of Zionism and the creation of Israel and have not gone into the details of the relatively well known events in the Middle East leading up to the 1967 Six-Day War. Rather, I have tried to give the informed reader a new perspective and a better analytical approach to known facts, and I introduce a growing degree of new evidence into the chapters relating to the post-1967 period.

As an Israeli political scientist, having no access to Arab—let alone Soviet—primary sources, I have refrained from offering an in-depth analysis of Arab, and Soviet, behavior, but concentrated upon their actions. I have suggested some explanations for them, emphasizing Israeli and American perception of the goals, motives, and methods of Arab and Soviet actors in the Middle East conflict. Where Israeli and U.S. foreign and defense policies are concerned, my analysis is based upon recently published and unpublished primary and secondary sources and intensive interviewing in Israel and the United States, and an assessment of the modus operandi of the participants. Most of the published material of Israeli origin used here is drawn directly from Hebrew publications, in order to avoid the abridged and sometimes distorting accounts often produced by translations.

For obvious legal and security reasons, and due to the positions of many interviewees (most of whom are still active in public life or are members of the public services in their respective countries), I am prevented from naming several of my sources of information. Therefore, some sources are quoted in general: "foreign ministry sources," for example, relates to the Israeli Ministry of Foreign Affairs; the same applies to "GHQ sources" or "intelligence sources." Highly complex issues, like Israel's nuclear option, are mostly described on the basis of Israeli and foreign interviews and press reports. In a case where I was unable to reach a verdict on differing or contradictory versions of an event or decision, these versions are cited jointly, allowing the reader to judge for himself. Events I have witnessed personally as Israeli state radio correspondent in West Germany, war correspondent in the Six-Day War and the Yom Kippur War, head of news and current affairs for Israeli television, and as a special information envoy for the government of Israel in Washington and at the Geneva Peace Conference after the 1973 war are also described as viewed through my own personal prism.

A large number of colleagues read my early papers and manuscripts and helped to balance my judgment and to correct historical and methodological errors. I cannot mention them all here, but I am especially indebted to Dr. Dan Horowitz of the Hebrew University in Jerusalem; Dr. David Schoenbaum of the U.S. Naval War College in Newport, Rhode Island, and the University of Iowa; Dr. Robert W. Tucker of The Johns Hopkins University in Baltimore, Maryland, and the School of Advanced International Studies at Washington, D.C.; and Dr. Barry Blechman and Mr. Robert Weinland of the Brookings Institution in Washington, D.C. The mistakes and dubious parts of the book that remain are solely mine.

I am also indebted to the Hebrew University for having financed a part of my research and to the Brookings Institution, which allowed me, as a guest scholar, to make use of its facilities and intellectual atmosphere during the last stage of my research and writing. Mr. Henry Tom, social sciences editor of The Johns Hopkins University Press, was firm and kind at the same time.

Mr. Yitzhak Bernstein of Jerusalem and Ms. Angela Smith of Washington worked very hard, as did Ms. Wendy Harris of The Johns Hopkins University Press, to make my English readable. Last but not least, my wife, Dalia, made this five years' work possible through personal sacrifice and wise advice. I thank them all very much.

July, 1977

Introduction

The Arab-Israeli conflict can be considered in several ever-narrowing dimensions. First, there is the national-ideological dimension, which relates to the clash between different types of old-new nationalism. The unique character of the conflict probably has most to do with this dimension; the substantive dimensions are sometimes reflections of it, being treated by one party as the most pressing problem, while the other party might treat them as symbolic behavior indicative either of an ideology that rejects its legitimacy or an ideology of expansion that threatens its tradition and legitimate rights. Zionism, or Jewish Nationalism, was largely instrumental, empirical, and entrepreneurlike. Jewish aggressive pragmatism and bargaining habits, combined with the deep-rooted ideological longing for Zion (the wish to create a new-old, sovereign, protected Jewish entity in Eretz-Israel) clashed head-on with emerging Arab nationalism. Arab nationalism seems to me, as a nonexpert, to be a mixture of traditional tribalism, state-nationalism, and a holistic supranationalism, more Gestalt-like and less entrepreneurlike. The very different characters of these two national movements have contributed to the psychological gap that prevented any measure of official compromise in the past between the parties.

Second, there is always the substantive dimension of the conflict, which cannot always be divorced from the ideological-nationalistic dimension. The political dimension, or the issue of Israel's legitimacy and of the Palestinians, which was treated until 1967 mainly as a refugee problem, is such a dimension. The substantive border issue, however, can sometimes be divorced from an ideology, especially with regard to former Palestinian territories, but not with regard to sovereign Arab lands captured by Israel from Arab states.

Third, different political systems, various elite behaviors, and domestic structures are involved in the conflict, giving it the character of a group conflict or coalition conflict. A relatively large number of partners are influencing each other, bargaining or competing with one another in the context of personal, group, and national interests within and outside the conflict.

Fourth, the Arab-Israeli conflict has an extraregional dimension of great importance: the role of third parties in the conflict, and the role of the principal parties in mobilizing, influencing, and playing these third parties against each other and against the adversary.

Fifth, many methods of conflict resolution, conflict reduction, or conflict control have been tried—sometimes half-heartedly, but since 1969, more seriously. Comprehensive or "substantive" solutions, "step-by-step" strategies, and a combination of the two have been implemented in the past in an effort to resolve the conflict or at least to reduce it to a low level. This fifty years' war is a relatively controlled war, with short outbursts of large-scale violence. Long periods of some mediation, relative low-level violence, and high-level bargaining took place in the area, and should be examined for the future.

In the following chapters I shall try to decode and interpret many Israeli patterns of behavior, psychological codes, and political signals, in order to explain what is, in foreign eyes, sometimes extremely aggressive and obstinate behavior. At the same time, I shall try to explain the positive role of Israeli nationalism, self-image, and self-respect, together with Israeli instrumental pragmatism and bargaining habits, domestic structures, group behavior, and personal approaches to the conflict in a quest for domestic power.

My book begins with the most influential, and least typical, Israeli statesman during the period between 1948 and 1960—David Ben-Gurion. I shall deal chronologically with all five dimensions of the conflict mentioned above, with more or less detail, depending on the vast amount of already existing literature. In the end, I shall try to venture into the future, suggesting several possibilities for developments in the Middle East conflict.

Conflict & Bargaining in the Middle East

1

David Ben-Gurion: Israel's Democratic Bismarck and His Heirs, 1949-67

THE CONFLICT

Lying at the heart of the Arab-Israeli conflict, and woven into the fabric of the domestic sociopolitical systems of the peoples involved and into that of the overarching international system, we find one of the basic concepts of the modern nationalist ethos: the concept of national sovereignty. People wish to participate in the historic process of liberation from a foreign yoke and to maintain an independent national existence. In the case of the Zionist ethos, national sovereignty involved a number of components other than the strictly political ones. Pursuing a national revolution, Zionism aspired to a political, psychological, cultural, and social revolution.[1] The Zionists wished to create a new Jewish man, to revive the historic figure of the sovereign Jew who would return to take possession of and to work his own land. National sovereignty was thus tightly bound up with the return to a specific territory that was declared to be the natural and historic right of the Jewish people; that is, Zionism regarded itself as historically legitimate, with Palestine as its legitimate territory. The Zionists saw their movement as their people's revolutionary liberation movement, of which they were the vanguard marking the historically correct path for Jews to follow. Zionism would restore to the Jewish people its land, long held by "foreigners" who had neglected and laid waste to it. To the historic right to the land would be added the justification derived from "making the desert bloom," while transforming Diaspora Jews into working people and fighting people, if necessary. The extermination of European Jewry would provide further proof, if any were needed, of the urgency of a refuge. To sum up, then, Zionism was perceived as a radical solution to the problems of national Jewish existence, of the crisis of values undergone by the Diaspora society (a rejection of the traditional Jewish way of life, economic, social, and mental), and of the people's physical security. Its three political and strategic compounds would thus be sovereignty, which was achieved in 1948–49,

1

legitimacy in the eyes of the outside world, which was partially achieved, and security, which was regarded as partially given.

From its inception, the Zionist movement tried to realize its aims in Palestine by working in two dimensions. It worked within the political and strategic framework of the external forces that controlled or influenced developments in the region: the Ottoman and British empires, the United States, the Soviet Union, and France. Internally, the Zionist elite tried to settle parts of the country, develop unique solutions to social problems, create instruments of political and social power that would enable them to absorb a large number of Jewish immigrants and take over an autonomous, and later independent, Jewish entity in Palestine. In the late 1920s, the Zionist leadership came to see the Palestinian Arabs and the Arab states as hostile to their aims. However, it was thought that some compromise might be reached with the support of external powers. So, until the establishment of the state, a great deal of effort was concentrated on recruiting support from extraregional parties (as the Arabs were doing) and on fending off any attempts to stop Jewish settlement in Palestine and thus foil the Zionists' economic and political plans. When the moment of truth came and the fate of Palestine would be decided by the mighty Jewish presence in the country, Jewish domestic achievements, sympathy for the plight of Jews abroad, and the hard-won Jewish power in Palestine would influence the decision to grant the Jews their state and would help to determine its borders.

The establishment of the Jewish state on May 15, 1948, in a part of Palestine was a major victory for Zionist policy. Independence had been attained upon the withdrawal of the hostile British and with Soviet and American support for the United Nations General Assembly partition plan in November, 1947.[2] To the Israeli leadership the dangers in the war waged by the Palestinian Arabs, their supporters in the Arab states, and Jordan (which had its own expansionist designs) lay in Western support of the Arabs. As it turned out, this support could be undermined. The United States favored partition.[3] Furthermore, Soviet-authorized military aid arrived at a crucial point in the 1948 war against the invading Arab armies and played a vital role in driving them back. Given the central role Zionist analysis assigned to the extraregional powers in the Middle East, it was logical for them to expect the positive attitude of the superpowers toward Jewish sovereignty in Israel to lead to a change in the Arab attitude. The General Armistice Agreements (GAA) signed in 1949 would, it was thought, quickly give way to peace treaties.[4]

Even with such a formal peace, however, the war was seen to have left a permanent scar on relations between the two peoples of Palestine. Since it was deemed impossible for these two peoples, demanding the same rights in the same land, to live together, the departure of most of the Arabs from Israeli territory was considered to be a reasonable solution to the problem. The Israelis felt that they had conceded much by agreeing to partition. The Arabs had been allotted extensive areas of the country previously designated for a Palestinian state, which they flatly rejected. The proposed border between the two states was twisting and complicated, and Jerusalem was internationalized. By going to war, however, the Arabs were seen to have violated the conditions of this eminently fair compromise and thus to have released the Israelis from their commitment to the plan. Israel felt that it could, therefore, legitimately change the partition boundaries, annex as much of Jerusalem as it held, and refuse to allow the repatriation of Palestinian Arab refugees.[5]

The Arab-Israeli conflict thus assumed a triangular form from an Arab point of view, with a problem at each angle. The first was the problem of sovereign Jewish existence in Palestine, and the second concerned the character of the Jewish territory there. The third problem involved the Arabs who had left and the commitments of the Arab states to them and to the future of the Arab world.

Arab positions and actual politics vis-à-vis Israel between 1949 and 1967 seem to me to be divided into the following manifestations:

1. On the inter-Arab level, a consensus was reached in the early 1950s that Israel could not be accepted ideologically and legally as an entity, as a neighbor, or as a partner for any official dealings that implied recognition or acceptance as a legitimate state, like the use of the Egypt Suez Canal or the "Arab waters" of the Tiran Straits.

2. Deviations from this consensus were publicly described in the Arab world as treachery. The only Arab political figure who tried, in the late 1940s, to negotiate peace with Israel—King Abdulla of Jordan—was assassinated after having recoiled from his bid for peace. However, some practical deviations from some specific rules were made.

3. All Arab states were engaged in varying degrees of activity against Israel's political and economic standing abroad, using social, economic, and political boycott measures based on their own relations with the third party involved.

4. On the level of separate Arab states, actual demands from Israel were raised mainly by Egypt, Iraq, Syria, and Saudi Arabia in their dealings with third parties and, through third parties, with Israel. The demands ranged from the return of the 1948 Arab refugees to Israel's return to the 1947 partition plan, and to the cession of the Negev—the land bridge between Egypt and the eastern part of the Arab world—or parts of it.

5. The refugee problem seems to have become the positive manifestation of both Arab claims on Palestine and of a concrete grievance and

injustice, as the Arabs perceived it, done to the Arab nation as a whole and to a specific Arab community in particular.

6. Yet, actual Arab behavior did not implement these ideological-political issues or transform them into an operational, all-Arab plan to destroy Israel. The refugees, on one hand, were settled in camps along Israel's borders and in this way demonstrated their own claim and misery and the all-Arab claim against Israel. On the other hand, Israel and Jordan partitioned Palestine, and de facto divided it between themselves; Israel's part was declared "occupied," and Jordan's share was also not officially recognized by the rest of the Arab world. No other Arab states had legitimate territorial claims to both parts of the former British mandatory territory. Jordan's presence in the West Bank of the Jordan River and Egypt's presence in the Gaza Strip were de facto recognized by the Arab coalition. Jordan's bid for integration of both banks and the populations of both territories, including Palestinian refugees, was a problem for changing inter-Arab coalitions and national regimes. De jure, however, spokesmen for the refugees, in cooperation with Egyptian or Syrian authorities, claimed the Israeli territory of Western Palestine with official support from the inter-Arab front, including Jordan, and/or demanded the right to return to their respective homes as individuals.

7. Several Arab states backed Palestinians and Palestinian organizations when they performed acts of violence against Israel: Egypt between 1955 and 1956 and Syria between 1965 and 1967. Both Arab states, however, refrained from allowing this activity to be pursued from their own territory and tried to achieve maximum control over Palestinian organizations, sometimes setting up organizations themselves. Arab states that took direct actions against Israel did so in a context of their claims against Israeli interpretations of the GAA, usually in connection with disputed territories along the Armistice Demarcation Line (ADL).

THE PEACE MYTH

Contrary to Israeli expectations, the 1949 armistice agreements were not replaced by peace treaties with any one of the Arab states. Despite what the Israelis saw as the clearly heterogeneous nature of the Arab world and the natural contradictions among the members of the Arab coalition, no major differences of opinion or attitude about the Jewish state emerged. The Hashemite Kingdom of Jordan, in particular, had been expected to enter into a peace agreement. It had annexed East Jerusalem and what remained of Arab Palestine on the West Bank of the Jordan

River and so had become Israel's partner in partition. Negotiations between the two states had reached an advanced stage, but finally Amman recoiled from an actual peace agreement.[6]

At the same time, conservative Arab leaders demanded from Britain and the United States that Israel make at least two concessions in exchange for some kind of coexistence: the cession of the Negev and the right of return for Palestinian refugees.[7] (They also mentioned a complete withdrawal to the 1947 partition line, above the Negev, which had been given to Israel in the partition plan.) The official rejection of Israel, as a matter of principle, was parallelly maintained. For the Israelis, all three demands combined to make an official denial of Israel's legitimacy. Territorial claims might reduce Israel's territory by two-thirds. The hostile Palestinian element, which had declared war on Zionism in the late twenties, then refused to accept partition and left because of Arab promises to return after Israel's destruction, could not return. Moreover, the refusal of Arab states to settle the Palestinian refugees in Jordan, Syria, Lebanon, and Egypt (where space, national fraternity, and a common heritage seemed to have been given) symbolized, in Israeli eyes, striking evidence of Arab hostility, denial of Israel's sovereignty, and threat to its security.

Meanwhile, a nationalist regime with great ambitions for Arab unity came to power in Egypt. The "Free Officers" seemed to have derived what was, to Israelis, Fascist ideology from the Arab defeat in 1948; unity and the liquidation of Israel were enshrined as their central national goals. To realize their aim, they would seek aid outside the region. Thus the Arabs had to be persuaded to reconcile themselves to Israel's existence and end the conflict. Such a peace became the expressed goal of Israeli foreign policy.[8] Without peace, Israel saw itself threatened with eventual destruction. Sometimes the danger seemed terribly imminent. Enough extraregional powers might be recruited against it or foreign aid might make the Arabs themselves strong enough to realize their ambitions to destroy the state. The conflict was thus taken as the datum-line for Israeli policy. The only way to end the conflict was through peace, which meant formal Arab recognition of Israel's rights; diplomatic, economic, and personal relations between Israel and its neighbors on the basis of the 1949 territorial status quo; and no repatriation of Palestinian Arab refugees of the 1948 war. Israel's legitimacy, sovereignty, and security within the 1949 borders had to be accepted by the Arabs. All three were included under the slogan "peace."

Many Israelis interpreted the absence of peace and the persistent, hostile acts of limited violence by the Arabs as a continuation of the war or as a potential war, liable to break out at any moment.[9] It seemed that this could be headed off by preventive actions or by a preventive war, but Israel's actual policy up to the 1967 war was much more subtle and adroit. Only once, in 1956, did the myth of peace and its absence bring about a full-scale war.

DAVID BEN-GURION AND ISRAEL'S FOREIGN AND DEFENSE POLICY TO 1956

The foreign and defense policy of David Ben-Gurion, founder and unchallenged leader of the Jewish state up to the early 1960s, was a complex response to a number of factors.[10] The first of these was the expressed ideological aspect of the Arabs' attitude to Israel. The second was the way the components of the Arab coalition actually behaved toward Israel. In the Israeli perception of this factor the conflict was taken as given. What Israelis feared initially was an Arab attempt, backed by their colonial mentors, the British, either to force the return of the Palestinian refugees or to force Israel to abandon its only vast, empty space—the Negev—or even to crush Israel militarily, using British weapons and military advisers while hiding behind British defense guarantees.[11] Later, they feared the unification of the Arab world under the banner of radical nationalism that posited the destruction of Israel as a function and a condition of Arab unity, led by the most powerful Arab nation, Egypt. Israeli perceptions of Arab political behavior were bound up with the following variables: foreign political assistance to or constraints imposed upon the Arabs in the conflict; foreign military aid, mainly arms supplies, that might tip the balance of power in the Arabs' favor; foreign economic aid in conjunction with the Arabs' own economic power and economic actions, such as the boycott against Israel; and Arab control of strategically important territories such as the Sinai, the West Bank of the Jordan, and Israel's southern maritime outlets, the Straits of Tiran, and the Suez Canal.

Another factor shaping Ben-Gurion's foreign and defense policy involved the practical politics of the Zionist-Israeli ethos in both the domestic and the foreign spheres. This factor had two facets of major importance: the wish to consolidate Israel as the working success story of Zionist ideology and the desire to create a Jewish man, qualitatively new in political, social, and cultural terms.

Yet another determinant was Israel's internal political structure. From its inception and at least partly as a result of the proportional representation system, the Israeli regime was founded on multi-party coalitions. The parties themselves were based upon closed lists that could not be changed by the voter. No formal constitution was ever adopted, but what emerged in practice was a parliament that was strong relative to the government; parties that were the only link between the voter and parliament but could never win a clear majority in the national elections; small parties that were strong relative to the large ones; and an eternal coalition administration. The cabinet would thus be made up of many ministers of roughly equal strength headed by a prime minister who was *primus inter pares*. To complete the picture one should note the lack of a tradition of independent polity or of conventional rules of behavior in many areas of political life, including foreign affairs and defense.

Israel's reaction to Arab attitudes and behavior may be outlined in the following form: it tried to obtain foreign political assistance and military and economic aid. It tried to develop weapon systems domestically, in order to lessen its dependence on the extraregional powers and to circumvent and overcome the Arab economic boycott. It took limited actions against Arabs in areas strategically vital to Israel's security and economy beyond the ADL,[12] in response to Arab provocations and in order to deter the Arab states from a general war. In 1956, Israel launched a preventive war against Egypt, hoping to bring about a change in Egyptian behavior and to control, if possible, certain spaces that were empty but strategically important in the context of the constant Israeli-Egyptian friction since 1954. It is no accident that I have mentioned empty territories of only strategic importance, not of historical and ideological importance. This latter aspect would become crucial for the governments after Ben-Gurion. He himself, however, had reached a compromise between the demands of Zionist ideology, which regarded all of Palestine as the historic homeland of the Jews and as the modern solution to their problems, and the movement's tactics and other goals in the mid-1930s, when he had accepted the Peel Commission partition plan.[13]

During the War of Independence, Ben-Gurion again proved willing to compromise on the territorial issue. His reasoning seems to have been along these lines: the main objective of Zionism was to establish Jewish sovereignty over territory in Palestine and bring it under Jewish military control, with the support and, if possible, aid of the extraregional powers. This territory would be settled by a growing Jewish majority composed mainly of the existing Jewish community and refugees and displaced persons in urgent need of the Zionist homeland. Later, other Jews would immigrate. At the same time, according to his experience and evaluation of emerging forces in the modern world, it was essential that there be as few Arabs as possible in the territory under Jewish control.[14]

Thus, before independence, the official Zionist line called for a coexistence of the two communities in Palestine and simultaneously demanded permission to create a Jewish majority in the country or Jewish sovereignty, through partition, over the areas where they already constituted a majority. After the 1948 war, Ben-Gurion's Israel refused to permit the repatriation of the refugees. Ben-Gurion argued that Israel was not responsible for their flight; they had been told to leave by the Arab governments to facilitate the suppression of Jewish sovereignty over a part of Palestine. Furthermore, the Palestinian Arabs' places were quickly taken by an equal number of Jewish refugees from the Arab countries. Returning the Arabs would mean Jewish rule over a very large, hostile minority, which would endanger the state's legitimacy as a Jewish country and create internal security problems of the first order.

Apart from West Jerusalem, the territory under sovereign Jewish control was not necessarily connected to any historic national borders.[15] Israel's boundaries were determined, instead, by the 1948 war, by external pressures, and by the desire not to rule Arabs. Ben-Gurion could have risked continuing the fight against Egypt in the Sinai to try to destroy the Egyptian army, which was almost surrounded and cut off from its bases across the Suez Canal. However, he yielded to British demands, seconded by the Americans, not to do so and was satisfied with the GAA.

Ben-Gurion also could have tried to capture large parts of the West Bank, but his cabinet stopped the Israel Defense Forces (IDF) from doing so. Most of the cabinet might have feared British, and American, pressures, which indeed were mounting at the time.[16] Ben-Gurion shared some of these fears, but he had another postulate—a matter of principle based on instincts, experience, and rational analysis—in mind: to refrain from ruling a large number of Arabs. Besides, the West Bank was controlled by a possible partner in a peace settlement—King Abdulla of Jordan, who had a powerful ally, Great Britain.

The prime minister did not tell the Israeli public all this in its exact meaning. The postulate of not ruling Arabs was not emphasized. Instead, he stressed that the borders were dictated by the military outcome of the War of Independence.[17] When it accepted partition, Israel gave up its historic rights to areas dear to the Judaeo-Zionist tradition. However, when the Arabs rejected partition and relieved the Jews of their commitment to the plan, Israel was kept from exercising its rights to improve the strategic situation caused by Arab aggression. Israel's right to expand its "historical" territory was restricted by pressures exerted by the extraregional powers, by Arab military strength, and by perceptions of Arab willingness to come to some agreement. Anglo-American pressure at the end of the war was enough to keep Ben-Gurion from expanding into the Sinai. Instead, he annexed the Eilat region, which Israel had not captured during the fighting but which was allotted to the Jewish state under the Partition Plan.

Brigadier General Yigal Allon, commander of the southern front in the War of Independence, leader of the kibbutz underground during the Mandate period, and member of the leftist nationalist Achdut Ha'Avoda party, disagreed.[18] He claimed that by deciding not to encircle or destroy the Egyptian army and to accept no more than an armistice, Ben-Gurion missed a historic opportunity to impose a peace settlement on Cairo. The pragmatic decision not to attempt to impose peace on hostile nations, but instead gradually to create a framework of cooperation through a general armistice, while allowing Israel to recover from a bloody war and to concentrate upon domestic rehabilitation and absorption of immigrants, was described by the nationalist left and right as a national catastrophy.[19]

The decision not to extend Israeli territory in the east was also attacked as leading to "generations of woe." This historic error was attributed to Israeli military weakness and naïveté in believing that peace could be achieved under the circumstances. Achdut Ha'Avoda and the nationalist right led by Menahem Begin, which had never accepted partition, accused Ben-Gurion of a "historic failure" for not capturing the West Bank and East Jerusalem. Ben-Gurion, who privately did not think Arab control of the West Bank an unmitigated disaster, publicly blamed both Israel's objective weakness, which had influenced the cabinet majority against his own wishes,[20] and the extraregional pressures. In time, his version of events was accepted, and the debate over the lost opportunities of the War of Independence was closed. However, by casting the argument in these terms he legitimized the aspiration to revised borders for as long as the conflict continued and if and when Israel was forced to fight the Arabs again.

Ben-Gurion's policy provided only indirect affirmation of the territorial status quo. The prime minister attributed much importance to developing and populating Israel's empty south, the Negev. He argued repeatedly that the 1949 boundaries gave Israel enough space to realize Zionism's main goal: providing a refuge for persecuted Jews and concentrating as many Jews as possible in a sovereign Israel. He hoped this would create the socially, psychologically, and culturally new Jewish type. However, there was a glaring contradiction in the argument. The national ideology stressed full Jewish sovereignty over the state's territory, that is, its exclusive Jewish character. It also stressed securing the borders of the state and protecting Jews from persecution. Logically, then, it follows that the physical security of the inhabitants of the sovereign Jewish state must be ensured in the fullest sense of the word. Given the Arabs' constant provocations, their open hostility, and their relations among themselves, it could be argued that the 1949 borders secured neither Jewish sovereignty nor the physical survival of individual Jews, let alone Israel's legitimacy.

Ben-Gurion's arguments and aims imposed serious constraints on his policy. He attached supreme importance to realizing Israeli sovereignty over Israeli-held territory, whether or not it was compatible with the Arab interpretation of the GAA and the demands of the great powers. He also wished to create a new proud and sovereign Jew, beginning a new life after a long spiritual and political exile.[21] Ben-Gurion's priorities and the problems of security forced him to react to the Arabs' general policies and specific acts with a mixture of force and diplomatic and political measures. During most of his tenure of office as prime minister, the response was defensive and held to a level less than war; the sole exception was the 1956 Sinai campaign. Ben-Gurion's offensive style, his past achievements, and his arguments concerning extraregional—"the world's" —interests and pressures that could not be ignored helped support his defensive posture, at least for a time.

In general, Ben-Gurion succeeded in developing a political consensus about the pragmatic policy he was able to present in fundamental ideological terms. He maneuvered between the demands for unattainable peace and war, between territorial compromise and protracted conflict, between the exigencies of day-to-day security and the challenges of basic, long-range security.

Ben-Gurion did not see Israel's natural growing space extending beyond the 1949 borders into Arab-populated areas, but rather into the large, defensible, and unpopulated Negev.[22] He wished to transfer the center of gravity of Jewish settlement there. Then, as now, the Jewish population was concentrated in the twelve-kilometer-wide coastal strip near Tel Aviv. Militarily, this area was regarded as a constant temptation to Israel's external enemy. Besides his basic solution—the Negev—and the creation of an internally strong, new cultural and social Jewry, Ben-Gurion sought to deter the Arabs and to create an image of a strong Israel, while preventing a large-scale war without foreign aid. In other words, Ben-Gurion was a "postulative" statesman; guided by a strong sense of sequencing and timing, he cognitively arrived at a set of principles and priorities. His political method, at the height of his intellectual and political power, was based upon his instincts for power, his understanding of where power lay or what might determine one's sovereignty and defense, and his habit of studying matters in depth, gathering data and analyzing it over a relatively long period until his opinion was set. On May 14, 1948, when he decided, against the advice of many political friends, to proclaim independence and await the invading Arab armies almost empty-handed, Ben-Gurion knew that he took a great risk, but he regarded other possibilities as even more risky in the long run. History, he believed, does not repeat itself, and the rare moment of Soviet-American understanding in favor of Jewish sovereignty in a part of Palestine might disappear forever. It was up to the power of will— his own—and the power of his nation to fight to use favorable political circumstances against heavy military odds. This method created an image of an aggressive, "hawkish" leader. In reality, his postulates usually brought about a pragmatic compromise, mostly a territorial status quo, to the dismay of his most ardent followers.

Since there was no room for retreats within the country, Ben-Gurion, in his capacity as defense minister, developed a military doctrine based on carrying the war into enemy territory. The conclusion could be drawn that this doctrine meant resorting to preventive war under predetermined, specific conditions;[23] Ben-Gurion himself, of course, was never bound to it. To him the doctrine had only technical significance under extreme conditions that he hoped to prevent through military deterrence, foreign aid, and political measures. However, its psychological and political implications, the meaning attached to the Arab challenge, Israel's physical insecurity, and the potential strategic insecurity of the 1949 boundaries and some of Ben-Gurion's own postulates could lead his critics and followers alike to conclude that preventive war—and possibly territorial change—was necessary.[24]

BEN-GURION'S FOREIGN AND DEFENSE POLICY IN PRACTICE: DETERRENCE, REPRISALS, AND THE 1956 WAR

During the first years of Israeli statehood and later, when the Free Officers' regime in Egypt was just consolidating itself, security, though an important problem, was of secondary importance to Ben-Gurion. As many new immigrants as possible had to be brought to Israel; the country's population doubled very quickly. Furthermore, these immigrants had to be absorbed and integrated with as little disruption as possible. The prime minister thought it necessary to replace the prestate traditional, sectoral, and partisan public action bodies with state institutions. He therefore disbanded the separate armies attached to various political parties and sectoral (kibbutz) movements and liquidated the class-based educational system of the Mandate period. He even engaged in a Bismarckian *Kulturkampf* against the traditional religious elements, but failed. He also tried to strengthen his position in the cabinet by having the cabinet (in which his own party, Mapai, always had the relative majority) take collective responsibility for decisions. Mapai institutions sometimes rubber-stamped actions that Ben-Gurion had already taken. By enforcing collective cabinet responsibility, he was trying to force Mapai's coalition partners to submit to its, and his, authority and to accept its decisions as binding on them. Actually, though, Ben-Gurion had to bargain among his various coalition partners on the relatively narrow power base provided by Mapai.

With these problems and priorities at home, Ben-Gurion's foreign policy was aimed largely at shoring up and protecting Israel's sovereignty, immigration, and shaky economy with the help of any extraregional state willing to provide it, even what many Israelis regarded as Nazi-stained West Germany.

Under Ben-Gurion's leadership, Israel adopted a clear pro-Western orientation in the early 1950s. When the Stalinist regime became aware of the revival of Soviet Jewry's national consciousness after the establishment of the state of Israel, it imposed stringent limitations on Jewish emigration and embarked on a bitter ideological campaign against Zionism. Another consideration for the prime minister was that he should side with the forces of freedom and democracy against those of totalitarianism in the Cold War. The Soviet Union's earlier support of partition and military assistance were thought to be no more than a response to the global constellation of forces at the time, intended to drive Britain from the Middle East. Soviet hostility toward emigration and Zionism was seen as putting Israel in a position where it had to side with the West, not only on principle but in the interests of Zionism as well. Although it could not formally join the Western alliance, Israel considered itself a part of the Western camp. The West, meanwhile, was trying to mobilize Arab support in the Cold War. The Israelis' sense of "Westernness" was only reinforced when the Soviets began to penetrate the Middle East, extending support to members of the Arab coalition, particularly Egypt, against Israel. Their expectations from the West remained unfulfilled in the problems of Arab refugees, the borders, and an official, binding Western commitment to Israel's survival.[25]

Ben-Gurion's foreign and defense policy was thus founded on a compromise among three factors. First, there was the need to ensure Israeli sovereignty in the 1949 borders and to foil Western (mainly British and American) attempts to resolve the refugee problem by allowing the Palestinians the choice of repatriation or resettlement and compensation. Second, there was the need for Western support and, if possible, an alliance, either in NATO or in a formal or informal bilateral framework. An informal alliance with France was attained before the Sinai campaign. The third factor in Ben-Gurion's foreign policy equation was the need to repel Arab challenges to Israel's day-to-day security and to keep the strategic balance from tipping in the Arabs' favor because of Arab military coalitions and/or foreign aid to the most powerful Arab nation—Egypt. At the same time, Israel was engaged in several informal and highly secretive attempts to come to terms first with Jordan and then with Egypt under Prime Minister Gamal Abdul Nasser. These attempts were sometimes conducted under Foreign Minister (and later Prime Minister) Moshe Sharett and sometimes between Ben-Gurion and Nasser with President Eisenhower's personal envoy, Robert Anderson, as a go-between. The Anderson negotiations, conducted in early 1956, were a kind of overture to future negotiations. President Nasser demanded the right of the Palestinians to choose between a return to Israel and staying where they were. He demanded a partial cession of the Negev and Israeli withdrawals to the borders of the Partition Plan. There were repeated difficulties, due to Arab public opinion, in dealing with Israel directly.[26] Israel regarded Nasser's approach and his substantive demands as a manifestation of Egypt's real intentions: a political program to bring about Israel's doom.

Ben-Gurion's methods in response to Arab demands and behavior between 1955 and the Sinai-Suez campaign of late 1956 were complex. He accumulated military power through foreign aid and shaped a domestic (cabinet) power base that would enable him to make decisions. This called for personnel changes such as the forced resignation of former Prime Minister Sharett, who had become Ben-Gurion's foreign minister in August, 1955.[27] Typically, Ben-Gurion, did not disclose to the public the real reason for Sharett's ouster. The humiliated ex-foreign and prime minister accepted his fate passively, though some anxieties and disharmonies were created in the Mapai elite as a result of his forced resignation. Second, Ben-Gurion prohibited any serious attempt by the army, under Chief of Staff Moshe Dayan, to launch a preventive war against Egypt or to become involved in serious fighting with British-protected Jordan (and its natural ally, Iraq). At the same time, he tried to develop the Negev and absorb new immigrants, while preventing the Arab regular forces from exploiting their advantage over Israel's reserve army and territorial inferiority. The Israelis' relative weakness meant that early warning and deployment were necessary; this led to the development of the doctrine of carrying the war to the enemy.

Ben-Gurion hoped to make the permanent state of war in the region unpleasant and uncomfortable for Arabs as well as Israelis. Basically, between 1951 and 1956 Israel tried to deal with these problems through deterrence and through retaliatory acts. It threatened ambiguously to act if its rights or interests were endangered, through Security Council actions and limited demonstrations in the Suez Canal, hoping to show to the international public Egypt's illegal acts against Israeli ships.[28] At the same time, Jerusalem tried to isolate the Arabs in the non-Arab Middle East and black Africa (mainly Ethiopia).

The retaliations carried out[29] were part of a response to, and attempted deterrence of, what the Jerusalem government considered a permanent Arab provocation as well as specific provocative acts. Israeli territory was infiltrated continuously, either by individual Palestinian refugees or by Palestinian organizations in Jordan and the Gaza Strip. In 1955 they began to receive official Egyptian support. The infiltrators came to gather intelligence and to commit acts of sabotage, and sometimes they reached the outskirts of Tel Aviv. These operations were seen as a challenge to

Israel's sovereignty, to its promise as a country or immigration, and to the physical security of the inhabitants.

The retaliations that followed such acts served a number of purposes. First, they were intended to punish Arab governments for allowing the infiltration to occur and to deter them from supporting it in the future. Second, they were also intended to help create the image of a strong and effective IDF in the eyes of the outside world, domestic citizens, and the IDF itself, without risking a full-scale war. Ben-Gurion was skeptical about the performance of a reserve army in general and had doubts about the IDF in particular. Third, the Israeli government wished to show the Arab governments that Israel would not be the only state to suffer from a continuation of the conflict. Fourth, the government wanted to show the population that it was looking out for their security and property without keeping large forces permanently mobilized to defend a fortified border. In fact, the border was left open, for the most part with a minimal amount of fencing and obstacles, and the IDF continued to be a reserve army. Fifth, the reprisals were meant to keep alive Israel's image as a "success story" and a safe land for immigration and, thus, to avert opposition attacks on the unsatisfactory territorial outcome of the War of Independence and the lack of internal security. Last, the government wished to avoid the rift with extraregional powers that would have resulted if Israel had resorted to stronger military actions than short night raids.

During this period, Israel tried to legitimize the ADL as its final border and to refrain from letting Arabs return to Israeli territory. The Western powers and the Soviet Union considered the possibility of giving the Palestinian refugees the choice of repatriation or compensation. The ADL was never accepted as Israel's international frontier and the West was inclined to cut off territory in the south of Israel to permit direct overland passage between Egypt and Jordan.[30] The United States was trying to induce the Arab states to join Dulles's cordon sanitaire around the Soviet Union and was offering them arms. No one recognized West Jerusalem as Israel's capital. The retaliations may thus have been meant to distract the great powers away from these vital considerations to the more marginal ones of reacting to the reprisals themselves. There is no proof that this is what Ben-Gurion intended when he ordered operations on a scale that both the extraregional powers and the Arabs considered escalatory, but such a policy was not beyond Ben-Gurion's capabilities. He was a master at mixing basic principles with sharp political tactics, camouflaging his rather pragmatic policy while mobilizing the nationalistic sensibilities of the public, creating a mood of activism, and exploiting it for domestic purpose.

Ben-Gurion's basic approach to Egypt until late 1956 was defensive. He hoped to deescalate the growing conflict along the Gaza border, in the Tiran Straits (closed by Egypt to Israeli shipping since 1955), and to reopen the Suez Canal to Israeli ships (barred from the waterway by President Nasser before he nationalized it in 1956) by acquiring arms in the United States and France to balance Egypt's supplies from the West and later from Czechoslovakia. Retaliatory acts seemed preferable for the time being, until arms could be acquired and thus a balance of power reestablished upon large-scale operations forcefully advocated by Chief of Staff Major General Moshe Dayan.[31]

The young Chief of Staff Dayan and his civilian colleague, Shimon Peres (at the time director general of the Defense Ministry), tried to influence Ben-Gurion to adopt a harder line toward Nasser, if possible in cooperation with France, otherwise, using newly acquired French weapons. (Dayan's perceptions of the Arab-Israeli conflict will be treated at length later, as he became a highly influencial policy maker himself.) With Ben-Gurion's consent, which was mixed with a large degree of skepticism toward Paris derived from French behavior in World War II,[32] Peres had developed a growing chain of secret contacts in Paris since mid-1955 and since France's involvement in the Algerian war. When Ben-Gurion failed in his attempts to acquire U.S. arms—Washington still hoped to come to terms with Nasser within the framework of the containment strategy toward the Soviet Union—he endorsed, in principle, Peres's suggestion to create a political-military alliance with France.

The aim of this informal alliance, in Peres's perception, should have been larger French weapon supplies and a possible Israeli-French action against Egypt.[33] He indeed suggested such a collaboration to the French in May, 1956, yet Ben-Gurion did not endorse the idea of a preventive war. Dayan, on the other hand, argued that Israel was steering toward a strategic impasse. He said that a militarily weak and passive Israel would encourage Egyptian aggression, which might culminate in a full-scale attack. In order to prevent that, both the United States and Britain would suggest that Israel consent to Nasser's territorial demands. Therefore, Israel should improve its borders with Egypt and occupy Rafah, the area separating the Gaza Strip and the Sinai. It should take the Tiran Straits and demonstrate to the Arabs that it would not accept unilateral Arab changes of the status quo, meaning the naval blockade of Israel's only access to the Red Sea, through the Tiran Straits. For Dayan, Arab behavior, if not contained, was bound to lead to escalation.

Dayan's strategic thinking was focused on "the Arabs," whereas Ben-Gurion's strategic-postulative thinking was more complex. Ben-Gurion wanted to avert a large-scale and costly war, in terms of casualties both civilian and military. The domestic price of full-scale hostilities frightened him, and he attached supreme importance to air cover—unavailable at the time—for Israel's cities.[34] Moreover, Ben-Gurion was seriously concerned about possible interference by the British on Egypt's behalf as a "typical" British trick to regain influence in that country. He feared British-backed Jordanian and Iraqi operations at Israel's rear during a unilateral Israeli action against Egypt, he resented a possible Israeli isolation in the world and the resulting total embargo on weapon supplies. Thus, he told Dayan and his general staff in late 1955, "There is one historical difference between us and the Arabs—that we cannot destroy [get rid of or annihilate] them. . . . This is adversely the case with our neighbors. They can suppose that . . . they may . . . get rid of that problem. . . . Therefore, after any war, any victorious war—we shall face the same problem as we face now."[35] Israeli-initiated war, in other words, might be an instrument of policy only when (1) foreign political and military aid had been obtained; (2) domestic moral and military preparations made; (3) limited, concrete war aims outlined; (4) flanks and air cover secured; and (5) involvement with extraregional "European" armies prevented.

Dayan's preventive war against Egypt was thus considered and rejected. Ben-Gurion agreed later to the joint French-British-Israeli action against Egypt in October and November, 1956, because several of his preconditions seemingly were met, even if not the way he wanted them to be.

1. An arrangement with France and Britain was concluded, which neutralized Jordan and Iraq and secured some kind of cooperation with the British against Nasser.
2. Quantities of French weapons were acquired. The public was gradually prepared for war by the worsening situation along the Gaza border and the retaliatory acts. The retaliation policy itself seemed to have reached an impass. Instead of deterring Egypt, the retaliatory acts provoked Nasser even more. Dayan was demanding large-scale daylight operations, instead of night raids.
3. A number of concrete war aims were put forth by the end of 1956: Ben-Gurion wished to put a stop to the fedayeen operations that had grown more extensive and serious with the retaliations policy. He wanted to head off a decisive shift in the regional balance of power, the result of Egypt's arms deal with the Soviets. In launching the attack, Ben-Gurion also wished to hamper the formation of an effective Arab military coalition. Such a coalition seemed possible when Egypt, Syria, and Jordan founded a Joint Arab Command on October 25, 1956. Ben-Gurion also wanted to open the Suez Canal and mainly the Tiran Straits, the only maritime access to what he considered the most important region to Israel's future—the Negev. At the same time, together with Paris and London, he hoped that more congenial ele-

ments might take over in Egypt as a result of the combined attack.

4. Air cover was provided by French planes stationed in Israeli air bases.

5. A "trick" was devised by Dayan to push Ben-Gurion to his final decision that the Israeli part of the combined operation should assume the character of a larger retaliatory action. It would be large enough for the French and the British to "intervene" but also small enough that the whole endeavor could be called off if they (especially Britain) would not live up to their obligations. [36]

This point represents a major element of Ben-Gurion's foreign and security policy in general. Such a policy left no room for *casus belli*, committing the state to go to war under certain predetermined conditions. The policy did lead to a search for allies, however, so that Israel did not need to start a war alone. The extraregional constellation of forces was so important a factor that when the United States and the Soviet Union demanded Israel's withdrawal from the Sinai and the Gaza Strip after the 1956 war, Ben-Gurion did not see much sense in arguing. He withdrew gladly from the Strip, which was heavily populated with Arab refugees, and regretfully from the unpopulated Sinai and the reopened Straits of Tiran. This was done, however, after receiving general assurances from the American administration about freedom of passage in the Straits and after U.N. buffer forces were stationed on the Egyptian side of the ADL and at the Straits for an indefinite period.[37] The rapid withdrawal could be carried out despite opposition by key political and military figures (particularly the chief of staff, Moshe Dayan),[38] because of the prime minister's firm leadership and unchallenged authority. Dayan's arguments were ignored, and the prime minister refrained from consulting him.

Early in 1958, Dayan resigned as chief of staff and entered politics. He eventually became, with Ben-Gurion's blessing, the representative of the young, Israeli-born elite in Mapai and joined Ben-Gurion's coalition as minister of agriculture. A relatively low-key, civil-servant-type pair of chiefs of staff, General Haim Laskov and General Zvi Zur, followed Dayan, in a period in which the prime minister returned to his old postulates: strengthening Israel's domestic structure and fostering its economic development, seeking any possible support abroad, including in West Germany, and developing Israel's own deterrent in cooperation with France. This led Ben-Gurion, in October, 1957, to accept Mr. Peres's suggestion to build a nuclear reactor at Dimona, in the central Negev.[39] France supplied a 24,000-kilowatt reactor to Israel in complete secrecy until 1960. The Dimona facility should have become operational by then. No separation plant for the plutonium produced was planned, however. Testifying before leading Israeli editors in 1958, Ben-Gurion stressed that he could not avoid the responsibility of giving Israel an option that might secure its future survival. Yet until its completion in 1962, the Dimona reactor did not play a major role in Israeli defense thinking. The U.N. buffer zone along Gaza and U.N. presence in the Tiran Straits contributed to a complete truce in these areas. Egypt's general foreign policy during that period—its union with Syrian and radical politics elsewhere in the Arab world—did not influence Ben-Gurion in his defensive approach toward Israel's neighbors and his preference for the territorial status quo. As long as Nasser refrained from resuming hostilities, directly or indirectly, against Israel, seemingly far-reaching strategic changes in the area (the Egyptian-Syrian bid for unification, the revolt in Iraq, and the Nasserite-Syrian plot against Jordan) did not move the prime minister to take any preventive or other actions. Even in the event of an Egyptian takeover in Jordan or a British action to save King Hussein's pro-Western regime, which might actively involve Israel with the British, Ben-Gurion's principles remained the same: "More than a million Arabs are living [in the West Bank] and this time they will not run away. . . . If we make them an autonomous region, they might decide to join Egypt." Otherwise Israel might have to occupy the land and deny civil rights. Since Israel would grant the Arabs their voting rights, as it granted such rights to Israeli Arabs, and since the Jews in Israel were politically divided, an Arab vote might become decisive.

Ben-Gurion also believed that Israel should not take over the Arab-held part of Jerusalem: "The Christian and the Moslem worlds will not accept our rule over the Holy Mosque and the Christian Tomb." A possible incorporation of Israel into a Western defense treaty would be a better guarantee against Soviet-backed Egypt than an Israeli autonomous game between the superpowers that would include ruling large numbers of Arabs and occupying Muslim and Christian holy places.[40] At the same time, Egypt refrained from massing troops in the Sinai or the Gaza Strip. The Egyptian army was steadily growing with Soviet aid, but direct Egyptian actions or Egyptian-backed Palestinian actions against Israel from Egyptian-controlled territories had stopped after the Sinai-Suez campaign. In public, Ben-Gurion related this change to Egypt's defeat in the 1956, which he presented as a smashing Israeli victory. He never publicly revealed his own doubts as to the IDF's preparedness and fighting quality, and the limitations he had imposed on Dayan before the 1956 war. His fears, typical of a Diaspora Jew, which he managed to control and disguise by iron will and discipline, did indeed remain disguised. Ben-Gurion became a symbol of Jewish bravery even if he remained very fearful. He developed an "active central" role between admitted soft-liners, no-risk-takers, and the brave, like Dayan, who did not fear the Arabs and so, in Ben-Gurion's opinion, might have run serious risks.

Ben-Gurion was creating gaps between his postulates and public expectations. He praised Israel's sovereignty, autonomy, and fighting qualities after the 1956 campaign, but withdrew quickly under foreign pressure, blaming the mighty powers and Israel's dependence on at least one of them—the United States. He blamed the United States for a shortsighted, self-defeating concession to Nasser, who would not refrain from pursuing his grand design against American interests in the future, as Ben-Gurion put it.

Thus, the Sinai campaign strengthened Israeli bids for autonomy, which Ben-Gurion had publicly pursued but privately rejected when it was manifested in Israeli-initiated wars and the occupation of Arab-populated territories. American-inspired arrangements after the war made the United States responsible, in Israeli eyes, for maintenance of the said arrangements. Many Israelis were still thinking in terms of a world ruled by the mighty, who, if it came to a moment of truth in Israeli's relations with its neighbors, would have to intervene and guarantee Israel's survival according to the United States' growing involvement in bringing about the 1957 status quo.[41]

Egypt refrained from massing troops in the Sinai, which became virtually a buffer zone between the two nations. The Sinai was fortified by the Egyptians, whose army and air force were steadily growing with Soviet aid.

The Suez-Sinai war was also an important precedent to be studied in preparation for wars to come. Israel learned that any hostilities, particularly a war it started, would be limited in time; the Middle East was too important and too great an energy supplier for the superpowers to allow an extended conflict there. Furthermore, the war showed that the great powers, particularly the United States, would not necessarily accept an Israeli response to Arab provocation as reasonable, in view of the increasing support for the Arabs in the Third World and the aid from the Soviet Union. The "first scene" of any Middle East war was, therefore, of great importance. It was not enough to prove provocation; the problem lay with the first party to start shooting and with the way his position looked to the superpowers and to the international public.

Top military leaders, such as Israeli air force commander General Ezer Weizman, combined the lesson of time constraints with the older doctrine of carrying the war to the enemy. The outcome was a blitzkrieg strategy: a short attack that would start with an air strike to destroy the enemy air forces on the ground. If need be, Israel could use this strategy alone, without the support of the extraregional powers that Ben-Gurion considered a necessary condition for waging war. The political problem of the "first scene" of a war was thus subordinated to military considerations and to the time constraint imposed by the danger of external intervention. A preventive strike was considered the optimum solution to the problems of the deployment and preparedness of the sides, the expected casualties, and a simultaneous Arab threat on a few fronts. These considerations stemmed from Israel's lack of a large standing army and the considerable growth of the Arabs' regular armies and fire power in the 1960s.[42] In other words, Israel had to mobilize its whole army in order to face up to and smash an offensive deployment of enemy troops with a lightning attack before the threat grew quantitatively and qualitatively.

ISRAELI'S DOMESTIC POLITICAL ORDER IN THE BEN-GURION PERIOD, 1949–60

Figuring out Ben-Gurion's actual, as opposed to his declared, political position is difficult for Israelis as well for foreigners.[43] Ben-Gurion was the product of the late-nineteenth-century, East European ghetto that was the cradle of various types of Jewish rebellion against the world as it was and against history. The rebellion took the form of Jewish socialist movements or of attempts to join non-Jewish revolutionary movements. In some cases, it stemmed from a mixture of messianism and moralism, self-pity and a sense of mission, a sense of the value of the national culture and history and a revolt against their structures, traditions, and ways of life. Also involved were populistic egalitarianism with a sense of self-righteousness, an inclination to treat others justly and equitably, and a certain degree of parochial arrogance.

In Ben-Gurion's prestate period, long discussions and innumerable reversals led the Zionist parties to develop a philosophy of how to operate. As applied by Ben-Gurion and his colleagues this philosophy provided the Zionist parties with the strict discipline needed to control the conflicting tendencies. At last, Mapai, the main socialist Zionist party, arrived at an internal consensus about how to accomplish its goals; Jewish social, economic, and political power would be accumulated slowly in Palestine. Relations with the Arab population there would be kept as friendly as possible, but no gains already made would be conceded in the name of better relations, which seemed to be impossible to achieve, particularly after the mid-1930s. Neither would the Jews risk a head-on clash with extraregional forces that were too strong.

Not all the East European Jews who joined the Zionist movement shared this typically pre-World War I social democratic conception. The Central European right of the interwar period had its counterpart in the radical Zionist right founded by Ze'ev Jabotinsky. In later years it was led by Menahem Begin, who had headed the Irgun Zva'i Le'umi (National Military Organization), or "Irgun," before Independence. The radical Zionist right shared the European right's apocalyptic vision of the dangers of the decline of national culture and of the nation itself. In Germany, this danger was seen in historical and cultural terms. For the Jews the danger perceived was to their very national and physical survival. Even before World War II, the radical Zionist right proposed direct action in order to exert pressure on the British mandatory power. The British, it was claimed, were not carrying out their commitments to Zionism as set forth in the Balfour Declaration and the League of Nations mandate, which, the right said, promised a Jewish state in all of Palestine in a short time.

Thus, another feature of the radical Zionist right becomes clear: The legalism and direct political action combined to reclaim Israel's rights; political and, later, military processes were more decisive, in Jabotinsky's eyes, than the piecemeal socialist settlement effort. A clear-cut, public Jewish claim on Palestine as a whole was the only viable political method to achieve independence. A disguised claim, merely a demand for a Jewish "homeland" in Palestine as agreed between the majority Zionist since the inception of the movement, led to a British mandate over Palestine under the terms of a Jewish "homeland" only. Palestine was later subjected to British political considerations and Arab pressures that led to a practical abandonment of the British obligation. Jabotinsky's basic approach toward politics was thus conceived in terms of working backward from declared goals to reality, using direct action to forcing either/or choices. Compromises on rights and a piecemeal settlement were marginal to the real political and military issue at stake. Compromises would lead to an increasing pressure on the compromiser to abandon his partial claims and withdraw from the disguised rights he would not claim openly. The basic compromise of traditional Zionism with regard to Palestine—the claim for merely a "homeland" under British protection—would lead the British to betray the compromisers and would not satisfy the Arabs, who claimed the whole country for themselves.

In 1925, Jabotinsky took his followers out of the Zionist organization and created the New Zionist Organization, endorsing a clear anti-Socialist program. He blamed the majority Socialists for funding only working-class, socialist-oriented settlements, and demanded that an open Jewish military system be established in Palestine to relieve British mandatory forces. After Hitler's rise to power and the Arab revolt against the British and Jews in 1936–39 (following British political concessions to the Arabs that could lead to the retention of an Arab majority in Palestine and the prevention of any significant growth in Jewish immigration) Jabotinsky went further and proclaimed a revolt or rebellion against the British.

Only an open, direct, mass action by the European Jews, threatened by Hitler and deprived by the British and Arabs of their hope to immigrate to Palestine, would achieve a sovereign state in historical Palestine. Both banks of the Jordan River were claimed, using the logic that one's right cannot be divided.

Jabotinsky's disciples, mainly in Poland, were organized in youth movements and "New Zionist" political parties, but their influence in Palestine itself was marginal. Their leaders waged a war of principles against the majority Socialists; he mocked the unique social achievements and he declared hard-working pioneers, underground defense organizers, piecemeal power accumulators, and hardened idealists to be traitors and soft-bellied compromisers. Jabotinsky's opponents were annoyed by the typical, radical right direct action methods, based on political and legal claims shared by no one else in the world at the time, and they were sure that a mass European Jewish onslaught on Palestine, which Jabotinsky had recommended in 1939, was a spectacular piece of nonsense, bound to be crushed by the British and to discredit Zionism and its serious personal, individual, social character for a long time to come. Parallelly, Jabotinsky authorized the establishment of his own underground organization, the Irgun, whose basic aim was to fight the British and to retaliate for the Arab acts of violence against Jews that were spreading rapidly between 1936 and 1939.[44]

The majority Zionists decided upon a political action to bring about the revision of British mandatory plans, hoping for Labor party support in Britain and later for American support in their bid for Palestine's partition. They thought the Jews in Palestine should fight Hitler, prepare for a possible political decision by the great powers, and be ready for an Arab military effort to nullify a possible great-power decision on partitioning the country. A Jewish terror campaign against the British and a retaliatory campaign against the Arabs by Begin's Irgun would confront the Jewish population with a world empire and would be self-defeating for Jewish moral claims to a part of the country. The Israelis would prove unable to live in peace with the Arabs and would contribute to a foreign perception that both sides—Arabs and Jews—could not control themselves as sovereign nations, thus justifying some kind of international or great-power control of Palestine. The debate between the Irgun and the majority Zionists led by Ben-Gurion's Mapai was escalated by Ben-Gurion and the nationalist leftist parties to the point of an open division and a public ban by the majority on the Irgun "dissidents," as they were called by Ben-Gurion in the mid-1940s. Ben-Gurion was ready for a "direct action" only if an international consensus was reached and the great powers decided to accept Jewish claims on a part of the country as a result of a complex political process at home and abroad (settlements to "create facts" in contested territories and preparations for a possible battle with the Arabs, rather than the British). A claim on the whole country, as Begin demanded, would meet with a rejection of that claim.

Ben-Gurion was quite willing to challenge the British indirectly, through the illegal immigration. The idea of Jewish sovereignty gained international publicity and sympathy because of the plight of those rescued from the European holocaust who wished to immigrate to Palestine. He was able to isolate the radical right by exploiting the majority held by the moderate left and center in the political institutions of the Yishuv (the Jewish community in Palestine) and the denial by the right of the authority of these institutions in matters relating to the struggle against the British.

Politically, the Yishuv was organized in party institutions. The Jewish community's great debates about how to achieve sovereignty and what risks to take occurred in bodies elected by the Zionist parties. The public voted for electoral lists made up by party apparatuses without the approval of the party rank and file. The party apparatuses were thus in effect self-electing; they presented the public with package deals of personalities and policies. After the election they discussed how to give a concrete interpretation to the mood that became apparent in the elections. The public or even the parties as a whole had little to do with setting the fundamental lines of public debate or discussions on normative issues and principles. The public and the party rank and file presented general outlines of views and articulated interests to smaller bodies, such as the Jewish Agency, unconstrained by constitutions or systems of checks and balances. Representation in these institutions was based on a proportional electoral system. Mapai, together with groups slightly to its left and right, usually had a majority of the seats.[45]

Because the radical right never acknowledged those bodies' authority in the struggle against the British, it deprived itself of any role in the Yishuv's decision-making system. It played into Ben-Gurion's hands; he could argue that the radical right did not accept the authority of the majority, and then banish it and the radical left to the political wilderness for as long as he led the Yishuv and the state. Thus, Begin's Herut party was always in opposition during Ben-Gurion's premiership.[46]

Mapai could be compared to a Central European Social Democratic party, with strong Jewish habits. Originally two pioneer organizations founded by a handful of idealists who immigrated to Palestine at the beginning of the century, Mapai became in the early 1920s the "United Workers party of Eretz-Israel."[47] Under Ben-Gurion's leadership, which became commonly accepted during the late 1920s, Mapai adopted the character of a strong, socially minded, non-Marxist reform movement (reform refers to the traditional Jewish way of life). It had an extremely strong vision of accumulating Jewish power in Palestine through piece-meal progress, as opposed to the spectacular fights and extreme demands propagated by the right. The Marxist, and at the same time more activist nationalist left, Achdut Ha'Avoda, which had been in Mapai since the beginning, was forced to secede from it in 1944. Ben-Gurion wanted a solid power base and a unified party before the end of World War II and the crucial events that would follow and determine Israel's future. Achdut Ha'Avoda seemed to him to be both too far left and pro-Soviet, yet too nationalistic and rigid concerning the inevitable territorial compromise that would be necessary to acquire independence. He thus provoked them to leave the united party and eventually join Hashomer Hatzair, a doctrinaire Marxist and pro-Soviet kibbutz movement, during the 1948–49 War of Independence. In the meantime, Mapai was able to work together with Achdut Ha'Avoda, the General Zionists (the moderate right), and the moderate religious block that became known later as the National Religious party (NRP). All these parties and Hashomer Hatzair joined forces under Mapai's majority in the Yishuv parliament, having no par-liamentary alternative. Thus, Mapai assumed its unique character in Israeli politics before 1965: too weak to win an absolute majority amid the mosaic of ethnic, class, political, and personal interests and views typical of Jewish politics, as reflected by the absolute proportional, one-constituency ballot system, Mapai became the biggest single party and the key to government. It held the blocking minority key to any possible coalition, such as the left and right, and the extreme left and the extreme right could not unite against it. Mapai achieved this role not only due to Ben-Gurion's leadership, which played a growing role after independ-ence, but also due to its secondary leadership and its party machine, which operated in all spheres of Jewish life in Palestine. The party helped establish the General Union Organization (Histadrut, whose first gen-eral secretary was David Ben-Gurion) and later had a majority in the governing bodies of this unique instrument of settlement, housing, job supply, and medicare. Mapai, with other socialist Zionist parties, chan-neled money raised from Jews abroad into the economy through Hista-drut enterprises that in turn financed the party itself. This was the most important instrument in developing the country before independence, since normal capital investments and market economic elements were missing, and it explains Mapai's central role in Jewish politics, as opposed to the nonsocialist right and the extreme nationalist right.

After Ben-Gurion's bold decision on May 14, 1948, to proclaim inde-pendence, against the fears of many secondary leaders in Mapai and the leftist parties, Mapai was a loyal, seemingly compact and cohesive polit-ical-economic instrument of power. Ben-Gurion's risky decision to change from a policy of slowly gathering strength to one of quick action was rewarded handsomely after its success. The membership included a large, heterogeneous number of individuals, who belonged to either the original pioneer generations that believed firmly in party socialism, egalitarianism, and piecemeal progress through physical labor, or to the middle-of-the-road, Jewish middle class that resented Marxism, nationalistic rhetoric, and dangerous anti-British terrorism.

Mapai's secondary leadership reflected this heterogenous character well; beside postulative emotional leaders (like Golda Meir, then minister of labor and later Ben-Gurion's foreign minister), whose goals were Jewish national survival and sovereignty and whose major premises were that party political power was needed to achieve and retain it and a general "activist" approach to a hostile world, bargaining leaders (like Levy Eshkol) controlled Israel's settlement effort and later Israel's economy.[48] Eshkol's approach to politics was basically economic; some sort of mutual gain must be found for everyone in the political process if a mutual goal were to be achieved. Israel's masses could not be expected to starve or to follow Mapai if the standard of living remained below a desired minimum. At the same time, Eshkol vigorously pursued large-scale settlement efforts in rural areas, pumping public money and his pioneer enthusiasm into them. In fact, since Israel's independence, a constantly rising standard of living was assured, through Mapai's give-and-take network of relations with labor unions and pressure groups by way of public investment in development areas, which created new vested interests. All of them influenced the party's economic policies, yet had no decisive influence on forign affairs and defense until the early 1960s.

Decisions made in party forums—a national conference that endorsed a national committee, which in turn endorsed a small governing body— were in fact debated in the governing body first. Thus, they were prepared by Ben-Gurion and overwhelmingly endorsed by the bigger forums controlled by the party elite and the small, but highly effective, party machinery. The public as a whole, including rank and file members of Mapai, was not able to, and usually did not want to, influence party leadership on foreign affairs. The leadership itself was in a way a self-recruiting and self-perpetuating bloc that offered itself to the electorate as a package, along with its broadly formulated middle-of-the-road policies. The parliamentary lists were closed, and as such were determined by the party leadership and were approved by the national committee. No primary elections took place; the list reflected a conglomerate of economic, regional, and social power interests as the party leadership recognized them or promoted them to be. At the same time, Mapai continued to control, through the disciplined members of its machinery, most of the state and Histadrut institutions, and thus played a significant role as an immigration absorption agency. Many new immigrants, who had doubled and tripled the country's population since 1949, were introduced to state or union services that were controlled, or regarded as controlled, mostly by Mapai agents in cooperation with NRP and other Zionist parties' representatives acceptable to Mapai. As a result, many of the immigrants joined the existing party structures or at least regarded them, and Mapai above the others, as a major domestic power that controlled their basic needs—jobs, medical care, housing, and identification. Thus, a prestate structure—Mapai and a given number of smaller parties—managed to retain its central domestic role in a rapidly changing demographic, cultural, and economic environment until the early 1960s.

The methods of this extraordinary achievement were, in the economic and social spheres under Mr. Eshkol and his dynamic lieutenant, Mr. Pinhas Sapir, basically bargaining methods. Yet the party had to reconcile its leader—a man of principles who devoted most of his energies to foreign policy, defense, and the creation of new Jewish habits and behavioral patterns, and who insisted upon transferring many party and union functions to the state—to the bargaining habits that, together with Ben-Gurion's popularity, had helped it to remain in power. It had to absorb two different kinds of new elements: its own Israeli-born young leadership, represented by Moshe Dayan and Shimon Peres (born in Poland and raised in Israel), and a relatively large number of new immigrants.

At cabinet level, Mapai had to choose among many coalition partners. Having banished the extreme right and the radical left, Ben-Gurion was suspicious of the not-so-radical leftist Mapam (United Workers' party). For most of the period that Ben-Gurion led Israel, Mapam was made up of two factions. One was the above-mentioned pro-Soviet kibbutz movement, Hashomer Hatzair[49] and the other was the leftist kibbutz movement, Achdut Ha'Avoda,[50] which followed an activist foreign and defense policy. Ben-Gurion abhorred the pro-Soviet stance maintained by Hashomer Hatzair until after Stalin's death. He was also repelled by Achdut Ha'Avoda's tendency to bemoan the territorial status quo, to aspire to Israeli sovereignty over a greater part of western Palestine, if not all of it, and to wish Jewish settlement everywhere within its "natural" historic and strategic borders. Ben-Gurion rejected its willingness to risk a high level of conflict without foreign assistance when sovereignty or vital interests were infringed upon in ways determined by hard and fast *casus belli*.[51] Ben-Gurion himself proclaimed *casus belli* after the Sinai campaign, but he believed that they committed him to action only in the proper circumstances. He thought Achdut Ha'Avoda's views on the issue were rather provincial and reflected no awareness of what could or could not be done in international grand strategy.

The multiplicity of parties during Ben-Gurion's first years in office was an advantage for him and gave him much room to maneuver. His own

Mapai never got more than 36–40 percent of the popular vote.[52] On this rather narrow base and with the help of an almost permanent partner, the National Religious party, he could turn to the moderates at his left or right as circumstances demanded. The NRP's views on foreign and defense policy were moderate and pragmatic. Usually they gave Ben-Gurion full support in this area in exchange for concessions in domestic policy on relations between religion and state, especially in the educational system. Ben-Gurion accepted the necessity for these concessions, albeit with ill-disguised unwillingness.

Ben-Gurion's charisma, drive, vision, and practical capabilities covered up the deficiencies in the Israeli political system. The proportional representation system, with practically no minimum percentage of the vote required for a seat in parliament, and the consequent multiplicity of parties were somewhat offset by Mapai's ability to maneuver among the other parties, by the ostracism of the extreme right and left, and by Ben-Gurion's firm control of Mapai itself. Parliament was subject neither to a constitution nor to precedent and could pass any legislation by a simple majority. Only coalition cabinets emerged from this system, and they tended, naturally, to become collegial bodies. The ministers' tightest bonds were to the parliamentary caucuses and to the nonparliamentary party power apparatuses rather than to the cabinet and the prime minister. Therefore, the prime minister could normally expect to be no more than first among equals, and the cabinet's decision making was liable to involve little more than determining the lowest common denominator of all the factions represented in it.

In fact, however, Ben-Gurion did hold some important cards that helped him to exercise control. During the mandate period, all political decision making in the Yishuv had been concentrated in a single executive body, the Jewish Agency, with no significant interference by the popularly elected assembly. The Israeli cabinets benefited from this tradition. Furthermore, in the first years of statehood, the structure of the political parties did not indicate any real policy differences from party caucuses or central committees that might bind his hands.

The potential of this political system was not realized. Despite its structures, the system was highly centralized and very conformist psychologically because of Ben-Gurion's great prestige with the party and the public and because his use of the compact power base Mapai provided enabled him to mobilize popular support. He could have the party institutions pass decisions binding on their members and representatives without much discussion or yielding to pressure from the membership. He could mobilize the public's support on most foreign and defense issues and thus neutralize any independent influence it might have on the content of a policy. With the permanent support provided by Mapai, Ben-

Gurion could approach other parties, enter coalitions in which Mapai held a majority, and demand collective responsibility, that is, unanimous acceptance of decisions passed by a majority of the cabinet. This system became less and less workable with time, however, when the other parties began to discover their own parliamentary strength and to demand personal, political, and ideological concessions and benefits.

Ben-Gurion exploited his authority in order to preserve the cohesion of the cabinet and the national consensus. He would sometimes use the defense situation to create a sense of great apprehension and attain the proper political atmosphere. Often he would adopt a very tough style in his policy statements or he would keep many of his ministers uninformed about forthcoming major decisions. The Sinai campaign, for instance, was decided upon and presented to the cabinet at the last moment. If these methods were not enough for him to control the course of policy, Ben-Gurion would sometimes form a new cabinet, engaging in bitter polemics against rival parties and factions. Before and after independence, he had no qualms about dismantling or splintering multi-party frameworks and purging people like Mr. Sharett. Apart from reflecting his quarrelsome nature, these methods were also a tool for keeping the party cabinet and parliament in line.

At his peak, Ben-Gurion basked in public acclaim and admiration that was cultivated by his colleagues and the media. By making crucial foreign and defense policy decisions in secret he contributed to the mystification of Israeli politics; he became the magus who knew better than others what was ahead. By concealing and camouflaging some of his major political goals he helped stunt the nation's critical faculty on foreign and defense matters. Not all the facts were known, and the executive, Ben-Gurion himself, enjoyed the people's confidence. The prime minister's past successes in these areas of policy led the communications media to accept his decisions. The conformity on foreign and defense issues of this multi-party system, with its strong parliament, is striking. Ben-Gurion at his peak stood so high that it is only natural that in time the criticism he and his heirs would suffer would be bitter and exaggerated.

After a while, Ben-Gurion's coalition partners refused to play his game. This started in the mid-1950s when Mapai's moderate right coalition partner, the General Zionist party, suffered a crushing decline in the polls. They had managed in a previous election to more than double their parliamentary representation, focusing on the nonsocialist middle class. Mapai abandoned its strict socialist-egalitarian, austere approach to economic and social problems and invited the General Zionists to join the cabinet. Yet economic, and foreign policy decisions remained in Mapai's hands and the tools remained Mapai-controlled instruments of power or state-controlled systems, rather than private initiatives. The credit for success went to Mapai and the responsibility for failures went to the General Zionists. As a result, that party preferred to stay in opposition, where it had been practically since 1955, and to remain an alternative between Mapai and the extreme right, Mr. Begin's Herut. Herut, realizing that Mapai had maneuvered it into irrelevance, started moving slowly toward the center, yet remained an anathema to Ben-Gurion. Deprived of coalition alternatives on the right, Mapai was left with only a small moderate right partner, the Progressive party, which joined the General Zionists first to form the Liberal party (the name remained) and then resumed its traditional coalition role with Mapai as the Independent Liberal party. Mapai had to continue an uneasy partnership with the nationalist left, Achdut Ha'Avoda, which terminated its union with Hashomer Hatzair. The latter retained the union's name, Mapam. Having lost his right-wing coalition alternative, Ben-Gurion was faced with a more demanding left wing. Political and emotional issues, such as Ben-Gurion's bid to sell Israeli-made weapons to West Germany or to buy German weapons, and his constant, almost humiliating efforts with President Eisenhower toward a treaty with the United States and joining NATO, were not easily acceptable to his leftist partners. They also resented the Sinai attack and withdrawal decisions made by Ben-Gurion without enough consultations with them.

Nasser's adventures in Jordan in 1958 and his supporters' revolt in Lebanon in the same year led the United States to supply Israel with small quantities of field weapons and to finance Israeli tank purchases in Britain. Britain also became more ready to support Israel, as a result of Nasser's activities against her allies in the area and the fall of the pro-British regime in Iraq. All this did not seem to be enough for Ben-Gurion, who feared a growing, Egyptian-led, Arab national movement with Soviet support. Yet he was not ready to endorse any military plan to occupy the West Bank of the Jordan River under Hashemite rule in the case of Hussein's seemingly imminent fall.[53] "I have explained [in a closed meeting] the danger of potentially a million Arabs to the State. . . . We shall become encircled again, [this time] an 'Algeria' will emerge from within that may destroy the whole state. . . . Our pressing problem is the lack of Jews, not the lack of territory." To Achdut Ha'Avoda this was an ideological, historical, and strategic blunder. Israel could be crushed if Arab armies attacked at its most vital and vulnerable area, the eight-mile bottleneck between Tel Aviv and the (in their perception, illegitimate and artificial) Jordanian border in the West Bank. They were also vehemently against any relations with West Germany. As a result, Ben-Gurion brought about a cabinet crisis when he pursued his German policy after his greatest victory in the 1959 elections. Mapam opposed his NATO efforts and both parties might have killed the nuclear deal with France, which was of the utmost importance to Ben-Gurion. So he presented them (and most of the Mapai ministers, who also resented the large investment and doubted its value) with a *fait accompli*. In return, the coalition partners were more than ever resolved to prevent such decisions in the future.

Coalition partners were becoming more and more demanding. In the late 1950s, Ben-Gurion tried to change the electoral system and put an end to the multi-party system that forced him to look for such partners. Fearing the emergence of a two-party, or few party system, most of the parties in parliament opposed the motion strongly. Ben-Gurion's colleagues in Mapai soon realized that electoral reform did not stand a chance and looked for other ways of stabilizing the political system. Gradually they turned to a solution that Ben-Gurion had opposed: the amalgamation of parties. In time, amalgamation expanded the narrow coalition base considerably, but it also lowered the common denominator needed to reach foreign and defense policy decisions. Ben-Gurion had always tried to keep control of these in his own hands. Although he paid lip service to the unity of the noncommunist left, he tried to keep Hashomer Hatzair and Achdut Ha'Avoda out of Mapai, separate from each other, and potential coalition partners.

Ben-Gurion sowed the seed of the destruction of his policy. Mapai's nationalist competition and his own views on the new Jew led him, through his statements, to create the image and mood of a strong and proud Israel, actively and determinedly protecting the life and property of the Jews. The content of his policy was more moderate than its form; it was a policy of active centrism, following the median line between the nationalist right and left and the Marxist left. Most of the public followed, believing deeply in the man and his methods. It was only a question of time, though, until the activist psychological climate he helped create had its effect on actual policy. His middle-of-the-road policy could last only until public opinion, which was so amorphous in the first years of statehood and which did not pay much attention to the substance of policy, began to crystalize around the conclusion drawn from the way the policy was articulated. The question is, then, not how long Ben-Gurion could go on playing Bismarck, but how long he could go on acting like Ben-Gurion?

THE "AFFAIR" AND THE RISE OF ESHKOL

Israel's domestic political system began undergoing substantial changes in the late 1950s that were to have an impact on the state's foreign and defense policy. These changes were manifested in what became known as the "Lavon Affair."

In 1954, after the Anglo-Egyptian agreement on the British with-drawal from bases in the Suez Canal zone, Israeli agents tried to exacer-bate relations between Nasser's Egypt and Britain and the United States. They placed bombs in public buildings in Egypt, including American and British institutions, and were eventually caught by the Egyptian authorities. Ben-Gurion was then in "retirement" at kibbutz Sdeh-Boker. His successor as defense minister, Pinhas Lavon, was forced to resign when the plot was discovered. Ben-Gurion returned to public life in 1955 to head the defense ministry; shortly afterward he resumed office as prime minister, replacing Moshe Sharett.

In 1960, Lavon demanded public rehabilitation.[54] He claimed that someone in the defense establishment had given the orders to proceed with the sabotage without his knowledge and that new evidence proved his contention. Therefore, he asked Ben-Gurion, the defense minister, to clear him publicly of all responsibility in the 1954 affair.

Pinhas Lavon was not an ordinary member of the "secondary leader-ship." He was a lone wolf, a moderate socialist youth leader who had been advanced by Ben-Gurion himself to the defense ministry because of his impressive personality and oratory. As a defense minister he became extremely "hawkish," and authorized harsh actions against Israel's neigh-bors even beyond the taste of Chief of Staff Dayan, operating sometimes behind his back. After Lavon's fall in 1954, nobody in the secondary leadership came to rescue him. On the contrary, his period in office was regarded as a regretable, if not irresponsible, tenure that led to the 1954 "Affair." Ben-Gurion, upon his return in 1955, helped rescue Lavon from disgrace and had him made secretary general of the Histadrut. In the meantime, the secondary leadership, already shaken by Sharett's dis-missal and Ben-Gurion's growing tendency to use secretive methods to achieve de facto decisions on sensitive issues like Germany and the nuclear deal, felt threatened by the very tools he used. Shimon Peres's defense ministry operated almost independently from Golda Meir's for-eign ministry. Peres seemed to them to incorporate in his person blind ambition, ruthless methods and technical qualities, rather than ideolog-ical and conceptual abilities. Moreover, Peres was young and seemed to be establishing, with Ben-Gurion's blessing, a personal network at the defense ministry, that the secondary leadership would not be able to con-trol if the succession question became a fact.

The main group in the secondary leadership consisted of Mrs. Meir, Mr. Eshkol, Mr. Sapir, and education minister Aran. They felt threatened by Peres and his formidable friend, former Chief of Staff Dayan. They felt that Ben-Gurion, an admirer of the "new Jew," was advancing Israeli-born military men before them. The moderate wing in the secondary leadership, headed by Aran and Sapir, had indeed feared Dayan's polit-ical style since his preventive war escapades. Meir might have been less concerned about the contents of Dayan's strategic thinking, but she had resented his political behavior since his entry into Israeli domestic politics and hated Peres, the empire builder. Before the 1959 elections, Dayan challenged the secondary leadership directly. He publicly denounced their bargaining methods, accusing them of bureaucratization coupled with a narrow, party political approach to Israel's basic challenges—the relationship with world Jewry, Israel's future development as a unique social experiment, and the future of Israel's empty spaces, now neglected in favor of a rising standard of living.

Ben-Gurion was forced to support Dayan in public, although he did not accept Dayan's tone, style, and some of his substantive remarks. Yet Dayan used precepts near and dear to Ben-Gurion's heart, and at the same time reflected a growing pressure by younger generation leaders to have their share in Mapai's closed elite. Therefore, Ben-Gurion invited Dayan to his cabinet after the 1959 elections, in a nonmilitary or foreign policy post, to calm secondary leadership fears, but promoted Peres to deputy minister of defense. Ben-Gurion promoted two other relatively young outsiders, including the former U.N. and United States Ambassador, Abba Eban, to cabinet posts. This "parachuting," as Israel's domestic political jargon calls promotions outside a closed party elite, brought about Aran's resignation, almost an open revolt by Mrs. Meir, and a continued battle between the "young" led by Dayan and Peres and the "seniors," with Ben-Gurion tending to support the young yet trying to balance between both groups so as to bring about a controlled process of transition over a relatively long period. The "Affair" exploded in the middle of this delicate process. Lavon, the lone wolf who became the head of the vast union bureaucracy, felt threatened by the "young," as did everyone else in the secondary leadership. Thus, they shared anxieties and interests. Moreover, he seemed to have a case against Dayan and Peres; he proved to be, due to the new evidence, innocent of the 1954 affair. Dayan and Peres were the next top executives of the defense establishment in 1954 after Lavon. They were nominated for the positions of chief of staff and director general of the defense ministry by Ben-Gurion upon his departure for Sdeh-Boker, and kept informal relations with the "retired" prime minister during the whole period. Their relations with Lavon gradually deteriorated as he tried to force his authority on them separately and bypass the chief of staff. When the "Affair" was secretly investigated for the first time, both gave a negative picture of their chief. The secret investigation could not prove Lavon's direct responsibility, but neither could they relieve him of an overall responsibility for the Egyptian affair that brought about the arrest and eventually the hanging of several Israeli agents.

The significance of Lavon's innocence, if proved in 1960, might have been that if he did not order the Egyptian action, Dayan and Peres might have done it behind his back. When it proved to be a disaster, they further plotted to cast the responsibility on Lavon, with Ben-Gurion's active or passive support. If Lavon did not give the order, then someone at the military intelligence branch, at the time in direct charge of the "Affair," should be made responsible.

Political "affairs," it seems to me, like the Dreyfus affair in France or the Watergate affair in the United States, are unique social conflicts. Sometimes they reflect latent tensions, changing expectations, or the decay of old rules in the society. Sometimes they help create tensions and expectations during a long process of escalating public debate. Usually political "affairs" have to do with facts, that is, with a public debate about deeds and misdeeds, whose political, moral, and personal significance becomes a part of the debate itself. Several versions of these facts become publicly known, interwoven with public perceptions of the people, social forces, and values involved. If one version is to be established and publicly accepted, an existing advantage by, or equilibrium of, people or social forces might be hurt when the parties to the debate, public opinion, and the media turn it into a battle on values and people who used to represent them.

Thus, the method of the inquiry into the facts at the root of the "affair" becomes a matter of great apprehension, especially in societies that lack established rules of inquiries, like Israel in 1960. The same may happen in societies that could liquidate such debates within the framework of a balanced system of people, social forces, and values when the nature of the "affair" or an imbalanced system, or both, prevent such an internal liquidation.

The Mapai system of people and values was already imbalanced before Mr. Lavon demanded his rehabilitation. Mapai still proclaimed pioneering values but rapidly abandoned them in practice. Ben-Gurion transferred his pioneering drive toward the empty Negev desert, without success. He tried to set a personal example, to lead the younger generation from a growing middle-class environment to a collective life in the strategically important empty space of Israel. Rather than accepting city life and its commercial values, the younger generation should serve the state and its unique social character, following Ben-Gurion, who had kept his residence in Sdeh-Boker. At the same time, Ben-Gurion tried to emphasize the state's own positive role in absorbing new immigrants, creating equal opportunities for them, and building a common ground between them and the established youth and the pioneering young members of the youth movements within the framework of the Israel Defense Forces. Lavon, the lone wolf, was speaking in terms of returning to old socialist values. He propagated a new effort by the "working masses" and their tools, the Histadrut, the network of Mapai's controlled unions, to take over society's spiritual and existential needs in times of decaying traditional values. The "masses," led by a proper spiritual and ideological leadership rather than the state, should take care of themselves; Sdeh-Boker and the army would not suffice. Dayan mocked Lavon's vast bureaucracy as an instrument to achieve these goals. Lavon generated interest in a group of Mapai intellectuals who were disappointed with what they perceived as Ben-Gurion's exaggerated reliance on the state and state tools—the army among them—to push forward Mapai's old values of egalitarianism, social reform, and a collective life within voluntary frameworks capable of balancing individual searches for the meaning of Jewish life with social and public benefits. Mapai was run by its secondary leadership, using political bargaining methods in order to retain power in a welfare, rather than pioneering, old-style socialist state. The principles of its main leader—the settlement of the Negev, a collective, social way of life, and strict moral behavior toward oneself, society, and state—were slowly given up as incompatible with Israel's resources, social reality, and lack of public interest.

Ben-Gurion's principles for foreign affairs, derived from a method of cognitive personal soul-searching, ceaseless reading, secrecy, and the refusal to accept compromises on crucial choices, were incompatible with the behavior of the secondary leadership, its group character, and open bargaining habits. Furthermore, the secondary leadership felt indeed threatened by Mapai's "young," who were groomed by Ben-Gurion but appeared to lack his experience, analytical power, restraints, and historical insight. As in the case of the Arab-Israeli conflict itself, this set of circumstances created a "Shakespearian tragedy" that could not be averted in time.

When Lavon claimed his rehabilitation, being a proud and imprudent man, he expected another proud and complex man to grant it to him at once. Ben-Gurion refused, at first, to grant the rehabilitation, claiming that he had not prosecuted Lavon at the time, so that a procedure should be devised to inquire into the 1954 events. Lavon expected Ben-Gurion to defend Dayan and Peres, and was very well acquainted with the prime minister's habits of dealing with delicate defense issues in secret. He therefore broke the new facts to the parliamentary committee of foreign affairs and defense and its opposition members, to the press, and to his Mapai colleagues. By so doing, Mr. Lavon created a triple crisis with Ben-Gurion. First, he fought his battle outside of the closed party club that was sometimes used by Ben-Gurion to bring about decisions on foreign affairs and defense issues. Second, he brought sensitive state secrets, which Ben-Gurion sometimes used to hide even from his own party and cabinet, to the attention of parliament, the press, and the public, thus making them partners to an internal rift in Mapai.

Third, Lavon's version of the affair, which escalated into a general offensive against Dayan, Peres, and Peres's regiment in Ben-Gurion's defense ministry, dealt with the hanging of Jews in Egypt because of an order that had been given in the defense establishment behind Lavon's back. It could be viewed, if accepted, as discrediting Ben-Gurion's defense establishment for being an idealistic instrument of social pioneering and defense. Thus the inquiry into the matter should indeed be nonpolitical and not public.

Ben-Gurion was not ready for such an open challenge by one of Mapai's leading comrades. He hesitated and deliberated, and allowed Dayan and Peres to start an anti-Lavon campaign, which automatically was attributed to Ben-Gurion himself by Lavon and a growing number of secondary Mapai leaders. Some of them were outraged by the shocking nature of the "affair," some were alienated by Ben-Gurion's long regime and his secretive manners that were not compatible with their own group behavior, and some, like Sharett, did not forgive Ben-Gurion for their own personal disgrace and the methods he used to get rid of them. Others were dragged into the campaign because it seemed to symbolize Ben-Gurion and Dayan's reliance on the state and the army as the tools to master Israel's social and existential problems, rather than on Histadrut, party or voluntary, socialist-oriented organizations that handled these challenges without state interference or guidance.

The facts seemed beyond contest. Lavon explained that he did not issue the 1954 order. No one else could be directly blamed for it, but a vehement debate and press revelations about the 1954 events were escalating as a result of Lavon's campaign. The story was militarily censored, and the astonished public learned about the details through code names and editorials. The press, especially a widely circulated afternoon paper, *Ma'ariv*, backed Lavon from the beginning. Later other newspapers supported his quest for rehabilitation or demanded a public inquiry.

Mr. Eshkol, the chief compromiser in Mapai's secondary leadership, realized that if Lavon were not granted an inquiry and then eventually rehabilitated, the party would be publicly discredited. However, he also realized that if Lavon's case were brought to the party for inquiry and a rehabilitation followed, Ben-Gurion might challenge this procedure or Lavon himself might not accept the results. Eshkol took a gamble; he brought the 1954 affair to the cabinet and initiated a ministerial inquiry. The majority hastily cleared Lavon, using Ben-Gurion's own methods of a majority cabinet decision. Thus an internal party debate was averted and Ben-Gurion was given a chance to use the pretext of a majority government decision, as he had in the past, to justify his own—different—opinion, while accepting the cabinet's verdict at the same time. The affair could be buried and forgotten; everyone could return to business, since the cabinet had cleared Lavon but had not blamed others. Lavon declared himself satisfied, of course, and the procedure was publicly accepted as correct. The outraged nation wanted the affair to be closed.

Eshkol, however, must have known that his compromise would not satisfy Ben-Gurion; the prime minister had usually accepted cabinet majority decisions against him when they suited his own, disguised, aims. Ben-Gurion had been happy with the majority decision against a possible occupation of the West Bank in the past, because he never intended to occupy the West Bank. He did not want any majority to make compromise decisions on delicate foreign and defense issues that he felt were either/or choices. The cabinet decision to clear Lavon was a compromise in this respect because it did not settle the question of who *had* given the order in 1954. But the ministers were not professional judges; they probably had in mind mainly an end to a devastating public and party debate.

Ben-Gurion was determined not to allow Lavon's campaign against "the sanctity of security"[55] to be sanctioned by the cabinet, or his use of parliamentary bodies and public opinion for his rehabilitation to become a practice. Lavon's mobilization of party leaders alienated from Ben-Gurion or at personal odds with Dayan and Peres should be exposed. The use of bargaining habits in the party should not be allowed to penetrate into cabinet procedure and thus establish those methods as new tools to determine Israel's foreign policy and defense choices. Ben-Gurion therefore denounced his own cabinet's majority decision to clear Lavon and started a personal campaign against his party colleagues. As the campaign gathered an alarming momentum, Lavon and his growing circle of followers returned to fight, and opposition parties became involved. Coalition parties that supported the cabinet decision were alienated, young and old established Israelis were pushed to the extreme in defense or defiance of the parties involved, and Israel's automatic confidence in the political system represented by Ben-Gurion was shattered. New immigrants were shocked and astounded by the internal rift in the seemingly cohesive power base that ran the country, even though they could not understand much of the code language allowed by the censored press.

Eshkol devised another compromise: remove Lavon from his Histadrut job yet retain his rehabilitation by the cabinet. Even if cleared by the ministerial committee, Lavon had damaged the party and discredited its leadership by using public campaign methods, said Eshkol to a shocked central party committee, and he had to be removed. The public reaction was as expected. Mapai yielded to its autocratic leader and sacrificed the persecuted man. Ben-Gurion, whose basic interest was not satisfied by this exercise since he wanted Lavon's case brought before a judicial commission of inquiry, was nevertheless blamed for Eshkol's compromise.

Meanwhile, the prime minister, having no other outlet, tried to repeat his past methods for times of crisis: he called for new elections, thus abolishing the hated ministerial majority that cleared Lavon. Mapai, however, lost several mandates in the elections as a result of the public scandal. Former coalition partners like Mapam, who resented Ben-Gurion's behavior in the affair, refused to join, sensing the supremacy of the state and the army over the Histadrut, socialist values and methods of social organization. Others refused to negotiate with the disgraced "prosecutor," so that Eshkol had to put together a coalition for Ben-Gurion based on Mapai, the NRP, and Achdut Ha'Avoda. (Achdut Ha'Avoda had gained in power and influence as Mapai lost it.) The crisis was theoretically over after Lavon's dismissal by the party, but Ben-Gurion's standing in Mapai, the party's own relations with its liberal intelligentsia, and the prime minister's position in the coalition were severely damaged. Ben-Gurion's personal relations with secondary leaders like Golda Meir were totally destroyed. Mrs. Meir resented Dayan and Peres and regarded Lavon's sacrifice as initiated by Ben-Gurion and as an act of authoritarianism. Accordingly, this act devastated the party's image almost beyond repair and poisoned the rules of group behavior in the party's elite. Mr. Eshkol became Mrs. Meir's favorite leader as he tried to save the party, whereas Eshkol himself knew well that the prime minister wanted him to initiate a judicial inquiry, rather than bring about a ministerial decision in Lavon's favor and then kill him politically. Eshkol moved away from Ben-Gurion, Dayan, and Peres, and established himself as the recognized leader of Mapai's emerging collective leadership, against the decline of Ben-Gurion and "the young." Eshkol developed growing ties with Achdut Ha'Avoda to balance out Mapai's alienated defense elite, whereas Dayan and Peres became totally identified with Ben-Gurion even though their approach to the Arab-Israeli conflict was very different. Both Dayan and Peres mobilized all possible support during the affair and were ready to end Mapai's boycott of the far right Herut party in their bid for help.

The significance of the affair in broader areas of public life in Israel cannot be exaggerated. The intelligentsia and broad sections of the established Israeli political body were alienated from Ben-Gurion.[56] Differences between Ben-Gurion's state methods and neo-socialist expectations, cleavages between young and old, the moderates' fear of Dayan and Peres, the imperfection of compromise solutions in an acute crisis atmosphere, the latent rejection of Ben-Gurion's secretive decision making and his formal use of majority decisions—all were blurred into the affair itself and were symbolized in the question of whether the cabinet majority decision that cleared Lavon should be declared invalid, and by whom. Israel did not possess a higher authority than the cabinet, which reflected parliamentary majority. It had not enacted a constitution and never reserved a standing for the courts in such disputes unless the attorney general, a cabinet officer, decided to bring the case before a court. In highly sensitive political matters, the attorney's decision would be influenced by political considerations.

Ben-Gurion had operated within this framework but now he refused to accept its "democratic" cabinet majority ruling. He wanted a "judicial procedure" to inquire into the case that seemed to have been resolved. Thus he was aiming at new procedures, rejecting a majority decision that did not suit him; he was aiming at Lavon and established procedures at the same time. Ben-Gurion's "judicial inquiry" was a pretext to deprive the cabinet of its majority ruling right. He used to do this often in the past, but this time he was exposed, being too tired to devise a more clever pretext and too much involved in supporting his dangerous lieutenants, as many Israeli intellectual liberals and neo-socialists thought.

Ben-Gurion hurled arguments of principles, law, and morality at Lavon's following, while ignoring the cabinet that had cleared Lavon. He declined collective responsibility—his own tool in ruling the cabinet—and thus seemed to be acting unfairly, dishonestly, and out of sheer quarrelsomeness or to be using irrelevant arguments to advance Dayan and Peres's interests. Both of them encouraged Ben-Gurion's wrath and became totally identified with him, although he differed from both in method and in substance with regard to defense and foreign affairs.

Ben-Gurion's persecution of his rival seemed to be contrary to other basic principles of his regime. He was always deeply concerned with social and cultural matters, with creating the new Jew. He had tried, unsuccessfully, to separate religion and state. He tried to create new moral and social patterns based on manual labor, the settlement of the country, and the absorption of massive immigration. The visions of the prophets and the Bible were a sort of spiritual guide, and he frequently referred to the Jews using the Biblical term, the "chosen people." Ben-Gurion wanted to change the ghetto characteristic of Diaspora Jewry and create a moral, sovereign Jew. The proud, working Jew with a universal social message, who had created such enterprises worthy of emulation as the kibbutz and the moshav (a smallholders' cooperative center), the image of Israel as just society—none of this fit in with the way he was treating Lavon.

In any case, a debate on Ben-Gurion's demand for a judicial inquiry was averted and he let up his attack for a while after Lavon was removed from the Histadrut. Yet Ben-Gurion was alienated from his party comrades and the opposition voiced by the press and the intelligentsia. Of course, he never could or would explain his methods in full. He could hardly say that defense was not always a subject for compromise and majority decision in cabinet, parliament, or the party institutions, or that the majority was sometimes "unqualified" in this field. Nor could he say that the "masses," even if they included intellectuals and a tame press, must not be allowed unqualified influence in these areas. He kept talking in symbols relating to the affair itself, implying that there was a basic flaw in political investigation of criminal acts committed when an incompetent served as defense minister.

The rift between the formerly accepted leader and his closest colleagues, parts of the intelligentsia and the media, and the confusion into which the public was thrown by Ben-Gurion's attacks on Lavon and the Mapai leadership helped bring about the final break in the old conformity on foreign and defense policy. Ben-Gurion had been fighting to keep these areas from becoming subject to debate in the formal political institutions and to the factional and personal considerations such debate involved. His campaign had just the opposite effect. To defend themselves, Lavon and the bargainers sought even more support of the majority in the cabinet, parliament, the party, the press, and the public. These factors were thus brought into the center of the political process and debate. No longer was the public's support of the leadership almost automatic. The public could be ignored only with difficulty, and the old methods of keeping it ignorant of many matters had to cease. Moreover, as a result of the internal rift in Mapai, the relative power of its coalition partners grew considerably. Ben-Gurion had to rely on Eshkol to round up his new Achdut Ha'Avoda-NRP-Mapai coalition. Ben-Gurion's grip on his junior partners weakened and the party followed Eshkol, the bargainer who seemingly brought about a reasonable compromise—Lavon's public death and personal clearance. Yet the prime minister had decided to reopen Lavon's case, through a judicial inquiry, and thus re-establish his authority while discrediting cabinet majority inquiries. At the same time he realized that the secondary leadership, afraid of Dayan and Peres, was capable of cooperating with other parties on cabinet level, against his foreign policy targets of Germany and the nuclear issue.

BEN-GURION'S FOREIGN AND DEFENSE POLICY, 1960–63

Ben-Gurion remained in office from 1960, when Lavon revived the "affair," until 1963. His resignation stemmed not only from his desire to revive the Lavon Affair but from spiritual and physical weariness combined with worrying developments in three areas: Israeli-German relations, internal changes in the Arab world, and Israel's nuclear option.

This weariness, however, did not mean the end of Ben-Gurion's political career. At 77, he felt in the minority in his own party and cabinet with regard to the "affair" and several defense issues, and he might have considered the establishment of a new power instrument for the 1965 general elections.

In the early 1960s, Israel received more military aid from the United States.[57] Israel's growing role in advancing economic, military, and political support to the nonmuslim peripheral states in the Middle East (Iran and Turkey) and Africa (Ethiopia and several new nations in black Africa), together with its passive support of Jordan and Lebanon during the 1958 events made it more acceptable to the Eisenhower administration. An American secret promise that was given at the time by Eisenhower to Ben-Gurion, that the United States "will not permit Israel's destruction," may also be interpreted as an effort to calm down Israeli anxieties. No binding commitments were made, however. As Egypt grew stronger with Soviet help, Washington, in 1962, began to help Israel directly by supplying it with defensive weapons and indirectly by allowing a deal with West Germany. Bonn was asked to supply Israel with offensive arms (mainly U.S.-made tanks), since Washington wished to avoid supplying Israel directly with such weapons. Chancellor Adenauer agreed to this deal, which was not to be made public, thus responding in other ways to Israel's attempts to establish full diplomatic relations, which he had declined for fear that the Arabs would retaliate by recognizing East Germany.[58]

Also in the early 1960s, German and Austrian scientists were in Egypt working on the development of a surface-to-surface missle and a fighter jet. Some of the heads of the Israeli security community, especially the chief of intelligence, Isser Harel, were deeply worried by this. Israeli politicians, particularly Foreign Minister Meir, tended to regard the German question as a moral issue and Bonn-Jerusalem relations as based on a German debt to the Jewish people and their state. They were, therefore, inclined to demand that the Bonn government take steps to get the German scientists out of Egypt. Bonn's sensitivity toward a possible Arab reaction brought about an initiative by Harel to launch a campaign of terror against the scientists in Egypt and Europe. Ben-Gurion and Peres, however, were more concerned about the arms deal than about the scientists. Ben-Gurion was afraid that the antiscientist campaign would wreck the deal and was surprised by the extent of Harel's widespread actions. Peres and he brought about Harel's resignation from office and put a stop to the terrorism against the scientists.[59] Under Ludwig Erhard the arms deal was ended in 1965, when word of it leaked out.

Foreign Minister Meir had meanwhile entered into cooperative action with the radical right-wing Herut faction in parliament in order to condemn Bonn's sins of omission and commission in the matter of the scientists. Besides, as a foreign minister, Mrs. Meir was excluded from Israeli-German (and Israeli-French) affairs. This used to be Mr. Peres' domain. Ben-Gurion had always been willing to establish relations with any foreign state as long as it was in Israel's economic and political interest. He thus must have seen this step, taken behind his back, as an instance of ghetto moralism. He had nothing against moralism so long as it served foreign policy and did not replace it, but Mrs. Meir's step did not serve foreign policy in his view. The German issue simply gave him another grievance against his old party comrades. American-Israeli relations, with regard to new Middle East initiatives and mainly the nuclear issue, became also a source for disputes and cleavages on party and coalition levels.

According to Ben-Gurion's biographer, Michael Bar-Zohar, the development of Israel's nuclear facility at Dimona until Ben-Gurion's sudden resignation in 1963, was as follows.[60] Until May, 1960, France continued to supply, in complete secrecy, the needed components to complete construction of the reactor in about two years. Yet on May 14, several months after the ousting of Israel's most ardent supporter in de Gaulle's cabinet—M. Jacques Soustelle, who happened to be minister of science and atomic energy—France's foreign minister, M. Couve de Murville, summoned the Israeli ambassador and advised him that Paris would not supply Israel with uranium for the Dimona facility. France demanded that Israel make its nuclear effort public and open the Dimona facility to foreign, possibly international, inspection.

Ben-Gurion decided to go to France and speak personally with General de Gaulle. The visit (to which the prime minister refrained from inviting his foreign minister, Mrs. Meir, to accompany him), in which Mr. Peres played a significant role, took place in June, 1960. Ben-Gurion reiterated to the French leader his traditional fears that the Arabs, and especially Egypt, were engaged in a nationalistic bid for power, unification, and radicalization. They might be tempted to attack a weak Israel—a symbol of their past humiliation and an easy diversion from domestic problems—if Israel lost its deterrent power. Deterrance meant, under the circumstances, better weapons. Israel, contrary to the victorious image that he more than anyone had created, was not unbeatable, especially if the enemy could attain air superiority and prevent mobilization through mass bombing. Paradoxically, here Ben-Gurion faced one of the outcomes of his own "active centrism." He had created in the Arab world the image of an arrogant, perhaps expansionist, leader trying to encircle them peripherally after occupying part of their heartland. On the other hand, France regarded Israel as so strong that de Gaulle could not figure out what Israel was aiming at. Ben-Gurion suggested an "Israeli solution" to the Algerian question—a large transfer of French Algerians to the empty Sahara—maintaining that "people may create geographic facts as geographic facts may create people," and adding to it the key sentence, "history taught me two things: . . . Free nations will never again agree to foreign rule; [and] . . . basic, final facts influence history much more than empty declarations." The general then understood that Israel did not want more space, as he had feared, and would not, if given weapons, disturb the delicate balance created in the region after 1956. On the subject of Dimona, Ben-Gurion told the general that Israel did not intend to separate its plutonium to build bombs. De Gaulle agreed to a compromise: France would supply the remaining reactor parts, Israel would continue constructing by itself, France would not demand foreign inspection, and Ben-Gurion would make the reactor construction public and would disclose peaceful research programs for it.

The French must have informed the United States about Dimona, for two U-2 spy planes were sent to photograph the facility, which at that time was disguised as a textile plant. American press disclosures, French public denials, and a public warning by Nasser that he would mobilize "millions of soldiers" to destroy Israel's nuclear capability brought about a public statement by Ben-Gurion in late 1960, in which he admitted construction of a "research reactor," stressing its peaceful character. Yet in January, 1961, the United States submitted to him five questions: (1) What are Israel's intentions with regard to the Dimona plutonium? (2) Is Israel ready to safeguard the plutonium, for instance with foreign inspections? (3) Is Israel building or planning another reactor? (4) Is Israel ready to allow scientists, either from the International Atomic Energy Agency (IAEA) or other friendly bodies, to visit Dimona? If so, when? (5) Could Israel definitely state its intentions to refrain from producing nuclear weapons?

Ben-Gurion refused any international safeguards but promised to allow American inspection visits, although not immediately, because the Israeli public was angry at American leakages and public pressures. He repeated his public promise of the reactor's peaceful character and denied any construction of another reactor. In the meantime, the Kennedy administration took over. It combined a renewed effort to find a common language with President Nasser with an effort to solve the Palestinian refugee question.[61] The nuclear issue was raised again by the new administration, and in May, 1961, Ben-Gurion went to the United States to meet the president. Kennedy failed to impress the 76-year-old leader; he seemed to Ben-Gurion to be a "politician," a bargainer who might make stupid concessions on Israel's account as a result of naïveté and hopes for short-range successes. Indeed, later in 1961 when Egypt's union with Syria failed, while the Soviet supported Syria's bid for independence, the president and Nasser embarked upon better relations. The United States then tried to negotiate, through Dr. Joseph Johnson, an American U.N. official,[62] a solution to the refugee problem, even in the absence of peace. He said that the refugees should be given the freedom of choice between returning to Israel and integration in Arab countries, and that most of them would probably choose to stay in Arab countries. Arab official attitudes, including the permanent threat to destroy Israel, were not serious.

For Ben-Gurion, the basic questions, besides Arab military effort, which had grown constantly since 1956 with Soviet aid, were Arab official attitudes and declared policies. The Arabs, he informed the United States in mid-1962, should stop their rejection of Israel, that is, abandon their will to destroy it. This meant a peace agreement, with Arab readiness to absorb most of the refugees. The United States suggested in January, 1963, a new plan to solve the refugee problem. Israel would absorb 10% of the refugees and the Arab states would integrate the rest. Negotiations to this effect would take place between the United States and Israel, because the Arabs refused any contacts with Israel, with the United States giving Israel a security guarantee. The plan would be carried out in phases over ten years. Ben-Gurion, as did many Israeli statesmen after him, argued that the United States might not adhere in the future, under a new president, to the guarantees suggested by Kennedy. Only a NATO-type treaty would be useful, he added, having developed suspicions toward Kennedy's "naïve experiment" with Arab good will. Moreover, since Eisenhower's second office, Ben-Gurion had become more and more skeptical toward the United States. He feared that Washington might have become too passive in its relations with the Soviets, and regarded Kennedy's experiments with Nasser as a possible manifestation of a poor analytical capability of international realities in general.[63] As long as they were not officially a party to Kennedy's plan, the Arabs would remain free, in ten years, to keep the conflict open, while Israel would retain the 100,000 hostile Palestinians. The Arab states rejected this refugee plan altogether. Kennedy agreed to supply Israel with air defense missiles and made a declaration of American support of Israel's security.[64]

In early 1963, the Ba'ath party came to power in Syria and Iraq, and on April 18, 1963, Egypt concluded an agreement to establish a federation with the two new radical nationalist regimes. One week later Ben-Gurion wrote an appeal to President Kennedy.[65] He declared that the new federation posed a severe threat to Israel's security and he quoted the treaty in which the signatories proclaimed their intention of establishing a "military alliance that will be able to free the Arab homeland from the Zionist danger and imperialism." He stressed his fear that as the Soviets helped strengthen the Arabs, Israel might lose its ability to deter an attack. The result would be a war that Israel would win, but only with heavy losses. As always, casualties were a major consideration in Ben-Gurion's assessment of a war. In his letter Ben-Gurion also insisted that the United States and the Soviet Union deny aid to countries refusing to recognize their neighbors or maintaining a state of war against them. He also suggested a secret meeting with the president to discuss the issue, but sent similar urgent letters to de Gaulle, the British, and half a dozen other world leaders.

Israeli diplomats in the three capitals recall that the British, French, and Americans were astonished by Ben-Gurion's forebodings. Given the conflicts of interest among the Egyptian, Iraqi, and Syrian regimes, it hardly seemed likely that anything would come of the tripartite federation agreement. Ben-Gurion's colleagues, however, maintain that his vision of Israel's future was apocalyptic. He seems to have become more and more convinced that Israel faced a long and increasingly dangerous struggle with the Arabs as countries traditionally hostile to each other, such as Egypt, Syria, and Iraq, joined forces under the banner of radical socialist Arab nationalism. At the same time, he might have tried to divert Kennedy's attention from Dimona to the Arab Federation or to justify Dimona in that way.

In his reply to Ben-Gurion's letter, on May 5, 1963, Kennedy defined some of the fundamental aspects of the American approach to the Arab-Israeli conflict. First, Israel's existence was important to the United States, but there seemed to be no immediate cause for alarm. Washington distinguished between official Arab ideology and Arab actions, and the federation did not yet represent a real challenge to Israel or America. Second, Soviet influence in the region, particularly through its support of radical Arab regimes, was indeed a destablizing factor. Israel, however, should not do anything that might bolster the Soviet Union's presence and influence. Joint American-Soviet guarantees would imply Washington's recognition of Moscow's position in the region. Third, the United States strongly opposed "a mutual race in developing weapons . . . in a way that endangers the safety of the area." Fourth, improved American-Arab relations were good for Israel too, since an improvement would "basically strengthen . . . our influence on Arab leaders." Kennedy rejected Ben-Gurion's request for a meeting and reiterated his demand for American or international control of the Dimona reactor. In 1961, Ben-Gurion allowed one visit by American experts to Dimona, but refused to grant regular inspection rights. In May, 1963, Ben-Gurion received a strong letter from Kennedy demanding more American visits to ascertain the true nature of the Dimona reactor. Golda Meir and Pinhas Sapir were extremely afraid of a major showdown with the United States. The finance minister, Mr. Eshkol, maintained that Israel could not go on financing the giant project. Ben-Gurion approached resourceful Jews all over the world, who granted regular donations for Dimona. Yet the coalition situation—the combination of Meir, Sapir, and Achdut Ha'Avoda ministers, who opposed the nuclear project altogether—forced Ben-Gurion, or so it seemed, to accept one American inspection visit annually.[66] A couple of weeks later, on June 16, 1963, soon after the Ben-Gurion/Kennedy exchange of letters about the Egyptian-Syrian-Iraqi federation and the nuclear issue, the prime minister realized that he had lost his grip on his party in substantive foreign and defense affairs and that he was in a minority in his coalition. He resigned calmly, as if his time had come, and recommended Levi Eshkol to succeed him as both prime minister and minister of defense. Dayan and Peres remained in the government as minister of agriculture and deputy minister of defense, respectively. Mapai's secondary leadership, led by Mr. Eshkol, Mr. Sapir, Mrs. Meir, and Mr. Aran, became Mapai's collective leadership. The "young" remained a minority in their party and on the coalition level.

THE ESHKOL GOVERNMENT AND
ITS FOREIGN AND DEFENSE POLICY, 1963-66

The government passed, apparently with Ben-Gurion's blessing, into the hands of the collective leadership headed by Mr. Eshkol. Mapai's coalition partners were the religious, moderate NRP, a fixture in Israel's cabinets, the independent liberals, and the nationalist leftist Achdut Ha'Avoda, led by Yigal Allon and Israel Galili. Later Mapam, the leftist kibbutz movement that had left the government because of Ben-Gurion's role in the "Affair," joined Eshkol's coalition. There began a period of adjustment in the internal structures of Israeli politics to the institutions of governance and decision making. In other words, the actual importance and influence of Mapai's coalition partners increased greatly in direct proportion to their parliamentary power. Eshkol needed his partners and was willing to pay a higher price for their collaboration than Ben-Gurion had.

The former prime minister was partly responsible for this development. Immediately after resigning, he once again demanded a judicial inquiry into the Lavon Affair and attacked the Mapai leadership, and later Mapai as a whole. He claimed publicly that his successor, who in 1960 had acted both to clear Lavon and to destroy his political career, had acted improperly in doing so. Ben-Gurion, therefore, doubted whether Eshkol and his colleagues were fit to manage the affairs of state. In fact, some sort of a vicious circle emerged in elite politics during 1964. Eshkol was determined to consolidate a new power base, in the party and on coalition level, against Mapai's "young"—Dayan and Peres. An alignment with Achdut Ha'Avoda, traditionally feared by Ben-Gurion and aimed at isolating Dayan and Peres, was pursued by Eshkol. Achdut Ha'Avoda itself, led by Yigal Allon and Israel Galili—both more or less of the same generation as Mapai's "young"—maneuvered toward Eshkol cleverly and slowly. It did not want to merge with Mapai and lose its identity and influence against the vast majority; the small, compact, nationalist leftist party was interested in a deal. Achdut Ha'Avoda wanted a shared access to power, based on an agreement to guarantee its autonomous status in an alignment that would suggest one party to the electorate yet would retain Achdut Ha'Avoda's relative strength in the alignment after the elections. Mapai's coalition partners would not agree to any change in the absolute proportional ballot system, so Eshkol dropped what had been a central issue in Ben-Gurion's days from the party's agenda. Eshkol was, furthermore, determined to end the extreme polemic and sharp personal style of Ben-Gurion's period. He made several gestures toward former political enemies, such as Begin's Herut, who had been banned by Ben-Gurion. Last, but not least, the prime minister tried to respond to the pressure of a group assembled behind Lavon to incorporate them back into the party. Most of them were intellectuals who had resented Ben-Gurion's style and came to regard Lavon's persecution as a symbol of authoritarianism.

This was too much for Ben-Gurion. His concepts of power, his compact and loyal power base, grew autonomous and, in his eyes, forced him out of office on issues of substance (Germany and the nuclear issue) and form. The new leadership was drifting toward Achdut Ha'Avoda, whose leaders, mainly Mr. Allon, were strongly opposed to a nuclear deterrent, yet who were thinking in terms of territorial-conventional safeguards and who were ready to go alone, under certain circumstances, to counter Arab threats. Moreover, Eshkol proved to be a "compromiser" —toward Lavon, whose dismissal he, Eshkol himself, had engineered in the party's governing bodies, and even toward Herut. Ben-Gurion believed that politics, when it came to crucial choices, could not be a compromise. Thus Lavon's rehabilitation acted as a test case for the new leadership, and a judicial inquiry into the 1954 affair was even more pressing. Ben-Gurion carried his case to the party's governing bodies, which were controlled by Eshkol and the old party machinery. Public opinion was firmly against the revival of the affair, whose details still remained officially secret. Ben-Gurion's fight seemed to be a simple bid to discredit a popular, easy-going politician, who had, at last, freed Israel from the long reign of a dominant father. Eshkol decided to prevent an inquiry that might, indeed, being "judicial," prove the cabinet's treatment of Lavon's too hasty and procedurally weak. In such a case Lavon might lose his rehabilitation. Ben-Gurion might be proved right at the time and ever since, and Eshkol's own compromise on the issue might be proved wrong. Neither Eshkol nor the whole secondary leadership was ready for that. They took the power the way they usually did things, on a bargaining, compromise basis, and they succeeded, using Ben-Gurion's own methods (threats to resign, actual resignation, and quick formations of stronger government coalitions) to mobilize party support after a crisis atmosphere and an either/or choice.

In October, 1964, Ben-Gurion submitted to the minister of justice a documented inquiry into the Lavon Affair, conducted after Lavon's dismissal by several researchers and lawyers. The bulk of the evidence related to the 1960 cabinet inquiry, which was sharply criticized by Ben-Gurion's lawyers. Endorsing a judicial opinion by the attorney general, Eshkol's minister of justice suggested a new inquiry into the affair, which, ipso facto, might have brought about the collapse of the cabinet inquiry of 1960. Eshkol seemed to agree, but at the last moment he resigned. This brought about a party endorsement of his regime in general, and he refused to deal with the affair in his new cabinet.

In February, 1965, the "affair" was brought to the party's convention, controlled by the secondary leadership, which was in direct power over the party and the state. Ben-Gurion was publicly criticized by Eshkol, Sharett, and Meir, who rejected his political style and related it to the inquiry into the "affair." Meir publicly criticized Ben-Gurion's tendency to make secret decisions on sensitive issues during his last seven years in office, particularly in contrast to his previous apparent willingness to discuss crucial choices with his colleagues. Yet she forgot that most of these choices had been acceptable to her, or at least that she had not protested against them. She, rather than Ben-Gurion, became more independent and politically ripe to have her own way, which was more simplistic, emotional, and hard-line vis-à-vis the Arabs and Germany than Ben-Gurion's, and also more American-bound. Eshkol, too, was determined to try his compromise methods with Arabs and Americans alike, instinctively deploring Ben-Gurion's clear choices and his no-bargaining method, as reflected by his handling of the "affair" as "nonpolitical." Ben-Gurion was forced to choose between accepting the new method passively and a new effort to enforce his old authority and method alike.

In June, 1965, Ben-Gurion resigned from Mapai and created a new political party—Rafi (Israel's Workers List). Shimon Peres resigned from Mapai to head the new body, and Moshe Dayan, who shortly before had resigned from Eshkol's cabinet, joined later. Both preferred to stay within Israel's center of power and build an internal, "young," "state-oriented" (rather than socialist) opposition to the middle-aged bargainers and moderates (with the exception of Meir) around Eshkol. Yet Ben-

Gurion's decision forced them to follow him, along with several other "young" and "etatists" who could not hope to retain any influence in a Mapai-Achdut Ha'Avoda alignment. Peres (rather than Dayan, who delayed his decision until the last moment) followed Ben-Gurion because of personal loyalty. He lacked Dayan's political substance, which in turn was different from Ben-Gurion's. The whole new body seemed to be a conglomerate of former establishmentarians, who tried to portray themselves as a new leadership, led by the oldest political veteran in the country. Etatistic slogans (devised by Peres) and welfare state principles were proclaimed by a new body lacking financial resources or any influence on the mother party's instruments of power—the unions, their economic enterprises, the state budget and its priorities, imported money, and Mapai's control over state institutions.

Ben-Gurion had some hopes that his cause, his old regiment, and his method might be followed by enough voters to create a blocking minority of about twenty to twenty-five seats in the Knesset, to prevent any coalitionary arrangement without Rafi. Peres and his aides, frantically putting together a party in the last moment before the elections, were pessimistic from the beginning. They were sorry for having been forced out of Mapai, the real power base, which would explain their ability and desire to join it again later. Yet the structure of Rafi and its campaigning against Mapai were of the utmost importance to Israel's domestic atmosphere and foreign policy, in the most devastating manner to Ben-Gurion's own principles. A political grouping of mostly Israeli-born former members of Mapai's executive establishment, Rafi, first led by Ben-Gurion and then by Dayan and Peres, became a legitimate instrument of opposition in foreign affairs and defense matters. This role was reserved for Achdut Ha'Avoda and Herut, the banned and irrelevant extreme right-wing opposition that used Begin's legalistic and ideological terms against the successful pragmatic fundamentalism Ben-Gurion pursued with Mapai. When Mapai preferred pragmatism over fundamentalism and open democratic bargaining over Ben-Gurion's autocratic methods, it gained even more popularity over Rafi's acceptance of the old regime. When it accepted Achdut Ha'Avoda as its defense-political semi-independent adviser, Mapai replaced Ben-Gurion's defense postures with those of Allon and Galili. It opened itself up to a double attack by Ben-Gurion, who feared Achdut Ha'Avoda, and by Dayan, who pushed even further than Allon and Galili on foreign policy and defense issues and principles. This double attack by established defense experts would play a growing role in Mapai's own foreign and defense policy and would, at the end of the process, give Dayan, rather than Ben-Gurion, an instrument of power to pursue his own policy in the conflict.

In the 1965 campaign Rafi's attacks on Mapai centered around three main issues.[67] The first was Mapai's handling of the Affair; it was, according to Rafi, compromising, political, illegal, and unfitting for a state. The second accusation was that Mapai was so concerned with hanging on to power that it was making Israel's economy and society subject to political dealing and horse trading, and it was not taking the state's "real" needs into account. The third line of attack was Rafi's claim that Mapai was led by people incapable of handling foreign and security problems properly.

Mapai was thus pressed to agree with Achdut Ha'Avoda to go ahead with the above-mentioned joint list (the alignment) in the forthcoming elections. Eshkol and his comrades moved clearly toward the nationalist left, which had long opposed Ben-Gurion and his activist centrism. The political hostility between Achdut Ha'Avoda and Rafi was reinforced by the personal rivalry between their respective defense experts, particularly Allon, and Dayan. This personal hostility became inextricably entwined with the political differences between the groups.

The Eshkol cabinet, increasingly dependent for its survival on the smaller parties, tended quite naturally to become a collegial body. More and more influence accrued to each minister and to his party. The prime minister became more like the *primus inter pares* that the formal political structure would led one to expect. This trend, which suited Eshkol's compromising and easy-going personality, combined with the greater importance that the elite now attached to the mass media and public opinion. The Eshkol leadership needed and used them in its struggle against Ben-Gurion, just as Ben-Gurion himself had tried to do during the controversy over the Lavon Affair. Yet Ben-Gurion, at his peak, had kept tight control of the state radio, had prevented the introduction of television to Israel altogether, and had scorned the independent press. Eshkol, characteristically, decided to set up a largely independent broadcasting authority. Later, he and Galili sponsored the introduction of television. His government regarded the printed media very seriously and would leak them information or seek out their views on political issues.

Part of the intelligentsia and the public greeted these changes as evidence of democratization. Rafi considered them evidence of the weakening of the regime, detracting from the centralism and supremacy of the state that Ben-Gurion had managed to create despite its formal structure. In any case, in the future the elite would not be able to ignore the arguments of the press and the public's mood of dissatisfaction, particularly in the new security situation that would emerge. In his search for support against his formidable predecessor, Eshkol thus unleashed forces that Ben-Gurion had tried to ignore or had exploited while ignoring their opinions. The new prime minister, however, did not try to ignore these forces; his regime accepted them and tried to respond to their opinions. At the same time, the Israeli right and center, the liberals and Herut faced with the Mapai-Achdut Ha'Avoda alignment, agreed to join forces in order to create their own political federation—the Gahal bloc. Thus, Herut finally succeeded in a long process that began in the mid-1950s. It moved slowly out of its total isolation and managed to suggest a relatively moderate image to nonsocialist voters. It kept its promise, as an established opposition, to protest voters. It played down its tradition foreign policy, the claim to the whole of Eretz-Israel, which now seemed to be irrelevant. Yet Herut never totally gave up this claim. It waited in the background, and then became relevant indeed when Mr. Begin became politically relevant and joined forces with others who shared his approach to territory outside Israel's ADL. The creation of Gahal was a step in this direction, as Herut was delivered by Mr. Eshkol of its status as a political pariah.

THE ESHKOL CABINET DEFENSE POLICY, 1963–67

Since its inception, the Eshkol government was faced with a number of major foreign and defense policy problems. Upon assuming power it inherited the unresolved issue of the nuclear option, with all the implications it had for American-Israeli relations. There is no primary written material available about Eshkol's response to American pressure to accept regular inspection in Dimona. Oral testimony and secondary sources indicate that in the second half of 1963 the Eshkol cabinet decided to prolong the process of nuclear development and to opt instead for American aid to strengthen Israel's conventional forces and shore up the political status quo. The United States made a stronger commitment to the status quo, albeit not publicly. In 1964, moreover, it undertook to supply Israel with Skyhawk attack aircraft, and President Johnson supported in public the territorial integrity and political independence of all Middle East countries. Eshkol managed to be officially invited to Washington as the president's guest, and in their joint communiqué both emphasized "the firm opposition of the U.S. to aggression and the use of force or the threat of force against any country."[68]

Was it a basic change in American policy toward Israel and the whole region, or was it a deal? Undoubtedly, the arms supplies were linked to an American bid to supply arms to Jordan, which emerged more and more isolated in a radicalized Arab world while Britain played no role there after the 1958 events. Arms also figured in Egypt's involvement in Yemen, with Soviet support, which endangered Saudi-Arabia, and with the pro-Soviet stand of the Syrian regime. But it seems, according to my research, that Eshkol, indeed, made a deal with Washington on the nuclear issue in exchange for American political concessions and conventional arms supplies. Though no formal connection was made, it appears that the Israeli part of the bargain involved an undertaking to allow some kind of inspection at Dimona. The American inspection of the Dimona reactor was permitted on an *ad hoc* basis; no long-term arrangements were made. The relevant documents concerning the status quo, the fighters, and the reactor were separated and exchanged with a lag of a day or two between them.[69]

More circumstantial evidence in support of this scenario is provided by the Israeli government's decision in the second half of 1963 not to go ahead with the development of a delivery system, the Jericho missile, capable of carrying a nuclear warhead. The order for the development of the system was given to Dassault in France, apparently over the protests of some of the heads of Israeli security, who wanted the work done at home.[70]

The available documents provide no proof of Michael Brecher's contention that in 1963 "a written assurance from Kennedy to Eshkol contained a virtual guarantee of Israel's territorial integrity" in exchange for Israel's giving up the nuclear option, as one may deduce. It seems that, in return for permitting some American inspection of the Dimona reactor, Israel received from the United States a commitment to maintain the status quo that would be the basis for later Israeli claims on Washington. Eshkol would thus acquire better leverage for later bargaining with the United States. The alleged secret American commitment, however, was not a treaty or even an executive agreement,[71] and it did not specify any *casus belli* accepted by both Jerusalem and Washington. For the defense establishment under the newly appointed chief of staff, Major General Yitzhak Rabin, and Eshkol's Achdut Ha'Avoda partners, this may have meant the adoption of the conventional first strike doctrine in a case of direct threats to Israel's security or strategic changes in the neighboring countries that might endanger it, or in the case of Israel's loosing it deterrence power due to the Arab violation of agreed norms and *casus belli*. Such an approach differed widely from Ben-Gurion's tradition and was not necessarily adopted by Eshkol or the whole cabinet. On the face of it, the Eshkol-Kennedy agreements and subsequent understandings with the Johnson administration indicated that Israel was moving toward cooperation with the United States and away from attempts to realize its nuclear option, while also trying to preserve a special relationship with France.

However, as de Gaulle developed his grand strategy in the early 1960s, certain developments bodied ill for Franco-Israeli relations. The Algerian problem was resolved by Algerian independence. France could thus enter into cooperation with Algeria, the other Maghreb states, and the whole

Arab world, to Paris's economic and political benefit. France developed an independent foreign policy as a great power with nuclear weapons of its own, without the collaboration of the European Atomic Community (Euratom). After the Suez War, de Gaulle's predecessors had concluded that France needed an alternative to Middle Eastern oil, and so it wanted to hold on to Algeria and its petroleum and to cooperate with other Western European states to develop an alternative energy supply. These conclusions were no longer valid once the main impediment to improved Franco-Arab relations, the French presence in Algeria, was removed. France could thus do what de Gaulle in any case preferred—develop an independent nuclear potential while making sure of the supply of petroleum from the Middle East. Further difficulties for Franco-Israeli relations would stem from the growing differences between Paris and Washington and the concomitant rapprochement between Paris and Moscow.

Changes in Jerusalem's relations with its ally of the Suez war were thus inevitable, especially when de Gaulle was no longer convinced as he had been under Ben-Gurion, that Israel's stance was defensive and that Jerusalem would remain very careful not to contribute to a crisis in the Middle-East. The differences between the two countries were made all the more dramatic when they burst into the open in the crisis atmosphere that preceded the June, 1967, war. The final break, however, was anticipated by a serious incident in October, 1965: the kidnapping of the Moroccan opposition leader, Mehdi Ben Barka, in France by the Moroccan security services with what appeared as some kind of collaboration with the Israeli secret service. De Gaulle ordered an investigation. The findings were that there was a high level of cooperation that the general had been trying to regulate and control since 1960 between the French and Israeli security establishments. He ordered a sharp cutback in these joint efforts. The French did continue to work on the Jericho missile, or as they called it, MD-660 (MD for Marcel Dassault). The Israeli were, after all, providing funds for the project and the French themselves were benefiting.

The Ben Barka Affair and the damage it did to the Franco-Israeli cooperation provided Rafi with ammunition for the then-current election campaign. The Eshkol government could be attacked for incompetence in the foreign and security sector on a concrete, though very sensitive, issue. Rafi also attacked the government obliquely for having given in to the United States on the nuclear inspection issue.[72] Formally, Eshkol did not "give in," but retained an option—a reduced nuclear research program that could bring about a nuclear capability in the future if such a decision were made. Ben-Gurion's deterrent fell victim to the objection of the majority in his own cabinet in 1963, when Mr. Allon—Achdut Ha'Avoda strategist and military thinker—advanced a large number of arguments against nuclear deterrence and convinced many Mapai ministers, who had their own doubts about it and resented Peres's independence and secretive methods in dealing with the issue. They did not block Dimona altogether, but pressed Ben-Gurion to accept American inspection, to which he reluctantly agreed as described above, then resigned immediately afterward.

It seemed to Ben-Gurion that a year later Eshkol's coalition adopted Allon's strategic concepts without knowing it.[73] They probably accepted his basic arguments against the viability of nuclear deterrents in the Middle East and opted for a large conventional effort that might have been the same. Allon argued, in public and mainly in private, against nuclear deterrence in the following terms: (A) Arab challenges to Israel could be, and should be, deterred by conventional methods because of their strategic and political flexibility (B) Nuclear deterrence is rigid, an "either/or" choice that might neutralize itself if the other side chose to ignore it. In other words, the credibility of nuclear deterrents is doubtful and the freedom of action of the enemy is, therefore, higher—not smaller —if one's strategy is based mainly on nuclear threats. (C) The political price that Israel would have to pay for becoming a nuclear power would be enormous. The great powers might even mount a "gun boat" diplomacy to dismantle Israel's nuclear facilities. (D) If Israel introduced nuclear weapons into the region, the Arabs might be pushed to a crash program of their own to acquire nuclear weapons. Israel would thus loose its relative advantage and freedom of action against conventional threats or "salami tactics" against its vulnerable borders. (E) Israel's conventional potential was not mobilized yet. A strong Israel, conventionally, might deter the enemy long enough or hit him sure enough, whenever it was needed, without taking the risks involved in a nuclearized environment. Yet a nuclear option—a reduced research effort—might be maintained and advanced if the Arabs chose to become a nuclear power.

This indeed was one, maybe the only, substantial difference between Dayan and Mapai's "young," and Allon. It remained until much later. Allon clearly moved from his early underground days toward the center and adopted some of Ben-Gurion's principles with regard to ruling Arabs and understanding the necessity to refrain from a major clash with foreign powers. Yet he, his close political friend, Galili, and Dayan shared the same approach to Israel's long, indefensible borders, to Jordanian-occupied territories in the West Bank, and to Arab challenges that should be contained in advance: accumulating power and using it, if necessary, to prevent a growing escalation on the Arab side as a result of Israel's territorial weakness. Dayan added to it a nuclear safeguard; Allon opposed it.   Ben-Gurion advocated power accumulation too, but he would not use it if many preconditions (such as foreign support, arms supplies,

and a clear-cut military political target short of ruling many Arabs)
were met. Being basically satisfied with Israel's territory, his stance was
defensive; a nuclear deterrent would suit it and maybe help convince the
Arabs that their chance to destroy Israel and get away with it was gone
altogether. Ben-Gurion therefore followed Eshkol's cabinet decisions on
the nuclear option and the conventional effort with dismay. This was not
true of Dayan and Peres, who shared Eshkol's cabinet decisions until late
in 1964 but wanted a nuclear option *and* a conventional effort too. They
followed Ben-Gurion to Rafi, then, because Mapai's leadership and Achdut
Ha'Avoda never trusted them and their influence in Eshkol's cabinet
was limited.

Another aspect of Eshkol's foreign policy at the time was his attempt
to improve relations with the Soviet Union. Eshkol tried to persuade
Moscow to moderate its position on the Middle East conflict and assume
a policy similar to the mediatory one it had adopted in the Indo-Pakistani
conflict of 1965. He also tried to convince the Soviet Union to permit
some Jewish emigration, however limited, to Israel. There was thus a
change in style in Jerusalem's approach to the Soviet Union, and, following its lead, some of the East European states moderated their public
treatment of Israel. These changes did nothing, however, to change the
Soviet Union's basic policy or to decrease its interest in the Mediterranean and the Arab world, an interest bound up with Moscow's relations
with Washington, Peking, the Third World as such, and the Arabs.[74]

The Mapai-Achdut Ha'Avoda-NRP coalition acted carefully and mod-
erately toward the Arab world at first, in a rather striking change from
the Ben-Gurion period's publicized activism. With the fading of the
threatened tripartite Arab federation, the main dangers that Israel faced
were the establishment of the Palestine Liberation Organization (PLO)
in 1964, the resumption of fedayeen attacks, by the Syrian-backed Fath,
on Israeli territory, and the direct clashes with Ba'athist Syria over the
Jordan waters.

Israel had wanted to draw water from the Jordan River to irrigate the
Negev as early as the 1950s. In the face of American-supported Syrian protests, Israel gave up the plan to take water from the Jordan and its tributaries, which were located partly in Israel, its neighbors, and demilitarized
zones along the Israel-Syrian border that Syria had claims on. The water
was drawn instead from the Sea of Galilee, which lay entirely in Israeli territory. At the 1964 Arab Summit Conference in Cairo, the Syrians claimed
that the water project would strengthen Israel greatly by allowing it to settle the Negev. They demanded the help of the other members of the Arab
coalition to divert water from the Jordan and its tributaries and deprive
Israel of the water needed for the development of the Negev. Egypt was
not particularly enthusiastic about the prospect of a confrontation with

Israel at that time; it was involved in the war in Yemen and its general arms build-up was planned as a medium-range project. Nor did Nasser consider that the Israeli water project was so serious that it required a sharp and immediate Egyptian response. Instead, the chiefs of state of the thirteen Arab League nations agreed in their summit on January 17, 1964, to establish a unified military command, and they devised a limited plan to divert the water sources flowing to Israel from Syria, Lebanon, and Jordan. The main effort was laid upon Syria itself.[75] The Eshkol government responded with sporadic, small-scale tank attacks on the Syrian diversion equipment whenever a routine border incident provided a pretext for retaliation. Given the Israeli-Syrian conflict over the status of the areas demilitarized under the terms of the 1949 GAA, there was no lack of such pretexts. When the Israelis succeeded in inflicting serious damage on the Syrian project, Damascus reacted with artillery barrages on Israel's northern settlements from the fortifications on the Golan Heights that gave it a strategic command of Galilee. Israel succeeded in disrupting the Syrian diversion project with limited and strictly controlled measures. Dayan, the former chief of staff and now Rafi's defense critic, recommended that Israel use stronger measures against Syria and other Arab partners to the water diversion project.[76] However, the government could find no solution to the continual Syrian shelling of the Galilee settlements in connection with Israeli civilian works at the demilitarized zones and the water diversion project; neither did they have any solution to the Fath terror.[77] Moreover, it regarded the takeover by the more radical Ba'athist group in Damascus in January, 1966, as a potential source of more trouble.

In the face of the Arab military build-up, a great deal was invested in Israel's air and tank forces. These developments were purposely concealed both in order to avoid stimulating some sort of response by the Arabs and the superpowers and because of the penchant for secrecy that the Israelis had developed during their underground struggle against the British. Mainly, however, Eshkol wanted to project a sort of intermediate image abroad, the image of a "poor Samson," as he put it. This course succeeded so long as the government did not face a security problem with serious domestic psychological and image ramifications. However, this was the very problem that Israel faced as its self-image began to crack under the blows of Syrian shelling and Fath terrorism. Eshkol's Israel was thus much stronger militarily than its domestic and foreign image. The incongruence between image and reality is all the more striking in view of the precedents Ben-Gurion had set in the style of foreign and security policy. Unable to put a stop to the shelling and the terrorism, the government began to look weaker and weaker. The cabinet's position and the public mood were not helped by Rafi's constant attacks on the government's general, day-to-day conduct of foreign and security affairs. The entire situation becomes paradoxical when one recalls that under Ben-Gurion, Israel was not as strong militarily as the image it projected and that actual policy was much more defensive than it seemed at first glance.

The 1965 election campaign thus saw Rafi breach the old conformity on foreign and security policy. It exploited the government's decisions on the nuclear issue and the Ben Barka Affair to make them suspect of a "major security error" and a "minor security error," although it could not state explicitly (because of the sensitivity of the issue and the military censorship) what was involved. However, the adjustment of internal structures to the formal structures of government that had begun with the Lavon Affair, Ben-Gurion's lack of public support, and Rafi's inability to suggest itself to the voter as a new, postulative leadership that would do away with Mapai's bargaining and party machinery tactics, limited Rafi's appeal down to a minority of technocrats, Ben-Gurion's own very much reduced constituency, and few "young" who could not hope for power in Mapai. In fact, the public was interested in a bargaining political framework and not in a postulative leadership. Jewish mentality returned to old, now legitimized, habits of compromise, give and take, and common gains. As always in election years, economic benefits for the whole electorate were deliberately used by Mapai to maintain loyalties and a status quo syndrome in voting behavior. The party machinery, as usualy, used power instruments such as the Histadrut and related economic institutes to finance a large-scale campaign and block Rafi's campaign. Moreover, the general security situation, which was perceived to depend more on Egyptian than Syrian or Fath policy, helped bring about the victory of the Eshkol coalition in the elections. Rafi did not win enough seats to become a blocking minority in parliament, without which no coalition would be possible, as Ben-Gurion hoped. Ben-Gurion, although still rejecting Eshkol's leadership, began to withdraw from public life. Rafi, more and more, became the party of Dayan and Peres.

THE SIX-DAY WAR: EXTERNAL AND INTERNAL CAUSES

From the time it came to power, the Eshkol government assumed that there was no danger of war for a short term. It was estimated that Egypt would take three to five years to complete Nasser's projected build-up of the armed forces. It was also thought that Nasser would not risk a war with Israel while involved in the fighting in Yemen. The armistice demarcation line with Egypt was quiet and no terrorists infiltrated Israel across it.

In the Israeli government's perception of regional relations there were four strategic changes that would be cause for worry. The first was the restoration of Egypt's blockade of the Straits of Tiran. Ben-Gurion had declared such a blockade a *casus belli* in order to deter Egypt from attempting it. Allon, the Eshkol government's leading defense spokesman, also declared it a *casus belli* and made the credibility of Israel's general deterrent capability dependent on it. This view was shared by many of the senior officers of the IDF. The chief of staff was Major General Yitzhak Rabin, an Achdut Ha'Avoda protégé, who was educated in the spirit of the national left. The chief of operations at GHQ, Brigadier General Ezer Weizman, was Rabin's deputy. Weizman was educated in the tradition of the national right.

The second of the four strategic changes was closely connected to the first: the withdrawal of United Nations Emergency Force (UNEF) from its positions along the ADL and at Sharm-el-Sheikh where it controlled the straits. Egypt was liable to bring about the United Nations forces' removal despite the General Assembly's instructions that they be stationed indefinitely. As long as UNEF was there Nasser could point to it as an obstacle to the resumption of fedayeen raids or the blockade of Eilat. If UNEF were removed the Israelis feared that Nasser could no longer justify his inaction in the face of pressure from other members of the Arab coalition.

The third strategic change was a large concentration of Egyptian troops in Sinai along the ADL. The Sinai desert, although recognized as sovereign Egyptian territory, was also a natural buffer zone between Israel and Egypt. Cairo fortified key areas along the border but did not station large forces in Sinai; troops were generally based in the populated areas of the country west of the Suez Canal. There was, therefore, no real Egyptian military presence in the Sinai desert. When troops were introduced in February, 1960, the object was to relieve Israeli pressure on the Syrian border; moreover, the troop movements were carried out in secret. Ben-Gurion ordered a secret partial mobilization,[78] and the Egyptians withdrew after a while. Ben-Gurion publicly announced his intention to go abroad, then left Israel.

The 1960 incident created a precedent for Israeli mobilization in case Egyptian forces were deployed in the Sinai. This precedent was an important one and can best be understood in terms of Israel's basic security. The IDF is a reserve army that requires advance warning to give it time to mobilize and organize. The Arabs, on the other hand, have standing armies that can be stationed along Israel's borders indefinitely and can shift from a defensive to an offensive deployment. Naturally, Israel would want to keep the Egyptian and Syrian armies, which had grown and strengthened with Soviet arms since 1956, as far away as possible. The

Egyptian army did, in fact, keep its distance on the other side of the Sinai, although Cairo had made no binding commitments for the future. Israel, meanwhile, got used to the idea of mobilizing reserves whenever Egyptian forces crossed the canal into the peninsula.

The fourth strategic factor deemed crucial by the Israelis was a total or partial, operative Arab military union. Such a development, which would permit a concerted attack on Israel from several directions, would change the situation in the region drastically. Jerusalem was particularly apprehensive about the possibility of an Arab army's being deployed in Jordan, which bordered on Israel's most heavily populated region and was so close to the Mediterranean in some places that it almost cut the country in two.

The Six-Day War broke out partly because all four of these strategic changes came about. However, the strategic and tactical steps leading to the war were preceded by a political and psychological process of great importance inside Israel.

In 1966, the newly elected Eshkol government embarked on a restrictive economic policy: the state's balance of payments situation was grave, because the standard of living was rapidly rising and the economy, as a result of election gifts, had been expanding much too quickly. Since there appeared to be little danger of war until at least 1969 or 1970, it seemed like a good time to dampen the economy. The government, however, lost control of the situation and the economy quickly slid into a serious recession. The great internal political and ideological cohesion that Ben-Gurion's activist foreign policy had helped to create had been destroyed in the early 1960s; the extreme conformity had given way to equally extreme criticalness. That situation was aggravated when the deteriorating economy combined with public grievances over Syrian shelling and Fath terrorism.

The semipublic debate about the nuclear option, which Israel had apparently exchanged for U.S. economic, military, and political aid, continued. In 1966, Jerusalem and Washington signed the first deal for the supply of offensive weapons—Skyhawks and tanks—from the United States. This replaced the deal with the Federal Republic of Germany. When the details were leaked, Bonn cancelled the deal for fear of an Arab reaction. At about the same time, Dr. E. D. Bergmann resigned as head of the Israel Atomic Energy Commission.[79] The IAEC was "civilianized" and Eshkol himself replaced Bergmann, who believed in an autonomous Israeli arms production capability. Ben-Gurion and Dayan attacked the government continually throughout that year, hinting at the abandonment of the nuclear development program. Their criticism merely fanned the fire fed by Fath raids, Syrian shelling, and the economic and psychological situation. Under these circumstances the Eshkol government began to vacillate between their moderate foreign and security policy and moods and patterns set in the past, between their fears of the public and the opposition and the changes and challenges abroad. On November 4, 1966, Syria and Egypt signed a military pact, causing alarm to Israel. Its fears of a strategic change, an alliance between Arabs, particularly radical nationalist Arab states, seemed to be coming true. On the same day the Soviet Union vetoed a U.N. Security Council resolution concerning Fath attacks in Israel by groups that had set out from Syria. The General Assembly had long been considered useless as a forum for defending Israeli interests because of the communist and Arab majority there. After the veto in the Security Council and the lack of international concern for blatant Arab provocations, Israel felt particularly humiliated.

The Eshkol government, therefore, decided that a firm response to the Fath attacks emanating from Damascus was in order, but it was wary of attacking Syria itself. Since coming to power in 1963, the Ba'athist regime had been getting more and more support from the Soviet Union. An attack on Syria could lead to a tough Soviet response of behalf of its client and could impede Eshkol's attempted rapprochement with Moscow. On November 13, 1966, an Israeli armored column attacked the Jordanian village of Samu' in retaliation of a raid by a Fath unit that had passed through the Samu' area on its way from Syria to its objective in Israel. The Jordanian forces rushing to the defense of the village suffered heavy casualties.[80] Strictly speaking, the raid was in accord with Israeli retaliation doctrine, which held responsible the country that initiated or permitted raids from its territory. However, the Israeli action triggered a chain reaction of unexpected magnitude, in an extremely complex and unbalanced Arab environment.

Initially, the action justified requests by West Bank dwellers for weapons to help themselves and the Fath warriors, whose presence in Jordan could not officially be denied by King Hussein. He had made commitments to a common Arab cause and a consensus in the Arab coalition that "Palestinian resistance" to Israel should, at least officially, be supported. In fact, the king tried to control Fath operations from his territory, if not to prevent them altogether, because Palestinian claims for entity and sovereignty could have led to a delegitimization of his rule over the West Bank and even to a Palestinian claim over the East Bank, which was a historical, integral part of Palestine under the British and the Turks. PLO and Fath agents agitated in the West Bank, and the Egyptian-sponsored PLO called for a Palestinian take over in Jordan. Amman moved against both the Syrian-backed Fath and the Egyptian-backed PLO, bitterly accusing Nasser of initiating a campaign against Jordan rather than leading the Arab nation against Israel, while hiding

behind UNEF and preventing any action against the "prime enemy"—
Israel—from Egyptian-controlled territory.

President Nasser, who was generating a credibility gap in his Arab
allies and foes concerning the Palestinian refugees, was caught empty-
handed in this issue. Since the late 1950s, pretenders to Arab leadership,
like Iraq's President Aref, raised the question of a "Palestinian entity" and
challenged Nasser to commit himself publicly to the refugees and their
right to regain their homeland, by force if necessary. Yet, in fact, Egypt
did nothing to allow Palestinian action against Israel from its territories,
according to the post-1956 status quo. Moreover, at the 1964 Arab summit conference, Nasser said that Egypt was not ready for war over the
Jordan water question. This created "something of a scandal" in the Arab
world, which he averted by setting up the Palestinian Liberation Organization, under Egypt's strict control. Thus Nasser's tactics, as Dan Schueftan suggests, stemmed from the need to extricate himself from the tangle
of constraints placed on him in the inter-Arab arena rather than from any
definite conception, however long term, of the "Liberation of Palestine."
His problem, when Syria took over as the contender for Arab leadership,
the chief champion of the Palestinian cause, and the most active supporter of an all Arab military effort, was to isolate Damascus without
being blamed for neglecting the Palestinians. Nasser spoke in public in
July, 1965, of a "final reckoning" with Israel that would take place within
five years. He concluded a military pact with Syria (probably to restrain
it) but was immersed in a campaign against Arabs in Yemen, at odds
with the conservative ally of the Yemenite royalists—Saudi Arabia. He
was exposed, after the Samu' raid, as having offered empty promises to
the Palestinians.

Given these inter-Arab pressures, the enormous gap between Egypt's
style and bold gestures, and the substance of his foreign policy, Nasser
was forced by Syrian and Fath initiatives and by Israel's reaction to do
something rather indefinite to save face and extricate himself from the
impasse in Yemen.[81] His solution might have been some gain at Israel's
expense—a prestige gain, probably—to be achieved, as Schueftan suggests, through a repetition of the 1960 concentration of Egyptian forces
in the Sinai, in the context of Israeli pressure on other Arab neighbors.
He might have also considered a reduction in the significance and role
of the UNEF troops without losing control, thus winning a prestige victory, keeping the conflict open, and retaining unspecified options for the
future. Even if Nasser realized that Israel's military capacity grew considerably, he might have hoped that Eshkol's cabinet would be less ready
to take risks than Ben-Gurion, as Eshkol's regime seemed to be far
weaker, attacking a civilian Jordanian target rather than punishing the
stronger, Soviet-backed Syria, who sponsored the Fath attacks. At the

same time, Nasser might have been provoked by Israel's official stance on the nuclear question. Since late in 1964, Eshkol had adopted an official formula that had remained unchanged: "Israel will not be the first to introduce nuclear weapons into the Middle East," yet Israel would not allow its adversaries to win a nuclear race once they chose to start it. Thus, Israel adopted an ambiguous strategy; the Arabs were to regard a future Israeli capability as possible or a a risk that they should calculate into their strategy in a restraining manner. Washington should be calm, and the decision to produce nuclear weapons should be shelved without losing freedom of action. Israel's domestic nuclear debate might have brought Nasser to repeat his public warnings that Egypt would launch a preventive war against Israel if it realized its nuclear option. According to Mr. Mohamed H. Haikal, Nasser's intimate friend and adviser,[82] the Egyptian ruler tried, in 1964–65 and later, to "acquire" nuclear weapons, but failed. Haikal's report coincides with a *New York Times* dispatch from Cairo on February 4, 1966, according to which Soviet Deputy Defense Minister Gretchko reportedly refused to provide Egypt with nuclear weapons but pledged protection if Israel developed or obtained such arms. Thus, a potential Israeli nuclear capability might have provoked and alarmed Nasser in the sense that such a capability might "freeze" the conflict and create final decisions on Israel's borders, the refugees, and Israel's very existence. It might have been a contributing factor in his decision to challenge Israel right away, and also a contributing factor to Israeli fears that the Egyptian president was indeed serious about a full-scale war.

As the Syrian-inspired Fath operations and the shelling continued, Israel began issuing public warning that there was a limit to its patience. Late in November, 1966, a new dimension was added to the Israeli-Syrian struggle: using a border incident as a pretext, the Israeli government for the first time sent the air force into action and destroyed most of the Syrian water diversion equipment in a precision airstrike.[83] After this precedent it was natural that the sporadic infiltration, incidents, and shelling of that winter should culminate in a serious air battle on April 7, 1967. The air force was sent to support ground forces in a border clash, but this time the Syrians sent their own fighters to intercept the Israelis. In the ensuing dogfight, six Syrian Migs were shot down over the outskirts of Damascus.[84] On April 11, 1967, the Israeli chief of staff, Yitzhak Rabin, warned the Syrians to stop helping Fath with its operations and proclaimed the Ba'athist regime in Damascus responsible for them.[85]

The Israeli cabinet viewed the military steps they had taken as suitable measures for punishment and deterrence. The retaliations were more severe than usual but were deemed to be an adequate response to the culmulative provocations. The Israelis were, in fact, careful to reply only after several incidents. There was no feeling that the fighting would escalate into war.

Fearing a massive Syrian artillery attack after the April air battle, the Israelis deployed some troops along the Syrian border.[86] The Israeli troop concentrations were not very large, but, taken together with the earlier fighting, they could be interpreted or represented as evidence of Israel's sharp change of course and an intention to attack Syria and bring down the Ba'athist regime. The Soviets and Egyptians used this argument to convince themselves and each other. There is no way of knowing to what extent they actually believed this claim or whether it was simply a cover and a pretext for decisions already made. At the same time the weak Israeli government would not dare risk a two-front confrontation if Egypt came to Syria's help.

It was at this point that the escalatory process leading to the Six-Day War started. No Israeli without access to authoritative Soviet and Arab sources can pretend to be able to describe this process adequately from the standpoint of the other side. The official Arab version of events is, however, well known.[87] According to Nasser and Sadat, Moscow pointed out Israel's warnings and troop concentrations on the Syrian border and pressed Egypt to come to the aid of the Damascus regime. There is, however, no proof that the Kremlin pressed Cairo to go to war.

On May 14, 1967, Egyptian troops in large numbers began crossing into the Sinai Peninsula. The troop movements were widely publicized; in fact, there was something of a parade atmosphere about them. The Israelis at first thought the Egyptians were muscle-flexing, like the 1960 troop concentrations that ended in an Egyptian withdrawal. Two days later, however, the Egyptian chief of staff asked the UNEF commander to assemble all his troops in their bases, that is, to withdraw them from the ADL and Sharm-el-Sheikh. The UNEF commander transmitted the request to U.N. Secretary General U Thant, who in turn appealed to Nasser: if the UNEF were restricted to bases it would be unable to carry out its duties and would, therefore, have to be withdrawn entirely. The president should consider if this was what he wanted.[88] Nasser was in a dilemma whether to retreat from his demand for something less than a withdrawal or to demand a total withdrawal. He took the latter course, and the secretary general complied. The Arab coalition's pressure on Nasser not to hide behind the UNEF seems to have been a decisive factor in his decision. Thus two more of the strategic changes feared by Israel materialized: an Egyptian army in the Sinai and the withdrawal of the UNEF buffer. The question remaining was whether Nasser would take the next step and try to reimpose the status quo before 1957 by blockading the Straits of Tiran.

The Eshkol government decided on a combined diplomatic and military approach to the problem.[89] It attacked U Thant for taking ill-considered action, asked the Americans to keep the withdrawal from being carried out, and demanded a public declaration of American support for the territorial integrity and security of Israel. On May 15, the government had also ordered a partial mobilization like the one ordered in 1960. In the face of an apprehensive public and the usual demands for "firm action," the Eshkol government was trying to keep the fire from spreading.

On May 18, 1967, Jerusalem had learned that U Thant accepted Nasser's demand to withdraw the UNEF. Egyptian forces in the Sinai had been reinforced by troops from Yemen. This move was interpreted as an Egyptian attempt to find an honorable way out of south Arabia and to add military weight to the threat against Israel. The Eshkol government's earlier optimistic assessment of Nasser's actions gave way to rising anxiety. It therefore decided, on May 19, to order an almost general mobilization.[90] If it wanted to deter Nasser, the Israeli government had to consider that deterrence measures can backfire. The side using the potential resort to force to deter an enemy may find that the deterrence measure, particularly a general mobilization, assumed autonomous force in later considerations. The "deterred" side, meanwhile, was liable to disregard it in the general political context and to perceive the measure as an unacceptable provocation that it must not respond to in order not to lose face. The main reason for the general mobilization, however, was the creation of an Israeli bargaining position vis-à-vis Egypt. According to Israel's foreign minister, Abba Eban, Israel proposed, on May 19, to the Soviet ambassador in Tel Aviv to help bring about a deescalation process through a mutual reduction of forces. Israel would demobilize when Egypt withdrew from the Sinai. The ambassador flatly refused[91] to mediate on this basis.

The call-up by Israel was later described as affected by the government's view of the basic security situation and by precedent. In 1960, Israel had ordered a partial mobilization and the Egyptians withdrew; on May 15, 1967, Israel ordered a partial mobilization and the Egyptians did not withdraw. They even reinforced their troops. The logical conclusion was that now, in 1967, the Egyptians intended to take action or, even if they did not they could be pushed into action. Israel had no large standing army to guard its southern border.[92] Therefore, it must now mobilize its reserves on a large scale, lest the Egyptians be tempted to exploit their numerical advantage of regular troops and their deployment along the armistice demarcation line to launch a surprise attack once the UNEF withdrew from the ADL on May 19. However, once mobilized, the reserves were liable to see action unless they could be quickly demobilized, that is, unless the reason for their mobilization were quickly removed and the Egyptians returned to their bases west of the canal and the UNEF returned to its stations. If the Egyptians stayed where they were—the regular army could encamp in their own territory indefinitely—Israel would have to keep its reserves mobilized to fend off a surprise attack. Meanwhile, the state's social and economic life would be paralyzed and the government would face increasing criticism and demands that they "do something."

This situation would be hard to control because too many factors had to be taken into account. Psychologically, the government would have to contend with a popular feeling of siege and strangulation mixed with injured pride and old habits of thought, created by retaliatory acts and the Sinai campaign. Mobilization would also force the economy to grind to a halt and would bring about drastic changes in everyday life.

Ben-Gurion had criticized very sharply the Samu' action, the aerial attack on Syria in November, 1966, and the April, 1967, air battle over Damascus. He had been opposed to the mobilization from the start, recognizing how much pressure would be exerted on the government to take military action, even unaided. He had always tried to avoid acting under pressure and without foreign support.[93] His bitter criticism of Eshkol and Rabin may also have been due to an awareness that a publicized general mobilization was a useless measure in an attempt to get Nasser to back down. Egypt's military build-up was taking place within its sovereign territory and there was no political reason for Egypt to withdraw its troops, even if faced with an Israeli demand in the form of a general mobilization. Moreover, since Israel could not keep its army mobilized for long, war was likely to break out, and with war would come the heavy casualties that the former prime minister had always feared.

Thus, Ben-Gurion's traditional fears that the Achdut Ha'Avoda-Eshkol combination would stupidly maneuver itself into war were materializing. He, therefore, strongly advocated Eshkol's removal, and perhaps his own return. If this were not possible, then General Dayan should become prime minister and minister of defense and he, Ben-Gurion, should become Dayan's adviser. Ben-Gurion realized that his former protégé had become an independent political personality, by a process that had begun much earlier, when Dayan entered politics on his own and started his campaign against the secondary elite. Ben-Gurion should not have been surprised when he learned that Dayan waited for his turn, without advisers; that Dayan would be ready to join the existing coalition, not to fight for both the premiership and the defense portfolio; and that Dayan did not share Ben-Gurion's gloomy forecast of fighting alone with possible high losses. Dayan did not even believe in Egypt's intentions to attack Israel.[94] His perception was strategic-political: Egypt should be stopped or deterred, and taught that it could not unilaterally change rules in the Middle East.

Chief of Staff Rabin also estimated that Israeli casualties in a war would be high, particularly as a result of aerial attacks. The human costs of an armed conflict began to be a consideration in government decisions as the possibility of war made the practical problems it entailed more immediate. At first, the politicians' assessments of casualties tended to be as gloomy as the chief of staff's.[95] So, while the mobilization was ordered, Israel also explored the option of mobilizing Western support for a settlement. Another reason for trying the diplomatic approach, and one quite in line with Ben-Gurion's thinking, was an unwillingness to get involved in a war to which the United States did not agree and for which it would accept no responsibility.

The government did not want to call for a Security Council meeting about the withdrawal of the UNEF or to warn the Egyptians publicly that, if they made the situation more acute by closing the Straits of Tiran to Israeli shipping, Jerusalem would respond militarily. By ordering a general mobilization, Israel had, however, imposed certain psychological constraints on the time it would have to manage the crisis, without knowing what Nasser's response to the move would be. It did not leave itself enough leeway if, instead of being deterred, Nasser took a tougher stand. Nor was the government ready to state publicly their objections to Egypt's next likely move, a blockage of Eilat; one could thus have thought that they might countenance such an action too.[96]

Unwilling to try to use the Security Council to pressure Egypt and unable to get the American public declaration of support for its security and territorial integrity that it sought, Israel was faced with a difficult diplomatic situation. Nasser had encountered no diplomatic or political obstacles either in the U.N. or in public U.S. policy, and he was assured of active political support by the Soviet Union. His military deployment in the Sinai seemed sufficient to him to deter Israel from attacking, and Ben-Gurion had taught him that Israel would not attack alone. Nor did he see any reason to withdraw in the face of Israeli general mobilization, particularly since to do so would involve a loss of face. If, despite his expectations, Israel should attack, it would, as in 1956, be branded the aggressor, this time a lone aggressor without support from France and Britain. Furthermore, with Soviet support in the Security Council, the length of the war could be controlled to Egypt's benefit. The deployment in the Sinai was deemed sufficient to hold the Israelis in check, drag out the conflict, and bring about a draw in the field. The Soviet Union would, therefore, have time to work out some compromise with the United States that would be favorable to Egypt. An isolated Israel, not victorious in battle and deemed an aggressor, would be forced to accept a total or partial revision of the status quo of the last ten years. Egypt might even win another plume—take over the Eilat area and thus have an overland route to Jordan and the Arab East. Cairo had regarded this area as disputed territory since its occupation by the IDF in 1949 after the 1948–49 war.

Nasser's status in the Arab world seems to have been a major consideration in his thinking. The Yemeni adventure and his conflicts with the radical and conservativeArab camps, both of which attacked his inaction regarding Israel, had hurt him. A successful outcome to the current gambit would have done much to restore his prestige and status as the principal Arab leader. Thus, on May 23, 1967, President Nasser announced that the Straits of Tiran were barred to Israeli shipping. The Israeli government were convinced that war was inevitable. The blockade was an act of war that demanded a military response both on principle and as a practical measure to lift it. The IDF's deterrent capabilities had clearly not been great enough. The Eshkol government was apprehensive that Nasser, with his political advantages and his army deployed in Sinai might want or be pushed to take even more serious action. From now on, the diplomatic alternatives discussed in cabinet were viewed mainly as tactical measures; war was thought inevitable and necessary.[97]

The public, most of the Achdut Ha'Avoda and some of the Mapai ministers, many of the IDF's top-ranking officers,[98] and perhaps the Arabs expected the Israeli government to act as Ben-Gurion had acted in his time and to react immediately to the Egyptian provocation. However, on May 24 the cabinet decided not to go to war yet. A gulf was opened between the public expectations, the army doctrine, and the government behavior, although the government's mood was not too different from the public's.Eshkol and his ministers had managed to isolate themselves despite the fact that they identified with the popular fears. Eshkol's personal tragedy, which later brought about his forced resignation as minister of defense, was that he followed popular "given" feelings on deterrence, *casus belli*, and Arab aims. He did not study the situation thoroughly, as Ben-Gurion used to do, but took it for granted. He obviously had some good reasons to accept Arab positions and actions as a manifestation of an Arab program to destroy Israel; Israel's neighbors should be deterred from attacking or putting an unbearable, constant pressure on it. Moreover, Eshkol had endorsed tough actions against Arab countries in the past, following suggestions put forward by General Weizman and General Rabin. He thought in terms of autonomous action if necessary, typical of the army, and in terms of bargaining to prevent this necessity. This combination of bargaining when firm action, even a gesture, was needed, and yet of bold autonomism (retaliations and general mobilization) destroyed him, because the enemy was not ready to respond positively but rather was provoked by these traits.

Tactical differences within Mapai, and between Eshkol and Achdut Ha'Avoda, were added to a general atmosphere of crisis. Some of the Mapai ministers expressed doubts about the goals and nature of diplomatic action and were afraid that the longer war was delayed, the higher the costs would be. The Achdut Ha'Avoda ministers, meanwhile, all demanded that Israel force its way through the Straits. Most of Mapai's ministers and NRP leaders followed Eshkol in his bid for further diplomatic efforts. The ratio in the cabinet was almost one to one. The post-Ben-Gurion defense policy elite—Eshkol, Allon, Rabin, and Galili—thus split at a critical moment, cracking the center of decision making on fundamental foreign policy and defense issues. Into the fissures flowed groups whose importance was now greatly enhanced: the high command, public opinion, small coalition parties that had had no say in defense matters before, and, finally, Rafi and the right-wing Herut party.[99]

The decision to postpone the war was due mainly to an American demand to refrain from any action, so as to give Washington time to resolve the crisis Nasser had created over the Straits. Israeli Foreign Minister Abba Eban was sent to Washington, London, and Paris to find out how far the Western powers were prepared to go in defense of Israel's freedom of passage. Eban's mission and the continuing mobilization, meanwhile, led to a grave crisis in the Eshkol cabinet and in parliament.

It was, of course, unrealistic to expect that in this emergency Eshkol should act as Ben-Gurion would have done. The structure of politics had changed; the coalition government and the disagreement among ministers over the great powers' likely reaction to a war and over the timing of it prevented immediate decisive action, even though no one doubted that force would have to be used. Eshkol acted within these constraints and tried to exhaust diplomatic channels before going to war. He did not act as forcefully as "Ben-Gurion would have done"; he could not act quickly and firmly, or circumvent institutional majority decisions or mobilize public opinion in support of his own decisions. He thus lost his legitimacy as a leader in times of emergency. Having accepted the majority decisions in Mapai and the coalition when they agreed with his views on postponing the war, Eshkol was obliged to acquiesce in their decisions when they opposed his views, and so he had to give up the defense ministry. His endeavors to exploit Israel's bargaining advantages vis-à-vis Washington—advantages gained also by bargaining with the nuclear option—could not be carried on in full public view. Nor could he explain persuasively that he needed time to exhaust this approach while the public and some members of his cabinet pressed in on him hysterically.

Eshkol did have some advantages in bargaining for America's active support. Together with Britain, the United States tried to initiate joint action by the world's maritime nations in order to break the blockade. This bargaining position was based not only on the nuclear deal but also on past promises concerning Israel's free shipping through the Straits and the acknowledgement of its right to use force to retain this right, given to it by Western maritime powers in 1957. President Johnson promised substantive action on the issue within two or three weeks; in the meantime he conducted secret consultations with the Soviet and U.S. allies to discover the extent of their support for Egypt.

Unlike the United States, France was in a dilemma forced upon it by what it viewed as Israel's extreme reaction to the closure of the Straits. President de Gaulle thought that it was not to Israel's benefit to make the blockade a test case for deterrence or for general relations with the Arabs. Such an approach would, necessarily, raise the profile of the conflict a great deal and inevitably lead the Arabs to mobilize their political and economic potential and their ties with the U.S.S.R.; France had already felt the bite of this potential realized during the Algerian war. Moreover, France, as Israel's ally and main arms supplier, was thus liable to find itself in confrontation with the Arabs and to see its relations with the Soviet Union suffer. Furthermore, a sharp deterioration in the Middle East situation was liable to lead to a superpower confrontation. After the closure of the Straits, Paris repeatedly voiced to Jerusalem its opinion on the issue and even imposed an embargo on arms to Israel during the crisis. The French suggested that they, together with Britain, the United States, and the Soviet Union, represented the only political framework to deal with the crisis and bring about a solution.

In Israel the French shift in position was regarded as an outright betrayal and another demonstration of Israel's abandonment and isolation among the nations. Ben-Gurion was the only Israeli political figure who understood and defended de Gaulle's position. He recognized the political logic and sophistication underlying it and maintained that it was a perfectly legitimate position for France to hold.[100]

By late May, the United States was the only extraregional power from which Israel could expect any help. Eshkol wanted to wait and see how Washington fulfilled its promise of action. On May 28, the cabinet again discussed whether to go to war right away, and the ministers were divided evenly on the issue. They hesitated not only because of the United State's promises, but also because of its warnings to Israel not to take unilateral action at this stage. The waiting, therefore, continued. Members of the IDF command clashed with Eshkol about this; they were growing impatient because the Egyptian army's strength was growing as it dug in and improved its positions in the Sinai. The army, too, became an active, though not decisive, factor in Israeli politics. The political parties were in turmoil, the media were spreading gloom and demanding action, and increasing pressure was brought to bear on the prime minister to shuffle and expand the cabinet in order to provide the state with "suitable" leadership for the emergency.

Eshkol contributed to this rising pressure with a radio broadcast about the government's decision to continue waiting and to exhaust all diplomatic and political channels in order to restore the status quo. He formulated Israel's demands on Egypt regarding the straits and troop concentrations in rather conciliatory, moderate terms and delivered his address in a voice and manner that were interpreted as indicative of vacillation and weakness. Many people did not believe in the content of his speech and did not think the wait-and-see policy stood much chance of success because "the world" did not compel Nasser to retain the UNEF and reopen the straits. The form of the address and the disappointed expectations in Israel were further sources of popular dissatisfaction. Eshkol's stature with the public fell drastically.

Most of the mass media and large sections of the public had welcomed the changes in the structures and rules of the political game that followed Ben-Gurion's resignation. Yet they expressed great disapproval of the government after Eshkol's "stammering speech" announcing a decision made in conformity with the new rules. They demanded the inclusion of Rafi and Gahal, the right-wing Herut-liberal bloc in the cabinet, and Eshkol's transfer of the defense portfolio to a more suitable candidate—Ben-Gurion or Dayan. Achdut Ha'Avoda, however, demanded the defense ministry for Allon. The policy debate among the national leadership consequently became entangled with partisan and personal rivalries.

The possibility of Ben-Gurion's restoration faded quickly, as he made known his views on the crisis to several ministers and his own party, Rafi. He regarded the general mobilization as a mistake, arguing that the IDF was not prepared to go to war on its own, and he suggested digging in and waiting for foreign assistance. This was simply a restatement of the policy he had followed as prime minister. Furthermore, Ben-Gurion thought that if Israel did go to war, it should aim mainly at reopening the Straits of Tiran. He wanted to restrict any confrontation with Egypt on issues in which Israel had strong arguments in its favor, and he did not think it desirable to raise the profile of the general Arab-Israeli conflict. No one listened to him, however. His views seemed diametrically opposite to those he had expressed as prime minister, and the apparent change was attributed to age or to his hatred of Eshkol.

The supporters of Ben-Gurion's restoration—an alliance of the Shimon Peres and Menahem Begin, of all people—cast about for another candidate and settled on General Dayan. He was ready for war without foreign help and did not think that the aims of this war should be restricted to lifting the blockade, for he saw the troop concentrations in the Sinai as the main problem. His views on the issue did not differ greatly from those held by his personal rivals in Achdut Ha'Avoda. Both considered it absolutely necessary to restore the strategic balance in the Middle East by a war in which the Egyptian army in the Sinai would be neutralized unless Egypt was ready to resume its obligations. Their opinions and fears seemed to be confirmed as Nasser continued to escalate the conflict. On May 29, the Egyptian president publicly demanded the cession of Eilat and other territory along the armistice demarcation line that Cairo had long claimed. He stressed the Palestinians' right to return to their homeland and Egypt's desire to return to the status quo of 1947. Nasser also emphasized however, that it was up to the Palestinians themselves to regain their rights and that Egypt would not initiate war operations against Israel, although he rejected any form of peaceful coexistence with the Jewish state.

From the Israeli standpoint this statement could be interpreted as a double trap. Nasser was demanding the cession of territory that Israel had long considered its own and that had been internationally recognized as such. He also committed himself to allowing the Palestinian organizations freedom of action against Israel from Egyptian and Syrian territory (there were no UNEF troops on the Egyptian border to restrain such action). He had voiced public support for these operations, was competing with Syria for the leadership of the Arab world on this issue, and was also committed to supporting the Damascus regime. An Israeli reprisal against the Palestinian organizations or an attempt to punish states that permitted Palestinian attacks would be considered an attack on Egypt or Syria or both. Thus, not only would the fedayeen attacks be resumed with greater violence but, because of the strategic shift in Egypt's position, Israel's ability to respond to the raids would be severely restricted. The continual Fath attacks would make civilian life in Israel hell and, once Israel was exhausted and had disintegrated internally, there was no way, apart from a general war, to keep Egypt from backing the operations or from going to war whenever it wished. With its forward deployment of forces in the Sinai, and arguing that it was responding to Israeli reprisals on Egypt's territory and population, Cairo could easily initiate and find a pretext for war. Israel, on the other hand, would have to demobilize soon and be ready to call up the reserves again from time to time in order to provide strategic cover for its reprisals, because of the Egyptian forces permanently arrayed along its southern border. The combination of attrition by the fedayeen and continual mobilization would weaken Israel drastically.

Thus the government's view that it was obliged to protect the state from terrorist attacks was an independent variable in its considerations. This atttiude resulted in a domestic political problem of the first order when it seemed that the government would be unable to perform this task. For, in order to do so, it was considered that Israel had to be free to carry out reprisals, and this freedom was now seriously restricted by the presence of Egyptian forces in the Sinai.

Time, always an important consideration in Israeli military calculations, was a large consideration in the constraints of general mobilization and of keeping the called-up reserves idle. Actually the time was used to build up the supplies of the various arms of the IDF for last-minute training and unconsciously for creating a readiness for battle and sacrifice. It seemed to the Israelis to be working against them. War with Egypt was increasingly seen as the only way to restore the strategic balance, that is, to remove the constant Egyptian threat. The political and psychological environment seemed bound to lead to an Egyptian attack once Nasser had completed the strengthening of his lines in the Sinai. Casualties would be very high in these circumstances and were, indeed, unavoidable. Since little could be done about them, they came to be considered less of an impediment in the debate over whether or not to go to war immediately. In fact, since the Egyptians had not finished digging in, it was argued that the sooner war came, the fewer losses the IDF would suffer. The wish to limit casualties thus gave added impetus to an immediate Israeli full-scale attack. The only real obstacle left was American opposition. The Jerusalem government was afraid to go to war immediately unless Washington's attitude changed, for if the Arabs should receive extensive military and political support from the Soviet Union there was always the danger that the United States might do nothing to counter it.

On May 30, the Arabs further escalated the situation. Jordan and Egypt signed a pact putting the Jordanian army under Egyptian command in case of war. Israel saw itself totally encircled. At best this military ring would be able to squeeze concessions from it by threatening war and forcing it to mobilize and demobilize its reserves frequently.

The conservative King Hussein, Nasser's mortal enemy, had been saved by external support (including Israel's indirect aid) from Nasserite-Syrian plots against him in 1958. When he joined Nasser's "progressive" camp, took up the war cry and the daily mass rallies of hatred, and staged anti-Israeli parades the same as in the other Arab capitals, the Israelis began to feel that they were indeed in immediate, mortal danger.

Associations with Munich in 1938 and with the destruction of European Jewry in World War II sharpened the tone of domestic criticism of what was seen as the Eshkol government's vacillation and impotence. Nevertheless, on May 31, Eshkol once more appealed to President Johnson to lift the blockade. If he succeeded, Nasser's prestige would suffer somewhat and he might be restrained from taking more risky gambles. If Johnson could not keep his promise of action, however, the Israelis expected some compensation from the United States. Most of the Israeli political parties thought that time was running out and that nothing would come of an American initiative. They, therefore, demanded an immediate change in the government in preparation for war. They wanted Dayan to be given the defense portfolio and a broad coalition government including Gahal to be established. Leading those demanding this change was the moderate head of the NRP, Minister of the Interior Shapira. He wanted a "government of national unity" for this time of emergency, and he felt that Dayan should be defense minister because he was a victorious military commander and the representative of a political party that should be included in the broadly based cabinet.

The Americans' response to Eshkol's appeal indicated a clear retreat from the idea of joint action by the maritime nations. These states' enthusiasm for the project had diminished; instead, the possibility was raised of bringing the question of the Straits of Tiran before the International Court of Justice at The Hague. While the case was pending, the Straits would be open to the shipping of all countries, except perhaps of Israel. The United States also refused to make a public statement in support of Israel's independence, territorial integrity, and position in the conflict. The Americans preferred to keep a low public profile so as not to provoke Soviet and Arab reactions which would only aggravate the situation. The Israelis, however, thought that a public statement would be more binding than a secret one and that, far from provoking the U.S.S.R. and the Arabs, it would deter them from escalating further. The United States feared that a public American position might drive the Soviets and the Arabs to harden their own public stand.

The Israelis were growing uneasy as the Arab leaders and media adopted a more and more aggressive style and tone. The impression in Israel was that an operative Arab decision to destroy the Jewish state was near. Israeli apprehension was reinforced by the next two escalatory steps taken by the Arabs in early June: Palestinian forces in the Gaza Strip opened fire on Israeli settlements for the first time in ten years and Iraq joined the Egyptian-Syrian-Jordanian ring around Israel.

Still, the balance of gross military power was not unfavorable to Israel so long as the reserves were mobilized. For example, the Egyptians and Syrians had a total of 1700 tanks to Israel's 1300, for a ratio of 1.3 to 1.[101] Moreover, the Americans argued that, given the differences in the quality of the forces, Israel's military situation was far from bad; the Pentagon estimated that a swift Israeli victory in a war was assured. Since the actual military threat against Israel was not so great, the Americans considered that Jerusalem could wait for a nonmilitary solution to the crisis.[102]

Jerusalem was less optimistic; the Egyptians were digging in and the feeling in Israel was that the state was under siege. Furthermore, the balance of forces that Washington interpreted so favorably was based on a comparison of a reserve army mobilized but kept idle for a long time and regular armies. Jerusalem wanted to be able to demobilize and change the strategic situation, the worsening of which had led to the mobilization. However, if the government had not decided on a publicized general mobilization so early, Nasser might not have taken an escalatory step of his own so as not to seem to be yielding to Israeli pressure. His escalation only provided greater justification for the mobilization. By ordering it the government also imposed time constraints on themselves. The expectations of a people mobilized for action limit the time psychologically available for decision making to days and hours.

The pressure inside Israel for a government of national unity to be established and for Eshkol to give up the defense portfolio was building daily. The Mapai apparatus began to give way. It was decided that Eshkol could not command the state in a war and that Dayan had to be invited to join the cabinet as the representative of Rafi. The party suggested a compromise, however: Allon would become defense minister and Dayan would be deputy prime minister. Dayan thought he could get a better deal, though, and rejected the proposal. Eshkol had not yet despaired of keeping the defense portfolio and tried to win Dayan over by offering him a military command. The NRP then issued an ultimatum demanding that Rafi should join the cabinet and Dayan be given the defense ministry. Eshkol gave in, agreeing to include Rafi and Gahal in the cabinet, and on June 1, he yielded to Mapai's demands. Mapai thus gave this key post to a man who had been a major rival of its leaders since 1960 and the party's mortal enemy since 1965. The party compromised again on one of Ben-Gurion's most important principles, that the decision making base must be kept compact and lòyal, especially in a crisis. Such a base must be sought and maintained even at the cost of political division, but must never be diluted by amalgamations that narrowed the area of agreement. It was the sense of crisis, the domestic pressure inside and outside Mapai and the wish to fulfill popular expectations that drove the party to take this step.

The Ben-Gurion period tradition of deciding alone on appointments to key offices, insulated from popular pressures, fell by the wayside after the "Lavon Affair." Dayan was appointed because the public applied direct pressure on the party institutions. Part of his power was thus derived directly from the public, and he held some very strong bargaining cards and a great deal of room to maneuver in the governing bodies he would join. It is ironic that those who raised him so high would also bring him low in the aftermath of the October, 1973, war.

On June 4, the government finally decided to go to war. Three immediate factors were behind this decision. First, Iraqi forces appeared in Jordan. Second, Meir Amit, the Israeli intelligence chief reported from Washington that the U.S. administration despaired of the plan for the maritime states to break the blockade and, therefore, would not stop Israel if it decided to take unilateral action. If Israel did not move now, the government concluded, Johnson would come to terms with Egypt, who proved to be the key-holder to the situation in the Middle East, in American eyes. Third, France put an embargo on all arms deliveries to Israel and publicly tied the question of the Straits to the Palestinian refugee problem. By making this connection, France seemed to express understanding for a limited Egyptian action (the blockade of Eilat) in the context of the broader Arab-Israeli conflict. It seemed that Israel's gains since 1949, and especially since 1956, including the shelving of the refugee problem and the maintenance of territorial status quo, would crumble one after the other.

To the extent that we can be certain what Nasser's position was, the Six-Day War seems to have been the outcome of a calculated political and military gamble by Egypt, in which Nasser continually raised the stakes in response to needs and pressures emanating from a number of sources. The political stance adopted was offensive and the military posture was defensive. When the fighting came, it became clear that the Egyptians could not militarily cover their political bets.

DAYAN AND THE SIGNIFICANCE OF THE GOVERNMENT OF NATIONAL UNITY UNDER ESHKOL

Dayan was publicly considered Ben-Gurion's disciple and heir. He had come by his key posts—chief of staff, cabinet minister, and leader of Rafi—not only because of his own abilities but also because of his patron's favor. Ben-Gurion regarded him as one of the most talented young men in Mapai and later became publicly identified with him, partially as a result of the "Lavon Affair."

In fact, however, Dayan was not a disciple of Ben-Gurion in either the style or content of his politics. He tended, to some extent, to manipulate symbols in his speech, as Ben-Gurion had done. He was often shockingly frank, however, in areas in which Ben-Gurion had been careful not to be too outspoken.[103] Ben-Gurion spoke of national symbols and general objectives in a visionary style, not going into detail about tactics; the assumption was that they were obvious. In fact, however, the presentation and practice of policy often contradicted each other. Dayan, on the other hand, sometimes spoke of the conflict and interests of Arabs and Israelis in clear, almost brutal, terms.[104] He did not always embellish his policy statements with moralism and prophecy as Ben-Gurion had done, so it is, therefore, relatively easy to study his political views and behavior.

Dayan did not follow Ben-Gurion's policy of limiting oneself to a relatively narrow party power base, nor did he think of creating a party power base of his own. He sought support, both inside and outside his party, for whichever policy he upheld at a given time, on the basis of agreement on the specific objectives he sought. For instance, in 1967, thinking that war was necessary, he and the Gahal leader, Menachem Begin agreed that they should both resign from the cabinet unless it voted for war. The desired decision was made and neither of them had to resign. There emerged between the two men a functional collaboration that obscured the commonly accepted boundaries between their parties in certain areas.

The customary procedures for decision making by party leaders and bodies that commit the party's cabinet ministers and the cabinet as a whole also became less clear-cut. The blurring of these boundaries became even worse when the great military victory and the ensuing euphoria inspired Rafi to join Mapai and Achdut Ha'Avoda in 1968 in the new Labor party. Mapam soon joined Labor in an electoral and parliamentary alignment but retained its separate party organization. All four elements retained their original parliamentary strength and factional behavior in the new framework. The machinery for creating political consensus, which had already broken down over the Lavon Affair, this had to tackle an even larger and more intractable amalgam. It was doubtful whether a consensus could be reached on some other basis than the lowest common denominator in the Labor-Mapam alignment and the even lower denominator in parliament and the national unity cabinet.

While Dayan had special status as a member of the ruling party and as a senior cabinet minister, the government as a whole often determined defense policy by majority decision. He refused, however, to construct a party power base of his own to help circumvent the compromise that this type of decision making entailed. Instead, he used his working agreement with the right-wing bloc and any other supporters in the cabinet and parliament. Even if the prime minister had a majority of the alignment on his side, he would have to take this connection into account before trying to force a decision.

In terms of the style and content of his policy, Dayan is quite typical of the new generation of Israelis, almost the symbol of the "new man" that Ben-Gurion and his generation had wished to create. Some of the latter, however, had little liking for this particular product of their labors, who had become a politician in his own right. Dayan was first of all a farmer, shrewd and wary, born on the first kibbutz, Degania, and raised in the large moshav, Nahalal. He was a fighter from his youth, first in skirmishes and later in full-scale wars with the Arabs. He believed that he understood their ways, their political behavior, and their political and military style. He had an inclination to poetry and to vague historical and ideological thinking. At the same time, Dayan was and remains a very ambitious politician. He is impatient, however, perhaps because of his wound and his strong impulses. His natural intelligence or cleverness and his extremely quick mind combined with his liking for power and the natural faith in his own right as a natural, national leader. Yet he never possessed the self-discpline and orderliness necessary for real greatness. From his youth, his path in the army and in politics had been smooth and in the spotlight of world publicity because of the popular image of his personality and because of accomplishments, not all of which were his, attributed to him.[105]

The fundamental aspects of his political views and behavior during the period under consideration can be set forth in the following manner. Dayan, and his patron before him, took the Arab-Israeli conflict as the basic given. Ben-Gurion described it as a conflict between Zionist rights —the Jewish people's moral, historical, and political rights—and dangerous Arab obstinacy, which could be overcome by the exercise of Israel's autonomous power, domestic, social, and moral strength with the help of extraregional powers. His protégé, however, stated bluntly that the Arab-Israeli conflict was a conflict between two national movements over the same plot of land. There was no absolute Israeli or Arab "right"; rather, each side, rightly, wanted its own right to win. Dayan often stated that if he were an Arab, he would act as the Arabs did, but since he was an Israeli he must try to advance the national interests of the Jewish people. Given these premises, it is possible and, indeed, probable that the struggle between the two national movements would go on for generations before Israel's ability to survive and the territorial and geostrategic framework for its survival in the Middle East would be finally determined. One could not expect the Arabs to resign themselves to the loss of their lands and watch from their refugee camp as Jews settled there. In this conflict, power and Israel's self-sacrifice and faith in itself and its ability, would be decisive.[106]

In Dayan's opinion, as circumstances changed, Israel must adopt the means and suitable measures to pursue autonomous policies and to respond to the Arab challenge. A manly-responsive leader (reacting to events and challenges emotionally, instinctively, and less cognitively) rather than a postulative-cognitive product of preWorld War I Zionist mentality (which was self-concerned, pessimistic toward Jewish presence, and hopeful toward Jewish future in Palestine, believing in progress and the effort one must exert to bring it about), Dayan was by nature more optimistic with regard to the present, more responsive to challenges from the outside, less self-concerned, and not interested in the founding fathers' internal quarrels with their own psyches. His clear, blunt mind functioned in terms of power, national interests, power games, and responses to Arab threats or power games, which might deteriorate because of the character of the Arab coalition and Arab mentality and would bring about unacceptable relations between Arab and Jew.[107] Dayan's approach to Arab handling of Israel's rights, formed by a combination of his own judgment of what these rights were or ought to be and historical and diplomatic precedents, was pessimistic unless based on Israel's own power and Arab recognition of the same. He was a man of action, rather than a man of disciplined cognition that sometimes arrested action, as in Ben-Gurion's case. He would do things according to his understanding of Arabs or any other foreign challenges or refrain from doing them according to his assessment of the power relations between Israel and the rest of the world or take action first and test reality, as he suggested to Ben-Gurion before the 1957 withdrawal, rather than accepting reality as a positive given.[108] If the test should be negative, one could, accordingly, try and return to a fall-back position instead of accepting it in advance. This commercial logic was far from Ben-Gurion's postulates, which dictated taking no risk if the situation were ambiguous or did not promise clear results. It concentrated on internal, social, and moral strength rather than on responding to Arab hostility or trying to force Arabs to change their historical patterns of behavior in times of enormous national upheaval in the Third World.

Dayan did not think that the Arabs were as formidable a military force as many Israelis feared. They should be treated with regard for their typical, historical characteristics: as deceivers who often deceived only themselves. At the same time their national pride and sense of honor should also be taken into consideration. Both characteristics dictated almost a continued struggle between the Arabs and any foreign element, such as the Jews.[109] In any event, it was up to Israel, and particularly its soldiering sons, to find themselves the personal bravery and exploit the advantages of having no alternative and of their national enthusiasm to make themselves superior soldiers. Dayan felt that Arabs must be taught to abide by binding norms of behavior in their relations with Israel. The relations among the peoples of the Middle East must be based on the observance of agreements, the honoring of commitments, and "playing by the rules of the game" customary among sovereign states. The Israeli Jew must not be treated as a "walad al-mit" (literally, son of death), as one condemned to die, who, therefore, had no rights and to whom one owed nothing.[110]

In Dayan's opinion, Israel's impossible borders (that is, the 1949 ADL, particularly the border with Jordan) constituted a standing invitation for the Arabs to attack or put an increased pressure on Israel. The boundaries must, therefore, be improved and revised. It was not only security that made Israeli control of the West Bank of the Jordan necessary, however, but also the realization of the historic vision of the Jewish people's return to the land of the Bible.[111] This vision was a political necessity, giving content and goals to a people involved in an historic struggle. Even if the West Bank were heavily populated by Arabs, Israel must take control of it and establish Jewish settlements there whenever this became politically and strategically necessary. Dayan thus diverged widely from Ben-Gurion's theories and practice, yet his behavior seemed to fit Ben-Gurion's own image of the "new Jew." After East Jerusalem was taken in the 1967 war, for example, he was instrumental in having it annexed, against Ben-Gurion traditional fears that "the world" would not allow it. At first, nothing of that sort happened.[112]

Dayan also believed that the behavior of the extraregional powers was a crucial consideration, perhaps of even greater strategic importance than the Arabs' actions for Israeli policy, and that various entanglements with the Soviet Union were to be avoided. Still, Israel could and sometimes must act alone, but without provoking the U.S.S.R. unduly. American counterbalance should be sought without accepting a decisive American say in Israeli affairs. In fact, his appointment as minister of defense a couple of days before the war did not influence the decision to go to war, but helped to widen the scope of it beyond Dayan's own intentions. Whereas Eshkol was considering a medium-scale operation to open the Straits and destroy the Egyptian army's main battle lines in the northern Sinai and the central Sinai-Israeli border, Dayan joined the majority in cabinet that was willing to chase the Egyptians to the vicinity of the Suez Canal. He warned against taking it, however, as the Russians might regard this as a challenge to their own supply routes to the Far East and as an unacceptable humiliation of their client.[113] Thus, backed by the entire cabinet, Dayan ordered the IDF not to go all the way to the Suez Canal in the Six-Day War. Nonetheless, the victorous army was carried to the banks of the canal by its momentum as it followed in the wake of the retreating Egyptians.

Dayan was also wary of attacking Syria, although the Syrians shelled northern Israel and even conducted some ground attacks. The northern Israeli settlements demanded the removal of the threat of bombardment once and for all, but Dayan dissociated himself from this direction. In a move characteristic of his political style, he took out an insurance policy, so to speak, in case the attack should fail because of a Soviet threat or direct intervention in defense of the regime in Damascus. Moscow contented with severing diplomatic relations and warned Israel not to move too close to Damascus.

After the 1967 war Dayan was able to exert decisive influence on the crucial problem of the West Bank and on the Palestinian problem as a whole. He felt that retention of the area was necessary, and argued publicly that the Palestinian refugees must be resettled elsewhere in the Arab world. As far as the Arabs of the occupied territories were concerned, he developed a "functional conception" for possible cooperation with Jordan: Israel would continue to occupy the West Bank but its inhabitants would remain Jordanian citizens and would cross the "open bridges" between the two banks of the river freely. He hoped this plan would foster economic integration and personal contact between Jews and Arabs in Palestine, while retaining Israeli control.[114]

Dayan had a number of natural allies in the cabinet on this issue: Menahem Begin and his rivals on the nationalist left, mainly Galili. They regarded the West Bank as of decisive importance to Israel's defense[115] and as a region of great historical significance. They considered Jordanian rule there hazardous to Israel because of the instability of the Hashemite regime and Hussein's extreme policy shift. The king's behavior in May and June of 1967 had discredited him in Israeli eyes: he had joined in a military pact with Nasser, responded to the Egyptian president's pleas for help, and attacked Israeli positions in Jerusalem on June 6, 1967. He had used American arms, which had been given to him on the understanding that they could not be used on the West Bank against Israel, and had consented to the deployment of Iraqi forces in Jordan. Furthermore, Begin, Dayan, and Galili were educated to see Palestine west of the Jordan River as a unit and they regarded the outcome of the 1948 war as a tragedy.

Allon was willing to return to the areas populated by Arabs to Jordan, for the most part, in exchange for a final peace agreement. Dayan did not regard such a deal as realistic. Begin was uncompromising: Palestine and Jewish rights to Palestine were indivisible in his view. For Allon and most of the government, the problem was more political and military. They feared Jordanian or local rule in the territories because of Jordanian irresponsibility or possible Syrian or radical Palestinian influence. Allon preferred direct Israeli rule as long as Hussein did not agree to an Israeli presence in the key strategic areas in the West Bank. Dayan did not agree even to that, and, as the minister responsible for the occupied territory, he opposed any local autonomy and also the encouragement of a West Bank leadership, which, he thought, inevitably would be anti-Israeli in character.

The old Mapai minister under Eshkol regarded these policies as dangerous, "hawkish," and too frank. Their own "dovish" stance was mainly negative, however: no Israeli rule over many Arabs and no external complications, which this might entail. Eshkol was not ready to yield any land for nothing. His basic approach to politics was and remained that bargaining assets should be acquired from second and third parties, so that a deal—a compromise of course—could be struck. This made Eshkol's policy in the future dependent totally upon Arab response; thus the initiative within his government passed to Dayan, Galili, Allon, and Begin. Later, when religious groups and Dayan, Galili, and Allon joined forces to establish Israeli settlements in areas of strategic and historic importance in the West Bank, the old Mapai ministers tried to restrict settlement as much as possible.

The doves' approach remained largely negative and they presented no alternatives. The result was a low common denominator of decision making in the cabinet and a split between hawks and doves in the Labor alignment. In theory then, Israel's rule of the West Bank was temporary, but no one in the government saw a realistic possibility of returning to Arab rule. The debate in the Labor alignment and the cabinet centered on whether Israel could avoid external, mainly American, pressure on this and other issues relating to the conflict.

One last word on David Ben-Gurion. After the Six-Day War, the "old man," as he was called years before, became old indeed, politically. He was caught in the contradictions that made up his foreign and defense policy between 1949 and 1963: his concepts of sovereignty and self-reliance could be interpreted as if they led toward an Israeli rule in Palestine *as a whole*, including Arabs. His pessimism, as far as the abilities of the IDF and pressures by foreign powers to return territories were concerned, proved false for the time being. When he spoke up and said that Israel should return all of the territories captured in 1967 in exchange for peace,[116] thus revealing his basic priority of not ruling Arabs, he was regarded as the fallen old leader who envied Eshkol's achievements.

Thus, Ben-Gurion himself started to correct his own traditional course. He added East Jerusalem and the Golan Heights to the territory that should remain in Israeli hands, yet, until his death in 1973, he kept arguing that Israel should return its conquests in exchange for peace. He found himself opposing a new national consensus created after June, 1967, and he lost his influence altogether. As a matter of fact, Dayan never consulted him before the war or after. Nevertheless, Ben-Gurion was fascinated by Dayan and his apparent success and was hopelessly at odds with the much more cautious Eshkol. He thus preferred to criticize Dayan indirectly, then left current politics behind altogether. Times had changed, but his instincts still told him that Israel's bid for autonomy, coupled with occupation of vast Arab lands populated by many Arabs, was an extremely risky exercise. Perhaps it was one that could be carried out by a real power, but not a tiny Jewish state.

Ben-Gurion had helped make many Israelis think of themselves as a proud, if possible autonomous, old/new brand of Jewishness. Dayan seemed a successful incorporation of that dream. Could Ben-Gurion tell them openly that he doubted it? He preferred silence.

2

Attrition and Mediation, 1967-70

ISRAEL, THE SUPERPOWERS, AND THE ARABS: THE TRANSITIONAL PERIOD, 1967-68

The crystallization of Israeli policy vis-à-vis the Arab states, the territory captured during the war, and the extraregional powers involved in the conflict was a very complex process. At first the Israelis were stunned by the magnitude and speed of their victory and they luxuriated in the sweet sense of having been rescued from destruction. Apart from the annexation of East Jerusalem immediately after the war, very few practical measures were taken to solve the new problems they faced. Since they thought that the Arabs would need many years to reconstruct their armed forces, the Israelis felt safe from attack for a long time to come.[1] The IDF reserves were demobilized; with the material and personal voluntary aid of Diaspora Jewry, the economic recession began to fade.

One factor in the formulation of post-war Israeli policy was the change in the political consciousness of a large section of the population, which began long before the war. Of particular importance was the change regarding the parts of Palestine not conquered in the 1948 war. Ben-Gurion had managed to restrain the desire for a revision of the strategic status quo and even for the conquest of all of Palestine. However, he had only maintained that this wish could not be fulfilled, not that it was illegitimate. The purportedly impossible had been realized, and Israeli attitudes about foreign and defense policy were affected. Many Israelis came to favor greater autonomy from extraregional powers. It had been customary to take the attitude of the Western powers into account and to hope for their assistance against the Arab states. When aid was not forthcoming, Israel would defer to their interests and judgment and would not act alone. Now that it had acted alone and had succeeded, Israel began to view its own strength and considerations as equal to, if not more important than, those of the great powers that had "disappointed" it on the eve of the war.

To use James Chace's distinction between innocence and experience, from his *New York Times Magazine* article, Israelis began to lose their innocence with regard to friend and foe alike and tended to lean heavily on their collective experience. Innocence, in Israeli terms, had domestic and foreign policy ramifications. Domestically, Israel's life style, egalitarian simplicity, the concentration on social and moral achievements that had already proved to be incongruous with the bargaining habits of a population demanding an ever-increasing standard of living, were slowly giving way. Guilt feelings toward the Arabs—typical of the left, especially Mapam and its followers—were replaced by a new-old set of "rights."

First, there was the "right of the lone defender" who had managed to help himself against open aggression. If he had not managed, he would have been totally annihilated for nobody would have rescued him. Slowly and logically, the "right of the lone defender" created "the right of occupation." Occupation of sovereign Arab lands and Palestinian-Jordanian territories could always be temporarily justified in terms of bargaining for peace (and self-defense in the absence of peace), but Israel's belief in a "historical" and strategic right to some of these territories was modified by its most recent experience. The role of the same territories as a bridgehead for a deadly attack against Israel's heartland, and a "humanistic" approach toward Arabs living under Israeli control (especially in comparison to the behavior Jews anticipated from the Arabs if they won the war) gained significance.

To this was added the "right of fear," or the methodical right to the worst possible case analysis. Israel was justified, in its own eyes, in making an almost unconscious decision not to take further risks and not to rely on any American promises, U.N. forces, or Arab concessions, which might allow a new escalatory process. It might have been the case with Egypt that Nasser had intended a limited confrontation at the outset of the May, 1967, events that led (by Nasser's definition, endorsed by all Arabs) to a war to eliminate Israel altogether when hostilities to deter Arab aggression commenced in June, 1967. Thus, a limited Arab aggression acted to trigger an all-out attack that included Jordan, almost an Israeli ally, Iraq, and, to an extent, Syria, the source of the truble.

I inject a speculation here as to the frame of mind of Jewish immigrants from the Arab countries. Normally absorbed by Mapai and the NRP, and having adopted the elite's foreign policy stance without much questioning during Ben-Gurion's reign, the non-Ashkenazi (non-Europeans) Israelis began slowly to develop a more autonomous view of the affairs of state in the early 1960s. Long-established egalitarian bargaining habits used by the secondary elite to approach them gave the immigrants a growing sense of their right to social benefits. "I deserve it," became a regular sociopolitical demand in Israel's domestic affairs after the mid-1950s, in the sense that the state (i.e., the political elite) owed its citizens, especially the less well-to-do (most of whom were immigrants from Arab countries), a fair, egalitarian treatment.

This growing autonomy could hardly coincide with Ben-Gurion's traditional defensive stance in foreign policy, when a moment of truth would challenge his bold style and offensive gestures and force a choice between his substance and his style. Accepting humiliation and possible destruction by their former Arab masters—who treated them sometimes as second-class citizens and sometimes as pariahs,—would have been too much to ask from Israelis who had lived for generations under Arab rule. As long as this political autonomy did not exist, Ben-Gurion could mobilize enthusiasm, using his bold style and old-new sovereignty by a subtle compromise that had not brought about war or territorial changes since 1949–56 and later between 1956–63. Yet Israeli fears of the Arabs, which might have gone back to the experience of living under Arab rule, influenced events after Ben-Gurion's resignation. Together with the bid for autonomy from an Ashkenazi monopoly on political wisdom (willingly granted in social matters), these fears eventually culminated in a bid for autonomy of opinion on foreign affairs. This autonomy might have expressed itself in a more "hawkish," hard line, and principled approach toward Arabs, as manifested by both Dayan and Begin. Israelis believed Arab behavior to be arrogant toward non-Muslim minorities and especially toward Jews; they thought the Arabs considered them "traitors" to the Koran who should never be trusted. The humiliating experience of living under Arab rule might have taught Jews that Arabs would never accept any form of Jewish sovereignty in Palestine, i.e., over Arab lands. If this was so, why make any concessions? If Jews had a right to Palestine, that right was exclusive, biblical, historical, and political in the sense that no other political choice could be made to supplant Jewish sovereignty. Arab rights could be compensated in the vast, twenty-one-state Arab world. Israeli scholars, like former General Yehoshafat Harkaby, who studied official Arab positions toward Zionism, Jewish rights to a state, Jewish history, and Jewish behavior as manifested in official publications and teaching materials, religious propaganda, and secular writings, painted to a pessimistic Israeli audience a very gloomy picture indeed.

The next right, the "right of the strong," who happened to be the just in Israeli perception, was enhanced by American and other Western enthusiastic comments on Israel's lightning victory and its new role as "a regional power." Many Israelis developed a consciousness of "the right of the Western bastion in the Middle East," after having defeated a heavily Soviet-armed Arab world. Special rights as a U.S. ally were derived, in Israeli popular and military thinking, from this perception, including confidence in Israel's military capabilities, far beyond Ben-Gurion's limited projections, in the event of a renewed Arab challenge.

Fear and the need for self-assertion, which dominated Israel's public psychology until June, 1967, and brought about a subtle compromise under Ben-Gurion, were replaced by a growing sense of confidence. However, fears returned when territorial changes (i.e., withdrawals) were mentioned abroad or at home because of the perception of the Arab regular forces' obvious numerical and strategic advantages when deployed along Israel's 1949 ADL. Another element started to play a role in Israeli public psychology—the sense of clever, high-stake, confident bargaining and smart use of force if necessary. Israelis felt these national characteristics were reflected in Dayan's public behavior. Dayan said to the public, though not in so many words, "Just let me handle these Arabs."

After the grand coalition was established, the elite became complex and diverse. The war and Dayan's public appeal as a clever victor who fooled the Arabs on the eve of the war and who symbolized decision and determination helped the elite to regain some kind of charismatic appeal. Public suspicions and doubts about Eshkol's "hesitations" were replaced with a growing faith in Dayan. The substance of Dayan's policy did not become a subject for public debate; the man enjoyed enormous popularity. Public attention was focused upon Arab activity, negligible though it was, and not upon Dayan's approach to the border question and the West Bank as a whole. Basically, he was supported in his opinion that the West Bank could not be returned to Arab sovereignty because Arabs could not be trusted, at least in the forseeable future, to be honest partners and because Israel had the right to settle there. Ruling Arabs became a necessary evil. In due course, a consciousness of new frontiers of Israeli-held territories—valid, from the point of view of historical claims and experience—was added to the above-mentioned "rights." It culminated later in the "movement for the whole of Eretz-Israel," which called upon the government with increasing urgency to settle the new territory, mainly in the West Bank, and to "create facts" there just as the Zionists used to do before the 1947 partition.

The altered consciousness, widely publicized in the mass media, did not have a direct effect on actual policy making during the summer and autumn of 1967, but it remained an important background factor.[2] The three main factors in determining Israeli policy during this period were American, Arab, and domestic Israeli politics. For the American factor, the relevant aspects of U.S. policy were the conceptions of the future of the Arab-Israeli conflict in general and of the specific steps to be taken in response to Soviet and Arab positions. As far as the Arab factor was concerned, the Israelis considered Egypt's position crucial. The third factor shaping Israeli policy was the new political order and public mood of the post-Ben-Gurion period. It is hard to determine the relative importance of each of these factors. However, it is clear that American and Arab attitudes contributed to the Israeli decision to hold on to the occupied territories until peace was negotiated, and even then to settle only for "secure and recognized boundaries" that would be different from the 1949 armistice lines.

The first U.S. action that influenced Jerusalem to adopt this approach was President Johnson's statement on June 19, 1967.[3] In striking contrast to Washington's policy after the 1956 war, this statement maintained that a resolution of the Arab-Israeli conflict was necessary and that until this was attained, Israel would not have to return the territory it had conquered. In private, the Americans stated the strategic and political condition under which this declaration held: Israel's ability to hold on to its conquests by itself without impairing U.S. vital interests.[4] However, since Washington wanted negotiations in which the territories would be bargaining points, it imposed an embargo on arms deliveries to the Middle East. Israel was the principal victim of this ban, which remained in effect for 135 days. The embargo was also connected with an American demand that Israel sign the Nuclear Non-Proliferation Treaty (NPT).[5] Simultaneously, in June, July, and August, 1967, the United States tried to resolve the conflict through a bargaining process at the U.N. which was basically aimed at an exchange of the occupied territories with a political settlement.[6]

In August, 1967, after Johnson's statement, the national unity government decided to offer Egypt a withdrawal to the international frontier between former British Palestine and Egypt, in return for a resolution of the problems of Straits of Tiran and of free navigation in the Suez Canal, for the demilitarization of the Sinai, and for a peace settlement.[7] To Syria, Israel offered complete withdrawal to the international border in exchange for demilitarization of the Golan Heights, guarantees of water supply from Jordan sources to Israel, and peace. A peace settlement would open the road to a "regional cooperation," both would contribute to a "regional and international resolution" of the refugee question. In other words, the refugees, as Israel always maintained, should be resettled outside Israeli boundaries.

Cairo and Damascus rejected the offer, demanding an unconditional Israeli withdrawal.[8] The cabinet decided to retain the territories; only as a result of direct negotiations would a withdrawal be justified.[9] The West Bank and the Gaza Strip were never included in the proposed deal because the center of the cabinet was not strong enough to stand up to the Rafi, Gahal, Achdut Ha'Avoda, and most of the NRP ministers who wanted to keep these areas, at least for the time being, for security and ideological reasons. Most of the government ministers came to agree on the Jordan River as Israel's "security border," in the sense that under no circumstances would Arab armies be allowed to cross it under the terms of a peace settlement. Most of the Mapai officials would have preferred to return most of it, especially the Arab-populated areas of the West Bank. In the course of the year, Allon formulated a plan that left most of the populated areas of the West Bank under Jordanian sovereignty and most of the unpopulated and strategically important areas and East Jerusalem in Israeli hands, in exchange for an overall piece settlement. Since no member of the Arab coalition seemed willing to negotiate and Hussein alone was regarded as too unreliable, the Eshkol government did not feel that it had to consider and make a final decision on the delicate matter of territory at this stage. The Allon Plan became a semiofficial cabinet blue print for Israeli settlements in the West Bank.

By postponing the decision, the cabinet left the way open for various groups to establish settlements in these areas. Religious groups settled in traditionally sacred parts of the West Bank, such as Hebron, and members of the moshav and kibbutz movements settled in areas of strategic importance, such as the Golan Heights. These party settlements did not have preliminary cabinet approval, but were supported by the Achdut Ha'Avoda and NRP ministers and later by the defense minister; such a development would have been unthinkable in Ben-Gurion's day. Yet shortly afterwards, a slow process of settling along the Allon Plan lines and in limited historical areas of utmost importance, like Hebron, became a response to Arab intransigence, a demonstration of Israeli territorial aspirations (as far as the whole cabinet could agree on them), and an instrument for partially filling the territorial and ideological vacuum that would have been created around areas dear to Jewish-Zionist traditions, had they not been settled. Other historical sites, like Shchem (Nablus), were not settled, in accord with Mapai's firm objection and Allon's principle of not settling in Arab-populated areas. The Arabs realized that Israel had resolved several points of contention over the West Bank (Allon's Plan), the Golan Heights, and Sharm-el-Sheikh. Israel's national consensus was reflected by an agreement between all parties to the grand coalition regarding the future of some occupied territories. However, Israeli leaders never said this in public and insisted upon direct negotiations without preconditions, maintaining, that it would not return to the pre-1967 lines. Moreover, they said that the Arabs should first make peace while the partial territorial vacuum still existed.

In the immediate postwar period the Israelis waited, as Dayan put it, "for a telephone call from the Arabs," that is for recognition, negotiations, and peace on Israeli terms. King Hussein became the only Arab leader willing to deal with Israel, but he was considered weak and unreliable as a negotiating partner, and the territory he wanted back was of major strategic, historical, and ideological importance.[10] While Egypt was rearming by a massive Soviet airlift, the first postwar Arab summit at Khartoum in late August, 1967, agreed on "three no's": no peace, no negotiations, and no recognition. The published version of the Khartoum decisions was less explicit than the internal talks, but the Israelis managed to obtain the original, radical decisions.[11] For them, this was further evidence of Arab determination to fight Israel to the end and of Arab double-talk used as a tactical measure. Israel's traditional fears that "the Arabs" would use such tactics to fool the gullible and to supply arguments to interested extraregional powers, which continued to guide Israel's attitude toward Arab "moderate" expressions vis-à-vis third parties, were nourished even more by its successful intelligence work on the Khartoum decisions. Yet Israel's demand for a public and final change in Arab policy might have helped bring about the Arab's total rejection of such a change. The gap between the two parties' positions left a political and diplomatic vacuum and helped keep the profile of the conflict very high. At the same time, the Arabs conducted a concentrated diplomatic effort at the United Nations, aimed at a Security Council resolution in support of the restoration of the status quo ante bellum, which would not require a concession by the Arabs or a renunciation of their rights as belligerents. In other words, not only were they unwilling to concede anything in terms of specific results of the 1967 conflict, but they also stood firm in the claims as to the problems arising from Israel's very existence. Fath warned Arab leaders at Khartoum that they might pay the price personally, if any concessions were made.

The United States, which sought a resolution of the conflict, could hardly support an Arab policy aimed at preserving it. The U.S.S.R. also tried, with little success, to moderate the Arab positions at the U.N.[12] After long bargaining, the British U.N. representative, Lord Caradon, came up with a compromise formula that was accepted as Security Council Resolution 242.[13] The preamble to the resolution affirmed the "inadmissability" of the acquisition of territory by force and the need for a just and lasting peace. The council laid down the following conditions for a resolution of the conflict: (1) the withdrawal of Israeli forces "from territories" or "from the territories" captured in the war (the first formulation is the English version, the second is the French; the Russian version does not distinguish between the two); (2) the renunciation of belligerency by all states in the area, and respect for the sovereignty, territorial integrity, political independence, and right to live in peace within secure and recognized boundaries of each state by all the others; (3) freedom of navigation in international waters; (4) a just settlement of the Arab refugee problem; (5) the fostering of the security and sovereignty of the Middle East states by various means, including the establishment of demilitarized zones; (6) the appointment of a special representative by the U.N. secretary general to promote an agreement in accordance with those principles. According to former U.S. Under Secretary of State Joseph Sisco,[14] Resolution 242 was an American concept, primarily devised by U.N. Ambassador Arthur Goldberg and sponsored by the British in the Security Council in order to demonstrate a large degree of understanding between western members of that body. Basically, the resolution was "constructively ambiguous" on the border question. American emphasis was contrary to the Arab-Russian demand, and to the future interpretation of the resolution if Israel were obliged to effect a complete withdrawal to the pre-June, 1967, ADL. According to Sisco, by the same token, the Israelis were not supposed to be given assurances for new borders.

Concerning the second, traditional issue of the Arab-Israeli conflict— the political problem, or Israel's right to exist at peace with its neighbors —Resolution 242 did not demand "contractual peace" from the Arabs (in Sisco's words), but some kind of end to the belligerency. The third, traditional element in the package—the Palestinian problem—was treated rather vaguely and generally, referring to the Palestinians as refugees.

President Nasser publicly announced his acceptance of the Resolution, while at the same time stating that "what was taken by force will be returned by force," and privately informing Egypt's own armed forces, and Fath, that his indirect acceptance of peace did not relate to them.[15] Thus, the problem of decoding Arab intentions became even more serious in Israeli eyes; they were usually informed about inner, and inter-Arab talks. The two or more faces used by Arab leaders when they approached different parties seemed to most Israelis to be typical Arab treachery, this seemed to General Dayan a typical Arab refusal to accomodate themselves to reality. More and more the cabinet insisted upon an official Arab recognition and acceptance of Israel, to put an end to the double talk and to pin Arab leaders down to their commitments. For Arab leaders this must have been a humiliating *Diktat:* the Israelis had forced themselves upon an Arab region, deprived the Palestinians of their homeland, worked together with Britain and France, tried to isolate Egypt from the non-Muslim periphial states and later from Black Africa, attacked them on June 4, 1967, won the war with U.S. support, and occupied vast Arab—including Arab-populated—lands, and now they wanted to dictate to the Arabs how to speak and behave, and to refrain from seeking every legitimate support from within and from without on an inter-Arab level in their bid to recover not only the land, but also their sovereignty, i.e., freedom of action and self-respect.

For most Israelis, this combination of Arab "rights" would mean their own destruction sooner or later. Jerusalem doubted Nasser's sincerity, suspecting him of wishing to interpret Resolution 242 in such a way as to retrieve the conquered Arab territories without committing himself to peace or to a settlement of the conflict that did not include an "acceptable" solution of the refugee problem. The official Egyptian position was that a resolution of the refugee problem meant a formula acceptable to the "Palestinians themselves," i.e. the PLO. The PLO's 1964 covenant, however, called for the destruction of Israel. Thus, Israeli government opinion was split over Resolution 242. A compromise was found when Israel's U.N. representative accepted the Resolution.[16] Yet, on December 1, 1967, Prime Minister Eshkol announced a new cabinet consensus that diverged from Resolution 242 on a number of points about the Arab position adopted at Khartoum.[17] First, Israel demanded secure and recognized boundaries that would be entrenched in a final peace treaty. "Secure" boundaries were explicitly stated to mean borders different from the 1949 ADL, since the latter was an invitation to Arab aggression. The second aspect of the consensus was that the settlement should be achieved through direct negotiations between Israel and the Arab states. Third, the refugee problem must be resolved in a regional and global framework, that is, outside Israel's final borders and with international help. Finally, Israel demanded freedom of passage for Israeli shipping through the Straits of Tiran and the Suez Canal.

All the coalition parties could join in this consensus partly because it did not define what the state's boundaries should be and it freed the parties from the need to discuss them, and partly because it stressed the negotiating procedure that increasingly became Israel's major criterion for judging Arab intentions. Still, and despite the fact that Jerusalem did not attach much importance to them, Israel did not object to the mediating efforts of the U.N. envoy Gunnar Jarring, a correct and careful Swedish diplomat who was entrusted with the implementation of Resolution 242.[18] Both sides regarded him simply as a tool for the advancement of their own interests, because he had little political significance or bargaining power of his own. The Soviet foreign minister was openly contemptuous of Jarring. "What divisions, ships at sea, or missiles in the air does he have?," Gromyko is quoted as having asked the Egyptians, hinting rather broadly that only the U.S.S.R. could help the Arab cause.[19] Indeed, even though, to the Arabs' only expressed disappointment, the Soviet Union did not directly intervene to help the Arabs, it threatened to do so if the Israelis got too close to Damascus. The Egyptians reported that, soon after the war, Secretary General Brezhnev said that if the Israelis ever threatened Cairo, they would bring the world to the brink of war. So, in the postwar period, the U.S.S.R. replaced Syrian and Egyptian arms lost in the war, seemed to have affirmed its protection to the capital cities of the Arab regimes close to it, and gave as much diplomatic support as it thought wise to give to Arab demands at the U.N.

Apparently, Egypt saw the restoration of its military option with Soviet strategic aid as a necessary condition for the recovery of all the Arab territory lost in the war. The recovery of this territory, however, was publicly proclaimed to be a phase in the Arab states' greater conflict with Israel. In the Arabs' view, the mere establishment of Israel had interferred with the rights of the Arab states both individually and collectively as limbs of the Arab nation. Moreover, they were politically and ideologically committed to the Palestinian cause.

Politically, militarily, and psychologically, there was no reason for most of the Arabs to concede the struggle after their defeat in the war. They initiated an examination of the strategic, political, and military causes for their defeat in order to correct the situation. With the possible exception of Jordan, which had not been able to fit completely into the populist and radical mainstream of Arab nationalism, it had also extended Jordanian citizenship to the resident Palestinians in its territory. The Arab states, therefore, wanted to continue their struggle against Israel, to negate the results of the Six-Day War without conceding any of their basic claims against the Jewish state.

Before 1967 the Arab states had often been split in their tactics, politics, and practice vis-à-vis Israel. They were now forced to combine all their claims in a single package, while the Israelis also raised their demands and called for a final settlement to include secure and recognized boundaries. The Khartoum resolutions provided an indication of the Arab consensus, yet Egypt remained the active power, Cairo's tactics were reflected in Nasser's combination of the acceptance of Resolution 242 with the military program and the expansion of strategic cooperation with the Soviet Union.

The Egyptians seem to have learned several lessons from their defeat in 1967, which would shape their policy in the ensuing period. First, Nasser concluded that it was necessary to balance American power in the Mediterranean with a Soviet presence great enough to neutralize it and to provide the Arabs with effective aid in the event of a general or limited war without fearing the U.S. reaction. In the Six-Day War, Soviet power in the area had proved insufficient. Furthermore, once the United States no longer had strategic superiority in the region, the threat of a confrontation with the U.S.S.R. would limit its ability to help Israel, and would thus limit Israel's own strategic capacity to fight the Arabs. Egypt might gain an advantage over Washington with Soviet support; indeed, it seemed that the Johnson administration would not take seriously a defeated gambler—President Nasser—without it.

Nasser's second conclusion was that using Soviet help was the only way to strengthen Egypt militarily. Egypt would, therefore, do well to give in to Moscow's requests for the use of military, principally naval, installations in Egypt. Not only would this serve Nasser's strategic objective of strengthening the U.S.S.R. in the Mediterranean, but it would also constitute repayment or a bargaining card for repayment for Soviet advisers and arms.

Third, Nasser decided that the diplomatic struggle in the United Nations should be combined with a three-stage plan, which would begin with military reconstruction and progress to "active deterrence." "Active deterrence" meant exerting political and military pressure on Israel (and the United States) from improved positions along the Suez Canal. Later, the liberation of the occupied territories by force of arms, political pressure, or both, would follow.

Fourth, it was decided to activate the eastern front against Israel, mainly with the help of the Palestinian organizations. These had, hitherto, been based largely in Syria and Lebanon and had been actively supported by Syria. Now they were to have Egypt's active support as well and would carry out operations against Israel from Jordan.[20] Indeed, for the time being, these guerilla attacks would be the sole expression of the Arabs' armed struggle against Israel. This struggle was directed against Israeli occupation of the areas captured in 1967 and also, according to the 1964 Palestine National Covenant, toward the liquidation of the Jewish state. The Israelis deemed Egypt's open support of organizations with these objectives to be incompatible with Cairo's acceptance of Resolution 242. Nasser's support of Fath was also considered to be qualitatively important by Israel in that it extended Cairo's political protection to the organization and created the first official link between Fath and Egypt's own sponsor, the U.S.S.R. Moreover, Fath's stepped-up campaign against Israel from the East Bank of the Jordan River and Hussein's assent to these operations in 1968 and 1969 made the king even less a negotiating partner for Israel.

In early 1968, Egypt itself opened hostilities, with massive artillery bombardments of the Israeli forces stationed along the Suez Canal. In 1969 the fighting developed into a continuous war of attrition, in the form of heavy shelling and commando raids along the Canal.[21] During that period, American policy toward the Middle East was based on considerations of its relations with the U.S.S.R., the Arab states, and Israel. In terms of relations with the Soviet Union, America's prime concern was to prevent a world war, while continuing a controlled struggle against the U.S.S.R. whenever it threatened U.S. interests, prestige, and allies. The global struggle against the Soviet Union was split into regional conflicts. It was desirable for these regional problems to be solved by compromise agreements with Moscow over each separate instance. If this could not be achieved, the United States must react using military, economic, and political measures wherever justified, and by exerting pressure on the U.S.S.R. in one region in order to influence Soviet behavior in other major crisis areas, such as Vietnam.[22]

U.S. relations with the Arab states involved problems on three levels. The first concerned relations with Soviet client states such as Egypt and Syria, who were strengthening the ties to their patron. Syria had not accepted Resolution 242 and had thus excluded itself from the diplomatic and political framework that the resolution entailed. Egypt, on the other hand, had accepted the resolution and could perhaps be influenced through controlled aid to Israel and proposals for settlements that would take Egypt's position into account. The United States might in this way establish a viable bargaining position vis-à-vis Egypt and the Soviet Union, which would contribute to the settling of the regional conflict and to restraining the U.S.S.R. in other regions, particularly Vietnam. The second level of consideration concerned the pro-Western Arab states, such as Saudi Arabia, Jordan, and Lebanon. Links with these countries had to be maintained and expanded and the radical Palestinian organizations in the latter two states had to be restrained. Washington should avoid identifying with all Israel's positions. Overidentification with Israel would have been detrimental to the pro-Western regimes' interests and status in the Arab coalition and could have pushed Egypt to opt for even more extreme positions and more Soviet aid, which would also endanger the pro-Western states. The third level was the conflict itself. The United States considered annexation or prolonged Israeli occupation of large Arab territories unacceptable, and looked for a way in which the Israeli-held lands might be exchanged for a general settlement that would include a resolution of the refugee problem.

In terms of U.S. policy considerations during this period, American relations with Israel could be divided schematically into the four areas. First was Israel's power within the United States; this involved specific domestic political concerns of the administration. Second was Israel's ability to reject and bargain over American views and claims; this was related, in part, to the domestic situation in Israel. Third was Israel's international standing; and fourth, Israel's positions, as opposed to those of the Arab states, in the context of U.S.—Soviet and U.S.—Arab relations.

Israel was reckoned a power inside the United States for a number of reasons. The first is the real or imagined political, economic, and electoral power that various administrations have attributed to the American Jewish community, particularly during an election year. Political power means the voting potential, and the ability to influence members of Congress, the mass media, public organizations such as unions, and the academic community. Economic power in this context refers mainly to donations to election campaigns by individual Jews acting in Jewish bodies or on the basis of considerations of Israeli interest. Even after the reform of political fund-raising legislation in 1974, considerable sums were raised by Jews in this way.[23]

Another source of Israeli power in the United States was the attitude of American non-Jews to the Jewish state. Americans identified, to some extent, with the people of the Bible trying to reestablish sovereignty in their land and carrying out exemplary pioneering enterprises while fighting off the Arabs. Americans also sympathized with Israel as a small Western democratic state fighting alone against forces tied to British imperialism and later to the Soviet Union and the "oil sheikhs." The destruction of European Jewry in World War II served to reinforce the popular feeling for Israel.[24]

A third source of Israel's political power in the United States was the relationship between Jews and gentiles there. Since 1949, American Jewry had come to identify more and more with Israel. Many Jews had previously been afraid to identify with Israel for fear of a clash with their gentile environment, or had not believed in Zionism's ideas and or chances of success; eventually they began to regard Israel as the major expression of their Jewishness, as a source of ethnic and personal pride, as an occupation for their free time and a refuge whenever one might be needed. This sympathy was mobilizd during the 1948–49 War of Independence, but it was not sufficient to prevent an American arms embargo on Israel during its gravest peril, in 1948. Jewish interests could not overcome a general U.S. foreign policy stance such as the strategy of containment. The Six-Day War reinforced Jewish support for Israel and silenced Jewish groups that were anti-Zionist or that had reservations about Israel.[25] At the same time, Israel proved to be a strong ally in fighting Soviet clients, who were no longer potential partners of the West.

Yitzhak Rabin, appointed ambassador to Washington soon after the 1967 war, made a conscious effort to organize and exploit these foundations of support for Israel, with the help of the well organized Israeli lobby in Congress and of other more or less representative Jewish bodies such as the "Presidents Club" of American Jewish organizations. During Rabin's term as ambassador, from 1968–73, the Israeli embassy began to profit from the potential Jewish influence and the ambassador himself tried to exercise leverage within the structures of the U.S. political system.[26]

During 1968, Israel found its bargaining position vis-à-vis the United States improved because of American global strategy. The Vietnam War was growing more serious at the time, the Soviets had invaded Czechoslovakia, and Soviet clients such as Nasser's Egypt were regarded as working against American interests in other regions as well. In the 1967 war, Israel had shown that it had the military capability to beat three of its neighbors without direct American assistance. It, therefore, had the "right" to be considered an autonomous political force in the future, as long as it did not use its power to pursue a policy detrimental to American interests. Israel also had the "right" to selective American aid, thanks to its political power in the United States and to a certain symmetry in Washington's and Jerusalem's interests; for reasons of its own, each wanted an end to the Middle East Conflict. Pursuing this end not on Arab terms meant pursuing it closer to Israeli terms.

At the same time the United States continued to show an interest in dealing with the U.S.S.R. over the Middle East and Vietnam, Washington did have reservations about President Nasser. However, it wanted to bring about an end to the conflict according to its own understanding, which was not necessarily Israel's. The Israelis, therefore, feared superpower deals to impose a settlement far different from their own formula of secure and recognized borders that were not those of June 4, 1967. Traditionally, they feared Soviet aid to the Arabs and a possible direct confrontation with the Soviet Union. Dayan made general public warnings about this danger during 1968, as the Canal War intensified with a growing Soviet presence in Egypt. At the same time, Israel was warned by American visitors, the foremost of whom was Professor Henry A. Kissinger, that the United States was not going "to lift a finger for Israel" if the Russians chose to intervene directly. In a meeting with Israeli scholars in Jerusalem, Kissinger talked about, "say, a Soviet missile attack against the Israeli air force bases in Sinai." Governor Rockefeller's adviser told the Israelis bluntly, that "the main aim of any American president is to prevent World War III. Second, that no American president would risk World War III because of territories occupied by Israel. Three, the Russians know this."[27]

Under these circumstances Dayan's dilemma was over how to bring a reluctant America behind Israel without losing Israel's autonomy; he might have supported even more strongly an Israeli autonomous nuclear program. At first, the three Arab "no's" at the August, 1967, Khartoum Conference and Egypt's escalated war against Israel along the Suez Canal helped Israeli strategic thinking by adopting a "territorial-defensive" approach to Arab challenges along the new cease-fire lines. A new chief of staff, Lieutenant General Haim Bar-Lev, replaced General Rabin, trying to use the new lines as best he could. These lines seemed to relieve most of the population from sharing, or being daily exposed to, constant defense risks, allowing Israel's heartland to develop and expand cautiously. Regular troops and the air force could contain the Arabs in remote border areas, thanks to Israel's own conventional strength and to limited American aid. This aid, however, was dependent upon U.S. global considerations, Soviet aid to the Arabs, and an inflexible Arab official stance. It was also linked, as mentioned above, to the Israeli consent to sign the future Non-Proliferation Treaty.

When Israel, which lost its "French connection" on the eve of the 1967 war, appealed to the United States for new warplanes, especially F-4 "Phantom" fighter-bombers, the decision was withheld at first because of the political process at the U.N. that should have brought about an exchange of territories in a political settlement. The key Arab states refused to negotiate such a settlement and turned to the Soviets for military aid and military presence, and the Johnson administration released "Skyhawk" attack planes and tried to link "Phantom" supplies to Israel's consent to sign the NPT. (The F-4 is capable of carrying nuclear warheads.) The Israelis could have argued[28] that the treaty would not prevent the Arabs from breaking it whenever they chose to "go nuclear," whereas Israel would not sign the agreement if it were only to transgress it. Having repeatedly declared their intention not to introduce nuclear weapons into the Middle East, the Israelis could see no advantage to opening their facilities to the international inspection that might be required by the NPT, unless there was an Arab quid pro quo, and the Arabs had no facilities of their own. International inspectors would have a political—and real— reason, if Israel were to develop a nuclear capacity, for condemning Israel for violating the NPT, and Israel would also lose the obvious political advantages of ambiguity in its nuclear option.

Dayan's frame of mind was traditionally different from the "conventional-territorial" school of thought that predominated Eshkol's Mapai-Achdut Ha'Avoda coalition and was reflected in the Allon-Rabin influence on defense thinking. Both Allon and Rabin lost their primacy in the defense establishment after the emergence of the grand coalition, while their successor, Dayan, did not feel secure as to foreign arms supplies. First there was the French embargo, which prompted an Israeli warplane production program, and the there was constant trouble with the United States over the Phantoms while the Russians were reequipping the Arabs with Mig 21s and sending active advisers to Egypt and Syria. At that point, Dayan's basic perception of foreign and defense policy could be summarized as "Gaullist," or "Gaullistic," not only in the simplistic terms of the supremacy of national interests and autonomy of action to enhance national interests first. This element in him, which was bound to his responsive behavior to Arab challenges per se as a matter of principle, and which made him a "manly leader," as opposed to the "postulative-cognitive" leader of Ben-Gurion's type or the "bargainer" of Eshkol's type, coupled with Dayan's new responsibilities, his reading of the past, and the international situation. For Dayan, at least until 1971, the actual defense political question was not Arab challenges, but the superpowers. Israel's ability to secure Dayan's main goal—"defensible and recognized borders"—after an inevitably long and hard struggle, was not a function of Arab net strength, or of an Israeli moderate stance that would not satisfy the Arabs in any case, or of territorial concessions that turned against Israel because of Arab coalitionary logics; rather, it was a function of superpower aid to Israel and superpower constraints upon Israel's autonomy of action against Arabs. Israel's "real enemies" in the struggle to achieve borders that, in Dayan's perception, were essential to Israel's security and development both politically and spiritually, were not the Arabs, whose behavior could be anticipated and understood, but the Soviet Union and the United States. The Russians were dangerous as arms suppliers, as military consultants with growing direct involvement in the Arab world, and as an empire with growing power and ambition. If intimidated by Israeli actions against Arabs, Moscow might come to the Arabs' aid because of Soviet prestige and global interests that might have nothing directly to do with the Middle East conflict but which were part of imperial Soviet interests in the area. The United States might support Israel or not, as happened during the 1948–49 war, when Washington imposed its deadly embargo on arms shipments to Israel, or during the 135-day embargo following the Six-Day War. American considerations were bound not only to the common cultural heritage, the holocaust, American Jewry, and Israel's democratic system, but also to those American domestic considerations and global and regional interests that might or might not coincide with Israeli interests. Since his journalistic mission to Vietnam in early 1967, Dayan had developed a growing feeling the United States might be a world power in retreat, unable to use its tremendous capabilities to subdue a determined little foe who enjoyed unlimited Soviet aid. Israel, as a result of this basic perception, should have developed every possible, even if marginal, measure of leverage over the superpowers and the Arabs at the same time. An Israeli nuclear capability might serve as an additional factor of uncertainty in restraining direct Soviet involvement in Egypt against Israel and an element of risk, limited though it might be, if Moscow chose to intervene in the Middle East conflict in the swift and crushing manner suggested above by Henry Kissinger. Kissinger's game, with Soviet IRBMs launched against Israeli air force bases in the Sinai, did not make much sense technically and politically. Dayan could have developed a sense of autonomy from the United States if Washington saw a slight advantage for itself, and a high risk of confrontation with Moscow, in opposing a Soviet action in the Middle East. Having no access to the primary sources in this case, since Israel has retained its official ambiguous stance on the nuclear issue ever since, some researchers suggest that, under Dayan, the early supporter of Israel's nuclear effort, incentives accumulated in 1968 to realize Israel's nuclear option.[29] During most of the same year, Israel was observing possible American moves to impose a solution in the Middle East because of the growing intensity of Soviet-backed Egyptian actions along the Suez Canal.

The seven-point document presented by Secretary of State Dean Rusk in November, 1968,[30] seemed to justify Israel's fears that an imposed solution was imminent. This document laid down the following principles: first, Israel would withdraw from Egyptian territory; second, there would be an end to the state of belligerency; third, the Suez Canal would be opened to the ships of all nations; fourth, the problem of the Palestinian refugees would be resolved in accordance with their own wishes; fifth, Sharm-el-Sheikh and the Straits of Tiran would be placed under international supervision, which could be removed only with the consent of the Security Council; sixth, the great powers would come to a general understanding on arms supplies to the area; seventh, Egypt and Israel would both sign an instrument of agreement. The most alarming term of this document, from the standpoint of long-established Israeli policy, was the fourth one, which provided for the repatriation of those refugees who wished to return. Israel would thus lose its Jewish character and would become a binational state with the old "impossible" borders.

Eshkol thought of using Israel's nuclear option as a possible trump card against a Soviet-American agreement to impose Rusk's program. The prime minister told his aides that Israel might be able to exploit the Johnson administration's sensitivity about nuclear nonproliferation—a sensitivity shared by McGeorge Bundy, the Rostow brothers, Defense Secretary McNamara, and other Kennedy intellectuals—to avert an imposed settlement or at least to have refugees clause struck from the document, and to secure the delivery of supersonic jets. In return, the prime minister was ready to consider allowing regular American inspection of Israel's nuclear installations; this right had never been granted the Kennedy administration, but such visits had become more frequent after 1966. At any rate, the prime minister was not ready to sign the NPT treaty.[31]

Eshkol's advisers thought such a proposal hasty and unnecessary. The refugee clause was, they felt, possibly just a bargaining ploy. Furthermore, the escalating Vietnam War was hurting Soviet-American relations, and the prospects of a superpower agreement on the Middle East were slim. Indeed, Egypt's Soviet-backed limited military strategy against Israel would probably stimulate American aid to Israel to contain Egypt and prevent a Soviet-supported military solution of the conflict. In any event, the Rusk proposals never became operative;[32] the Arabs, with Soviet support, rejected them. At the same time, Israel did not sign the NPT, as the U.S.-Israeli relations were influenced by the end phase of the Johnson administration and by the Canal War, which gained momentum as the U.S.S.R. stepped up aid to the Arabs. Israel repeatedly appealed to the United States for military supplies, especially F-4 Phantom fighter-bombers. Since launching the lightning attack on the Arab air forces at the outbreak of the 1967 war, Israel's air force had become its key military arm. In the absence of a large regular army supported by a large artillery force, the IAF became the principal tool for maintaining Israel's strategic superiority. Steps were taken to increase the regular army, mainly the armored divisions. The air force and the canal became a combined military-political asset.

Because a large reserve force could not be kept permanently mobilized, the canal sector was defended by only a very small land force. More regular units were stationed behind these. The IAF acted as Israel's flying artillery, providing tactical cover for the canal line. To perform these strategic and tactical tasks, Israel wanted a modern, long-range fighter-bomber. Washington was hesitant to supply this airplane. It did not want to increase its customers autonomy; a degree of dependence would give the United States leverage for extracting Israeli concessions to the Arabs and would help achieve the final settlement the Americans wanted. However, with the Vietnam war escalating, with no prospect of a political end to the canal war, and with the Arabs and the U.S.S.R. adamant in their demands for a restoration of the status quo ante bellum, in late 1968 the U.S. administration decided to supply Israel with fifty Phantoms and fifty ground support Skyhawks, with deliveries to be spaced over a long period. The Israelis, meanwhile, built up their standing military forces by extending the period of conscript service.

The Johnson administration drew near its end and the United States prepared to elect a new president. In early 1969, Levi Eshkol died, and changes had to be made in the Israeli government as well.

THE MEIR GOVERNMENT: DOMESTIC FEATURES AND FOREIGN POLICY, 1969–70

Mapai, the main faction in the Labor party, had not prepared anyone to succeed Eshkol. Nor did it want to see either of the leaders of the Rafi and Achdut Ha'Avoda factions, Dayan and Allon, as prime minister. Most of the Mapai leadership was composed of party activists whose main concern had always been the party machinery and the national economy. They were very powerful within the party apparatus and tended to hold moderate views on foreign policy. Led by Finance Minister Pinhas Sapir,[33] they looked for a successor to Eshkol among their own number. They were well aware that anyone who, like themselves, had no authority in foreign affairs and security would have a hard time as prime minister.

Thus they automatically arrived at the choice of Golda Meir. With the Mapai apparatus behind her, she was quickly nominated by the Central Party Committee and she assumed office in March, 1969.

Meir was one of the old Mapai leaders, a friend and opponent of Ben-Gurion, a former foreign minister and Mapai party secretary.[34] Of the generation of the founders of the state, she had already retired from active politics and was much older than the party activists who chose her. She differed with them on many matters. Most of the people who chose Meir thought pragmatically about the survival of the state and feared an extended period of Israeli rule over a large Arab population. They, therefore, favored making large territorial concessions in return for arrangements that would somehow ensure Israel's survival. However, they had no idea of how to go about obtaining these settlements or of what nature these settlements would assume. Meir, on the other hand, had been skeptical about the possibility of such arrangements; she was unwilling to make any concessions unless there was a drastic change in the Arabs' attitude, and these concessions should be limited to ensure Israel's security in the future.[35] In her opinion, the solution of the conflict depended primarily on the Arabs' acceptance of Israel's right to exist, manifested in total peace. Meir believed that Israeli-Arab relations should be established on the pattern of U.S.-Canadian or Belgian-Dutch relations.

A product of an eastern European Jewish ghetto, Golda Meir learned to fear and to hate as a young girl. Later she revolted against this pogrom reality and joined the Zionists to prevent pogroms or a second holocaust. She believed that if the Arabs did not accept Israel, they should be treated accordingly; hatred should be answered with a firm Israeli stand. Until total Arab acceptance was gained, and on the basis of past experience, she was inclined not to make any concessions. A settlement founded on something less than a change in the Arabs' basic attitude toward Israel was worse than useless and would, indeed, put the state in an even more unfavorable political position: Israel would be forced to make further concessions without any gains.

Meir and most of her ministers thought their position and problem to be substantially the same as the Eshkol government's had been before June, 1967: how to control possibly inevitable escalatory steps by the Arab coalition, which would endanger Israel's basic security and dictate how it acted in the whole range of issues of the Arab-Israel conflict. If Israel withdrew to the pre-June, 1967, borders, the escalation itself would be dependent solely on developments in the Arab world. No matter what Israel did, no matter what position it took on the issues, it could not control them.

The problem was much more difficult before the Six-Day War. Israel might have been able to stop the build-up to a war by accepting defeat in the Straits of Tiran. However, then it would have had to deal with more terrorist attacks backed by Egypt's operational military deployment in the Sinai. It would also have had to worry about the military alliance of Egypt, Syria, Jordan, and Iraq, which its own restraint and Nasser's successes in May, 1967, had made possible. Since no external power was willing to call the Egyptian president to heel or to stop the crystallization of an all-Arab coalition politically committed to the PLO and Fath, Israel felt that it was forced to take action itself.

Drawing her lessons from the earlier period, Meir concluded that to control such an escalatory process, Israel would have to control the territory captured in the war until a real peace was made. Any concessions to the Arabs might inevitably be followed by escalation and would leave Israel with less leverage to control the process. Thus, any Israeli concession would be an Arab gain: a real zero-sum game. Far-reaching concessions that were not traded for an end to the conflict could be followed by terrorist attacks on the populated areas of Israel, and such raids would give rise to domestic pressures that no Israeli government could ignore. Retaliations would ensue to act as a catalyst for escalation, and would give rise to extraregional pressures for further Israeli concessions in areas crucial to the state. In the end Jerusalem might be forced to accept the repatriation of Palestinian refugees, and its capacity for domestic control and for freedom of action beyond its borders would be severely restricted. Meir tended to see the Palestinians as an integral part of the Arab nation —as they themselves felt—and as such they could easily be resettled anywhere in the Arab world. She also remembered that in the 1920s Palestinian bodies had defined themselves as "southern Syrian Arabs." To her, the claim for a separate Palestinian national entity was simply a political demand for the liquidation of Israel.

The conclusion that Meir drew from this analysis of the situation was that it would be tactically unwise to present a detailed plan indicating Israel's willingness to make concrete concessions. The Arabs, the great powers, and international public opinion would accept the concessions, but then these would be taken as given and in the real negotiations attempts would be made to extort more concessions in exchange for something less than a termination of the conflict. Israel's tactic, she believed, should be to put up a hard and bitter struggle for every bit of territory in order to extract concessions from the Arabs. Following this course, moreover, would entail tough dealings with the United States so that Jerusalem might make minimal concessions in exchange for maximal changes in the Arab position. In general, though, it was assumed that such changes were highly unlikely. "Change" meant that the Arabs would have to undergo "reeducation" if they wanted any territory back. The focus of the conflict would be shifted from the Israeli heartland, from the problem of Israel's survival, to territorial reserves that Israel could parcel out as needed. Any withdrawal, however, would occur only after the contention over these "marginal" areas had fulfilled its educational function, and that would certainly take a long time.

Mrs. Meir regarded an Israeli-American understanding, or a recognized special relationship, as a basic parameter of her policy. She would always argue with, and even threaten, her American counterparts in times of need, but at the same time would try to maintain the Israeli-American dialogue. If she had no other choice she would yield to American pressures, not because of specific arguments or threats used by Washington, but in order to maintain a basic U.S.-Israeli framework of mutual understanding and cooperation. Her basic approach to both Arabs and Americans was stonewalling—standing firm, to "reeducate" the Arabs and prove to Washington at the same time that Israel was an American asset in a shaky Middle East. She wished to show that a strong Israel was the best guarantee for stability in the area (a major American aim) and the best instrument to bring about a political settlement.

Dayan, previously a bitter enemy of Meir, thought and behaved in terms of Israeli autonomous interest, as he understood it, in a world in which national sovereignty and national power prevailed, and in which Israeli interest might or might not coincide with American interest. Yet Dayan shared many views with Meir, as both of them soon discovered. He reflected her thinking completely when he used blunt terms for domestic consumption and to reeducate the Arabs. Her fear of Dayan's past escapades—preventive wars, retaliatory acts, and his association with Ben-Gurion's Rafi—diminished in the situation after 1967. Meir was as responsive to Arab negativism and concrete challenges as the "manly leader" used to be, and she agreed with Dayan that the Arabs must be taught to live with Israel in peace, even if she did not share his quest for the West Bank and she resented, as did every traditional Mapai leader, ruling a large number of Arabs. Yet these Arabs were given free access to Hussein's East Bank, in accordance with Dayan's relatively liberal occupation regime, and Israel did not annex their territories or grant them citizenship. Israel could wait, and Dayan and Meir could cooperate, until the Arabs changed their behavior.

With characteristic "manly" bluntness, Dayan, in 1970, used the biblical phrase "by the sword thou livest" in speaking of the process of "reeducating" the Arabs, which, he thought, would go on for generations. Such speaking in pure power terms gave the Arabs a great moral and propaganda edge. Egypt (and later Syria) learned to use positive terms when appealing to international public opinion, to speak about peace and the legitimate rights of a conquered people. Israel was maneuvered into the position of having to reply to Arab statements that often seemed quite reasonable. Jerusalem, however, would hesitate to put them to a test, for it saw the conflict as a zero-sum game and lacked faith in "moderate" Arab positions. The attitudes of the leadership and the general public in Israel tended to be mutually reinforcing, and they hardened this position.

The new prime minister's style was as firm and aggressive as Ben-Gurion's had been, and she soon created an atmosphere of public calm and confidence. Unlike Ben-Gurion's, though, Meir's actual policy toward the Arabs was more simplistic and fundamentalistic. It was based on the concepts of historic rights and past precedents—the wrongs Israel had suffered at the hands of the Arabs, their basic hostility to the Jewish state, and the wrongs done to the Jews by the "world" as a whole.

Meir was at the same time a careful and experienced parliamentary and party politician. Thanks to her firm and authoritative personality, she was able to overcome structural and personal divisions in the cabinet. The shocks of the Ben-Gurion period and the political rules of behavior entrenched after his retirement led her to seek as broad as possible a coalitional base for her government. The National Unity framework was, therefore, maintained until the 1969 general elections. These elections did not result in any change in the parties relative strengths, and the new government was very similar to the outgoing one. Rafi and Gahal, previously represented mainly by Dayan and Begin, gained greater representation in the cabinet.[36]

The new cabinet had the following form: at the center of the principal party in the cabinet—Labor—was the Mapai faction, headed by Golda Meir. Even though most of the members of the faction were inclined to a more elastic foreign policy than she was, they deferred to her personal authority in foreign policy, and regarded her firm domestic leadership as an asset in itself. The Rafi faction followed the popular defense minister, whose foreign and defense policy considerations were military, strategic, and ideological. Achdut Ha'Avoda held views similar to Dayan's in most foreign affairs, although it was strongly opposed to him personally, and it opposed a nuclear deterrent. Internally, the faction was split between Allon, who propagated autonomy for the West Bank dwellers as a first step toward realizing his plan, and Galili, who endorsed the territorial framework drawn by the plan as settlement lines for Israelis but had his doubts about further steps toward a Palestinian, rather than Jordanian, political entity in the West Bank. Yitzhak Ben-Aharon, another leading member of the faction and an outspoken Socialist "dove," became secretary general of the Histadrut and launched a bitter attack on the economic regime of Finance Minister Sapir, another leading "dove." Trying to revive old socialist-egalitarian values, Ben-

Aharon vigorously opposed Sapir's efforts to promote the free market through government investments and loans, and publicly denounced the new moneyed elite, the expanding services, and the cheap Arab labor used by many Israelis to advance their own standards of living. Ben-Ahraon's practical alternative was to support pressure and interest groups fighting Sapir for a better share of the national economic resources, thus spliting the "dovish" camp in the alignment and legitimizing even more bargains with interest groups to calm them down.

The National Religious party, the customary coalition partner of Mapai and now Labor, was beginning to undergo a process of internal faction and political and ideological radicalization. Its moderate leader, Shapira, had died in 1968. The old pragmatic leadership was being challenged by a younger generation with more fundamentalistic religious views, connected to territorial issues. Biblical concepts, particularly of the Jews' sacred right to all of Palestine, came to hold practical, operative significance for them.[37]

The small, moderate Independent Liberal party, which was also in the coalition, usually went along with the majority on foreign and defense matters. Mapam was, once more, in an electoral alignment with Labor and formed the left wing of the coalition. Gahal, the Herut-Liberal party alignment was the right wing of the government.

The center of the Israeli political stage thus continued to be held by two large blocs: the Labor-Mapam alignment and Gahal. Each bloc was split into factions often holding widely differing views on foreign and defense policy and the occupied territories. Especially strange was the pact between Mr. Menaham Begin's Herut party and the former General Zionists, or Liberals, who formed the Gahal block back in 1965. Begin was an ideologist with a unique legalistic approach to foreign affairs. His Central European, rightist background had led him to assume a catastrophic view of Jewish survival in the Diaspora, which proved to be even more accurate than he ever feared during World War II. The Jewish right to Palestine, inherited in Jewish tradition, as opposed to vast Arab lands that could accomodate any numbers, was for him indivisible, on both sides of the Jordan River. Moreover, this right was formally acknowledged, according to Begin's spiritual leader, Wladimir Ze'ev Jabotinsky, by the British in the 1917 Balfour declaration. It was cemented in the instrument of the British mandate for Palestine, authorized by the League of Nations. When the British failed to behave according to the spirit of the mandate—granting autonomy and later independence to the eastern bank Hashemite kingdom, limiting Jewish immigration, and then almost stopping it altogether during Hitler's extermination campaign—Begin derived from these political acts a historical-legal right to fight the illegitimate foreign ruler who did not live up to his obligations. This was a historical-legal right to the territory of the country as a whole, thus opposing partition, and a historical-legal *raison d'être* that allowed him not to accept Jewish majority decisions with regard to strategy and tactics of foreign policy.

After independence, Begin's Herut party, which merged his Irgun with Jabontinsky's political followers, gave up the claim to Trans-Jordan, which they had assumed at first as a matter of principle, but they stuck to their claim to the West Bank as a whole. Their legalistic approach was manifested in Jabotinsky's argument that one could not compromise on one's rights.[38] If Israel agreed to partition, i.e., disclaimed its own right to a part of western Palestine, the rest of the claims could be contested too. The ideology of the followers remained nationalistic, conservative, and highly responsive to Arab challenges, thus creating problems for Ben-Gurion on his right, which in these areas did not differ much from the nationalist left. At the same time, Herut managed, even though it had been banished to permanent opposition in Ben-Gurion's days, to attract a growing number of lower strata, non-Ashkenazi Jews, who felt alienated from Mapai's elite as a result of poor bargaining capabilities, neglect, or other individual reasons. Mainly slum dwellers in the big cities, Israeli-born, non-European Jews who were not given enough attention as new immigrants, they followed a Polish-born, mild-mannered gentleman who could speak like a national and social revolutionary and could fire their imaginations while denouncing Mapai's foreign policy compromises, Arab behavior, and the elite's unequal bargaining methods with regard to his particular social clients. Yet during Ben-Gurion's reign, Herut never managed to free itself from its image as an extremist minority that had not respected majority policy in the past and might not respect it in the future. Herut's antisocialist, free market economic policy did not fit with the egalitarian, state socialism of the day. Slowly, Herut managed to move out of isolation when it joined the General Labor Union, Histadrut. Herut accepted Histadrut as a decisive instrument of power to be conquered from within, and later made a historical deal with the liberals who joined Herut in Gahal in 1965 to fight Mapai's alignment with Achdut Ha'Avoda. The liberals were a middle-of-the-road, pragmatic white-collar and Central European Zionist party that had refused, since 1955, to serve Ben-Gurion as a junior coalition partner. The logic of Gahal was thus domestic and partisan. The moderate right and the nationalist right made a deal in order to create a real challenge to the alignment, and to survive together as a united block, instead of as a divided and frustrating, separate opposition.

No liberal leader in 1965 thought in terms of what was to become of the post-June, 1967, dilemma; most of them shared Mapai's pragmatic caution with regard to foreign and defense affairs. Yet they refused to adhere to Mapai's state socialism or to accept Mapai's social bargaining, which left the upper middle class and middle class (as far as property and private initiative were concerned) outside the realm of bargaining most of the period. They found themselves under Mr. Begin's uncontested leadership in foreign affairs, having maneuvered Gahal to the government on the eve of the war, and having assumed a popular stance with regard to Arab-held territories that the liberals could not challenge without suggesting a positive alternative. Begin argued that Israel was there to stay, mainly in the West Bank, and would return the rest in exchange for peace. The liberals did not see any peace at hand and did not argue with the Gahal leader's ideological, Biblical, and legalistic approach; arguing might have destroyed their partisan framework without any meaningful domestic and external result. Even if they did not accept Begin's reasoning, the liberals endorsed a formula, according to which "the West Bank [as a whole] should never be partitioned again." Israeli presence, one way or another, would be maintained there, though Begin himself pressed for more settlements and formal annexation. This was unacceptable to the Liberals, most of Mapai and Mapam. The outcome was a typical compromise—few settlements in the West Bank, and more in the Golan Heights—due to complete Syrian hostility and the strategic value of that narrow strip, and a constant struggle in the cabinet between widely different, pragmatic, ideological, partisan approaches to foreign affairs by different parties who had never shared the government bench before.

It was the pressure of war that brought these formerly hostile groups and leaders together in the coalition. The differences over issues and personalities were not forgotten; they persisted in the face of Arab intransigence, took root within the smallest parties in the blocs, and could be bridged by low-level compromises. Meir's approach to foreign affairs was, of course, influenced very much by this internal political structure.

The Meir government's foreign and defense policy can be divided roughly into three areas of concern: captured Syrian and Egyptian territory, the West Bank, and the Gaza Strip; relations with the Arab states and the Palestine problem, in the general context of the conflict; Israeli-U.S. relations, in the context of global superpower relations and of internal developments in the United States.

At the same time, Meir, as her immediate predecessor had done, had to obtain approval by a majority of the cabinet for policy decisions that were first formulated in a smaller forum of senior ministers. Modern analysis of events in the Arab capitals and Moscow, as well as in Washington, was not maintained. Thus the type of information gathered and the way in which (and the people to whom) it was reported meant that the cabinet could not always consider international politics as a whole liable to have substantive political and military consequences for the Middle East. To a great extent, policy making consisted of reactions to the initiatives of others and ad hoc government consultations whenever anything happened. The government's basic attitude was one of satisfaction with the strategic situation and of unwillingness or inability to take the political offensive. On the whole, a very complicated domestic set-up helped create a simplistic foreign policy. A great intellectual effort, mainly by Meir's most important adviser, minister without portfolio Israel Galili of Achdut Ha'Avoda, was invested in repulsing the initiatives of external powers. Meir herself would have remained satisfied with the status quo, but Begin, Galili, Dayan, Allon, and the religious bloc were interested in more settlements in the occupied areas, and in creating a counterbalance to the pragmatic Mapai majority and the leftist Mapam. The outcome was again a compromise tending to the right, since the center and left had no positive alternative in the face of the Arab position and the War of Attrition.

Before the 1969 elections the Labor-Mapan alignment had agreed, through Galili's mediation, on a so-called "oral law" regarding the occupied territories.[39] Israel would continue to rule united Jerusalem. It would also continue to control the Golan Heights, the Gaza Strip, and Sharm-el-Sheikh (control of Sharm-el-Sheikh entailed an Israeli corridor from Eilat to the southern tip of the Sinai). The Jordan River was again declared Israel's "security frontier"; even if Israel ceded parts of the West Bank in a final peace settlement, no Arab armies would be allowed to cross the river. There would be no withdrawal until the conflict was settled in the framework of a final and general peace. A solution to the Palestinian refugee problem was not considered Israel's concern, and so would not have to be included in the settlement. Meir was to repeat this point often after becoming prime minister, stating that there was no such thing as a Palestinian nation.[40]

A sort of ironic reversal of traditional Arab claims against Israel was adopted by Israel against Arab claims. Before the Six-Day War there was no doubt in Israel that Palestinians—former inhabitants of parts of the country—did exist as a group and after their departure were organized by their own extremely hostile leadership with the help of the Arab states that refused to absorb them, so that they might reclaim their "rights" to the country.

The pre-1967 traditional approach toward Arabs as a whole and toward Palestinians as a group—refugees or Palestinians living in Jordan, the only Arab state that offered to absorb them—was the official Israeli bid for peace. Palestinians, or any other Arabs, were expected to make peace with the pre-June, 1967, Israel, or to coexist with it in an armistice regime if they could not make peace. Israel's official business was not to intervene with Arab deliberations over their territory after having accepted the partition of the whole West Bank and having legalized Israel's existence at peace with them. Whether Jordan, which became largely Palestinian in population after 1948, or an independent Palestinian state in Jordan and a part of the West Bank, or a West Bank state and Jordan would make peace with Israel—all these possibilities were theoretically acceptable to Israel before June, 1967. Ben-Gurion's Israel had accepted a third, Palestinian state between it and Jordan when it agreed to the 1947 partition plan.

Mrs. Meir went a step further; she denied the Palestinians recognition as a nation because of the following political reasons (and because of her "historical" approach to them as "southern Syrian Arabs"):

1. For post-1967 Israel, only a Jordanian solution to the Palestinian problem seemed viable: the PLO, with its structure as a weak coalition of radical Arab functionaries and its 1964 covenant that denied Israel's rights as a state and withheld recognition from the Jews as a nation, was totally unacceptable to the prime minister, who seemed to read Russian czarist and Nazi slogans into the PLO claims and arguments.

2. If the whole Arab coalition would accept Jordan as a legitimate owner of Arab-populated areas in the West Bank, which might be returned to it under these circumstances, Jordan could absorb Palestinian refugees in *both* banks. Yet, due to its conservative and pro-Western character, Jordan could prevent radical Palestinians from assuming the uncompromising stance that must, in Meir's perceptions, become the official policy of a miniature PLO state in the West Bank.

3. Thus, recognizing "Palestinians" rather than Jordanians meant, for Mrs. Meir, accepting in advance a third state between Israel and Jordan, delegitimizing both. Since the Arab states had never accepted Jordanian sovereignty on the West Bank after 1948, Mrs. Meir did not, for her part, wholeheartedly accept Amman's sovereignty over that area. For her, a general Arab consensus was needed, to agree to an Israeli-Jordanian deal over that territory.

4. At the same time in 1969–72, the Israeli cabinet resumed negotiations with King Hussein over Allon's plan, i.e., returning Arab-populated areas in the West Bank to Jordan, while retaining the strategic areas and Jerusalem. As expected, Hussein refused again and again what was, from an Israeli point of view, this "minimal" offer, so that no serious debate in the cabinet was necessary on the "oral law" and its adaptation to a peace agreement with Jordan.[41]

5. Moreover, the Arab states accepted Jordanian presence in the West Bank after 1948 de facto only. Since 1967 they had moved clearly toward promising that territory—and the former British Palestinian

Gaza strip, governed by Egypt until 1967—to the PLO, an anathema to Israel, with its possible claims on both banks of the Jordan and its record of radical behavior. Israel's answer to this change in the PLO position was doubly negative; it did not accept King Hussein's demands for most of the West Bank (for which he had expressed his willingness to make separate peace) because Jerusalem did not believe in a separate Jordanian move outside an all-Arab consensus. At the same time, Meir publicly denied a separate Palestinian identity, with its claims on Palestine as a whole or a third state between Jordan and Israel. These claims were regarded as one tactical, interim phase in a PLO plan to reclaim the whole later.

Apart from the "oral law," the government implemented parts of some of the conceptions various ministers held about the West Bank. The cabinet never officially adopted the Allon Plan to retain strategic and unpopulated areas of the West Bank. However, since there was a sufficient degree of agreement about this in the cabinet, and particularly since Mr. Galili was the minister responsible for Israeli settlement in the occupied territories, settlements which comprised several thousand inhabitants were established along the plan lines, as well as on the Golan Heights and in the Rafah approaches on the border between the Sinai and the Gaza Strip. Earlier unofficial settlements by kibbutz, moshav, and religious movements now gained approval.

Egypt and Jordan, which, in contrast to Syria, had accepted Resolution 242, were officially considered partners in negotiations for a general peace. Israel's attitude to them was influenced by their demands on it by hostile acts by them against it, by their relations with the extra-regional powers (particularly Cairo's relations with Moscow), and by Israel's relations with the United States. The main focus of Meir's foreign and security policy, in fact, was not the Arab-Israeli conflict proper, but the Jerusalem-Washington relationship. The mediation efforts of the United Nations envoy, Gunnar Jarring, in 1969 and 1970 were regarded as of secondary importance, to be kept up in order to avoid a total diplomatic vacuum. What Meir wanted from Egypt was a change in its declared position on the Arab-Israeli conflict as a whole. This shift would be followed by direct negotiations over territory and freedom of navigation for Israeli shipping through the Straits of Tiran. In the absence of such a shift, Israel's basic terms of reference were the existing conflict and the U.S.-Israeli relations.

Egypt's willingness to enter into direct negotiations became the major criterion for determining Nasser's readiness to accept Israel's legitimacy. This also became a matter of domestic political argument of great significance in Israel. Direct negotiations and recognition could be justifica-

tion for yielding territory won at high cost in June, 1967, and still defended with daily losses, in the face of a relatively "hawkish" public
opinion.[42] The Egyptians' refusal to enter into direct talks with Israel
and Israel's sense of military power thus contributed to a deadlock.

The Meir government's policy was, therefore, an attempt to base foreign policy on Israeli power and autonomy of decision, as opposed to
external pressures, in order to bring about a basic change in the Arab
approach to the conflict. Meir regarded Israel's military strength as an
asset, not only to itself but also to the United States as well; a strong
Israel would contribute to the stability of the Middle East. Thus, under
Meir, the government's main concerns were reacting to the Soviet-backed
military initiatives of the Arabs and the political initiatives of the Americans. Ostensibly, this course was imposed on Israel by the Arabs and was
the only one it could follow.

THE AMERICAN INITIATIVES, 1969-72

From the vantage point of 1977 one can recognize changes in U.S. foreign
policy after Nixon's accession to the presidency and Kissinger's appointment as his national security adviser. Lyndon Johnson had wanted to
contain the U.S.S.R. in order to reach compromises with it about each
separate problem and local conflict. The Nixon administration had a
global conception of its relations with the U.S.S.R., and the Middle East
problems were not to be handled in isolation from other issues.[43] Few
public and explicit statements of this shift in emphasis were made in
1969 or 1970,[44] but Washington's inclination to a Soviet-American package deal was clear enough, and the Israeli government once again came
to fear a settlement imposed by the superpowers without sufficient regard for Israel's views and interests.

We now know that the United States was indeed trying to reach a
general settlement of its relations with the U.S.S.R., which was considered
the linchpin of American foreign policy, on the basis of the "linkage
approach." A relaxation of tensions was to be sought with Moscow on all
fronts at the same time. "The goal," say former Kissinger aids, "was an
overall understanding, not a selective détente." The Nixon-Kissinger team
wanted to defuse dangerous local conflicts through a multi-issue and
multiregional compromise: the United States would make concessions on
SALT and in Vietnam in exchange for Soviet concessions in the Middle
East, while other issues would be dealt with by mutual compromise.

In 1969 and 1970 this policy was being carefully studied; the United
States consulted with the U.S.S.R., France, and Great Britain about the

possibility of a package deal in the Middle East. The conflict in Vietnam loomed in the background and was escalating as the U.S.S.R., in American perceptions, showed no readiness to accept the larger deal Washington had proposed and as Hanoi continued the barren negotiations in Paris. The United States, then, was trying seriously to make a deal with the U.S.S.R. over the Middle East, while constantly pursuing its bid for an overall arrangement with the Soviet Union. According to former Assistant Secretary of State Joseph Sisco, the United States at first sought a general settlement of the conflict, at least between Israel and the Arab states that might have been ready for it.

During 1969, two factors arose that constituted additional incentives for the American objectives of a general settlement. Egypt's Soviet-backed war of attrition against Israel was becoming increasingly serious and endangering the whole international situation. Raids against Israel by the Palestinian organizations operating out of Jordanian territory were becoming more numerous and the organizations with Soviet as well as Syrian backing were becoming increasingly autonomous of King Hussein's pro-western regime.[45] Yet in the opening days of the Nixon administration, says Sisco,

> the president asked Secretary of State William Rogers to come up with recommendations to review the situation. Rogers asked me to take over. . . . In that very March [1969] we had several NSC meetings. . . . Three options were considered. . . . One, to continue basically the Johnson policy, based on . . . [U.N. Special Representative] Jarring mediation. The second, a more active policy based on bilateral discussions with the Soviet Union and on the assumption that the Nixon administration was embarking on a new turning point in Soviet-American relations. The Middle East would be one of the testing points in the broad, overall strategy also based on Nixon's assumption that, while he was dubious that the Russians were really interested in this, it was an area worth testing . . . [bearing in mind] that the Russians were making so many inroads in the area. So the second option was selected, namely, that it would be a strong probe of Soviet intentions, in the context of Israeli desire for a peace treaty.

In other words, the administration moved from the "constructively vague" formulation of Security Council Resolution 242, which equated Israeli withdrawals with the end of Arab belligerency toward Israeli demands for a more explicit peace arrangement.

The third option, which was also implemented by the Americans simultaneously with the bilateral Soviet-American negotiations, was the four-power talks in New York. Thus, in March, 1969, Sisco began regular consultations with the Soviet ambassador to Washington, Mr. Dobrynin. Soon afterward, Britain and France joined the United States and the

Soviet Union in a parallel framework, the four-power talks, initiated by de Gaulle. The new U.S. administration was interested, according to Sisco, in better relations with France and in creating a broader diplomatic framework to ease the passage of a decision in the Security Council if and when agreement on a settlement was reached.[46]

On June 5, 1969, Secretary of State Rogers stated that the United States and the Soviet Union had been engaged in Middle East peace discussions since February and were close to an agreement on proposals that would be submitted to the Arab states and Israel for negotiations.[47] The arms promised by the Johnson administration in 1968 continued to arrive in Israel, but Jerusalem's requests for new deliveries were not acted upon.

In September, 1969, Washington transmitted to Moscow a secret plan for a political settlement in the Middle East.[48] On December 9, Rogers made the plan public.[49] The main points were as follows: First, the United States would be as impartial as it could be toward the parties to the conflict, and would thus encourage the Arabs to accept a binding agreement for permanent peace and to demand an Israeli withdrawal from occupied territories. Second, Rogers stated that there could be no lasting peace without a solution of the Arab refugee problem.

Third, no unilateral action by Israel could determine the final status of Jerusalem; this would be settled only by an agreement by the two states directly concerned, Jordan and Israel, taking into account Muslim, Christian, and Jewish interests in the city. Rogers added that the city must remain united and that there must not by any limitations on access to it (such as those imposed between 1949 and 1967), denying Jews the right to visit the part of the city under Jordanian control. Both Jordan and Israel must have a role in organizing the civilian economic and religious life of the city's various communities.

Fourth, mentioning the talks the United States had been holding with the Soviet Union since March, 1969, Rogers proceeded to state the terms for a general Israel-Egyptian settlement. Egypt and Israel should make a binding commitment to peace with each other. This would entail undertakings to prevent hostile acts against each other from within their territories. The details of the security safeguards would be worked out under the guidance of the U.N. mediator. The procedure would be the same as for the U.N.-sponsored negotiations between Egypt and Israel in 1949, in which the parties held direct and indirect negotiations under the auspices of the U.N. The four great powers would help Ambassador Jarring during the negotiation. Security safeguards would relate principally to the Sharm-el-Sheikh area, to demilitarized zones such as those mentioned in Resolution 242, and the Gaza Strip. Peace and the safeguards would basically require an Israeli withdrawal to the international frontier. The Gaza Strip was not considered Egyptian sovereign territory and would be considered as a future Jordanian territory. Peace and the assurance of peace would require that the parties themselves conduct the negotiations over the practical measures for safeguarding it.

Rogers's package included some elements responsive to Israel's demands: commitments toward peace, safeguards on the ground, especially at Sharm-el-Sheikh, the unity of Jerusalem, and the assurance of Jewish rights in all parts of the city. Some aspects of the deal, though, were closer to Arab views; the secretary recognized that a resolution of the refugee problem was a necessary condition for lasting peace. He demanded an Israeli withdrawal to international frontiers on the Egyptian front and did not bind the Arabs to direct negotiations right away, but only at a later stage to discuss practical security measures under U.N. sponsorship.

On December 10, the Israeli cabinet held a special session and decided to reject what they called the "Rogers Plan" (although they well knew that this was the administration plan). They tried to open a gap between the secretary, who announced it, and the president, to avoid a prestige problem for Nixon if he considered dropping it. Israel rejected the plan on the grounds that the Arabs' attitudes and deed reflected a fundamental unwillingness for peace with Israel; if they were really interested they would negotiate in the manner customary among states. Israel was also angered by the U.S. failure to consult it before making the plan public and by its attempt to force Israel into largely indirect negotiations with the Arabs, setting the framework and substance of the talks in advance.[50] The government was most shaken, however, by the way the plan dealt with the Jerusalem problem, denying Israeli sovereignty over the city as a whole. Moreover, accepting Arab demands to solve the refugee problem as a guarantee for lasting peace meant, for the Israeli cabinet, accepting Arab rights in the Palestinian problem itself, as manifested by contradictory Palestinian and Jordanian claims.

Apprehension in Jerusalem mounted after the Yost document (named after the American delegate to the United Nations) was presented to Israel on December 18.[51] The plan was rejected at the cabinet meeting of December 21.[52] This document was basically an extension to the Jordanian front of the principles of the Rogers Plan. According to the plan the parties were to agree to a procedure, timetable, and map for the withdrawal of Israeli forces from most of the West Bank. Each party would commit itself to peace and to preventing aggression against the other from within its territory. They would agree on a permanent border more or less congruent with the 1949 ADL, with some changes for security, administrative, and economic reasons. The plan repeated verbatim the principles about Jerusalem expressed in the Rogers Plan. It also involved

Jordan in the settlement of the problem of the Gaza Strip and its Palestinian refugee inhabitants. They would become citizens of Jordan, and the Strip would be connected to the West Bank by a corridor. This would, of course, be subject to Israeli and Egyptian approval. The plan recognized the possibility of demilitarized zones in the West Bank after an Israeli withdrawal. The U.N. envoy would establish an international commission to poll the wishes of the Arab refugees for repatriation to Israel, but since this would be a long process, the other provision clauses would be implemented first. The documents would be adopted by the Security Council and the Big Four would help to carry it out.

The Israeli reaction to the proposal was hardly surprising. The plan denied Israel the possibility of maneuvering on the territorial issue and limited Israel's influence on the refugee problem. It made negotiations subject to a diplomatic framework that included the Big Four, most of whom Israel did not think very friendly. It did not dictate direct negotiations at the outset, and did not recognize Israel's bid for secure borders. On December 29, the Knesset voted to reject the Rogers and Yost plans by fifty-seven to three. Sisco maintains that the Yost document was submitted in a "context that everybody knew . . . was not operational:" Egypt rejected its part of the deal, and the more sensitive Jordanian package remained undiscussed. In retrospect, Sisco was right, not because of American unwillingnes to pursue the Jordanian plan, but because of Nasser's refusal to accept concrete American ideas on the Egyptian-Israeli agreement and the Jordanian-Israeli agreement.[53]

What was the "real" American plan, and the concrete context of the Sisco-Dobrynin-Nasser negotiations that secretly took place after the winter of 1969? Eight years later, Mr. Sisco described them to me in the following way:

> The substance of the Rogers Plan [was] Israeli withdrawal to the international boundary, subject to the following conditions.
>
> There would be direct negotiations between Israel and Egypt on the security features; those included Sharm-el-Sheikh and did not preclude the question of an [Israeli] access to Sharm-el-Sheikh, demilitarization in the Sinai, and the question of security and the question of sovereignty as it related to Gaza. Now that final position . . . we . . . quietly presented to the Soviets by September. No response for weeks. In the meantime, the Soviets were exploiting the position publicly in the Arab world, they were taking the total Arab position—total Israeli withdrawals to pre-June, 1967, lines and restoration of the rights of the Palestinians. We are being silent because of a formal proposal awaiting response—a . . . proposal which combined Soviet and American working papers that have been developed in the context of seven or eight months. . . . I concluded that we could wait no longer, because the situation was being distorted. We had no contact with Cairo, and it

became clear that the Russians were distorting our position not only in the Arab world . . . but also . . . in Cairo itself. . . . So we went to Rogers and said, "Most people don't know the far-reaching proposals we have made. The Russians are exploiting it; it is obvious that there is not going to be a positive response. We think that these proposals ought to be made public. . . ." The reason it was made public is that it was no longer considered negotiable; and secondly, it surfaced because the Soviets exploited the situation.

When asked whether, accordingly, the Soviets failed Nixon's test in the Middle East, or possibly failed to demonstrate good will in a broader Soviet-American context, Sisco answered:

No question. . . . Gromyko went to see Nasser; Nasser's response was that this was not enough. Both Nasser and the Russians agreed. . . . The Egyptian response was that the question of Sharm-el-Sheikh and [Israeli] access [to the Straits] could not be kept open [to bilateral Israeli-Egyptian negotiations.] . . . We even talked about, frankly, a 99-year lease, a joint Israeli-Egyptian lease for that particular area, among the ideas that we felt needed to be considered in direct, face-to-face, negotiations between Egypt and Israel. Their answer was that you have to fill that in; no negotiations. [Their demand was for] a U.N. peace-keeping force [in Sharm-el-Sheikh]; demilitarization of the entire Sinai—no, no—a small buffer on both sides of the international boundary, . . . security arrangements and sovereignty in Gaza, no, you could not keep that open [to direct negotiations.] There should be a U.N. peace-keeping force, and secondly there would have to be, explicitly, a commitment that it would be returned to Arab sovereignty. Remembering that Gaza had never been under Egyptian sovereignty but under Egyptian administration, at that time the conventional wisdom was that it would be returned to Jordan under the Jordanian-Israeli aspect of the Treaty. . . . What [Nasser] wanted was all of those security questions resolved in his favor without direct negotiations, and we turned that down flatly.

Sisco says that the United States indeed pursued an Egyptian-Jordanian deal with Israel, but no linkage was created to Syrian claims, because Damascus did not accept Resolution 242. Yet Nasser was not ready to accept concessions with regard to Sharm-el-Sheikh; he became increasingly committed to the PLO over former Palestinian territories like Gaza. The Rogers Plan was a disaster from Israel's point of view because of its territorial nature, especially in connection with the West Bank negotiations. The vague peace treaty that might emerge following U.N.-sponsored negotiations might lead only to a new armistice, as it had in 1949, rather than to peace, and the refugee problem would remain unsolved and outside the Egyptian-Israeli negotiations.

The plan was also unacceptable to the Egyptian president for the same reasons. It broke down the conflict into an Egyptian-Israeli negotiating process that might culminate in direct negotiations—even under U.N.

auspices—against the Khartoum "no" number one. Second, it might have forced Egypt to agree to a compromise over both Sharm-el-Sheikh and Gaza. Third, it might have left the refugee problem open, making Nasser concede recognition and territory to Israel. This would be short of a final peace, but enough to cause Nasser to abandon his belligerent rights without meeting Palestinian demands.[54]

Nasser, therefore, continued his policy of a limited, and periodically escalated, military confrontation with Israel along the canal, and he encouraged the Palestinian organizations to expand their operations from the East Bank of Jordan. Since the plan had already been rejected by Egypt and the U.S.S.R., Washington saw no sense in exerting pressure on Israel to discuss it. The Americans were apparently satisfied that the pro-western Arab states had accepted the essentials of the Rogers Plan as evidence of American even-handedness. The U.S. "package deal" for the Middle East with the Soviet Union in the context of a larger deal between superpowers failed largely because of Arab opposition, which Washington attributed to the U.S.S.R. as well.

In December, 1969, partly in reaction to the Rogers Plan, Ambassador Rabin was recalled to Jerusalem for consultations. His talks with the government also dealt with the situation along the Suez Canal, where the fighting was becoming harder. Israel already had some of the Phantoms sold by the Johnson administration. From various directions came the proposal to use the aircraft to respond to Egyptian artillery attacks by expanded bombing deep inside Egypt.[55] This was seen in the light of holding on to the canal area. Some members of the cabinet thought that Israel was doing the United States a service by keeping the Suez Canal closed. If it were opened, the U.S.S.R. could more easily send supplies to North Vietnam, and show the flag in the Red Sea, the Persian Gulf, and the Indian Ocean. With the canal closed, ships from the western and southern ports of the Soviet Union had to take the long route around the Cape of Good Hope. It was, therefore, in Washington's interest to have a continued Israeli presence on its eastern bank block the canal or to allow it to be reopened only as part of a general settlement favorable to the United States. This does not mean there was any prior collusion. After reaching the canal in 1967, without any previous planning the Israelis dug in and fortified their positions. Later, the canal became a strategic barrier and was used as a political trump card. As the situation in Vietnam grew more serious, the continuation of Israel's struggle in the canal area became, in Israeli eyes, an important factor in terms of the coordination of American and Israeli interests.

Rabin spoke on behalf of bombing deep inside Egypt. He said that, far from being opposed, the Americans would welcome such action.[56] He made a distinction between the positions of the State Department and the defense establishment about the Middle East: the latter was primarily concerned with southeast Asia. Rabin also thought that since the U.S.S.R. had not responded favorably to American proposals for a broad package deal, Henry Kissinger and others in the White House who dealt with U.S.-Soviet relations held views closer to Israel's than to the State Department's. He interpreted statements he had heard from members of the American defense establishment indicating that Washington would favorably regard deep-penetration bombing to mean that the United States would not be sorry if Israel helped itself in this way to win the canal war, as long as there was no settlement and the Soviet Union's main client in the Middle East was struck from the air or even overthrown. The U.S. conflict with the Soviet clients in southeast Asia in the absence of Soviet willingness to enter into the "grand deal" might thus mean a common U.S.-Israeli interest in Israel's conflict with the Soviet client in the Middle East.

Yigal Allon and other senior Labor party ministers also thought that Nasser might be overthrown as a result of deep penetration bombings. Allon doubted that the U.S.S.R.'s reaction to such bombing would be very strong; that would be "impractical" and against historical precedents of Soviet behavior. Dayan however, was convinced that Moscow was committed to come to Egypt's aid and that increasing Soviet involvement in the Egyptian war effort was inevitable, no matter was Israel might do. The defense minister regarded the Soviet intervention as the major threat to Israeli interests since early 1968. Yet he did not see any way to influence Soviet behavior without damaging Israeli interests. A Russian threat in Egypt might compel Washington to extend aid to Israel beyond its previously indicated intentions. His view was thus very different from that of Rabin and most of the Labor ministers; they were far more optimistic about the outcome of the bombings than the defense minister, who feared that increased Soviet assistance would soon put a stop to Israeli deep-penetration bombings. The IDF should, therefore, go ahead and try to derive whatever limited advantages it could from the air raids to ease the pressure on the Suez Canal line, and Israel should wait and see how the United States would react to the increased Soviet aid to Egypt before and after the bombing. His practical conclusion was thus the same as the other members of the cabinet. Meir usually accepted Dayan's military ideas if Allon and the other military experts in the cabinet did not oppose them vigorously.

If the Israelis had tried to follow the logic behind Washington's ostensible agreement to the bombing, they might have been less enthusiastic about it. There were, apparently, two reasons for the American interest. First, Israli raids might make Nasser more responsive to the American initiative that Israel itself had rejected. Second, the United States had bombed and was about to escalate its air attacks in southeast Asia and was expanding the war into Cambodia. Israeli raids in Egypt might make liberal Jewish critics of the Nixon administration hesitate before attacking American operations in Cambodia and Vietnam.[57]

Israel's deep-penetration bombings of Egypt lasted only from January to March, 1970. In response to Nasser's appeal for more military aid, the U.S.S.R. delivered improved SA-2 and SA-3 antiaircraft missiles and sent in advisers and personnel to operate the antiaircraft batteries. Apparently, the Soviet Union had assumed responsibility for the surface antiaircraft defense of the Egyptian heartland, but not of the canal zone.[58] For Israelis, Egypt's military power came to be regarded as a function of the presence of Soviet personnel as advisers and in combat roles. Thus, for the Israeli defense establishment the conflict had been escalated qualitatively. Against such a change something qualitatively decisive should have been done. According to some researchers,[59] this would have been the moment, if not earlier in 1968, in which Dayan might have decided to turn Israel's nuclear option into a real "bomb in the basement," meaning an existing nuclear capacity that becomes known to the parties of the conflict without an explicit, open nuclear policy. This speculation may be supported by Dayan's contempt for the Arab's military power and his traditional fear concerning the role of the Soviets in the conflict. Israel could not fight the Russians conventionally but it could have involved them in an unconventional risk: to confront them with the fact of supplying nuclear weapons to Egypt against the NPT, world public opinion, and Moscow's relations with the United States, or to have the U.S.S.R. face an Israeli nuclear potential against a conventional Soviet-Arab threat. If the decision to develop the nuclear option into a "bomb in the basement" were made or the presence of an already-existing bomb were implied, winter and summer, 1970, could have been the period.

The "bomb in the basement" policy has the apparent advantage of permitting one to possess nuclear arms and a nuclear threat without having to pay the full political price for an overt nuclear strategy. Israel would not immediately be faced with the consequences open nuclearization would have on the inter-Arab, Arab superpower, and global political planes. If a decision for a "bomb in the basement" was made at this time, such considerations must have figured in it. Yet Israel's foreign policy was not influenced by such a decision. On the face of things, Israel behaved as if it had no nuclear capability, and the issue was never raised by the Nixon-Kissinger administration.[60]

Washington, meanwhile, tried to exploit Cairo's distress, and with a great deal of publicity postponed a decision on the requests for additional aircraft that Israel had made in January. In late March of 1970, Rogers stated publicly that Israel had requested twenty-five more Phantoms and 100 more Skyhawks, but that this was not the time to fulfill this request.[61] Privately, however, Jerusalem and Washington agreed that the jet supply would be maintained at a slow rate in relation to IAF losses in the War of Attrition.[62] Israel thought that it had achieved "on-going talks" about arms supplies, that is, a firmer American commitment for on-going supply, subject to Soviet and Arab actions. In fact, though, Washington had embarked on a political and diplomatic initiative of its own and Joseph Sisco arrived in Cairo for talks on March 23, 1970. He planned to go on to Amman from there, but when he arrived in Cairo, PLO-inspired unrest broke out in Jordan and Lebanon. Apparently, the Palestinian organizations were trying to ensure that neither of the two states reached an agreement with Israel that did not take their interests into account. Sisco was forced to give up any idea of visiting Amman.

An Israeli commentator who was close to Gahal and Dayan at the time, writes that "Israel's chances for bringing about the failure of Washington's new efforts were centered on Yassir Arafat. . . . Jerusalem was afraid that these efforts would be made at the expense of its hold . . . on the secure, though not agreed, cease-fire boundaries and of its demand for lasting peace."[63]

In Cairo, Sisco tried to convince the Egyptian leadership that only America could help bring about an Israeli withdrawal without a general war. Moscow might be able to equip Egypt for a crossing of the canal by force, but such a crossing did not seem practical from a military standpoint at this stage. If the Egyptians changed their attitude to the Rogers Plan, however, Washington would be able to do what Moscow could not.

After leaving Cairo, Sisco visited Israel in an attempt to extract a more flexible public position vis-à-vis Jordan and Egypt. On the very day he left Israel, IAF pilots for the first time encountered Soviet pilots flying Egyptian interceptors in defense of the Egyptian heartland. (In time, Rabin would say that his assessment of the political value of the deep-penetration air raids had been the "mistake of his life." The U.S.S.R. was actively involved in Egypt and its armed forces so deeply that the political and strategic situation changed dramatically.) Washington began to consider the dangers it faced by a possible Israeli confrontation with Egypt and its Soviet backers. By his misreading of the situation, Rabin had helped bring about increased Soviet involvement and, consequently, a qualitatively changed strategic and political framework. Israel's reaction to this, apart from the nuclear speculations, was manifested in several areas: it tried to find out the geographical extent of the U.S.S.R.'s commitment. Had it assumed responsibility for the defense only of Cairo and other vital areas of the Egyptian heartland or of the canal front as well? In the latter case, Israel's air superiority—necessary to preventing a crossing—would be threatened or cancelled. Jerusalem asked Washington to warn Moscow, privately, not to extend its involvement. The Israelis did not want to publicize the Soviet presence for fear that the U.S.S.R. would feel it necessary to persist in its involvement or else lose face.[64] Washington, on the other hand, wanted to publicize the Soviet presence; the administration apparently thought that the Soviet escalation in the Middle East might lead some of the American liberal and Jewish critics to moderate their criticism of the imminent invasion of Cambodia by the United States. On April 29, the *New York Times* published a story about the Soviet pilots. Three days later American forces invaded Cambodia and Nixon ordered a "detailed survey" of all the political and military aspects of the Middle East conflict.

During the month of May the fighting along the canal grew worse and the IAF stepped up its raids on the canal zone and unprotected Egyptian flanks. At the same time, however, Prime Minister Meir made a moderate speech to the Knesset in order to deflect international pressure from Israel on to the Arabs. For the first time in parliament, she proclaimed Israel's acceptance of Resolution 242, expressed her willingness to agree to a negotiating procedure like that of the 1949 armistice talks, and called for a resumption of United Nations mediation efforts. The Gahal faction in the cabinet voiced bitter objections to this statement, because it indirectly entailed an agreement to withdraw from occupied territories, particularly the West Bank. Cabinet unity was maintained, however, by allowing the Gahal members of the Knesset to abstain from voting on the government statement.[65]

Foreign Minister Eban reiterated the statement on a visit to Washington, and the administration promised to continue the secret arms deliveries despite public statements to the contrary. On June 19, 1970, however, the United States publicly launched a new initiative to end the War of Attrition and its started new negotiations in the Middle East. Nixon privately indicated to Israel that continued arms supplies were conditional on Israel's agreement to the initiative. The American endeavor met with success in late July because of three factors: the first was that with American aid the IAF had partially succeeded against the Egyptian ground forces, while with Soviet help the Egyptians had some success in battle against the IAF. The second was a combination of American pressure on and promises to Israel and its war weariness and criticism of the Israel government. The third factor was the Soviet-Egyptian deliberations.

The June, 1970, "Rogers Initiative" differed from the "Rogers Plan" of December, 1969, in that it did not mention borders and thus, it was hoped, would not disturb Israeli sensibilities on the issue.[66] It suggested a procedure for resuming the U.N. envoy's mediation efforts on the basis of two principles: mutual recognition of each state's sovereignty, territorial integrity, and political independence by Egypt, Jordan, and Israel, and Israeli withdrawal from the territories conquered in 1967. Ambassador Jarring would recommend the procedures, location, and time, taking into account the parties' attitudes and past precedents about these elements.[67] To facilitate the mediator's task, Egypt and Israel would agree to observe a cease-fire for at least six months. Actually, according to the Security Council resolution of June 6, 1967, a cease-fire was supposed to be in effect in any case, but Nasser had unilaterally declared it void in March, 1969.[68]

In any event, the Rogers Initiative's "maplessness" did not have the desired effect; the United States had already made its views on borders known in the Rogers Plan. Furthermore, most of the cabinet ministers felt that Washington had accepted the Soviet and Arab view that the cease-fire could not be observed until Israel agreed to return most of the territories in question. The Americans were thus acquiescing to the Arabs' selective observance of U.N. resolutions, honoring those that suited them and violating others. For the Israelis, the main political problem was the Arabs' reliability in any negotiations and the value of their commitments. In terms of this specific cease-fire problem, the Arabs might claim that its maintenance was part of a resolution of the Middle East conflict as a whole. If, for example, the refugee problem was not resolved in accordance with Resolution 242 or the Rogers Plan, the Arabs might feel free to violate the cease-fire in order to extract more political and/or military advantages after having gained previous Israeli concessions. On July 21, therefore, the cabinet voted to reject the initiative.[69]

Washington did not press Israel for an immediate response to its initiative and preferred to wait first for the Egyptian reactions, which were not totally hostile, and the Soviet reply. Meir, however, was rather impatient; she wanted to transmit a negative reply in order to protest the manner in which Nixon had made continued arms supplies conditional on "progress" on the initiative, in apparent violation of earlier American promises. She sent Ambassador Rabin a harsh note to be delivered to the president.[70]

Rabin refused to deliver the note, however; Kissinger advised him that it was better not to challenge an American president directly. Israel should voice its objections to the demands and claims at the lower levels of the administration, leaving the president room to maneuver and reach a compromise. Rabin added that, because of his difficulties in Cambodia, Nixon wanted the Israelis to restrain their criticism of the administration. The ambassador thought that the president deserved this consideration since he was the only member of the administration who had consistently supported Israel's arguments and arms requests throughout the year. Rabin was afraid that American public opinion would not support the risk of another war abroad, in a time when there was some chance for negotiations in the Middle East based on the Rogers Initiative.[71]

Meir was supported in her tough line against the U.S. administration by Begin and Dayan. The latter argued that, given the administration's difficulties in southeast Asia, Israel should seriously consider opening a second front against American pressure inside the United States, where the Israelis had considerable bargaining power. He also argued that the alignment had not received a mandate from the electorate for a settlement that promised something less than peace in secure and recognized boundaries different from those of June 4, 1967.[72]

Between June 21 and July 22, the period in which Nasser considered the new American proposals, President Nixon and his national security adviser made two statements on the Middle East, which the majority of the cabinet regarded as pro-Israeli public declarations that should not be ignored. On 26 June, 1970, Kissinger made his famous remark in a background briefing, saying that the United States would "expel" the Soviets from Egypt.[73]

On July 1, 1970, Nixon asserted at a press conference that Israel was entitled to "defensible," not just "secured," borders.[74] This action should be understood in the general context of the Soviet-American relations in the pre-détente period, and also in connection with Arab-Soviet deliberations, which followed the Rogers Initiative. Clearly, the White House wanted to demonstrate to the Soviets and their Egyptian clients that Washington was ready to discuss the Middle East, or détente in general, but would not yield to Soviet or Arab demands. A general compromise was needed, and the Kremlin should consider it seriously. If Russia would not pressure its Arab clients for moderation, Washington might approach them directly, always retaining the ability to strengthen Israel in its military struggle against the Soviet-Egyptian war. Washington was not interested in such an open and dangerous game—not in the Middle East or elsewhere. It had presented the Rogers Plan to Israel in the past, and it was ready to pressure it again to accept a cease-fire and to start negotiations. Yet either Moscow or Egypt should demonstrate their willingness to compromise, and the best method would be a general Soviet-American deal.

After Nixon's and Kissinger's statements, Meir did not send the original note to the president, but did make tough public and private statements condemning the idea of a limited cease-fire.[75] This would only provide the Arabs with a controlled means for raising and lowering tension whenever it suited them, she believed. At the same time SA-2 missile batteries operated by Egyptians and SA-3 batteries manned, it was thought, by Soviet personnel were being moved closer and closer to the canal line and were having an impact on the fighting: on a single day two Israeli Phantoms had been shot down.

Moscow had, meanwhile, adopted a more moderate public policy line on the Middle East in the Big Four talks and in leaks to the press in various Western capitals.[76] The U.S.S.R. proclaimed its desire for a "situation of peace" in the region and the Arab states' obligation to prevent attacks on Israel from their territory. This, however, was conditional a resolution of the Palestinian problem and the withdrawal of the IDF to the 1949 armistice demarcation lines. Though this was far from Israel's position, it could be interpreted in the West as evidence of Soviet moderation.

Nasser arrived in the U.S.S.R. on June 29, 1970, for a long visit, and the Israelis began to be apprehensive that both superpowers were courting his favor. Washington was offering him Israeli withdrawal through American political and supply pressure and Moscow was proposing military aid and a plan similar to the Rogers Plan. After his return from Moscow, on July 17, Nasser, contrary to Israeli expectations and hopes, announced his agreement to the Rogers Initiative. Israel regarded the Egyptian move as a trick; Cairo was agreeing to a diplomatic framework that it would use to promote its interests but was not committing itself to terminate the conflict or to separate its terriorial claims from the Palestinian and Syrian demands. Nasser had not made any concessions in the vital areas of legitimacy and sovereignty. For the Israeli cabinet this meant that the bargaining process, mainly between itself and the United States, should have been tactically modified and adjusted to the new circumstances; the internal debate would be over how to adjust it without making any advance concessions in the territorial issue, which incorporated, in the eyes of the majority, both issues of legitimacy and defense.

Still, why did Nasser agree to a cease-fire? After all, his strategy was based on two confrontations, a military and political confrontation with Israel, against the backdrop of a possible superpower confrontation. In practical terms, his strategy called for increased Soviet power in the Middle East and for more active Soviet involvement in Egypt itself, to deter Washington and bring about American pressure on Israel. This appears to have worked after Israel's deep-penetration bombing. The answer seems to be connected with the limits of Soviet aid. Moscow's increasing conventional arms supplies to the Arabs in any case required larger investments in training and some infrastructure for the aid. Egypt was not a contiguous territory—the supplier and the receiver were separated by states and a sea that the Soviet Union did not control. Moreover, if Moscow strengthened Egypt, Washington would strengthen Israel, then Egypt would have to be supplied with even more arms, and so on in a vicious circle. The level of a conventional conflict would thus be raised, but an Egyptian victory, however limited, would still not be assured. As time passed, Egypt would demand more Soviet aid and more direct involvement. America would reply by increasing supplies to Israel or by taking some other action in the context of its general relations with the Soviet Union; in either case the superpowers' relationship would be complicated. Furthermore, the Arabs had never been satisfied with the aid they had received. The deliveries had always been a source of Egyptian bitterness and of Soviet-Egyptian contention over quantities and qualities. The Arabs had even voiced their dissatisfaction in public.[77]

An extension of direct Soviet involvement was liable to lead to clashes with Israel and harsh American reactions. Moscow's response, whether to retreat or to react more sharply, would be dictated to a great extent by Nasser's wishes and so would not necessarily be in the Soviet interest. Nuclear aid to the Arabs to balance the Israeli nuclear option would not be desirable in terms of Soviet global interests. The Kremlin proclaimed its belief in nuclear nonproliferation far and wide, and it is doubtful that it would violate this principle. To do so would disturb superpower relations, harm its international image, and perhaps even legitimize Israel's possession of nuclear arms.

At the same time, the Soviet leadership was very much interested in retaining its cooperation with Egypt, and it regarded Nasser personally as an ally. It discussed with him freely the Libyan coup, which had brought Colonel Khaddafi to power earlier in 1969. As Heikal reports, "Kosygin . . . [said] that according to his calculations the Libyians had the highest per capita production of oil in the world. . . . The figures seemed to fascinate him. . . . He was very interested when Nasser told him of the possibility of a complete union between Libya, Egypt, and Syria."[78] The Soviet Middle East policy had, thus, to be a compromise between assisting Nasser militarily and cooperating with him politically.

Moscow could have logically concluded that it was best to advise Nasser to accept the American cease-fire initiative, while securing for itself a political role as Egypt's representative vis-à-vis Washington and retaining its presence on Egyptian soil. By doing so Moscow would retain its leverage over Egypt as the sole arms supplier and main strategic asset without risking high-profile conflict. Even if the Soviets were not interested in an American-sponsored cease-fire, as Haikal reports,[79] and were very much surprised when Nasser informed them that he needed "a breathing space so that we can finish our missile sites," the slow process of Soviet approval of Egyptian military requests, which Nasser called "bureaucratic" and which one may call cautious, created a gap between his actual military situation and his growing potential. Nasser himself might have thought that the cease-fire was inevitable. But the Rogers Initiative did have its advantages: a cease-fire could be used to improve Egypt's military position on the canal front, by moving antiaircraft missiles closer to the waterline in order to deprive Israel of air superiority in that sector. The respite might also be used for military exercises and training under relaxed conditions and for repairing the damage caused by the Israeli bombing. Moreover, the cease-fire might be of political use; a wedge could be driven between Washington and Jerusalem over the question of the nature of the negotiations to follow the cease-fire and over the issues of the borders, Jerusalem, and the refugees. Egypt would, meanwhile, continue to receive Soviet political support and aid, principally arms aid.

Washington combined new public pressures on Israel and secret promises, exploiting the worsening military situation along the canal. On July 24, Nixon sent the government a special message, the main terms of which were as follows:[80] First, the United States recognized the need to preserve Israel's Jewish character. In Jerusalem this was interpreted to mean that Israel would not have to agree to the repatriation of Palestinian refugees as part of a general settlement with Egypt and Jordan. Second, the borders to be fixed by the negotiations must satisfy Israel. The Israelis understood this to mean that the boundaries could not be identical with the pre–Six-Day War ADL. If the Israelis were right, this provision was a clear departure from the Rogers Plan. Third, Nixon wrote that the United States would not join in imposing a settlement; in other words, it did not intend to reach a prior agreement with the U.S.S.R., as it had wished to do in 1969. This implied a great change in the political and strategic framework of the negotiations. Fourth, no Israeli troops would retreat from the cease-fire lines until a contractual peace settlement was signed by Israel and the Arab party concerned. Fifth, the United States pledged to maintain the balance of military power in the Middle East and to continue the arms supplies to Israel. This promise allayed Israeli fears that the cessation of military activity would be accompanied by an American arms embargo. Sixth, Nixon undertook to provide Israel with large-scale economic aid to ease the burden of the war on its economy.

The Israeli government began, neither immediately nor unanimously, to look upon the Nixon note as either an American retreat from the Rogers Plan or as grounds for an Israeli argument that the Americans were abandoning the plan. The government's diplomatic, military, and domestic political situation was far from good. Egypt and then Jordan agreed to the American proposals; Jerusalem could not evade a response to the president's appeal if it did not want a confrontation with the United States. Meir had always believed in the necessity of seeking an understanding and a common interest with the United States, but to do so now, on Washington's terms, would be to contradict Israel's own pessimistic assessments of Arab intentions. In light of Nixon's note, however, it seemed more important to cultivate relations with Washington than the permanent distrust of the Arabs.

Another factor that contributed to Israel's agreement to the Rogers Initiative was the worsening situation along the canal. Israeli losses were mounting as Soviet involvement increased. Until July, 1970, it had been thought that Soviet pilots were responsible for Egypt's defense everywhere but the canal sector. However, on July 25 Egyptian Migs piloted by Russian-speaking flyers intercepted and damaged an Israeli Skyhawk near Suez City. Israel replied to this expanding Soviet intervention on July 30, at the height of the debate in cabinet on the American initiative. In a dogfight between Israeli fighters and Soviet-piloted Migs near the Gulf of Suez, several Russian jets were shot down and some of the Soviet flyers were killed.[81] The incident, the only one of its kind, was not made public until December, 1970.

Egyptian artillery was, meanwhile, claiming heavy casualties on the ground. Inside Israel there was mounting criticism by leftist groups, intellectual doves, and the humanistically educated youth who failed to comprehend the gulf between the tough and intransigent line the government was taking and their oft-repeated claim that they were examining every possibility in their search for peace. Critics thought that Israel should have agreed to the initiative as soon as the Arabs did so. The black framed pictures of the casualties published every day in the press added to the criticism. For Meir, though, the casualties were a good reason *not* to make concessions to Egypt, which, by its continued military pressure, was refusing to end the conflict. Still, the fear of a confrontation with the United States and of a more serious entanglement with the Soviet Union and the promise of a favorable shift in American policy made acceptance of the initiative more appealing to her and to Dayan. The defense minister was concerned because of the military situation along the canal,[82] and did not wish escalated hostilities with the Soviets without enough American political and military aid, which was subject to some Israeli response to the Rogers Initiative. Allon and Galili tended to regard the Soviet threat as less crucial, but, together with Eban, wanted to preserve American aid and political assistance. Allon was perhaps the only Israeli leader at the time who also paid attention to the regional situation rather than occupying himself solely with the superpowers' intentions and behavior. He thought that Nasser had taken a risk, when he accepted the American initiative. Israel, he believed, should show good will by accepting the initiative itself, thus giving the Egyptian president a chance to demonstrate his intentions, and at the same time repairing Israel's image abroad, which had been damaged by its obstinate declared positions.

The Gahal leader, Menahem Begin, was firmly opposed to the Rogers Initiative.[83] By accepting it Israel would be agreeing in principle to a withdrawal on the Jordanian as well as the Egyptian fronts. He did not object to such a withdrawal from the Sinai if, and only if, Egypt was ready to withdraw from the conflict and conclude a peace treaty. Begin's legal mind resented mediations bound to lead to less than that. He wanted direct negotiations as a manifestation of legally mutually respected countries. He thought that the territory issue could be settled, but it had to be isolated from the other aspects of the Arab-Israeli conflict. The Sinai would be returned only in exchange for a termination of Egypt's conflict with Israel both individually and as part of the Arab coalition. The West Bank, however, was "the land of our fathers" and was not negotiable. Israel's acceptance in principle of withdrawal from the West Bank would lay it open to charges of undermining a settlement once the agreed negotiations with Jordan began and Jerusalem's objections to a withdrawal became evident. It was far better to clash with Washington early, since a clash was in any case inevitable. Israel could fight the issue inside the United States without worrying that the Americans could use Jerusalem's own statements against it. Clearly Begin's arguments were based on the "pessimistic" assumption that Egypt and the U.S.S.R. would honor the cease-fire agreement and that the U.N. mediator would soon appear to demand Israel's withdrawal from the Sinai and the West Bank.

In an attempt to preserve the National Unity Government and yet avoid a negative reply to Washington and to provide public justification for its change in attitude, the government dubbed the American proposals and promises of June 19 and afterward "the American peace initiative." This phrase also helped distinguish these gestures from the "Rogers Plan." The government asked Washington for some "clarifications" too:[84] it wanted the United States to supply more Phantoms and air-to-ground Shrike missles, to abandon the Rogers Plan, and to regard the Nixon note as the definitive statement of American policy on the conflict. Jerusalem also asked the United States to use its veto power to neutralize the Security Council as a forum for international pressure on Israel. The United States did not wish to isolate itself in the Council for Israel's sake, and up to now had refrained from using its right of veto as commonly as the U.S.S.R. used it. The United States made commitments regarding arms deliveries and reiterated and confirmed, though not publicly, the principles of the Nixon note. At the same time, it refused to abandon the Rogers Plan or to commit itself to using the veto.[85]

Most of the cabinet thought that it would be impossible to extract firmer commitments about borders and security arrangements than the rather flexible formulations of the Nixon note, although the 1969 plan remained an American public declaration of interest concerning the borders. These formulations, however, left Israel with some room to maneuver vis-à-vis the Americans and the Arabs.

On August 1, the cabinet secretary announced Israel's acceptance, with reservations, of the U.S. proposals.[86] In her statement to the Knesset on August 4 Meir[87] stressed the right of the parties to live in secure and recognized boundaries and announced Israel's withdrawal from territory captured in 1967 to secure, recognized, and agreed boundaries. This formula, composed by Dayan and Galili, emphasized Israel's wish to ignore the territorial principles of the 1969 "Rogers Plan." Israel's response, as the government spokesmen stressed, was thus only partially affirmative and entailed the prior establishment of a standstill cease-fire along the canal.

Washington was angered by Jerusalem's reservations and preferred to inform the U.N. mediator simply that Israel, Egypt, and Jordan had agreed to its initiative.[88] Begin's worst fears seemed to be confirmed. Israel had apparently accepted the initiative and the principle of withdrawal that it involved. A confrontation with the United States would thus be inevitable, because to Washington withdrawal meant in principle retreat to near the pre–June, 1967, borders. So, immediately after the Knesset's vote on Prime Minister Meir's August 4 announcement, Gahal withdrew from the coalition and the National Unity government was no more.

The Israeli government's main concern at this point became putting a cease-fire into effect on the canal front quickly and with American mediation. For as soon as Israel was maneuvered to accept the United States' initiative, Egypt and the Soviet Union were liable to begin a race to the canal line in an attempt to move their antiaircraft missiles as close to it as possible.[89] In the earlier stages of the War of Attrition, the Israeli air force had been able to clear the ground of antiaircraft batteries, but now, despite the constant air raids, the missiles were being moved forward, closer to the canal bank. These batteries consisted of newer, more sophisticated weapons operated with the advice of, if not directly by, Soviet personnel. Israel believed that the "American peace initiative" entailed a military standstill and that any change on the ground after it came into effect would be considered a violation of the cease-fire. Israel would be able to demand military or political compensation from the United States or to react in the context of the negotiations set to begin after the cease-fire came into effect. Dayan, therefore, insisted on a cease-fire as soon as possible, even if adequate aerial inspection arrangements could not be instituted immediately, and so the cease-fire came into effect on August 7, 1970.

It seemed that the American diplomacy had achieved at least a partial success in the Middle East, having demonstrated to Nasser that it could push Israel to make some concessions against its declared position and previous behavior. Yet these concessions were made by a unique combination of American pressures and secret promises and the Soviet military pressure. No agreement was achieved between the two superpowers themselves, and the local clients, mainly Egypt, probably made its decision alone. The ability of that client to continue using his superpowers' aid and backing for a different course of action, should he choose to do so, remained within the limits of Moscow's global considerations. Nixon, and Kissinger, were probably skeptical from the beginning of the effective extent of these pre-détente agreements, yet the White House backed the State Department in its Middle East efforts. It made far-reaching promises to Israel, probably because of its skepticism about the whole agreement and in order to promote it.

BLACK SEPTEMBER

Immediately after the declaration of the cease-fire, Israel accused Egypt of violating• the military standstill. Actually, the "standstill principle," which Israel considered an integral and explicit part of the agreement, consisted of American promises to Israel, not a formal, bilateral Israeli-Egyptian agreement.[90] According to Joseph Sisco seven years later, the "standstill principle" had been bilaterally and informally agreed upon between the United States and Israel on the basis of *different maps*, without adequate means to survey the canal area from the air. The Egyptians transmitted their agreement to the United States, and the Soviets were made partners to the cease-fire agreement, not to the "standstill principle," that was informally annexed to it on a bilateral (Egyptian-American) level.

The violation of the standstill involved the movement by the Egyptians and their Soviet advisers of antiaircraft missile batteries into the canal sector, which the IAF had previously managed to keep clear of these arms. Since battle conditions no longer prevailed, Egypt could deploy the weapon systems more easily in the quantity and quality necessary to challenge Israel's air superiority in the canal zone and deep inside occupied Sinai as well. Clearly, the Egyptians violated the "standstill principle" beyond an initial, limited point. The Russians assisted them, yet it is hard to tell whether even the Russians may justly be accused of bad faith. According to Kissinger's biographers,[91] Joseph Sisco was solely responsible for the negotiations with Soviet Ambassador Dobrynin that led to the cease-fire. In conversation with Kissinger, Sisco was described as very reluctant to produce "proof" of the U.S.S.R.'s agreement to a military standstill as part of the cease-fire, and Kissinger was skeptical that Dobrynin had ever explicitly made such a commitment. The same source states that Nixon later accepted Ambassador Rabin's claim that the State Department had hoodwinked the Israelis and that the Russians had outwitted the Americans. The Kalb brothers wrote that Nixon, "was angry at the Egyptians and reserved a special fury for the Russians. They had not accepted the 'Rogers Plan' of December, 1969. They had moved operational combat personnel into Egypt. And they had violated the standstill cease-fire. He wondered if they thought he was a pushover."

It may well be that the ten days of State Department silence, despite Israel's allegations, were due to the lack of an explicit Soviet commitment to the standstill principle. In any event, Washington was not eager to publicize the violation because there was no such commitment or because it was afraid that if the facts became known, considerations of prestige would force the U.S.S.R. to stick to the violations. Thus the possible reason for the silence may be that the United States, with Soviet diplomatic aid, tried in that period to convince the Egyptians, its partners to the standstill agreement, to move the missiles back. Both Moscow and Cairo refused.[92] Apparently, however, after some time of studying the situation in the Middle East and other regions, Nixon finally lost patience with the U.S.S.R. It seems that the Soviet Union, in a challenge to the United States unmatched since 1962, had built a nuclear missile base at Cienfuegos, Cuba. Along the Suez Canal, the U.S.S.R. was continuing to help the Egyptians strengthen their missile battery system. Moreover, the Kremlin had not yet responded to the public, and not-so-public, signals from Washington for a global "package deal" between the superpowers that would trade American concessions in Vietnam for Soviet concessions in the Middle East.

Dayan considered and presented the apparent cease-fire violation as part of a calculated and continuous Soviet program in several theaters of the world, not only in the Middle East. Unless some counter move were made, the U.S.S.R. (and its Arab clients) would simply be encouraged to take more dangerous steps in the Middle East and, perhaps, elsewhere. The defense minister and some of the NRP ministers threatened to resign unless Israel responded to the change in the status quo along the canal. Gahal, which had always opposed the Rogers Initiative, was quite happy at the prospect of seeing Dayan join the ranks of the opposition. The majority in the cabinet, though, hesitated to take a firm stand for fear of a clash with Washington. Dayan increased his pressure, and the press joined the chorus of allegations of Egyptian treachery and charges of the uselessness of agreements with Cairo arrived at with American mediation. On September 6, the government decided to suspend the negotiations with Egypt that were due to begin with the mediation of the U.N. envoy, Gunnar Jarring. The United States did not have time to respond. Within a week crucial changes occurred in the Arab world: bloody incidents broke out between the Palestinian organizations and the Jordanian armed forces, leading to a Syrian military intervention, and President Nasser died. The foundations for the status quo that would last until the outbreak of war in October, 1973, were laid.

The violence turned into open war between the Palestinian organizations and the Hashemite regime during the week of September 15–22, 1970 ("Black Sptember" to the Palestinians). This may well have been due to Palestinian fears of an Israeli-Jordanian deal at their expense. As before Sisco's projected visit to Amman in the spring, the Palestinian organizations apparently intended to demonstrate that no settlement involving Palestinian territory was possible without their agreement. Syria may have been involved too; it tried to use the PLO to dampen Egypt's and Jordan's apparent willingness to negotiate with Israel on the basis of the American proposals, which spoke of final peace settlements and ignored the Golan Heights and the Palestinian cause. Whatever the reason, the Palestinian organizations became embroiled in open conflict with King Hussein at a time when he wished to reassert his sovereign authority in the kingdom. His control had been imperiled by the presence of the organizations and by their operations against Israel and in Europe. He refused to allow the PLO to deny him the role of Israel's partner in negotiations about the Palestinian-populated West Bank and Gaza Strip. Moreover, the trans-Jordanian Bedouin and the middle classes, which, though of Palestinian origin, had an interest in law and order, thought it time to settle affairs with the Palestinian warriors; no compromise was possible.

As the civil war developed, the United States began to fear that radical leftist Syria might, with Soviet support, intervene in pro-Western Jordan. Kissinger had always feared a combination of local radical nationalism and Soviet support, which, in the absence of a global superpower package deal, was liable to threaten the pro-Western oil states of the Arabian peninsula and the gulf. It now seemed that such a coalition was about to topple the Jordanian regime and was endangering the one in Lebanon.[93]

On September 15 Washington demanded clarifications from Moscow as to whether Syria was about to invade (or had already invaded) Jordan. According to one source, Moscow's reply was negative. On September 19, however, both Jerusalem and Amman notified Washington that about 300 Syrian tanks had crossed into Jordan.[94] The United States put its forces at home and in Europe on partial alert. An American emergency staff, presided over by the national security adviser, was established. The Kalbs maintain that this was Kissinger's first experience as a "supercrisis manager," acting on the president's behalf.[95] According to the then chief of naval operations, Admiral Elmo Zumwalt, however, until the Watergate Affair Nixon was the strategist and Kissinger, the adviser.[96] Great importance was attached to the crisis because it was considered to be a superpower confrontation: The U.S.S.R. had assured the United States that there would not be a Syrian invasion, and Moscow was held responsible for Syria's military actions.

Damascus was apparently caught between its obligation to the Palestinian organizations, which stood in danger of annihilation, and the risk of an American-Israeli reaction. Syria chose to compromise, despatching some 300 of its approximately 1000 tanks to Jordan; its air force saw no action at all. The U.S.S.R., too, compromised in order to allay Washington's suspicions. Soviet advisers, the Russians assured Kissinger, would accompany the Syrian troops up to the Jordanian border and no further.[97] Hussein, however, was occupied with the Palestinians in Amman and could counter the Syrian move with only two armored divisions. Only one of them was actually on the border and was forced to fall back.

At this point, Kissinger is said to have led the power-oriented group. He argued that the U.S. positions could not become "credible" to the Kremlin in the Middle East or anywhere unless the United States stopped the open Syrian aggression that the U.S.S.R. was backing. Rogers and the State Department were more cautious and preferred diplomatic action. They also considered possible European opposition to American intervention; the west Europeans had learned a lesson from the 1956 Suez War and feared a general conflagration. A compromise would be to use Israel as the counter-weight to the Syrians.[98]

Nixon, it is said, agreed to a "stark and historical" course if the Syrians should continue their advance: Israel would move against Syrian forces in Jordan; and if Egyptian or Soviet forces then moved against Israel the United States would intervene against both. This agreement was "historic" in the sense that, for the first time, Israel was helping the United States uphold its position in the Middle East. A precedent was set for military cooperation between Washington and Jerusalem, based on a community of interests, though, and not on a formal treaty. Israel's American-backed military strength became an asset for the United States at least as a counter to a radical Arab actor receiving Soviet aid in order to change the status quo. The Israeli-American collaboration also set a personal or emotional precedent for the Israelis: Kissinger and Nixon, who ordered arms and funds released at this time, were considered "friends." In 1971, Ambassador Rabin told his aides that Israel should actively support Nixon's reelection.[99] This was not only done out of gratitude, but in order to create another level of mutual obligation.

Israel, meanwhile, openly transferred armored forces to the Syrian-

Jordanian border region and ordered a partial mobilization and reconnaissance flights over the Syrian forces in Jordan. Limited in number and
lacking air support, the Syrians had difficulty advancing and on September 23 began to withdraw. The "compromise" in the military operations
implemented by Salah Jadid's Ba'athist regime could not save the Palestinian organizations that were decimated and expelled from Jordan. The
Jordanian cease-fire line would no longer be disturbed by these organizations; quiet reigned because of an apparently durable joint American-
Jordanian-Israeli interest and despite Israel's continued occupation of the
West Bank.

Washington, having taught the Russians a lesson in Jordan, was apparently encouraged to indicate to Moscow that discussions on major global
issues were in order. As early as September 16, 1970, Kissinger told
the press

> Our relations with the Soviet Union have reached a point where some impor-
> tant decisions have to be made, especially in Moscow. . . . Events in the
> Middle East and *in other parts of the world* have raised questions of whether
> Soviet leaders as of now are prepared to pursue the principles that I outlined
> earlier, specifically, whether the Soviet leaders are prepared to forego tactical
> advantages they can derive from certain situations for the sake of the larger
> interest of peace.[100]

Indeed, the Soviet Union and its clients in Syria and Jordan seem to
have suffered a number of setbacks in September, 1970. At the height of
the fighting between the Jordanian forces and the Palestinian organizations, Nasser died and the Syrians withdrew from Jordan. Shortly afterwards, Salah Jadid was replaced by another Ba'athist general, Hafez
Assad.

In an interview in October, 1975, the U.S. chief of naval operations,
Admiral Zumwalt, described the resolution of the Jordanian crisis of
1970 in the following terms.[101] America's own military strength in the
region was insufficient to prevent the Soviet-backed forces in Jordan from
emerging victorious or to handle a conventional confrontation with the
U.S.S.R. Effective American power would have to be based on three elements: the U.S. Navy, mainly the carrier group of the Sixth Fleet and
reinforcements from the Atlantic Second Fleet; the marines and strategic
mobile units that could be transported to the area; and the U.S. Air
Force, to provide cover for the naval and landing operations and to give
Americans air superiority. The air force, Zumwalt continued, required
land bases and the political ability to use them. Thanks to the Soviet
naval build-up after the Cuban missile crisis and to the political situation
in the Mediterranean, the United States no longer enjoyed total superiority. The U.S.S.R. could use bases in the Crimea and possibly in Yugoslavia, Egypt, and Syria. The United States, on the other hand, could not

rely on Arab sympathizers such as Spain, Greece, or even Turkey. Ankara, or Madrid, might well hesitate to allow Turkish-based American forces to operate against a third party in a regional conflict in which the Turks or the Spaniards had no stake.

According to Zumwalt, the favorable outcome of the crisis was due to Hussein's power, to the capability shown by his armed forces, which had surprised the Americans, and to Israel's power. Thus the old Israeli argument that a strong Israel was an element for stability in the Middle East became more palatable to the United States partly because of the decline in its own power in the area. The Nixon administration tried to remedy this situation by considering more naval expenditures, but the democratic Congress was hostile, mainly because of the continued war in Indochina. Zumwalt says that, rather than try to mobilize public support for the budget increase by revealing to the public the naval situation in general, and in the Middle East in particular, and by fighting Congress on the issue, mobilizing it and public opinion, the administration proceeded along its course in the Middle East without enough American military power. It chose a policy more likely to be endorsed by Congress—to strengthen Israel militarily, within limits. Zumwalt maintains that the administration preferred not to tell the public the truth because Nixon and Kissinger considered Congress to be selfish and short-sighted and because they thought the general public weary of the war in Vietnam and inured to any arguments that might be raised. These views, Zumwalt claims, were typical of the Nixon administration's cynical and narrow attitude toward American democracy. At any rate, in late 1970 quiet descended on the Middle East, after the implementation of the cease-fire with Egypt and the cessation of operations by the Palestinian organizations in Jordan. For the first time since the Six-Day War many Israelis felt that they could breathe freely and that Israel had come into unchallenged possession of the territories conquered at the cost of so much blood. The Arab coalition was split: Egypt had not come to the aid of the Palestinian organizations, and Syria's assistance had been ineffective. Saudi Arabia, Iraq, and the gulf states acted in only an advisory role. The Israeli military and the mass media were maintaining that Israel had won the War of Attrition militarily and they wondered why it should yield anything politically.[102]

The Middle East was facing a transition period, caused mainly by the death of the most profound Arab leader—President Nasser of Egypt. He died before he could try to exploit his military gains along the canal, and continue his strategy of military pressure with Soviet aid, or try to negotiate with the Israelis with Soviet aid and American mediation.

3

The Yom Kippur War: Origins and Course of Events, 1970-73

ISRAEL'S DOMESTIC SCENE: SOCIAL, ECONOMIC, AND PSYCHOLOGICAL DEVELOPMENTS

The domestic Israeli situation following the August, 1970, cease-fire until the October, 1973, war could be characterized economically, socially, and psychologically as follows. Israel remained officially and politically an egalitarian society, a welfare state deeply committed to the absorption of new immigrants and to a rising standard of living for the lower strata, without connection to economic productivity. At the same time, Israel's free market was developing rapidly under Finance Minister Sapir, in traditional control of imported money from the United States (Jewish funding and U.S. government aid) and from West Germany. The free market industry and fast-growing service and leisure industries competed with the state-controlled economy. The state was constantly trying to bridge the gap between egalitarian values and lower strata demands, allowing a relatively high degree of inflation.[1]

A traditional Israeli political and social postulate—full employment, necessary to absorb new immigrants and to support the lower strata—was maintained. Employees, many of them in state- and Histadrut-owned services and industries, created political pressures for an ever higher standard of living while making good their inflation losses. The usual bargaining was intensified and carried to the extreme by pressure groups and employees in vital services. The public learned that the elite was responsive to threats or to the use of social force. This social and economic power, which became common after the early 1960s, became even more extensive following the cease-fire that proved to be a long armistice. Expectations and envy were growing, as a result of the unequal distribution of both defense burdens, which hit the younger generation more severely, and of the distribution of defense benefits, such as lucrative earth works hastily commenced along the canal line, in anticipation of a renewed war

135

of attrition. Imported money, heavy taxes, and inflation, together with a reasonable degree of foreign investments and a larger volume of production rather than productivity greatly strained the economy. The war itself, fought intensively after early 1969, suddenly terminated, creating contradictory feelings in Israel. Many Israelis were led to believe that Israel had won the war and that Nasser had been forced to accept a cease-fire because of the IAF bombing and because Egypt had not been prepared for a successful invasion. Thus a "status quo syndrome," a psychological satisfaction with the situation along the existing border, was progressively enhanced. Contempt for the enemy, including the PLO, which had been uprooted and banned from Jordan, was mixed with a high degree of attention to terrorist actions from Lebanon, both from the highest military level and from the man in the street. Lebanon was the only base of operation left for the Palestinian organizations under the 1969 Cairo accord.

This "status quo syndrome" combined with traditional fears (the rejection of an imposed settlement, based on U.S. or superpower interests rather than on Arab concessions, and the fear of American naïveté and lack of understanding of Middle East realities that had brought about the 1957 withdrawals without terminating the conflict). Egyptian behavior with regard to the "standstill" clause in the August, 1970, cease-fire agreement was commonly understood as a typical manifestation of Arab treachery, American naïveté, or worse—U.S. interest in gaining influence in the Arab world at Israel's expense. The Gahal block, free of coalition obligations and back in an active opposition, vigorously exploited Egypt's behavior. The "standstill" breach happened to be linked to the criticism expressed by General Ezer Weizman—former IAF commander and second leader of Gahal after Begin—of the cabinet's strategy during the 1969–70 canal war. Weizman, who remained in the minority in the cabinet within this issue, wanted to fight and destroy Nasser's SAM missiles rather than to accept a cease-fire that was exploited by the Egyptians in order to bring their missile sites to the canal. When this happened, against Nasser's obligations, Weizman recommended "sending in ground forces to seize footholds on the western bank of the canal, including the capture of [the city of] Port Said, and by intensifying and extending our bombing raids."[2] Israel, according to his public outcry, found itself instead under considerable U.S. pressure not to let these violations by Egypt upset the cease-fire. Israel lost strategic points for no gains and Egypt gained points, in Weizman's and very many Israelis' perceptions. This would directly influence Israeli behavior in the future.

Very many Israelis developed tendencies toward conservatism in foreign policy and feelings of alienation from the traditional Labor-dominated elite over economic and social matters. Full employment, inflation, a growing, unstable economy, and permanent bargaining with the more powerful social groups moved vast numbers of young, non-European voters away from the once mighty Mapai. The Labor party's foreign policy, under Meir and Dayan, satisfied their conservative stance in style and substance, if not in detail, during most of the period.

This trend toward a "conservative-hawkish" behavior, which started before the Six-Day War, demanded an equal and opposite reaction from adversaries in the bargaining process. However, since the hawks' bargaining assets in this case were real and tangible, such as territories, and the adversaries' were less tangible, like political concessions, the hawks tended to hold on to their real estate instead of trading for questionable benefits. In other words, because the conservatives were pessimistic from the start about the "real intentions" of the adversary and because the Israelis were faced with a whole group of enemies competing with each other against them, the hawks preferred "self-reliance" over deals, and they retained even those bargaining assets that they had been prepared to trade. Furthermore, the "conservative hawks" tended to assert themselves internationally from "a position of strength," which entailed a double-edged postulate of strength. The hawks either regarded themselves as strong enough not to yield to the adversaries' pressure, or as too weak to yield to it, or as bound to weaken their strategic, legal, or historical claims if they yielded.

The "doves," who advocated concessions per se or were afraid of provoking the other side to a greater effort as a result of the "hawkish" philosophy and behavior, were publicly denounced as cowards. They were maneuvered, in public debates, either to argue that the adversaries (i.e., "the Arabs") were not serious about their declared intentions, value system, and education slogans that clearly called for the destruction of Israel, or else they were maneuvered into a relatively passive role, waiting for a change in the official Arab position while limiting "hawkish" initiatives (settlements) as far as they could. This syndrome, which engulfed Israelis during three years without war, was accompanied by the decline of former Jewish-Socialist ideals. This gave Mapai an initial ideological lead and discredited Israel's right for two generations. Against Diaspora habits and values—commercialism, and survival at all costs—on the one hand, and Begin's sweeping ideological-legalistic-heroic claims and method of fighting back from indivisible rights to reality on the other, against religious fatalism and fanaticism, Labor Zionism suggested a national secular and socialist vision. Physical labor, individual pioneering, in terms of collective life on the land and collective social efforts, and fighting, if necessary, were to replace traditional Jewish habits and ideological-legalistic indivisible rightism, and were linked with a large amount of pragmatism. During Ben-Gurion's time, some of these goals proved to lack real substance when implemented. Others, like egalitarian expectations, remained.

A growing psychological and cultural demand for new-old values was created, as Israel turned to be just another, less efficient, westernized state. Socialism, which had generated some unique social experiments in Israel, had been confined since the early 1950s to a minority in kibbutzim. The Histadrut grew to be both a giant union and an entrepreneur. Bargaining for the sake of political survival became Labor's motto, and it survived as long as its machinery and economic tools were thought to deliver social and economic benefits. Yet the monopoly over a promising, meaningful, and imaginative political, cultural, social, and historical thinking slipped away from the labor group, as manifested by the Lavon Affair. A spiritual and cultural vacuum existed after the decline of the secular-Socialist pioneering values. First it was covered up by Eshkol and Sapir's welfare free market spirit, which helped Israel develop into a consumer society, yet brought with it typical grievances—growing cities, environmental maladies, and fierce competition. Old characteristics of the bureaucratized, party state remained, however; a vast state and union bureaucracy free from pioneering puritanism and politically identified with the ruling coalition was running a less dependent society living in a spiritual vacuum.

New forces started to fill the vacuum. Religious groupings headed by "Gush Emunim" (Block of the Faith) combined demands for a meaningful life with a search for puritan, Jewish moral life in Eretz-Israel as a whole.[3] Pioneering, still in demand by the younger generation, particuraly young kibbutznik's, yet absorbed by the War of Attrition until now, started to look for national, territory-oriented, and religiously inspired groups, like "the Movement for the whole of Eretz-Israel." Labor started to lose more of its support in the liberal, "dovish" intelligentsia that tended toward socialistic values and resented the constant bargaining that created, in their eyes, a "valueless society" in a conservative Israel.[4] Conservative intelligentsia moved to the right, toward territorial-pioneering-ethical Zionism. Still, Dayan and Meir satisfied more of their demands; the foreign policy of Dayan and Meir was conservative and "hawkish," as demanded by the growing "hawkish" popular feeling inspired by right-wing intelligents. Some of those who could find refuge in Ben-Gurion's Mapai now joined the former far right in their bid for self-righteousness and self-pity, and in an existential quest for a meaning to their Jewish life.[5] The masses, to an extent satisfied with newly acquired economic benefits, to an extent uneasy about it, lost old loyalties to Labor and were sure to become autonomous of the leadership, if Dayan and Meir failed in their defense and foreign policy.

Television, the first mass circulation media comprehensible to very many Arab-speaking immigrants and to the lower, Israeli-born strata, was first introduced to Israel in 1968. It made politics more tangible to these people, and probably helped create a growing demand for participation and a tendency to follow events more intimately and thus critically. The old magic of the Israeli elite, shaken by the "Lavon Affair" and revived by Dayan and Meir, became more vulnerable than Ben-Gurion's, and both leaders knew it. At first, Dayan demonstrated his old shrewdness; yet at the same time he developed a hesitant, prudent approach toward Egypt, aware of domestic expectations for a prolonged calm along the borders without making far-reaching concessions to the Arabs.

THE SUPERPOWERS, SADAT, AND ISRAEL, 1970–72

Egypt's violation of the standstill cease-fire and the civil war in Jordan led to the suspension of the talks about a general settlement, which were supposed to have begun after the implementation of the cease-fire at the Suez Canal in August. In October, 1970, diplomatic activity resumed on two levels: the United Nations' envoy tried to bring about a general settlement, and Defense Minister Dayan proposed a partial settlement that would involve only Egypt and Israel. The United States pursued an agreement on both levels.

Dayan had been behind Israeli decision to suspend the talks with Jarring. After the Egyptian violation of the cease-fire and Nixon's attack on the U.S.S.R.'s global and Middle East policy, and with the fighting in Jordan, Dayan was able to make some major gains for Jerusalem in its relations with Washington. Israel received a great deal of military and financial aid during September. Still, when the fighting in Jordan ended and a new president came to power in Egypt, Israel faced the possibility of a new American initiative. The resumption of negotiations about a comprehensive agreement meant dealing, sooner or later, with the problem of the West Bank. To prevent such a development, on October 3, 1970, Dayan suggested publicly that Jarring need not be the sole channel of negotiations between Israel and Egypt; he did not mention Jordan.[6]

After some hesitation, Dayan came to agree with the proposal of some of his aides[7] to try to split up the Arab claims and Israeli counterclaims by offering a gradual withdrawal from the canal. Some of Egypt's national goals might thus be satisfied and severed from the package of all the Arab demands. Traditionally, Dayan had been against the degree of provocation that Israel's presence along the canal constituted for Egypt, but he refused to make any concessions—responding with force to the Arab use of force—as long as Nasser was applying military pressure on Israel. When Egypt stopped the fighting, the minister of defense was ready to negotiate. "Egypt cannot live without the Suez Canal," Dayan used to say, "and we cannot live without an access to the Red Sea," meaning without direct control over Sharm-el-Sheikh. Thus, he tended to withdraw, as a result of a deal with Egypt, from the canal zone and even further. On the assumption that the U.S.S.R. had a strategic and political interest in the reopening of the Suez Canal, a separate deal with Egypt might meet this need, while America's interest in quiet in the region might also be satisfied. Israel would be left with the West Bank and the expanses of the Sinai to bargain for future deals with Egypt, which would develop a vested interest in a reopened canal and in rebuilt canal cities, while staying in Sharm-el-Sheikh.

Specifically, the plan called for a gradual withdrawal from the canal toward the Giddi and Mitla passes, which were considered the strategic key to the Sinai and which controlled the eastern bank of the canal. While the Israeli forces retreated, the Egyptians would begin clearing the waterway to prepare for its reopening. Resumption of navigation through the canal would be accompanied by political arrangements aimed at taking Cairo out of the conflict without final peace.[8]

Dayan should have been aware that there was an interrelationship between Israel's claims and the Arabs' demands. By demanding all ("real peace and defensible borders") or nothing, the Israelis thus encouraged the Arabs to demand all the occupied territory and the Palestinian rights, or nothing. The only outcome could be political deadlock, a stepped-up Arab war effort, increased Soviet aid for the Arabs, American fears of a war, and Soviet-American deals over Israel's head without regard for its territorial and procedural demands. Dayan wanted the cease-fire with Egypt maintained; the War of Attrition had cost Israel many casulties, hurt it economically and socially, made it more dependent on the United States, and had not brought any of its political objectives any nearer. He tried to make Israel's position more acceptable to Egypt and the superpowers on a marginal level and to see if Egypt would agree to the resultant strategic change in its position as a temporary outlet.

Prime Minister Meir was at first opposed to Dayan's suggestions.[9] Egypt, which had violated the August, 1970, cease-fire and other agreements, was not a reliable negotiating partner. Israel would make concrete concessions for Egypt's worthless signature on documents that did not entail an end to the conflict. What was needed, in Meir's view, was a change in the form and content of Cairo's position on the conflict as a whole. This meant acceptance of direct recognition, liquidation of the conflict, a final and full peace, and diplomatic, commercial, and economic relations.

During the "War of Attrition" Dayan, in his "manly responsive" fashion had been thinking in military terms. It is contended that Soviet involvement in Egypt, Jordan, and Lebanon (through the PLO), its support of Syria, and its strong position in Iraq could have led him to concentrate upon fighting the Arabs. It mattered little how moderate or immoderate a line Israel took toward its neighbors; the Arab-Israeli conflict was considered constant, a fact of political life, a permanent subsystem of the global system. The Arabs, and therefore Israel, would try to achieve their objectives with whatever foreign aid they could muster. A general settlement was consequently even more unlikely, since each party would try to attain its goals in the context of the global conflict.

Thus Dayan was expecting American aid, in the global context of the Middle East Conflict, without sacrificing Israeli interests as he understood them. This aid was given during "Black September" because of an American-Israeli community of interests, an important asset that might be expected to last for quite a while if Washington were not confronted with a new Soviet-Arab war. Dayan felt that a resumed canal war, or any other kind of Israeli-Egyptian-Soviet confrontation, should be prevented or delayed. An Israeli political initiative was important to prevent a political deadlock—a renewed war, or an American political initiative to which Israel would react as a passive client or else risk troubles with Washington.

At first, Dayan's idea of a partial settlement met with a cool reception in Washington. The Americans feared that the Arabs and the U.S.S.R. would see it as an attempt by Israel to evade a comprehensive agreement. The United States was not particularly interested in reopening the canal except in the context of a final settlement; as long as the canal was closed it was a bargaining point to be used against the U.S.S.R. and Egypt.[10]

Egypt's new president, Anwar Sadat, surprised both Washington and Jerusalem, however. On February 4, 1971, Sadat announced a "new Egyptian initiative";[11] he demanded an Israel withdrawal from the canal under the cease-fire as a preliminary step toward agreeing on a timetable for the terms of Resolution 242. Once a timetable was accepted, Egypt would be willing to start clearing the waterway in order to reopen it. In an interview with Newsweek a few days later, Sadat narrowed his terms.[12] A "partial Israeli withdrawal" meant a pullback to a line east of El-Arish in northeast Sinai. The cease-fire would be limited in time; if Egypt agreed to an indefinite cease-fire it would not be able to exert pressure on Israel or the superpowers, and the situation would be deadlocked. The canal would be reopened six months after the clearing work began. Israeli shipping would not be allowed through the waterway until it had fulfilled all its obligations under the U.N. resolutions, that is, until it withdrew from all Arab territories and the refugee problem was settled. Israel was assured of freedom of passage through the Straits of Tiran and a U.N. force would be stationed at Sharm-el-Sheikh.

Sadat's public position was now more gradual and diversified in comparison to the line Nasser had taken after the Six-Day War. Egypt's motto then had been, "What was taken by force shall be restored by force," and it had demanded a restoration of the prewar status quo or a general settlement that would include a resolution of the Palestinian problem according to PLO demands. Still, Jerusalem could interpret this shift as purely tactical and as consistent with Egypt's commitment to the general Arab and Palestinian cause. Sadat's move could be seen as an attempt to extract the maximum Israeli withdrawal in a diplomatic and political framework that would not liquidate the conflict and all the Arabs' demands on Israel. Sadat did, in fact, connect the partial settlement along the canal front and the timetable with the other terms of Resolution 242 as it was understood by Egypt: a total Israeli withdrawal to the 1949 armistice demarcation lines and a solution of the refugee problem in accordance with their choice.

Meanwhile, Gunnar Jarring, the U.N. envoy, was making a move of his own, which, because of its timing and consequences, resulted in the final collapse of his mission. Assuming that Cairo and Jerusalem were preparing for partial settlement, in an attempt to obtain the general Arab-Israeli settlement called for by Resolution 242, on February 8 he sent notes to Egypt and Israel that differed in content but were identical in diplomatic significance.[13] Jarring asked Israel whether it would be willing to pull back to the international frontier and he asked Egypt whether it would be willing to make peace. Thus he openly raised the two crucial questions of the Egyptian-Israeli conflict just when Sadat seemed willing to discuss a *partial* agreement. Had serious negotiations about a limited Israeli withdrawal taken place, Jerusalem would have been temporarily freed from the need to consider a comprehensive approach and all that implied, i.e., withdrawals in all fronts. The United States, too, came to regard a partial settlement as the more realistic option, because Sadat seemingly endorsed it and because the United States could see some political benefit for itself in assuming the mediation role toward such a settlement.[14] Instead of the U.N., where the Soviet Union had a say, the United States might be able to become the sole mediator, with Egyptian consent. Moscow would hardly be able to raise public objections to the American role under these circumstances. Up to now, the United States had been involved in several mediation efforts under U.N. auspices that permitted the Soviets to retain some degree of control. The Arabs preferred this arrangement as a means of balancing "pro-Israeli" Washington with Moscow. The U.N. envoy had been charged with achieving a full settlement. Once the parties opted for something less than a full settlement, he was superfluous.

On February 15, 1971, Cairo replied to Jarring's note. For the first time in a diplomatic message the Egyptians stated that if all the terms of Resolution 242 were implemented as Cairo interpreted them, Egypt would agree to "salaam" with Israel. The word "salaam" is usually translated as "peace"; to the Israeli cabinet, the press, and most of the public it meant no more than a political settlement that could be abandoned under changed circumstances and did not entail reconciliation. Peace-cum-reconciliation would have been expressed in Arabic by the word "sulh."[15]

On February 26, 1971, Israel sent Jarring its reply, stating that it could not envisage a total withdrawal to the 1967 lines. Jerusalem reiterated its demand for secure and recognized boundaries that, by definition, had to be different from the earlier ones. Meir saw Egypt's proposed "salaam" as an empty slogan, for it continued to speak of satisfying its and the Arab coalition's old demands—the restoration of all Arab land captured in 1967 and a resolution of the refugee problem on Israel's account.

Washington hurried to dissociate itself from Israel's reply, which was not in line with traditional American ideas about a general Israeli-Arab settlement. Jarring, however, did not exploit the proximity between Cairo's and Washington's views and Jerusalem's isolation. February passed and he did nothing. Soon Israel discredited him as "one-sided"; he had asked it for a complete retreat and had involved it in a diplomatic defeat, when he allowed Egypt to offer an empty word ("salaam") for Israeli real estate. The United States then assumed the role of mediator, and Jarring made his final exit from the Middle Eastern stage.

On March 1, 1971, Sadat paid a secret visit to the U.S.S.R. to seek greater military assistance, and upon his return on March 7 he announced that he had been very successful. Much of his speech that day, however, dealt with the United States, which, he claimed, had promised him, "particularly during this past month," that it opposed and would continue to oppose the acquisition of territory by force. He demanded that Washington impose its views on the Israelis.[16] Later, Sadat would reveal that his visit to the U.S.S.R. had been a failure and that he had been denied the weapon systems that the chief of staff, General Sadek, considered necessary if resumed fighting were to be successful.[17]

When he assumed power in the summer of 1970, President Sadat had several theoretical ways to attain the goal of recovering all Arab land without submitting to Israeli political demands and still solve the Palestinian problem: (1) a political solution imposed by the superpowers without war; (2) political "progress" imposed by the superpowers, yet linked to his, and the Arab's, common goals; (3) an overall military offensive with active Soviet aid, including a nuclear guarantee; (4) a partial military effort with active Soviet aid; (5) an overall offensive without active Soviet aid, but with some kind of a Soviet nuclear guarantee; (6) a partial Arab (Egypt, Syria, and other Arab states) offensive to bring about American pressure on Israel to withdraw from the territories and to agree to a solution of the Palestinian problem.

Sadat tested most of these options, and his final choice was dictated by a combination of Soviet (and American) behavior toward him and his domestic and inter-Arab considerations. At first, during the March, 1971, visit to Moscow, Sadat seemed to have considered the option of a Soviet-backed general offensive. He was not interested in another war of attrition, but in a general campaign to cross the Suez Canal and fight Israel at least to the former ADL, thus endangering its vital heartland. The War of Attrition had not been an unequivocal success; it had been very costly economically and politically, it had increased Egypt's dependence on the Kremlin without any substantial military achievements. For a general offensive, Sadat needed surface-to-surface missiles with enough range to strike Israel's centers of population and so deter Israeli deep-penetration bombing of Egypt and any aircraft with a range and payload similar to the Phantom.

There is evidence that the Egptians asked for nuclear arms or for at least a Soviet nuclear guarantee against Israel. According to Israeli sources,[18] General Sadek demanded from the Russians nuclear weapons, delivery means, and the permission to use both according to Egypt's autonomous judgment. A political faction in Egypt that was critical of Sadat might have regarded Israel's nuclear option as a basic given of the conflict. (One of this group's leaders was Muhammad Hassanein Heikal, Nasser's friend and confidant and the editor of Al-Ahram.) This might have been one reason that the group was so suspicious of Sadat's departure from Nasser's policy of seeking common ground solely with the U.S.S.R. and of Sadat's public overtures toward the United States. They might have felt that these deviations would endanger the chances of getting Soviet aid to counter Israel's conventional might and nuclear option. At this point, Sadat did not have to bother trying to justify his actions, since the Soviet Union refused to give him either the arms or an automatic nuclear guarantee, according to Israeli sources. The Soviet refusal to give conventional arms may have stemmed, in part, from considerations of relations between the superpowers, which were the subject of much diplomatic action at this time. Apparently, Moscow did not want to disturb the rapprochement that would eventually lead to SALT 1 and the other 1972 détente agreements by providing Egypt with the military capability to go to war. A war that Egypt would start when it wanted to do so might be blamed on the U.S.S.R. by the Americans.[19]

In Washington it was thought that after the Polish unrest of December, 1970, and perhaps because of the failure of the Soviet coalition with the PLO, Syria, and Egypt in September, 1970, the U.S.S.R. might be more responsive to the ideas of the global package deal that Nixon and Kissinger had been proposing for the past two years. This deal implicitly or explicitly entailed a Middle East settlement based on a decrease in

Soviet military involvement and support for Arab extremism. Further-more, at the April, 1971, congress of the Communist party of the Soviet Union, Brezhnev made a speech that was considered in Washington to be a breakthrough toward the proposed package deal.

An affirmative Soviet answer to Sadat's requests might have been detrimental to the Soviet Union's interests whether or not it was sincerely interested in the American proposals. Even if the U.S.S.R. intended only to exploit the agreement and not to fulfill its part in the bargain, it still had to be careful about the timing of its actions. Supplying Egypt now was not in its interests, as a large number of Soviet advisers were stationed in Egypt, implying Soviet responsibility for Egyptian actions. The Soviet refusal to supply arms may also have stemmed from complications in relations between the U.S.S.R. and Egypt. Egyptian factions critical of Sadat claimed that he was moving away from Nasser's heritage, and particularly from the Soviet orientation in foreign, social, and economic policy that had characterized Egypt since 1956. These opposition group-ings, headed by Vice President Ali Sabri, had strong support in the civil-ian bureaucratic establishment. Actually, the differences over policy might have been no more than a cover for a power struggle, a fight for the succession. On May 1, 1971, Sadat used the army to crush his domestic enemies.

The U.S.S.R. might have regarded this outcome as a victory for the Egyptian national bourgeoisie, which was less interested in keeping the connection with Moscow as close as Nasser had kept it. Even before the Six-Day War Nasser had supported Soviet policy in North Africa, South Arabia, Aden, and the neighboring Arab states. After the war, he came to see a strong Soviet military presence in the eastern Mediterranean as necessary to balance American power in the region, to exert pressure on Washington, and to maintain Egypt's bargaining capacity vis-à-vis Israel. The Soviet had their difficulties with this strategy too, yet Nasser was, during most of the period, a conscious ally. Sadat became an uneasy, semiautonomous client.

A third possible reason for the Soviet refusal of arms to Egypt may have been, quite simply, that it did not yet have some of them, like a conventional surface-to-surface missile and the Phantom-like jets, in its arsenal.

Sadat's troubles at home, which led to the purge of the Ali Sabri group, did nothing to improve his bargaining capacity in Washington, particu-larly as all was quiet at the canal and the other fronts. A global settle-ment with the U.S.S.R. became the highest priority of U.S. foreign policy. Until one was achieved, Washington wanted to ensure quiet in the regional theaters. The local conflicts at least would be kept from spilling over into the global system by the larger settlement.

On April 1 Nixon replied to Sadat's address of March 7,[20] and on April 4 he expanded on his ideas at a press conference. He said that it was a good idea for the parties to the conflict to come to an interim agreement, and that the United States would not impose its views on them. Washington would maintain the military balance in the region. He stated that the cease-fire must not lapse and that the discussions between Israel and Egypt must go forward. On April 2, 1971, Egypt answered Nixon publicly: Sadat said[21] that peaceful coexistence with Israel and Israeli occupation of Arab territories and the continuation of its expansionist policy were incompatible. As far as interim agreement between Egypt and Israel were concerned, Cairo made the following specific points. First, an Israeli partial retreat in the Sinai would not be a partial solution to the conflict, but rather "an administrative move" in the framework of U.N. Resolution 242. Second, Egypt would be ready to start clearing the Suez Canal parallelly to the beginning of the Israeli retreat. Following the Israeli retreat, Egypt would agree to a "limited cease-fire" to enable Ambassador Jarring to arrange for a "timetable" to implement Resolution 242. Third, Egyptian forces would follow the retreating Israeli army, but Egypt would be ready to take "practical steps" in the field for the "separation of forces" and the continuation of the cease-fire. Egypt would not be ready to accept the demilitarization of the Sinai, nor any Israeli presence in Sharm-el-Sheikh.

At the same time, Cairo began a political offensive in western Europe. By the end of March, Egyptian Foreign Minister Riad had visited western European capitals and informed them that Egypt would be ready to start clearing the canal after an Israeli partial retreat, yet its opening to the benefit of European shipping, for example, would wait until a final Israeli retreat. The State Department became active in the region again and pursued its own course, parallel to that of the White House. In an effort at direct mediation in the field, Rogers and Sisco toured the Middle East, arriving in Egypt on May 4 and in Israel on May 6. Sisco went back to Egypt for two days and in August returned for another visit. The Americans were trying to demonstrate their presence in the region and to prevent a political deadlock. Word reached Jerusalem that the Americans were saying one thing to the Egyptians and another to the Israelis.[22]

On the whole, the Rogers-Sisco visit seems to have been rather hastily and poorly planned. The proposals they made were not detailed enough to serve as a basis for either a general or an interim settlement; nor did they present any alternatives when the parties raised objections to their suggstions. Furthermore, instead of concentrating on Sadat, Rogers and Sisco wasted some time talking with other Egyptian officials. They did not have enough time or knowledge to bring about the crystallization of a new position in the various factions of the Meir cabinet.[23]

On May 25, the president of the Supreme Soviet, Nikolai Podgorny, came to Egypt and signed a "Treaty of Friendship"[24] between the U.S.S.R. and Egypt, which astounded the Israelis and Americans. The main points of the treaty were contained in articles 7–10. The parties undertook to coordinate their activities in the international arena. Military cooperation was to be developed to strengthen Egypt's defensive capability and to increase its capacity to reverse "the results of the aggression" and to withstand further aggression. Undertakings and agreements or international commitments by the signatories to third parties were not to give rise to contradictions between the two of them or to run counter to the spirit of the treaty.

Later, after the expulsion of the Soviet advisers in July, 1972, Sadat explained why he had signed the treaty.[25] Before May, 1971, the U.S.S.R. had not lived up to its promises of arms for Egypt. Sadat had proclaimed 1971 the "year of decision," yet by midyear had no political movement or military accomplishment to show for it. The Egyptian public was growing frustrated and angry.

It seems that the treaty was regarded by both Egypt and the U.S.S.R. as a means of binding each other's hands in relations with the United States. The strategic arms limitation and other détente-related talks were gaining substance. The U.S.S.R. may have wanted to create a formal political framework for discussions and shared interests with Egypt for two reasons: to keep Cairo from feeling at a disadvantage because of the superpowers dialogue and Egypt's trying to sabotage it, and also to represent Egypt's interests to Washington. The timing of Soviet refusals of arms supplies to Egypt was, it should be noted, certainly subject to global considerations: Moscow's relations with the United States, western Europe, and China, and the aid committed to India.[26] So if the Soviet Union did promise Egypt the arms it wanted, they did not necessarily need to be delivered immediately, as Sadat complained later.[27] In the meantime, the Soviets wanted to formalize Soviet-Egyptian diplomatic and political relations, in order to synchronize and coordinate the various interests of the two states and to keep Cairo from turning to the United States.

Sadat made it clear that he did not think the treaty would be an obstacle to a rapprochement with the United States if Washington should pressure Israel to agree to an interim arrangement on Egypt's terms. In Cairo it was argued that Israel's demands were unimportant; it was Washington's attitude that was crucial, since Jerusalem depended on the United States for everything from bread to Phantoms. In any case, only external pressure could dislodge Israel, which was, by its very nature, aggressive and expansionistic.[28]

Israel was very suspicious of Egypt's demands and of the ways in which it was trying to advance its interests—the treaty with the Soviet Union, the appeal to the United States, and the activity in western Europe. Egypt seemed to be looking for diplomatic and military tools that would help it retrieve territory without having to end the conflict with the Jewish state. The charges of Israeli expansionism and aggressiveness were viewed with anger and contempt, and the existing boundaries were deemed secure enough.

In April, 1971, Meir was convinced by Dayan and by her own, newly appointed political adviser, Simcha Dinitz,[29] to try and negotiate with Washington an American-Israeli understanding on an interim settlement with Egypt. The idea was to negotiate directly with Kissinger—a "friend" since "Black September"—and Nixon himself, thus avoiding the State Department's machinery and what Israel considered its traditional, hostile approach. Bypassing Secretary Rogers, the Israelis suggested a deal to Nixon: the United States would shelve the Rogers Plan in its entirety, including the Jordanian component and the 1967 borders component, in exchange for an Israeli withdrawal from the Suez Canal zone. Meir was finally ready to discuss the idea, which detached the "interim settlement" from an overall discussion of the other elements of the Arab-Israeli conflict (meaning an American acknowledgment that the Rogers Plan was dead and buried), so that no Arab demands would be acceptable to Washington for less than peace and defensible borders. However, most of the Israeli cabinet also argued that increased Soviet military involvement on Egypt's behalf in the canal sector and the Sinai following an Israeli pullback would have to be balanced by a significant level of American guarantees.[30] The government's decision reiterated a traditional Israeli stance that they did not want a single American soldier to die for Israel. As always, they wanted the United States to deter the Russians from intervening in renewed Arab-Israeli hostilities and to counterbalance Soviet military aid to Arab states and the PLO.

Kissinger, and later Nixon, tended toward a favorable response to the Israeli suggestion, with the exception of automatic military guarantees to Israel. This, Nixon and Kissinger said, would be considered in the light of Soviet aggression, which would trigger an American response. President Sadat seemed not to be very serious, twisting as an emotional child between threats to and simple bargaining of Moscow and Washington alike; moreover, Nixon and Kissinger believed Sadat was weak, and could not deliver any serious commitment to peace or any Egyptian concessions short of peace. An interim settlement could have given him, had he been strong enough, a reopened canal, a respite from the refugees who fled the canal zone to the main cities during the War of Attrition, and a possibility to rehabilitate the whole area—clearly preferable to the formal guarantees toward Isreal that he might not willingly accept. This advantage, obvious to both Kissinger and Dayan, seemed to them beyond Sadat's capabilities. Both Israel and Washington thus agreed that interim settlements should be discussed, rather than an overall, comprehensive (Rogers) solution, yet they were very skeptical about it.

Meir presented Israel's proposed terms for an interim settlement to parliament on June 15, 1971. Always skeptical of making "concrete concessions for a mere signature," she demanded an indefinite Egyptian commitment not to resume hostilities, no Egyptian troops permitted east of the Suez Canal, effective inspection arrangements, the severance of Sadat's agreement from other Egyptian demands, and no further Israeli withdrawals until a full peace settlement was reached. Meir had told this to Rogers and Sisco during their visit in May and had repeatedly stressed Israel's demands for an ongoing arms supply. Since "compensating" Israel for the Egyptian standstill cease-fire violation in September, 1970, the Americans had not agreed to new arms agreements; requests for sophisticated equipment to offset the antiaircraft missiles in the canal sector remained "under study." Ambassador Rabin mobilized Congress against this with a reasonable degree of success. Senatorial letters to Nixon to safeguard Israel's security were signed by an overwhelming majority, yet jet plane deliveries were blocked, pending Sadat's response to the interim agreement suggestions.

When Sisco again toured the region in August, 1971, Meir reiterated Israel's terms for a partial settlement, which were supported by most of the cabinet. Dayan, however, was quite willing to concede to Egypt the right to station troops east of the canal. He was sensitive to the importance that the Egyptians attached to their sovereignty over the territory to be evacuated, and he assumed that Sadat would not be satisfied with a withdrawal that was not followed by the introduction of Egyptian troops. In Dayan's talks with Sisco, the figure of 750 Egyptian soldiers and policemen was mentioned as the maximum to be permitted across the canal.[31]

Sadat attached the interim settlement to a general settlement on the Arabs' terms. It was not Dayan's style to assume risks, domestically or externally, when the chances of success were slim and there was no military pressure on Israel to make the risk seem worthwhile. In fact, Sadat's "year of the decision" was half over and Egypt did not resume hostilities.

On September 16, 1971 Sadat gave vent to his anger with American policy, saying that Washington was acting as a letter carrier between Cairo and Jerusalem rather than clarifying its own position, which, he argued, would determine Israel's position.[32] "1971 will pass and 1972, when the U.S. presidential elections take place, will too, and then we shall enter ten more years until the day when everything becomes a lasting fact."

There is no doubt that after April, 1971, the Egyptians began to feel that time was fast running out. This was due in part to Sadat's personal position; he was a new, uncharismatic president, mocked by the Egyptian public and under pressure from the Arab world to accomplish *something* in relation to Israel.[33] He seemed also to have feared a global Soviet-American rapprochement. An agreement on Vietnam seemed more viable, and once this stumbling block was removed superpower relations could improve. Meanwhile, the Israelis were liable to grow so strong that it would be impossible to dislodge them. For, owing partly to the aid the Egyptians had been getting from the U.S.S.R. and to Israel's bargaining power inside the United States, Jerusalem had received a great deal of American aid. Egypt was in a dilemma; it could not give up Soviet aid if it wanted to retain its military option, but it did not get all it requested and what it did receive gave Israel grounds for requesting more arms from Washington. If Egypt should ask the United States for political backing, Israel's bargaining capacity in the United States might prove to be great enough to frustrate any steps the State Department might take in the direction desired by Cairo.

The Arabs' calculations of Israel's strength seem to have included an IDF nuclear option. In 1971, an Arab writer, Fuad Jabber, published a book stating that Israel must develop its nuclear power in order to gain a decisively advantageous position for the advancement of its expansionist ambitions.[34] This book reflected a mood in the Arab world, even though Cairo was very careful not to make public reference to an operational Israeli capability. Only Heikal, Nasser's intimate friend and minister of information, made, in July, 1970, a statement in the foreign press that Israel was able, in his assessment, to produce the bomb.[35] This capability was, however, at the back of the Arabs' mind, and their growing impatience in the summer of 1971 may have been due to the Israeli nuclear challenge as well as to the political deadlock and the conventional arms balance.[36] This does not mean that the Arabs were unanimous in their attitude. General Sadek, Heikal, and the purged "pro-Russian" Ali Sabri group, might have thought that Egyptian possession of nuclear arms or a Soviet nuclear guarantee was a necessary condition for full-scale war. Such a war would be fought in order to recover "all the territories," as well as some rights for the Palestinians that would be politically attainable. The military planning for "Operation Granite Two" under Egyptian Chief of Staff Sadek, involved a canal crossing, storming the Sinai passes, and a sweep toward the 1949 ADL. "Granite Two" was further expanded into "Granite Three" to include the Gaza Strip, forty kilometers from Tel Aviv.[37] At the same time, rumors were coming from General Dayan's vicinity with regard to possible Israeli nuclear capability, either to deter the Arabs directly without admitting a capability in public or to increase the ambiguity and doubt in the Arab-Soviet camp as to Israel's nuclear effort.

Libya's Muammar Khaddafi, Nasser's young admirer, seemed to have been caught in Dayan's net. He apparently saw no way of dealing with Israel unless the Arabs had nuclear arms to regain the strategic flexibility necessary to conduct a full-scale war and to determine where the fighting would take place. This line of reasoning is the only explanation for Khaddafi's decision in 1970 to ask China, unsuccessfully, for a nuclear bomb.[38] Conventionally, too, the Egyptians did not regard themselves as prepared for a full-scale war that would push Israel out of the occupied territories and dictate some sort of a solution to the Palestinian problem. Heikal summarizes the confused military-political thinking in Egypt by the end of 1971 as follows:[39] "Egypt was so obsessed with Israel's successful preemptive strike of June 5, 1967, that, to begin with, all thoughts were concentrated on how to achieve the degree of air superiority that would enable Egypt in its turn to neutralize Israeli bases. Egyptian planning was complicated by a mixture of frustration and hope, as the projected attack was put off while the planning for it ground on. We were impatient. It was a long time before Egypt became ready to accept the idea of a limited attack aimed primarily at opening up political possibilities."

One may assume that the "all-out offensive" strategy at least to regain all lost territories and dictate a solution to the Palestinian problem, which President Sadat inherited from his late predecessor or decided upon himself, could not have been implemented, in Arab eyes, without a decisive conventional advantage *and* an answer to Israel's "bomb in the basement." The Soviet Union was the only source of conventional weaponry needed to resume hostilities on a very large scale; a smaller scale might have brought Israeli counteractions without a decision. Moscow was also the only source of nuclear guarantees. Arab radicals, who opted for the "all-out offensive" concept—most of them had to accept a Soviet orientation as a result—were thus forced to accept no war at all until the Soviet Union agreed to supply the needed conventional weaponry and until an answer was found to what they perceived as Israel's nuclear threat. Other, more pragmatic leaders, like Sadat, who happened to carry the responsibility, slowly developed, after 1971, a more subtle strategy of limited war on Israel's occupied margins. Sadat finally aimed at successful conventional war without securing total superiority, conventionally and unconventionally, in advance.

After 1967 Israel pursued a strategy of fighting stubbornly, both politically and militarily, for the margins, in order to bring about a substantive change in the Arab position, to safeguard the Israeli heartland, and to secure "defensible borders." A properly conducted Arab limited war in the same margins would cause Israel political problems merely by breaking out and continuing for some time. Israel's security doctrine was based on short wars and on obtaining decisive military superiority at the time and place that Israel wanted. Arab military cooperation concentrated in limited areas for limited objectives could help the Arabs fight a relatively long, hard war with many Israeli casualties, which could lead to intervention by the superpowers. At the same time, Sadat realized, as he hinted in his 1977 Arabic version memoirs,[40] the enormous political usefulness of the word "peace" if intended for European or American audiences. He kept repeating that Egypt wanted peace in exchange for the occupied territories and the rights of the Palestinians. Sadat, as opposed to Nasser, used that word extensively, though the Israelis interpreted "peace," simple as it sounded, as if Egypt did not really mean that when it demanded the "rights of the Palestinians" in the same terms. For the Israelis, Egypt indeed refused peace when it asked for all territories and the rights of the Palestinians as defined by the PLO, as Mrs. Meir and General Dayan publicly kept saying.[41] Even if Sadat came to the conclusion that the PLO would have to accept a miniature state in the West Bank and Gaza, he did not say so in public, and the idea itself was unacceptable to the Meir-Dayan coalition. Yet Sadat, the less charismatic leader, the more traditional, Egyptian villager, gained more points against Israel internationally with his "peace" strategy than Nasser had with his inter-Arab commitments as a "manly hero." Nasser, who represented the all-Arab, Gestaltlike nationalism, was forced to an extreme rigidity with no outlet positions, as is shown by his behavior in given periods during his presidency.

Sadat, his memoirs reveal, was more a postulative-cognitive leader, who tried to make Egypt's goals compatible with his studies of history and his understanding of reality. Thus, he became capable of instrumental, and hence by definition limited, political and military strategy. Nasser's Gestaltlike, pan-Arab duties and images wasted both his time and Egypt's limited resources. Israel's leadership did not make any distinction between Sadat and Nasser, just as Arabs were incapable of making distinctions between Begin and Ben-Gurion at the time, or between Eshkol and Dayan. It seems that the United States, and less so Moscow, was also incapable of penetrating Sadat's mind at that time. Yet Washington kept trying, while sticking to its traditional perception of Sadat's relations with Moscow and Egypt's military strength against Israel's seemingly clear military advantage.

In October, 1971, Secretary of State Rogers made what turned out to be his final attempt to propose a formula that would meet Egypt's demands part way, without alienating Israel. Speaking at the United Nations, he summarized the American position on a partial settlement.[42]

First, he stated, an interim settlement was not an end in itself but rather a step toward the implementation of Resolution 242 within a reasonable amount of time. One could not expect partial settlement to lead to changes in the basic concept of an overall settlement or to bring a permanent end to belligerency. In practice, however, the interim settlement would lead to a long cease-fire period. The issue of the depth of the Israeli pullback could be settled; the essential point was to realize the principle of withdrawal. The agreement would be supervised by U.N. forces, which had been in the area since 1967 and which would be reinforced for their expanded duties. Rogers also stated that a compromise over an Egyptian military presence east of the canal was not out of the question and that while all nations had the right to use the Suez Canal, a compromise might be reached about timing, that is, about when Israel might be able to use it.

Rogers privately suggested to Egypt's foreign minister, Mahmud Riad, that Egypt and Israel should engage in "proximity talks" at the Waldorf Astoria in New York with Sisco acting as mediator, on the basis of these points.[43] On October 11, 1971, Sadat left for a visit to Moscow, and after his return an increasingly hostile attitude to the idea of "proximity talks" took shape. This response was probably due to Soviet objections to exclusive American mediation, and to the absence of any promise on Washington's part to exert pressure on Israel to realize Egypt's objectives. The U.S.S.R. had also supplied more military aid, which had been refused until then, though not all the Egyptian demands—mainly ground-to-ground ballistic missiles, modern ground-to-air missiles, T62 tanks, etc.— were met.[44]

Ambassador Rabin's reactions to Rogers's proposal, which seemed to approximate the Arab position more closely, became increasingly sharp. He objected that, by yielding to Arab demands, the United States would harden rather than soften Cairo's stand. He also bitterly complained of the traditional ban of arms deliveries that existed during the period of Rogers's resumed activity.

On November 11, Sadat declared that an Israeli withdrawal from the land occupied in 1967 was not the only problem.[45] He attacked Washington and said Egypt was not willing to discuss a Suez Canal agreement. The real issue, he said, was the occupied territories *and* the rights of the Palestinian people. Since he again put all the Arab demands into a single condition and rejected proximity talks under American guidance, he cut away his common ground with the United States.

In late 1971, according to Kissinger's biographers, Nixon ordered his adviser to go into the Middle East issue in the following way. "Kissinger got the president's permission to assure Rabin that plane deliveries would continue and State Department pressure would stop. That intercession paved the way for Mrs. Meir to visit the president in early December and set the stage for Israel's sympathetic view of his candidacy in 1972. Rabin spoke undiplomatically about his admiration for Nixon and Kissinger and his fear of McGovern, and he helped swing many traditionally Democratic Jewish votes into the GOP column."[46] The effectiveness of Rabin's campaign on behalf of Nixon is debatable, and not a few liberal American Jews probably regarded his intervention as stupid and liable to backfire on Israel. In the short run, however, the Arabs might have been impressed with Israel's ability to establish its position with the Republicans while retaining the support of the Democrats, one of whose leaders, Senator Henry Jackson, would soon lead the fight for free Jewish emigration from the U.S.S.R.

Prime Minister Meir herself might have had an impact on her hosts. This personable woman, the last of the Zionist "founders," might have charmed Richard Nixon (and his national security adviser), who loved to rub shoulders with the great. At any rate, during her December, 1971, visit, Meir was assured, privately of course, of an ongoing supply of weapons.[47]

President Nixon seems to have agreed that a strong Israel was a guarantee of the status quo in the Middle East, in the sense that it would ensure quiet in the region for the time being. He also accepted the Israeli bid for direct negotiations toward a complete and final resolution of the conflict, and Israeli demands in case of an interim agreement, disconnected from the general Arab package.[48] Assured of a continued supply of arms, Israel agreed to the proximity talks on February 2, 1972.[49] Egypt had hoped that the arms agreement would be disrupted so that it could extract concessions from the Israelis.

On February 2 Sadat again went to Moscow, to strengthen his own arms supply agreement with the U.S.S.R. and to discuss with the Soviets a common ground before Nixon's visit to the Soviet capital.[50] He announced that he had terminated discussions with the Americans.[51] Washington continued to try to obtain Egyptian agreement to the proximity talks during February but received no response. Five months later, Egypt suddenly expelled Soviet advisers serving there and tried its luck again with the United States.

THE ROAD TO WAR: THE INTERNATIONAL ENVIRONMENT

After February, 1972, there was a noticeable decline in American Middle East mediation efforts; finally they ceased entirely. The change in Washington's attitude seems to have been due to a number of factors: Sadat's policy underwent rapid and sharp twists and turns, which were perceived as a result of a mixture of weakness and crass cunning. There was no fighting, apparently due to Israel's strength and Egypt's weakness. The presidential election campaign was in full swing. But perhaps of equal importance to an understanding of the shift in American policy are the changes in the global system after February, 1972.

In 1972 and 1973 great changes occurred in four areas of international politics that had an impact on one another and, evidently, on the Arab-Israeli conflict as well. First, changes occurred in Chinese-American relations, which affected Soviet-American and Soviet-Third World relations. The second area of change was Soviet-American relations, which influenced the U.S.S.R.'s relations with the Arabs. The third area was U.S.–West European relations. The fourth—Vietnam—still drew much attention and apprehension in Washington, as the war was to be concluded without a total American defeat. Changes in each of these areas were likely to have an effect on the other three, but there is no way of knowing the extent to which the actors were themselves aware of these linkages. This point must be kept in mind as I describe and analyze those developments and their possible influence on the Arab decision to go to war in October, 1973.

In February, 1972, when the United States made its last official efforts to encourage Egyptian-Israeli proximity talks, Richard Nixon also made his visis to China.[52] In May he visited Moscow; he and Brezhnev signed the first strategic arms limitation treaty and other agreements for Soviet-American cooperation and proclaimed their common desire to help resolve local conflicts.[53] A timetable was established for negotiations on European affairs (a European Security Conference and talks on mutual and balanced force reductions). Moscow and East Germany also signed agreements with Bonn, with the participation of the Western powers, on the German question in the fall of 1972.

The Moscow accords constituted de facto recognition of the Soviet Union's nuclear equality with the United States, and left the way open for the U.S.S.R. to improve its status through developments in areas of nuclear technology, in which it lagged. It seemed too that a consensus was reached on what was to be permitted in this area. The U.S.S.R. obtained recognition for the German Democratic Republic. These agreements were supposed to lead toward and constitute part of the Soviet-American global package deal that the Nixon administration wanted. The objective was to forge a link between Soviet and U.S. interests, between Soviet calculations of what might be gained or lost by yielding to the temptations of gain in areas of tension such as the Middle East.[54] This "linkage theory" was thus concerned with creating the "rules of the game" for the nuclear arms race, and with tying the U.S.S.R. to the

United States through American proposals of economic and technological benefits. The value of such ties to the U.S.S.R. was demonstrated in 1972 when there was a drought in the U.S.S.R. and the United States exported vast amount of grains.

Washington's Chinese initiative and its attempt to reshape relations with the Soviet Union were presented as two dimensions of a three-dimensional American foreign and defense policy. Nuclear deterrence still constituted a basis of American policy, but it was a policy fraught with dangers and of only limited effectiveness in averting conflict in the world's "grey areas." The superpowers' mutual nuclear deterrence also left a great deal of room for middle powers and even small states to maneuver and to exploit the superpower stalemate to their own ends.[55]

The United States tried to balance the Soviet Union by reaching some sort of understanding with the U.S.S.R.'s great rival, China, while making rapprochement with Washington desirable to Moscow too. New "rules of the game" would be proposed for Soviet-American relations in this process of creating a new strategic and psychological global equilibrium.[56] In 1973 it seemed that agreement on some rules was reached; the sense of accomplishment in this area reached a peak during Brezhnev's American tour in June of that year.

After signing the 1972 Moscow agreements, the American president and the Soviet party leader agreed on five more cooperation accords.[57] Their final communiqué was intended to reflect the new relations between the two superpowers. In Kissinger's briefings he stressed that the most important achievement was the *momentum* of détente.[58] Thus the superpowers did agree, at least, to such rules as averting military confrontation that might lead the United States and the U.S.S.R. into nuclear war either with each other or with another country. They promised not to exacerbate relations with any state to the point of provoking a nuclear war.

The most significant development, according to the contemporary news analysis, was the superpowers' undertaking to enter into "urgent consultations" of relationships between them or between one of them and a third country that "appeared to involve the risk of nuclear conflict." This accord was preceded by a decision to accelerate the strategic arms limitation talks; the target date for SALT 2 was advanced from 1977 to 1974, and the international timetable as a whole was rearranged. An agricultural agreement was signed to regulate Soviet grain purchases over the long run so as to avoid upsetting American prices.[59]

Did this series of agreements mean that the superpowers had agreed on a set of rules for conducting their international affairs? Nixon and Brezhnev both stressed that the consultation procedure and the pledge to avoid military confrontations liable to escalate into a nuclear war did not detract from their right to self-defense or from their obligations to their allies. In their talks on the Middle East they agreed to continue their efforts to promote the quickest possible settlement, and that the solution itself should be in accordance with the interests of all states in the region. They should be consistent with existing independence and sovereignty and take into account the legitimate interests in the Palestinian people.[60] The "legitimate interests of the Palestinian people" had already been mentioned by the two parties during Nixon's visit to Moscow in 1972. According to Nixon's 1977 TV interviews, the Soviet Union had warned him repeatedly during the May–June, 1973, summit that Arab territorial and political demands should be met; otherwise, a war in the Middle East was imminent.[61] Thus, Moscow remained loyal to its Egyptian client in accordance with the May, 1971, Treaty of Friendship. Kissinger publicly said at the time that the Middle East was one of the most complex issues discussed and that it was fair to say that the United States and the U.S.S.R. disagreed on how it should be resolved. They concurred, however, on the need to avoid superpower conflict there and again stated their desire to prevent war in the region.

In the summer of 1973, State Department officials often stressed that the superpowers had basically agreed to avoid confrontations between themselves in local conflicts.[62] If this was true, then any revisionist regional power would have had cause to worry. The problem is whether the Russians actually did commit themselves to such a rule at least temporarily, whether the Arabs forced them to change their minds, or whether the Arabs feared that such rules might emerge as a fixture in U.S.-Soviet relations in the future if they remained passive.

Several factors were to throw a shadow over this Soviet-American détente from the beginning: first, the Chinese-American rapprochement, and second, the Jackson amendment to the American trade bill, which would have granted the U.S.S.R. "most favored nation" status. The amendment made this status conditional on free (Jewish) emigration from the Soviet Union and so became a bone of contention between the administration and Congress.[63] Kissinger, who feared hurting the Russians and who adopted "closed style confrontation tactics vis-à-vis Senator Jackson,"[64] helped stoke the flames of controversy, and the bill's passage was delayed.

China, at the time, was not only engaged in a territorial and ideological conflict with the Soviet Union, but was also the U.S.S.R.'s principal rival in the Third World. The Chinese distinction between the poor "south" and the wealthy, industrialized "north," led by the United States and the Soviet Union, found much support in the Third World. Peking, naturally, saw itself as the moral leader of the South. The American move toward China may have forced the Soviets to reconsider their long-term strategic and political relations with Peking and Washington and the strategic isolation of China in the neighboring areas of the Indian subcontinent and the Middle and Far East. Moscow had to take into consideration the new ties between China and the United States or to give aid to southern world nations so that the Chinese ideological challenge would be neutralized. The very reordering of relations between the superpowers seems to have forced Moscow to demonstrate a degree of noncompliance with the linkage theory and the new "rules of the game" in particular areas of the Third World for ideological and political reasons. Strategic considerations led it to try to contain developments emerging from Washington's relations with Peking.

At the same time, it is possible that the rules of the game were not as clear as they had originally seemed, as Professor Alexander George puts it. "These rules, or norms of behavior, carried, or must carry, with them certain imperfectly understood and unexpected risks, for they are not unambiguous; they are not easily 'operationalized;' the two sides will not necessarily agree on how the norms, or rules, apply in a particular situation; there may be a certain amount of wishful thinking on Kissinger's part regarding the extent to which verbal adherence to the norms will in fact constrain certain kinds of Soviet behavior."[65] The Arabs, however, might have feared that the opposite was the case, that some rules were set and the norms determined, or bound to be determined soon.[66] Even worse, from that aspect, was a "momentum" strategy, based on creating "linkages" and images of superpower détente, which should have moved Moscow toward real cooperation. Without any rules agreed upon in advance in Moscow or San Clemente, the "momentum" strategy itself angered the Arabs without being supported by any Soviet obligations toward Washington. At the same time, the Soviets might have felt compelled to show the Arabs and the Chinese that détente did not deprive the Third World of Soviet aid. The U.S.S.R. started massive arms shipments to Egypt in the winter of 1973, after the conclusion of the first round of the détente agreements, and the departure of the Soviet advisers from Egypt. The arms deliveries might also have been intended as compensation for the relatively large number of Jews allowed to emigrate from the Soviet Union.[67] The emigration was in part aimed at extracting economic benefits from the United States, where the trade bill was then inching its way through Congress. The Russians could then claim that this part of the "grand deal" was not honored by Washington.

In other words, even if the United States and the Soviet Union did agree on new rules of the game, the practical foundations for these rules —concrete benefits for the Soviet Union—were not firm enough to justify the spirit of détente and the manner in which it was perceived as an accomplished fact. America's Chinese move (over the head of the Japanese), the state of relations among western countries, and the Jackson amendment provide ample grounds for doubting the existence of such a solid system.[68]

Considering the nature of the rules of the game, one must also see the rules as a framework of excuses and interpretations. In such a framework a party could derive value and promote its own interests by accusing the other party of not observing the rules or by interpreting its behavior in such a way as to put it in a bad light. The Kremlin could represent the Jackson amendment in this way, for example, or derive from it a tacit reasoning to advance its interest in regional conflict because of developments in the region itself. Furthermore, a party to the agreement on the rules would have to compromise somewhat in observing them. The Soviet Union, for instance, subject to pressures from the Arabs, the Third World, and China, would have difficulty in adhering strictly to the rules, even if it wanted to do so, and would have to compromise in implementing them. In the final analysis one can only expect such rules, insofar as they are adequately defined, to be obeyed if they are based on a common interest or on a clear-cut military and political balance.

Actually, the situation in the Middle East was far from clear-cut. The rules of the game seemed imprecise and intangible enough to give each superpower freedom to maneuver in certain areas, especially where the regional actors tried to manipulate the superpowers to their own ends. In his writings, Kissinger noted the room that the strategic balance between the superpowers left for the regional actors and suggested that the United States try to mobilize their support by creating common interests with those regional actors.[69] After May, 1972, however, the Nixon administration was concerned primarily with establishing a common interest and a bond of dependence with the Soviet Union itself.

SOVIET-ARAB AND U.S.-ARAB RELATIONS, 1972 TO OCTOBER, 1973: ARAB PLANNING DILEMMAS

Although we cannot be certain of the reasons behind the Arab decision to go to war in October, 1973, it is clear that the protracted stalemate in the region was feeding the Arabs' fears and frustrations. The superpower that Egypt felt was capable of dislodging Israel—the United States—had given up its official diplomatic efforts in the Middle East in February, 1972. In July, the Americans neglected to respond properly to Sadat's expulsion of the Soviet military advisers. It seems that Sadat, subjected to many pressures inside his own country and in the Arab coalition, had acted out a series of considerations.[70]

Soviet military presence apparently had not sufficed in the past to influence the United States in the desired direction. Moreover, the U.S.S.R.'s active involvement in Egypt would appear to have made the Kremlin very wary about raising the profile of the conflict.

In 1971 and 1972 the U.S.S.R. had already imposed certain limits on its aid and had not given Egypt all the types of weapons it wanted. Global considerations and relations with Sadat seem to have played a part in this decision. The Kremlin might have feared an interminable arms race in the Middle East combined with a military presence in Egypt, which might disturb the Soviet-American dialogue and lead Washington to expand its aid to Israel. The Soviet Union's freedom of action would thus be narrowed by supporting an Arab strategy designed to advance Arab interests at the cost of certain Soviet global interests and by once again raising its own level of involvement in response to American aid to Israel. If Soviet aid and direct involvement were to lead the Arabs to the conclusion that they were strong enough and secure enough by virtue of Soviet backing to launch a new war, then Soviet-American relations would seriously be damaged. A Soviet-American confrontation might follow—a risk that Moscow was never ready to take, at least in the Middle East. Direct Soviet involvement thus contained a self-limiting factor; it was in the U.S.S.R.'s interest to restrict its entanglement in Egypt. Because of these drawbacks, Sadat seemed to have learned that direct Soviet involvement had to be terminated, but indirect aid for conducting an Arab war had to be assured. The war was not to be a Soviet-Arab war but an Arab war with Soviet aid. Moscow would probably agree to this formula, after the expulsion if not beforehand. What the Egyptians wanted was arms, not soldiers, a minimum of advisers, and a Soviet political and military backing to neutralize the United States military influence and limit Israel's freedom of actions. Modern weaponry would be the price the Soviets would pay for their release from active involvement on the Egyptian front, though they would retain the naval and air bases that Nasser had granted them. Moreover, the internal pressures and frustration in Egypt would ease somewhat, since the expulsion would excise a source of tension between the Egyptian army and its Soviet patron. There was even a prospect that the United States might reward Egypt for sending the advisers packing. In the final analysis, the expulsion may have actually ensured the continuation of Soviet aid for a war on Israel, since such a war no longer presented the certain danger of Soviet physical involvement. Sadat's decision may also have helped ensure massive arms supplies during the war itself.

If the foregoing analysis is correct, a high level of superpower involvement in a regional conflict is likely to constitute a constraint on both client and superpower. The patron may then try to find some substitute for its involvement in the local conflict, and this substitute aid, which had not hitherto been granted, might then serve to exacerbate the local conflict. It is ironic that, by freeing it to go to war, the superpower should allow its client to set new rules of the game for the conflict, particularly when the war might enable the client-state to turn to the other superpower for support.

At the time (the end of 1972) Washington feared that Sadat's aims were to retain his Soviet support and to receive American support without moderating his claims against Israel. For this reason and in order to make the Egyptians decrease the level of their demands on Israel, Washington responded coldly to Cairo's attempts to extract an American reward for the expulsion.[71] Washington's wariness may have been due not only to the fact that 1972 was an election year, but also to Israel's bargaining ability inside its political system. Moreover, the United States seemed to have expected Sadat to make more concessions over his relations with the Soviets. Indeed, he should turn fully to the United States for aid, and lower his demands from Israel if he could.

Sadat wanted to force the United States to exert pressure on Israel without lowering his demands. After some secret overtures with Kissinger, he realized that the United States had adopted in the meantime significant Israeli positions: territorial demands with regard to the Sinai, especially Sharm-el-Sheikh; the quest for peace and direct negotiations,[72] or an interim Egyptian-Israeli deal, separated from the seemingly insoluble Jordanian-Palestinian complex; and no American interest in Syrian claims (Syria retained, for the time being, its traditional anti-Resolution 242 stance and its close ties with the Soviet Union.) In order to extract concessions from Israel, direct pressure on the United States was needed; only a war—a limited, Soviet-backed, Arab war—could change Israel's standing with the United States and secure direct military gains against the Israelis. A war required Soviet aid and should carry a superpower political involvement. While a military victory was hardly undesirable, the Arabs could still accomplish a great deal if they managed to keep Israel at bay, prolong the fighting, involve the superpowers, and throw in an oil embargo at the proper moment. Since Egypt (and Syria) were not really aiming at a decisive victory, Israel's military power was not enough to deter them from war: it merely imposed constraints in terms of timing and the external aid they would need in order to conduct a limited and long war. The Egyptians might thus have felt that they did not need Soviet nuclear weapons and could settle instead for a questionable guarantee in case of an Israeli threat of nuclear attack, as the Soviets retained the power of decision in this hypersensitive area.

Egypt's basic aim was a limited war for the territorial margins in order to achieve limited successes in the field, the reconquest of the eastern shore of the Suez Canal, including the fortified passes that controlled them. The political objectives were to force the superpowers, particularly the United States, to reconsider Arab strength and Arab claims. The impetus for such a reconsideration would be the risk that Washington might lose control of its relationship with Moscow during a prolonged war founded on Soviet aid and backed up by Soviet power in the Mediterranean and elsewhere. The limited war aims and the fact that Israel itself had chosen to fight for the margins in order to avert damage to the core of its homeland would ensure that the war would be limited and conventional.

In Israel, a sense of overall military superiority reinforced the psychological and political inertia. The existing situation often came to be believed the desired situation; inferences were drawn from the past, unappealing options for the future were examined, and the status quo seemed preferable to both. Decisions entailing a change in policy were postponed to some point in the future when a reconsideration might be unavoidable.

Military and political choices seem to be bound to economic and psychological considerations. Since Israel's 1967 victory, which was understood to have given it a "strategic depth" and a "territorial safety belt," Israel's military costs soared to unthinkable heights in comparison with the military expenditures during its period of relative vulnerability and "impossible borders." Israel's defense budget in 1966 was about 1.222 billion Israeli pounds, much more than ever under Ben-Gurion; in 1972 it reached the figure of 6.119 billion.[73] The strain on the economy and the unequal distribution of the defense burden, and of defense benefits, created pressures on the political leadership. Costly mobilizations, even arms purchases, were judged in these terms. Moreover, as long as the enemy did not clearly move, so it seemed, the leadership was domestically constrained from launching large-scale precautionary measures. The Israelis enjoyed a third consecutive year of practical peace, retaining the territories and making no concessions. How could a leadership justify alarms, emergency moves, or concessions, especially in an election year? The Israeli cabinet did not think it desirable, or indeed possible, for a reassessment of the Middle Eastern deadlock to be imposed during the year between the November, 1972, U.S. presidential elections and the October, 1973, elections to the Knesset. Egypt's insistence on combining all its claims on Israel into a single package and on the resumption of Soviet aid also made it easier for the Israelis to maintain the conservative line described above. Meanwhile, the Americans were helping Israel in certain selected areas. The Israel Air Force was promised aircraft,[74] although not the equipment needed to counter antiaircraft missile batteries that it had requested.

The Israeli leadership did not press the Americans for the more sophisticated weapons.[75] Indeed, a reexamination of the policy of investments in the IDF's conventional arms was begun, because of the huge economic burden that the arms supplies entailed. Even a reduction of the regular service was considered.[76] Such a reconsideration was deemed possible because the Israelis retained air and tank superiority and, therefore, thought that they had a decisive strategic advantage. Assuming that the Arabs lacked a "reasonble military option," General Dayan turned to a longer range military planning; he brought about changes in the high command personnel, in order to develop a new generation of military leaders. Some of these changes, insisted upon by Chief of Staff David Elazar, proved to be fateful, especially in the southern front. However, the old and new army generals thought in precedents; in 1967 the Egyptians were rooted, even if their problems at the time seemed to be less serious than a crossing over a major water barrier without air superiority. The gap between the two armies seemed to have grown, rather than declined. Moreover, if Egypt did not go to war, and it had every incentive to do so after "the year of decision," it probably could not go to war. "Sadat does whatever he can; if he does not go to war, he knows that he can't win it."[77] Moshe Dayan, a political general rather than a military-technical expert, relied on his general's advice, which seemed to be a total consensus with regard to Arab chances.

Starting in March, 1973, new weapon systems began to flow into Egypt and Syria from the Soviet Union. Yet Israel considered Egypt weakened after the expulsion of the Soviet advisers in the summer of 1972. Israeli military establishment regarded the deep Soviet military penetration of Egypt in 1970 to have constituted a shift in the strategic balance; the Soviets' withdrawal weakened Egypt by the same degree that their presence had strengthened it.

Israel's view of the situation did not change even after the U.S.S.R. began delivering Scud surface-to-surface missiles and the more advanced SA-6 missiles to Egypt and later to Syria in 1973. Although Jerusalem knew about these deliveries, Israeli military intelligence estimated that the Scuds would not be operational for another year because it doubted the Egyptians could operate them without direct Soviet aid.[78] Moreover, these missiles could not be of decisive strategic value in a war but would at most limit an Israeli threat of deep-penetration bombing. The SA-6 missiles, the multibarralled, radar-guided, antiaircraft guns (ZSU-23/4), and the vast number of Sagger antitank missiles that arrived in Egypt were considered to be problematical but not to constitute a qualitative change in the balance of forces, because the Egyptians still lacked air superiority and Soviet advisers.[79]

Israeli military intelligence did keep a close watch on the Arab armed forces though. As they were reinforced with new weapon systems and completed their training with the antitank weapons, large quantities of equipment were concentrated along the canal in preparation for a crossing. At the end of the winter, Dayan ordered Chief of Staff Major General David Elazar "to prepare for a war at the end of the summer." Yet at the same time, he proceded with his long-range plans, based on a "no war" assumption. Suspicious by nature, Dayan always sought to share responsibility in delicate situations; despite the intelligence assessment that there was no danger of war, he did not oppose a cabinet order for partial mobilization in May, 1973, because of Egyptian and Syrian troop concentrations along the cease-fire lines. War did not break out, and military intelligence could boast of being right all along.[80] The mobilization was very costly and hurt Israel's economy.

The possibility of a general war was not discounted entirely, though it was thought adventurous on the part of the Arabs. The Arab's military weakness and Israeli military intelligence assessments of Sadat's personality led to the conclusion that war was highly unlikely.[81] Israel had an impressive record of discovering secrets about the private statements and actions of the Arab leadership; it thought Sadat too eager to hang on to power to risk losing it as a result of a war that he had little chance of winning. Sadat was well aware of the effectiveness of Israeli intelligence and so must have been very careful not to let those close to him know about his preparations for war. He continued public sabre rattling and made very mild, and thus misleading public statements.[82]

To offset the danger of a new war of attrition of the 1969 style, Dayan adopted a public deterrent stance, founded on the emphasis of Israeli superiority and the opposition's inferiority. He tried to deter the Arabs with public declarations about Israeli might and with threats of a massive Israeli response to isolated or limited Arab actions.[83] Dayan's statements fed the Israeli public's sense of self-confidence and complacency; indeed, this attitude had not been in short supply since the victory of 1967 and the cease-fire of 1970, which was also represented as a victory even if serious challenges to Israel's air force and close support methods by airplanes had become evident by then.[84] The negligence that accompanied the complacency should have been obvious in some of the service units, yet war seemed unlikely.

Dayan's contempt for Arab combat ability was not only for public audiences; he stated both publicly and privately that he did not foresee a war in the next ten years.[85] One cannot, however, tell the extent to which his confidence was founded on Israel's nuclear option, but it may well have been a consideration. The Arabs treated it, or "the bomb in the basement," seriously. They had no nuclear option of their own and Israeli estimates were that they needed at least ten more years to develop one. Furthermore, before the 1972 expulsions of the Soviet advisers from

Egypt, information reached Jerusalem that the U.S.S.R. refused to supply the Arabs with nuclear arms. If the Israelis continued to believe this after the expulsion of the Soviet advisers, then those, such as Dayan, who had seen their entry as a qualitative change in the conflict would regard their exit as a substantive change in conventional and nuclear military terms.

The "bomb in the basement" concept, which might have been conceived to deter growing Soviet involvement in Egypt, continued, and could have been regarded as an additional element of Israeli military superiority over the Arabs. Israel's basic security was ensured by its possession and the Arabs' lack of the "bomb." Its conventional power meanwhile allowed it to negotiate and to fight for distant margins of territories in order to bring about a change in the Arab attitude to the conflict. The mere existence of a nuclear option limited the area in which the Arabs would dare to fight; any attempt to carry the fighting to and do serious damage to the Israeli heartland was liable to trigger a warning signal in Israel's nuclear cellar. The Arabs were thus forced to fight for the margins only, and Israel's conventional power could swiftly turn such a limited war into an Arab defeat.

If this is a faithful description of the thinking of Israel's "nuclearists," such as Dayan, then they made both a practical and a conceptual error. The practical error was that Israel's conventional power was *not* adequate to prevent a long and bloody war in the margins. The "bomb in the basement" concept meant that there was no overt nuclear strategy and that there was no legitimate political framework in which Israel could threaten to use it. Since no one accepted the legitimacy of Israel's conquests, it is doubtful that Israel could make meaningful use of its threat outside the 1949 ADL. Nevertheless, if Israel should carry out its threat, the Soviets might activate a nuclear guarantee, whether or not they were committed to do so in advance, to protect a legitimate Arab war on the margins. Thus, Israel's "battle for the territorial margins" would indeed take place conventionally, in the margins. Israel's "territorial depth" or safety belt, would be used—safely enough, from an Arab point of view— to deprive it of that "territorial safety belt" through a military-political process that would not allow Israel to enjoy its possible unconventional advantage. Israel, in Arab eyes, developed the advantage to protect its heartland. In that sense, the occupied territories presented an area designated by Israel itself to protect the heartland. If the war was to take place in the territorial "safety belt" and not over the heartland, Israel could be dragged into a long and bloody conventional war, which might be followed by a political process to remove it from the occupied territories without being threatened directly. A nuclear response by Israel would not be justified in the eyes of Israel and the third parties.

This meant a conscious reduction of Arab war aims by Sadat, and probably also by Hafez el Assad, a pragmatic, tough, and calculating officer who removed Ba'athist radicals from power in Damascus following the 1970 fiasco in Jordan. It is not clear whether Assad and Sadat in fact agreed upon some kind of coexistence with a pre-1967 Israel, which would have to agree to a Palestinian state in the West Bank and in Gaza as a result of a combined military-political process. Yet it seems that both of them did dismiss the "all-out offensive option;" even the recovery by force of all Arab territories captured in 1967 does not seem to me to have been Egypt's and Syria's military plan for 1973.

To sum up, if the "bomb in the basement" theory is correct, Israeli's nuclear options proved, from its perceptions, to be productive. It prevented an overall Arab offensive and split the Arab camp into a radical group that wanted an "all-out offensive"—Libya, Iraq, and the PLO—but had to agree that such a strategy must wait until an Arab countermeasure was found; and second group—Sadat, Assad, and later King Faisal of Saudi Arabia—which opted for "a limited war" that could not be prevented by an Israeli "bomb in the basement." From this point of view, if Israel's Dayan indeed counted on that option as a deterrent, it proved to be counterproductive. Thus the "bomb in the basement," which might have been devised to add an element of risk and uncertainty to Soviet calculations and to help prevent a Soviet-backed "all-out offensive," might indeed have influenced both Moscow and Cairo. The U.S.S.R. had to be even more careful in the Middle East as a result of several considerations that might have included Israel's nuclear option, and to refrain from a high level of involvement and from supplying conventional weapons in qualities and quantities that might have influenced the Arabs to go to war as long as Soviet troops were involved in Egypt. Egypt had to reduce its war aims and decide upon a limited war rather than an all-out offensive.

Yet two other contributing factors might also have influenced Egypt and its newly won Syrian ally to adopt a "limited war option." First, Israel's conventional strength dictated, so it seems, a concentrated Arab effort in assault areas protected by ground-to-air missiles and AA gun systems to neutralize Israel's air force. The range of these systems was limited at the time to thirty kilometers, enough to cover the Golan Heights and the Sinai area up to and including the strategic Mitla and Giddi passes. Moreover, aware of Israeli advantages in a fast and complex armored warfare, which might expose the flanks of a deep Arab penetration to a devastating counterattack, Egyptian planning, once Sadat reduced his war aims, seems to have been based on a limited infantry offensive to capture and seal off a relatively narrow strip along the Suez Canal and on an immediate change to a defensive posture in order to repulse an expected armored counteroffensive. Later, an armored assault to capture the strategic passes controlling the canal zone and the Sinai itself should have been launched. Assad planned an armored assault with his mechanized divisions against the relatively narrow occupied Golan.

The second contributing factor to the Arab decision to launch a limited offensive, besides the nuclear speculation and Israel's own conventional strength, was probably an anticipated American reaction if the Arabs managed very well in an all-out offensive. Even if Nasser and other Arab leaders felt wounded by the growing U.S. commitment to Israel since President Eisenhower's days and could never accept them, nevertheless these commitments were a reality. Nasser might have tried, after 1967, to balance Americans with Russians in order to retain his freedom of action and learned that this process was not easily controlled by Egypt. Sadat learned this and knew enough about superpower behavior to believe that the United States would let the Arabs win a Soviet-backed, decisive Arab victory over an American client. To him, the key power was the United States, rather than the Soviet Union, if he wanted a political process favorable to Arab interests. Yet Soviet military aid was needed at first, and as long as that aid was needed, Sadat's overtures toward the United States were doomed to fail if not accompanied by a war.

At this stage, the U.S. policy was roughly the same as Israel's: to preserve the status quo in the Middle East. After all, Egypt's military and political bargaining power did not seem to be very great. Nor did Sadat's sabre rattling after the winter of 1973 seem to require any immediate action on Washington's part. There were three reasons for this lack of sense of urgency: Sadat had already expelled the Soviet technicians and had not even asked for an American reward before doing so; the détente agreements seemed to have lessened the risk of a superpower confrontation in local conflicts; and finally, Israel's military power and its parliamentary elections apparently ruled out any change in the status quo until the end of October, 1973, at the earliest.

Meanwhile, however, attacks on the Palestinian organizations in Lebanon, the suppression of terrorist activity on the occupied territories and abroad, and the changes in the status of parts of the territories helped increasingly to isolate Israel internationally. Jewish settlement was expanding around Jerusalem, land was expropriated for Jewish settlements in the West Bank, and in the Yamit area, between Gaza and northern Sinai, preparations were underway for the construction of a city. The Labor party's 1973 election platform stressed a continued Israeli presence and settlement in the West Bank, the Golan Heights, and the Yamit area,[86] and Sadat used it fairly convincingly later as a *casus belli*.

ISRAEL'S GROWING ISOLATION: ISRAEL AND KISSINGER
BEFORE AND AFTER OCTOBER 6, 1973

Israel's growing international isolation was also a function of the interests of the western Europeans, the Japanese, and the black Africans. Western Europe and Japan were totally dependent on the Middle East for their oil imports. Furthermore, they did not consider themselves always bound by the United States' considerations, which helped inspire Washington's support of the status quo in the Middle East. Inter-European politics, too, must have led the members of the European Economic Community to take into consideration France's pro-Arab policy. Western European states were opposed to prolonged Israeli rule over a large Palestinian population and doubted that Jerusalem could in fact maintain it. Just because America supported it, temporarily, Europe did not have to follow suit. These interests and attitudes, though, had not yet given rise to the formulation of a full-fledged new European policy toward the Middle East conflict. The differences became well-known during 1972 and early 1973.

Israel's isolation increased in the summer of 1973, during the conference of nonaligned nations at Algiers. Cuba, the last communist state, apart from Rumania, to maintain diplomatic relations with Israel, announced that it was breaking them off. The U.S.S.R. found itself under attack in Algiers; the Chinese delivered a long diatribe against Soviet-American détente and the San Clemente agreements of June, 1973. Moscow was forced to assume a defensive posture in the face of an angry "southern world."

The changes in the Arab coalition in the early 1970s also played a role in Africa. Khaddafi's radical regime, which had been established in Libya in 1969, joined the radical regimes in Syria, Iraq, and Algeria. Arab efforts against Israel were stepped up in Africa, and more Arab financial resources were diverted to supporting these efforts. Israel thus became isolated from Black Africa because of Libyan efforts with Saudi support, which were combined with a growing bid for African solidarity. Apparently, at Algiers, the Black African states agreed to sever relations with Israel in the event of a war "over the occupied territories." Earlier in 1972, mediation efforts by five moderate African presidents had, like Jarring's mission, ended in failure.[87]

The growing political isolation made little impression inside Israel, which concentrated upon its American ties and on military deterrence. However, military deterrence can persist only so long as one of the parties to the conflict accepts being deterred. If war broke out and Israel could not win an immediate crushing victory, its political situation would put the superpowers' détente and the relations among other states to a severe test. When there is no war, a small, isolated state usually has more room to maneuver than during a war. In the case of the Middle East, hostilities would force the west Europeans and perhaps even the Americans to reorder their priorities. The relatively large number of dilemmas tolerated during periods with no war would become unendurable for third parties, and for the United States, and an unequivocal decision would be sought.

A small, politically isolated country, whose international position even in quarters that are not hostile is very delicate, should do its best to prevent a war, or to win it quickly. One of Israel's mistakes was its failure to evaluate accurately the global political situation in 1973, and to comprehend the extreme political and economic vulnerability of the West, its internal strifes, and contradicting interests. The oil companies and King Faisal began to exert pressure, sometimes overtly, on the United States. The Nixon administration, however, seems not to have regarded the Arab oil options seriously. At the same time, it was already beginning to be mired in the Watergate Affair. Even had its situation been better, it is doubtful that the administration would have exerted pressure on Jerusalem. With the logic of members of a democratic pluralistic society, the U.S. decision makers thought that the American Middle East initiative could be resumed only after Knesset elections, having in mind a strong, even if isolated, Israel as a partner to negotiations.

Late in the summer, Henry Kissinger was appointed secretary of state, and it seemed that Washington was preparing to resume its diplomatic activity after the Israeli elections. In their meetings with Kissinger, Israeli diplomats had the impression that the new secretary of state was skeptical of whether or not he should deal with the Middle East crisis very energetically.[88] Kissinger met a special Egyptian envoy by the end of 1972, and discussed with him for the first time a distinction between Israeli "security lines" outside Israel's sovereign borders and "recognized borders" relating to parts of the Sinai and Sharm-el-Sheikh. Sadat was not interested, and Kissinger believed the area was "not ripe" for diplomacy. Kissinger also thought at the time that war was unlikely because of Israel's overwhelming military power, the prevention of hostilities being traditionally an American aim per se.

War did break out, however, and it soon proved that the Egyptians would not be pushed back across the canal with a mere wave of the hand. The maintenance of the Middle Eastern status quo depended on American aid in time of war, and not on the autonomous might of Israeli forces selectively supplied with American arms in a cease-fire. As the war dragged on, Israel's military autonomy and its community of interests with the United States in preventing a war in the Middle East were undermined. America's military aid had not prevented the war, as Israel had hoped and proclaimed. The assistance had even failed to end the war quickly. The community of interests between Israel and the United States in preventing war or in winning one very quickly, the community of interests upon which the status quo was based, was now over.

Furthermore, certain fundamental concepts that the Americans had held since 1967 combined with some of Kissinger's views on the nature of the conflict to lead to a substantive shift in U.S. policy. American support for Israel since the Six-Day War had been always based on Israel's retaining the territories by itself, with selective U.S. support (until the resolution of the conflict) as long as U.S. interests were not hurt. The prolongation of the fighting in October, 1973, meant that two elements of this basis were changed: Israeli military power had not only prevented a war, but in the course of the fighting Israel began to demand more and more military aid. Secondly, the U.S. interests were likely to suffer during the war, and particularly as it gave aid to Israel. The Arab coalition would turn against the United States, and the U.S.S.R. would present itself as the savior of the Arab cause. The attitudes and interests of the west Europeans and the Japanese might drive them to an open rift with Washington. Within the United States itself, difficulties would emerge as a result of these developments. A superpower confrontation might take place.

As a national security adviser and as secretary of state, Kissinger tried to "link" the Soviets to the United States to prevent regional conflicts from assuming the dangers described above. He was led to accept the view that a strong Israel could contain them by itself. Never, however, did Kissinger support long-term Israeli rule over the territory of Arab states or over a large Arab population. He was certainly unlikely to be really impressed by Israel's arguments about its security needs. Both as a scholar and a statesman, Kissinger maintained that one state's absolute security was another's absolute insecurity.[89] In other words, demands for security by one party to a conflict would probably be perceived as a threat by the other party.

The Arab states had not recognized Israel's right to exist even before it occupied their territory in 1967. Israel had the advantage of a trained and educated population, but it had limited manpower and its other resources were stretched to the utmost. The Arabs whose sovereignty had been infringed upon and who felt threatened by Israel, could mobilize far greater resources and power. To Kissinger the Middle East was then not only a dilemma, it was also a powder keg. Israel's survival depended on its ability to deliver a swift crushing blow to its enemies. In a similar conflict, elsewhere, one could visualize stabilizing the region by creating a military equilibrium. However, such an equilibrium would, he maintained, mean certain death for Israel; in a prolonged war of accelerated activity on both sides, Israel would be ruined first. Israel must, therefore, seek not equilibrium but superiority.[90] But that complicated the conflict and implicated the United States as the source of Israel's superiority. A clearly superior Israel, however, would be a greater provocation to the Arabs, so Israel must seek even greater superiority. It would be a major feat to break out of this vicious circle. The longer Israel maintained its superiority without being drawn into a real war of attrition, the better. Kissinger doubted that this was possible over the long run. Yet his pre-October, 1973, plans for the next stages in the U.S. mediation efforts were based on the recognition of Israel's military superiority, and consequently its relative political autonomy, to decide for itself what suited its survival most.

However, once a war broke out with Soviet help, there was a danger that the United States might be forced to react to Soviet behavior. It was quite possible that the global superpower deal had not, after all, had the desired effect on the local conflict. Indeed, Kissinger has said that the Soviets made their calculations and figured out that they could have the war and détente too.[91]

The Yom Kippur War would not only be important for superpower relations, but for Israel as well. "Ever since the . . . War shattered so many illusions, including several of his own, Kissinger felt a growing conviction that Israel was pursuing a foolish, shortsighted policy, clinging to Arab lands that brought little security and tremendous resentment."[92] Thus, the war might have forced Kissinger to reconsider Soviet-American relations *and* American-Israeli relations. In other words, in the beginning both Nixon and Kissinger expected a swift Israeli victory without American aid; later they were still determined to prevent a Soviet-backed Arab victory. Their world perception, primarily founded on power relations, common interests, and the rules based on them dictated to the administration a policy of supporting Israel toward a "reasonable" victory (in their eyes, rather than Israelis') so that the Arabs would have to turn to Washington after the hostilities were over. The Israelis gained in the field whatever advantages they could without involving the two superpowers. In this sense, Israel indeed lost its autonomy from the United States—an autonomy based on American recognition of both its strength and its judgment—to decide for itself what suited its interests best. Yet Israel did not lose the American interest in its victory, a "reasonable" victory, as a result of its inability to gain a decisive one soon.

An analysis of Kissinger's complex character leads me to the conclusion that, being basically suspicious, especially toward adversaries like the Soviets, Kissinger indeed tried to "link" the Soviets to the United States, and yet never really believed them. The above-mentioned "rules of the game" were devised to bind the Soviets, while creating an image of cooperation that might later materialize as a result of its own momentum, threats, and benefits. Kissinger was surprised when a Soviet-backed Middle East war broke out because the "rules" proved to be differently interpreted by the Soviets, yet in a way he had always expected the Kremlin to cheat. He turned his attention to the Israelis, expecting them to win and then become "reasonable" according to his understanding.

ISRAEL'S DILEMMAS, OCTOBER 6–13, 1973

Israeli thinking before October 6, 1973, and during the first days of the war was influenced by many factors, among which the American position was crucial in many ways. Precedents were very important in shaping the ideas of the Israeli cabinet. Particularly important were the precedents of 1956 and 1967. From their experience in those two wars the Israelis concluded that the U.S.S.R. must be neutralized so that it did not intervene directly in the fighting. They must, therefore, obtain American political and strategic balance without loosing their autonomy from the United States.

Another lesson drawn from their war experience was that the "opening scene," the way the situation looked at the brink of war, was of paramount importance. On both occasions, but most vividly in 1967, Israel suffered the pangs of the dilemmas of general mobilization and of a preemptive strike. The Meir-Dayan government thought that receiving the basic American support depended, to some extent, on the "opening scene" of the war. Washington would ask: Who started it? Was there provocation? Was there a pretext for the Russians to extend aid or threaten to intervene? Had there been a threat that could justify a preemptive strike militarily and, more important, politically?[93]

This point was discussed on the morning of October 6, when it was known that war was only hours away. Meir and Dayan decided not to attack first, despite Chief of Staff Elazar's pleading. Elazar suggested, drastically, several air strikes against Syrian and Egyptian antiaircraft missile batteries.[94] The political damage Israel would suffer by striking first, it was thought, would be greater than the military damage it would suffer by waiting for the Arabs to attack.[95] Israel's borders were at this time much more secure than they had been in 1967, when, according to Israeli military doctrine, they had made a preemptive attack necessary. Moreover, if one had confidence in the relatively large regular military force built up since 1967, one need not be rash and order a general mobilization in reaction to the Syrian-Egyptian threat evident on the eve of Yom Kippur. At least this was Dayan's attitude, which he had expressed already in a smaller cabinet meeting on October 3, 1973.

Even when the danger became almost a certainty, Dayan refused to give in to Elazar's requests for a general call-up, and passed the decision along to Prime Minister Meir.[96] Dayan must have thought that a general mobilization might disturb the opening scene that Israel wanted to project; third parties were liable to see the call-up as a provocation for the Arab attack that would follow. On the other hand, nothing at all might happen, since the military intelligence continued to predict that the Arabs had never intended to attack.

Dayan's reluctance to mobilize can also be explained by a conceptual distinction he made between the power needed for defensive, as opposed to offensive, action.[97] Because he thought in defensive terms, he was ready, during the heated debate with Elazar on the morning of Yom Kippur, to call up two reserve divisions at the utmost. Elazar did not accept this distinction, arguing that the best defense should be an attack, and he got Meir's permission for a general call-up. The Egyptian-Syrian attack was expected, owing to a mistake in communicating intelligence reports, to begin at 1800 hours, local time. In fact, it began at 1350. The decision to mobilize the whole reserve army, which was delayed until the very last moment because of political-strategic reasons, could not influence the military scene in time.

The IDF was surprised strategically and, after it was finally known that war was imminent, tactically as well, in terms of the actual timing of the attack. The full brunt of the first attack had to be borne by regular forces, mostly the tanks of two regular divisions, which, because of the enemy's technical and operational progress since 1967, were inadequate to block the Egyptian and Syrian advance. The mobilizing reserves made their way hastily and in confusion toward the fronts; the 72 hours needed for an orderly call-up and deployment of reserves were lost because military intelligence had not given warning of the attack in time. Even had such a warning been given, political and military considerations had led Dayan not to order a general mobilizatiton on October 3. Thus, Israel, who mobilized too early in 1967 and did not prevent a war by doing so, mobilized too late this time and again did not prevent war.

The government decision not to mobilize in time was, moreover, influenced, as one of the ministers later admitted, by electoral concerns.[98] At the back of their minds, the ministers all feared that a full-scale mobilziation in a period of total calm already three years old would seem a hollow election device and an unnecessary heating up of the border. Dayan had even spoken, three days before Yom Kippur, of not having a mandate from the electorate for "big moves."[99] The government wanted to preserve the calm and avoid the economic costs of a large-scale mobilization. Furthermore, during the period that preceded the immediate attack, when orderly mobilization was still possible, Meir had been preoccupied with the highjacking of a Jewish immigrants' train coming from the Soviet Union to Vienna, Austria. This diversion, which might have been a Soviet-backed action, worked well to shift the cabinet's attention from the forthcoming attack, described by the IDF intelligence branch as "an exercise," to a minor incident.[100]

Here I should also discuss some of the purely military aspects of the Israeli failure in the opening days of the war. A full description is beyond the scope of this study.[101]

Since June, 1967, the so-called Bar-Lev Line had been intended as a concrete manifestation of Israel's presence along the Suez Canal. It evolved into a system to provide shelter for Israeli forces from shelling during the War of Attrition. To prevent an Egyptian crossing, it was constructed according to a defensive military plan formulated by a consensus in Chief of Staff Bar-Lev's GHQ for combat on the shores of the waterway. Thirty strongholds were built at intervals along the canal line, manned by crack military units—regular army paratroopers—and supported by armored forces. The idea was that an Egyptian attack would have to be directed against each of the strongholds and so would be fragmented.[102] The tanks would fight crossing boats on the water line, and would handle any Egyptian troops that managed to cross. Both would be supported by the IAF. This combined operation would limit the depth of an Egyptian invasion so that the invading forces could not get a firm foothold before Israeli reinforcements arrived. The air force's first task would be to knock out the Egyptians' antiaircraft missile system by catapulting bombs from a considerable distance so as to avoid the missile barrage.[103] Accomplishing this mission necessitated observation from the stronghold to report on hits.

Israel's dilemma in the canal line after 1968 was whether it should trade territory for time—let the enemy across while assembling its forces, pinpoint his main thrusts, and maneuver him into fast, mobile battles on preplanned battle grounds in the Israel-held territory, or else fight him on the water line. General Bar-Lev's GHQ adopted a mixed strategy: fixed strongholds on the water line, a regular tank brigade to rush in and be stationed between them to fight crossing enemy troops in the water, and two regular brigades to support the line in immediate preparedness.[104] This plan, known as "Operation Pigeonhole," was supposed to be the first phase in a much larger effort, "Operation Rock." That plan called for two additional reserve divisions to be stationed behind the three regular brigades and to be prepared for a large-scale defensive-offensive effort, including a countercrossing to the west side of the canal. Based on the assumption that at least a 48-hour warning would be given in advance, the regular troops should be given adequate support by mobilizing reserves.

Basically, both plans reflected Israel's constant shortage of manpower, which prevented a solid, wide, and deep permanent defense system on the water line and even kept the regular troops, most of them tanks, in training and fighting duties alike. Due to permanent financial and manpower shortages, investment priorities were given to the tank corps and the IAF. Israel's relatively large infantry was deprived of a mechanized vehicle comparable to tanks; it relied upon obsolete vehicles that could not cope with tanks, and so the infantry was organized separately from the armor. The IDF's artillery fell victim to heavy investments in tanks and planes. As a result of these priorities, the whole army was unbalanced. Yet the IDF retained a typical aggressive-offensive spirit. It expected the enemy to behave the way it would, and push to the utmost in the event of a successful, or partially successful, crossing. Both GHQ and Southern Command, under the newly appointed General Shmuel Gonen, were again taken by surprise. The attack and its timing surprised them at first. The character of the attack—infantry carrying vast quantities of antitank weapons, supported by armor and vastly deployed artillery batteries—surprised them further. Gonen still believed in the original "Operation Pigeonhole," even when the Egyptians made the crossing and dug in on Israeli territory three to six kilometers deep along the whole line, isolating most of the strongholds and capturing several that had no protective armor because of the incorrect timing estimate. Gonen hastily ordered his regular brigades to fight the crossing Egyptians between the strongholds; he lost half of them during the same night—October 6–7, 1973—to the dug-in enemy infantry.[105]

Gonen then tried to determine where the enemy's main thrusts were, as they must have been toward the depth of the Sinai. There were no principal thrusts; the whole canal front was assaulted by roughly even Egyptian forces covered by artillery and dominating tank and Sagger positions on the other side of the canal. Behind them, a strategic reserve of armored divisions covered their back. The Egyptians thus carried out a limited offensive combined with an immediate defensive formation. They were able to create a solid strip of defenses along the Israeli side of the canal; they expected an automatic tank attack, which they were able to defeat and, without trying to exploit their victory, they refrained from undertaking a deep penetration effort outside the immediate canal zone. This "strategic halt" was aimed at a renewed offensive effort, when the bridgehead was widened, enough AA missiles moved to the Israeli side, and enough armor moved toward the strategic passes.

Gonen was still thinking offensively when Operation Rock's two tank divisions started to arrive without artillery or enough mechanized infantry. The general first planned a limited counteroffensive, under Chief of Staff Elazar's instructions, for October 8. Both veteran tank generals agreed to refrain from approaching the canal itself, but, if enough air and artillery support were ready, to try and sweep the whole area beyond the three-kilometer deep Egyptian-held box and destroy the enemy armor that was expected to push toward dominating areas. Later General Gonen changed the original plan, and obtained permission from Elazar, owing to a bad general staff supervisory error, to cross the canal on "a captured Egyptian bridge." Elazar was of the impression that, as his limited attack proved to be a success, why should Gonen not cross? Gonen was pressing for it constantly, and understood that Elazar approved his new plan, even if he lacked enough air support and artillery. Gonen, it seems, was totally devoted to a crossing; he abandoned Elazar's tentative and cautious counterattack, still relying on his tanks and limited air cover.

The IAF was unable to provide effective close support to Gonen after October 6. It was hastily called to help relieve pressure from the strongholds and to interrupt with enemy supplies through the canal, so it could not strike first at the enemy's antiaircraft missile batteries. It lacked the whole range of "smart" bombs and electronic devices to handlle the missiles and the ZSU guns, and its "toss bombing" tactics in missile areas proved to be ineffective. Even so, Gonen pressed his northern division under Major General Avraham Adan to clear Egyptian "deep penetrations," push to the canal, achieve a crossing, and thus retake the strategic offensive. Hoping for Adan's success in clearing the north central canal sector and achieving a bridgehead, at the same time, he ordered his southern division, under Major General Ariel Sharon, to withdraw from the central canal sector and make a crossing in the southern sector, while relieving the besieged strongholds there.

Sharon, an aggressive and egotistic war leader, hurried to "his" mission, even if he was supposed to leave some of his division in the area to support Adan. In the meantime, Adan developed growing difficulties on his mission, not fully realizing that Gonen had changed Elazar's original order. He tried to "clear" Egyptian deep penetration and found none; he then found himself with Egyptian forces in the immediate vicinity of the canal, trying to follow Gonen's order to cross, and fully exposed to the enemy's missiles and artillery. His own artillery, mostly reserve, arrived on October 9. Tanks were easier to mobilize and he had tanks. Hard pressed to achieve a local break through over the canal, Adan was twice bloodily repulsed, then he realized that Sharon had exposed his flank. A bitter hatred emerged among Gonen, realizing that he must call Sharon back from the south to reestablish the center canal front, Adan, and Sharon. Rivalries over operational-technical matters between them and Deputy Chief of Staff Israel Tal took place before the war. Gonen, Sharon, and Tal sought scapegoats for the failure on October 8, which included a piecemeal surrender of all the hopelessly encircled strongholds except one.[106] Israel's reserve army, and later the whole nation, was shocked. The enemy's surprise attack, the fall of the "Bar-Lev Line," the failure of the October 8 counterattack, and a defensive posture toward the south taken by Israel on the 9th were almost unbelievable. Dayan's behavior added more confusion and anger to the popular feeling. Most of the nation was mobilized, and rumors, true stories, and allegations penetrated through the military censorship.

Dayan's perception of the Middle East conflict was always determined not only through Arab military threat as an isolated factor. The role of the superpowers, as a result of a possible military conflict seemed to him always to be of the utmost importance. After the fall of the Suez Line, when a short "war on the margin" developed into prolonged war of attrition, he prepared to move the southern front back to a natural defensible area behind the water line. This would prevent a continued offensive over a heavily defended enemy front that could be breached, if at all, only with very heavy losses after a prolonged attrition, which might prove to be politically very costly. When enough power was accumulated, Israel should retake the strategic offensive. Typically, Dayan gave "ministerial advice" to General Gonen to retreat without assuming direct responsibility.[107] Gonen agreed first, but then returned to the above-mentioned counteroffensive. Dayan presented his retreat ideas to the cabinet, and they were spread at GHQ. Most ministers and generals thought he had lost his nerve; they were determined to hold on to the territory and resume the offensive. Meir herself was amazed to realize that her "manly" defense minister was a cautious, even relatively "pessimistic" strategist.[108] Yet the cabinet tended to stick to a strategy that was based on three elements: holding on to as much territory captured in 1967 as possible until the other side had changed its basic attitude and behavior toward its existence and interests; punishing the enemy for its behavior, in this case by pushing back beyond the cease-fire lines; and negotiating a bargain. Yielding territory might mean endangering Israel's basic security and undermining its bargaining capabilities with the Arabs and the United States if this happened under Arab military pressure and not as a result of a negotiated bargain. Here "doves" and "hawks" in the cabinet agreed, including Dayan, whose defensive posture was based upon the assumptions that Israel might not succeed in its thrust to recapture the canal area and thus would lose its bargaining position later. He did not oppose the counterattack of October 8 openly, but his "pessimism" undermined his standing in the eyes of Meir, and served his personal enemies in the cabinet. One may say that Dayan lost his almost exclusive influence upon Israel's defense policy during the first days of the war. Even if he continued to exercise a large degree of influence later, he lost his decisive public standing as a "manly" military and political leader.

In the southern sector of the Golan Heights, meanwhile, masses of

Syrian tanks succeeded in pushing through a tiny Israeli defense, almost to the pre-June, 1967, armistice line. Some of the regular forces defending the line were annihilated, and the others continued to hold the northern half. It took the first reserves 12–24 hours (instead of the normal 72) to reach the front and start stabilizing it. Yet the Syrian initial success opened the way for them to Israel's pre-1967 border and even to the Israeli heartland in the upper Galilee. Syrian commandos captured the Israeli intelligence gathering station on Mount Hermon. They could repeat the same tactics and capture the few bridges leading from Israel's heartland to the Golan Heights, or at least damage them, try to blow them up, and halt the whole Israeli military traffic to the front. Why indeed did Assad not exploit his initial success in the southern sector? Why did the Egyptians stop their successful offensive and remain dug in at the narrow canal sector after having defeated Gonen's counteroffensive? Two considerations might have dictated this cautious strategy; first, the inability, or unwillingness, to risk a mobile warfare in the Sinai without securing one's flanks; second, the Egyptians preferred to capture a wide sector, which they covered and sealed off effectively at the begining, so that no outflanking or maneuvering against this broad but shallow bridgehead seemed possible. They did not take the risk of a deep penetration with uncovered flanks; this might have given them, once they surprised the Israelis, crossed the canal, and destroyed most of the available Israeli forces there, an opportunity to pentrate into the Sinai and open a classical "armored fan." Israeli reserves would be disorganized on their way to the battlefield, and many would have been annihilated. Communications, supply depots, and headquarters would be rendered useless; perhaps the occupation of the Sinai as a whole could be secured. The reason behind that, in current Israeli military perceptions, is twofold. First, Israel's conventional power in the canal zone seemed to the Egyptians strong enough to make the crossing a costly operation. They never planned a deep-penetration assault, and were too slow to exploit their own success. Second, both Egypt and Syria were determined not to risk a deep-penetration assault without covering their flanks, while preventing aerial attacks by enemy fighter bombers in a limited area close to their surface-to-air missile bases. Accordingly, Israel's nuclear threat did not influence Arab planning and actual operations, but rather Israel's conventional power forced them to behave they way they did.

This might have been the case. Yet the evidence of Arab doubts and actions as to an Israeli nuclear option, and of their appeals to Moscow, may lead to a different speculation, that Arab war aims were reduced in advance because of an Arab perception of an Israeli "bomb in the basement" that could have been realized by a hard-pressed Israeli leadership without a credible Soviet counterguarantee. In fact, the Syrian army, which theoretically could easily send several armored groups into Israel's pre-1967 heartland after its initial success on October 6, 1973, without risking its uncovered masses, refrained from getting too close to the old armistice line.[109] The reason might have been the shock of success, battle confusion, and rigid preplanning. Yet it seems to me that this preplanning might have been influenced, among other things, by the fear that the pre-1967 lines were guarded by a nuclear threat and that the other side might panic and be driven to materialize his nuclear capacity, especially if Israeli civilian settlements, cities, and communications were to suffer. The Israelis had taught the Arabs over twenty-five years that even small-scale Arab attacks on centers of Jewish population were bound to bring a violent reaction. Instead of triggering such a reaction, Syria and Egypt preferred to battle with Israel on the margin of the occupied territories, conventionally, drawing much blood from the Israeli army. The occupied territories were regarded by the Arabs as safe, in this respect, yet as sufficient to achieve important goals—to inflict heavy losses upon the Israelis, and to involve them in a large-scale war of attrition in which larger masses and fire power might achieve significant advantages in a limited battlefield and force a political process from an advantageous military standpoint. The fighting on the Syrian front was indeed of strategic importance, since it tied up part of the Israel Air Force. The air force had to provide ground support for the army there, and so its efforts were split between the two fronts. Furthermore, after the initial setbacks in the Golan Heights, the GHQ's armored reserve was sent north and remained there for most of the fighting.[110] The IDF's flexibility was thus drastically reduced. The pre-1967 borders had given the army relatively short internal lines of communication, which generally enabled a concentration of forces on one front. Now, in October, 1973, Israel's armed forces were, for all practical purposes, split into two separate armies, each fighting a war of its own along very long supply routes. Israel's reliance on air superiority proved to be excessive, for the Arabs forced the IAF to assume an extensive ground support role in areas bristling with antiaircraft missiles. Still, the IAF later managed to foil Egyptian efforts to move forward beyond their stationary missile cover.

On October 10, the crisis in the Golan was over; the Syrians were pushed back along the northern sector with heavy casualties. The cabinet, almost in a permanent session, approved Dayan's suggestion to try and push them further toward Damascus. The attack started on October 11, achieved some territory beyond the June, 1967, line, but then died away as Iraqi and Jordanian troops joined the Syrians, who offered a fierce and costly battle of retreat. Damascus, however, came into the range of Israeli artillery on October 12, 1973. In the south the Egyptians were trying, on October 9, 10, and 11, to widen their bridgehead and capture the Abu-Rodeis oil fields. The IAF foiled that attempt, because the oil fields lay outside the missile umbrella. The initial unbalanced nature of the Israeli forces started to improve. Artillery and infantry joined the tanks, and more tanks, mostly repaired units, returned to the front. Thus, Egyptian efforts to capture a six- to ten-kilometer wide box along the canal largely failed. Israel's problem seemed to be a major military supply emergency, which drove the whole cabinet into an atmosphere of crisis. The actual situation, as it proved after the war, was much less alarming. However, the Israeli cabinet did not know this, and it pressed for more American supplies, to be flown at first by Israeli planes. At the same time, Kissinger told the Israelis "to use whatever they had" to achieve a victory soon. Replacements, he is quoted to have said, would arrive too late.[111] The Israelis adopted other, much more cautious, thoughts; they were struck in both the north and the south, facing an Egyptian defense system that should be breached when enough power was accumulated. Their ammunition, tank, and plane situation seemed catastrophic, even more so on October 10, when the Soviets started a massive air lift to Egypt and Syria. A sea lift had been under way since October 6. As Washington deliberated, between October 10 and 13, Israel's ambassador in Washington, the newly appointed Simcha Dinitz, was instructed to ask for a "cease-fire in place" on October 12, much to Kissinger's dismay. "You don't ask for a cease-fire with your back to the wall," he is quoted as having told Dinitz. The Arabs, meanwhile, rejected a British-sponsored cease-fire bid on October 13.

EGYPT AND KISSINGER: SOVIET BEHAVIOR, OCTOBER 6–22, 1973

One of the problems Sadat had to resolve before he could establish the strategic framework that would enable him to breach the regional status quo, was that of how to obtain the support of the largely conservative and anti-Soviet oil states *and* the assistance of the U.S.S.R. The Soviet aid came first; in the winter of 1973, Egypt began to receive the needed modern weaponry from the Soviet Union. Once these supplies were assured, Sadat set out to obtain the cooperation of King Faisal of Saudi Arabia.[112]

Saudi collaboration was obviously necessary to increase Sadat's financial and, more important, political leverage in Washington. The United State's had always been sensitive to the views of the Arab world's most important oil producer and most zealous anticommunist state. Still, the United States rejected Faisal's advice to pressure Israel to withdraw "so as to be rid of the Soviets in Egypt." Sadat's expulsion of the Soviet advisers in 1972 had greatly pleased Faisal and may well have made the Saudi King more amenable to Egyptian requests for help in the event of a war. The best way for him to help, clearly, was with an oil embargo. The continuous rise in petroleum consumption in the west, the current low price of oil and the economic rivalries in the west provided fertile ground for the Arabs to exploit. Yet according to Sadat, the king made an oil boycott pending on a prolonoged war.[113]

Saudi cooperation during the fighting and their aid after the war was important to Sadat's general plans. After the war, Sadat and other Egyptian politicians stated a number of times that before October, Egypt had been in a hopeless economic situation.[114] These difficulties were an added incentive to fight, since the Arab states would then be more open with military and economic aid, and in time the United States might begin to help. The U.S.S.R.'s capacity to provide the necessary economic assistance was limited, and the Soviet model did not suit Sadat's own social and economic views. Egyptian hints about the inadequacy of the Soviet model were, one should note, in accordance with the views of Kissinger, the theoretician. One of his basic tenets was the need to create common interests between the United States and other states on the basis of "coordinated structures."[115] Cairo tried to persuade Washington to exert pressure on Jerusalem to withdraw from the occupied territories if it wanted to pursue a policy of cooperation with Egypt. Egypt was economically and socially ready for this, yet would not make any move in this direction unless there was a change in the Arab-Israeli status quo.[116]

Heikal hints that Kissinger the theoretician and Kissinger the diplomat were both studied in depth in Cairo, and that before October, 1973, the Egyptians had pinned their hopes on the methods and diplomacy Kissinger had practiced in Vietnam and in connection with Taiwan.[117] The American Administration's initial cool reception to their moves disappointed the Egyptians, however, and they concluded that only a war would turn U.S. views and interests into an operative policy favorable to the Arabs. War, though, meant enough Russian arms, which did not materialize until March, 1973. Once war broke out they needed a continuous supply of Soviet arms. Then they had to choose the right moment to break off hostilities while establishing a dialogue with the Americans, without—if possible—giving up Soviet diplomatic and military aid.

The Soviet fleet still had port facilities in Egypt. The Kremlin was also ideologically committed to Syria, Iraq, Algeria, and the other radical Arab states. After the distressing challenge launched by the "southern world" at the Algiers Conference, the U.S.S.R. must also have felt it necessary to prove itself. Israel's political isolation and the economic disarray in the West also could figure in Moscow's calculations. Furthermore, the naval construction program begun in the aftermath of the Cuban missile crisis resulted in Soviet strategic parity with the American Mediterranean fleet. The U.S. Sixth Fleet still possessed a mighty nuclear force, but it is doubtful that it retained the conventional superiority it had had in 1967.

When war broke out, there was no proof of the allegations made in some quarters that the U.S.S.R. had actively encouraged the Arabs to begin hostilities. The Arabs themselves initiated the idea and made the decisions, though the Russians knew of the attack and provided help. The Nixon-Brezhnev talks in May, 1973, had resulted in an agreement that the superpowers should not intervene directly in the Middle East. Accordingly, the U.S.S.R. did not interfere directly and did not dispatch troops or advisers to the region. It thus was actively involved to a lesser degree than in 1970 during the War of Attrition. The Soviets even hurriedly evacuated their personnel from Egypt and to a lesser degree from Syria before October 6.[118] Formally Moscow could not be accused of anything more than providing superpower services to clients whose patience had been exhausted by Israeli obstinacy and American support of the status quo. During the war, on October 10, 1973, the U.S.S.R. began arms deliveries in large quantities.[119]

After the war, Egyptian sources claimed that the U.S.S.R. had tried very hard to obtain a cease-fire after the initial Arab successes.[120] Egypt and Syria had rejected it. The Soviet policy was thus divided into various manifestations: military aid (but no combat troops or active advisers) to Egypt (more advisers were active in Syria); and diplomatic activity to secure Arab initial success and continue to isolate Israel. The U.S.S.R. wanted to restrain Arab enthusiasm from bringing about an American reaction that might harm Soviet interests or develop into a confrontation, or an Israeli reaction that might develop into a dangerous complication for the Arabs and the Soviets. Thus, the Russians were ready to accept damage to their property, and probably casualties too, when the IAF bombed Damascus and hit the Soviet embassy there.[121] The IAF also destroyed one or two huge Antonov transport planes without incurring an angry reaction from Moscow. First, when a Soviet cargo ship was attacked and sunk in a Syrian port, the Kremlin warned Israel in tough terms against repeating such actions.[122] Soviet-made Scud ballistic missiles, which had been supplied to Egypt and later to Syria, were not used against Israeli targets beyond the 1967 cease-fire lines, and probably remained under Soviet control. Soviet-made *subsonic* Kelt missiles, and short-range Frog missiles, were launched on October 6 against Israeli targets in the Sinai, and one of them was sent into the general direction of Tel Aviv. It was intercepted by the IAF long before arriving in the vicinity of any meaningful target, but it served its possible aim: to warn Israel against deep bombing and aerial attack on Egyptian cities.[123] Thus, the ground-to-ground missiles served Egypt, through their mere presence, in its initial bid to protect its cities while fighting a limited ground war. If Egypt or Syria had used them, they might well have risked not only an Israeli conventional bombing raid, but also an unconventional answer to a ballistic missile attack, since Israel could not identify the warheads to make sure they were conventional before they hit their targets.

By pursuing their cautious policy during October, 1973, the Soviets were trying to benefit from the war and its side effects as much as they could. They tried to avoid confrontation with the United States, while also retaining some of the spirit of détente, strengthening their links with Egypt, and tightening their relations with Syria (and Iraq, which rushed to Assad's aid). Their assistance to the Arabs was, moreover, proof to the Third World that they would provide their clients with substantial aid while the Chinese could offer only empty words.

AMERICAN AID TO ISRAEL AND THE CEASE-FIRE OF OCTOBER 22, 1973

When the Middle East crisis broke, Washington had to deal with the problem on two levels: the management of the local crisis, and its possible impact on global relations. At first, the administration saw the crisis as an Arab outburst that Israel would soon be able to contain by itself.[124] The United States would then be able to deal with the conflict as a whole and could also study Soviet behavior during the crisis. Kissinger was, therefore, very careful to maintain a moderate public tone regarding the Soviet Union, while warily examining its actual behavior.[125] Assessments of Soviet aid to the Arabs up to this point, the continuation of the arms lift, and the Arabs' rejection of a cease-fire on October 13 would be important considerations in later American decisions.

When the war dragged on and no decisive conclusion was in sight, other questions too came to figure in American thinking: to what extent had the Soviet aid damaged the superpowers' global relations and to what extent would it do so in the future? To what extent would an American reaction, or the lack of one, damage or reinforce the foundations of these relations? To what extent would U.S. aid to Israel lead to a Soviet reaction that would deviate from established rules of behavior? Taking into account Soviet aid to the Arabs, Israel's military situation and demands, and the possible Arab reaction, what would be the correct time to resupply Israel? Finally, to what extent would internal (Jewish and Israeli) pressure be exerted in the United States, and how might it be neutralized so that the correct decisions for managing the crisis could be made?

These last questions related mainly to the management of the crisis per se. Only after the situation was stabilized could conclusions be drawn from it and a more basic treatment of the Middle East conflict be implemented.[126] Given these concerns, it was reasonable for the United States to delay overt arms shipments to Israel until October 13, when the Arabs rejected the cease-fire proposal and the Soviet Union continued its weapon supplies to Egypt and Syria. The course the United States chose was to stabilize the crisis by providing enough aid to Israel to stave off a Soviet-backed Arab victory, yet the timing of the resupply effort was dictated by domestic bureaucratic considerations, by the character of Israeli demands, and by Soviet and Arab behavior.

Until the collapse of the counterattack on October 8, Israel had not requested massive aid from the United States; it asked only for approval of certain items on an "unimaginative" and relatively short list of arms.[127] President Nixon approved the list on October 9 and even approved flying the material to Israel. (Jerusalem initially wanted the supplies flown in Israeli or chartered aircraft).[128] Some of Kissinger's supporters and detractors have accused him, or alternatively Defense Secretary Schlesinger, of intentionally trying to delay the airlift by waiting for civilian carriers to transport the goods.[129] The Israelis themselves were thinking at first in these terms rather than in terms of an airlift.

When a stalemate came about on the Syrian front, and an Egyptian armored attack was predicted for October 14, Jerusalem started to press for more supplies to be delivered as quickly as possible. The administration deliberated for three days after receiving the expanded list of arms that Israel wanted. The delay in resupply was due to the assumption, mentioned above, that the supplies would arrive too late to influence events in the field. When Israel asked for a cease-fire on October 12, and was told by Kissinger not to pursue such a move with "their backs to the wall," he was asked to bring about an airlifting. The situation indeed seemed to justify a dramatic injection to aid a hard-pressed client; the Russians had been aiding theirs since October 10. On October 13, Nixon decided to start the airlift to Israel.[130]

On October 12, Egypt had begun moving its armored divisions across the canal; a general Egyptian offensive was expected for the 14th. This time the Egyptians could not repeat the tactics they had initially used to cross the canal and capture a salient along the canal zone, mainly dug-in infantry. In order to capture more territory—possibly the Mitla and Giddi passes—against the present Israeli regular and reserve forces, they had to use masses of tanks in addition to infantry, which could not advance against Israeli artillery and infantry. But when they moved most of their armored divisions, practically their entire strategic reserve, across the canal, the Egyptians uncovered their back. Most of their second and third armies were deployed in the Sinai. If the IDF could break through between them and cross the canal, while destroying the AA missile batteries and securing IAF supports, it would encounter no significant opposition on the western side. Previous attacks on the invading Egyptian forces in the formerly Israeli-held eastern side of the canal had been costly. The "stitch" between the two Egyptian armies seemed adequate for a crossing attempt, and Elazar ordered his Southern Command to await the Egyptian tank offensive, which he was sure to meet because of the IDF's traditional advantage in armored warfare, and then he would start the crossing.

On October 14, the Egyptians suffered their first serious setback in an armored attack on the line Israel had stabilized not far from the Suez Canal. On October 15, small Israeli units began crossing to the west bank of the canal and later began to destroy the surface-to-air missile systems there. The IAF was given increased freedom of action over the southern section of the canal zone, and the ground forces could establish a solid bridgehead on October 18.[131] In retrospect, the breaking off of hostilities on October 13 would have been better for Egypt, but not for Syria. Assad, having lost territory, demanded aid from Sadat who had gained it. Sadat seems to have responded cautiously by launching a limited attack toward the Sinai passes on October 14. Thus Egypt opted for the continuation of the war, and made it possible for the Israelis to cross. Egypt's behavior might be explained by three reasons: Sadat's interest in a prolonged war per se, which might mobilize King Faisal's oil; Cairo's wish to capture the passes; and Egypt's obligation to Syria.

On October 16 the Soviet premier, Alexei Kosygin, arrived in Cairo. "The Russians were in favor of a cease-fire, and were obviously in close touch over this with the Americans," said Heikal.[132] Kosygin said that the battle, with its current scale of material losses, was very risky. Kosygin knew more than the fighting was just "risky;" there were spy satellites and a spy ship permanently stationed off the coast of Israel to keep him and his colleagues informed. During the three days he spent in Cairo, the Israeli forces west of the canal became a real threat, at least in the southern sector of the front, where the Egyptian Third Army was located.

Kosygin returned to Moscow on October 19 and the next day Secretary Kissinger flew there for "urgent consultations on the Middle East" at the request of the Soviet leadership. If the dialogue between the superpowers were not kept up there might be grave political and even military complications. With the Syrians forced back toward Damascus and the Egyptian front in danger of collapse, Kissinger concluded, according to his biographers, that "the Russians were getting very anxious and very upset" and that they gave vent to their anxiety in a number of ways, both politically and militarily.[133] In fact, the center of the Egyptian front had been breached and the Egyptian forces in the southern sector of the front were in danger of being surrounded. There were not enough Egyptian forces between the canal and Cairo to detain the Israelis, should they choose to advance on the capital. Thus, it seems that before leaving Cairo on October 19, Kosygin agreed with Sadat upon a cease-fire, which would enable Egypt to retain its territorial gains and prevent a total change in its strategic position. This must have included Russian backing for Egypt's positions when the cease-fire went into effect.

The Soviet anxiety may have been connected to concern for one of the invisible "red lines" that the superpowers drew to protect their clients in the Middle East. The U.S.S.R.'s red lines were apparently the capital cities, Cairo and Damascus, and possibly also the annihilation of large Arab ground forces. The Americans spoke as if the 1949 armistice demarcation lines were Israel's "red line." Indeed, after the outbreak of fighting Nixon warned the Arab ambassadors in Washington not to violate these lines.[134] However, in a "grey zone" of the world where the superpowers' spheres of influence are not clearly defined, "red lines" are different. The great powers seek first to avoid a confrontation between themselves. The clients may fight between the "red lines," and when one of them (in this case Israel, whose interests were not identified with American interests) succeeds in changing the balance in his favor, the patron would consider not only his own interests first, but would not help his client push a Soviet client behind a "red line" unless Moscow were militarily neutralized; otherwise, vital American interests might suffer. Since the Soviets were powerful enough to intervene in the Middle East war, an American intervention would be made necessary. Thus, a Russian demand for consultations should at least be respected.

If the United States had not agreed to consultations, the U.S.S.R. could have proposed an immediate cease-fire at the Security Council and received the support of all the other members of the Council, including Great Britain and France. The United States, if it opposed the resolution, would then seem to be the guardian of an isolated Israel in a divided western alliance and the only supporter of the war. Yet, according to Dinitz's version, supported by his former aides, Kissinger was still basically interested in an Israeli victory, and at least hoped to provide Israel with more time to achieve it. When asked how much more time they needed, the Israelis told Kissinger, according to this version, "as much as possible," as they had not yet achieved a swift breakthrough or fully developed their encirclement move against the Third Egyptian

Army. Israel left Kissinger to decide for himself how much more time was indeed available. The secretary set out for Moscow on October 20 to direct the negotiations with the Kremlin and, as he told the Israelis, to gain time for the IDF to improve its position in the field. He gave them 72 hours: 24 hours of flights plus 48 hours of discussions, including the time for consultations with Washington and final confirmation by the president.[135] On the eve of Kissinger's departure, Nixon asked Congress to grant Israel 2,200 million dollars in emergency aid.[136]

On his way to Moscow the secretary of state was informed of the Saudi announcement of an oil embargo. America's aid to Israel had already justified, on October 17, an Arab announcement of a ten percent cutback in petroleum production and to Abu Dhabi's and Libya's imposing their own oil boycott of the United States.

Kissinger's biographers report that the president later authorized the secretary of state to negotiate and conclude an agreement in Moscow; he would not have to come back to Washington for presidential approval.[137] There are two possible and not mutually exclusive explanations for this arrangement, if indeed it was made. First, Nixon was so busy with the Watergate scandal that he could no longer pay sufficient attention to foreign affairs. In fact, while Kissinger was off on his mission, Nixon dismissed the Watergate special prosecutor, Archibald Cox, during "the Saturday Night Massacre." The other possible explanation was that Nixon was worried by the Saudi action and sought, while proposing aid for Israel, to stop the fighting and leave Egypt with some military gains. By relieving Kissinger of the obligation of consulting him, Nixon considerably reduced the time necessary for the secretary's mission.

Immediately upon his arrival in Moscow, the secretary went directly to the Soviet leaders and began intensive negotiations. The Israelis still believed that they had enough time for extensive military moves in the field[138] and were very surprised the next day, October 21, when they received a message from President Nixon urging acceptance of an immediate cease-fire, which would be followed by direct negotiations between the parties. The Meir government complied. The cabinet did not see any realistic way of flatly refusing Nixon's request. American political and military aid, let alone financial help, were considered essential.

Which conclusion seems in retrospect to be more justified with regard to the administration's interest in an Israeli victory? It seems that the administration was interested in a quick Israeli victory. A Soviet-backed Arab victory might have dictated an American intervention in the Middle East. An Israeli victory did not mean any more a continued territorial status quo, but rather a degree of confidence in Israel that would allow

Israeli concessions later, and a degree of Arab dependence upon U.S. mediation toward a political process, rather than upon Soviet military aid toward a military process. When the war dragged on, with no decisive Israelis victories in sight and Arab–Soviet–Third World pressure mounted for a cease-fire starting October 19, the administration had to consider Soviet patience, Soviet military "capability in place," and the parliamentary situation at the U.N. The administration reduced its timetable, and instead of allowing the Israelis four more days of fighting, which might have brought a total encirclement of the Egyptian Third Army, it brought about a cease-fire three days after Kissinger's departure for Moscow. As Kissinger realized in Moscow, Israel should have been satisfied with whatever it might have gained in the field; it might even be allowed to add some territorial gains to its bargaining arsenal in the northern canal sector, rather than in the highly sensitive Third Army (southern) sector.[139] At the same time, the secretary also presented to the Israelis some Arab political concessions.

An agreement on the principle of direct negotiations in Security Council Resolution 338 of October 22, 1973 was put forward to the Israelis by Kissinger as a major gain for Israel. Resolution 338 called on the belligerents to cease fire twelve hours after passage of the resolution; immediately afterwards, they would commence implementation of all parts of Resolution 242 through negotiations between the parties concerned under suitable auspices to attain a just and lasting peace in the Middle East. The formula was not unambiguous.[140] The Security Council called upon "all parties to the present fighting to cease all firing . . . no later than 12 hours after . . . the adoption of this resolution, in the positions they now occupy. [The Security Council] calls upon the parties concerned to start immediately . . . the implementation of Resolution 242 . . . in all of its parts; [the Security Council] decides that immediately . . . negotiations shall start between the parties concerned under appropriate auspices aimed at establishing a just and durable peace." According to the available sources, when he arrived in Israel, the secretary of state soft-pedalled the equivocal formulation of Resolution 338 and said that direct negotiations between Egypt and Israel were self-evident, since no mediator was appointed by the Security Council, yet "negotiations between the parties" were to start "immediately."[141] Kissinger spoke contemptuously of the Arabs' lack of a sense of proportion for having rejected the cease-fire offered on October 13 when their situation was so much better. He described the situation as fundamentally different from the pre-war diplomatic deadlock. The Russians accepted for Egypt the principle of negotiation to implement Resolution 242, without timetables for an Israeli total withdrawal and without an Israeli commitment in advance for such a withdrawal. These traditional Arab demands, which were repeated by Sadat several times during the war, were abandoned for a more subtle process of negotiations, although Resolution 242 was mentioned in Resolution 338 as the ultimate goal of the negotiating process. Kissinger also raised the possibility of a peace conference at Geneva, in accordance with Resolution 338, where Israel and the Arab states would finally sit down together to negotiate. However, such a conference would necessarily touch upon the whole conflict and the West Bank, and the prime minister replied that she would need a mandate from the people to attend such a conference; in other words, that it could take place, if at all, only after the parliamentary elections postponed to the end of the year. The secretary did not press the point. On the contrary, he said that the Middle East conflict could not be resolved all at one time; it was impossible to move from the current level of conflict directly to a final settlement, so interim arrangements were necessary.

In discussing the contents of the new American strategy he said that Egypt would have to be the main focus of the new approach, that the road to peace first ran through Cairo. This idea, too, may have signalled Washington's recovery from the notion of the global arrangement with the U.S.S.R. After all, the war had clearly demonstrated that arrangements with Moscow did not lessen the danger of violent local conflicts. Kissinger, therefore, recognized that the United States itself would have to come to some understanding with the regional actors, and he told the Israelis so.[142]

During Kissinger's conversations with the cabinet ministers, members of the IDF command joined the talks. The secretary asked the officers how much time the Israeli forces would need to destroy the two Egyptian armies east of the Suez Canal. Chief of Staff Elazar and most of the other officers said that they would need at least ten to twelve days of hard fighting. This assessment supported Kissinger's contention that a cease-fire in place was the best course of action, given the apparent impossibility of an immediate crushing victory for Israel.

On the other hand, Major General Binyamin Peled, the commander of the air force, is quoted as having said that since the Egyptian armies' antiaircraft wall had been breached, no more than two or three days would be needed to inflict heavy damage on the Egyptian armies. Kissinger may have misunderstood and thought Peled meant that only air strikes would be necessary to do the job. In any case, according to one version of the conversations, Kissinger is reported to have said: "Really? Is that all? In Vietnam the cease-fire didn't come into effect when it was supposed to either."[143] According to another version, one of the Israeli army men said this while Kissinger remained silent.[144]

A similar construction could be put on Kissinger's reaction when the Israelis asked about the arrangements for the supervision of the cease-fire, since there was nothing about supervision in Resolution 338. Sisco immediately grasped the significance of the question: without super-vision it would be very hard to maintain the cease-fire. He replied that the U.N. observers, who had been stationed along the cease-fire lines since June 14, 1967, and had evacuated when the fighting broke out in October, were in Cairo and Cyprus and that there would be no problem in getting them back into position. Kissinger, however, is described as having interjected sharply and impatiently that he had no intention of dealing with that "damned problem" now.[145] It is useless to try to guess why he said this. He may have wanted to please his hosts, or was angry with Sisco for speaking out of turn, or was afraid to tell the Israelis out-right that he wanted to end the war at that time. In any case, his military interlocutors understood this remark as a hint that they could do whatever circumstances allowed.[146] According to Dinitz's version, Kissinger explicitly agreed, in talks with Meir and Dayan, to some Israeli gains in the northern canal sector *after* the cease-fire went into effect.[147] This version is not supported by Dayan's actions on October 22, and the impression of the southern front commanders was that the political level was wearing out.

Dayan did not believe, under the new circumstances, that the "Ameri-cans will allow us to draw a new map" in the west side, nor did he think that even if the Egyptians gave Israel a chance, a far-reaching strategic change on the west side would be tolerated by the super-powers.[148] Yet General Gonen and the southern front command agreed upon a continued thrust to encircle the Third Egyptian Army by a deep strategic move behind it.[149]

On October 22, the fighting stopped. However, the Egyptian Third Army, a unit about the size of a western army corps and one of the country's best fighting units, was partially surrounded. The commander wanted to improve its position. He particularly wanted to open some of the access routes that the Israelis had blocked in their advance on the west bank on the canal.[150] Kissinger might have been willing to let the Israelis respond to an Egyptian violation of the cease-fire by gaining some more territory. It is hard to believe that he wanted the Israelis to respond by continuing their full-scale offensive to encircle the Third Army and destroy it. Instead, Israel was beginning to change the way in which the war had ended. Egypt raised an outcry, and demanded that the U.S.S.R. fulfill its obligations to help maintain the cease-fire under the terms of the agreement with the United States. The Soviet Union threatened to take action.

ON THE BRINK

The cease-fire came into effect at 1855 hours on October 22, 1973, and was violated locally by forces of the Egyptian Third Army at 2100 hours. On October 23 the IDF ground troops, which had already partly surrounded the Egyptian force in the southern sector, advanced, reached the city of Suez, and went on toward the port of Adabiah on the Gulf of Suez.

The United States and the Soviet Union together pushed a new cease-fire resolution through the Security Council.[151] Sadat did not want just a cease-fire, though. He demanded a joint Soviet-American intervention to impose a cease-fire in the October 22 lines. The United States, of course, did not intend to let the Russians gain a foothold in Egypt, nor to sanction this action, and did not wish to be involved in direct confrontation with Soviet troops in the area. Thus it seems that President Nixon promised to President Sadat that the Third Army would live,[152] and that the United States would take care of it, without superpower troops in the area. In his 1977 T.V. interview, Nixon said that he handled the Israelis like a "godfather," advising them very strongly to let the Third Army survive. On October 23, the Security Council passed Resolution 339, based on their previous resolution, and called on the parties to return to the positions of October 22. In other words, it called on the Israelis to pull back to where they had been the day before. U.N. observers were to be sent in immediately to supervise the cease-fire; the "supervision vacuum" left by Resolution 338 was thus filled. The cease-fire was to go into effect at 0700 hours on October 24.

Israel agreed to the cease-fire. During the day and on October 25, however, Israeli forces reached Adabiah and Suez City, though not taken, was surrounded. The Third Army was encircled. Jerusalem had no intention of returning this unexpected gain without suitable compensation. After all, the IDF had only managed to acquire these spoils after a relatively long and bloody war.

Moscow began to act.[153] On October 24, Soviet air-mobile forces in Europe were reported as having been placed on alert. Some of the advance staff units of these divisions were reported to have been sent to the Middle East, although not to the real area of danger, Egypt, but to Damascus. In violation of common rules of safety, fueled and armed tanks were reported to be loaded on Soviet freighters at Nikolaev.

The U.S.S.R. was also active on the diplomatic front. On October 24, third world delegates at the U.N. headquarters began to discuss a proposed Security Council resolution that would direct the United States and the U.S.S.R. to dispatch a joint military force to the Middle East to implement Resolution 339. In Washington, Ambassador Dobrynin made it plain that the U.S.S.R. would support this resolution; Secretary Kissinger threatened to veto it. The passage of such a resolution was unacceptable to the United States: it would mean that the Soviet and non-aligned majority would dictate policy to the United States or, if America did not comply, would publicly isolate it. The United States did not insist upon an Israeli pullback to its positions of October 22, but Kissinger stressed that the United States would not go beyond the brink with Israel.[154]

A couple of days earlier, a Soviet vessel was reported southbound in the Turkish straits. The same freighter was located there on October 13, carrying a deck cargo of pontoon bridge sections. On October 22 it carried no deck cargo, but nuclear material inside, according to highly sophisticated American monitoring methods.[155] The ship arrived in Alexandria a few days later. If the same ship contained nuclear material during its first trip through the straits on October 13, her freight might have meant a signal to Israel, via Washington, not to play with nuclear fire. If non-Israeli press reports are to be believed,[156] the danger of Syrian breakthrough on October 9 might have driven Dayan to order Israeli missiles armed with nuclear warheads to be positioned and targeted for the first time in Israel's history; until then, says the same source, the warheads had been stored and were never mounted on missiles.

A Soviet "nuclear ship," i.e., some kind of nuclear guarantee for Egypt, might indeed have been sent out from Nikolaev on October 10 or 11, reaching the straits on October 13, as a result of semi-overt deployment of an Israeli "bomb in the basement." I did not verify Israel's actual behavior in this respect during the 1973 war; yet if the Soviet vessel returned to the Mediterranean on October 22, carrying the nuclear materials that were picked up by sophisticated, secret U.S. monitoring stations, and having carried pontoon bridges on the 13th, the speculation about a Soviet nuclear signal to Israel on the 13th (which indeed fits well with the press stories about nuclear deployments in Israel on October 9) seems to collapse. Since the radiation was *not* meant to be picked up, according to my Washington sources, the "nuclear ship" was not, therefore, a signal or a response to Israeli action. It was understood to be a shipment intended to provide nuclear "teeth" for Soviet intervention in the fighting, if necessary, following Sadat's acceptance of a cease-fire on October 19. It might have been a signal in that direction, unless Israel was forced back to the October 22 lines. The Soviet navy, having already a "capability in place" in the eastern Mediterranean, indeed assumed a much more aggressive pattern toward the Sixth Fleet after 1967, and especially after October 22.[157] The "nuclear ship" might have been a component in a Soviet contingency plan to intervene in Egypt; it seems, according to the results of my inquiry, that the "nuclear ship" remained in the Alexandria harbor under strict Soviet guard and its cargo was not unloaded; it "disappeared" from the monitoring devices sometimes, but probably remained on the vessel until early November, when the ship and its freight returned to Nikolaev.[158] The "nuclear ship," about which the United States informed the Israelis after October 24, when it arrived in Alexandria, might have supplied ammunition to the "conventionalists" in the Israeli cabinet, headed by Mr. Allon, at the same time as the relative decline of Dayan's public and cabinet position. The minister of defense was more of a "nuclearist" and a "nuclear deterrence" minded strategist than most of the cabinet. For them, especially Mr. Allon, the Yom Kippur War itself might have proved, if the "bomb in the basement" speculation holds, that a nuclear threat was not credible if the other side chose not to be deterred and obtained some sort of Soviet nuclear presence. Yet for Washington, as Nixon put it in his 1977 T.V. interviews, the "nuclear ship" was another demonstration of Soviet behavior that dictated a strong American response.[159]

On October 25 the Kremlin sent a note to Washington. According to Admiral Zumwalt, the note was similar in style to the American ultimatum to the Soviet Union during the Cuban missile crisis.[160] The Soviet leaders stated that a Soviet-American military force must be sent to the Middle East immediately to force the Israelis to withdraw to the October 22 cease-fire lines. If the force was not sent, Moscow would have to consider unilateral action to put an end to the IDF's continued violation of the cease-fire.

At this time the Israelis were busy assembling about 8000 Egyptian troops to be sent to prisoner of war camps. The IDF and the Egyptian forces in Suez City were exchanging fire. The encirclement of the Third Army was maintained.

The United States reacted to the situation on the battlefield and to the U.S.S.R.'s threats on three levels: on the intersuperpower level, it declared a global nuclear alert; on the level of relations with Israel, Washington warned Jerusalem that the United States would not engage in a third world war for its sake (however, Washington was evidently taking steps to deter the Soviets, so the credibility of the warning was partial at best); on the level of relations with the Arabs, Washington apparently repeated the promise to Sadat that the Third Army would not be annihilated. Before it could get down to the step-by-step method for a settlement, the United States had to resolve the unexpected crisis that had resulted from the Israeli advance; it had to avert an Arab victory due to exclusive Soviet aid. It also had to prevent an Israeli victory, after the October 22 cease-fire, that would be attributed to American backing. A confrontation with the Soviet Union had to be avoided. Several versions were published or disclosed after 1973 concerning the

American nuclear alert; since this issue belongs to the sphere in which I could not gain access to primary sources, I shall deal only with the versions themselves.

Admiral Elmo Zumwalt and others claim that, at about this time, Henry Kissinger was becoming the ultimate arbiter of American foreign policy, as Nixon became increasingly concerned with Watergate.[161] Zumwalt says that Kissinger sold out Israeli interests at the start of the crisis, when he kept vital military supplies from Israel. Even the admiral thinks, though, that once Moscow threatened unilateral action, the United States had little choice but to consider the Soviet demands very carefully and to come to some understanding with Cairo in order to avert a confrontation with, or too blatant a success by the Kremlin. Zumwalt contents that the United States and the U.S.S.R. applied a lesson learned during the Cuban missile crisis; that the super-power that is politically and militarily weaker in a specific region will back down during a high-profile crisis if it confronts the other superpower. However, the stronger one will not try to achieve too great a victory.

Of the two superpowers, the U.S.S.R. was strategically as strong in the Middle East as the United States—and even stronger, says the admiral—after the Jordanian crisis of September, 1970. It had air bases relatively close by in the Crimea and Odessa and permission to use the airspace over Yugoslavia, Iran, and Turkey. Moreover, Turkey, Greece, and perhaps Italy were inclined to support the Arabs, so they might not have allowed the United States to give the Sixth Fleet the air support it needed from air bases on their territory if a direct confrontation developed between the United States and the Arabs and Soviets over Israel. Apart from Caetano's Portugal, none of the west European states officially allowed the airplanes carrying arms to Israel to land and refuel on their territory. In such circumstances the Soviet naval and air forces could cut off the Sixth Fleet.

It was partly in order to avoid such an eventuality that the Nixon administration had provided military aid for Israel when domestic pressures ruled out the reinforcement of the Mediterranean fleet. Such assistance should have been given in large quantities after the war broke out, adds Zumwalt. Instead, after having delayed it, the United States found itself confronted with a stronger Soviet presence, and had to yield to Soviet demands. Its naval forces elsewhere were overstretched and also attached to other danger spots—North Korea, Guantanamo base, and the southern Atlantic route, now heavily used by the Soviets to resupply the Arabs—and as no effective U.S. air force support was available.

Professor Zbigniew Brzezinski considered Zumwalt's view of the situation typically narrow.[162] The Soviet air force, the main trump against the American fleet, had to use Greek, Turkish, and Yugoslav air space.

These countries had granted the U.S.S.R. overflight rights for logistic support missions to Egypt and Syria, but not to support a direct clash with the United States. If the Soviet Union had landed troops in the two Arab states, it would have had very serious logistical problems of its own because of the long shipping lines without air cover. The U.S.S.R. was aware of the problem and was very cautious about how it was handled; it did not, for example, retaliate against Israeli air force attacks on Soviet aircraft carrying supplies to Syria and Egypt. Moreover, Brzezinski maintains that a purely regional confrontation by the superpowers in the Mediterranean was not possible; the United States could have responded to a Soviet threat there with a threat of its own somewhere else, in the Skagerrak Straits, for instance. If Brzezinski's analysis of the situation is correct, then there are two explanations for the U.S. nuclear alert. According to him the affair should be seen in the context of the Nixon administration's domestic difficulties, particularly Watergate, and possibly also as an attempt to jolt the Middle East onto a more stable course in order to prepare for later compromise negotiations.

In conversations with senior naval officers at the Pentagon after the second cease-fire of October 24, 1973, I received the impression that they were very worried about military risks in the Mediterranean. Kissinger himself was reported to be very much influenced by considerations of a possible escalation.

The director of the U.S. naval intelligence told me on October 30, 1973, that some members of the American defense establishment were afraid that general turmoil might develop in the crowded waters of the Mediterranean and that an Egyptian, Syrian, or disguised Soviet submarine might sink an American aircraft carrier. The United States command would be unable to ascertain the cause of the clash, who had started it, who had fired the first shot, and what it was all about. The scenario seemed like a formula for a third world war, but the admiral said, "Oh, no, not at all. On the contrary, since we would have feared precisely that, we would have deliberated, we would have sat down and talked it over with the Russians to clarify the situation. But in the meantime a costly vessel . . . might have come to grief and our prestige might be terribly impaired."[163]

Apparently, the administration's main concern at this moment was not to lose control. Nixon and Kissinger realized that the rules agreed upon in Moscow and San Clemente had proved inadequate in preventing Soviet aid to the Arabs, threats of intervention, and enthusiastic encouragement of the oil embargo. All these moves might have been foreseen in terms of Soviet commitments to the Third World, and formally they did not violate the San Clemente agreements. Formally, again, Moscow rushed to the aid of a client, according to a specific cease-fire agreement between itself and Washington and two Security Council resolutions. Yet the Soviets undermined the "spirit" of détente, or could be accused of having done so, when they dispatched the "nuclear ship" to Egypt and threatened a unilateral intervention.

On October 25, when the United States armed forces around the world were placed on nuclear alert, Kissinger publicly warned the U.S.S.R. that a nuclear war might result from the Middle East confrontation.[164] The alert might also have been intended as a response to the ship loaded with nuclear devices anchored in the Alexandria harbor. The Americans, it is reported, were keeping a close watch on the ship to see whether it was unloaded; and were greatly concerned when they lost track of the radiation for a few days and did not know what had happened.

At the same time the U.S.S.R. was threatening to intervene. A public ultimatum to deter them from intervention (and remove the ship), such as the one in the Cuban missile crisis of 1962 was not possible, given the relatively weak American sea power in the region and the fundamental political differences. The United States might, therefore, have decided upon a world-wide nuclear alert to deter the U.S.S.R. from intervening and to hint to it to get rid of the ship, without turning the issue into a public warning over which the Kremlin might lose face.

It should be noted that Kissinger thought that Russian policy makers tended to move rather slowly, that they never took more than one step at a time, with long intervals between each step.[165] Therefore, since Cambodia, the usual American response to a Soviet challenge has been a multidimensional political and military challenge to force the Soviets into as many decision dilemmas as possible, to overload the Soviet decision making system. At the height of a confrontation Washington may engage in violent and dangerous maneuvers to make it clear to the other side that it is playing with fire. Secretary Kissinger's contempt for the Soviets was apparently combined with great apprehension and the determination not to lose control over a very complicated military, political, and economic crisis.

KILOMETER 101: EGYPT, THE UNITED STATES, AND THE STEP-BY-STEP APPROACH

On October 25, the Soviets gave up their demands to send a joint Soviet-American force to the Middle East. The Security Council adopted Resolution 340 to reestablish and expand the United Nations Emergency Force.[166] The force would be composed of troops from the member states of the U.N., with the exception of the permanent members of the Security Council, particularly the superpowers. However, U.N. observers from the United States and the Soviet Union were stationed there, and blue-helmeted Soviet soldiers appeared in the area to satisfy the Russians' demands, though not on the level they had originally wished. Washington agreed to this compromise as the smallest possible compensation that Moscow could accept for the supposed breach of an agreement with its client and itself by an American client. Within 48 hours of the proclamation of the alert, the level of U.S. military preparedness was reduced to its usual peacetime status.

Meanwhile, the siege of the Third Army continued, and Israel did not pull back to the lines of October 22 as called for by Resolution 339. However, Israel was well aware of the political and military complications the encirclement might give rise to, and so proposed direct military talks with Egypt about the implementation of Resolution 338. These talks would fill the political vacuum and Israel would also be able to find out what it could obtain from Egypt, and the United States, for lifting the siege. At the same time, Israel agreed to allow limited supplies to reach the Third Army through Israeli lines.

At this point, Syria was a secondary concern, because the cease-fire had been in effect since October 23 on that front. The front had stabilized even earlier, with the IDF about thirty kilometers closer to Damascus than it had been on October 5, 1973. In fact, Egypt seems to have accepted the cease-fire on October 22 without consulting Assad, forcing him to accept it as well. Syria quietly accepted Resolutions 338 and 242 at the same time. Cairo agreed to Jerusalem's suggestion, and negotiations began on October 29, 1973 at Kilometer 101 on the Cairo-Suez road.[167] The belligerents remained in their positions, but supplies and medical aid were allowed to pass, from time to time, through the Israeli blockade to the Egyptian Third Army.

At the first meeting at Kilometer 101, the Israeli representative, Major General Aharon Yariv, demanded an immediate exchange of prisoners of war, the lifting of the blockade of the Bab al-Mandeb at the entrance to the Red Sea (threatened by Egypt when the hostilities began), and the recovery of the bodies of the Israeli dead. The Israelis tried to avoid a retreat to the October 22 lines by demanding an exchange of the banks of the canal—in other words, a return to the status quo ante bellum— as an opening position.[168]

The Egyptian delegation, led by Lieutenant General Abd al-Rani Gamassi, the chief of staff, asked for regular supplies to the beseiged Third Army and an Israeli retreat to the October 22 lines. Further Israeli retreats would follow: first to the Mitla and Giddi mountain passes in the Sinai, and then to the El-Arish–Sharm-el-Sheikh line Sadat had proposed in 1971.

At this stage of the talks, Israel's main concern was the prisoners of war, particularly the wounded ones in Egypt. Jerusalem presented Cairo with a complete list of the approximately 8000 Egyptian soldiers it had captured, permitted the Red Cross to visit them, and allowed medical assistance to the Third Army and Suez City. Egypt did not reciprocate, but demanded that the wounded be allowed to leave the blockaded area, maintaining that there was a difference between its besieged troops and wounded Israeli POWs. After some bargaining Egypt agreed to evacuate the Third Army's wounded, release the wounded Israeli POWs, send medical aid to Suez City, deliver a list of the other Israeli prisoners, and allow Red Cross officials to visit their prison camps. In the meantime, General Gamassi was appointed an aide for political affairs to the Egyptian war minister. His role as negotiator thus assumed a certain political dimension.

The problem of regular supplies for the Third Army was still not resolved when, on October 31, Prime Minister Meir decided to visit Washington to find out the extent to which she could hold on to Israel's prize—the Third Army—and what price she could extract for letting it go. She also wanted to secure more arms. Her talks, most of which were with Kissinger, were very complicated. He demanded the lifting of the siege, the surrender of Israel's trump card, and subsequent step-by-step negotiations.[169]

Meir regarded such a move as a strategic and political mistake if Israel could not at least secure the release of its POWs in exchange for a regular life line, under U.N. control, to the Third Army. She feared the political and psychological consequences in Israel. "Why was so much blood spilled?," the mobilized nation would ask, and the opposition leaders would loudly echo the same question. The enemy's successful surprise attack had already caused the government a lot of trouble domestically. Ariel Sharon, one of the opposition leaders who served as a reserve divisional commander on the southern front, gave an aura of military knowledge and charisma to his personal and professional criticism of the handling of the war.[170]

The Americans exerted a great deal of pressure on Meir to agree to lift the siege. President Nixon himself requested it; the pressure was often aggressive and almost crude. However, the greater the pressure, the stiffer Meir's resistance became. She refused to give in to the secretary of state, who, her aides say, was still in shock from the near confrontation with the Soviet Union.[171] After several days of heated discussion, however, Meir agreed to open a regular line of supply to the Third Army, provided that the supply corridor would be completely under Israeli control. A United Nations observation post might be placed at the entrance to the corridor. The POW problem was not resolved during this visit and no agreement was reached on further steps. Meir returned to

Israel without an agreement on further military aid beyond that already promised.

Immediately after Meir's departure, Kissinger left Washington for Cairo, on November 6, 1973. On that visit a "special relationship" developed between Kissinger and Sadat. The Kalbs quote Kissinger as having said that this was one of the major breakthroughs of his diplomacy: "It brought about . . . a major turn in the foreign policy of Egypt and therefore in the whole orientation of the area." "Kissinger was full of praise for the Egyptian leader. Sadat showed 'great wisdom,' he said. 'You have to give him a lot of credit.' "[172] After a break of more than six years, diplomatic relations between Egypt and the United States were restored. The Egyptians "linked" this to the plight of the Third Army, having obtained a regular supply line to it because of American pressure on Israel. Sadat showed the Soviets at the same time that he could deal with the Americans on his own. But was there a basic change in Egypt's policy and orientation? Was Sadat abandoning the strict pro-Soviet line in foreign policy or the socialist orientation in internal and economic policy, which had been the two main pillars of Nasserist Egypt? Was there an Egyptian initiative to make a basic change, or was Cairo responding to American enticements regarding an Israeli withdrawal, at the expense of Soviet standing?

The simple answer seems to be that Sadat's policy had remained unchanged since the summer of 1972. After assuming power in late 1970, he had learned that if his foreign and defense policies relied solely on the Soviet Union, he would force the United States to support Israel. He had also learned that the expulsion of the Soviet experts would not necessarily bring American aid against Israel. American aid should be forthcoming, however, after a war.

Moscow would naturally be backing the Arab coalition in this war. Nasser had tried to bolster Soviet power in the Mediterranean; by 1973 this power was great enough to serve Egyptian interest, so that Cairo could use it as the basis on which to turn to the U.S. opinion. To what extent, however, would the U.S.S.R. continue to support a client groping its way westward in collaboration and cooperation with America's firmest client and communism's staunchest foe in the region—King Faisal of Saudi Arabia?

In moving westward, it was possible that Sadat would effect a social and economic change away from the state socialist bureaucratic system. Kissinger could see such a change as the beginning of a "coordination of structures" and the formation of real common interests of the type that should prevail in America's relations with other countries. This shift might be possible if Sadat intended to institute a new economic and social regime, to return to a market economy, and to stabilize Egypt's deteriorating standard of living. To outflank the existing bureaucratic system with all its vested interest and to establish a new competitive economy, he needed huge investments, western technology, conomic guarantees, and good terms of credit from the industrialized states.

This might have been seen as a "once in a lifetime" opportunity for the United States. Egypt was one of the key countries of the Third World, burdened by a "socialist" orientation in its domestic affairs, its foreign policy bound up with the aims of the main "socialist" state and shaped by extreme emotionalism and a sense of deprivation. Yet this country seemed willing to be linked with the United States on the basis of common interests and to coordinate its internal structures with America's. The willingness of a moderate Egyptian leader to cooperate with the United States thus constituted a real change. Sadat seems to have convinced Kissinger that an Egyptian-American linkage could be forged.

From now on, the secretary of state would tell the Israelis that "Sadat said that he has turned towards peace and that it was possible to bind him to this course by pushing the Russians out of Egypt and entrenching the United States there."[173] But the "coordination of structures" and the formation of "real common interest" is a long-term process, a step-by-step" process. The Arab-Israeli problem, too, could be better controlled one step at a time. To Egypt the restoration of its territories was more important than the new western orientation, and Syrian and Palestinian claims also had to be satisfied. From Washington's standpoint it was preferable if progress on these issues was made in stages. The time between the stages would be used for the "coordination of structures," to strengthen American-Egyptian links.

The "phased" or "step-by-step" approach was essentially in keeping with Kissinger's views on the need for coordinated structures, or linkages, between the United States and other countries. The big package deal he had tried to reach with the U.S.S.R. had proved too narrow and vulnerable to pressure from third countries. Later, he told a closed meeting with Israeli newspaper editors that he had also thought of an overall settlement for the Middle East. However, the Vietnam negotiations had taught him that partial settlements and interim agreements, for all their inherent difficulties, seemed preferable now. Kissinger attached supreme importance to time, which was necessary for the coordination of structures. Moreover, a discussion of final aims in negotiations for an overall settlement was very dangerous, because the final aims of the parties in conflict tended to be diametrically opposed. A linkage might be created, though, between the partial aims of the adversaries. Time could thus be gained, and used to link the adversaries' interests and/or structures to those of the United States.

The secretary of state sought to divide the Middle East conflict into its various components and to begin trying to control it by treating the Egyptian component. He hoped that, slowly, the resolution of more peripheral problems might lead to a resolution of the heart of the issue.

One can see this step-by-step approach as an expression of the structural-functionalist variant of positivist-evolutionary thinking on the future.[174] According to Professor Robert Cox, such thinking differs from other types in that positivism is based on data, on externally observed givens. Some other approaches to understanding the social world deal with facts, with events or institutions that are intelligible to man because they are made by man. Positivism, in seeking objective data, fragments what Cox defines as a subjective totality into a number of distinct observations that can be classified as variables. In the simplest case, changes in one variable are observed to be associated with changes in another; casual inferences can be drawn from this observation if one assumes that other factors are either irrelevant or constant.

Generally, social life is too complex to be reduced to two variables. One must, therefore, devise a linkage among a number of ostensibly relevant and interacting variables; this leads to the development of the device of a *system*. Cox denotes two variants of the system model; it seems that Kissinger's methods fit, with occasional deviations (emphasis upon specific actors and a historical approach), into the structural-functionalist type, in which social roles are conceived of as linked together by the performance of complementary functions that result in an equilibrium at the systemic level. The system is thus not merely a framework for organizing data; it is, implicitly, a real entity with ends of its own: the maintenance of its own equilibrium. There are homeostatic mechanisms in the system countering the destabilizing effects of dysfunctional activity and restoring equilibrium. The normative consensual content of the system is an important regulatory mechanism that socializes the actors in the system and restricts deviant behavior.

Obviously, the concept of equilibrium involves a latent bias in favor of the status quo.[175] The bias is modified somewhat by the conception of the development of the system in terms of its progressive "integration." This notion of social change is derived from nineteenth-century sociological thought, particularly from the work of Ferdinand Tönnies and Emil Durkheim. They conceived of social evolution as a movement away from a traditional, rural, organic community (the "Gemeinschaft") toward a more complex urban and industrial world. In this framework, integration is seen as being capable of ensuring the harmonious complementarity of functionally specific roles in a society (or world) in which the parts are highly interdependent. The problems to be overcome during the integration process can be defined deductively and their solution planned in order to facilitate the process. Functionalism lends itself to problem solving, to the diagnosis of technical obstacles and the engineering of appropriate adjustments.

In general, Cox concludes, the view of the historical process in this positivist-evolutionary approach is based on a projection of tendencies observed in contemporary society. The existing distribution of power, the existing forms of social relations, and the currently dominant norms are taken as given, and the future is thought of as the fulfillment of the tendencies inherent in these phenomena. A basic problem for political thinking in these terms is to observe and define the existing powers correctly.

Kissinger's thinking and methods can be linked with Professor Ernst Haas's neo-functionalism,[176] or with Karl Popper's piecemeal social engineering. Kissinger is not a political sociologist like Haas, but rather a politician educated as a historian. Still, some of Haas's definitions seem to explain Kissinger's views as a scholar and statesman.

Kissinger's "systemic" thinking is evident in what he himself later felt was the too-heavy stress laid on the "big package deal" between the superpowers. By concentrating too much on this problem, other forces were able, if not encouraged, to strike out when they felt that their vital and legitimate interests were being sacrificed on the altar of superpower harmony. The Arabs asserted themselves by going to war and imposing an oil embargo, and from then on they were actors with autonomous power to be reckoned with in the international system. They had brought on a crisis that had endangered the entire system's equilibrium and the consensual rules of the game that were supposed to keep local conflicts within bounds.

Thus, the superpowers' deal did not create adequate structural mechanisms to settle conflicts dysfunctional to the global system. Insufficient attention was given to the Arabs' interest and to their ability to influence the system as a whole. The Arab elite did not undergo the necessary socialization that would have prepared them to participate in the maintenance of the system's equilibrium. Washington had to stabilize the situation and end the global crisis and the "crisis of the west." The decline in Nixon's international stature as a result of the Watergate scandal and the relationship between the shaky Republican administration and the Democratic Congress also made corrections of U.S. foreign policy necessary.

Kissinger's first priority was the Middle East conflict itself. He had to deal with it initially, not as the outcome or function of a prior settlement with the U.S.S.R. but in relation to a global crisis, to serious problems inside the United States and in the western world. These difficulties could be handled properly only after the Middle East crisis was stabilized. The stabilization of the Middle Eastern situation would be made possible by a change in U.S.-Egyptian relations. Such a change was possible because Sadat was ready for it.[177] Kissinger thought that Egypt could be bound to the United States by the diplomatic and economic aid that only the Americans could provide, in coordination with the traditionally pro-western Arab states, especially Saudi Arabia.

Riyadh gained much greater international importance as a result of the oil embargo. It held the key to lifting the embargo, since its vast oil reserves made it the world's most important oil power. There was also a large area of agreement between Saudi Arabia and the United States because of the former's uncompromising hostility to the Soviet Union.[178]

Thus, Kissinger would try to apply something akin to the linkage approach, first applied to relations with the U.S.S.R., to relations with Egypt, in order to stabilize the situation in the region and, perhaps, to change the character of the conflict. The secretary of state's premise was that a "victorious" Egypt tied to the United States, which was itself committed to Israel, would no longer be free to make the same extreme demands that it had made with Soviet backing. More than the regional problem was involved in Washington's attempt to seek common ground with Arabs who demanded and received Soviet backing in their local disputes and were also among the most important actors in the now-recognized Third World.

As we have already seen, the course chosen to attain a growing community of interests—a "link" between Washington and Cairo—was the "step-by-step" approach, which can be substantially understood in structural-functional terms. The approach aims at the integration of the internal structures of states (Egypt and the United States) and the socialization of their leaders, maintaining an equilibrium in the Middle East and the international system. This process should, it was thought, be carried out slowly; the failure of the too-hasty global package deal was fresh in Kissinger's mind.

The structural linkage between the United States and Egypt should combine both bilateral relations and the "progress" in the Arab-Israeli conflict, which would honor Arab interests but at the same time would take Israeli basic interests, as Kissinger understood them, into account. In the conflict, the integration process should move from the periphery to the center. The coordination of structures between Cairo and Washington was linked to the slow advance from the margins to the core of the Arab-Israeli conflict. At the same time, an awareness or consensus was created among the actors of the necessity for the process, particularly as it brought them benefits that they might lose if it stopped. In overly simplistic terms, this was the core of Haas's neofunctionalism, at its theoretical beginning.

In conservative Israeli perceptions, Sadat, familiar with Kissinger's functionalistic modes of thought, proposed a course that he knew the secretary of state would understand. He himself would try to relinquish as little as possible of the Soviet aid he received and of his own commitments to the Arab cause or would try to advance it with American aid to his economy and later to his armed forces, while continuing the political and economic struggle against Israel. The "link" that would be created between Arab (oil) assets and American economic interest might serve the general Arab cause later, to bring about a growing rift between Israel and its main source of power—the United States. Economic and "low political" benefits might not prevent, or change, the pursuing of "high political" (as Haas's critic, Professor Stanley Hoffmann, defined them)[179] national aims of an elite involved in an "integration" process by its ambivalent political character.

By adopting this approach, each party—the United States and Egypt—could hope that the *other* would become bound to its interests. The Americans could think that Sadat would be bound so tightly that, in time, he would abandon his ideological obligations to the destruction of Israel, if he had not abandoned them already. On the other hand, conservative Israelis thought that Sadat might hope that he had not robbed himself of his freedom of action vis-à-vis Israel; he would rather obtain everything he could from Washington and weaken the enemy to such an extent that, in time, the Arabs could deliver the *coup de grace* to the Jewish state. Or, they thought, he might leave Israel alone, a weakened and isolated state beside a Palestinian one, until it would cease to exist because of internal troubles. Thus Israeli conservatives like Dayan and Meir were resolved to negotiate very thoroughly with the Egyptian president to extract the most far-reaching concessions possible from him in exchange for the Third Army and the Israeli-held territory in "Africa" (the Israeli salient on the west side of the Suez Canal).[180]

THE SIX-POINT AGREEMENT AND SYRIA

Dayan showed a strong and "manly" reaction to the daily Egyptian harassment of Israeli troops in "Africa" that began in early November. He was extremely annoyed when he realized that Israeli POWs were not exchanged, as an Egyptian quid pro quo, for Israeli consent to allow supplies to pass to the Third Army. The Third Army seemed an easy prey; deprived of an extensive missile coverage, low in ammunition, food, and water, it could be attacked from the air and then assaulted from the land if the Egyptians continued their new war of attrition and did not return the POWs. Plans were drawn up along these lines and stronger retaliatory acts were considered,[181] but the new southern front commander, Major General Israel Tal, was firmly against them, fearing heavy casualties. The cabinet was too weary to consider renewed hostilities without American support.

The nation as a whole seemed not to be able to cope with Dayan's double-edged character: his cautious and "pessimistic" assessment of strategic changes, which brought him at first to assume a defensive stance (unheard of by most Israelis) after the enemy's initial success, and his later aggressive, "manly" behavior. General Tal, for example, had to be relieved of his post by Dayan, as a result. The mobilized nation regarded Dayan as responsible for the disasters of the first days of the war, and later also saw Meir as liable. The nation was behind its quick minded defense minister, who seemed too trigger happy and eager to achieve a final victory. The Israelis might have agreed that such a final victory was necessary, but many of them mistrusted Dayan's motives. The cabinet seemed to mistrust him too, except for Meir, who slowly returned to a close relationship with the defense minister, yet her preference for American-Israeli cooperation moved her away from the war option. The cabinet preferred to bargain, even if Egypt's war of attrition greatly provoked it. The relatively "dovish" element which had been largely influenced by Dayan and Meir since 1969, opted for negotiations even if the Egyptians had transgressed the cease-fire agreement and used the POWs as bargaining points.

Meanwhile, Kissinger was in Egypt formulating the first stage of his step-by-step strategy. He sent his deputy, Joseph Sisco, to Israel to report on the talks in Cairo and then report back on the Israeli reaction.[182] Sisco found that Israel was interested in a partial settlement with Egypt along the lines of the 1971 proposals: Israel would try to extract maximal political concessions from Egypt in exchange for minimal territorial concessions on its part. Jerusalem wanted to make the conflict less salient for Cairo, to make Egypt no longer a party to the demands presented by the Arab coalition. In order to reach these ends it wanted to use the encircled Third Army and the territory it held west of the canal as bargaining points.

In any event, Israel was not interested in a comprehensive deal: Meir and Dayan did not believe in Arab ability to accept such a deal without total Israeli withdrawals and some solution to the Palestinian problem acceptable to the PLO and thus unacceptable to the "hawks" and "doves" in the Israeli cabinet. The government had not been able to reach an agreement on the content of an overall settlement since 1967 because of domestic structural factors and security and ideological concerns. The shock of the October war and the crisis in the national psyche that followed it, as well as the imminent general elections, constituted further barriers to ministerial agreement.

The United States was certainly expected to reject the idea of restoring the status quo ante bellum or of a peace settlement, in which Israel would retain some of the territories, leading toward a general settlement which might be based on foreign guarantees.[183] No matter who was the guarantor, Israel's political and military maneuverability would be restricted; to the Jewish state such constraints constituted an attack on its sovereignty, security, and national ethos. Almost instinctively, the Israeli government tried to stave off this eventuality by returning to Dayan's 1971 ideas about a partial settlement.

Kissinger's immediate task was not easy. He had to solve Egypt's pressing problems: how to free the Third Army without giving anything substantial for the Israelis in return, and how to extract the largest possible territorial concessions from Israel in exchange for some Egyptian concessions, without conceding to other Arab demands. The whole process could not seriously begin before the Israeli elections took place in early December, but until then some pressing problems had to be solved: the POW exchange and the control over the supply line to the Third Army.

The solution Kissinger arrived at was a six-point accord formulated during his tour of the Middle East in early November. The agreement was signed by Egypt and Israel at Kilometer 101 on November 11, 1973.[184] The parties agreed, first, that they would observe the cease-fire strictly in accordance with Security Council Resolution 338. The second point was an agreement to begin immediate talks on the return of the forces to the positions of October 22, in the framework of a U.N.-sponsored agreement on the separation and disengagement of the forces. The third provision concerned daily supplies of food, water, and medicine to Suez City and the evacuation of wounded civilians. Fourth, there was an agreement on the immediate transport of nonmilitary supplies to the Third Army. The fifth point dealt with joint U.N.-Israeli supervision of the supply route to the encircled Egyptians. The sixth point provided for the immediate exchange of all POWs when the control points at both ends of the supply corridor were installed.

The "separation of forces" concept in the second point was drawn from the Egyptian-Israeli lexicon for the proposed partial settlement of 1971. For the Israelis, the term was meant as a substitute for the hated word "withdrawal." Now it could be used as an over-arching concept in negotiations that would simultaneously settle the question of the October 22 lines and provide for a larger Israeli pull-back. What Israel might get in return would be determined after the elections by a concatenation of forces: the U.S. attitude; what the United States might be willing to give in place of concessions by Egypt; the domestic situation in Israel and the results of the forthcoming general elections; Egypt's difficulties over the Third Army and Suez City; pressures inside the Egyptian armed forces for a more or less tough posture; Cairo-Moscow relations; and pressures inside the Arab coalition. When he left Egypt, Kissinger went to Saudi Arabia, Syria, and Jordan to explain the second point of the accord. The Saudis told him that the start of an Israeli withdrawal on both fronts would lead to an easing and then a lifting of the oil embargo.[185]

The Israeli POWs began to come home on November 15. Their return presented the public with a scene that they had not seen since the 1948 War of Independence. Once more stories were heard of IDF positions overrun by the enemy; once more the public was told of troops taken prisoner when no way was found of extricating them from their stronghold. According to Israeli traditions, none of these things should have happened; they were all contrary to the IDF's tactical doctrine, the high command's pretensions, and the convention that the IDF did not let its men be captured. The number of prisoners was not large—a few score, in comparison with the thousands of Egyptians—but shock at the outbreak of the war, the shame of not having attained a decisive victory, and the very high number of casualties in both fronts fed the fires of criticism of the government.

The reserves were still mobilized, manning their positions west of the canal, in the Sinai and on the Golan Heights. The circumstances in which the war broke out and the manner in which it was conducted gave rise to a feeling of great bitterness, and they discussed the reasons for the government failings that led to these difficulties. The reserves would not be released until the disengagement agreement was signed; meanwhile they reflected and talked.

The separation of forces agreement was the subject of direct negotiations between Yariv and Gamassi at Kilometer 101.[186] These negotiations became less and less important, however, as Kissinger, by his mediation, established a diplomatic and political framework for the dealings between Cairo and Jerusalem, in which Israel was more interested than in direct talks. Yariv said later that he had suggested what amounted to almost a total settlement, which would involve Israeli withdrawals and a thinning out of Egyptian forces.[187] Dayan and Meir were worried that after that pull-back, Egypt would return to the Palestinian and Syrian issues; it was, furthermore, interested in American commitments arising from Kissinger's mediation.

The Israeli public, both at home and at the front, was angered by the government's failures in the war. Confused information and silly censorship policies had kept the news of the initial setbacks from the public during the early stages of the war. When the gravity of the situation was made known,[188] many sectors of the public attributed it to governmental mismanagement and to the very nature of the regime. Much of the criticism was military and technical in form, in part because high active and reserve officers participated in public discussions of the war. Much of the criticism was directed against the political elite. An Israeli newspaper editor used the term "earthquake" to describe the extent of the psychological shock produced by the war, and the public was gunning for the ones who had caused it.[189] The list of the guilty was headed by Dayan and Meir; Chief of Staff Elazar, his predecessor, Haim Bar-Lev, and other generals also came in for a share of the blame. Criticism was leveled at the ruling party and at the economic and social system represented by Finance Minister Sapir. Also attacked were the nation's prewar calm and complacency, the alienation from historic ideals, and the corruption of pioneering values and ideals of public service. The image of a fearless, fighting Israeli, whether realistic or not, was damaged. This perception of self-righteousness and military and technical efficiency had celebrated its greatest triumph in June, 1967. Now military efficiency was shaken, as was the faith in the efficiency of the Meir-Dayan elite.

The crisis atmosphere was aggravated by Dayan's public arguments that Israel's initial setbacks were caused by an improved Arab fighting spirit. Neither the missing tanks of "Operation Pigeonhole," which had not been posted in time between the strongholds, nor the cabinet's decision not to mobilize "Operation Rock's" divisions on October 3 were to blame for Arab success, as many Israelis were openly told by Likud leaders, rival generals, and an outraged press hinting at Dayan's own responsibility. The minister of defense explained Arab gains, pointing out a better Arab military performance, Soviet aid, and Israel's dependence on American strategic support and military aid, which prevented preemptive action. These arguments were partially relevant to Dayan's initial decisions but partially not. They did not influence Dayan's "defensive" attitude toward mobilization, his reluctance to mobilize on October 3 because of the intelligence estimate ruling out an Arab offensive, his thoughts in 1967 on mobilization risks, or his reliance upon a structurally unbalanced army supported by an IAF that relied, for its part, on an untested anti-SAM plan that could not be carried out without a preemptive strike to which Dayan objected.

In current Israeli military thinking this imbalance would have probably brought about a successful Egyptian crossing, with more losses, even if "Operation Pigeonhole" had been carried out in time. Egyptian foot soldiers would have been able to destroy "Operation Pigeonhole's" tanks and even "Operation Rock's" divisions would have faced serious problems fighting new Egyptian tactics. Dayan was not ready to mobilize them anyway in the period that could have brought them to the field before the crossing. Yet the minister of defense did not elaborate much on these issues in public. He said that the Arabs had become better fighters—an established fact for Israelis who encountered them—and repeated his arguments on the quality and quantity of Soviet arms and on Israel's dependence on American weapons. These arguments seemed to justify, when repeated again and again, less territorial concessions to the Arabs, in order to prevent a repeated Arab attack under similar conditions; a gap could be opened between Dayan's own strategy of partial agreements with Egypt and public apprehensions. A gap was also created between Israel's self-image, sovereign and fearless behavior, and growing threats from outside: Arab fighting qualities, Soviet aid, and U.S. intervention. "Two mighty powers are sealing my fate, without my being able to determine it myself anymore," said a young reserve officer to me in the Israeli-held salient in "Africa" in those days.

The result of this crisis was to free large sections of the public, mainly the mobilized youth, from the networks of political affiliation that had emerged after Eshkol's death and to foster the spontaneous emergency of protest movements. The situation could have led to more increasing charges against the Meir-Dayan government in terms of issues and personalities, which could have ended in an overhaul of the Israeli political system. The elite was well aware of the dangers. Meir, therefore, thought it essential to hold elections soon, on December 31, and to establish a legal commission of inquiry into the war. The commission would be headed by the chief of justice, Shimon Agranat, and he would appoint the other members. By calling the elections and setting up the commission, the storm was calmed somewhat.

The talks at Kilometer 101 continued but were of little practical significance. They were bitterly attacked by Syria, which condemned them on ideological grounds and because it feared that Egypt might make a separate deal with Israel.

Kissinger was apprehensive about pressure from within the Arab camp; he visited Israel and pro-western Arab capitals in mid-December to prevent a political impasse. He knew that the Meir government would have trouble coming to any firm decision until the elections in Israel.[190] He proposed holding a "short run of the Geneva show," that is, holding talks before the elections about an overall settlement, under U.N. auspices and with the Soviets present. The conference, it was agreed, would open and then be adjourned until late January, until after a new government was installed in Jerusalem.

Sadat understood that Israel's internal problems made some delay in substantive action inevitable. Indeed, he claims that he also initiated the idea of opening the Geneva conference before any movement took place in the field, in order to reach an interim consensus in the Arab coalition. It was preferable to Egypt that Syria participate in the conference, as an expression of continued cooperation between the wartime allies and as evidence that a Soviet-backed, leftist regime committed to the Palestinian cause agreed with Sadat's policy,[191] Sadat has said.

> We were surprised that the Syrians refused to go to Geneva and they asked me to postpone going there because they thought [that an Israeli withdrawal] had to come first. I am no one's keeper, and I also wish no one to be my keeper. I said [to the Syrians], "The person handling the separation of forces [Kissinger] is not able to carry out this task in December. He will do it in January, and that's not far off." I thought that it would be a mistake for us not to go to Geneva, but the Syrians said, "We have decided . . . that is, the Ba'ath party decided." I, for my part, also came to a decision: to go to Geneva. But what was the result? The Syrian foreign minister went to the emir of Kuwait and to King Faisal with a message. The message said that Egypt had given up the fight, . . . that Egypt was in agreement with the Israelis and was going to Geneva to declare this publicly. The aim was obviously to foster dissent in Egypt and to make it accept the decision of the Ba'ath party. . . . I said to the envoys [from the emir and the king] that we were going to Geneva in order to state our position that we want peace. So we went to Geneva and did not proclaim what the Syrians claimed [we would]. We agreed on it wits the Americans.[192]

In other words, there was a prior agreement that the parties would proclaim positions but that the real negotiations would not start until later.

The Egyptian regime was in the firm grip of an individual policy maker, while the one-party Syrian government was made up of a very complex group ideologically committed to the Palestinian organizations and to a national Syrian bid for leadership. They grew suspicious of Egypt's cooperation with the United States; remembering how Sadat had consented to the cease-fire of October 22, probably without consulting them. The Syrian president, General Assad, could ignore this grouping only at his own risk, but if he did not ignore it he risked isolating Syria from Egypt. For if Egypt should make a separate agreement with Israel, he must consider following it, against other Ba'athist commitments, if he wanted Israeli concessions.

Sadat needed Geneva as a platform from which he could proclaim to the world his desire for peace, but he also promised Syria that no substantive settlement with Israel would come out of the conference. Egypt would honor its commitment to the other Arab states and to the Palestinian cause. This was the "catch" in Sadat's policy as Israel saw it: declarations of peace got a yes, but an actual peace settlement received a no unless it could include Egypt's obligations vis-à-vis the greater Arab coalition; a gradual Israeli withdrawal later without real peace received a yes. The Americans hoped that once the Israeli withdrawal began, "common interests" and the "coordination of structures" would prod Egypt in the desired direction of an American-influenced conflict rather than toward an open war in the condition of a free competition between the two superpowers. On the other hand, the Israeli cabinet, under Meir and Dayan tended to agree to some withdrawals in exchange for a real political gain, or to lesser withdrawals for lesser gains. They did not want to hold on to "Africa" and retain their complicated and costly grip on the canal. They agreed with Kissinger that the Geneva "show" should take place first, then the elections, and later a serious Egyptian-Israeli bargaining process should start.

Thus, the "peace conference" scheduled to begin in Geneva in late December was nothing but a framework for maintaining momentum for the time being. The real effort waited for Kissinger's shuttle diplomacy. Another gap was created between Israeli popular expectations, this time from Geneva, and reality, but this time the gap was also a result of Kissinger's diplomatic method. Moreover, direct negotiations—an official Israeli goal in its relations with the Arabs—were abandoned by the leadership in favor of Kissinger's mediation after the "show" was held in Geneva.

4

Shuttle Diplomacy, November, 1973-February, 1974

THE INTERNATIONAL AND AMERICAN BACKGROUND

Shuttle diplomacy is a very rare form of international negotiation; it is dramatic and dramatizing and necessarily involves heavy time pressures. Moreover, both parties to the conflict might develop relatively strong bargaining positions with the mediator if his interests were involved, since the negotiations would divert a great deal of his time from other vital tasks. Such diplomacy creates expectations that might influence the bargaining process itself. However, a dramatic and unorthodox approach seemed necessary and possible in the winter of 1973–74.

The breaches among the western states stemming from the trade and economic problems of the early 1970s and perhaps, too, from détente began to widen in November, 1973. During the war contradictory interests and Europe's critical attitudes toward the United States led all the western European states, except Portugal, officially to deny U.S. aircraft headed for Israel during the October war the right to land and refuel on their territories.[1] The Arab oil embargo was more threatening to the Europeans than to the Americans.[2] In response to the embargo, the European Community accepted the Arab interpretation of Resolution 242. In November, 1973, the Community's council of ministers called for the restoration of all the territory Israel had captured in 1967 and agreed to start a political dialogue between the Community and the Arabs.[3]

Before the October, 1973, war, the Europeans had held consultations on the Arab-Israeli conflict, usually on the level of foreign office political directors general and sometimes on the level of foreign ministers.[4] The issue was analyzed in preparation for the discussion and formulation of proposals, but the talks never led to any substantive conclusions or common proposals contrary to Washington's own views on the conflict. However, the outbreak and prolongation of the war and the oil embargo may have been the proverbial straws to break the camel's back, already bent under the burden of European anger with U.S. economic and foreign policy over the 1970 dollar crisis, Vietnam, and the bilateral American-

212

Soviet dialogue of 1972-73, and over U.S. policy in the Middle East in particular. The result was the formulation of a Community political position independent of and contrary to America's.

The maneuverability of the European governments was affected by an apparently serious lack of petroleum and by economic and political problems within the individual states. Italy, the Netherlands, and Denmark were beset by difficulties in the ruling coalitions and by rampant inflation. Britain, too, suffered from political instability and an economic crisis. Even in the Federal Republic of Germany, people began to speak of the end of the Age of Abundance under the impact of the energy crisis and the damage suffered by part of German industry, particularly the automobile industry.

At the same time as this "crisis of the west," there was a domestic crisis in the United States. The Watergate scandal engulfed Nixon and all those associated with him, except Henry Kissinger, whose role as the prime mover behind United States foreign policy became stronger. Before he could reorder the relations among the western states, Kissinger first had to deal with the Middle East, giving it a great deal of personal attention. He had to bring the United States, Egypt, and Saudi Arabia closer together and maintain the United States' close links with Jordan. He also had to take into account the fact that Israel was growing increasingly isolated, not only in the Third World, where the black African states had broken off diplomatic relations with Israel during the war, but in Western Europe as well.

The strategy chosen, as we have seen, was the step-by-step approach, which would advance Egyptian interests but not satisfy them all at once, and would coordinate internal structures in Egypt with those in the United States. The technique for carrying out this policy, under time pressures resulting from Watergate, the "crisis of the west," and the oil embargo and under the pressure of controlled competition with the Soviet Union in the Middle East, was shuttle diplomacy.[5]

The secretary of state was certainly aware of Israel's powerful position in Congress and in the Jewish community. Yet Kissinger had better bargaining advantages in this respect than before. America's public opinion leaders, especially the television networks and the press, tended to treat the secretary very carefully, if not actually to favor him. They probably had no wish to appear to be indiscriminate persecutors of the Nixon administration, and their criticism of the president might seem more credible if they simultaneously praised a member of the administration unsullied by the Watergate scandal.

Furthermore, the media had accepted détente as a wise and realistic policy in the wake of the Vietnam war, and Kissinger was, after all, the man who had "ended" the war. Even after the October, 1973, war, the press continued to see the man and his policy in terms of détente. No conclusions were drawn from the Middle East war and pre-war U.S. policy; it was as if the policy should continue as before. Thus, while Kissinger did reexamine the idea of the global package deal with the Soviets, especially as a measure to deal with regional conflicts, much of the media did not and continued to back the secretary and détente.[6]

Many journalists accepted the secretary of state's views on the necessity of rectifying the Middle East status quo but did not consider the outbreak of the war as a consequence of an erroneous American global policy. The blame was tacitly laid on Israel, and Washington was criticized to some extent for having relied too much on Israeli power. Many of these critics had long tended to see Israel's status quo policy as leading to dangerous problems in the not too distant future. Somehow, Israel had managed to hold its 1967 gains through its military power, but the Yom Kippur War proved its policy a failure and showed it to be undermining the U.S. position in the region[7] and American domestic interests and foreign policy in general.

The press, predisposed in the secretary's favor, could be exploited to further the aims of the shuttle diplomacy. A select group of journalists was attached to Kissinger on his trips to the region. He also gave important columnists and top journalists, like Joseph Alsop, detailed briefings during and immediately after the war and enlisted them to influence their readers and Israel's representatives in Washington.[8] These reporters were more exposed to Kissinger and his briefings than to the events themselves, which necessarily moved at breakneck speed. The journalists were totally dependent on the secretary for all their information before they discovered the system, or nonsystem, of leaks in Israel. Kissinger's iron grip on State Department affairs and his personal and secret handling of everything important there were enough to make the reporters consider very carefully before risking a conflict with their only source of information and making trouble for their editors.

The secretary had a certain freedom of action vis-à-vis the Congress, Israel's principal bastion in Washington. Congress was still wholeheartedly in favor of détente and there were very few members who would accus Kissinger of a conceptual error in policy toward the U.S.S.R., although this error had led to or helped bring about Soviet aid to the Arabs. There were complaints about the global nuclear alert, but there was general support for the secretary's attempts to deal with the conflagration in the Middle East. In other words, it seemed that the fire in the region had to be put out so that the United States could *return* to the earlier concept of foreign policy.[9]

Kissinger had excellent personal and working relations with Senator Fulbright, the chairman of the Senate Foreign Relations Committee.[10] Fulbright agreed with Kissinger on the need for a change in the Middle Eastern status quo and could help prevent the emergence of bitter criticism of the secretary's entire philosophy of foreign policy. This happened later, in 1975 and 1976, following Kissinger's success in the Middle East. Kissinger's philosophy could be accused of being detrimental to the United States in its relations with the U.S.S.R. and the Middle East, in the sense that the Soviets broke the rules set by détente, or that détente could not set clear and binding rules. Senator Jackson, who maintained a hawkish posture toward the Soviet Union and was sympathetic to Israel, had grounds for attacking this policy, but his criticism was regarded by many liberals as old fashioned. The secretary of state could thus brief Fulbright and the plenary committee without fear of decisively influential hostile members and public criticism. In this way he could maintain the constitutional backing he needed to pursue his work at the height of the Watergate crisis, and develop a new Middle East policy seemingly without abandoning the essence of détente and without a public debate on the principles of his foreign policy. The debate on détente only emerged after the earlier policy underwent some fundamental changes, at least as regards the Middle East, and after Kissinger had already rejected the value of the global package deal in regional conflicts.[11] Other aspects of détente, particularly the need to restrain the nuclear arms race, were unaffected.

The secretary of state was able to achieve some freedom vis-à-vis the sources of Israeli power in the United States—individual Jewish voters, Jewish organizations. Congressional lobbying groups and the presidents of the Jewish organizations tended to exchange opinions at the Israeli Embassy in Washington. Kissinger developed special relations with Ambassador Dinitz and was assisted by presidential statements and messages to Israel[12] and by other branches of the administration, who seemed to be less cooperative in specific areas.[13]

Even if Israel was suspicious of some of his methods, Meir was reluctant to risk a major crisis with Kissinger.[14] She had to consider the constraint of a possible confrontation between Jewish and non-Jewish interests and the administration, especially during a serious economic recession and oil shortages publicly attached to the Middle East war. Since Rabin's days, the Israeli lobby could mobilize Congress to put pressure on the administration; it repeated this in October. Even so, the parameters within which the administration could act had changed. The Vietnam War was over for the U.S. armed forces, so the administration no longer had to be so concerned with neutralizing liberal (often Jewish) criticism of the Indochina war. Furthermore, important sectors of the public backed the administration's policy of détente, and at the same time were impressed by the oil crisis.[15] However, the energy crisis was not purely a result of the embargo; it was also related in public to the fixed oil price policy of the U.S. administration, to a shortage of refining and storage capacity, and to environmental protection legislation.[16] The Arabs and the Americans themselves were blamed for the crisis, and Israel avoided becoming a major target of popular criticism in that issue. Yet during November, 1973, Israel still had to be careful about it.

In general then, Kissinger had a relative freedom of action inside the United States; he could give top priority to a gradual change in the Middle Eastern status quo by concentrating first on the Israeli-Egyptian negotiations not aimed at a general settlement. An economic recession in the United States and Europe was regarded as imminent because of the energy crisis and other, structural, stagflationary problems.[17] The embargo at least had to be lifted. The United States could have tried to exploit certain differences within the Organization of Petroleum Exporting Countries (OPEC). For instance, Iraq, Libya, and probably Algeria had never restricted oil production, even though they were politically radical states; they simply needed the money. They, and also Iran, were most interested in getting the highest price possible for their oil and were trying to realize this objective in the framework of the oil cartel. Saudi Arabia, on the other hand, could efficiently invest only part of the huge dollar surplus it could expect from a price rise. Thus the Arab radicals, who were breaking the terms of the oil embargo, actually stood to gain most from it because it created a demand for more expensive oil. The Saudis seemed to observe the embargo and had an interest in easing it and bringing about the more moderate prices created by more supply. Although he was not a direct party to the oil embargo, Sadat had been involved in starting it, and the Arab cause could be served in making it politically easier for the Saudis formally to lift the embargo.[18]

Kissinger wanted to hold the Geneva Conference as soon as possible to fill the political vacuum between the signing of the Six-Point Agreement and the Israeli elections and to help get his shuttle diplomacy started again. He had determined as early as October 22 that active and exclusive American mediation should be the framework for U.S. policy in the Middle East. The Geneva Conference would allow the parties to bide time without seeming to do so; it would create the appearance of Soviet-American cooperation and then permit exclusive American mediation. Publicly, however, the gathering was proclaimed to be a "peace conference."

GENEVA

Until a few days before it opened, the Geneva Conference seemed one of the most illprepared international conferences ever to take place.[19] There had been strong differences of opinion among the United States, the Soviet Union, and Israel before the conference was convened on December 21, 1973, by U.N. Secretary General Kurt Waldheim. Washington regarded the Geneva Conference as a means of maintaining the appearance of political movement, not as a means of achieving a final resolution of the conflict. The Americans, therefore, wanted to convene the conference in December but postpone substantive negotiations until the end of January, after the Israeli elections. The United States would then be able to resume its mediating role to bring about a partial settlement. Moscow, however, wanted the conference to be the permanent framework for substantive negotiations under joint Soviet-American-U.N. auspices. Kissinger and Gromyko held discussions on the matter in New York until just before the conference convened, and the United States succeeded in obtaining Soviet consent to a formal opening of the conference, with the interested parties present, to be followed by narrower Israeli-Egyptian negotiations in accordance with Cairo's expressed wishes, in which the Soviets hoped to be present. This procedure would allow, Moscow believed, a discussion of the whole conflict, with *all* parties concerned, in the framework of the conference.[20] Israel was, as always, interested in excluding or at least neutralizing the U.S.S.R. Jerusalem also wanted the United Nations' role at Geneva to be as small as possible, since it felt that the Arabs could exploit the U.N. to increase their bargaining leverage. The Arabs had broad support in the organization; there was a permanent anti-Israel majority in the Security Council and the General Assembly. The shift in Western Europe's public posture made the international body even less acceptable to the Israelis.

It was not clear what the U.N. role at Geneva would be until opening day; the invitations were not sent to the participants until the very last minute. The conference was called jointly by the American and Soviet foreign ministers who acted as cochairmen. The U.N., represented by the secretary general, was asked to convene the conference sessions in accordance with a Security Council resolution.[21] As stipulated by the resolution, the secretary general played only a limited, largely symbolic, role. Another disagreement that was not resolved until the very eve of the conference revolved around Egypt's request to invite not only the belligerents of the October fighting and Jordan, but also the PLO. Israel objected to PLO participation and secured an American promise that in the future no other parties would be invited to the conference without

Jerusalem's consent.[22] In the end, Jordan and Egypt were the only Arab parties to attend.

Syria was reluctant to attend. Israel, too, however, was hesitant about sitting down with representatives of a state that had not yet delivered a list of names of the Israeli POWs and did not let the Red Cross visit the prison camps. Dayan was inclined to make any further political moves dependent on a resolution of the POW problem. Meir was willing to go to Geneva in any case; she recognized the significance the superpowers attached to the conference. She also knew that Kissinger would not back an Israeli boycott over the POW issue. In her conversations with him, he had compared the Syrian tactics in the matter to those of the North Vietnamese, and the Americans had negotiated with them for years. Meir suggested to her cabinet that Israel attend the Conference but refuse to attend the opening session with the Syrian delegation unless Damascus complied with the Geneva Conventions.[23] Syria solved Israel's problem by not coming to the conference at all.

The opening of the conference provided the superpowers with a platform from which they could proclaim positions in the conflict. Soviet foreign minister Gromyko stressed that the U.S.S.R. would be willing to recognize Israeli sovereignty within the 1949 Armistice Demarcation Lines, which both Moscow and the Arabs had never accepted as final. The Soviet foreign minister also said that his government was ready to agree to the demilitarization of occupied areas to be evacuated by Israel. Israel had advocated demilitarization since 1968.[24] At the same time Gromyko insisted upon Israeli withdrawals from *all* territories occupied in 1967 and upon the "rights of the Palestinians." The Soviet position seemed to have changed since the seemingly total support of Arab territorial claims and demands on behalf of the Palestinians in the late 1960s. The recognition of the 1949 ADL was a substantive public change, repudiating PLO claims to Palestine as a whole, and thus officially interpreting "Palestinian rights" in terms deviating from the official Arab consensus. Secondly, Gromyko emphasized a political process, rather than belligerency, as the appropriate method to resolve the Middle East conflict, quoting détente. In fact, some clear-cut differences between Arab positions (rather than Arab behavior) and Soviet positions became publicly known through Gromyko's speech: Israel (in the 1949 boundaries) was there to stay, occupied territories were to be returned, and "Palestinian rights," among other things, had to be secured. The superpowers should guarantee this comprehensive solution.

Gromyko also had an informal private meeting with his Israeli counterpart, Abba Eban. The Israelis' impression was that the Soviets were mainly concerned with satisfying the specific Egyptian interest—an Israeli pullback as soon as possible—and with the maintenance of the Geneva framework so that Moscow would have a role in the negotiating process. Eban was concerned chiefly with discussing the possibility of reestablishing diplomatic relations between Israel and the Soviet Union (diplomatic relations had been severed by Moscow on October 10, 1967). Gromyko was not interested in this issue; the Arab world would have regarded such a change in Moscow's official hostility to Israel as an act unfriendly to the Arabs. The reestablishment of diplomatic relations would have to come at the end of the political process in the region. The Kremlin's uncompromising demand for total Israeli withdrawal was understood to demonstrate that it could serve its clients' interests. Such services, however, were conditional on the clients' own wishes.

In private conversations with western observers and even Israelis, the author among them, the Egyptians at Geneva spoke of a strong desire to limit Cairo's dependence on Moscow. The basic Egyptian strategy seemed to be to achieve as much freedom of action as possible vis-à-vis the superpowers, while simultaneously cooperating with both of them but more with the United States, in order to win their combined support. Cairo would, however, not forget its commitments to the all-Arab cause, and particularly to Syria.

Kissinger had to make sure that the opening of the conference helped the forces in Israel that he wished to see strengthened in the forthcoming elections. His treatment of Israel was based on one of his fundamental principles: that a country's foreign policy cannot be divorced from the domestic political conditions there. The principle was valid for the United States as well as for Israel; for instance, pro-Israeli elements in the United States could not be ignored. In his address at Geneva, the secretary of state repeated again and again the "historical" significance of the peace conference, and skirted issues on which Israel was especially sensitive; he did, however, refer to the rights of the Arab states and of the Palestinians.[25]

The Egyptian and Israeli foreign ministers, Fahmi and Eban, made statements in accord with the official lines of their governments.[26] In the closed sessions, Kissinger, Gromyko, Eban, and Fahmi agreed that an Egyptian-Israeli military working group should start talks on the disengagement and separation of forces under the chairmanship of the commanding officer of UNEF, General Ensio Siilasvuo. The Egyptians thus achieved the desired appearance of continuity in negotiations, while the Israelis got the respite they needed to hold their general elections on December 31, 1973, without anything in the talks that would require a government in Jerusalem to obtain a new mandate from the electorate.

The plenary session of the conference was adjourned on December 24, 1973. The military talks between Israel and Egypt begun at Kilometer 101 were continued in Geneva, although there was not much hope anything would come of them until a new government came to power in Jerusalem. Kissinger had already suggested that both sides send delegations to Washington very soon.[27] In the meantime, Egypt resumed small-scale hostilities in the canal zone, and inflicted daily casualties on the Israeli forces. Thus, many Israelis were still thinking that some kind of a peace process was taking place at Geneva, while at the same time they were being mobilized and exposed to daily Egyptian pressure in the field.

BETWEEN ASWAN AND JERUSALEM

The Israeli General Elections

On December 31, 1973, with most of the reserves still mobilized, the general elections were held in Israel. The opening of the Geneva "peace" conference had an important impact on the elections and compensated the Labor-Mapam alignment to an extent for the shocks of the war and the mobilization of most of its active members. If there was confusion or a strong challenge to its authority at home, Labor had managed to get out the vote with the help of its party machinery. The party apparatus was closely linked with the economic organizations such as the Histadrut and other bodies that provided employment and services, particularly medical and health services. Although there had been a shift in the political loyalties of Israelis after Ben-Gurion's resignation and although many immigrants, particularly those from Asia and North Africa and the young, were more inclined to vote for right-wing parties, the party machine still had a great deal of influence on the voters. Its influence stemmed from the fact that it represented a ruling elite, under Meir and Dayan, that in any case had broad popular support, and also from the fact that it dispensed, or was thought to dispense economic and political patronage. The mobilization, however, had largely paralyzed the party apparatus at a time when the elite's public image was severely damaged by the outbreak of the war and its military outcome.

As the election drew near, the alignment managed to close ranks behind Meir and Dayan even though the old Mapai leadership, particularly Pinhas Sapir, who ran the party apparatus, blamed Dayan for the policy of maintaining a high profile of the conflict with (as it turned out) inadequate military and political backing. Meir herself was at first absolved of blame in this matter. Her position in the party was still regarded as decisively important if the alignment wanted to avert a fight among Mapai, Rafi, and Achdut Ha'Avoda over the succession problem, which might have endangered the delicate balance between the factions. Sapir thought Meir was Dayan's victim in the defense policy because she relied on his advice and on the judgment of the military apparatus under his control; she had to reckon with the pressure he and his supporters inside the party exerted in the matter of past behavior toward the Arabs. The old Mapai moderates also had doubts about the feasibility of Dayan's autonomist orientation toward the United States. Like Meir, they were wholeheartedly in favor of maintaining a wide area of agreement with the United States. On the eve of the elections, though, Meir and her colleagues saw no political reason to get rid of Dayan and thus admit to responsibility for the war troubles, while alienating his small, but highly important, Rafi faction. Moreover, Meir, emotional as she was, did not officially blame the "young soldiers" around her—Dayan, Elazar, and their generals—for the Yom Kippur disaster. She was not an expert in these areas; she resented Dayan's behavior during the opening phase of the war, his pessimism and the "ministerial advice" he used to give to the fighting generals, and his practice of sharing responsibilities with her, the nonexpert, or with the rest of the cabinet, when the risk was too high. Yet, after the initial shock, this practice made her Dayan's partner in many decisions. Some of them, like the shift from direct negotiations at Kilometer 101 to an interim agreement, she fully endorsed. Others were made by the whole cabinet on the advice of Chief of Staff Elazar. In her own eyes, for all practical purposes, Meir shared responsibility with them.

The appointment of a commission of inquiry into the Yom Kippur War, the Geneva "peace conference," and the elections themselves, provided channels to divert the pressure of criticism from the government to some extent. Yet the moderate Labor ministers and party activists demanded a revised election platform that would stress Israel's desire for a peace settlement based on territorial compromise *and* defensible borders. The former election platform—Dayan and Galili's document, which stressed Israel's settlement policy in the occupied territories—was diluted somewhat, yet the document remained a compromise among all the party sections.[28] Thus, the alignment elite managed to close ranks under the banner of peace through the Geneva Conference and the negotiations that would follow.

During the campaign the alignment spokesmen, particularly Dayan, represented the outbreak of the war as a tactical surprise, not as the political, strategic, and tactical surprise it really was. The perseverance in battle until the Third Army was surrounded and the repulsion of the Syrians from the Golan Heights were described as a brilliant military victory. In this version of events, the victory was not completed for the same reason that there was no Israeli preemptive attack on October 6: the need for the military and political support of the United States. Because Israel had received such aid during the war, it could now take the road to a negotiated peace, even though it had been denied a complete military victory.[29]

The nationalist opposition accused the government of the "blunder" that resulted in the surprise of the outbreak of the war, but basically it accepted the alignment's claim that the "blunder" was tactical and technical. According to Begin, the main reasons for Israel's setbacks during the war and the subsequent political problems were that the reserves had not been called up in time and that there had been no regular armored forces stationed around the strongholds on October 6,[30] as "Operation Pigeonhole" designed them to be. Dwelling on what were essentially military and technical points about past errors, even though many accepted this analysis of events, was not enough to make the expanded right-wing alignment, the Likud, seem a positive political alternative for the future.

The right-wing conglomerate was composed of four parties: Gahal; the State List (former Rafi followers, who refused to join the Labor alignment or to stay there because of Labor's bargaining habits and compromising approach to the West Bank); the Free Center (a nationalistic, free enterprise group who first belonged to Herut but later preferred independence because Begin's authoritarian regiment in his party limited their influence in Herut and Gahal as a whole);[31] and the Movement for the Whole of Eretz-Israel.[32] The spirit behind the new alignment was Reserve General Ariel Sharon, who resigned from the army shortly before the war and publicly pressed the right to join ranks and challenge the Labor-Mapam regime. Many voters indeed seemed willing to punish Labor for the war and were psychologically more ready for it as old loyalties and affiliations were rapidly vanishing. Yet Labor asked them to wait for the report of the commission of inquiry, and to opt for peace in Geneva. The Likud platform called for a hard line toward the Arabs with regard to such crucial issues as the West Bank and the occupied territories in general, including the "African" territory. They demanded peace in exchange for any withdrawal from Egyptian territory.

Thus the very beginning of the bargaining process, in which most Israelis hoped to retain some important territories, but not all of them, in exchange for peace at Geneva, seemed impossible. They wanted to give the conference a chance, to see how Kissinger would enhance peace and/or make U.S. aid to Israel possible as a result of Arab intransigence at Geneva. Labor was more flexible, on the face of things, regarding the West Bank, and offered a reasonable compromise with Egypt, using the Third Army and "African" territory as trump cards for peace. Likud propagandists kept repeating accusations about the war. Likud thus did not offer a realistic alternative to the peace conference at Geneva, because very few Israelis realized that Geneva was never intended for peace with Egypt and Jordan, but instead for gaining time for separate negotiations with Egypt. Most of the still mobilized nation did not want the war to start again and considered aid from the United States vital. The alignment refrained from proposing extensive concessions, which the public opposed with the same vigor that it opposed going to war again, and so it maneuvered between the electorate's two main apprehensions. Consequently, despite the ostensible earthquake brought on by the Yom Kippur War, the alignment won the elections, or, more accurately, the losses it expected to suffer were not so great that a government could be formed without it.[33] Although the rightist opposition was significantly strengthened, the alignment held a large enough block of seats to prevent any other grouping from forming a viable coalition. In the election campaign, the alignment had made promises of peace and American support. The expectations and beliefs among the public regarding these two points, if disappointed, could open a serious gap between the Labor leaders' promises and reality.

In fact, Dayan and Meir did not believe that peace and defensible borders were attainable at this point. What they were seeking was an interim settlement along the lines of the 1971 proposals to use the encircled Third Army and territory captured west of the canal, plus some territory on the east side, as bargaining cards. They wanted to draw Cairo out of the circle of conflict as far as possible, in exchange for territorial concessions and the decrease of the danger of war and of escalation in the future. These objectives would be negotiated through the American mediator. Other ministers, like Eban, might have indeed pursued a comprehensive peace settlement at Geneva, but Meir and Dayan still had a decisive influence over the alignment, and the Arab position at Geneva itself appeared to be incompatible even with the moderate alignment view (total withdrawals and "the rights" of the Palestinians, in exchange for doubtful and unclear Egyptian definitions of peace).

Kissinger began discussing an interim settlement with the parties even before the Geneva Conference, during a visit to the Middle East in mid-December. The talks resumed after the conference, when Dayan arrived in Washington on January 3.[34] Discussions about a comprehensive settlement meant negotiations about an unmanageable number of claims and counterclaims. Israel in particular had good reason not to want to broach such talks. Another aim of the negotiations was to lift the oil embargo, which intensified Israel's isolation and invited pressure from Western Europe and Japan on Jerusalem and Washington. The embargo also promoted Soviet interests, to the detriment of the oil states.

When the secretary of state came to Israel on December 16, 1973, he said that Sadat demanded a pullback of Israeli forces but was willing to settle, for the time being, for a more limited one—about 30 kilometers into the Sinai, beyond the fortified Mitla and Giddi passes. These passes not only dominated the canal, but they were also the geostrategic key to the great expanses of the Sinai.[35] The Israeli and Egyptian forces were to be separated by several strips of land: a central strip, to be held by

U.N. soldiers, flanked on both sides by forward and backward Israeli and Egyptian-held strips, in which there would be a restriction of forces and equipment. Another point Kissinger made in outlining his ideas about the negotiations was that the international strategic situation was in Egypt's favor. Sadat had the advantages; the secretary of state thought it odd that he should settle for no more than an interim settlement, when he could just as well have demanded an overall settlement, an Israeli withdrawal to the 1967 borders. He would have had extensive international and domestic American support for such a demand, and he could have risked a resumption of hostilities. Sadat had two options: he could either try to obtain an agreement with American help, in a controlled international atmosphere, or he could try to incite the West Europeans, Japanese, and Soviets against the United States, in an atmosphere of global crisis, in order to pressure America to support Egypt's claims. Sadat really did not have to start hostilities again; the continuation of the oil embargo and odd incidents at the front would be enough.

Kissinger expressed wonder that Sadat did not exploit such obvious advantages. He urged the Israelis to agree to pull back from the canal, in return for promises by Sadat to limit his forces and military equipment in the areas evacuated by the IDF and in areas that the Egyptian army already held near the waterway. He also reported that Sadat had promised to lift the blockade at the Bab al-Mandab and allow Israeli cargoes through the canal, which would be reopened after the disengagement agreement was reached. Sadat also spoke of normalizing life in the canal zone and of rebuilding the canal cities, which had been evacuated and destroyed during the war of attrition and were of greater concern for economic reconstruction and development. The Egyptian president thus developed ideas for an interim settlement that he and Dayan advanced in 1971. This time, too, he refused to separate the proposed agreement from the whole package of Arab demands. He was unwilling to make any political concessions in terms of the actual substance of the conflict and spoke of it only as a military agreement, limited in time. Yet he dropped his demand that the interim agreement be made in the framework of a timetable for a total Israeli withdrawal from all territories, on the basis of an advance Israeli formal obligation to withdraw from the territories according to the timetable.

Meir, at first, rejected the idea of an Israeli withdrawal without a suitable qid pro quo, i.e., "peace and defensible borders." She did not see Sadat's promises to reopen the canal and normalize life in the battle zone as a substantial gain for Israel. Sadat, after all, could easily break his promise, but a withdrawal would be irreversible. Furthermore, if Sadat's strategic and political situation were really so good, he had no incentive to keep any of his promises. If the oil embargo were lifted, he could always threaten to reimpose it. His aggression had gone unpunished, for no one cared if Israel were the victim; in an unjust world where only might and oil were of any consequence, the Arabs could force Israel back to the 1949 borders and give nothing in return. Because the balance of power was so much in their favor, they could disregard their commitments and the world would still be on their side. Consequently, Meir said, the confrontation between Israel and the "world" was inevitable. The only relevant question was whether it should come now, when Israel had military advantages in the field, or later, when it had lost its advantages and with the international situation no better. Why should Jerusalem not demand peace for territory *now*, instead of temporary arrangements from which it gained nothing, which did not resolve the conflict, and which limited its future bargaining power? The question, of course, was really rhetorical, since Meir was not interested in a comprehensive deal; she did not believe in a deal that might bring the enemy directly to Israel's heartland. Nor was there the domestic consensus and the political apparatus to permit a substantive discussion of this possibility.

Kissinger did not care for a comprehensive deal either. In structural terms, such a deal would have to involve a coalition of all the Arab states, some of which were Soviet clients and some of which denied Israel's right to exist. In terms of content, it would have to deal with the West Bank, Jerusalem, the Gaza Strip, the Golan Heights, and the Palestinian refugees; some of these issues were taboo in Israel. The Arab coalition would probably agree on a radical common denominator unacceptable to Washington. The U.S.S.R. would have to participate in the negotiations; it was strategically obliged and ideologically closer to Arabs with more extreme demands, such as Syria, Iraq, Algeria, and the PLO. The whole Arab coalition would move in the direction of the official, radical demands, whereas in private, said Kissinger to the Israelis, Sadat seemed to be much less interested in the PLO than Assad. Kissinger clearly wanted a "moderate" agreement between Israel and the "moderate" Sadat, arrived at with American mediation and without Russian participation. The secretary of state claimed that a second oil embargo would not be so great a bargaining weapon for the Arabs once the first one was lifted as Faisal promised. A second embargo would not catch the Western Europeans and Japanese unawares. Nor would Saudi Arabia hasten to impose one again; it was well aware of its dependence on western money and goods.

Therefore, Kissinger argued, Israel had to gain time, which might decrease the Arabs' greater bargaining power, help bind Egypt to the United States, and make it easier for Israel to obtain American support. Gaining time meant American military and political assistance, and such

aid would not be forthcoming if there were no agreement. Most of the
Israeli cabinet ministers were susceptible to these arguments, yet they
saw no way to turn Washington down without risking war again, and
that would in any event certainly entail more casualties. Nor did they
want to negotiate about a comprehensive deal; in such talks the U.S.
position would necessarily be far different from Israel's. Instead, Dayan
wanted the 1971 interim deal, which would take Egypt out of a military
conflict by a guaranteed agreement to end the state of war between the
two countries in exchange for the canal zone. He realized that Egypt
would not agree to end its belligerency in exchange for the canal territory, which Sadat already partially held in his own hands. Israel's "African" territory was an asset, but not enough to obtain far-reaching political concessions, due to the relative dubious outcome of the war.

Meir, always skeptical about such deals, could not offer any positive
alternative, and accepted the idea of an interim agreement just as she had
in 1971—under Dayan's pressure. Then she limited Israeli concessions a
great deal; after a bloody war, she could not deny Egyptian military
presence in the canal area, and she realized that "nonbelligerency" was
unattainable in exchange for the Yom Kippur War gains. Thus she
agreed with Dayan to negotiate a pullback from "Africa" and parts of
the east side of the canal, short of Sadat's war aims—the Sinai passes—
for domestic military and political gains—demobilization, a shorter front,
and a lesser economic strain—for the sake of American-Israeli relations
and for the most viable deal with Egypt that might be obtained and
guaranteed. Furthermore, typical of Israel's political tradition, there was
a strong tendency in Meir's psyche to believe in the "imponderability of
the future," that is, a tendency to avoid looking at the future in terms of
the present. Unlike Kissinger's systematic positivism, in Israel's national
ethos there is a tendency to doubt that knowledge of the present will
give one an idea of the future. The Zionist enterprise was largely based
on ignoring the dry and unpromising facts of the present; it succeeded
despite this. This attitude made it easier for Meir and her colleagues to
accept the lesser evil: there would be negotiations on a partial settlement,
in circumstances unfavorable to Israel. Circumstances might change for
the better in the future, for total withdrawal was the worst possible
alternative.

After the elections, Defense Minister Dayan went to Washington at
Kissinger's invitation and brought proposals for a partial or interim
settlement. The Israeli proposals called, first of all, for a limited exchange
of territory on both sides of the Suez Canal. The defense minister mentioned informally a unilateral Israeli withdrawal some twenty kilometers
into the Sinai to a line between the Mitla and Giddi passes and the canal.
Second, the Israelis proposed a significant reduction and thinning out of

the Egyptian forces east of the canal and on part of the west side of the canal. The aim was to move Egypt's antiaircraft missiles and artillery as far back as possible, to prevent a new war of attrition or full-scale hostilities. Third, the Isrelis wanted preparations to reopen the Suez Canal to shipping, and the reconstruction of the cities on the waterway. This would constitute a certain guarantee against the immediate resumption of fighting, by removing the military bridges over the canal and starting a civilian traffic there. The presence of civilian shipping and rebuilt cities would also inject an element of peace and normality into the former combat zones. Fourth, the Israelis called for freedom of passage for Israeli ships and cargoes through the canal, in due course, and the final and formal lifting of the blockade of the Bab al-Mandab. Fifth, U.N. forces would be stationed in a demilitarized zone between the parties to oversee the implementation and observance of the agreement. Sixth, Egypt would end the state of belligerency as a political guarantee of the agreement. Finally, Israel wanted American arms supplies and other political and military assistance, including the neutralization of the U.S.S.R. if necessary, in case of an Egyptian breach of the accord.

The January, 1974, Shuttle

One week later, on January 10, Kissinger came to Egypt and set about the task of narrowing the gaps between the parties' positions.[36] Negotiating the agreement involved a number of political and substantive difficulties for the secretary of state. First, he had to ensure that the Soviets had no part in the negotiations, but at the same time the bilateral relations between the superpowers could not be exacerbated. Kissinger was in a good position to achieve this; he had been invited to mediate by the Kremlin's Egyptian client, so the U.S.S.R. had no pretext to voice public objections to his role. Still, he is reported as having tried to compensate Moscow by asking Jerusalem to use its influence on Senator Jackson to mute his opposition to giving the U.S.S.R. most favored nation status. Israel promised nothing in this regard.[37] Kissinger may also have hoped that the U.S.S.R. would be partially satisfied because the agreement involved the reopening of the Suez Canal, and the U.S.S.R. would certainly benefit from it. The canal is the shortest waterway between Russia and the Soviet Union's provinces in the Far East, and it is the most convenient approach to the Indian Ocean and to East Africa.

The second problem the secretary of state faced was that of coordinating America's global concerns with the parochial concerns of the parties, particularly in the face of the asymmetry between the political muscle of the Arab coalition, as he said he saw it, and the Jewish and Israeli influence in the United States. He resolved this difficulty by obtaining greater concessions from Israel in exchange for temporary Egyptian commitments guaranteed by the United States and for purely American commitments to Israel. Third, how was Kissinger to balance Cairo's demands for tangible concessions and the political concession of nonbelligerency that Israel demanded? If Egypt declared an end to the state of war, it would cut itself off from the rest of the Arab states and their claims or would lay itself open to the accusation that it had abandoned the Arab cause. Nonbelligerency could be interpreted as Cairo's giving up its military option, that is, giving up the leverage it needed to obtain the remainder of its objectives in the conflict.

The fourth problem related to Egyptian sovereignty. Sadat agreed to limitations on troops and armaments in the forward areas and to the reopening of the canal. Yet the problem with including these points in an Egyptian-Israeli agreement was that they implied a renunciation of sovereignty. Although Sadat wanted to do what the Israelis preferred he would do, he would not accept a formal Israeli say in Egyptian affairs. This sort of problem would recur during the negotiations; Israel wanted certain steps taken that Egypt did not really object to but that it did not want to commit itself to publicly. Kissinger and Dayan were able to smooth out these difficulties by finding techniques acceptable to both sides.

Egypt's limited renunciation of sovereignty over both banks of the canal, implied in its agreement to the U.N. presence and to the reduction of its forces, would be generally incorporated into a purely military arrangement backed by secret annexes and undertakings toward the United States. The formal disengagement agreement was not signed at Geneva, in the political framework of the "peace" conference, but at Kilometer 101, the scene of the military talks between the signatories. Israel, however, had the satisfaction of having arrived at a direct agreement with Egypt signed by high-ranking representatives, the two chiefs of staff. The secret annexes to the same documents, signed by the generals, were cosigned by the chiefs of state.

Kissinger was able to still Cairo's objections to significant restrictions on its forces by having Israel also agree to reduce its forces in the forward zones. Egypt agreed to a significant reduction of forces and to the withdrawal of heavy artillery and missiles because Israel was adamant on the subject in the face of General Gamassi's strenuous opposition. Kissinger had at first said that Egypt would not agree and tried to convince the Israelis that they were being unnecessarily rigid. A compromise on the political character of the agreement was reached when Egypt agreed to "scrupulously observe" the cease-fire, without mentioning its traditional claims and other Arab demands in the conflict. Instead, the disengagement agreement was referred to as a "first step toward peace."

The territorial problem (i.e., the depth of Israel's withdrawal) did not arise as a subject for much bargaining, as Israel had agreed in advance to a unilateral withdrawal to the fortified Sinai passes. Cairo did not try to achieve more, for the time being.

To satisfy Israel, the test of Egypt's intentions—that is, whether its actions were compatible with its promises—would begin immediately. However, the reopening of the canal might be conditional on Israel's behavior, since Egypt did not agree publicly to Israel's "dictation" on this matter. Provisions for Israeli cargoes through the Suez Canal were included in a secret Egyptian promise to the United States; fulfillment of this point could also be made conditional on Israel's subsequent behavior. Israel agreed to waive its demand for an explicit agreement on the Bab al-Mandab blockade after receiving a secret American promise of support in any test of Egypt's sincerity, as Cairo maintained that the straits were outside Egyptian territory.

In conclusion, the following aspects of the Egyptian-Israeli agreement should be stressed: First, the Egyptians insisted that the mandate of the U.N. forces in the Sinai be limited in time, in order to stress the interim character of the agreement. The period agreed upon was thus only six months. Later, every renewal of the mandate became a trump card in the hands of the party interested in further negotiations and/or a controlled crisis, meaning Egypt. Second, the parties guaranteed their commitments to thin out their forces, and resolved doubts about the validity of their promises by signing secret documents to this effect, backed by undertakings to the American president. Third, Egypt refused to undertake to reopen the Suez Canal in the context of the official agreement with Israel. Instead, in a bilateral Israeli-American "instrument of understanding," the United States promised that priority would be given to the reopening of the canal, the rebuilding of its cities, and the implementation of the separation of forces agreement upon further negotiations between Egypt and Israel.

Fourth, the Israeli-American protocol stated that in order to prevent a repetition of the events of May, 1967, the U.N. force could be removed during its mandate period only at the request of both Egypt and Israel. In case of a unilateral attempt to do so by Egypt, the United States would veto it in the Security Council. Fifth, Washington and Jerusalem agreed to regard the Bab al-Mandab as an international waterway in which there was freedom of passage for all, including Israeli shipping. In the event of Egyptian interference with navigation there, the United States and Israel would enter into consultations about how to guarantee this right. Sixth, the depth of the Israeli withdrawal would be about 20 kilometers east to the Suez Canal. Israel would thus lose its direct presence in the canal zone, yet maintain its control over the fortified

Mitla and Giddi passes. Finally, the American-Israeli protocol—which was, of course, a secret document—included an American assumption of responsibility for maintaining Israel's defense capability.

It should be noted that different kinds of documents were signed and exchanged by the three states. There was the official agreement signed at Kilometer 101, including secret annexes signed by Sadat and Meir, Sadat's letters to Nixon, and Nixon's letters to Meir. Finally, there was the Israeli-American instrument of understanding (there may also have been a similar document signed by the United States and Egypt). The system of documents was implicitly limited in time by the U.N. mandate provision, to be prolonged every six months. Egypt had not arrived, yet, at its limited war goals—the Sinai passes. It had to accept less, for the time being, because it accepted Israel's presence in "Africa" as an Israeli trump card, and did not try to risk full-scale hostilities to remove the IDF from that area. Kissinger's argument that Sadat had altogether better cards, was not shared by the Egyptian president himself, who proved to be cautious and patient. A new war might involve the United States against him, and he would need Soviet aid. The chances of quick Egyptian gains were not great, just as the chances of quick Israeli gains without heavy casualties were slim. Both parties—Egypt and Israel—opted for a fair deal for the time being, the future pending on their relative power and influence with Washington. The bargaining procedure was thus plain and simple, no inflated demands to be dropped later, no "Oriental bazaar" methods, mostly real demands to be modified. Even if this procedure encountered several difficulties, especially with regard to public and secret commitments, Kissinger and Dayan proved to be excellent technicians in overcoming them. Kissinger told the Israelis openly that another round would have to take place "in a year or so," after the 1974 agreement, even if nothing to this effect was agreed upon or stated in the agreement itself. He did not try to paint glowing pictures of Sadat, but rather spoke in terms of an academic, observing data and organizing it into a viable, functional system, while always having in mind the whole global system.

Kissinger's technique of personal shuttle diplomacy was important in bringing about an agreement in a strategic framework that was created before. By hopping back and forth between Jerusalem and Aswan, he was able to dictate the timetable of the talks to each party. For example, it seemed that Kissinger could not spend much time in the Middle East, so the parties were under pressure to reach an agreement within the limited time allotted to his tour if they wanted to prevent an explosion in the field. Furthermore, the parties had to deliberate and make decisions in the short intervals between the secretary of state's return trips. In order to maintain the momentum this technique created, Kissinger postponed talks on major obstacles to an agreement until the other issues were settled, and he dealt with each issue separately. It should be noted, though, that he had previously reached a "conceptual" if not a "strategic" understanding with the Israelis, at least about the necessity for an interim agreement. By the time these major obstacles were reached, an agreement would be in sight; it would then be difficult for one of the parties to sabotage the entire endeavor by a sudden display of obstinacy over a specific detail. To expedite the process further, the secretary spent time in Jerusalem talking with various cabinet ministers in order to help them arrive at a consensus. He spoke of Sadat's realism and stressed the Egyptian president's desire to devote his country's resources to social and economic development, yet he never committed himself to Sadat's intentions. Instead he repeatedly said that a structural-political change in the Middle East was the objective of the negotiating process: Egypt's ties with the United States and the reduction of Soviet influence were the targets of his diplomacy. Sadat would go along willingly because of his realism, after having won back his country's honor, if Israel played the game properly.

The text of the agreement signed at Kilometer 101 was published on January 18. Entitled "Egyptian-Israeli Agreement on Disengagement of Forces in Pursuance of the Geneva Peace Conference," its provisions were general.[38] The existence of secret annexes was leaked to the Israeli press later.[39]

The disengagement agreement had the following consequences for the parties: the military option was restricted but not formally eliminated for both sides, and became dependent on subsequent political and military-political developments; Israel got a short front line that was relatively easy to defend; Israel would be in a position to demobilize part of the reserves and would not have to worry about a war of attrition on the bank of the canal; Egypt would have the siege of the Third Army lifted, and would retain its territorial gains on the east side of the canal.

In more general terms, the observance, rather than the nonobservance of the agreement, would be Egypt's trump card in the short run. Should Israel refuse to continue negotiations after a reasonable period of time had elapsed—a year, as Kissinger told the Israelis—it would find itself in renewed difficulties with the United States. The Israelis could hope that they might extract real political gains from the forthcoming round in 1975, in exchange for the Sinai passes.

The Israelis did not think that formal American guarantees approved by Congress were necessary; if Cairo breached the agreement with Soviet help, American assistance would, it was thought, be forthcoming as a matter of course. Nixon's secret guarantees to the Saigon regime had not yet been tested, so there were no negative precedents to disturb Jerusalem's thinking. Furthermore, the Israelis still regarded the American president's role in the making of foreign policy as decisive.

Kissinger now had to deal with the problems on the Syrian front with Israel, and the situation was different. The Syrian attitude to Israel, stemming as it did from the internal ideological and political logic of the Ba'athist regime, was radically hostile. At the same time, Damascus showed no sign of renouncing its close ties with the U.S.S.R. Syria had, moreover, made no territorial gains in the October fighting and had in fact lost ground. There was little incentive for Israel to make any great concessions. Still, the Syrians were capable of enlisting the support of other Arab states, such as Saudi Arabia, and of exerting pressure on Egypt. Kissinger held the key to any Syrian territorial gains—his leverage on Israel, which had reached an interim agreement that satisfied Egypt's national demands. Thus Syria had to consider the possibility of becoming isolated from Cairo if it insisted upon radical aims at once.

Kissinger seems to have thought of compensating the U.S.S.R. elsewhere, outside the Middle East. This compensation might take the form of economic, technological, and commercial concessions provided for in the foreign trade bill that was blocked by the Jackson amendment.[40] The SALT, MBFR (Mutual and Balanced Forces Reduction), and the European security conference talks were to be continued in spite of Soviet behavior in the Middle East. It seems that Washington developed a more limited concept of détente as a result of the Middle East war. The "global package deal" was abandoned for a "controlled competition" in the Middle East, in accordance with the interests of former Soviet clients, mainly Egypt, and with their actual wishes in the negotiating process. Formally the U.S.S.R. could not argue against this, as it had helped the same client outside the "spirit" of détente. Yet, Washington did not return to the cold war. On the contrary, it maintained its dialogue with the Soviets on the arms race and in Europe,[41] and tried to pursue the "linkage" approach in the areas of technology and trade. Yet, the Jackson amendment continued to block the trade agreement, and in the meantime Soviet patience with regard to the trade bill was running out.[42]

THE FALL OF THE DAYAN-MEIR CABINET

The continuing hostilities on the Syrian front (Damascus launched a war of attrition in February, 1974) became of great concern in the regional and global context. Sadat was anxious for a Syrian-Israeli agreement to be concluded to release him from his uncomfortable and exposed position as the only Arab leader to have signed an agreement with the Israelis since the October war. He encouraged Kissinger to try to bring about a Syrian-Israeli disengagement agreement.

King Faisal of Saudi Arabia was also an interested party, as he was the key actor in the oil embargo that continued to wreak political and psychological havoc in the West. The Saudis wanted to lift the embargo formally but also wanted a substantial political gain by doing so, namely, another Israeli withdrawal from Arab lands.

The Syrian-Israeli negotiations were important for the Soviets too. They were becoming increasingly worried about America's exclusive role in directing the postwar course of events in the Middle East. They had agreed to Kissinger's solo performance in engineering the Egyptian-Israeli accord because they had no other choice. Now they were worried that a repeat performance on the Syrian front might lessen their influence in Damascus. Moscow's greater anxiety led to several visits to Syria by Foreign Minister Gromyko and to a meeting between Kissinger and Gromyko on Cyprus to create the appearance of Soviet-American cooperation.[43]

Kissinger was aware of the anxious spectators watching the Syrian-Israeli talks from the sidelines and tried to deal in form or substance or both with the problems they raised. He met with Gromyko and made visits to Egypt, Saudi Arabia, and Jordan. In Amman the secretary of state tried to allay King Hussein's anxieties at being left out of the negotiating process but did not make any concrete proposals.

Another factor that affected the timing and conduct of the negotiations was the political crisis in Israel. The popular disenchantment with the Meir-Dayan government calmed somewhat before the national elections of December, and enabled Meir to start negotiations on the formulation of a new coalition in January, and to conclude, in the meantime, the interim agreement with Egypt. This agreement brought about the demobilization of a large part of the Israeli reserve army. After the initial shock of the surprise attack and the three weeks of war in which several habits, legends, expectations, and past experiences had to be abandoned or at least reconsidered, many reserve soldiers, who had served almost six months in the field, became politically active. The national elections did not reflect the antiestablishment mood of these groups, because at the time they voted for established parties, largely in the context of a possible settlement with Egypt, and possibly also with Jordan, or at least in relation to their demobilization. As a result, the alignment, which promised a peace conference and a less militant formula for future compromises with the Arabs than the right-wing Likud opposition, was able to remain in power. But once the Geneva Conference yielded no peace and only an interim agreement had been signed (which was vehemently attacked by the Likud[44] as an Israeli renunciation of a position of strength with nothing in return), and the reserves were demobilized as a result, many reservists were free to criticize both the "blunder" of the war itself and the interim agreement. Most of them, however, were still concerned with the outbreak and the conduct of the war. Popular criticism against Dayan mounted daily, despite the Agranat Commission of Inquiry, which started its work in November. Dayan was physically assaulted several times by the relatives of the fallen; very quickly Meir and her foreign minister, Eban, who in fact had no influence upon Israel's foreign policy under Meir, and sometimes the minister without portfolio, Galili, were nicknamed "the blunder government." Dayan's personal and political party opponents, such as finance minister Sapir, would have preferred to get rid of him altogether. Yet Meir realized that if Dayan fell, she would become the next target for public criticism, because the defense minister's resignation would not solve Israel's domestic and foreign political problems. At the same time she respected his cleverness and alert mind and agreed with his strategy as a negotiator, remembering his unshaken control over the Rafi faction of the alignment. Doing away with Dayan would mean an internal party dispute that might end with a split: Rafi might walk out and join the Likud, thus making the rightist opposition, for the first time, a real candidate for power in Israel, also influenced by the swing to the right in the NRP since 1968. If the "hawkish" Rafi left, the NRP might regard this as a change toward a "dovish" coalition in which the religious party would remain in the minority.

The popular argument against Dayan was that he was "parliamentarily responsible" for the preparedness of the army and morally responsible for the psychological and political background that led the Israelis to believe that no war was expected "in ten years." Yet the formal argument concerning Dayan's parliamentary responsibility was far from the traditional truth. Israel never developed a concept of sole responsibility in public affairs. The cabinet as a whole was responsible, and even the prime minister could not be personally regarded as responsible. Moreover, there was never a clear-cut chain of command in military affairs after Ben-Gurion, who had combined both the offices of prime minister and minister of defense by his strong personal position and uncollegial methods. But even then there was no single commander in chief of the Israeli armed forces, but only the cabinet as a whole. The chief of staff was nominated by the cabinet. The defense minister was formally subjected to it before the October, 1973, war, and more so when the outbreak of the hostilities and the failure of the first counterattack shattered his position internally and publicly. Dayan tried to capitalize on these formal traditions, and bluntly refused to resign. Under these circumstances, he retained his marginal influence over the alignment's party leadership, which would not risk an open breach with him because of his key parliamentary position and his close cooperation, in substance, with Meir after the initial shock was over. However, Dayan was openly criticized by secondary Mapai leaders and the public.

In March, 1974, Dayan announced his decision not to join Meir's new coalition. Because Dayan asked for it under heavy public pressure, his Rafi followers could not blame the alignment's majority for removing their leader from the cabinet on the grounds of a substantial foreign policy issue dispute and did not expect Mapai to beg him to join. For a while it seemed that Dayan had maneuvered himself out of the cabinet without any political gains, and with no substantive excuse for Rafi to leave the alignment. Meir, under these circumstances, did not ask him to stay, and neither could the NRP follow Dayan to a new coalition, because his case seemed to be related to his "parliamentary responsibility" for the war rather than to his policy toward the West Bank, which most of the NRP shared with him.

The alignment's majority, mainly old Mapai's leaders, were again in a dilemma as to who should replace a key minister influential in foreign and defense matters; they had no candidate of their own. Yitzhak Rabin, a former chief of staff and ambassador to Washington, and a protégé of Achdut Ha'Avoda, Mapai's closest ally, had returned to Israel before the war, hoping for a minor cabinet job. He was hastily presented by the two factions as their candidate, because he had no connection with the October war. Rabin's candidacy reflected two established facts: first, no civilian, without reputation and experience in defense matters, dared to assume the position of minister of defense; second, even an outsider, who did not formally belong to any internal party grouping but was regarded as "clean" and free from the Yom Kippur "blunder," was preferable to the shaken alignment majority.

Dayan understood his mistake, and announced his decision to join the government. Yet his public position was affected even more; he used an intelligence report on a possible attack along the Golan front to explain his decision.[45] Dayan also had hopes that the inquiry commission under Chief Justice Agranat would clear him. In April the commission published an interim report, which cleared Meir and Dayan from "immediate responsibility" for the mobilization, or rather the decision not to mobilize in time, because both lacked an independent source of information and depended on the army intelligence. The commission felt, however, that it should not deal with the broader aspects of policy, strategy, and preparedness, returning the issue to the political institutions to be dealt with.[46] At the same time, it explicitly blamed chief of staff Elazar and the chief of the army intelligence branch for the intelligence failure and lack of preparedness along the front lines, and praised Elazar for the conduct of the war later. The chief of staff immediately resigned, but his half-cleared political superior remained in office. The commission continued its work, though the basic political and strategic questions remained unanswered; no other procedure to deal with them elsewhere was opened.

Public debates and protests movements filled this vacuum. Scenes, reminiscent of the street rallies of June, 1967, which had forced Dayan, with the support of hysterical party bodies, upon Prime Minister Eshkol, were now reversed against him.[47] Lower-echelon Mapai leaders, with the passive consent of Dayan's opponent, Yigal Allon, who was more moderate than his Achdut Ha'Avoda colleague, Galili, demanded Dayan's resignation.

Criticism engulfed Meir. Because the Agranat Commission left the question open, she was held "parliamentarily responsible," with Dayan, for the nonmobilization decision of October 3, 1973. The fact that her senior ministers, and not the whole cabinet, had made this decision was described by her personal opponent, Shulamit Aloni of the Civil Rights Movement, as a contributing factor to the content of the decision. Her continued cooperation with Dayan after the war caused Meir public political damage and shattered her authority over the lower-echelon Mapai leaders, who mostly held a moderate approach to foreign affairs and resented her continued alliance with the Rafi leader. Dayan's relative flexibility toward Sadat's demands in 1971, as opposed to Meir's less compromising position, was not forgotten, but it discredited Meir in the eyes of the moderates and did not help Dayan out of the October, 1973, events. Moreover, Meir was described by the protest movements as a symbol of a closed, almost semiauthoritarian elite regime, which refrained from holding primaries for party offices and controlled the party organization from above, thus contributing to a power euphoria also in foreign and defense affairs. This argument was at least oversimplistic, since it mixed military preparedness with the party regime and the cabinet decision making procedure. Moreover, Meir and Dayan shaped public opinion and were shaped by it in return. They were very alert to the public mood in foreign affairs. The structure of their regime produced, of course, the very political and diplomatic deadlock that led to the war, but the mixture of "hawkish-conservative" postulates with old bargaining habits could be attributed to Mapai's Sapir by the same token, and a foreign political alternative had to be suggested. Yet public criticism remained vague and general as to a better foreign policy. Criticism was directed more against structures and forms of policy making and against personalities, but basically the deep cleavage between "hawks" and "doves" remained.

Since January, 1974, the "hawkish" approach had temporarily lost some of its ideological, nationalistic character, and had assumed a typical conservative power-security approach to foreign affairs. The traditional Israeli fear of the Arabs made many no more ready for far-reaching concessions. As expected, the criticism of the alignment's regime, and mainly of the party's apparatus and *apparatchiks* (party functionaries), damaged Dayan's most outspoken opponent, the party's strongman, Pinhas Sapir, who held moderate views in foreign affairs. It reduced his influence considerably, just when Meir, his choice for the premiership in 1968, began rapidly to lose hers. Both of them were losing their party and public support. Whereas Dayan was able to continue to control his small minority faction, which remained loyal to him personally, and a relatively closed power grouping made up mostly of "hawks," Meir's support in Mapai, the larger, less cohesive grouping, could not be maintained under an attack against the structure of the party, the decision making system in her cabinet, and Meir's "parliamentary" responsibility for the war. After some maneuvering, Meir announced her resignation on April 11, 1974. Facing Ben-Gurion's dilemma when he lost both his dominating public position and his primacy in the party, Meir, who had never held that kind of predominance, was unable to force Dayan alone out of the government, but was also unable to rule with him. Criticized by lower echelon Mapai leaders, Achdut Ha'Avoda leaders, and Mapai "doves" alike because of her alliance with him, Meir preferred simply to quit. The party's strongman, Sapir, preferred to resign too. He could have become prime minister himself, but public criticism against his party regime was now combined with criticism against his economic policy, and he, of course, did not enjoy Rafi's support. The economic expansion before the war, which was financed largely through inflationary measures and imported capital, deepened social differences, while trying to retain some egalitarian principles and to raise the standard of living in the lower strata. The outcome was a new money elite, a less efficient public service system, a deficit budget, and a low rate of productivity. Yet the money elite, the flourishing consumer market that was created for them, and the general rush for better living that became a by-product of this system were now described by the protest movements and by many individuals who were eagerly a part of it, as partially responsible for the lack of preparedness before the war.

The Central Party Committee, with Sapir in his last role as Mapai's boss, was summoned to elect a candidate for the premiership and for the post of the minister of defense. Meir's resignation forced Dayan to follow her. Had he remained, his position as the one key public figure left who had been held responsible for the "blunder" would have become intolerable publicly, and his influence, always based on both his public's support and his parliamentary power base, would have been considerably reduced. As an outsider, he might profit by the mistakes of the new government. Dayan was forced to declare his personal wish to stay out of the government, while Rafi as a whole remained in the alignment. Dayan himself would retain his parliamentary seat, but Rafi's cabinet representation passed to Peres and a younger Rafi politician.

Shimon Peres, until now Dayan's junior partner in the Rafi leadership, sensed the vacuum in the alignment, and offered himself for the premiership. The old Mapai leaders were strong enough to prevent a Rafi man from this; they still could mobilize a marginal majority for Yitzhak Rabin, who advanced from the Defense Ministry offer to the prime minister's office because no other candidate in Mapai qualified for defense and foreign policy making in the traditional sense.

The regime was not changed, as the protest movements demanded, but substantive personal changes were agreed upon. The public storm calmed again; the changes were enough, at least for the time being, for the silent majority. This majority did not organize itself in new political formations, but joined the protest movements passively and sometimes actively in its demands for punishment of those responsible for the "blunder." When Meir and Dayan resigned, popular support for the protest movements, which had remained loose, ad hoc organizations, diminished rapidly, and after a while most of those groups disappeared. The demands for more active party and popular participation in the political process seemed to have been fulfilled by the vote in the alignment's Central Committee. Rabin, an outsider who was challenged by another competitor, won; Peres ably mobilized a much larger number of supporters than his Rafi constituency would have given him, because of the relative weakness of the party apparatus, Peres's own tactical skill, and efficient public appearance. Thus, for the first time in Israel, something like a primary took place before a candidate for the highest state office assumed responsibility. The basic features of the regime remained unchanged, as party blocks and their parliamentary representation had been elected in December, 1973, the collegial cabinet remained and the new elite was even more sensitive to public opinion and opinion makers than the former leadership, though it lacked an established public record. The prime minister was relatively unknown. He had no power base of his own in his party, and had to negotiate with the alignment's potential coalition partners first. But until Rabin and Peres (who automatically became defense minister as Rafi's representative when Rabin won the premiership on Mapai's ticket) could start negotiations on a new coalition, Meir's government remained as a caretaker cabinet, and carried on the talks with Syria.

BETWEEN JERUSALEM AND DAMASCUS

Over four months passed from Kissinger's first exploratory visit to Damascus on January 20, 1974, until the agreement was actually signed. The secretary's first visit was unsuccessful, and, at his suggestion, preliminary talks were held in March with high-ranking Israeli and Syrian representatives in Washington.[48] Kissinger talked with each delegation separately. The discussions, however, proved unproductive, so Kissinger decided that a round of shuttle diplomacy was in order. The shuttle lasted 32 days, and the agreement was signed on May 31, 1974.

When Syria failed to enlist the support of a united Arab front to try and force a total Israeli withdrawal, or at least an Israeli commitment to total withdrawal, including a major gain for the Palestinians, it became more amenable to the idea of an interim agreement. Syria had come out of the October war at a clear territorial disadvantage, with apparently none of the military bargaining advantages that Egypt had won. Damascus's one trump card seemed to be the Israeli POWs. It refused to produce a list of the prisoners or to allow Red Cross visits to the camps. It hoped to wear down Israel's resistance by a war of nerves and to ensure that Jerusalem would enter substantive negotiations about territory.[49] The Israeli government and public's anxiety over the unknown number and fate of the POWs was painfully obvious; it invited a Syrian attempt to exploit the issue.[50] Syria feared that, since Israel held better territorial bargaining points, it would find a pretext to evade negotiations about withdrawal once it was assured that the prisoners were safe.

Despite their possible anxiety to move the IDF back out of range of Damascus, the Syrians were careful not to display their fears openly and thus invite Israeli or American pressures. The Assad government adopted extreme positions during the talks and allowed them to lurch to the brink of failure before relenting, and then only minimally. The Syrians also fired, parallel to Kissinger's shuttle, artillery barrages against Israeli troops and civilian settlements on the Golan Heights. The continuing casualties and the mobilization of reserves stemming from this helped pressure Israel in favor of an agreement.

Kissinger and, no doubt, the Israelis were never sure what the minimum and maximum Syrian positions were, or what was negotiable and what was not. Thinking of first that the Syrians were following the North Vietnamese model of bargaining,[51] Kissinger pressed Israel to make concessions he considered essential for the continuation of the talks. When Israeli intransigence forced the secretary of state to call Assad's bluff, he found that Syrian concessions were usually forthcoming in order to keep the talks going. The Syrians had no wish to remain isolated against Israel and in a disadvantageous strategic situation, and they could not be sure of Egyptian military support or of joint military action in the event that a deadlock led to new hostilities.

A point in Syria's favor was that Kissinger expected Israel to make concessions similar to those it had made to Egypt, that is, to give up territory in the pre-October, 1973, occupied areas. Still, Syria did not want to follow the Egyptian model of plain bargaining. Israel itself adopted, then, an "oriental bazaar" approach.

The secretary of state's repeated habit or technique was to dwell on what would happen if Israel persisted in a particular course of action and refused to yield to Syrian demands. If there were no agreement, there would be a deterioration of the situation on the Syrian front and possibly a larger war involving Egypt. A new war and a continuation or reimposition of the oil embargo would make Israel's international position (already at a nadir) absolutely intolerable. The world would then use any pretext to force an Israeli withdrawal to the 1949 ADL; America's gains in the region would evaporate and the U.S.S.R. would return, its position enhanced.[52]

The Israelis formulated a set of maximum and minimum objectives—what they would like to achieve and what they had to achieve—and stuck doggedly to these parameters throughout the talks, often in the face of intense pressure from the secretary of state.[53] Israel's basic concerns were the strategic military situation in the Golan and the security of the civilian settlements there. The settlements were, it should be recalled, a major issue of domestic politics; settlement of occupied territories, particularly in the Golan, was the declared policy of the Rafi and Achdut Ha'Avoda factions of the Labor party. It was backed by the National Religious party, a large section of the public, two influential daily newspapers (*Ma'ariv* and *Yediot Aharonot*), and the population of Galilee, which remembered all too well the Syrian bombardments that preceded the 1967 war.[54] The Israeli negotiating team's basic goal was not to agree on any step that would weaken Israel's strategic position on the Heights or threaten the safety of the settlements there. Jerusalem's maximum position called for the entire disengagement and separation of forces to take place inside the salient captured during the October War. Thus, the goals on which the talks eventually concentrated were essentially negative. Israel knew what it did not want to happen in terms of its security and settlements, and it was not overly concerned with the wider issues of the United States' global and even regional position and the oil embargo, which Kissinger constantly asserted were valid considerations for Jerusalem. The Israelis did not expect any serious political concessions from the radical Syria.

An agreement was essential to Israel, however. It needed a respite to rebuild and resupply its armed forces, which the war and the continued mobilization had greatly strained. The POWs were one source of weakness that affected Israel's initial posture in the talks and were the first of the Israeli negotiators' concerns during the talks. The casualties and the continued mobilization of large numbers of reserves resulting from the war of attrition helped make Israel's bargaining position more flexible.

At the preliminary talks in Washington, the Syrians had demanded half of the Israeli-occupied Golan Heights, while the Israelis insisted that the disengagement be carried out entirely in the salient captured in October. Kissinger exerted pressure on Israel to treat Syria more like Egypt and to offer to pull out of land west of the 1967 cease-fire line. Assad tacitly accepted Israel's now somewhat modified proposals as a basis for bargaining once the negotiations began.[55]

The first touchy point in the negotiations over the depth of the Israeli withdrawal was the town of Kuneitra, which was one of Syria's major political goals in the bargaining process. Kuneitra was the regional capital of the Golan and from 1949 to 1967 had been the headquarters of the Syrian army's southern command. The town was deserted and in almost complete ruins following the fighting in 1967 and 1973. In addition to Kuneitra, Syria demanded the three hills overlooking the town and more Israeli concessions beyond the 1967 cease-fire line, including several formerly Syrian villages captured in 1967.

It took a great deal of prodding by Washington to get Jerusalem to agree, informally at first and then formally, to discuss withdrawals beyond the 1967 line. Once he opened this wedge, Kissinger came down forcefully on Assad's side, demanding an Israeli pullback from Kuneitra, the hills, the villages, and along the entire 1967 line. At first Israel was willing to give up only part of Kuneitra, and to partition the ghost town. The Israeli team refused to consider a withdrawal to a line parallel to the old one in the Golan, and was especially stubborn about the three hills. Either move would have clearly endangered the civilian settlements in the area, but ceding the hills would also have meant abandoning an important strategic position. The hills were essential to the maintenance or achievement of military control of the Golan. Kuneitra was of negligible strategic value to Israel but had prestige value for Syria, so Jerusalem was willing to cede the town, but bargained hard on its partition first, in order to avoid bargaining on the hills and the entire line.

Kissinger set a deadline for the completion of the talks, and Syria made its demands in the form of an ultimatum. The Israeli cabinet met to reconsider their position.[56] Kissinger was exasperated with the Israelis' narrow concern for the settlements and the military balance in the Golan. He stressed repeatedly that neither the United States nor any other country supported Israel's settlement policy and that an agreement was Israel's best guarantee of security because it would neutralize the Syrian military option, for the time being at least. He constantly denigrated the strategic importance of the hills, calling them "Gur's Himalayas" after the Israeli chief of staff.

The turning point in the talks came when Israel agreed in principle to cede all of Kuneitra plus one village. In return, it demanded that Syria drop the demands for the hills and the other villages and accept a very limited pullback beyond the salient captured in October, 1973. At the same time, Syria should begin meaningful discussions on force reductions, disengagement zones, and the like. Kissinger was not satisfied and demanded greater concessions in the Kuneitra area, including the hills. The problem of Kuneitra and the hills was resolved when Israel agreed to withdraw 150 meters from Kuneitra and to have the least significant of the hills included in the U.N. demilitarized zone. Syria dropped its demand for an Israeli withdrawal from the other two hills, but secured an Israeli promise and an American guarantee that no heavy weapons would be placed there to threaten the town.

The next phase of shuttle diplomacy was devoted to discussions of the disengagement zones, mutual force reductions, the U.N. role, and terrorist activities. Futhermore, although the issue had apparently been closed, Syria made new territorial demands. An Israeli proposal for the separation and reduction of forces served as the basis for the discussions. The original plan called for a U.N. buffer zone flanked by reduced force zones. Each party's reduced force zones would be divided into two. The limited forces zone closest to the United Nations buffer would be ten kilometers wide, and the second zone fifteen kilometers wide. Heavy artillery and surface-to-air missile installations were not to be permitted in the limited force areas. The level of forces permitted in the zones would be adequate for defensive purposes. It was Israel's interest to keep the force levels low in order to prevent a massive Syrian surprise attack, but not so low as to deprive itself of the capacity to withstand an attack and to keep from being swept off the Heights.[57]

The issue of U.N. presence in the buffer zone proved to be relatively easy to handle, though some unexpected Syrian demands did crop up. Israel initially sought 3000 to 5000 U.N. troops, while Syria wanted only 500. This wide gap stemmed in part from the differing conceptions of the U.N. role held by each side. Syria wanted the U.N. presence to bear the label of "disengagement observers" instead of "U.N. force." This demand was due partly to Syrian sensitivity about its sovereignty in the buffer zone and partly to its desire for the U.N. to play a lesser role in the field as a human barrier between itself and Israel. Israel wanted a larger number of U.N. troops to serve as a physical and a political obstacle of significance to the Syrians should they surprise attack Israel again and to ensure that they could perform their job of supervision properly. The parties eventually compromised on 1250 U.N. troops and decided that they would perform the same functions as the U.N. force in the Sinai agreement but would bear a different name, the U.N. Disengagement Observer Force (UNDOF).[58]

A last minute crisis erupted over an Israeli demand that Syria undertake to prevent terrorist activities being launched from its territory. Here, as in other provisions of the agreement, Israel's concern was for the safety of the Golan settlements. Syria argued that because of its commitment to the Palestinian cause it could not assume such an obligation either publicly or privately. Israel refused to relent, however, and a compromise was reached: Israel would be able to retaliate against terrorist activities launched from Syrian territory, and the United States would not regard the retaliations as violations of the cease-fire provisions of the agreement.

Kissinger described the Syrian-Israeli round of talks as the last one before full peace negotiations. He also said that the Israelis would not have to make any more concessions for a long time because of the fundamental difficulties in reaching a final Syrian-Israeli settlement. He concluded that one should always negotiate with Damascus from a position of strength.

CHANGES IN THE ARAB COALITION, 1974–75

After the Syrian round of talks, in early June of 1974, the Arab oil ministers formally agreed to lift the oil embargo.[59] Kissinger could then attend a NATO conference in Ottawa and meet his European colleagues in Brussels in a much improved atmosphere.[60] I cannot, of course, treat the energy crisis and its global economic ramifications in any depth here, but it should be mentioned that the various western countries were each affected differently by the oil price increase, which turned out to be the most important problem after the boycott and the immediate supply problems. Because of its own resources and the domestic price of oil, the United States could better accept the substantial rise in the international price. Western European countries suffered serious balance of payments deficits and their exports declined while domestic demand also dropped in some sensitive sectors. The United States could thus reassume the economic leadership of the West, because no European country could match American financial capabilities and relative independence from Arab oil. The new situation in the West was connected to political relations between some (conservative) Arab oil producers and Washington regarding the Middle East conflict. Saudi Arabia, the wealthiest Arab state, where the largest proven reserves of crude oil in the world were located, began accumulating a huge surplus of capital that could not be invested in Saudi Arabi itself. The smaller gulf states, such as Kuwait, were in a similar situation. Other Arab producers, particularly Iraq and Algeria, were committed to large-scale development schemes and military expansion that absorbed the new financial resources. Iran, leading the non-Arab member of OPEC, was also able to spend everything it earned. OAPEC, the Arab members of the international oil cartel, was thus divided into two economic groups, Iraq, Algeria, and, to a lesser degree, Libya, which, because of its monetary reserves, could afford some periods of lower production, were interested in the highest prices obtainable. Saudi Arabia, however, was less interested in converting its natural resources into money that could not be invested in national development projects and whose values was constantly being eroded by inflation. Iran wanted to sell as much as possible at the highest prices possible. Through cooperation with Riadh, Washington could hope to secure Saudi help in restraining the prices for its own, and its allies', benefit. Politically, Saudi Arabia retained its American orientation, but was also committed to the general Arab and Palestinian cause; Saudi policy laid particular emphasis on the exclusive Arab right to East Jerusalem.

As early as January–February, 1974, Washington made it known that it was trying to set up a "western axis in the Middle East" that would link Cairo, Riyadh, and Teheran.[61] The creation of such a system would purportedly help relax tension in the entire region by linking the changing Egyptian-Israeli relationship to inducements to Egypt to concentrate more on domestic development with the help of Saudi and Iranian investments and American aid. The United States' role would involve financial guarantees, technical know-how, direct food aid, and budgetary financing. David Rockefeller, the president of the Chase Manhattan Bank, had discussions about this in Cairo and Riyadh in February and March of 1974.[62]

Thus Egypt, once the political and military leader of the Arab world, would develop working "linkages" with the emerging economic power, Saudi Arabia, to the benefit of Egypt's "internal structures," and Saudi surplus money, with some Iranian aid, would be invested in Egypt's economy. The recycling of Arab oil money, now the major international economic problem, would be enhanced by such arrangements, including Arab purchases of western goods and technologies and Arab investments in the West. The Saudis themselves, on the other hand, seemed ready to support Egypt, but extended limited economic aid, while embarking upon a giant economic and military program themselves. In Israeli perceptions, Riyadh's interests always lay in preventing its erstwhile enemy, Egypt, which has the potential to dominate the Arabian Peninsula, from becoming overly strong, economically and militarily. It was in Riydah's interest to divert Cairo's attention elsewhere. Furthermore, as the most conservative rulers in the Arab coalition, the Saudi royal family had to fear the radical elements in the Arab world and so find common grounds with them, perhaps by extending political support, financial support, and military aid to Syrian and the various PLO groupings.

The Israelis became increasingly suspicious when the Cairo-Riyadh-Teheran axis was mentioned to them as a "structural-functional" change in the Arab coalition. As before, they feared the "high political" logics of the different Arab regimes and thought the common Arab political cause against Israel to be by far more dominating in Arab national and coalition politics. Saudi Arabia's emergence as a new Arab power did not calm Israeli fears; on the contrary, they noted enormous Saudi weapon purchases in the West after mid-1974 with growing anxiety. In the meantime, the PLO, backed primarily by Syria, was pursuing official inter-Arab recognition as "the sole representative of the Palestinian people," trying to gain an internationally recognized status.

In September, 1974, Egypt, Syria, and the PLO issued a communiqué in Cairo, recognizing the PLO as the sole representative of the Palestinian people. Yet Jordan turned down an invitation to join the Cairo talks, thus challenging the "sole representation" doctrine. Particularly after the Six-Day War, the Hashemite regime had had close ties with Saudi Arabia because of their common traditionalism and pro-western leanings. In its relations with Cairo and Damascus, Amman had to strike a delicate balance between Hashemite interests and the interests of the Trans-Jordanian Bedouin population, on the one hand, and the regime's view of itself as the guardian of the Palestinians in Trans-Jordan, the West Bank, and the Gaza Strip on the other. Jordan wished to maintain its position as one of Israel's bargaining partners, but it also had to take into account the attitude of the other Arab states toward the PLO.

King Hussein was totally opposed to the PLO. After the September, 1970, bloodbath and the expulsion of the various elements of the PLO from Jordan, the king saw the Palestinian organizations as competitors for his claim to the West Bank, Jerusalem, and the Gaza Strip as well as a challenge to his authority over the East Bank. They could demand a foothold there in order to carry on the war against Israel or they might try to take over Trans-Jordan in the name of its past Palestinian heritage and of its Palestinian inhabitants, who by the late 1960s constituted about 50 percent of the area's population. In Israeli perceptions, the east bank Palestinians were, to a growing extent, middle-class people, well established in the country, opposed to the radicalism of the PLO, and loyal to the Hashemite regime. Their preference became clear when they rejected the PLO in 1970 in favor of the strong, established rule of Jordan's Bedouin army and of Hashemite law and order. Until 1970, the most fertile ground for the Palestinian organizations in Jordan had been the refugees who had fled the West Bank after the Israeli conquest. After September, 1970, the political influence of this group was neutralized, and Hussein would still have been happy to repatriate them to a Hashemite-ruled West Bank as soon as possible.

The differences between Jordan and the PLO were the cause of much diplomatic activity in Cairo during 1974. Sadat tried a number of formulas to keep Jordan from being deprived of its status as a claimant against Israel; Jordan had the advantage, in Sadat's view, of being a sovereign state with belligerent rights vis-à-vis Israel since 1967. Furthermore, much of the world, particularly the West, recognized Amman's role in the West Bank. On the other hand, the Egyptians wanted the PLO to be the de facto claimant—a status which could be interpreted as being the exclusive claimant—to the land Israel should evacuate in the West Bank and Gaza. The formulas Egypt adopted regarding the PLO and Jordan were contradictory, until October, 1974.[63] By then Egypt seemed to have officially adopted a final Palestinian doctrine: the PLO was to be the sole representative of the Palestinian people outside the east bank of the Jordan River, i.e., the territory under the direct Hashemite rule. A Palestinian state should be created as a part of a solution to the Arab-Israeli conflict. The territory of that state should, for all practical purposes, be comprised of the Israeli-occupied West Bank and the Gaza Strip, since Israel's pre-1967 borders were internationally recognized as such also by the Soviet Union.

The PLO itself did not renounce its claims to Palestine as a whole, but set forth to enhance its international position with inter-Arab support. During October it achieved a practical observer status in the U.N. General Assembly, where Arafat repeated the official doctrine on the future of Palestine as a "democratic and secular" (i.e., non-Jewish) state to be ruled by a repatriated Arab majority. Syria seemed to have endorsed the third state doctrine, coupled with immediate Israeli withdrawals to the 1967 lines. Iraq, Libya, and Algeria gave the PLO "secular state" doctrine firm public support. Washington was considering a new step in its Middle East strategy: an Israeli partial withdrawal from the West Bank, which might strengthen Hussein's position in the Arab coalition.

THE STEP-BY-STEP STRATEGY: THE MIDDLE STAGE, JUNE, 1974–MARCH, 1975

On June 12, 1974, President Nixon began a tour of the Middle East and visited Egypt, Israel, Syria, and Jordan. Whatever the status of his administration in the United States, Nixon's visit reflected the introduction of new elements into the relations among Washington, Cairo, Damascus, and Jerusalem after the Yom Kippur War.[64]

According to information received in Israel immediately after the tour,[65] Nixon had promised Sadat and Assad that Israel would withdraw completely from their countries.[66] This view constituted a reversion to the policy maintained by every administration since the 1968 Rusk Plan. As we have seen, for various reasons, this policy was never carried out. Nixon himself had tried a number of approaches to the problem; for a time he had responded to the cooperation of key Arab states with the Soviet Union backing a "strong Israel" policy. America's position on the desirable borders in the region had never changed, but there was now a qualitative change in its relations with key members of the Arab coalition in terms of the overall strategic framework of the American foreign relations. The operational framework for U.S. policy continued to be the step-by-step approach, and until after March, 1975, shuttle diplomacy continued to be the method by which it was accomplished.

Nixon told his interlocutors in Jerusalem that there was no returning to the status quo ante bellum, and that Washington would not tolerate a political and diplomatic deadlock that could lead to war and to the end of the process set in motion after the October 22 cease-fire. In other words, the United States was not about to risk losing the gains it had made so that the Soviet Union might recover its earlier position.

Nixon stressed that, with the disengagement agreements with Egypt and Syria out of the way, it was time for a similar arrangement with Jordan. Unless an agreement was reached on the Jordanian front, Hussein's standing in the Arab world as a partner to the negotiations with Israel would be weakened, and the Soviet-backed PLO's standing would be enhanced. The deal with Amman would be followed by a second round with Cairo and Damascus.

To soften the blow, Nixon offered Israel more economic and military aid, American investments, and economic and commercial cooperation. Israel, whose economy had been in poor shape before the war, was now totally dependent on American financial aid. Furthermore, one of the lessons the IDF learned from the 1973 war was that it needed more American arms of all types. Sometimes, American arms aid did not suffice for the United States to retain enough control over Israel. Instead, Israel succeeded or did not succeed in obtaining arms by a very complex set of domestic and American-Soviet and Soviet-Arab considerations. The case was the same with Egypt and the U.S.S.R. Economic aid seemed to have created a new leverage, for unlike arms, which could be stocked until war broke out, economic aid to Israel would be consumed almost immediately. The president also spoke of supplying nuclear reactors for peaceful purposes to both Egypt and Israel. Jerusalem tended not to oppose the idea, so as not to drive Cairo to turn to Moscow or Paris for nuclear development assistance.

Apparently, the Israeli government took the same approach to the nuclear option, as far as the majority was concerned, as it did before Dayan's appointment to the Defense Ministry in 1967; that is, it was very skeptical about its deterrent value, and seems to have viewed that option as "a last resort bomb in the basement," whose military deterrent value was nullified when the other side chose not to be deterred. The political dangers to Israel were obvious. This option did not rule out the possibility of limited war. Conventional arms and the occupied territories became even more important from a purely military standpoint in the view of the new defense establishment.[67] The occupied territories were still regarded as Israel's greatest political asset, making possible negotiations with the Arabs and the United States in order to retain and/or change Israel's position in the Middle East: to make the Arabs change their attitude to Israel's right to exist in borders it thought suitable and to extract aid from the United States. The West Bank of particular importance, lying as it did along Israel's vulnerable heartland. The domestic sensitivity of the territorial issue was undiminished in Israel. Indeed, with the changes in the Israeli government and the rise of a new weak leadership group sensitive to criticism inside and outside the cabinet, the importance of the territories in domestic politics rose. Moreover, as Geneva proved to be a diplomatic trick, the PLO was suddenly admitted as an active partner to U.N. deliberations, and American pressure was mounting for concessions in the West Bank, amid daily diplomatic-political gains for the PLO in Western Europe, very many Israelis developed their old, holocaust-inspired siege syndrome. "The World," which until October, 1973, was not ready to negotiate with the PLO and denounced its "Nazi" covenant and terrorist acts, and did not try to force Israel out of the West Bank because of Arab intransigence, was now ready to sacrifice Israeli security interest and ideological-historical claims in favor of the PLO or Hussein, who might later be forced by the Arab coalition to yield these concessions to the PLO anyway.

This "crisis of the West" was manifested in Western Europe and Japan's modification of attitude toward the PLO (inspired by France) and Kissinger's pressure on Israel to make concessions to Hussein. Coupled with oil interests and Israeli perceptions of a strong Soviet block, it was perceived by right-wing publicists like Eliezer Livne as a moral crisis of the western middle class culture, which social Zionism deplored and tried to set an ideological alternative to. Livne's arguments in the popular afternoon press, even if they were derived from his experience with western and central European Jewish experience in the 1920s, were falling on a fertile public soil. The protest movements, which represented an antiestablishment mood outside the political parties in connection with the war "blunder" and a vague rejection of a closed elite and a bargaining regime, never succeeded in becoming a political factor themselves, yet they played a part in bringing Dayan and Meir down in early 1974, then disintegrated afterwards. Their role was taken, in a way, by another grouping—Gush Emunim—the militant religious and nationalistic movement operating outside the parliamentary and party political framework, yet closely associated with the radical NRP wing and some Rafi and Herut circles. Gush Emunim wanted to offer a moral-historical-religious alternative to domestic bargainers and power politicians without enough faith and moral-religious substance, and to show the "materialistic, Christian West" its moral-religious substance, demonstrated also in forming religious settlements in the whole West Bank and Golan Heights. Its illegal settlement efforts gained a growing public support after mid-1974. The coalition had, thus, to reckon with Gush Emunim's actions and popularity, which was enhanced by the decline of the alignment and protest movements.

After Nixon's departure, discussions were held to clarify a number of issues, including the West Bank problem. In the midst of these talks, on August 8, 1974, Nixon resigned and Gerald Ford became president. In Israel the new government took office on June 3 with Yitzhak Rabin as prime minister, Shimon Peres as defense minister, and Yigal Allon as foreign minister.[68] Israel Galili, the minister without portfolio who had helped Meir formulate her foreign policy, retained a role as adviser to the prime minister.

Rabin had been appointed to the office by the central committee of the alignment, with only a slim majority over his nearest rival, Shimon Peres, who was appointed to the defense ministry. Yigal Allon, regarded as Rabin's patron from the days as his commander in the underground Palmach, and who represented the relatively small Achdut Ha'Avoda faction, became foreign minister. Despite their personal connection, Rabin avoided being identified with Achdut Ha'Avoda or with Allon personally. He chose to follow a line midway between Peres and Allon, who developed a more moderate stance than most of his faction, but Rabin could not rely on the old Mapai machine that had backed his predecessors so efficiently. The Labor strongman, Pinhas Sapir, resigned from the government when Meir did and would not return to office. With him went his vast network of personal connections and his party control over some sectors of the economy. For the first time, Mapai did not nominate one of its number to office of prime minister and instead accepted an outsider who had made a reputation for himself as a soldier and a diplomat but was a member neither of Rafi nor of Mapai itself. The military reputation was challenged by Herut's General Ezer Weizman, Rabin's deputy during the 1967 crisis. Weizman published his version of Rabin's apparent collapse in May, 1967, which had, at first, a boomerang effect: it drew public and party sympathy for Rabin in and outside Labor.

Rabin's main concern on assuming office was to gain time to consolidate his grip on power. He had no interest in negotiating with Jordan; such talks could only lead to dissension within the party. For example, his new colleague and erstwhile opponent, Peres, held views about the West Bank not very different from Dayan's—that Israel should continue to rule the territory for reasons of security and ideology and perhaps should offer the Jordanians some share in responsibility for the Arabs there, without any direct territorial presence.[69] Some formal ties might be suggested to Amman and West Bank Arabs might maintain their informal economic relations with Amman.

Rabin and Galili both regarded the government's parliamentary base as too narrow. The National Religious party refused to join the coalition; the party's aggressive younger members of the Knesset, led by Zevulun Hammer and Yehuda Ben-Meir, were able to keep the party out of the coalition by refusing to concede their demands on religious issues or on the formation of a national unity government, that is, a wall-to-wall coalition, which would include the right-wing Likud block and would automatically strengthen the weight of the "hawks" in the cabinet.[70] Rabin's slim majority was dependent on the support of the Independent Liberals and Shulamit Aloni's Citizen's Rights Movement, a small, new liberal "anticlericalist" party that held moderate views on foreign policy. Rabin could have tried, in Ben Gurion's tradition, a bold maneuver: since Dayan, the most extreme "hawk" in the Rafi faction, was practically neutralized for the time being as a public figure, and since two other Rafi members joined the cabinet, thus developing vested interests in the new coalition, the others, no longer subjected to Dayan's strong influence and predominance as their faction's leader, were divided on foreign policy issues, and Rabin could have tried to force Dayan out of the alignment altogether. Rabin could have used Dayan's "manly responsive" manner and forced him to choose between a rather flaxible formula for future negotiations on the West Bank, which Dayan had announced in advance he would not accept, and a final departure from alignment's politics. The maneuver would have been bold indeed; Mr. Peres would have to choose between a rather "dovish" formula and his defense ministry—a chance to join a Likud-NRP coalition with some Rafi members who would follow the disgraced Dayan—or a chance to remain in the alignment and try to work together with Rabin as the alignment's recognized leader. Rafi would have been eliminated, and the alignment pushed clearly toward a "dovish" approach to future negotiations with Egypt, Jordan, and Syria. A clear-cut distinction would have been created between the Likud and

NRP right wing members (and Dayan) and the alignment. Rabin accepted the alignment's framework as given.

Rabin and Galili, following the post-Ben-Gurionite style of broad-based coalitions, did not want to alienate the NRP, so negotiations with Jordan were out of the question, because of this party's sensitivity to any withdrawal there. Furthermore, the prime minister publicly committed himself to bring any agreement on the West Bank to the nation for approval by calling a general election. This public promise was also aimed at the United States; Rabin was warning the Americans that negotiations with Jordan might lead to an electoral victory for the right and the formation of a government that would be much harder for Washington to handle.

On July 28, 1974, Yigal Allon, the only member of the alignment triumvirate to favor negotiations with Jordan, visited Washington. Allon assumed already in July, 1967, a negative approach to ruling a large Arab population. At the same time he feared that if Israel refused to deal with Jordan, it might well have to deal with the PLO. Kissinger suggested that in an agreement with Amman, Jerusalem would concede a limited area of the West Bank, for example, Jericho and its vicinity, which were of no military significance and had a large Arab population.[71] This notion fit in with Allon's own plan of late 1967, which called for Israel's retention of the strategically important and unpopulated areas of the West Bank and for the reversion of the remainder to Arab authority.[72] During Allon's visit, Rabin wired Washington that he was not ready to discuss the Jericho plan because general elections would then be necessary. Kissinger and Allon agreed to maintain ongoing consultations; the Israelis regarded this accord as an American commitment not to adopt a new position on the issue without first informing Israel and discussing the new approach.[73]

With the idea of negotiations about the West Bank seeming less realistic, the secretary of state and the foreign minister discussed the possibility of a new interim agreement with Egypt to preserve the momemtum of the step-by-step strategy. Kissinger wanted to know what Israel would demand in return for a further pullback; he assumed that Egypt would ask Israel to evacuate the oil fields on the Gulf of Suez and the strategic mountain passes in the Sinai. Allon mentioned two conditions, one political and one military: a public Egyptian commitment to non-belligerency and the demilitarization of the evacuated areas. Kissinger said that a public renunciation of belligerency was a very sensitive point, and it would be very hard to make Cairo take such a radical step. Instead, he suggested, Israel should ask for the practical components of nonbelligerent behavior, that is, substantive moves to lower the level of Egyptian hostility.[74] In August Allon gave Washington a list of possible

"practical components of nonbelligerency:"[75] free passage of tourists between Egypt and Israel, limited commercial links, and a loosening of the
boycott regulations against Israeli goods and against third parties dealing
with Israel. Jerusalem stuck to its political demands too though, in order
to create two bargaining positions: one for a greater withdrawal and one
for a lesser.

In September, 1974, Rabin arrived in Washington for his first visit
there as prime minister. On his arrival, final approval was given to the
supply of arms that had been promised earlier; when President Ford
mentioned this during his meeting with Rabin, the latter replied, "Big
deal! Those things [the arms] were already promised [to us]."[76] In any
case, it was clear that the United States received little political profit
from the arms deal, once it was approved. Rabin proposed to Ford that
Israel and the United States adopt a common strategic approach: they
should agree in advance on the areas to be evacuated by Israel and to
the Arabs' concession at each stage until peace was established. This
notion called for a long-range timetable and a gradual process that would
end with formal peace and the total eradication of the Arab-Israel conflict.[77]

Washington would not accept such a strategy: Kissinger could not believe in Washington and Jerusalem's ability to plan peace in advance or
to work backward from the final goal to the present under such uncertain conditions with so many different factors playing so many different
roles. The United States might bind itself to some course of action that
would recognize Israeli demands for formal Arab political concessions,
which the United States might view as unattainable and less important
than its own growing influence in the area. Israel might make territorial
demands too, which Washington was never ready to endorse. Kissinger
returned instead to the step-by-step strategy, which, in its next phase
should focus on Jordan and aim, in general terms, toward a future when
the conflict might be resolved through the linkage of as many members
of the Arab coalition as possible with the United States. This process
required time and Israeli concessions.

An Arab summit conference was due to be convened at Rabat in late
October, 1974. Earlier in the month Kissinger returned to the Middle
East to promote the Jordanian case. He wanted King Hussein to remain
an active representative of at least some aspects of the Palestinian cause.
He also wanted to enhance Egypt's position in Rabat. The PLO, backed
by Syria, Iraq, Libya, and a reluctant Saudi Arabia, might challenge
Hussein and any moderate Arab strategy or tactic regarding the conflict
at the conference. To avert or counteract such an eventuality, Kissinger
again argued that Hussein should be given at least a symbolic Israeli
concession in the West Bank so that he might remain a factor to be

reckoned with in the Palestinian question. In Israel, however, the secretary realized that the new government simply could not be confronted
with so difficult and delicate a foreign and domestic political issue. He
returned to another round of talks with Egypt and let Jordan know that
its turn would follow.[78]

Later, Israel and the United States were shocked by the Rabat summit decisions publicly recognizing the PLO as the sole representative of
the Palestinians and depriving Hussein of any standing in the matter,
seemingly with the king's helpless consent.[79] The Arab heads of state
further agreed that there should be no more separate agreements with
Israel. Egypt and Saudi Arabia agreed to both resolutions. The step-by-
step strategy seemed to have reached the end of the road. The Arabs
had appeared to raise the profile of the conflict by stressing its ideological
aspects and by such operational moves as legitimizing the PLO as an
autonomous actor in the conflict. The summit reiterated the official Arab
position with regard to the right of the Palestinians to return "to their
homeland" and their right for self-determination. Since the PLO's official
line called for the liquidation of Israel, the summit resolution seemed to
link even moderates like Sadat, who spoke of "peace," to this uncompromising demand.

The secretary of state's strategy of driving a wedge between ideology
and practice seemed to have suffered a hard blow, and he hinted that
Israeli intransigence vis-à-vis Jordan was to blame. However, after sound-
ing Egyptian opinion, Kissinger told the Israelis that Sadat had not, after
all, renounced the step-by-step strategy. Cairo would enter negotiations
on a new interim agreement, but the delicacy of its position in the Arab
coalition meant that it would have to make some very clear-cut gains.
Thus, a clear-cut feature of Arab political behavior was manifested again:
an Arab regime paid tribute to a common Arab cause in public, yet it
was not entirely bound by public commitment; it sought to achieve
national aims at the same time, trying to derive benefit from this devia-
tion from the Israelis and a third party (Washington). For the Israelis,
this was the source of one of their basic dilemmas. They wanted an Arab
public and official position that would recognize their rights, but they
mistrusted such public positions from the beginning. A public Arab recognition of Israel would have been accepted as a major political change,
yet even such an unattainable declaration would still have been regarded
as a weak foundation to balanced relationships between Israel and its
neighbors.

It is instructive to examine Kissinger's arguments with American scholars
about his policies in this period after Rabat.[80] In general, he claimed that
his strategy meant that more time would be gained to the benefit of both

Israel and the United States. If two years were gained, the United States would be able to increase its freedom of action, which was restricted by the complexities of the international situation in 1974 and 1975. The Europeans would return to the American fold and take part in a joint western effort to overcome the energy crisis. Furthermore, an American president would be elected in his own right. Without the fetters of an unelected president faced with a hostile Congress[81] and seeking reelection, he would be able to act more freely concerning possible new obligations in the Middle East and would be able to shape public opinion more easily.

Another device Kissinger deemed beneficial was a Cairo-Riyadh-Teheran axis, which he probably thought would contribute to stability in the region. The basic aspect of the system was to provide Saudi, Iranian, and American support for Egypt's development. The administration, however, was having a hard time persuading Congress to appropriate the full 250 million dollars that Nixon had promised Egypt during his visit shortly before his resignation. If Israel agreed to a further withdrawal, Egypt could present this as a major gain, and Saudi Arabia might be politically induced to give Cairo more aid. The United States would gain Saudi support for its role as the promoter of moderate Arab interests in the region.

Kissinger argued that his strategy was continually eroding Soviet influence, in Egypt at least, and that both the United States and Israel benefited from this development. He repeated his argument that the U.S.S.R.'s support of the Arabs has nothing to do with the substance of the Arab-Israeli conflict but was dictated by its interests and considerations as a superpower. An Arab state or group could always be sure of Soviet military support no matter how extreme its attitude to Israel, and the only "goods" the Soviet Union could deliver to the Arabs in the conflict were military aid. Kissinger also told American supporters of Israel that he was "the best secretary of state Israel can hope for in Washington." He and his strategy were made independent variables in the complex of Israeli considerations.

The substantive defect in this strategy, as some American critics of Kissinger put it in January, 1975,[82] was that territorial concessions made in separate partial agreements with Egypt and then Syria and perhaps Jordan neither resolve the Middle East conflict nor create a better "atmosphere" for resolving the main issues of the conflict. Such partial or marginal moves merely make the resolution of the central problems of the Israel-Arab-Palestinian conflict even more difficult. These moves were isolated from the "high political" logic of the Arab-Israeli conflict. They were marginal, rather than substantive, and a "neofunctional" progress from the margins to the core was methodologically impossible. Conflicts cannot be resolved if the "high political" substance in them is not tackled or discussed and a consensus is created with regard to them, if possible, by compromise. Linkages between the United States and the parties in the conflict created in time without tackling the substance of the conflict might remain irrelevant because of the high political logic of the conflict. Moreover, as far as Israel was concerned, these scholars argued that Washington, not Jerusalem, was benefiting from the step-by-step approach, for it was Washington that had a clear political and economic interest in resuming its position of influence in and tightening relations with the Arab world. During the course of 1974, they claimed, this interest began to clash with Israel's position and political influence inside the United States. This change was largely due to Washington's changed orientation toward Cairo, its cooperation with Riyadh on the oil price problem, and Cairo's increasing independence from Moscow. Furthermore, in the context of the Arab-Israeli conflict itself, there was a reversal of popular images: the Arabs, particularly with Egypt speaking of its readiness for peace, began to look more moderate, even to those who were not dazzled by their growing economic and political power. Israel, on the other hand, seemed to be insisting on absolute security, an untenable and unattainable objective in the view of post-Vietnam, détente-oriented Americans. If, despite its insistence, Israel knew absolute security was an impossible aim, the obvious conclusion was that Israel was more interested in retaining territories that did not belong to it than in relative, attainable security.

These arguments voiced by critics of the secretary of state might have contributed later to a "substantive approach" to the Middle East problem—the Brookings Institution Middle East program that became President Carter's platform vis-à-vis the Arab-Israeli conflict. Yet paradoxically enough, the same criticism helped Israel develop a growing suspicion toward Kissinger's step-by-step approach. When American critics of Kissinger meant Israeli withdrawals from most of the territories captured in 1967 as one of the "substantive" solutions to a "substantive" conflict, Israelis developed a tendency to keep territories while demanding far-reaching Arab political concessions as a "substantive" solution.

5

The Breakdown of the March, 1975, Negotiations: Built-in Constraints on Diplomacy in Complex Conflicts

THE STEP-BY-STEP APPROACH AND ISRAEL'S DOMESTIC SITUATION

As I have already pointed out, Rabin's domestic political problems contributed to Kissinger's decision to continue the step-by-step approach with Egypt. There were also other aspects of domestic politics in Israel important to its foreign relations and policy.

In late 1974 and during 1975, Israel faced four types of internal difficulties, which had ramifications in its foreign policy. The first of these was the nature of the post-Ben-Gurion political regime. It was a multiparty parliamentary system with a collegial cabinet in which the prime minister was primus inter pares. The other ministers were his equals, representing and drawing support from many factions—from outside the government and, in most cases, from outside the parliamentary factions as well. Yet, at the same time, the premiership had been traditionally perceived by the public as a much stronger position. The prime minister was thought responsible, even more so after Mrs. Meir's resignation, for members of his cabinet whom, politically, he could not always fully control, owing to the factional and coalitionary situation. In the public eye, Rabin was now even more "parliamentarily responsible." Since he had failed to dissolve Rafi by forcing Dayan out of the alignment, he still had a relatively compact, effective, and hostile power group at his back, whose leader, Mr. Peres, was himself constantly aiming at the premiership. Second was the normative structure of the regime: there was a lack of conventions, of customary "rules of the game," in many sectors of public life relating, after October, 1973, to foreign and defense policy issues.

The third domestic difficulty was the ideological and institutional crisis of the old party system. Differences over foreign and security policy, based on ideological political, personal, and factional considerations, cut

256

across party lines and gave rise to innerparty rather than interparty controversies. Consequently, a large part of the public no longer felt itself bound by the customary party frameworks, and the typical Israeli attitude of benign passivity vis-à-vis the elite continued to recede. The old system permitted parliamentary debates between the majority and the minority. These became increasingly irrelevant, however, because the small minority in a party block could join a larger minority outside the coalition, and both could become a majority. An active, floating public voiced its opinions outside the party frameworks in demonstrations, rallies, petitions, and settlement campaigns in the occupied territories, timed to coincide with Kissinger's visits.[1] The new government, for its part, was forced to recognize the groups behind these actions as legitimate interest groups.

The fourth problem was the economic crisis, which had social, ideological, and political ramifications of great importance. As we have already pointed out, the largest block in parliament was a union of three parties (Mapai, Achdut Ha'Avoda, and Rafi) cooperating with a fourth (Mapam). The platform of this grouping has always included sometimes incompatible political, social, and economic planks: full employment, economic growth, equal opportunity, and social security.

Within the alignment, there were two main schools of thought on the security issue. Some tended toward the minimalist pragmatic views formerly associated with Mapai, particularly in relation to the occupied territories. They were against a prolonged occupation and rule over too many Arabs. On the other hand, there were those whose attitude on the territories was shaped by defense-oriented and maximal bargaining considerations and who maintained Israel's right to establish settlements there. The same people sometimes held both views, swinging from one to the other in accordance with Arab statements or political and terrorist action.

Mapai, meanwhile, no longer had so much political and economic power. After the October, 1973, war came the economic crisis, increased defense spending, the political crisis, and the rise of actors who were not members of the old Mapai to the posts of prime minister, defense minister, and foreign minister: all these factors contributed to Mapai's decline. The power of the minimalist pragmatic school of thought declined, partly for economic reasons and because of the party's inability to realize the four planks of its platform simultaneously. Even before October, 1973, the government had a hard time trying to attain the four contradictory objectives. The party had already been shaken by quarrels over "how to slice the pie," prolonged inflation, social unrest, and the demands of deprived social groups for a better deal. The party's power had always been based to a very great extent on its ability or the image of its ability to distribute livelihoods, housing, health services, and political and social status positions, with the help of imported funds. As its capacity to do so declined, so did its political power.

Developments after the Six-Day War led to the strengthening of the two smaller factions of the Labor party and to the further decline of Mapai. The appointment as prime minister of Yitzhak Rabin, who lacked any real base of political support in the party, meant that compromises had to be reached with the different party factions that could not agree among themselves on foreign policy initiatives or when they meant withdrawal, and that public opinion should not be neglected. Rabin, as long as he accepted this framework, could not sponsor any initiatives of his own; he could only react to the initiatives of others, particularly to those of the American secretary of state.

ON LAYING DOWN A FOREIGN POLICY IN THE CONDITIONS FACED BY THE RABIN GOVERNMENT

We shall, for the moment, take leave of the history of the Rabin government on the eve of the negotiations on a new Sinai accord and look at the problems that exist in principle in this complex type of negotiating and in the formulation of any sort of foreign and defense policy under conditions of stress and uncertainty. These problems are particularly important in the case of the apparently shaky and inexperienced Rabin government.

The first difficulty is the absence, in conditions of uncertainty, of a direct link between the making of a decision and its results. Researchers generally agree that in conditions of uncertainty any decision is something of a gamble and should be assessed in terms of its reasonableness at the time it is made, rather than in terms of its outcome.[2] The interim and final outcomes are often determined by unexpected and haphazard events. Still, the political decision maker must take into account that the public's evaluation of his decision will be based primarily upon precisely these unanticipated outcomes and that he will have to devote a lot of effort to explaining his limited responsibility for the outcome, should it be failure. Much, therefore, depends on the public's ability to understand and accept such an explanation and on the personal and political attitudes of the decision maker's opponents.

A second and related difficulty stems from the need, in a democratic system, to mobilize political support just to make the decision itself. To obtain this support the decision maker may promise to the public, parliament or any other element whose help he might need that the outcome will be "successful." Or he may create an atmosphere of "success in advance" based on the public's confidence in him, his talents, his abilities, and luck. In other words, he may enlist support by creating or exploiting a popular belief that he is a "sure winner." A third possible condition for obtaining the support needed to have a decision made is to mobilize party support and/or the support of interest groups and the press on the basis of their interests and other factors. Of course, none of this guarantees that the outcome will be the desired one.

A third common problem is that the political decision maker and the other actors whom he must take into account, particularly the public and the press, do not have access to the same levels of information. Some information often is and must be privileged if the decision maker wishes to preserve his own freedom of action vis-à-vis the other side in, for example, international negotiations.[3] He must, however, take into account that public opinion and attitudes may well be based on incomplete or even false information.

A fourth problem is the decision maker's assessment of "public opinion" when he comes to make a decision.[4] The decision making system's evaluations and images of public opinion, one should note, affect how the outcome of the decision is discussed in and outside the parliamentary framework.

The fifth problem of decision making in conditions of uncertainty is often inherent in the complexity of the political and/or military issue considered and of the proposed solutions. For example, the Israeli public might see withdrawal from the occupied territories as clear concessions, while the "gains" proposed in exchange may seem too abstract or may simply not include a visible "substantive concession." The argument against the deal may thus be very simple, but the arguments needed to obtain the support of the public and of various political groups are complex and difficult. The political opposition clearly has a right to exploit this weakness in the complex argument, and its use of the simpler counterarguments certainly help it gain support.

The decision maker can tackle this problem in any of a number of ways. He can simplify the arguments he uses when dealing with the public and even with the various constitutional institutions dependent on the public. He can try to manipulate public opinion and refrain from telling the "whole truth" for a time. By doing this he risks creating a gap between the actual decision and the way it is presented, in the hope that he will be saved by the outcome. Another possibility is for the decision maker to harmonize his bargaining position vis-à-vis the external actor, for instance, with the public's attitudes. This course, however, limits his freedom of action and may even cause him to act in a manner contrary to his assessments and his understanding. The decision makers may also try to mold public opinion to fit their views, information, and considerations without relying too much on arguments. Their ability to shape public opinion may be a function of leadership, of a public image based on charisma or on some concatenation of events that all contribute to widening the room to maneuver in the traditional, rule-based political system. The ability to mold public opinion may also be a function of some past successes that gave the decision makers public credit and political power.

This last possibility (of molding public opinion) is not of concern to us here. Israel under Rabin lacked, initially at least, charismatic or any other kind of traditionally accepted leadership. Nor were there, in many sectors of public life, any conventional or obligatory formal and constitutional rules of behavior in foreign and security affairs that would give Rabin a credit—some degree of freedom of actions at the beginning. The state was going through a transitional period that started with the decline of the founding generation and became more critical with the shock of the Yom Kippur War.

The sixth and last of the common difficulties of decision making concerns the possible clash between two types of norms that exist concurrently in parliamentary democracies of the French, Dutch, or Israeli variety. One of the basic norms of parliamentary democracy concerns the nature of representation: on the one hand the representative has the autonomy to act according to the dictates of his conscience for the benefit of all, of the society, the state, and his party; on the other hand, working within a party means working according to the logic of party politics. This second area concerns also the norm that the representative must maintain his dialogue with the public after the election, even disregarding for the moment his need to work for reelection, and must give the public reliable information so that it can judge issues as they develop. The difficulties of explanation have already been mentioned. From a normative standpoint these problems can be overcome with suitable parliamentary tools and a political consensus among the public about the proper methods for dealing with serious issues of foreign and defense policy. Such a consensus can arise through a consociational elite able to bargain within itself on every issue that emerges in a fragmented society through a permanent coalitionary compromise, as was Israel's case after Ben-Gurion's departure. Sometimes, though, unbridgeable differences of opinion among the public, the parties, and the decision makers themselves make it impossible to sustain a working consensus.

Confronted with these difficulties, Rabin and his cabinet had a marked preference for the territorial status quo. Before the October, 1973, war, Meir and Dayan had pursued a policy of maintaining the status quo out of a basic distrust of the Arabs, a positive approach toward parts of the occupied territories (those that must remain in Israeli hands), and a bid for autonomy from foreign powers; they and their policy had firm popular backing. The Rabin-Peres government was no more trusting of the Arabs, but their domestic base was weaker, and the relations between the alignment's components were unclear. Peres's component had almost won the premiership and could now assume a strong rear position toward Rabin, with Dayan's support or criticism at his own rear. The alignment's 1973 election promises of peace at Geneva or negotiations on a separate peace with Egypt, and perhaps with Jordan too, were not kept; it became clear to everyone that negotiations would resume about Israeli concessions to Egypt in exchange for something less than peace. Peace referred to Arab territorial demands, which were unacceptable to many Israelis. It was also linked to "the restoration of the rights of the Palestinians"—i.e., "Palestinian rights" acceptable to the PLO, and thus unacceptable to all Israelis. Moreover, "peace" itself depended upon Arab willingness to embark upon relations with Israel similar to the U.S.-Canadian or Dutch-Belgian relations, as demanded by noted "doves" like Mr. Abba Eban. As the hopes of peace receded, the public became less and less willing to make concessions for no substantive quid pro quo except the promotion of America's interests. The public, and particularly some mass media, did not consider the reinforcement of Washington's standing in the region to be a contribution to a fundamental favorable change in Israel's position in the conflict.[5]

The former leadership, especially Dayan, could now press its own case freely and argue that Kissinger had imposed a draw on the 1973 fighting just when an Israeli victory was imminent.[6] The autonomist conception of a strong Israel acting to serve its own interests and to maintain its position of strength in the Middle East led to the claim that Kissinger was simply not interested in Israel's interests. He should, therefore, be pressured to make Egypt renounce belligerency, to take Cairo out of the framework of the conflict, and to break up the package of Arab demands if real peace were unattainable and both the Arabs and the Israelis could not agree on the substantive and ideological concessions necessary to make "real peace." Israel, therefore, should negotiate separate agreements between the Arab party ready for it and Israel on partial withdrawals in exchange for nonbelligerency. This offer was relevant to Egypt alone (perhaps to Syria), as the West Bank remained, in Dayan's eyes, ideologically and defense-politically nonnegotiable, and King Hussein remained a nonpartner due to his weakness and dependence on coalitionary Arab developments.

Dayan himself was apparently destroyed as a figure of major political consequence but his Rafi colleague, Peres, still had to reckon with the ex-defense minister's parliamentary position as a leading Rafi member, and with his arguments, which struck a responsive chord in the public. It is hard to know what Peres himself thought. The impression is that, in general, he shared Dayan's autonomist ideas. Furthermore, he was an experienced and clever political technician, and his primary concern was for the public's mood or for political consensus in the public, parliament, and the government. The center of political gravity was "conservative-hawkish," and this was what interested Peres in his day-to-day activity.[7]

He did, however, say, as Dayan had, that the Arabs had to be brought to change their attitude toward Israel, and that Jerusalem, recognizing that Israel's and America's interests were not synonymous, must "fight" Washington to help bring about this change. Dayan and Peres both considered structural changes inside Egypt—clearing and reopening the canal, and developing the economy of the canal zone and its cities—changes for the better. They did not, however, see the American-Egyptian "match" as beneficial to Israel per se. Quite the contrary; the common interests of the two states might dictate Israeli concessions. The problem, as Dayan and Peres perceived it, was how to make Egypt recognize Israel's existence and autonomy in the region, its national objectives, and its "rights" in Palestine as a whole, or how to live in a situation of relatively no war with Egypt if it does not fully recognize Israel and its "rights." For that purpose they were ready to make large territorial concessions to Egypt in the Sinai. A guaranteed non-belligerency treaty would be the conditio sine qua non for them, in exchange for the Sinai passes and the Suez Gulf oil.

Before becoming prime minister, Yitzhak Rabin had mainly been a man who was supposed to carry out policies; as chief of staff and ambassador his job had been more or less to execute the diplomatic and security decisions of others. He had played an important political role as Eshkol's chief military adviser, until his deterrent posture collapsed in May, 1967, but he did not know then how to proceed further from that point. As ambassador to Washington, Rabin had used domestic American power triggers more vigorously than his precedessors, yet he had always warned against Israeli-American confrontations, and (wrongly) assessed U.S. determination to pursue a "Rogers," or comprehensive, strategy in the Middle East until the administration dropped that framework itself. A historian would, therefore, have a hard time evaluating what Rabin's personal attitudes on the conflict were before he became prime minister. It seems that on the whole he held traditional Achdut Ha'Avoda attitudes: the Arab-Israeli conflict was a fundamental given; the occupied territories were strategic and bargaining assets that must be disputed long and hard so that as much as possible would be retained, at least in the West Bank. In Washington he had heard Kissinger and Sisco expound on and present their arguments about the broader political and strategic aspects of the conflict, and he developed a growing tendency to approach Israel's foreign affairs and defense problems from the viewpoint of American-Israeli relations, a traditional perception of old Mapai, which made him a better choice for Mrs. Meir and Mr. Sapir than the autonomistic Rafi leader, Peres. Yet, being an operator, by experience and nature, rather than a strategic thinker, a director of operations in a postulative or ideological framework conceived by others, Rabin just did not know what to do on the eve of the Six-Day War, when his deterrence and tough warnings strategy failed to deter Nasser. As an ambassador to the United States, he managed to exploit bargaining potentialities in a given system, relying on the expertise of very knowledgeable lobbyists. But now he found himself as Israel's prime minister, a position he never dreamt he would be able to hold, and he could not resist the temptation. He chose different perspectives on the conflict from time to time. At this point, he regarded the conflict chiefly in terms of the Egyptian positions in the general context of the Arab coalition's attitude toward Israel and in the terms of his domestic situation.

THE STEP-BY-STEP STRATEGY: THE ARAB POSITION, ITS DEFINITION, AND THE INTERPRETATION OF ITS IMPLEMENTATION

The fundamental problem of negotiations between democracies (open societies) and nondemocratic coalitions or components of them is so complex that it is difficult to lay down any hard and fast rules: can the public, expressive aspects of the policy of the leadership in a nondemocratic state possibly be separated from its actions? Can one assume that either the action or the expressive aspect is the more important determinant? In the Arab-Israeli case, the form and content problem is even more complicated because there are a greater number of actors involved, holding a number of public positions and following the debating many different kinds of tactics and strategies.

An Arab state, such as Egypt, may make a verbal concession; it may use the word "peace" as its target, but make no step toward it at present. It may agree to verbal concessions to a third party in order to attain political and strategic advantages. The actual, or the potential behavior of its military-political elite, though, may stand in clear contradiction to such a verbal concession and to the conventional positions of the heterogeneous Arab coalition as a whole. Then again, in the course of the negotiations a state may insist on making no public verbal concessions, but subsequent substantive internal structural changes may serve the other side's purposes and justify meeting the publicly recalcitrant state part way. However, such developments may not seem certain enough during the negotiations to justify large concessions. The Arab side may view the negotiations as a way of strengthening its position without making any substantive changes in its goals. This attitude or domestic and all-Arab concerns may lead it to reject any demand by the opposing side for public verbal commitments. Moreover, after the negotiations, its actual behavior would have to take into account its position as a member of the Arab coalition.

The Arab coalition itself seemed to be divided into several parties: Egypt, Syria, and Iraq and Libya. Egypt, which was willing to negotiate a separate deal with Israel against the spirit of the Rabat summit decisions, yet was committed to a PLO state in the West Bank and Gaza and to Syria's territorial claims on the Golan Heights. A PLO state was out of the question for Rabin's cabinet; it would install between Israel and Jordan the most radical enemy of Israel—a coalition of professional nationalists with radical revolutionaries who always deplored any step taken by nationalist and "moderate" Arab regimes toward some kind of coexistence with Israel. This West Bank-Gaza entity would become an established, PLO-ruled base for further claims against both Israel and Jordan, strategically capable of launching attacks against Israel's heart and would cause, even if a minority radical group used it for that purpose, a general escalation process, since other Arab states would rush to the aid of that PLO entity when Israel retaliated. Such an entity was bound to become friendly with the Soviets who would then protect it. It would not solve the refugee problem in Syria and Lebanon, as the refugees were educated to demand their return to the pre-1967 Israel, but rather it would create a forward base for this claim, and would unite the West Bankers with the refugees in trying to achieve it. If Egypt was committed to that entity, backed by Syria, which was not ready to give Israel anything in exchange, and yet the entity was unacceptable to the totally hostile Iraq and Libya, Cairo was perhaps more subtle than Damascus and Tripoli. Nevertheless, Cairo was still committed to a totally unacceptable, short-lived "solution."

These then were the problems of substance and method faced by Rabin in trying to assess the Arab position. He did get another perspective on the Arab world during the negotiations, however, because the American mediator had reported on some aspects of the Arab position. The mere fact that one or both negotiating parties are to some extent dependent for information on the mediator influenced how they regarded the information they received from him as compared to their own sources and/or how they dealt and argued with him.

Since Kissinger had come to the Middle East as an active mediator in November, 1973, and with the substantive change in U.S. policy in the region marked by this entry, American officials and State Department envoys had increasingly tended to argue that Cairo was concerned with internal economic development and with social problems. The American appraisal was that the extreme Arab demands were not identical with Egypt's perception of its national interests. The Americans claimed that Sadat was aware of the severity of his country's economic and social problems and wanted to tackle them with American, European, and Middle Eastern aid.[8] Sadat recognized that the U.S.S.R. could not provide such assistance; it could give him military equipment, though, because Soviet interests were served by the Arab-Israeli conflict.

Furthermore, Sadat realized that only the United States could make Israel yield to some of his demands in the conflict and that any link with the United States aimed at achieving his objectives assumed a respect for Israel's existence. The U.S.S.R. could still be of use to him, but only in keeping his military option open. The Soviet Union might retain some influence in Cairo, but Sadat would try to dilute it with American help as far as possible when his domestic and foreign political interests were served through American aid.

Egypt's leading role in the Arab world did not mean that it could freely ignore all-Arab goals, particularly when Syria, always a contender for the leadership of the Arab nation, was behind them. There were also the other radical Arab capitals to be reckoned with, as well as the fact that the relatively moderate Saudis tended to recognize radical interests vis-à-vis Israel. Egypt would thus be risking isolation during and after the negotiations and so would have to be rewarded.

As "proof" of their arguments about Egypt's new attitude, the Americans pointed to the rise in U.S. influence in Cairo and the concomitant decline in Soviet influence there. Certain Egyptian demands and actions were interpreted as honest expressions of disappointment over the unkept American promises.[9] Public and other statements by Sadat were compared to the more extreme Arab demands, and Egypt's cooperation with Saudi Arabia was also pointed out.

These claims and proofs of Egyptian intentions were not necessarily complementary and, from Israel's standpoint, might even be contradictory. As we have already noted, Dayan and Peres did not think that closer ties between Cairo and Washington were necessarily in Israel's interest. Moreover, although Sadat was supposedly "resigned" to Israel's survival, Egypt and the other Arab states kept up their political and military pressure on Israel in relation to the current conflict and future agreements. Even if the demands of Egypt and the other Arab states and some Palestinian claims were met, Egypt was unwilling to establish normal relations with Israel.[10] Meanwhile, Egypt would accept parts of the Sinai in military agreements that would not end the conflict; if Egypt was indeed ready to coexist with Israel, why shouldn't it make political concessions?

Because of its position in the Arab world, Egypt was dependent on a consensus among more or less extreme Arabs in other states and in Egypt itself; and this consensus might well clash with its own national interests. The result was likely to be a compromise, an ambiguous Egyptian position with regard to the conflict as a whole embodying its national interests and the extreme Arab demands. It might be in Egypt's national interest to lower the profile of the conflict and to recognize and coexist with Israel, de facto. Other Arab demands, however, required keeping the profile of the conflict high as long as Israel did not yield to them and allowed no ideological coexistence with a Zionist Israel, ever. The position would remain ambiguous as long as Egypt was negotiating for the passes and the Suez Gulf oil. When it got them, it will return to other Arab grievances. Therefore, a political concession was essential. Mr. Rabin, usually much more aware of American interests and inclined to negotiate on the basis of a common U.S.-Israeli ground (which was less relevant to Peres and Dayan), was thus led to reconsider his public stance. He could not ignore Peres's and Dayan's arguments, and indeed, he had his doubts about Egypt's "real intentions." Still thinking in terms of Israel's domestic power in the United States which he had helped exploit during his term as ambassador—he hoped for a reasonable bargaining with Kissinger, because the acute crisis atmosphere of 1973–74 was over. The mere fact of mediation encouraged the parties, particularly the one that thought it held the lesser hand, to make ambiguous and equivocal statements and to leave it to the mediator to bring about a working agreement through hard bargaining. Each party to the conflict hoped that the mediator would respond to considerations not related specifically to the conflict but to its bilateral relations with it and would find a compromise closer to the one it had already made among its contradictory objectives.

THE RESUMPTION OF AMERICAN MEDIATION, JANUARY, 1975: DILEMMAS AND BASIC THESES

The positions of the parties at the start of the Egyptian-Israeli negotiations in March, 1975, were compromises between contradictory goals and various pressures on a number of levels. The United States itself had several different goals in its foreign policy and had to contend with various internal and external pressures. Its goals seem to have been five in number.

First, the United States wished, as always, to avert an uncontrolled conflict with the U.S.S.R., which might escalate into a superpower confrontation. Second, there was the desire to maintain elements of the détente with the U.S.S.R. Third, there was also the wish to advance specific American political and strategic interests in various parts of the world, and to prevent damage to America's position as a superpower because of commitments to clients in conflict with each other and directly or indirectly supported by the Soviet Union or because of commitments to clients in conflict with semiindependent Soviet clients.

Fourth, the United States wished to advance its own specific economic, political, and strategic interests against the backdrop of the international economic crisis and America's psychological withdrawal into itself.[11] From this standpoint, the role of more or less prowestern, semiindependent actors (Saudi Arabia and the gulf states) in the Arab world was crucial. They were bound to a major political and military Arab power that had no oil (Egypt), and they also cooperated politically and militarily with another major Arab actor that was quite close to the Soviet Union (Syria). The Arab oil states had a moral and political commitment to back Moscow's problematic protégé, the PLO, as well. All of these actors were, furthermore, involved in a high-profile conflict with Israel, although since October, 1973, the conflict had been directed into political and diplomatic channels. The role of Western Europe and Japan, which were dependent on Arab oil, was also an important factor in terms of a modified American foreign policy after October, 1973.

The fifth objective of American policy was to promote the interests of a Republican administration facing the 1976 presidential election campaign and a hostile Democratic Congress. During an exploratory visit to Israel in January, 1975, Kissinger sought some agreement with the Israelis on a number of basic points.[12] First, the negotiations would not be about a general settlement. This was not the time to tackle all the territories, all the interested parties, and all the problems. Therefore, neither "peace" nor "an end to the state of war," both of which are functions of a general settlement, were to be discussed, despite Israel's public insistence on nonbelligerency as the price for a substantial pullback in the Sinai.

Second, the negotiations would be about another Israeli withdrawal in the Sinai as part of an interim Egyptian-Israeli settlement. In return, Israel would demand political and military undertakings by Egypt that were less than peace or nonbelligerency. Third, an Egypt with close links to the United States would be an asset to both the United States and Israel. An American-oriented Egypt would be good for Israel too, because Israel's survival and security were fundamental to U.S. policy, and Egypt would have to abide by this fact of life, if it did not accept it already.

Fourth, the step-by-step negotiations should be continued so that Egypt might obtain more of the territory important to it in the Sinai. The profile of the conflict would consequently be lowered and Cairo could concentrate more easily on solving its domestic problems with American help. Syria would then have to decide whether to maintain the high profile of the conflict and risk losing Egyptian support or to accept interim agreements in the Golan with Egyptian and American help, perhaps in exchange for decreasing Soviet influence in Damascus. Once this hurdle was passed and agreement or agreements reached, there might be room for the continuation of the negotiations with Jordan, Egypt, and Syria. In any event, a careful distinction would have to be made between the declared positions of the parties, especially of the Arabs, and their deeds. The words would probably remain more or less hostile, but there would be de facto coexistence. Israel's demand for a political quid pro quo for its territorial concessions was quite understandable, but it would necessarily have to be something less than peace and nonbelligerency, as long as there was no final resolution of the conflict, and its exact nature would be decided in the practical bargaining. The main thing to be secured was another agreement with Egypt.

The fifth of Kissinger's apparent ground rules was that the government of Israel, for all its domestic difficulties, was an active partner of the United States; both states must help promote each other's interest. Indeed, Israel owed the Ford-Kissinger administration understanding and consideration. Rabin, Allon, and Peres should accept the opinions outlined in the ground rules for the talks, but even if they did not agree with them, they should meet Ford and Kissinger part way because the Americans had fulfilled all their political, financial, and military commitments to Israel. Similarly, the Israeli government was, or should have been, aware that if the talks failed, Jerusalem's relations with Washington would be endangered. A political and diplomatic vacuum would be another consequence of the breakdown of the mediation efforts, and that could lead to war or to a return to Geneva, At Geneva, a key role was reserved for the U.S.S.R., and an overall deal would have to be considered. Israel, as everyone knew, wanted nothing to do with the Soviet Union and was domestically incapable of negotiating about the territories as a whole, should the step-by-step strategy fail.

ISRAEL AND EGYPT: BASIC POSITIONS
BEFORE THE NEGOTIATIONS

After Kissinger began his shuttle between Aswan and Jerusalem in March, 1975, he said he thought he had reached a basic agreement, with Rabin and Allon at least, about the five ground rules and so there was room for his mediation efforts.[13] Later, the secretary of state would hint that Israel had deceived him during these preparatory talks.[14] Actually, it seems that "deception" is not really the right way to describe Israel's behavior. What happened was that some of the built-in constraints in negotiations undermined the talks. Rabin had accepted some of Kissinger's ground rules both publicly and privately; American influence in Egypt was a good thing. Israel would be compensated for its withdrawal not only by verbal commitments but by Egypt's deeds. It was important to lower the profile of the conflict with Egypt. Still, Israel did not give up its demand for some sort of public commitment from Egypt to end the state of war. It was ready to give up a very small, and useless piece of the Sinai, yet Rabin publicly created the impression that he was ready to withdraw from the passes and the oil fields. A public outcry held him to the nonbelligerency claim in exchange for these assets, although he well knew that Egypt would not agree to it. Knowing this, and yet inviting Kissinger to a new shuttle round signalled to the secretary a departure from nonbelligerency, while accepting in advance the necessity to withdraw from the passes and the oil. This vicious circle involved Rabin in trouble with Kissinger, Peres, Dayan, and with the public opinion in Israel.

Egypt demanded the two strategic mountain passes in the Sinai (the Mitla and the Giddi) and the Abu Rodeis oilfields on the Gulf of Suez. Israel exported most of the oil to the European country that was Egypt's original partner in discovering and producing it. Its financial value had run to a few hundred million dollars. Both passes are dominant physical features about thirty kilometers from the canal. Withdrawing from them would mean a redeployment of the Israel Defense Forces along a longer, winding line in the Sinai. In other words, what was involved was seemingly a concession of substantial "goods" with rather easily exploitable strategic and economic value in return for a subtle, complex, and "intelligent" settlement, based on structural probabilities.

Each party had the following advantages in the bargaining. Apart from the passes and the oilfields, Israel had other territories in the Sinai and a military option that had grown, physically, thanks to improvements in the Armed forces after October, 1973, and to American supplies after the disengagement agreements. In addition, there were its ties with the United States: its dialogue with the administration and its links to Congress. As always, a key role was played by American Jewry. Egypt's advantages were the political and economic interests and attitudes it shared with the United States in the context of interbloc competition and petroleum. Another advantage was its ties with the U.S.S.R., which had not been completely broken.[15] Indeed, they were quite strong enough for the Soviet Union to resume limited arms shipments to Egypt in January, 1975, and to continue to give Cairo political support until it violated the Rabat resolutions and began separate talks with the Israelis.[16]

The long public debate in Israel about the passes and the oilfields created the impression that Israel would be conceding a great deal militarily and economically if it pulled back from them. One of those responsible for creating this attitude was the Likud member of the Knesset and reserve general, Ariel Sharon.[17]

There were differences of opinion in the IDF itself as to the importance of the passes and the value of the 1974 disengagement line.[18] These issues were judged in terms of the lessons drawn from the last war. There was general agreement that Egypt's advantage in the fighting was due to its masses of men, equipment, and firepower, and its absorptive capacity on a relatively narrow front, and to Israel's lack of numerical equality. Some of the members of the Israeli general staff also thought that it was desirable for the regular Arab armies to be kept away from the Israeli line, which could then be manned by a relatively small Israeli regular force during periods of less tension. To tackle the mobilized Israeli reserves, the enemy would have to advance into a no man's land where they would not have the excellent missile cover they had had in the 1973 fighting and would have to tangle with a flexible Israeli force. The attacker's own forward line could be breached rather easily because of the difficulties of attacking with uniform strength along a long front. The canal line and the 1974 disengagement line were both relatively short and it was relatively easy to concentrate enough forces for a general offensive along them and to provide them with adequate missile cover. According to this school of thought, then, the IDF, because of its mechanized and offensive character and the ability of its field commanders to improvise, would obtain the flexibility it needed if a relatively large buffer zone were established between the two armies; that is, if the territory Israel evacuated were demilitarized, and the battle lines lengthened. The best way of handling the territorial problems then would be to provide for effective demilitarization and to separate the regular Egyptians from the Israeli line, to make mobilization easier until the Egyptians arrived. Yet many other members of the defense establishment thought that Israel's control over the passes, close to the canal zone, enabled it to reoccupy the whole eastern canal area and to threaten the canal cities again. Sadat would not easily risk hostilities so close to the canal and lose his already established "historical victory" of October, 1973, in Arab eyes.

As public debates continued, more and more demands were raised for at least "far-reaching" Egyptian political concessions in exchange for the passes. Unless Cairo undertook suitable political commitments it could encroach militarily on the territory evacuated using various pretexts and arguments. Furthermore, with petroleum, petrodollars, and its tightening links with the United States, Cairo had time on its side, so its incentive to uphold any agreement was sure to decrease.

The problem that the Israeli government thought that it faced during the prolonged public debate that accompanied the shuttle process was how to obtain from Egypt a concession on the belligerency issue, its severance from radical Soviet-backed Syria, and a longer-term dissocia-iton from all-Arab concerns. To many members of the cabinet these demands were not only justifiable in terms of foreign and defense policy, but they were also of great domestic importance. The government *had* to show the public some gains if it did not want to be thought to have abandoned some of the state's great political and military achievements for nothing. They could hardly argue that these achievements had not been unequivocal but dependent for their value on Israel's overall political and strategic situation. Nor could they let it be known that they thought that Israel's territorial advantages were of doubtful value; many of them thought the territories were very valuable bargaining assets. Certainly an admission that Israel's position was not really that good would be seized by the opposition, which could claim that the Israeli government had itself undermined its bargaining power with the Arabs and the United States. Consequently, the value attributed to the territories subject to negotiation was continually increased, but as their importance grew in the public mind, it became increasingly difficult to justify abandoning them.[19]

The ruling Israeli triumvirate was split by personal and political differences. Peres had lost the Labor party leadership race by a very small number of votes. Sapir, the old Mapai strongman who had mobilized the few votes needed for Rabin's election in order to avert a victory by Peres, had left active politics. Without his strong guiding hand, Labor's central body became more exposed to all kinds of influences. The mechanisms Mapai had established to influence broad sectors of the population were in an advanced stage of decay. Since the Lavon affair the party's economic and patronage frameworks had lost much of their control over individuals, and the process was hastened by the Yom Kippur War.

In such an unstable situation, a mistake by Rabin in the talks with Kissinger would be a point in Peres's favor among the public and in the central bodies of the party. If Rabin made political concessions to Egypt and looked as though he had lost a lot of Israel's autonomy, he might not obtain a majority in the cabinet, and Peres would benefit. Peres might also benefit if Rabin took too firm a line and the Americans reacted strongly; the public's fears about complications in the relationship with the United States might count against the prime minister, not the defense minister.

Inside the cabinet itself, the balance of opinion shifted in the winter of 1975 in favor of a firmer, more autonomous position. When he set up his government, Rabin had the support of the moderate left, which was in the coalition, and could count on the support of the more extreme left outside the coalition. The National Religious party did not join the government because of differences between its extreme right wing and its moderate factions over foreign, security, and religious issues. Acting on Galili's advice, Rabin sought to expand his coalition by bringing the NRP into it on the evening of the resumption of negotiations in March. The reasoning behind this attempt was simple; if the government decided on a policy of concessions, it was assured of the support of the moderate left whether it was in the coalition or not. The NRP's support was more important, however, since it had more seats in Knesset and greater public support than the Citizens' Rights Movement. The prevailing mood in the public and in the main coalition parties was, moreover, somewhat right of center, favoring firm bargaining for substantial gains in exchange for minimal territorial concessions. After some deliberations, the NRP decided to join the coalition and thus influence the negotiating process, having realized that Rabin was not, after all, an American-influenced "dove."

The Rabin government adopted a firm bargaining stance because it was acceptable to the important factions in the coalition, because the prime minister was afraid of losing influence if he let Peres obtain political advantage from public displays of firmness, and because Rabin's main focus in the negotiations at this time was the Arab attitude and the value of Arab promises. This last point seemed to him at the time to be the most relevant to Israel, the government, and his standing in it. Rabin, therefore, continued the bitter battle for Israel's territorial periphery and for substantial changes in Egypt's attitude to the conflict. He would let Kissinger worry about the general background of the conflict.[20] Still, Kissinger did agree that an Egyptian political concession was necessary,[21] and Rabin hoped to bargain on that.

The Israeli government viewed its position in a way very similar to Sadat's view of his situation. Sadat neither could nor wanted to cut himself off publicly from the package of Arab demands and would find it very difficult to make declarations or sign documents ending the state of war. Similarly, the Israeli government would have great difficulty explaining the abandonment of real estate like fortified passes and oil wells without a substantive concession from Egypt. Since Egypt had no such material assets to trade with Israel, the Israeli government would have to justify its action by arguing on a more abstract and complex level than the opposition ("Who abandons a line of fortification for nothing?"). Thus, even if Rabin and Kissinger agreed on the ground rules outlined above, the Israeli government would still have to demand a political concession from Egypt. If Kissinger accepted Sadat's refusal on the grounds that he feared public opinion and rivals and critics in the Arab world or that he was suspicious of the other side's intentions, he would have to accept such agruments as being valid for Israel, too.

This was the stand-off that the secretary of state tried to overcome when he came to the region. His mere appearance led to an increase in public tension and sensitivity, and to discussion about the issues; this sensitivity in turn tended to make the issues simultaneously more complex and more simplistic.

Sadat remained throughly consistent in his goals—the passes and the oil. Washington held the master key to achieving these goals. Egypt's main foreign and security policy objective must then be to enlist U.S. support and, if possible, to drive a wedge between the Israelis and the Americans. This assessment of the U.S. role had been behind Sadat's decision to go to war in 1973 and the series of political and economic moves Cairo made toward Washington.

Egypt and the United States had a common interest now. Once they shared such interests, Jerusalem could not obtain what it wished from Washington by presenting the conflict as one with an Arab —Soviet client— state. Henceforth, the conflict would be with closer American clients (Saudi Arabia) and more independent ones (Egypt). Until the Egyptian armed forces were reequiped, Cairo could safely treat its military option, which was weakened somewhat by strained relations with Moscow, as of secondary importance. Egypt probably also considered that if it could obtain the Sanai passes, their strategic value would compensate it for the loss of Soviet arms supplies and the military threat against Israel would not be weakened.

Two other factors were in Egypt's favor from October, 1973, on. The first was the problem of keeping control of escalation in the Middle East. Unless this effort was successful the superpowers might be dragged into direct or indirect confrontation and the humiliation and/or backing down of one of them in the face of the political and military superiority of the other. Seemingly, the power to back down would be the United States; Soviet military strength in the Mediterranean and the political restraints on American operational capacity since Vietnam were enough to restrain Washington from risking a military confrontation or taking limited military action. Thus, even though their influence in Egypt had declined, the Soviets, because of their mere political and military presence in the Middle East, were an asset to Sadat. The Americans would do their utmost to prevent escalation and all that might ensue. Furthermore, the

United States would curry favor with Cairo in order to drive the U.S.S.R. out of the region.

The second factor benefiting Egypt was that the western states were deeply engrossed in studying and trying to rectify their relations with each other in the light of the 1973 crisis. Since the war, Washington had tried to deal with its allies in several ways. During and immediately after the war, the Americans had chosen the approach of verbal confrontation, voicing threats about dire consequences for the Europeans if they did not cooperate with the United States in tackling the oil crisis and the Arab states.[22] The Federal Republic of Germany and Britain were the chief victims of these threats, which, in the final analysis, might have helped retain the European Community from being dragged into following the French autonomist and pro-Arab line. The Europeans had been alienated by American bullying in 1970–73, but they may actually have been brought back by the same tactic, since they needed economic cooperation with the United States to fight the outcomes of the energy crisis.

When, in 1974, the energy crisis turned from a crisis of supply to a price crisis, the economic and political bases for cooperation among the western states expanded. Despite the differences among the European states regarding supply and their economic interest in the price of oil, it was impossible to imagine that they might try to overcome the price crisis on their own. It was very unlikely that they could control the complex of inflation, unemployment, structural damage to various parts of their economy, and the requirements of importing fuel without cooperating with the United States and all industrial states.

In 1974 the United States tried to correct some of its past mistakes and base its policy on the interests common to all western industrial countries. All of them wanted to avoid a fatal constriction of international trade and a return to the protectionism of the 1930s. The United States proposed that they adopt a common policy on the energy crisis and that they coordinate their policies on the Middle East crisis; the United States would have the responsibility for managing the crisis but would take the Europeans' interests into account.[23] Thus, particularly after Harold Wilson returned to power in the U.K.,[24] the Americans did not have too much trouble in entering into cooperation with the Germans and the British and isolating Pompidou's France in its splendid autonomism.[25]

American verbal threats against the oil producers[26] gave way to talks between the leading industrial states and the oil producers and the Third World as a whole. This paved the way for a dialogue between the West and OPEC and the Third World about global economic issues and the development of the poorer states.[27]

After Giscard's election to the presidency,[28] the United States could begin a rapprochement with France and could take French interests into account in its own policy. The rectification of relations among the western states was proceeding quickly when Kissinger returned to the Middle East in March, 1975. To a great extent the success of this process depended on the success of American mediation in the region, since it would make the Arab-Israeli conflict less of a disruptive factor in the international system. A more stable international system based on American-European-Japanese cooperation and a dialogue between rich and poor states would also make it easier to control local conflicts.

In early 1975 the international system was somewhere in the middle of this process; this fact too was to Egypt's advantage in the negotiations with Israel. The West German foreign minister told Kissinger in the summer of 1974 that a forthcoming European-Arab dialogue would not be concerned with the Middle East conflict or the energy problem.[29] In return, however, Kissinger would have to take Europe's interests into account in dealing with the conflict and to consider that the stability of the international system might suffer if mediation efforts failed.

While the reordering of relations among western states and the overall superpower strategic ratio in the Middle East worked to Egypt's benefit, Egypt itself had to worry about the reactions of Syria, the PLO, and other radical Arab states to separate Egyptian-Israeli negotiations contrary to the resolutions of the Rabat Summit. It seems that at this point, Egypt started publicly to advise the PLO to accept a miniature Palestinian state at the West Bank and Gaza as a reasonable solution to the Palestinian problem for the forseeable future. This was to be pursued after the interim agreement in the Sinai was to free Arab land without Egypt's renouncing a public commitment to Syria and the PLO. The PLO and Syria angrily responded that Cairo was breaking the rules set at Rabat while entering into a new round of negotiations separately. Still, Sadat could cite his inter-Arab difficulties vis-à-vis Kissinger as an argument for not making concessions to Israel and as reinforcement of his need for clear-cut achievements. Thus Egypt's general international position was favorable, and inter-Arab and domestic Egyptian pressures certainly helped Sadat to formulate a fairly tough position in the talks, with no Third Army and "African" territory to relieve.

Other factors, too, would affect the course of the negotiations. A new, unelected president had recently assumed office in Washington, and, in the wake of the Watergate scandal, there were strong domestic pressures on Kissinger himself.[30] Cambodia and later South Vietnam were rapidly disintegrating. In such circumstances, both the president and his secretary of state would welcome a new and rapid success in the Middle East. This factor also thus weighed in Egypt's favor in the negotiations.

KISSINGER AND RABIN: THE KNIGHT
OF THE WOEFUL COUNTENANCE DOES BATTLE
WITH THE WINDMILL

In his Harvard days, Kissinger became known for his personal acquaintance with many important politicians and often every promising "second string" politician in most of the countries of the world, particularly in Europe. Moreover, he liked to evaluate these people, to give them marks, and he was proud of his ability to pinpoint what he considered to be their characteristics, talents, and failings.[31]

Later, as an active politician one cornerstone of his thinking was an appraisal of a political strategic situation based on the real power relations of the sides, that is, on their existing political leverage and their potential ability to mobilize other powers or superpowers. A second cornerstone was his personal acquaintance with the leaders of the states and his assessments of how they would behave. Kissinger had known Yitzhak Rabin in Washington. Apparently, because of his past affiliations with Washington, the secretary's opinion of Rabin was similar to that of the Israeli moderates who had supported his appointment as prime minister. Kissinger and the Israeli doves were both wrong.

From 1968 on, the Israeli ambassador to Washington had spoken of the need to drive the Russians out of Egypt and had given the impression that he thought that American penetration of Cairo was an asset to America and to Israel.[32] This was one of the basic theses that Kissinger might have thought were accepted by the Israeli cabinet before the discussions started. The second thesis was that this was not the time to discuss peace, or even nonbelligerency. In this respect, Kissinger might have thought he was doing Rabin a favor. It seemed that Rabin wished to lower the profile of the Egyptian-Israeli conflict and saw the lessening of the Israeli "challenge" in the Sinai as an incentive to Cairo to look after its affairs. Rabin often argued in this vein both in public and in private during that period.[33] To the members of Mapam, to Israeli writers, and to other intellectuals he is even reported to have said that in due course he would negotiate with the Syrians and discuss the Palestinian problem.[34] The situation was such that, just before Kissinger's arrival, Rabin's policies seemed to be a reflection of the secretary's assumptions.

The prime minister continued to demand an end to the state of war even though he knew he could not get it.[35] He spoke in the same breath of a settlement with Sadat, of driving a wedge between Egypt and Syria, of preventing a rift between Israel and America, and of the great importance of the mountain passes in the Sinai. These four points were certainly not compatible and publicly Rabin appeared confused, at best. During the negotiations it became clear that he was not confused but had only been "presenting" various positions in public and had not arrived at the final position. He left this to the negotiations, hoping that Kissinger woud work some miracle or that Sadat might back down.

Kissinger began his negotiations with the Israeli team by giving a comprehensive survey of the international situation and of the problems the United States faced because of the Cambodia and Vietnam crises and in the aftermath of Watergate.[36] Referring to the U.S. role in a number of the world's explosive areas, he emphasized that "America is going through a critical period." Alluding to the U.S.S.R.'s power in the Middle East, to the United States' inability to rely on European (Portuguese and Italian) support for American conventional intervention in another local war, and to the difficulties the administration would face at home in such an event, Kissinger repeatedly stressed that it was Israel that was "entering a period in which its very survival was at stake." He claimed that Israel's position in Congress and in American public opinion had been eroded and would grow even worse if Israel were to be "intransigent" in these negotiations. Again and again he warned that a deadlock would involve the threat or imposition of a war and an oil embargo.[37]

The secretary then proposed a "method" for conducting the substantive negotiations: each side must be willing to make concessions, but it must also keep some of its bargaining points out of the present round, so that it had something more to offer at a later stage. When a member of the Israeli team proposed a withdrawal far beyond the Mitla and Giddi passes in exchange for the longed for "large political concession," the secretary of state remarked, "Don't rush. Keep something for later." Kissinger would also emphasize repeatedly how "tired Israel is of wars" and, at the same time, would agree with the Israeli team that a "political concession" from Egypt was necessary.

The "political concession" that Egypt proposed was an undertaking not to resort to force as part of a military agreement valid for one year: Cairo would not commit itself to extend the UNEF mandate for more than a year. Israel, however, wanted a "political agreement" that would take Egypt out of the conflict for a few years. If this could not be accomplished, Israel argued that it would still have to worry about a war in which Egypt would hold militarily advantageous topographical features. Kissinger claimed that an agreement more in line with the Egyption stand would immediately act to mitigate this danger; while the lack of an agreement would surely bring about a risk of war, an agreement would not.

Jerusalem could not accept this view. Its basic position was that the passes in the Sinai were bargaining advantages that it felt should enable Israel to obtain some "substantial quid pro quo," because a bargaining process must bring a "substantial return" in exchange for a "substantial concession." If the bargaining did not accomplish this, it furnished clear proof of the other side's "true and bad intentions." The Israeli view was that the other side's opening position in the negotiations was a compromise between contradictory goals, and the object of negotiating was to force it to reveal its real intentions or to proclaim its good intentions (even if they were not its real ones). Political declarations and practical steps, however limited, would, perhaps, lead to criticism from the radical Arabs, thus driving a wedge between them and Egypt and/or adding a more moderate dimension to the Arab-Israel conflict. Furthermore, the Israeli public and the various political parties would see such a declaration as the substantive gain to which the Israeli negotiators had publicly committed themselves.

One could argue against the Israeli team that in seeking such a declaration they had publicly painted themselves into a corner. The Israelis could say in rebuttal, however, that the momentum Kissinger was trying to create was only a dubious and complicated substitute—one that would become increasingly hard for Israel to control—for a clear, precise, and meaningful bargaining situation in which Israel and Egypt were the partners to the negotiations and America was the mediator. If Israel did accept a deal based on exchanging Israeli "goods" for the reinforcement of America's power in the region, and Sadat did not decrease but possibly even strengthened his own political-military option, Jerusalem would become dependent on the Washington-Cairo axis.

Kissinger returned to Egypt and, it was later revealed,[38] managed to extract "twelve points" from the Egyptians, which, he argued, fulfilled Israel's political and military demands to a reasonable extent, particularly given the pressures Sadat had to face and his basic strategic advantage.[39] The first of the twelve points was permission for Arab students and families from Gaza to cross the cease-fire line in the Sinai. Such an arrangement had already long been in effect. Israel wanted a sort of open-bridges policy, which it had had with Jordan since 1967, with non-Israeli tourists and normal Arab traffic able to cross the line freely. This arrangement, Jerusalem thought, would contribute to the overall normalization of life in the region.

Israel also mentioned a much more advanced arrangement than such a limited "substitute for peace:" a final, "peacelike" agreement in exchange for a withdrawal from most of the Sinai. Failing that, Israel offered a smaller withdrawal in exchange for a binding declartion of non-belligerency for period of seven to twelve years. Another alternative Jerusalem suggested was a political arrangement that would not end the state of war but that would keep war from breaking out for a reasonable length of time; the territorial concession in this case would be quite small. The second of the twelve points was Egypt's response to these proposals: the passes and the oil fields for a declaration that the conflict would be resolved by peaceful means. The third and fourth points were a variation on the second: a declaration that Egypt would not resort to or threaten to use force and would settle all its differences with Israel peacefully, by negotiation. A weaker form of such a declaration was already included in the 1974 disengagement agreement, with a commitment to observe the cease-fire and to "refrain, from the time of signing of this document, from all military and paramilitary actions against each other." Kissinger argued that the Egyptian proposal contained a stronger and more binding form than in the earlier agreement. Since this undertaking was part of the 1974 agreement, the Israelis saw it as no gain if it remained general and divorced from a time commitment.

Fifth, the Egyptians proposed that the agreement would remain in force as long as a new agreement was not reached. The decisive time element for the Israelis was the U.N. mandate that embodied Egypt's acceptance of an actual "no war" situation. Sixth, Egypt agreed to keep the U.N. forces in the region and to renew their mandate annually, thus hinting that it could be extended beyond the first year. The Israelis wanted more. They felt that if the Egyptians agreed not to resort to force, what difference could it make to them if the UNEF mandate were extended in advance for a much longer, even unlimited period. Furthermore, the Israelis considered that the Egyptian armed forces would be in no condition to go to war for another one or two years, because of the limited volume of Soviet support, and that an election year was approaching in the United States. Relative diplomatic calm and a military lull were thus inevitable, yet the Egyptians seemed to be trying to present those developments as a concession.

The seventh point that Kissinger included in Cairo's package of concessions was a reiteration of one of the understandings included in the 1974 set of agreements: ships bearing Israeli cargoes would be allowed through the Suez Canal. The Israelis thought that Egypt was trying to sell them the same goods twice. The eighth point was similar: the assurance of freedom of navigation in the Bab al-Mandab. Kissinger and Sadat could, of course, see this as reconfirmation of earlier, temporary agreements.

The ninth point concerned the implementation of the military aspects of the agreement. Egypt proposed that the agreement (i.e., the Israeli pullback) be implemented in stages. Israel would be able to prepare a new defensive line while withdrawing from the old one. Jerusalem did not see this as a concession; a withdrawal in stages was in its view an objective, technical necessity. The tenth point was in response to the Israeli demand for some elements of direct cooperation with the Egyptians, such as joint patrols for the inspection of demilitarized areas. The Egyptians suggested establishing an Israeli-Egyptian technical-military committee (like the mixed armistice commission set up under the 1949 armistice agreement) under United Nations auspices, tô handle problems that might arise in the implementation of the agreement. They suggested no demilitarization. The Israelis were, of course, interested in much more: demilitarization and direct cooperation, with the limited U.N. presence.

In response to Israel's demand for a cessation of Egypt's anti-Israeli propaganda, Egypt suggested, as the eleventh point, an undertaking to "limit" such propaganda in the communications organs under its direct control. (One could see in this a reservation about PLO organs in Egypt). An Israeli demand that Cairo should cease its diplomatic warfare in third countries was flatly refused.

Israel had demanded that Egypt enter into trade and economic agreements with it, or at least that it withdraw from the boycott system. As the twelfth point the Egyptians instead proposed a selective easing of the boycott companies dealing with Israel, primarily three American corporations—Ford, Coca Cola, and Xerox. The Israelis could claim, however, that the boycott against these companies had already been lifted, since Egypt was interested in doing business with the three firms in any case.[40]

Israel's reaction to these proposals was that they still constituted no more than a military agreement, lacking any significant political elements that could be portrayed as terminating, or at least freezing, the conflict. Kissinger suggested a technical device, already used in Middle East negotiations, whereby each side could view and present the *form* of the agreement however it liked, while its *content* would, hopefully, act to lower the profile of the conflict. Egyptian and Israeli representatives would meet face-to-face for the final elaboration and signing of the agreement. The Egyptian delegation would be headed by a military man with a diplomat or politician as his deputy, while the Israel delegation would be headed by a diplomat or politician with a military man as his deputy. Doubtless, Rabin was inclined to see this exercise as proof of Egypt's willingness to endow the "settlement," in which Israel would lose strategic positions and gain only one year or two, with no political significance.

An important element in Israel's considerations was the delimitarization of the areas it would leave and the eventual total demilitarization of the Sinai Peninsula in the overall settlement with Egypt. The Egyptians demanded that the Israelis withdraw beyond the passes (and from the oilfields and a strip along the Gulf of Suez), so that the Egyptian army could move further east. A U.N.-controlled buffer zone would be set up between the forces. There would be no formal demilitarized zone, since that was a matter for a final settlement and would have to cover both sides of the international frontier.[41] The second possibility for Jerusalem was to divide the passes between the two sides with practically a small buffer between them. As a third possibility, Israel proposed a smaller withdrawal, which would still increase the distance of its artillery from the canal, for less political and military concessions from Egypt. In any case, it demanded the right to maintain electronic warning installations in the passes because of their strategic topographic signifinance. Egypt should also be permitted such installations.

At the beginning of the shuttle, the Israeli negotiators seemingly abandoned their demands for "nonbelligerency" and, together with Kissinger, laboriously drafted a "tortuous and convoluted acceptance" of Egypt's proposed alternative formula, "non-use of force."[42] Kissinger was dumfounded, then enraged when the Israeli team told him, after all this work was completed, that for the watered-down terms they would evacuate only a part of the passes and an enclave around Abu Rodeis.

When the Israeli team decided that the twelve points did not indicate a turnabout on Cairo's part in favor of peace, Rabin asked Kissinger: "Why must we give Egypt back something of strategic value if there is no change of orientation there?" All the secretary of state could argue, over and over again, was that the very agreement was a significant device for bringing about the desired change of orientation (mainly toward the United States) and that one should not expect a major political commitment at this time. Changing circumstances, due, among other things, to this agreement, would lead to the change of direction. Of course, Kissinger said that this was his hope and expectation, and refused to commit himself to final outcomes. The Israelis side, though, was all to ready to grab at the straw of such a commitment.

The secretary of state's basic pessimism with regard to Israel's international position and his great wariness in assessing the actions of dictators like Sadat led him to adopt a formula that was not enough and yet too complex for the Israelis' taste: help Sadat bind his own hands by decreasing the Israeli challenge in the Sinai. The twelve points were a satisfactory means to this end. Here, then, we have a clear and outstanding built-in constraint: Kissinger spoke of a continued change of orientation by Egypt, to be enhanced by the agreement, though he did not commit himself to such an outcome and only pointed out its probability. Rabin, however, wanted the agreement itself to be an expression of the change in orientation.

Why, in any case, should Egypt threaten Israel? Partly because of the persistent linkage between Egypt and Syria (and the PLO). This meant also that after any agreement, Damascus and the Palestinian organization would demand their share. Should Israel fail to move in this direction, Sadat might be forced to act under Syrian (PLO) pressure, with Saudi backing. Indeed, when asked what would happen if the Syrians made their demands immediately after the agreement with Egypt, Kissinger answered: That "depends on how wise you are."[43] He hinted that another pullback in the Golan would be well worth considering if the Israelis were wise enough to understand that, as a consequence, Soviet involvement in the region would probably decline even more. Significant time would be gained in the north; Sadat would more easily be able to bury himself in Egypt's domestic affairs; there would be an improvement in the United States (because of the election of a new president) and in the international atmosphere, and all these factors would help to moderate the conflict as a whole, when seen in the context of a growing structural linkage between Washington and Cairo.

THE BREAKDOWN OF THE NEGOTIATIONS

If Sadat was consistent in his opinion that only Washington held the key to forcing Israel out of the occupied territories and even to bringing about a "reasonable solution" of the Palestinian problem, then in the March, 1975, negotiations as well, he was trying to enlist Washington to obtain another Israeli pullback. Sadat hoped that if he could not get a withdrawal he would still be able to drive a wedge between Washington and Jerusalem. This hope was based on the fact that the symmetric conditions of a conflict between the superpowers (in which the United States, combatting "purely" Soviet clients, supported Israel) no longer existed, for Egypt had, in the meantime, become an American client as well. Thus, he would gain no matter what happened. Israel's strategy could be perceived as trying, as Rabin publicly said, to drive a wedge between Egypt and Syria, or alternatively, between Egypt and America. Alert to this danger, Sadat agreed to the declaration not to resort to force, so as to show political flexibility without actually abandoning his firm territorial demands and without committing himself to a long time limit.

Apparently, Peres thought that Egypt was trying to mobilize American pressure on Israel to withdraw toward the 1949 borders and to restore the rights of the Palestinians; there was thus no meaningful difference between Cairo and Damascus. Both states' policies were simply different manifestations of the Arab wish to be rid of Israel. They were both working toward the same objective from different directions and were inextricably bound and committed to each other and to the PLO. Whatever Sadat gained in negotiations with Israel was no more than the minimum that Assad would demand. In due course, with his strategic positions improved as a result of the talks, Sadat or his successor would join in hostilities initiated by Syria or instigated by the PLO.

Consequently, all that Israel stood to gain from yielding the oil fields and the passes was a temporary and illusory truce in its relations with the United States, which would ease its pressure for a while. In the next phase of the negotiations, though, Sadat would induce the Americans to obtain more for him and would also firmly support Syria's demands. The Americans would have to back the Syrians too in order to preserve their entente with the Egyptians. Washington's mediation would then be a hindrance to the Israel and Kissinger would become more and more an Egyptian and then a Syrian-Egyptian envoy.

Given this analysis, the logical policy for Israel to follow was to play on America's fear of another Middle Eastern war. Since Israel, in its present boundaries had no reason to go to war, the only quarter from which war could come was Egypt, which, after all, still had a military option.[44] It would thus be more reasonable for Washington to extract concessions from Egypt too. Cairo's military option should be turned to its own disadvantage. It seems that, during the course of the March negotiations, Rabin came to accept this view that was so contrary to his public statements. Even if he had not, he would not let Peres, and perhaps too many cabinet members, emerge as a clear opponent to a bad deal, as most of the public might view it.

Israel, therefore, rejected the twelve points proposed by Egypt and backed by the United States even though doing so could lead to a crisis in its relations with Washington. The Israeli leadership seems to have felt that the end of the shuttle would mean a temporary cessation of the step-by-step strategy, a return to the Geneva framework, and later perhaps a return to the step-by-step approach with Israel in a better position. To Peres at least, the Geneva framework was not without its attractions, and when the talks were suspended he forcefully proclaimed Israel's willingness to go to Geneva.[45] He thought that at Geneva the U.S.S.R. would play a major role and that Syria would try to bind Sadat to a more ideologically correct policy. Since Geneva would be a public forum, all the Arab participants would have to voice a unanimous and extreme policy, the only one that they could agree on and proclaim publicly. The step-by-step strategy, intended to create a cleavage between what at least some Arabs said and what they did, was founded on the moderate views Sadat had expressed in his contacts with the Americans. Peres did not seem to believe that there was or could be such a cleavage, and said that Sadat's moderation was phony unless the Egyptin president was ready for serious political concessions. If Sadat were to participate in a forum in which the expressive side of the conflict was highlighted, he would say things he would not say in private to the Americans and *he* would appear to be the intransigent party. Moreover, typical built-in constraints influenced Peres and the whole cabinet in their relations with Kissinger.

Peres would not tell Kissinger openly what they thought of the common denominator between American and Israeli interests, their own bid for autonomy, and their perception of American fears of war, which they felt should be used against Egypt. Second, the Israelis also had a problem of when to say what to whom. Although they considered an evacuation of the passes a serious change in the strategic situation, they did not want to argue this point at length with Kissinger and the Egyptians. Because Egypt had few forces and little territory in the Sinai, the Israelis did not think that Sadat would risk hostile action so close to the canal if there was some possibility that Israel could reoccupy the area and erase all the gains of Egypt's "historic victory" in October, 1973. An Israeli pullback, however, would improve Egypt's strategic position and Sadat might try to exploit the better conditions to start a war of attrition or a general war when it suited him. There was little sense in making this point to Kissinger or the Egyptians; it was an internal evaluation, not a subject for negotiation. It was far better, from this standpoint, to talk and bargain about assets, which in fact were also manifestations of Arab and Israeli goals and fears than about the substance behind the symbols. For, in the final analysis, if Israel responded to the American-Egyptian demands, it would do so or not because it wanted to avert or was afraid of a future war. This was also Kissinger's main fear, and as a result he would press the Israelis to make concessions; they should show him that they were not afraid of war.

Peres, like Sadat, was willing to risk the breakdown of the talks. Deadlock could mean the resurrection of the threat of war, and each side hoped the United States would then exert pressure on the other party to prevent hostilities. On the other hand, the Geneva Conference might be resumed, and Israel might be isolated (as Sadat hoped) or Egypt's "true" extremism would be exposed to the world (as Peres is said to have thought). During the March shuttle, Rabin apparently accepted or was forced to accept the views attributed to Peres. The defense minister was thus a major force behind the policy, while Rabin bore the burden of public responsibility.

Kissinger's Middle East policy was founded on an assessment of the real power relations between the superpowers, the ability of the local clients to enlist superpower support, and the United States' global and regional interests in the Middle East. From this standpoint, Israel's power was limited and what small capacity it had for imposing its will on the Arabs depended on its political initiative, and maneuverability, and on making the other side look guilty or potentially guilty. After October, 1973, it was no longer in America's interest to maintain the status quo in the region, but rather to cooperate with Egypt, Saudi Arabia, and the gulf states, and to enter into controlled competition with the U.S.S.R. in the region as a whole, and even in Syria and Iraq.

Kissinger's negotiating habit was to portray the forces as he understood them, to make up scenarios of what might happen if the talks failed, and to point out the probable positive results if the talks succeeded. In March, 1975, all the scenarios he drew for Israel were the worst ones possible. Under no circumstances would he go further than to indicate probabilities of positive outcomes and he never committed himself to specific results. Kissinger's negotiating techniques were also based on his assessment of the personalities of his interlocutor and on his belief in his ability to judge and influence people.

The characteristic (positivist-structuralist) "bleak scenario" approach that Kissinger had used in his contacts with the Israelis as early as 1968 had been superseded by a tough and aggressive approach in the negotiations of October, 1973. The Israelis attributed this change to the threat of global confrontation raised by the Yom Kippur War. Once this danger passed, though, he returned to what the Israelis saw as lamentations, overly pessimistic evaluations of the situation, and a worst-case strategy. This approach was foreign to the Israelis' national ethos and to their opinion that bargaining meant taking risks and "fighting it out." Kissinger, far from wanting to "fight it out," sought to lower the profile of the conflict. Thus, at the crucial moment, the intellectual, Jewish professor of government from Harvard faced a team of Israelis who saw themselves as "men of action" and who were annoyed by a gloomy, talkative diaspora Jew who was too consistent in his fears and his pessimism.

Kissinger had dramatized the negotiations a great deal merely by coming to the region and by the time pressures his presence created. Now, however, he could not persuade Peres and Rabin, who had the strong behind-the-scenes support of Golda Meir and Moshe Dayan, to agree to complex temporary arrangements based on probabilities of lowering the profile of the conflict, on the one hand, and on delivering Israeli "goods" to the Arabs via the Americans on the other. In return for this deal Washington would supposedly have become a more influental actor in a few Arab capitals. The Israelis feared, however, that instead of America exerting influence on the Arabs, the Arabs would make even stronger demands for greater Israeli concessions with even more American support in the future. The secretary of state also angered the Israeli negotiators with his style, his endless prattle, and his indiscretions about Arab and other world leaders. The Israelis feared that he was similarly indiscreet about them when he visited the Arab capitals and other places.[46]

Kissinger erred in his assessment of his interlocutors; Rabin was not basically "moderate" nor was it his greatest wish to see the Russians expelled from Egypt. Yet this is what Kissinger might have thought from the years of their acquaintanceship in Washington. Rabin proved to think of the Arab-Israeli conflict in regional-historical terms and to consider that its fundamentalistic nature could not be affected by what seemed to him to be tricks of forms of words and short-term arrangements. He also thought about his own role in the long, fateful struggle over the borders of the country, the value of topographical features, the next war, and, of course, his partisan position and influence vis-à-vis Peres.

Kissinger might have thought of himself as a Jewish knight assisting his brothers in distress, but his brothers saw him more as the "Knight of the woeful countenance," who could not conceive of Jewish pride and statehood or of "fighting it out" for all this statehood entailed. Kissinger's *Realpolitik* meant, to them: accept your weakness as a fact of life, maneuver with great flexibility, and change your image so as to survive until the difficulty passes. The Zionists, the former army men he spoke to, thought such an attitude unrealistic and an invitation for the conflict to go on in conditions worse for Israel. Therefore, when the Israelis considered the "twelve points" during the last two weeks of Kissinger's stay, they rejected them. Sadat remained firm.

By this time, the secretary had spent three weeks in the Middle East, and South Vietnam was beginning to collapse. The final defeat of the Saigon government and the fall of Pnom Penh were imminent. There was criticism on all sides in the western world to the effect that Kissinger could not go on conducting the world's affairs from his suite at the King David Hotel; he could stay in the region for only one or two days more. With all this external pressure on Kissinger, both Cairo and Jerusalem must have thought that their leverage with him had increased while his own had declined.

President Ford's message to the Israeli government during the final phase of the talks must also have affected the Israeli decision.[47] Ford wrote in harsh, almost brutal terms, warning the Israelis that unless they accepted the Egyptian-American suggestions, Israel would be totally isolated and would no longer be able to count on American assistance. The message (Kissinger may have known about it, since he used to request such presidential intervention sometimes) exploded like a bombshell during a crucial cabinet meeting and apparently had the opposite impact of that it intended. Rabin and his colleagues not only looked at the substantive issues the note raised but also reacted to it as a challenge to and test of their political autonomy.

Since he was very inexperienced in delicate domestic political matters, Rabin reported the contents of the president's note to the Knesset Foreign and Defense Affairs Committee. His wish was to obtain the committee's support of the cabinet's decision to refuse Ford's request and so deadlock the negotiations. The message was leaked to the press. The press and most of the public endorsed the government's decision, but, as Kissinger later told Israeli newspaper editors, Ford was placed in a very delicate position. He had to choose between defending the message and continuing his attack on Israel in public or renouncing the message and being on the defensive against Israel. "The president was forced, by the leak . . . to defend himself and attack you."[48] The leak of a document that was a tactical move in a different context thus forced the president into an official attitude of reserve toward Israel; this attitude would later dovetail with the final breakdown of the talks.

Before leaving Israel, Kissinger asked his interlocutors to put off announcing the breakdown of the talks until after he had left the country. He threatened that if they blamed Egypt for the failure of the talks, he would come to Sadat's defense.[49] The Egyptians were thus able to be first with the news of the end of the shuttle and they laid the blame squarely on Israel. The secretary of state joined in the accusations while still aboard the airplane bound back for Washington.[50] A new phase in the United States' Middle East policy seemed to have begun: pressure would be exerted on Israel publicly and an attempt would be made to isolate in from American public opinion. Furthermore, the administration declared that it would reassess its policy on the conflict; during this study phase, Washington was not committed to any specific diplomatic course of action.

LESSONS AND OUTCOME

In this international negotiating process, the following constraints and difficulties arose. First, the formula for the deal was asymmetric. One side of the equation was made up of substantive concessions and the second was composed on probabilities. Under the circumstances such a deal could be seen as giving away something for nothing.

A second built-in constraint involved the reversibility of the agreement. If Egypt violated the accord, Israel could not go back on its concessions unless it was willing to go to war. Egypt, on the other hand, could exploit its improved strategic situation and use "salami tactics," political pressure, and the new interests it shared with the United States to evade its commitments. Third, in a state like Israel there was the added difficulty of "selling" a deal of this sort to the public and to a coalition government that represents a broad spectrum of strategic and political views. The arguments against such a bargain, however, can be made very easily and find support in factions of the government, the rightist opposition, and the public.

Fourth, if negotiators reveal in public or in the negotiations (where, though information is held in secret, it will soon be leaked) their real reasons for accepting an interim agreement (fear of war, for example, or fear of a confrontation with the United States), they have given the other side information that can be used against them in future phases of the talks. The enemy will draw the correct conclusions and will continue to exert political and military pressure. If the negotiators' own public hears about their reasons, its morale can suffer. The negotiators are, therefore, forced to negotiate about symbols (kilometers and topographical features) and to avoid using the arguments that really bother them. The symbol becomes the concrete expression of their fears, and so their position looks petty, weak, and narrow, to third parties, yet is unchangeable. Because the negotiators cannot talk about what is really important to them, the symbols become the heart of the negotiations and assume a separate importance of their own.

The norms and national ethos of the particular society were also an important consideration. There was a broad consensus among Zionists of the left and right that the Arab-Israeli conflict was a protracted conflict. To Kissinger the relevant span of time was only one or two years, until after the American presidential elections. His view of Israel's long-range capabilities was more *realpolitisch* (and, to the Israelis, pessimistic); Israel would soon have to make compromises and concessions for its own good.

The breakdown of the negotiations was also related to some of the antinomies of democracy. The elected representative had to obtain popular support and give the electors reliable information. He had an autonomy of conscience and must fulfil his duties to his party and faction. Even if conscience inclined him to accept Kissinger's probabilities as valid, he must still operate within a political framework that did not consider such probalities adequate. The political system also required that he tell the truth and admit that everything offered was a probability. He thus risked supplying ammunition to his domestic political rivals, who sincerely opposed the deal and/or who could exploit this argument for their own political advantage. He was faced with similar problems regarding the admission that one of his basic considerations was his fear of troubles with the United States.

Another built-in contraint in this negotiating process was the asymmetry between Kissinger's global, superpower view and Rabin and Peres' parochial perspective. The latter were not interested in the "globe" and did not think the United States' great, world-wide problems were decisive considerations in these negotiations. There was little common conceptual ground between Israel and the United States and no agreed common approach before the talks began. The creation of such a common denominator was a very complex process, given the differences in mentality, perspective, habit, and the spaces and times in which they operated. The paradox is that Kissinger thought that there was in fact such a conceptual common denominator, that there was an agreement on the basic harmony of American and Israeli interests in the region and that Israel took the United States' and the administration's views into consideration. In any case, the lack of a common conceptual approach when one side believed such an approach existed led to particularly bitter reactions by the "disappointed" or "deceived" side when the talks broke down.

As I have already mentioned, the step-by-step strategy bears some relation to the neofunctionalist theory developed by Ernst Haas with reference to European unification. Stanley Hoffmann has criticized this theory in both the European and Middle East contexts. In the early stages of the construction of the theory, the essence of Haas's neofunctionalism was that step-by-step economic decisions were preferable to crucial political choices. In the case under discussion, Kissinger apparently assumed that step-by-step political moves (and an economic scene changing correspondingly) were preferable to crucial political choices. Both Haas and Kissinger attempted to erode the edges of crucial political choices, which Hoffmann calls "high politics." Debates on fundamental political decisions, such as the West Bank or resolving the Palestine problem, were avoided because they had no chance of succeeding. It was preferable to deal with more marginal issues of the conflict in the hope that the continuous erosion of the edges would influence the crucial choices of high politics when they arose.

Such an approach entails some belief in a spillover effect from the periphery to the core. Hoffmann has voiced doubts about the validity of such an approach in the West European context and took issue with a strategy based on spillover in the Middle East, during his visit to Israel in January, 1975, and in an article later published in *Foreign Affairs*.[51] He argued, in other words, that erosion of the outer edges of the conflict did not affect the problem of high politics at all. Indeed, the step-by-step strategy simply made the crucial political choices more acute for Israel. Israel slowly divested itself of its bargaining assets in negotiations on interim settlements, and there was no movement on the basic problems at issue between itself and the Arabs.

Another difficulty was Kissinger's tactic, whether by choice or habit, of always predicting the worst possible outcome if the talks should fail. The Israelis did not necessarily agree with his assessments and they certainly resented his positivism ("pessimism") and very worst possible case strategy. They felt, but could not prove, that this was no basis for political decisions. Moreover, the Israelis could also think of frightening scenarios of what might happen if they did accept the agreement he proposed and the probabilities were not realized. Furthermore, the Israelis did not agree that a bargaining process should be an incentive to a process of political and ideological change, but thought it should be the expression of such a change.

Another of the difficulties of the negotiations was that the Israelis tended to think in terms of precedents. The precedent of Kissinger the miracle worker led the Israelis to leave the determination of the course and agenda of the talks to the secretary of state. They left the political initiative to him and to Sadat, hoping, on the basis of the secretary's qualifications and their past experience with him, that a compromise "somewhere in the middle" would be found as the talks progressed. There was also the precedent of the tough Arab opening bargaining position that became more flexible as the talks continued. This had been the pattern in the Kilometer 101 talks, and the Israelis hoped that Sadat would become more flexible and could be compelled to make substantive concessions.

Another constraint of precedents involved the contents of the previous agreements. The Israelis thought that all their gains, even if they took the form of Egyptian undertakings to the United States, were still valid and they did not want to pay for them again. Kissinger apparently thought that there was nothing permanent in these earlier gains and that reinforcement and reconfirmation were required. We can see here the contradiction between a static, formalistic view of such gains and the dynamic view that casts doubt on their value and makes their preservation conditional on continual diplomatic and political movement.

The complexity and imbalance of the system of relationships among the actors was a constraint. Faced with the tangle of dyads—Israel-U.S., Israel-Egypt, Egypt-U.S. (U.S.-Saudi Arabia, Egypt-Syria, Syria-PLO, Syria-U.S.S.R., PLO-U.S.S.R., U.S.S.R.-Egypt, U.S.S.R.-U.S.) the parties were apparently inclined to try to simplify and cut through the Gordian knot with sharp and straight lines of thought. Thus, Israel decided to concentrate on obtaining an Egyptian concession while the United States worked on an Israeli concession.

In 1974, Kissinger's presence and the consequent time contraints and dramatization of the issues had helped make the disengagement talks a success; this time they boomeranged. Both the Israelis and the Egyptians refused to "yield under pressure," since they were not under the same degree of military, economic, and domestic political pressure as they had been in January and May of 1974. The old rule that diplomacy cannot work unless backed by political, military, and economic inducements was reconfirmed. The only way out of the impasse was that the very failure of the talks might create a political vacuum, which both parties feared and were willing to fill with a new agreement. This accord, however, would be reached less dramatically, in long, quite discussions outside the Middle East. The deadlocked shuttle would then be a step in a more complex negotiating process leading to another interim agreement.

During the March talks, the U.S.-backed regimes in South Vietnam and Cambodia collapsed. Paradoxically, Cairo and Jerusalem both saw this development as improving their bargaining power and diminishing Washington's vis-à-vis each of them.

Negotiations such as those between Israel and Egypt begin in a certain international situation that might change during the negotiating. There is, then, always the danger that the parties to the talks will not feel obligated to continue following a course of action dictated by the situation at the outset. The superpowers' problems and need though may make the semiindependent clients see the international situation as more fluid and their ability to exercise influence upon the superpowers accordingly greater. Being indeed pessimistic and suspicious by nature, Kissinger tried to "link" Sadat as he was trying to link the Soviet Union, but yet he remained suspicious of Sadat's intentions and delivery capabilities. The secretary seemed very worried about Sadat's future course, and expected the Israelis to be "reasonable." The Israeli negotiating team, especially those who were more shrewd and pessimistic toward the Arabs and Kissinger and those who were less exposed to public criticism or American expectations (i.e., Mr. Peres, who was just a member of the cabinet, not the prime minister), learned from this that Sadat was bound to gain *because* of his being domestically constrained, or "unreasonable," in Kissinger's eyes. Peres would not yield to Sadat or to Kissinger, if these were the reasons. Many Mapai followers and the public criticized the government for having invited Kissinger and allowing a major crisis with the United States. Peres believed, furthermore, that Rabin would suffer because of the crisis, whereas Peres himself could suggest for the future a less "reasonable" Israeli behavior, to extract more concessions from the United States.

The breakdown of the March, 1975, shuttle demonstrated another dimension of client-superpower relations. Kissinger's image of the speed (as well as the direction) of events was incorrect; he thought in terms of an inevitable explosion, or a war, of Egypt's immediate return to Soviet patronage. He foresaw a "Greek tragedy," as he put it when he left

Israel after the talks broke down.[52] During the period since Sadat acceded to the presidency in Egypt, however, international politics in the Middle East have generally moved at a slower pace. The secretary's fears and "pessimism" proved to be false, yet they dictated a renewed effort to put pressure on Israel and to offer American aid instead of major Egyptian concessions.

Another problem in this set of negotiations was a technical one: the inexperienced Israeli team did not seriously prepare alternative maps, or fall-back positions, in preparatory negotiations with the United States. No alternative formulations for the set of different, mostly secret, instruments of agreement were prepared before the shuttle, and the Americans later cited this oversight as evidence of Israel's bad faith. Whether or not they acted in bad faith, the Israeli negotiators were divided among themselves; each member of the team—Rabin, Peres, and Allon, wanted to put himself forward, to increase his public support.[53] During the shuttle, Rabin's popularity in the public opinion polls sank to the lowest level for any prime minister in the history of such polls.

6

From the Sinai 2 Agreement to Begin's Victory, March, 1975-May, 1977

AFTER THE BREAKDOWN OF SHUTTLE DIPLOMACY: WASHINGTON TO THE VIRGIN ISLANDS TO BONN AND BACK (MARCH–SEPTEMBER, 1975)

When the March, 1975, talks broke down Israeli-American relations entered a period of confrontation or "reassessment," as the administration dubbed the campaign it conducted, wittingly or unwittingly, against Israel inside the United States.[1] Sadat's calculations about the wedge that would be driven between Washington and Israel in the event the talks broke down at first proved accurate. He did not want a political vacuum to come about, however, for such a vacuum might have raised the profile of the conflict, and he could still make respectable gains if the profile were kept relatively low. So, on March 26, 1975, Sadat proclaimed that the Suez Canal would be reopened on June 5 of that year. This move was likely to be politically profitable to him. It was a gesture to Washington that he had no intention of exacerbating the conflict. It was also likely to be economically profitable, because of the levies on passage through the canal. Psychological and political profit could be gained inside Egypt, and Sadat portrayed to his people the opening of the canal under Egyptian sovereignty as one of the achievements of the October War.

Sadat did not think he would be able to extract another Israeli concession for the reopening of the canal at this stage. He probably decided instead to use it to signal Washington that Cairo had no intention of reverting to Moscow's patronage or raising the profile of the conflict sharply.

We cannot know for certain why Kissinger and Ford attacked the Rabin government publicly and privately inside the United States in March–April, 1975.[2] They might have been afraid of a total political deadlock in the region, but Sadat dispelled that fear to some extent in late March. They might have felt personally injured or insulted or have been worried about their commitments to Europe and Japan. Israel's obstinacy over the interim agreement might have convinced them that they should deal with Israel's power base inside the United States in order to soften Jerusalem for the next round of talks. The secretary also might have become aware of Mr. Peres's tactics: demonstrate Israeli "unreasonableness" in order to be compensated, reconvene the Geneva forum in order to expose Arab intransigence, and demonstrate to the Israelis that neither was going to work.

In private talks, the secretary of state argued that the Israelis had been told that there was no hope of Egypt's renouncing belligerency and that Egypt wanted the deal to include at least the passes and the oil fields. Israel had, however, agreed to begin the talks and thus implicitly agreed to be flexible on these issues. Ford criticized Israel in public on a number of occasions. In general, though, the campaign against the Rabin government took place in behind-the-scenes briefings and conversations between members of the administration and the mass media.

Kissinger had always warned the Israelis that they would acquire the image of being obstinate and irrational if any round of talks should fail; now he actively set out to make sure this happened. In fact, the administration organized and legitimized criticism against Israel's "intransigence" that was widespread in the liberal media and among many civil servants. As usual, the Americans used arms supplies to exert pressure: they "froze" Israeli requests for new and sophisticated items, particularly F–15 fighters and laser-guided bombs for use against missile batteries.[3]

Rabin responded as he had when he was ambassador in Washington. According to one version, he sent the Jewish lobby into action at the suggestions of the lobby itself, to have most of the Senate sign a petition to the administration not to take action detrimental to Israel's needs and security.[4] The letter, signed by seventy-six senators, was thought by some observers in Washington to have stopped the momentum of the administration's "reassessment."[5] In other words, the direct clash with Israel was replaced by a more subtle, traditional approach—a continued dialogue with an eager Egypt, coupled with "linkage" benefits, and a resumed dialogue with Israel, aimed at American compensations for Egyptian demands and at a bargaining process between Israel and Egypt themselves. Geneva, or any other form of all-Arab-Israeli comprehensive talks, was considered and dropped again, because that framework would have brought about public discussions of too many contradictory demands by all parties in a radical atmosphere. Step-by-step remained the only viable strategy and a new Sinai deal with Egypt the only possible course, as Sadat was still willing to negotiate. Rabin analyzed the situation during the "reassessment" period in the following terms.[6]

a. Israel's strategic and political aims could not possibly be served by a new Middle East war. Even if, as he assumed, Israel won the war, its victory would not be translated into strategic political gains; American interests and Soviet aid to Arab countries would prevent a clear-cut, definite regional change in Israel's favor. Therefore, the prevention of a new Middle East war was in the interest of Israel.

b. The American national interest in promoting U.S.-Arab relations could not be ignored, even if Israel would have preferred a break-through in Arab-Israeli relations as the key to stability in the region. Israel should, therefore, use this American interest, which could be promoted also because of its concessions to Arabs, and get American aid and political obligations on concrete issues—PLO, West Bank, future negotiations, etc.—if Egypt was incapable of making them.

c. Thus, the retention of strategic territorial-political vital assets in the West Bank and the Golan Heights, northern Sinai, and Sharm-el-Sheikh should be pursued by prolonged, phased, separate bargaining on the rest of the occupied territories with Egypt and Syria, while retaining possible control over the bargaining process. If Egypt was incapable of delivering political concessions, at least a wedge should be driven between Cairo and Damascus, Cairo and the PLO, and Cairo plus Saudi Arabia and Damascus and the PLO.

d. An American-Israeli confrontation, as the "reassessment" proved to be, was damaging to Israel politically and psychologically inside the United States. Even if it could have been limited and contained with Congressional aid, such a dangerous path should be reserved to protect vital Israeli interests in the future, like West Bank assets and fighting the PLO.

Mr. Peres seemed not to have shared some of these strategic assumptions.[7] A "no war" doctrine might push the other side to display its war option in order to apply pressure on the United States. One might reject war as a viable solution, but one should not formulate, in public, as Rabin did, a "no war" approach on the eve of negotiations that are based upon the relative ability of the parties to go to war and thus endanger U.S. interests. Israel should be ready for war, the Arabs should be confronted with its military risks, and the United States should apply pressure on *all* parties, and aid Israel, if it wanted to prevent war. At the same time, Mr. Peres realized that some benefits to Israel that might have emerged as a result of the March failure—a Geneva conference with publicly intransigent Arabs or a more balanced American approach to a "less reasonable" Israel—did not materialize. Instead, weapon deliveries were upheld, and Sadat seemed to score points with Washington and American public opinion. The diplomatic-strategic framework, the step-by-step approach, seemed to have been kept by both Kissinger and Sadat. Reluctantly, the defense minister accepted it as the only given framework for further negotiations, to be conducted with Egypt in exchange for minimal territorial concessions and maximal U.S. military and political aid. To Dayan's and the Likud's dismay, the cabinet basically moved back to accept U.S.-Israeli relations as a major variable in its overall assessment of future negotiations.

In June, 1975, Ford and Sadat met in Salzburg for talks.[8] The full details of their talks are not known, but apparently Ford offered the Egyptians economic aid: grain supplies, increased financial aid (from the $250 million appropriated for 1974 to $750 million for 1975), and help in setting up a western consortium to raise more direct financial assistance and investments in Egypt. The United States repeated its offer of nuclear reactors for peaceful purposes.

The large-scale American economic aid could very possibly have been connected with the administration's disappointment over Saudi and Iranian investments in Egypt up to then.[9] The Saudis proved to be very conservative in their foreign investments in general. Instead of helping to modernize the Egyptian infrastructure, Saudi Arabia and the gulf states began to buy more and more arms. Increasing numbers of increasingly sophisticated weapons were purchased in the United States, Britain, and France; Israeli sources estimated the orders placed in 1974–75 by the whole Arab coalition in the West for the next five years at $17,000 million.[10] The weapons bought by Saudi Arabia were regarded by Israel as a strategic arsenal for the Arab coalition. They might also serve to give the Saudis leverage over Egypt, to keep the U.S.S.R. from coming back as weapon suppliers and to provide Egypt with a modern military option if Riyadh decided one was necessary. Because Egypt did not have enough Arab aid to overcome its pressing infrastructure and supply problems, the United States did its best to fill the gap. Washington, of course, was trying to create a linkage between Cairo's economic and technological needs and broaden American-Egyptian cooperation. It was also trying to link the Egyptians' more urgent needs and a new interim agreement.

It was reported that at Salzburg Sadat suggested some compromises concerning some basic Israeli demands on the duration of the UNEF mandate, and the staffing of the warning stations that Israel wanted to maintain in the Sinai passes. The Israelis wanted their installations to be manned by Israelis; Sadat categorically refused to allow an Israeli presence in the passes, suggesting that Americans staff the warning stations instead.[11]

Israel's defense minister, Shimon Peres, regarded an American presence in the passes as a much better guarantee than the U.N. force that supervised the existing agreement. The Egyptians would be more wary of the American force in the event of war than they had been of the UNEF in 1967 and 1973. They would also have to consider the U.S. reaction if they fought their way through the American positions. Furthermore, an American presence would commit Washington more directly to maintaining the agreement.[12]

The Americans were not interested in an American presence in the passes, particularly since Congress and the public would probably be very cool to any kind of direct presence in conflict areas. Kissinger told the Israelis, though, that it might be possible to staff some installations with a few American technicians. Washington also studied the map very carefully and suggested a solution to the problem of the passes: since the Mitla and Giddi gradually ascend into hills and higher peaks at both ends, Israel might give up the western hills and peaks and try to retain part of the eastern hills.

When Rabin visited Washington in early June, 1975, he agreed to cede to the Egyptians more territory along the Gulf of Suez and to allow them the continuous strip of land to the Abu Rodeis oilfields that had been refused in March.[13] The Israelis did try to haggle over the Sinai line suggested by the Americans, but mainly they tried to reach an agreement with the Americans on a common strategic concept of the whole negotiating process and on American concessions to Egypt. Jerusalem also tried to use the warning station systems as a justification for as large an American, and Israeli, presence as possible. The IDF would maintain the existing warning installation at Umm Hashiba in the Giddi Pass, but six more stations would be built in both passes, which would be staffed by American technicians and would supply information to both Egypt and Israel.

At a meeting in the Virgin Islands in early August, Ambassador Dinitz and the secretary of state apparently agreed in principle on a number of points.[14] First, Israel would pull back to the lower part of the eastern hills. Second, there would be an American presence in the passes. Third, the United States would be committed to support Israel in case of active Soviet intervention. Fourth, there would be no Jordanian-Israeli interim agreement for the period of the interim agreement with Egypt. Fifth, there would be no major Israeli withdrawal in the Golan, though "cosmetic changes" could be considered. (Of course, Jerusalem would be willing to reconsider this point if there were a final Syrian-Israeli peace agreement, but since Damacus was not speaking in terms of peace acceptable to Israel, this could not be attained in the foreseeable future.) Sixth, Israel would receive over $2,000 million in military and economic aid annually for the period of the Israeli-Egyptian agreement; the United States would remain committed to Israel's security and would continue military and economic aid later. Sophisticated hardware, such as the laser-guided bombs, whose delivery was now prohibited or blocked, would be released. Seventh, Israel—and the United States—would not negotiate with the PLO.

Soon afterward, Rabin and Kissinger met in Bonn and agreed on a new round of the shuttle to begin in August, 1975.[15] The date was important because the annual U.N. General Assembly session was scheduled for September and the PLO and Syria might try to suspend or expel Israel from the assembly. A second interim agreement with Egypt might keep Cairo from giving such an attempt its full support.

The Americans thus changed their diplomatic techniques but not their aims. Instead of conducting dramatic negotiations in the area under the pressure of time and with the full attention of the world's media, Kissinger first reached an understanding with Sadat, after his statement about reopening the canal. The secretary of state then secretly resumed negotiations with the Israelis. The negotiations, which began in May and took place in Washington, the Virgin Islands, and Bonn, were not understood as such in Israel and the public could not follow them with the same degree of awareness and sensitivity as they did the shuttles. Thus, when Kissinger arrived in Israel on August 21, the parliamentary opposition (groups like Dayan's, within the alignment that opposed an agreement that would not take Egypt out of the conflict, or the young religious groups that were interested in the West Bank and the Golan and were determined to fight any withdrawal in order to delay and prevent, if possible, future changes in the occupied areas most important to them) demonstrated against his presence, but the negotiations had already gathered too much momentum for their opposition to have any impact.

The pragmatic leadership of the National Religious party, which was cautious in foreign policy and economically dependent on participation in the government, endorsed the new Sinai accord. The militant NRP leadership had to consider splitting the party without Rafi's joining them, if Mr. Peres accepted the new accord. General Sharon, the most ruthless and popular exponent of the rightist opposition, was offered and accepted a job as adviser in the prime minister's office. Thus, the most outspoken and popular opponent of the interim agreement was silenced just as the agreement was being signed.[16] A wedge was driven between Dayan and Peres when the defense minister accepted the new deal.

The Israeli public was still hostile to the interim agreement, just as it had been in March. The government had not prepared it for the territorial concessions agreed upon over the spring and summer. However, over the six months that had elapsed since the breakdown of the talks, the incomplete and contradictory news about the ongoing secret negotiations, the precedent of Israel saying "no" during a crucial shuttle, Washington's "reassessment," the deteriorating economic situation, and the acknowledged need for U.S. aid seem to have led to the attrition of active public hostility. Rabin's stubborn refusal in March had won him enough support and had strengthened his domestic position enough so that he could now afford to say "yes."

Indeed, Rabin had committed himself so firmly to a new agreement, based mainly on American political and economic commitments, that when Kissinger told him that some of the terms decided in Bonn and the Virgin Islands were no longer tenable, Rabin behaved as if he, Rabin, had better accept the others to prevent another American-Israeli show-down.[17] Both Rabin and Peres would not block a new agreement because Washington did not go to Geneva and did not press Egypt; the administration threatened Israel from within the United States and made some direct concessions to Israel with regard to U.S. technicians and American military and economic aid. Egypt accepted what Israel thought of as a better line in the Sinai, which gave the IDF control over the eastern approaches to the passes. Israel retained a warning station at the Giddi pass, and Egypt was ready to extend the UNEF mandate automatically for the next three years. Israel became, however, increasingly disappointed with the political promises Kissinger had made during the secret talks at the Virgin Islands and Bonn. The secretary of state told the Israelis that Congress would not approve an automatic American commitment against Soviet intervention. Other reservations could imply to the Israelis that American commitments regarding Syria, the PLO, and Jordan would not necessarily be binding either but would be subject to Syrian pressure and to possible changes in Syria's pro-Soviet orientation and in the PLO's expressed position.

Kissinger also suggested an informal general conference on the Middle East conflict. The conference was apparently intended as an interim diplomatic feeler that would at least fill the gap between a second Sinai agreement and the American election year of 1976, even if it did not succeed in bringing about another agreement with Syria.[18]

The Israelis tended to regard these maneuvers with dismay, and for the first time Jerusalem accused Kissinger of having lied.[19] At the same time, Israel had to adapt to several changes in the domestic American scenery, and to make use of them as far as possible. Congress wanted to restrict American commitments in the world's trouble spots, or at least to receive an exact and public description of any direct, indirect, moral, or immoral promise of intervention that the administration planned to make. The Ford-Kissinger administration was thus deprived of an important tool of diplomacy; the president would no longer be fully free to make secret promises, sometimes with only the limited knowledge of key members of Congress. Such promises did not constitute formal American commitments, but could encourage the state to whom they were made to take political steps that, it was hoped, would remove any need for the Americans to fulfil their promise.[20]

Congress' insistence on being informed about all foreign commitments was due in part to another change in U.S. politics. Since the fall of the American-backed side in South Vietnam and because of a growing criticism of his détente policy, his approach to the SALT 2 and his rivalry with defense secretary Schlesinger, Kissinger's relations with the Senate and the House had deteriorated. Furthermore, after Senator Fulbright lost the elections in 1974, Kissinger could no longer count on a direct link with a sympathetic, discreet, and powerful chairman of the Senate Foreign Relations Committee.

Meanwhile, Israel came under fire because of Syrian initiative at the United Nations.[21] The United States would help Israel at the U.N., and an attempt to expel Israel might be foiled. However, Egyptian help, too, would be necssary to fend off the attack, and Cairo would demand its reward.[22]

It was under these circumstances, then, that the Israel government agreed to the final shuttle in August, 1975.

THE 1975 SINAI AGREEMENT

On September 1, after ten days of the shuttle, Israel and Egypt initialed the new Sinai pact in separate ceremonies in Alexandria and Jerusalem.[23] Secretary Kissinger initialed the U.S. proposal concerning the early warning system and the provisions for the stationing of American technicians in the Sinai. The agreement was then officially signed by representatives of both sides during a brief ceremony in Geneva on September 4.

The agreement between Israel and Egypt comprised nine articles and was accompanied by a detailed map of the new lines in the Sinai. In the first three political articles, both sides agreed that the conflict should not be resolved by military force but by peaceful means, and expressed their determination to reach a final and just peace settlement through negotiations on the basis of Security Council Resolution 338. In addition, the parties pledged not to resort to the threat or use of force or military blockade against each other, to continue scrupulously to observe the cease-fire, and to refrain from all military or paramilitary actions against each other.

Articles four, five, and six dealt with the exact position of the forces of the parties and established the following areas: a limited-forces zone, like the one agreed on in the 1974 accord; a buffer zone where the United Nations Emergency Force would function on the same terms as those outlined in the agreement; and an area where there would be no military forces at all. Both parties undertook to extend the UNEF's mandate annually and to establish a joint commission for the duration of the agreement to discuss problems that might arise in connection with the agreement and to assist the UNEF.

In article seven, it was stated that nonmilitary cargoes coming from or destined for Israel were permitted through the Suez Canal; the last two articles confirmed that the parties saw in the agreement a significant step toward a just and lasting peace and that the agreement itself was not a final peace agreement. After again stating their intention to continue their efforts to reach a final peace settlement within the framework of the Geneva Conference and Resolution 338 both sides confirmed that the agreement should remain in force until superceded by a new agreement.

In the Annex to the Egypt-Israel Agreement, certain principles were established to help the parties' representatives prepare a detailed Protocol in the Military Working Group at Geneva. These guidelines, an integral part of the agreement itself, included the establishment of an early warning system by U.S. civilian personnel in the buffer zone, the continuation of aerial reconnaissance missions by the United States, limitations on arms and forces, and the details of a de facto demilitarization of an area on the eastern shore of the Gulf of Suez.

The provisions for the early warning system were contained in a formal American proposal that constituted an addendum to the agreement. There would be two strategic warning surveillance stations, staffed by Israeli and Egyptian teams of no more than 250 to carry out electronic and visual surveillance. The United States would establish three stations for tactical early warning, operated by American civilian personnel and located near the Mitla and Giddi passes. These stations would be supported by three unmanned electronic sensor fields at either end of each pass, near each station and along the roads leading to and from each station. The U.S. personnel would have to check on operations at the Egyptian and Israeli stations and immediately report any unauthorized use of the stations. The Americans would also have to give immediate notification of any movement of forces other than United Nations' troops into the passes or of any preparation for such movements. Only small arms for personal protection would be allowed at the surveillance posts.

The American personnel could number no more than 200 and could be evacuated by their government whenever their lives were thought to be in jeopardy or when their tasks were no longer necessary. In the latter case, both sides would have to be given sufficient advance notice to make other arrangements. If Egypt and Israel both requested the termination of the U.S. presence, the Americans would be withdrawn. At a session of the House of Representatives international relations committee on September 8, 1975, Kissinger elaborated on this aspect of the agreement.[24] He said that Israel, which already operated an early warning station in the western approaches to the Mitla and Giddi passes, insisted on keeping its installation and offered Egypt the opportunity to build a similar one on the other side. The United States at first refused to staff these two stations because so many Americans would then have had to be present in the area. Finally the United States agreed to assume the supervision of the two stations when it became obvious that no agreement would be reached unless the problem of early strategic warning were resolved. Israel had also insisted—and indeed made it a condition for the agreement—that the United States should be responsible for tactical warning; it was this provision that made the presence of 200 American technicians necessary.

On October 3, the House international relations committee passed a resolution agreeing to the stationing of 200 American technicians. A number of conditions were attached to this approval, though. The technicians would be removed immediately if fighting should break out or if both houses of Congress directed their removal in a veto-proof concurrent resolution. The technicians must be civilian volunteers. The president would report semiannually to Congress on the status of the force.[25]

During the committee's deliberations, American newspapers published secret American assurances to Egypt and Israel that had been reported in an executive session of the committee. On September 17–18, the *New York Times* printed four documents containing three "assurances" to Israel and one to Egypt. The Times claimed that the documents had "been authenticated by officials who had seen the original" ones. In reaction to these revelations, several senators demanded the official release of all documents including U.S. commitments to the parties and demanded a Congressional vote on the undertakings. The administration claimed that it had in fact submitted all the relevant documents to Congress under the terms of the Case Act, which provides for the submission of executive agreements to Congress with "an appropriate injunction of secrecy to be removed only upon due notice from the president."[26] In his testimony to the Senate foreign relations committee on October 7, Kissinger stressed that "no assurances or undertakings beyond those submitted to the Congress are binding upon the United States. We will make no contrary claim in the future; nor can any other government."[27]

In his Senate testimony, Kissinger also stated that not all the provisions of the documents were "binding undertakings." Many of the terms were statements of intention, provisions subject to rapid change, or undertakings conditional on the prior authorization and approval by Congress or which fall within the president's constitutional authority to conduct the foreign relations of the United States. Still, Kissinger went on, having agreed to these provisions Washington was not morally or politically free to act as though they did not exist. "They are important statements of diplomatic policy and engage the good faith of the United States so long as the circumstances that gave rise to them persist." Representative Lee Hamilton submitted the documents published by the *New York Times* as an appendix to the House international relations committee report, *To Implement the United States Proposal for the Early Warning System in Sinai;* the provisions thus obtained a semiofficial character.

The first of the four documents was entitled *Memorandum of Agreement between the United States and Israel* and contained sixteen provisions relating to American aid to Israel and to diplomatic action in the Middle East. The Americans promised to make every effort to be responsive to Israel's long-term defense, energy, and economic needs beginning with the 1976 fiscal year. Congressional approval, of course, would be necessary. The United States viewed Israel's request for advanced weapons sympathetically and agreed to a joint study of Israel's military needs, including agreement on specific items in a special U.S.-Israel memorandum, "Addendum on Arms." The addendum declared Washington's determination to maintain Israel's defensive capacity by supplying advanced equipment, such as F-15 and F-16 aircraft. The Americans also agreed to undertake a joint, and sympathetic, study of sophisticated, high-technology items, including Pershing ground-to-ground missiles with conventional warheads.

To make up for the withdrawal from Abu Rodeis and in the event that Israel could not buy the oil it needed through normal channels, Washington agreed to sell and help ship petroleum to Israel for the next five years. If an oil embargo were imposed on the United States, the U.S. would make oil available for purchase through the International Energy Agency. The administration also took Israel's oil expenses into consideration in determining the overall figure of aid to Israel. Furthermore, the United States would make available funds for the construction of storage facilities to allow Israel to keep one year of reserves on hand.

The memorandum's diplomatic and political provisions included a statement that the United States would not expect Israel to implement its part of the agreement unless Egypt permitted Israeli cargo through the Suez Canal. Israel would be consulted on any action the United States might take in response to an Egyptian violation of the agreement. The United States would veto any Security Council resolution that might be detrimental to the agreement and it would prevent all attempts by third parties to consider proposals detrimental to Israeli interests.

There were also more general political provisions: the next agreement with Egypt should be a final peace agreement. In the event of a threat to Israel's security by a world power, Washington would "consult promptly with the government of Israel with respect to what diplomatic or other support or assistance it could lend Israel in accordance with its constitutional practices." Jerusalem and Washington also agreed to prepart a contingency plan for a military supply operation within two months.

The Americans stated that they recognized that the Egyptian-Israeli agreement entailing withdrawal from vital areas in the Sinai was a very important move by Israel in the pursuit of an overall peace agreement. The United States expressed the view that Egypt's commitments under the agreement were not contingent on any developments in Israel's relations with other Arab states. Furthermore, the United States shared Israel's opinion that negotiations with Jordan were to point toward an overall peace settlement. This provision was aimed at indefinitely delaying negotiations on the West Bank, as the step-by-step strategy, rather than an overall peace settlement, remained the common U.S.-Israeli negotiating framework.

America, furthermore, declared that it regarded the Bab al-Mandab and the Straits of Tiran as international waterways and that it would support Israel's freedom of passage and overflight in the straits and the Red Sea. Finally, Israel and the United States agreed to regard the Israeli-Egyptian accord as binding even if the UNEF were withdrawn and no other agreement replaced this one. This provision was intended to cover the possibility that the U.N. force might be withdrawn without prior agreement of Egypt, Israel, and the United States.

This memorandum and the "Addendum on Arms" comprised seventeen provisions, while the "Assurances to Egypt" comprised only three items. The United States promised to make a serious attempt to bring about another round of negotiations between Syria and Israel. Egypt would be consulted through diplomatic channels if Israel violated the agreement (this provision corresponded to one in the memorandum to Israel). Finally, the Americans would give the Egyptians technical assistance to establish their early warning station.

On September 18, the *New York Times* published the text of a document entitled "Memorandum of Agreement between the United States and Israel with Regard to the Geneva Peace Conference." In it the two states promised to cooperate in planning the timing of the conference and in ensuring that the conference promoted a negotiated peace between Israel and its neighbors. The United States stated that it would not recognize or negotiate with the PLO so long as the PLO did not recognize Israel's right to exist or did not accept Security Council Resolutions 242 and 338. Jerusalem and Washington pledged to coordinate their strategy and positions regarding the PLO and the participation of other states at the conference. The United States undertook to ensure that all substantive negotiations at the conference would be on a bilateral basis and promised to veto any Security Council Resolution that would change the terms of reference of the conference or of Resolution 242 and 338. The United States also promised that it would try to make certain that the role of the conference's cochairmen (the United States and the U.S.S.R.) would be consistent with the understanding reached by Israel and the United States on December 20, 1973.

RESULTS OF THE SINAI AGREEMENT AND OF THE STEP-BY-STEP STRATEGY, 1975–76

U.S.-Israeli Relations, and Israel's Domestic Situation

An analysis of the Sinai accords from the perspective of 1977 should examine three aspects of Middle Eastern politics: American-Israeli relations, the relations of the superpowers and the Arab coalition, and relations within the Arab coalition.

Congressional approval of the Sinai agreement and the implementation of the commitments entailed in the accord led to arms and money for Israel and to friction between Israel and some of its power bases in the United States: the media and both houses of Congress. This friction then relieved the administration of the need to fulfill some of its commitments and permitted it to dilute others.

The agreement's financial provisions and, particularly, the provision for American technicians led to a long, drawn-out debate. Kissinger and Sisco testified on behalf of the administration to the various committees and joint committees of both houses of Congress. Because of the Case Act, the great sensitivity to foreign involvements since the Vietnam War, and the increasing public criticism of the Nixon-Kissinger administration's secret deals, all aspects of the Sinai accords were discussed in closed sessions of both houses.[28]

Kissinger had testified that parts of the agreements were less binding than others and that they would be interpreted in light of future circumstances. This provides a good illustration of the special nature of the Sinai agreement, Israel's relations with the United States and the administration's ability to reach agreements with foreign countries in the aftermath of Vietnam and Watergate. The Sinai agreement was no ordinary international treaty ratified by Congress. Senators Javits and Case suggested that Congress vote to approve all the agreements included in the accord in order to commit the administration more deeply to the accords. Their fight for formal ratification ended in an odd compromise: the non-monetary sections of the agreements were discussed in executive sessions of both houses. Their contents were leaked to the press and Lee Hamilton read the reports into the Congressional Record to give them semiofficial significance.

The provisions regarding 200 American technicians, whose number reminded some Americans of the early days of the U.S. involvement in Vietnam, caused apprehension in Congress. The discussions exposed the administration difficulty in undertaking long-term commitments to Israel, in the framework of a step-by-step strategy, which kept the conflict open. Kissinger's and Sisco's testimonies highlighted America's interest in Egypt and the other moderate Arab states as a means of keeping the profile of the conflict low and avoiding new foreign entanglements by the United States. Congress was willing to help Israel and to provide political and economic aid to Egypt, but insisted on clear-cut obligations. Nevertheless, the U.S. political commitment to Israel was formulated in such a way that it remained subject to the interpretation of the administration. The Israelis, on the other hand, could hope to be able to use the political commitments, especially with regard to the PLO and Jordan in the future, working together with their Congressional friends. A "step" toward Jordan could be fought over, because Kissinger agreed to no further negotiations with Amman short of peace "as circumstances allow." The same could be applied to another "step" toward Egypt, unless Cairo agreed to far-reaching concessions, and the same might have been said to Congressional leaders with regard to Syria, apart from "cosmetic changes" in the Golan Line. Yet the Israelis knew that their deal was limited in time. Sadat told the Americans privately that the agreement would be binding for three years. The next round of Arab-Israeli negotiations would have to take place in 1977 (after the American presidential elections) toward implementation in 1978.

In the meantime, some American promises were not kept, and the Israelis were closely watching U.S.-Egyptian relations. Ford and Kissinger introduced the idea of direct American military aid to Cairo to replace Soviet supplies.

The Pershing deal was "killed" in discussions between the Israeli and American defense establishments, with the active participation of the U.S. media.[29] After signing the Sinai agreement Israel presented a long list of the arms it wanted. Some of the items were far-reaching in scope and sophistication; they were supposed to give Israel an autonomous strategic early warning capacity to make up for the loss of the passes and the limitations of the proposed American stations.[30] The Americans refused them, making comments about the client's sense of proportion.

Other Israeli arms requests were approved: laser-guided bombs, artillery rockets with a range of eighty kilometers, conventional warheads (specially developed models of the Lance missile), unpiloted aircraft, electronic jamming devices, large numbers of armored personnel carriers, artillery, and tanks (American tank production was accelerated after the 1973 war.) The debate that erupted in the United States over Israel's list and its arms needs was viewed against a background of leaks about requests rejected and deals approved.

The CIA was active in all these maneuvers during the winter of 1975–76 and argued that, after the Sinai accord, Israel was stronger than ever. It circulated an assessment that the balance of forces had improved sharply in Israel's favor.[31] Israel sent its own experts, notably General Aharon Yariv, to the United States to refute this claim. The CIA calculations were based on the IDF and armed forces confronting Israel directly, excluding Saudi Arabia, Algeria, and Iraq. Indeed, while the debate over arms for Israel blazed, the United States was deciding on massive arms sales to Saudi Arabia and the beginning of supplies to Egypt— deals which involved some very important American economic, industrial, defense, and political interests.[32]

Meanwhile, the CIA also leaked a report that Israel had operational nuclear weapons—ten to twenty atom bombs. *Time* magazine claimed that Dayan had ordered the bombs to be made operational during the Yom Kippur War.[33] Israel's attempts to prevent the beginnings of American military sales to Egypt and the huge sale to Saudi Arabia were engulfed by news of how strong in conventional arms Israel had become since the disengagement agreements and of how it had acquired a nuclear capability as well.

There was no detailed formal link between the second Sinai agreement and the promises of American funds to cover Israel's economic and military needs. Kissinger told Congress that Washington had not "bought" the interim agreement. In fact, Israel lost the income from the oil wells in Sinai, had to construct a new military line in Sinai, and had to pay higher prices for American arms. Jerusalem ended up absorbing all these costs itself, contrary to its expectations that it would receive at least a few annual payments to compensate it for the loss of the oil fields. Still, Congress did appropriate more than two billion dollars for the 1976 fiscal year. A similar sum was expected for 1977 and 1978, and military purchases were ordered from the United States accordingly by Israel in advance for the whole period.[34] In American if not Israeli terms this was a vast sum, constituting the lion's share of the entire foreign aid budget.

In the 1977 budget estimates, which were discussed in 1976, Ford cut $500 million from the amount Israel was promised. Rabin preferred not to clash openly and directly with Ford. The president faced tough competition from Ronald Reagan for the Republican presidential nomination, and foreign aid was not popular with the conservative American voter. Rabin visited Washington in the winter of 1976 and received confirmation in principle that further arms supplies would be released. He chose to assume that approval of the arms meant approval of the money to pay for them and thus left the actual fight to restore all or part of the $500 million of the budget to Israeli lobbyists in Congress.[35]

The fight for the money was part of an Israeli attempt to compete for arms with the Arabs, to attain conventional, technological superiority, and to maintain a relatively high standard of living in Israel, with Congress' help. This attempt was itself the best illustration of the qualitative change that had taken place in Jerusalem's relationship with Washington; it left the Administration more room to maneuver vis-à-vis Jerusalem, at least with regard to aid to Egypt (and Syria) and arms deals with Saudi Arabia. From 1969–73, Israel had been dependent, though not overwhelmingly so, on American conventional arms and, to a lesser extent, on American financial aid. Congress' greater support for Israel influenced its relations with the administration, while the extent of support from the administration itself tended to grow. (In 1976, Israel was substantially dependent on American arms supplies and overwhelmingly dependent on American economic assistance.) The administration's relations with Congress, too, had changed, largely because of Congress' wish to avoid extensive foreign commitments and to respond to the voters' desire to reduce foreign aid. Caught as they were between Israel's requests for aid and the general antiaid mood of the public, the members of both houses could not but arrive at a compromise, which was based upon their wish to prevent a new Middle East war and which took into consideration the need to extend financial and military aid to Egypt and military supplies to Saudi Arabia. Without a commitment to Israel alone in this matter, the administration assumed the role of initiator and ultimate arbiter of foreign aid, placing itself above the fray so that it could use aid to serve its objectives in the Middle East.

Thus, many of the built-in constraints influenced Israeli public judgment of the Sinai 2 agreement. First negotiated in secret and later published as a set of complicated provisions, some of them admittedly open to different future interpretations, and lacking a tangible Egyptian quid pro quo except a minor concession with regard to the free passage of Israeli cargoes in the Suez Canal, the agreement seemed after a while to many Israelis to be similar to Egypt's proposals turned down by the Rabin government of March, 1975. If the government was ready to accept a limited, nonpolitical agreement with Egypt, why had it not agreed to it in March, instead of risking a devastating showdown with the United States, asked traditional Mapai, American-oriented doves. The hawks, autonomists and conservatives, were alarmed by the complex compromise, based on American military and economic support promised for the duration of the agreement (three years) but not firmly dictated by U.S. and/or Egyptian obligations in terms of the conflict as a whole. American political obligations in these terms were watered down, during the Congressional debate, and thus their temporary and vague nature was exposed as a result of Rabin's maneuvers to make them more binding. At the time, while trying to nail Kissinger down to his commitments, the Israeli government was publicly admitting its doubts about them, arousing Kissinger's contempt and doubts as to the political skills of Rabin's cabinet. Domestically, then, the whole procedure seemed to be deprived of political depth and clever maneuvering.

Outcomes of political decisions made under conditions of uncertainty could hardly be questioned by the decision makers themselves without publicly undermining their own decision. The Likud opposition was given plenty of simple, easy to follow arguments against Sinai 2 for having failed to take Egypt out of the conflict. It had won some time, but no changes in the overall conflict patterns, thus paving the way for Syria and other Arab powers to exercise pressure on Israel through the United States and Egypt itself. Sadat was perceived as a clever, sly, and dangerous manipulator, working behind another manipulator, Kissinger, who was sometimes accused by the Israeli government for being untrustworthy and who had to be nailed down to his own commitments. Many Israelis felt that they were being swept away, losing control over their own destiny, while converting real estate and American public support into financial aid and conventional weapons. This further undermined Israel's position in the United States. Instead of standing by Israel's principles and explaining their grievances "properly" so as to enlist American Jewish support, these Israelis felt that their clear and "just" cause had become a commodity for bargaining, and they were not sure whether Rabin knew where Kissinger was leading him. The growing domestic American criticism of Kissinger's "linkage" methods and his conservative, power-oriented approach to international affairs also alienated many Israelis from him. Israel's collegial cabinet seemed to lack a clear-cut viable foreign policy and defense concept after Sinai 2. It seemed to "fight on the territorial margins," but the fight was influenced by the government's fear of new "reassessments," by Kissinger's own successful campaign against Israel's image in American media since March, by Israel's domestic economic strain, by the leadership's economic and social obligations, and by the conventional arms race.

The arms race, coupled with a growing dependence on the United States, seemed to some influencial Israelis to be a self-defeating formula. Since Israel's conventional territorial defense doctrine was now based

on occupied territories and conventional weapons acquired through diplomatic bargaining with the Arabs and the United States, Israel could
not have both territories and U.S.-made weapons. It was Dayan, again,
who publicly criticized Israel's dependence on U.S. conventional weapons and the domestic strain imposed on Israel by a giant conventional
arms acquirement program dependent on U.S. supplies. Instead he suggested territorial concessions to Egypt and Syria, if they were ready to
renounce belligerency, and a nuclear deterrence posture, adopted by
Israel with regard to its heartland and the West Bank.[36] Likud experts
like Professor Moshe Arens suggested a national austerity program, production of arms without American aid if necessary, and that no further
concessions be made to Washington for less than real peace with Egypt.
The cabinet itself seemed skeptical about Sinai 2: Mr. Peres did not object to it, but he refrained from hailing it, sensing public objections; the
NRP reluctantly accepted it, but feared future ramifications with regard
to the West Bank; Rabin himself became openly worried about Syria
and the PLO, and yet was regarded by the public as the chief architect
of the agreement, both as prime minister and an "American expert."
Washington's behavior concerning the financial aid, its refusal to supply
the "Pershings," and its increasing military aid to Saudi Arabia (and the
beginning of supplying Egypt) contributed to a growing public criticism
of Rabin. Rabin, with his lack of polish and his neurotic difficulties in
expressing himself in public, felt threatened by Peres in the cabinet and
Dayan outside it, and helped turn himself into an object of criticism,
mockery, and contempt.

The economic strain, too, began to show. U.S. aid was insufficient to
maintain the standard of living, and the economic and social conventions,
similar to those of the British welfare and trades union state, were an
obstacle to economic efficiency and savings. There was increasing competition for the government's dwindling income from foreign and domestic sources. Emigration was decreasing, and immigration from the
U.S.S.R. dropped sharply. The change in Soviet-American trade and commercial relations after the 1973 war and Moscow's rejection of a flexible
interpretation of the Jackson Amendment led, in 1974, to the cessation of
talks on granting the Soviet Union most favored nation status.[37] The
Russians then no longer considered it worth their while to permit the
Jewish emigration that they had allowed from 1971 to 1973.

The situation led to an atmosphere of gloom in Israel, which affected
Israel's image in the United States. The Jewish state was no longer as
great a source of spiritual inspiration and ethnic pride for American
Jews, nor was it regarded as firmly as a potential refuge as it had been
after the Six-Day War.[38] Arab money and organization in the United
States also eroded Israel's image. The increasing international political

gains of the PLO, the continual attacks on Zionism, and its condemnation as racism at the U.N.[39] with the support of the entire Third World and the communist states synchronized with demonstrations in the occupied territories, and helped erode Israel's image in her own eyes.

Egypt, acting in a manner contrary to the spirit of the Sinai accord, took part in the Arab anti-Zionist campaigns in U.N. institutions. Syria, with the support of radical Arab states, initiated such a campaign, and Egypt sometimes assumed responsibility in the Security Council for conducting it. Usually the Egyptians tried to emphasize the positive aspect, enhancing the status of the PLO rather than the strictly anti-Zionist points. Cairo took this course to keep from being totally isolated from the rest of the Arab coalition, which mostly deplored the second Sinai agreement as a breach of the Rabat conference accord. Thus, during his American and European tours in 1975 and 1976, Sadat repeatedly stressed to the non-Arab world that the PLO was the only authentic representative of the Palestinian people that could accept a national entity in Palesine on behalf of these people.[40]

During the winter of 1976, the PLO received de facto recognition by most of the states of the world and was given an observer status in most U.N. bodies.[41] Washington, too, began to move toward recognition of a role to be played by the PLO. Still, the Americans made careful use of their power of veto in the Security Council in order to keep the U.N. from granting the PLO full recognition and from voiding all the Council's Middle East resolutions that had provided the framework for whatever Arab-Israeli rapprochement had taken place. The American attitude to the PLO was also affected by the wish to help Sadat keep from being isolated by the radicals in the Arab coalition. Yet, the PLO, in the administration's opinion, could not be totally ignored; all local forces had to be involved, slowly, in a stable settlement in the Middle East, while the Russians had to be driven out of the region.[42] Since Egypt seemed to have adopted a clear, unchangeable obligation to a reduced PLO claim over a part of Palestine and Syria was committed to a PLO state, the separation of Egypt and Syria from a PLO-connected solution to the Palestinian question (which Kissinger was talking about in Jerusalem in late 1973 and early 1974, with regard to Egypt, at least) seemed not to hold any more. The two questions that remained to be answered, were whether the PLO itself was capable of accepting Israel and would commit itself, in word and deed, to live in peace with it, and whether Jordan should be given a role in guaranteeing a PLO connected solution to the Palestinian question. The administration seemed not to be in a hurry about it. A process had just started, and the PLO, Jordan, and Israel should address themselves to a possible compromise.

The Rabin government protested against the American moves toward the PLO. The Israeli press even went so far as to accuse the administration of breaking the promises it had made in the Sinai agreement. However, these commitments did not exist in a vacuum; they were meant to help implement the United States' strategic concept and that meant recognizing local forces in the region. In the course of 1976, the implementation of the American strategy began to approach informal dealings with the PLO, but the organization would not get full recognition until it recognized Israel and settled its differences with Jordan.

The Arab Coalition and the Lebanese Civil War

I shall now turn to the second important aspect of the aftermath of the Sinai agreements: developments in the superpowers' relations with the Arab coalition. These relations are divided into a number of facets related to developments inside the coalition in 1975 and 1976.

U.S.-Egyptian relations continued along the path that Sadat and Kissinger started to follow when the latter visited Cairo in November, 1973. Political cooperation at the expense of the U.S.S.R., economic aid, and the beginnings of military aid were the essential aspects of these ties. The most striking external evidence of these tightening bonds was Sadat's visit to the United States in the spring of 1976.

It seems, however, that one of the aspects of the new relationship, the Cairo-Riyadh-Teheran axis that American diplomats spoke so much about in 1974, did not fulfill its expectations. The economic and financial dimensions of the axis remained underdeveloped. Instead of Saudi and Iranian financial aid guaranteed by the United States, Egypt received direct American aid—$750 million in 1976 after $500 million in 1975.[43] Given the domestic constraints on aid in the United States, it seemed unlikely that much more would be forthcoming in following years. The Saudis, meanwhile, were as wary as ever of giving much financial aid to other states. The assassination of King Faisal in 1976 and the accession of King Khaled did not change much in this regard. Riyadh preferred to invest most of the money that did not go into its own development programs into buying arms from the United States for itself and for what Israelis believed to be an emergency arsenal for the Arabs.

In Egypt, meanwhile, the continually expanding population nullified any gains in gross national product and foreign aid.[44] The financial resources needed to stem the decline in the standard of living were simply unattainable; Sadat was forced to go on emergency fund-rasing tours of Saudi Arabia and the gulf states from time to time. Egypt's standing in the Arab world declined from what it had been under Nasser, at least until 1965, and the positions of Saudi Arabia and Syria were enhanced.

Politically, Egypt was able to maintain a relatively balanced and strong bargaining position vis-à-vis both superpowers from October, 1973, until the January, 1974, disengagement agreement. Later, as it continued to negotiate separately with Israel through the exclusive mediation of the United States and its relations with the United States became closer, its military and political ties with the Soviet Union were weakened. The U.S.S.R. sent massive arms supplies to Syria. Egypt then accused Moscow of refusing to deliver adequate quantities of weaponry, while the Soviets sided with Damascus and the PLO against Cairo's separate deal with Israel. The Russians reportedly refused to reschedule Egypt's debts and made personal propaganda attacks on Sadat and his regime. Thereupon Sadat unilaterally renounced the 1971 Treaty of Friendship with the U.S.S.R. and closed Egypt's naval bases to Soviet ships.[45] Washington greeted this move with great public satisfaction. The U.S.S.R. was forced to turn more to the Arab periphery, to Libya and Somalia, to shore up its position in the Arab world. It also continued to give Syria strong support until Damascus' intervention in the Lebanese civil war.

During the course of 1975, even Ba'athist Iraq, which also was bound to the Soviet Union by a formal treaty of friendship and isolated from the rest of the Arab world, because of its exceptionally radical regime began to draw away from the U.S.S.R. Economic and political considerations led it to begin a dialogue with France and the United States. Baghdad succeeded in isolating the Kurdish rebels and liquidating the uprising with Iranian cooperation and without American opposition.[46] Cooperation with Washington and Paris was also necessary to further the Iraqis' extensive economic program. France, moreover, was asked to help in the construction of nuclear reactors in Iraq.[47]

In 1976, Saudi-American collaboration was successful in driving the U.S.S.R. out of North Yemen, which the Russians had managed to penetrate during Nasser's intervention against the Yemeni royalists in the mid-1960s. The Kremlin was forced out into the Republic of South Yemen and established a base at Berbera in Somalia. In late 1975, the Soviet Union signed a massive arms supply deal with Libya, Egypt's radical enemy. Moscow maintained its links with Algiers, which came into conflict with Morocco and Mauritania over the Spanish Sahara in 1976.

The Arab world had changed since 1973. That was only to be expected, since it was a sort of formless mass made up of a number of shifting nuclei that were very unlike each other in terms of their economic resources and political and military power, and that lacked a fixed external orientation. Syria in 1975 and 1976 is a good illustration of these changes. Assad's postwar behavior indicated that he had learned that political and military cooperation with Egypt must necessarily be limited. Sadat had not hurried to Assad's assistance when Syrian forces were pushed back during the Yom Kippur War and carried out only limited operations on the Sinai front as part of his limited war. Sadat then agreed to a cease-fire after consulting Kosygin and Kissinger, but not Assad, who seems to have been presented with a *fait accompli*. The Syrians, then, apparently concluded that they could only depend on themselves and that if they wanted to further their own interests in the Arab world they needed autonomous military power and political freedom to maneuver. Power and maneuverability were necessary to exert pressure on Israel and to make up for the lack of Egyptian support if Cairo's political and economic links with Washington and its lack of military aid from Moscow rendered such support unlikely.

America's "Egyptian" policy and Egypt's separate deal with Israel in 1975 thus helped create a new political and military center of gravity in the Arab coalition. Syria and Jordan drew closer together and established a limited partnership founded on massive Soviet backing for Damascus and on American support of Amman. The wedge Rabin had hoped to see driven between Egypt and Syria before the March, 1975, shuttle became a reality after the signing of the second Sinai agreement. The Arab coalition split; on on side was Egypt, bound to the United States and supported, to some extent, by Saudi Arabia, and on the other was the rejection front that opposed any negotiations with Israel. The second group was led by Iraq and Libya, with Syria and some PLO leaders objecting strongly to separate deals with Israel and advocating a common Arab front to negotiate a total Israeli withdrawal and the establishment of a Palestinian entity in the West Bank and Gaza. Other PLO groups were totally opposed to any negotiated arrangement, thus working together with Iraq and Libya. Jordan, who opposed the PLO, became Assad's political and military ally. Such splits in the Arab world are not symmetrical or internally homogeneous. Yet they were bound to terrify both Egypt and Saudi Arabia, who did not want to risk open isolation from the rejectionists, the PLO, and Syria.

Assad was, in fact, trying to isolate Egypt in order to enhance Damascus's inter-Arab status and to create a multiple threat to Israel while protecting his own flanks. Damascus's prestige in the Arab world would then certainly rise and Syria's leading role would be a growing consideration for Saudi Arabia and the other oil states. Saudi financial aid to Syria would be increased and Riyadh might join in the Syrian-inspired pressure on Cairo not to foresake the Arab, and the Palestinian, cause.

Yet Assad was willing to cooperate politically and militarily with the PLO's historic enemy, King Hussein, in order to protect Syria's southern flank. This collaboration allowed Assad to speak in behalf of Jordan as well. He also tried to negotiate with his hostile Ba'athist neighbor, Iraq, in order to create an autonomous northeastern military front against Israel that could carry on the struggle without Egypt.

Hussein was ready to collaborate with the Syrians because any Arab partner was desirable to end Jordan's isolation among the Arab states and to undermine the PLO's claims to being the sole representative of the Palestinian cause. So Syria and Jordan, which were ostensibly diametrically opposed to each other on the Palestinian issue and each of which looked to a separate superpower for support, could agree on limited cooperation.[48] The Syrian-Jordanian rapprochement was progressing when the UNDOF mandate was due for extension in May, 1976. In December, 1975, Syria had exploited the extension to show up the PLO's status; it had made the appearance of PLO representatives at a Security Council debate on the Palestine problem a condition for the renewal of the U.N. forces mandate.[49] In May, 1976, it seemed that Damascus would again exploit the issue to obtain something for itself—a territorial gain in the Golan, perhaps, despite Israel's sensitivity to any concessions there. The actual course of events was different.

By this time the American presidental election campaign was in full swing and was having its effect on the administration's Middle East policy. To his surprise, president Ford found that he needed the Jewish vote more than he had thought at first, because of the close competition of Ronald Reagan and the appearance of Jimmy Carter. Had Humphrey or Jackson stayed in the race, the Jewish vote would have gone to them no matter what Ford might do. But with the Democrats opting for Carter, the Jewish vote was uncommitted and, because the competition was so stiff, an asset to any candidate. Ford tried to curry favor with the Jewish electorate more than he had when the primaries began.

During the spring and summer of 1976, the Lebanese civil was was exacerbated, Syria intervened in Lebanon and members of the Arab coalition changed partners again. There was, therefore, no longer any chance of movement in Israel's negotiations with its neighbors before the elections in the United States.

The Muslim/Christian, left/right, oppressed majority/privileged minority conflagration in Lebanon forced Assad to turn his attention to his western flank. The PLO contributed to the conflict out of sympathy for the Muslims and from a desire to extend its autonomy in Lebanon. The Muslims had disturbed Lebanon's communal status quo.[50] The new Lebanon might prove to be an autonomous nest of PLO operations that might drag Syria into an uncontrolled conflict with Israel. The PLO would then, in effect, be dictating Syria's reactions and Syrian policy would be subject to the internal logic of the competing groups in the PLO. There was no assurance that the United States would react vigorously to an Israeli attack on Lebanon, as it would if the communal balance there were maintained. What is more, a new Lebanon would require a redeployment of the Syrian armed forces from the Golan to defend Damascus and the country's western flank,[51] because Israel would have fewer qualms about attacking Syria through Lebanon if war broke out.

Consequently, in May, 1976, Assad dispatched part of the Syrian army to Lebanon to restabilize the country. It would once more be essentially neutral vis-à-vis Israel, the Christians would not be deprived of too many privileges, and the PLO would not obtain too much autonomy there. The United States had an opportunity to draw closer to Syria while pulling it away from the Soviet Union. It helped Israel decide that inter-Arab strife in and around Lebanon was none of its affair so long as there was no decisive military change on the Israeli-Lebanese border, that is, as long as there were no Syrian or PLO forces south of the Litani River. The Israelis developed a strategy of indirectly aiding Christian troops in Lebanon and directly supporting them along the Israeli-Lebanese border, so that a kind of buffer zone would be created between unfriendly Muslim areas and a Christian-dominated area. This process was enhanced when the Syrians developed growing difficulties in Lebanon in the spring and summer of 1976.

One military strike was not enough for the Syrians to restabilize the situation in Lebanon. They became bogged down in bloody battles with the Palestinians, who feared losing autonomy, were committed to the Muslims, and tended to resort to force when threatened by force. The Syrians stayed in Lebanon through July despite Assad's agreement to evacuate his troops to make way for Arab League force.

At first the PLO seemed to do well against the Syrians and its political prestige was enhanced. Soon, however, it found itself on the defensive, as it had been in Jordan in 1970. The Palestinians suffered heavy losses and Arafat appealed for help to Libya, Iraq, and Egypt. Egypt and Libya had been in open conflict since Sadat had turned from Khaddafi to King Faisal on the eve of the Yom Kippur War and then went on to negotiate separately with Israel. The PLO's base of support in the Arab coalition was thus split: Libya and Egypt were in conflict and each relied on a different superpower, while Iraq stood somewhere in between. Egypt's official policy called for a Palestinian state in the West Bank and the Gaza Strip, while Libya backed the official PLO position of a single democratic, secular state covering all the territory of Palestine. Both were too far away to intervene against the Syrians. Iraq, though nearer, was content to conduct a propaganda campaign against Assad and to concentrate troops on its border with Syria.

The Syrian army's Lebanese adventure cut Damascus off from the rejection front, particularly Libya, Iraq, and the PLO, while Saudi Arabia tried to mediate between Egypt and Syria. Changes in the Arab coalition's group behavior became necessary for Assad, Sadat, and the Saudis. Assad was determined at first to restablish Lebanon as a neutral, Syrian-influenced element at his strategic rear. Syria fought its way to the strategic centers of the country, and cooperated with the Christians against the PLO. Syrian-dominated PLO units fought autonomous PLO units, while Assad was threatening to bring about personal changes in the PLO leadership if Yassir Arafat would not yield to his demands to restore Lebanon's domestic unity and accept Syrian influence in Lebanon, as opposed to total PLO-Muslim predominance. Shortly before the winter of 1976, and before the lull in the U.S. domestic politics created by the presidential elections was to be over, Syrian troops conquered most of Lebanon's strategic area and threatened, together with the Christians (and the Israelis, who partially blockaded Muslim-held seashores, with Kissinger's support)[52] to encircle the remaining PLO-Muslim-held regions. At this moment Saudi Arabia intervened, and brought about a series of Arab coalitionary consultations with regard to Lebanon and the conflict as a whole. Syria, which firmly established itself in Lebanon, agreed to retain its presence there under the cover of an "Arab peace-keeping force," together with small Saudi and other Arab states' police forces. The PLO standing in Lebanon, its last autonomous base, was considerably reduced but not abandoned altogether. PLO units were transferred back to the south, where they continued to fight Israeli-supported Christians during 1977. Syrian units supported them, but did not approach the Israeli border. Israel's "buffer zone" in southern Lebanon was reduced to a Christian-controlled and a PLO-dominated area. Direct contacts between Lebanese Christians and Israelis continued along the "open fence" in the Israeli-Lebanese border, much to the dismay of radical Arabs and against the official tradition of total Arab boycott of any personal contacts, let alone defense arrangements between Arab and Israelis.

In October, 1976, Egypt, Syria, and Saudi Arabia held a "mini summit" at Riyadh. Events in Lebanon (meaning Syria's deep military and political involvement there, which could not be terminated until the rival factions agreed to coexistence) were regarded by Israelis as a good reason for General Assad to return to some degree of cooperation with Egypt, and Saudi Arabia, in terms of the conflict. Assad was at total odds with Iraq, the rival Ba'athist regime always behind radical PLO groupings, and Libya, whom all denounced Syria's intervention in Lebanon. The "rejection front," an anti-Egyptian constellation with which Assad cooperated following Sinai 2 in order to isolate Sadat and reclaim Syrian leadership in the Arab coalition, split as a result of the Lebanese affair. Syrian-PLO relations and common interests declined, because the PLO was interested in its autonomy in Lebanon, and in its autonomy to decide for itself what would best suit its interests in the conflict. Syria had officially backed this bid for autonomy in the past. It criticized Egypt's separate deal with Israel, and did not officially endorse Sadat's bid for a Palestinian state in the West Bank and the Gaza Strip in exchange for a de facto settlement with Israel. The PLO never endorsed it officially, not having arrived at a consensus among its internal groups with regard to a "mini solution" of their total claims over Palestine as a whole, and their future relations with Israel.[53] Yet PLO intransigence concerning a greater autonomy in Lebanon, as a result of the internal Lebanese problems that brought about Syria's intervention, opened a gap between the PLO and Syria on other issues, especially as Iraq and PLO radicals were using the Lebanese affair to denounce the Syrian regime.

Assad agreed with Sadat and the Saudis that they should strive for a Palestinian state in the West Bank and the Gaza Strip at the new round of negotiations with Israel. The key Arab states thus combined Assad's traditional demand for a coalitionary Arab strategy toward Israel and for a solution that would be comprehensive and would include the "rights" of the Palestinians, with an Egyptian notion that these "rights" should be satisfied in the West Bank and Gaza, at least for a generation. Real peace, as Sadat repeatedly said to western visitors, which meant normalization and reconsiliation, would have to wait for the next generation to decide.

The PLO's National Council was now expected to meet in Cairo to discuss the new strategic political environment. On March 20, 1977, the PNC, largely dominated by Fath representatives, adopted, against the votes of the radical Marxist Popular Front for the Liberation of Palestine, a fifteen-point resolution that reaffirmed the PLO's strategic aims: the liberation of Palestine as a whole, the "democratization" of the country as a whole (i.e., the return of Palestine to Arab majority rule), and the traditional methods to pursue these aims (i.e., armed "revolution" against the "racist Zionist" entity). At the same time, the council adopted two points in the political declaration that sounded like the beginning of a change toward the acceptance of a West Bank–Gaza state. Paragraphs 15a and 15b of the declaration confirmed the PNC's care for the PLO's "rights to participate in an independent manner and on an equal footing in all the conferences and international forums concerned with the Palestine issue and the Arab-Zionist conflict," and declared "any settlement or agreement affecting the rights of our Palestinian people in the absence of this people . . . completely null and void."[54] The Popular Front, which voted against two points in this declaration, might have had these two paragraphs in mind, as they dialectically referred to the possibility that agreements with Israel, as a result of joint conferences with it, might be possible. Since the other paragraphs were totally uncompromising, the resolution could be interpreted, as Israeli official spokesmen did, as a repetition of the 1964 covenant. In fact, this declaration seems to be a typical Middle Eastern compromise, which should have secured the PLO further international recognition as a future participant in any comprehensive conference and given it the discretion to decide whether and which tactics to employ in order to gain most of its aims at the conference, at the inter-Arab level and within Arab states, or to modify—if necessary—its goals and be satisfied with whatever was possible to gain in territory and sovereignty. Arafat himself was busy in the meantime acquiring U.S. and Soviet support. In Moscow he was received several times during 1976–77 as a chief of state, an honor that was never bestowed on him before the Lebanese civil war. Yet the Soviets were reported as having told him that the PLO would have to accept the West Bank-Gaza state,[55] as Israel's pre-1967 borders were internationally recognized, de facto, since the 1949 armistice agreements. Moscow would be ready, as the Soviets told Washington repeatedly, to guarantee these borders. The PLO did not commit itself publicly, however, to any borders, to any acceptance of Israel and to any withdrawal of homeland rights for the Palestinians with regard to the pre-1967 Israel. Arafat gave hints to the western press, though, that he might be willing to accept a "mini solution" for the next twenty years if the United States accepted PLO rights first.[56] He complained about obvious problems with the "rejectionists" who might break the whole Palestinian organization if he went further.

Thus in the winter of 1977, the key Arab states and the PLO, in its peculiar way, seemed to be moving toward a common concept: a comprehensive conference was to take place in 1977 (no "step-by-step," separate deals with Israel were tolerable any more) including PLO representatives, to bring about Israel's withdrawals from all territories occupied in June, 1967, and the establishment of a "mini" Palestinian state in the West Bank and Gaza. The Arab quid pro quo seemed to be split along the following lines: Egypt was speaking "peace," sometimes interpreting it as nonbelligerency, sometimes as a more positive state of no war short of any normalized relations, "like the U.S.-Communist China relationship" before Nixon's opening, as Sadat openly said.[57] Syria was talking about Israeli withdrawals and Palestinian rights to a state of their own.[58] Arafat was less outspoken, and stressed the "victim's rights to recognition and sovereignty." Jordan was included by Sadat as a partner to the Palestinian entity that should somehow be "linked," according to the Egyptian president, to Jordan.[59] For the first time it seemed that, following the Lebanese war, the key Arab states and elements in the PLO agreed on a formula that might sound viable to a new American administration if the PLO moderated its public stance toward Israel and found a common language with Jordan. As a result of this, Rabin's Israel would have to accept such a modified formula at least as a bargaining framework. While reestablishing itself as the political leader of the key Arab states, at least for the time being, Egypt was suddenly shattered, in January, 1977, by violent domestic upheavals. Trying to implement economic measures recommended by western experts and creditors in order to tackle Egypt's economic stagnation and introduce some market elements into it, Sadat encountered almost a popular rebellion. The regime hurriedly canceled the suggested measures, and remained totally dependent on Arab and foreign aid, facing a deteriorating economic situation and domestic unrest.

Developments in Jimmy Carter's Washington and in Israel in the spring of 1977, all related to each other and to Israel's domestic situation, created in the meantime a change in the Middle East in May–June of the same year.

THE FALL OF THE LABOR ALIGNMENT

The Decline of Rabin's Rule

Yitzhak Rabin's political end in April, 1977, and Menahem Begin's electoral victory, which followed it in May, surprised many Israelis and foreign observers alike. Yet Rabin's decline and fall and the Likud victory were rooted in some basic features of Israel's domestic, socioeconomic, and foreign political situation, as both related to the leaderships' actual behavior and policy choices and to external developments related, to an extent, to their own behavior.

It is too early to weigh the relative importance of every factor in the process that brought Labor down after a rule uninterrupted in Israel since 1948. It seems to me that the following basic features and contributing elements played a role in the process:

a. Israel's socioeconomic structures in a period of economic crisis were influential, together with conscious policy choices made by the alignment's leadership and the growing credibility gap that emerged following these decisions.

b. There was the inability of the alignment's elite to supply moral and political leadership in a period of extreme domestic tension with an ideological and cultural vacuum. An atmosphere of domestic stress, cultural and ideological expectations that went unfulfilled, a growing competition with American material and political-cultural values and examples, and increasing emigration to the United States combined with a growing friction between individuals fighting for bigger shares of the dwindling economic resources.

c. An extreme sensitivity to external—including American—challenges, typical of a stress behavior, played its own role in Mr. Begin's favor.

d. Growing demands for new domestic rules of the game, following the Yom Kippur "blunder" and public assessments of the reasons for it, were partially imposed on the alignment by public opinion and the press, and were partially met by the leadership. These demands helped undermine the party machinery and expose it to further criticism.

e. Tactical, political, and foreign political mistakes, incorrect assessments of the public's basically conservative mood, and incorrect timing calculations were immediate causes of Mr. Rabin's and later Mr. Peres's failure.

f. The emergence of new political parties, as a result of the above-mentioned factors, also contributed to the Likud victory.

g. President Carter's actions and statements with regard to Israel, coupled with Arab demands and reactions to Carter's initiatives, were other concrete contributing factors.

Israel's economy, and mainly its standard of living, were constantly growing since the early fifties. The process was not harmonious, nor was it egalitarian: a gap was parallelly growing between official socialist (later welfare-state) ideologies, expectations, and realities. The Labor leadership managed to bridge that gap with imported funds, foreign investments, high taxation, and inflation. The responsibility of the political state leadership, which was at the same time identifiable with union bureaucracy, was enormous, and yet its real power was declining rapidly when scarcity of resources forced hard policy choices on the state leadership. The leadership itself was divided between Mr. Rabin, the contested prime minister, Mr. Peres, the contender, Mr. Rabinowitz, a Mapai choice for the finance ministry, Mr. Haim Zadok, a Mapai minister of justice, and Messrs. Allon and Galili, Achdut Ha'Avoda representatives.

The leadership adopted a conventional territorial defense policy, which seems to have been a complex compromise between almost contradictory demands in a period of scarce resources, strategic traditions, and lessons drawn from the Yom Kippur War. First, Israel was to enlarge and modernize its conventional forces, in a more balanced manner. A sort of a crash program was initiated in 1974, the needed purchases abroad financed to a large extent by U.S. appropriations connected to the diplomatic bargaining. Second, Israel tried to maintain a high degree of preparedness as a result of the 1973 lesson; it had to build a new defense line in the Sinai and needed large investments in Israeli pounds to train its new army and take care of the borders, especially in the north. At the same time, it was decided to enhance and develop Israel's own conventional arms production, already boosted following the French arms embargo of 1967. The economic impact of the military situation in general and of huge investments in this sector (which produces, among other things, jet fighters and a heavy tank) on Israel's socioeconomic structure is worth studying, yet the data is not all available.[60] A speculation with regard to the military crash program's impact upon prices, employee treatment, and salaries, or vice versa, the impact of a consumer and services market upon state-run military industries in inflation times, could be mentioned. It seems that an ever growing tension and competition between the salaried state and the free market employees must deepen when the hard pressed state cannot compete with the free market. In the case of special preference for state-owned, but publicly run, military-civilian enterprises like Israel's aircraft industry, a gap must have opened between their employees, who were treated more like free market workers, and state-run industries and services. Besides the conventional military effort, it would have been hard to believe that minister Peres, the first promoter of Israel's nuclear option, would have neglected that option altogether.

Third, Israel's objective economic situation had deteriorated since 1974 due to higher oil prices and the 1975 loss of the Abu-Rodeis oil fields. Fourth, the alignment's ideological and political obligations to maintain a welfare state, attract and absorb immigration, and supply universal services remained unchanged. The budget was inflated to fulfill most of them; large subsidies for commodities and services, education, and social security services were consciously financed by printed money and by ever growing taxes to relieve the pressure of a deficit budget and to prevent the runaway consumption of foreign currency resources. Even if impressive gains were made in exports during 1975–76, foreign currency reserves were used in an alarming ratio to finance these contradictory demands. The quality of most of the services, run by a huge state and union bureaucracy, had not improved since the pioneering days, whereas the bureaucrats themselves demanded egalitarian treatment, meaning higher salaries. Since the salaried middle class were traditionally alignment voters, the party tried to appeal to the lower strata as well. However, the young nationalists were not satisfied, and they joined Begin's supporters.[61] The government had the choice, of course, of declaring a national emergency, suspending some spendings, reducing others, and freezing wages and prices for at least some time. Yet Mr. Rabinowitz, a typical Mapai bargainer, was not made for such harsh choices; instead he introduced many semiausterity measures (the first Israeli government to do so since 1952) but maintained full employment, services, and free market competition for his state-run economy while permanently inflating and devaluating the Israeli pound. The outcome was a permanent bargaining on compensations to the middle and the lower strata, followed by constant frustration of both, as stronger interest groups won more in the open bargaining game.

The elite's spiritual and inspirational role was nonexistent altogether under Rabin, Peres, and Rabinowitz. Rabin, a director of military and diplomatic operations, behaved as a prime minister, the most important, but least tangible Israeli power position, as an American president, and as a political analyst. Having a strong tendency to follow foreign events— especially in "his" fascinating Washington—and always trying to press the pedals of power there, as Kissinger and Nixon taught him, Rabin simply never exactly understood all the premises of Israel's domestic power or the extreme changes in the public's mood since "his" 1967 victory. Enjoying his unexpected rise to the premiership, Rabin was incapable of sharing power with Peres because he, rightly, suspected Peres of indirectly undermining his position. But Rabin was incapable of forcing a showdown in his own favor, and so he gave vent to his frustrating experience with the sly minister of defense in public outbursts, many of them concerning Peres's relative lack of military expertise. Peres himself was not used to that sort of public, military-technical, and personal criticism, but instead to a more subtle game of leaks and indirect press campaigns against his enemies since the "Lavon affair," and was forced to react publicly. Both men were hurt, in the public eye, as a result of their rivalries. Rabin could not develop any working team of aides around him, since he trusted nobody and preferred to concentrate on the diplomatic game and a "direct contact" with the nation. Being a poor speaker, an arrogant and yet introverted, cold, and egotistic man, his public campaigns remained of not much avail, yet they consumed much of his time.

Peres tried to capitalize on Rabin's weaknesses, but remained too sly, political, calculating, and general in his public statements. He was trying to please Israel's bid for love, care, understanding, meaning of life and struggle, self pity, and self-righteousness, as expressed in concrete, and many times contradictory, demands. No one could fill Golda Meir's and Moshe Dayan's vacant chairs, as Eshkol failed to fill in Ben-Gurion's vacancy. Yet Eshkol was ready to fight his terrible predecessor, and being the embodiment of Israel's political middle-of-the-road, compromising, very Jewish bargaining nature, he failed when this nature collided with Israel's "manly" sovereign, fighting and fearing substance. Rabin did not fail, because he never succeeded. He occupied a central political position, but did not manage to become Israel's spiritual, political, or moral leader. The demand for such a leadership grew more and more after the war. Credibility gaps created by the war, by the Geneva "show," by Watergate, by Sinai 2, by a growing U.S. and Israeli criticism of Henry

Kissinger,[62] by fears of weakness symbolized by U.S. behavior in Angola helped drive many Israelis to a state of cynicism and nihilism. They had lost confidence in their own leadership and system, the American system, and U.S. treatment of their interests, as most of them understood these interests in terms of a renewed and strengthened conservatism.

This moral, psychological, and cultural vacuum was, to an extent, filled by Gush Emunim, the religious group that combined traditional religious Jewish virtues like piety, Jewish social humanism, strong catechistic discipline, and religious studies with proud nationalism manifested in settlements in occupied Arab territories.[63] The younger NRP leadership was very much influenced by the "Gush," as were young Herut activists. When all three elements defied a government regulation on settlements in the West Bank and demonstrated in forbidden Arab populated territory, asking for permission to settle, many established Israeli groups— kibbutzim and cooperative farm members, members of the intelligentsia and quasi-intelligentsia, middle-of-the-road yet acutely, culturally, and existentially antinomical Israelis tired of crowded cities, diminishing quality of life, and the constant friction with each other created by envy and competition for scarce resources—hailed the Gush activists as Israel's new pioneers. When they finally settled, illegally, in Kaddum, outside the area authorized for settlements by cabinet instructions, in order to demonstrate Israel's "right" to the West Bank as a whole, and its fighting and autonomous spirit in an insecure world, the Gush settlers manipulated Zionist values that usually were politically and substantialy controlled by a legitimate elite. The alignment seemed at first to be fully aware of the Kaddum challenge to its authority, the authority of the government in general, its West Bank policy, and its standing in the United States.

At the same time as the Gush escapades in the West Bank, defense minister Peres authorized free, municipal elections in the Arab communities there, hoping to create a local, elected elite that would become an alternative to the PLO. Peres thus deviated from Dayan's tradition of not enhancing any local Arab autonomism that was bound, in Dayan's conviction, to be hostile to Israel. But since Dayan's early days as occupation minister the PLO had managed to enhance its international standing as the "sole representative" of the Palestinians, including West Bank dwellers, who were left without any representative, semiautonomous leadership of their own. Peres tried to rectify this situation through free elections in the West Bank, intended to encourage local, popular forces to emerge and later display their own interests as opposed to PLO "foreign" and radical interests and habits. Even if most of the elected Arab municipal officers expressed public support of the PLO as their "sole representative" according to an inter-Arab official consensus, they were now believed to be bound to their regional and local interests,[64] and thus potentially more open to a future dialogue with Israel, in comparison to the PLO leadership. The PLO leaders were perceived as representing 1948 refugees in Syria and Lebanon and as by nature willing to ask for their return to the pre-1967 Israel while demanding at some time exclusive rights to the West Bank. Arab local leadership might thus be developed and encouraged to resist PLO ambitions in the West Bank and to prefer cooperation with Israel and Jordan. Kaddum disturbed that delicate process, helped PLO-inspired and locally antagonized Arab youth to stage noisy demonstrations, and damaged Rabin's government image in Washington. Yet Peres sensed that public opinion was leaning toward the settlers, at least emotionally, and, being a Rafi representative in the government, he felt the factional-political logics of his position dictated a slightly rightist, nationalist approach to the settlement question. Mapai, Mapam, and more dovish Achdut Ha'Avoda minister, Allon, or his colleague Galili, who insisted on government authority in the Kaddum question as a matter of principle, might be confronted with a largely conservative, emotional public opinion. Consequently, Peres remained vague about Kaddum and stressed Israel's right to settlements in the West Bank, in the spirit of past Rafi-inspired party platforms. The NRP ministers went further, and threatened to quit the coalition if Kaddum was to be removed, under the pressure of the young NRP leadership.

Gush Emunim mobilized a small army of supporters from Mapai's traditional bastions and Achdut Ha'Avoda kibbutzim, idealists kibbutzniks, and Moshavniks expressed their support for "creating facts" on Arab territory quite near to Israel's 1949 "impossible border" in the heart of the country, thus giving a new-old meaning to spiritual and material Zionism, in their eyes. Rabin was forced to accept Kaddum, at least as a "temporary arrangement," and thus he outraged many liberal and left-wing Israelis, who wanted him to impose the state's authority and to prevent troubles with the West Bank dwellers and the United States. The NRP, meanwhile, and the Gush, forced a reluctant majority to its knees through cooperation with Herut officials, including the Likud leader himself, who joined his young followers publicly in support of Kaddum.

This precedent helped dissolve the "historical cooperation" between the NRP and Labor, and enhanced events that led to the emergence of a Likud-NRP coalition in the summer of 1977. The details of the process were connected with two other features of Israel's domestic crisis: the demand for new public rules of the game, and the demand for better public participation in the political process. Both demands were linked to the Yom Kippur "blunder," which was perceived by many opinion makers and the general public as a result of closed elite deliberations without any institutionalized public criticism. Elite social behavior since 1967 (and principally since 1970), the overconfidence of many generals and generals turned politicians, and the excessive behavior of some of them—all were connected to the "blunder." An eager press was busily exposing this trend. It had started before the war but could not damage Dayan, for example, as long as his policy seemed to be working. Dayan was among the victims of that mood, but his enemies, "dovish" Mapai apparatchiks, suffered no less. Old Mapai machinery methods such as political favoritism, financial favoritism, and kickbacks used to finance party operations (and sometimes individual party members) were exposed largely by the independent press, radio, and T.V., which had managed to acquire a large degree of freedom from the partisan Broadcasting Authority since Eshkol days. Israel's masses were disappointed with the machinery's inability to supply their demands, and even if most of them knew of its methods they were amazed to hear about them in public, in a period of acute competition resolved by state party bureaucrats in favor of stronger interest groups. New rules were demanded; a moral code for public and civil servants was loudly supported by Israelis who as individuals might have forced the same civil servants to yield to their wage demands because of the open bargaining system, realizing that some rules of the social game must be introduced to force others to behave themselves; then they might follow. Many Kaddum sympathizers were ardent followers of strict legalism with regard to dovish, Mapai functionaries exposed by the press as less legal manipulators. The Rabin-Zadok government hurriedly adapted itself to the new mood, authorizing legal inquiries into the behavior of Mapai appartchiks exposed by the press. They dealt another blow to the decaying machinery and its legendary strength, thus creating an even greater power vacuum and adding to the decline of Mapai's dovish power base.

Rabin hoped to create a new, relatively pragmatic, middle-of-the-road majority for himself in the alignment. Unwilling and unable to outflank Peres to the right he hoped to insulate him, on the party level, and contain him in Rafi. Peres was preparing to contest Rabin again in Labor primaries before the 1977 November elections. The new rules—a public demand for participation and party democracy that manifested itself since the Yom Kippur War—forced Rabin to accept the challenge reluctantly. The primaries were to take place in a large body, the party's national convention, mostly elected this time. No single machinery existed any more to secure Rabin's victory. Mapai's apparatus, still powerful enough to swing the vote in his favor in 1974, was partially in the hands of new regional bosses and partially in the hands of Peres's followers, who preferred a more articulate and more political leader over Rabin. To an extent, it disintegrated altogether; its former boss, finance minister Sapir, resigned, and died shortly afterward. Sapir's successor,

Rabinowitz, did not operate along Sapir's lines; he refrained from using party channels and his personal authority to acquire economic power and retain it, but was caught between contradictory demands and compromised on them with inflation and austerity measures, bargaining and yielding to growing wage demands.

Rabin was forced to enter an open, free contest. His choice was to opt for a more dovish, traditional Mapai ticket in the primaries, to isolate Peres at the right and secure Mapam's support. At the same time, Rabin had to reckon with a new challenge; the demand for new public rules, more democratization, and less wild bargaining helped the last surviving protest movement of the aftermath of the Yom Kippur War, Shinuy (change), to break free of its relative insignificance. It backed a potential national leader when Professor Yigael Yadin, Israel's second chief of staff and the actual director of operations in the 1948–49 war, decided to enter public life and create with Shinuy a new "Democratic Movement for Change" (DMC). The danger seemed to be serious because the DMC could offer an alternative to Labor if it could implement its slogans about personal ethics, a democratic structure, and rules of participation and if it could use the former Labor-affiliated business and administrative leaders who defected daily from the alignment to join Yadin. Without swinging too far right, the average Israeli could, for the first time, vote for a middle-of-the-road party block that was trying to demonstrate a democratic organization and made concrete suggestions with regard to domestic reforms; first, the introduction of a new ballot law that should bring about a two-, or three-party system based on constituencies and proportional representation alike; second, the strengthening of the prime minister's position vis-à-vis his cabinet and the Knesset; third, a parliamentary reform to enhance public participation in Knesset affairs and better supervision by parliament of the government's work.[65] The DMC's foreign policy platform was vague, as was the alignment's, yet its main concern was Israel's domestic rehabilitation rather than a continued high-level conflict. The DMC could therfore, be regarded as an old Mapai-type party, free of personal rivalries. As Yadin and his colleagues were preparing for a long election year, trying to implement their new party rules and to set up a party apparatus, Rabin tried, in early 1977 to regain the initiative. He first fired two NRP ministers from the cabinet when they followed a censure motion in the Knesset against the government in which they participated, in connection with a minor religious affair.

Thus the alignment–NRP–Independent Liberal coalition came to an end. Rabin dissociated himself from the NRP and its Kaddum adventure, and yet he remained as prime minister, heading a caretaker government until the new elections, which he rescheduled for May 17, 1977. The DMC was supposed to be caught unprepared and off balance, having not yet organized according to its program. In the meantime, as Israel's acting prime minister and having defeated Peres in the forthcoming primaries, Rabin was scheduled to meet President Carter in Washington and demonstrate to the voters that he was, and remained, Israel's chief negotiator with a friendly United States. Yet the double maneuver brought about unexpected developments. Rabin had to decide quickly who was going to head the alignment's election campaign. An old Mapai election organizer, housing minister Avraham Offer, was pressing for a decision while under legal investigation for political and personal corruption. As Rabin waited for the investigation's results, Offer, who indeed had helped the party all his life to acquire, legally and illegally, its election funds and to exercise influence through housing projects, felt deserted and humiliated. Shortly thereafter he committed suicide, realizing that the rules had changed and that under the new rules nobody would back him or share responsibility with him. The nation was shocked again and yet was sure that Minister Offer was corrupt and that his party machinery, now totally in disarray, was corrupt, as revealed by Offer's personal friend Asher Yadlin.

This former Histadrut boss, who became Rabin's candidate for the governorship of Israel's central bank, was exposed before the Offer affair as a Mapai financier who took good care of himself while supplying the party with kickback moneys. After Offer's suicide, Yadlin admitted most of the charges of kickbacks in order to disqualify the party that had sacrificed Offer and him. Rabin and Zadok tried to capitalize on a clean-up campaign initiated by the press and run by their own apolitical young attorney general. In Israel's tradition the attorney general was supposed to defend the political system, to prosecute or not to prosecute according to complex political considerations that played different roles in decisions made by former attorneys, all of them members of the elite's clubs, either as Ben-Gurion's followers or as politically oriented "don't rock the boat" lawyers. Rabin and Zadok themselves were aware of the new rules or rather of the expectations of the new rules—no cover-ups and no kickbacks—and the attorney general proceeded along the same lines. Having won the Labor's primaries with an extremely marginal vote, which instituted his rivalry with Peres instead of disqualifying the defense minister, as a large margin would have done, Rabin and Peres were dividing party institutions between their supporters according to the vote when the prime minister went to visit President Carter.

Rabin knew that the moratorium on further talks, given to Israel by Sadat in 1975 for three years, was almost over. Israel used this time primarily to acquire military and economic aid from the United States, to intervene indirectly in Lebanon, and to create some kind of local leadership in the West Bank. It followed with concern an apparent emerging Arab consensus with regard to a comprehensive solution to be negotiated in 1977, and Carter's ideas about a substantive, comprehensive Middle East conference in late 1977. Rabin was not thinking in terms of a final peace conference; his perception of Israel's defense requirements in the West Bank, the Golan Heights, and northern Sinai plus Sharm-el-Sheikh were traditionally somewhere between Dayan's and Allon's. The difference between them was over strategic approach and order of priorities. Whereas Allon resented a prolonged Israeli rule over Arabs and was ready in principle to negotiate the return of Arab populated territories to Arab control in exchange for a stable peace, Dayan, and hence Peres, did not see any strategically balanced peace or stable, ready to cooperate, Arab entity to absorb these territories. His solution was to retain the West Bank (and Gaza) as a whole, perhaps until such a strategically balanced peace became feasible, and to settle parts of it as Israel's historical rights allowed without formally annexing the area.

Rabin and Allon were both more anxious than Dayan to avert a showdown with the United States. They were aware of Israel's economic and military dependence on Washington, Rabin having in mind available Congressional support for Israeli suggestions. Both Allon and Rabin shared a profound dislike for Dayan's nuclear deterrence and feared Carter's much publicized sensitivity in this area.[66] They condemned Dayan's public suggestions to Israel to try and negotiate nonbelligerency with Egypt and Syria in exchange for most of the Sinai and the Golan Heights while retaining the West Bank, and to "develop" a nuclear capacity.

Rabin preferred that the Republicans win in the November, 1976, presidential elections. He shared Kissinger's opinion that the area was not yet "ripe for peace," and preferred a Republican president, checked and balanced by a Democrat pro-Israel Congress. Rabin backed President Ford publicly in his race against Carter, and parallelly obtained new weaponry shipments. Yet Carter won, and Carter was known to consider a comprehensive, immediate Middle East solution. Allon therefore considered a curious combination of the "step-by-step" approach and a comprehensive solution: Israel should bargain on withdrawals on all fronts (no total withdrawals and no PLO state), in exchange for nonbelligerency and for a very long period of no further withdrawals. The next, and last, step would be made under terms of a stabilized peace. Thus, the Sinai 2 provisions regarding a further step in exchange for a final arrangement with Egypt and Jordan (and Syria) would be replaced by a long-range, comprehensive, three-front political-territorial agreement. Rabin and Galili deliberated and hesitated.[67] In the end, Galili insisted upon "real peace" agreements in exchange for further withdrawals, especially in the West Bank, and upon an American-Israeli understanding of "real peace" (or the substance of peace, in the Israeli political jargon). He also insisted upon separate negotiations between Israel and its neighbors, to attain that peace, so that no possible concessions to Egypt would automatically include the West Bank and so that no deals with the PLO would be possible by negotiating with a common Arab delegation (including PLO representatives). Rabin adopted Galili's stance, especially with regard to the West Bank, hoping to attain some kind of an understanding (with Congressional aid) with the United States on a more comprehensive and durable agreement with Egypt, capitalizing upon Sadat's inability to make "real peace" under any circumstances. He hoped to preserve American aid and to avoid confrontations with the administration, working toward a combined "step-by-step" and comprehensive approach while making verbal concessions concerning the West Bank. On the coalitionary level, once the elections were over, he would become dependent again on Peres and exposed to Dayan's and Likud's criticism; he would need further coalitionary arrangements either with the alienated NRP or the DMC, and then would bargain on an operational decision with his future partners and the United States, blaming his domestic constraints while negotiating with the Americans. The party endorsed a platform[68] making retreats on all fronts possible, while Rabin negotiated with Dayan—still a leading Rafi member with some support— a complicated compromise that did not rule out new elections to sanction a West Bank withdrawal.

In Washington, the prime minister encountered a new president, a new open style, and a much more comprehensive and far-reaching Middle East program. Rabin and Carter did not hide their mutual disappointment. The former ambassador, rude in his style and used to bargains with former administrations, failed to impress a "no bargain," popular, and inexperienced Baptist from Georgia. The Israelis realized that the alignment had no special privileges in Washington any more; Kissinger's direct election aid to that party in 1973 was replaced by a new, threatening Middle East plan that might, the Israelis thought, have been devised either by fools or by scoundrels.[69] Back home, Rabin realized that an illegal bank account held in Washington since his days as an ambassador had been exposed during his visit by the Israeli press. Trying to minimize the damage, he admitted having illegally kept a small sum of money in a foreign bank and volunteered to have the case investigated by the attorney general. The attorney realized that the real sum was far higher than disclosed, and decided to prosecute Rabin's wife, formally in charge of the common account. Sensing a disaster to his party and himself under the "new rules" he personally had helped to introduce, Rabin resigned from the alignment's candidacy for the premiership, and Peres became the No. 1 candidate.

Carter's Middle East Program and General Foreign Policy Concept

The new administration's Middle East program was taking shape during the winter and spring of 1977 along two lines. First, there was a comprehensive Middle East concept, suggested by a study group at the Brookings Institution in Washington following Kissinger's March, 1975, shuttle failure.[70] Several members of the Brookings team, Zbigniew Brzezinski and Henry Owen, shared another, more conceptual foreign policy "think tank" with the future president—the "Trilateral Commission."[71] Brzezinski assumed, in January, 1977, the key position of national security adviser. His choice for the Middle East desk was another member of the Brookings Middle East team, William Quandt, the most outspoken advocate of a Palestinian state in that team.

The second line along which the president operated until the Israeli May elections, was a round of talks with Middle East leaders conducted first by Secretary of State Cyrus Vance and later by the president himself, who at the same time addressed himself to several Middle East issues in public.[72] Mr. Carter seemed to have drawn support for the original Brookings program from an updated analysis of the Middle East situation following events in Lebanon, while focusing mainly on two issues: (a) a methodical criticism of Kissinger's "step-by-step" strategy, together with a general criticism of the "linkage approach" as a foreign policy method; and (b) inter-Arab and domestic Arab relations as affecting the conflict and OAPEC's role in OPEC, and Arab grievances in the conflict. He paid less attention to Israel's domestic disarray, even if Israel's grievances were well known to him; an American commitment to Israeli survival and development in peace was taken for granted by Mr. Carter.

The basic features of the 1975 Brookings formula,[73] published and unpublished, were as follows:

1. The U.S. basic interest in the region itself lies in a stable Middle East and good relations with both Arabs and Israelis.
2. Kissinger's "step-by-step strategy" in the Middle East is rejected as methodically wrong; it excluded the "basic elements" of the conflict— peace (normalization), withdrawals (borders), the Palestinians, and Jerusalem. Thus, possible rising tensions in the area "will generate increased risks of violence."
3. The assumption is that the "key Arab states" (Egypt, Syria, and Saudi Arabia) are basically interested in a conflict resolution. These "moderate" Arab countries are involved in economic development, having a clear-cut interest in cooperation with the West. They fear Arab Radicalism and are aware of their inability to destroy Israel militarily be-

cause of the U.S. commitment to Israel and because of Israel's own conventional (and unconventional) might. Yet, the same Arab countries will not accept any conflict resolution short of Israeli withdrawals from occupied Arab lands and some kind of a solution to the Palestinian question. At the same time, if no solution is quickly pursued (to be implemented later), Arab "moderate" regimes will face severe domestic and inter-Arab radical pressures. These "moderate" regimes might thus be endangered, toppled, or would resolve to cooperate with the Soviet Union again or to pursue a radical foreign policy.

4. A method of conflict resolution, which could be described as a controlled process of lowering the conflict's profile provided that final targets are known and agreed upon in advance, is suggested against Kissinger's "linkage" and "structural change" method. Kissinger's method operates from the givens of the present and moves toward an unknown future; while trying to avoid tackling "unsolvable problems," it creates at the same time, "structural linkages" between the United States and the parties due to partial Israeli withdrawals achieved by Washington and American aid to the parties in separate deals.

5. A bargaining procedure should take place at the outset of the process, especially with regard to the borders. The U.S. official position should, however, be that the basis for that bargain is the June 5, 1976, ADL. Only minor rectifications would be supported by the United States. Since the border question is linked, in Israeli perceptions, to the problem of its security, this question may be handled through a phased withdrawal strategy.

The basic elements of the Brookings formula are:

1. A comprehensive solution to the Middle East conflict, rather than interim, "step-by-step" measures is desirable from an American point of view, and in order to achieve it, the "basic elements" of the conflict should "soon" be addressed.

2. A "fair and enduring settlement" should contain "a commitment to respect the sovereignty and territorial integrity of others." The Arabs undertake "not only to give evidence of progress toward the development of normal international and regional political and economic relations." This feature would be called later the "normalization" element of the Brookings package.

3. Israel "undertakes to withdraw by agreed stages to the June 5, 1967, lines with only such modifications as are mutually accepted." Boundaries will probably need to be safeguarded by demilitarized zones supervised by U.N. forces.

4. There should be a provision for Palestinian self-determination, sub-

ject to Palestinian acceptance of the sovereignty and integrity of Israel within agreed boundaries. This might take the form of either an independent Palestinian state accepting the . . . peace agreements, or of a Palestinian entity voluntarily federated with Jordan, but exercising extensive political autonomy."

5. The Jerusalem problem is regarded by the authors as "particularly difficult;" therefore, the report does not suggest a specific solution to it. It recommends some minimum requirements to be met by any possible solutions: "unimpeded access to all of the holy places, and each should be under the custodianship of its own faith;" "no barriers dividing the city;" "each national group within the city should, if it so desires, have substantial political autonomy within the area where it predominates."

6. After having agreed in advance upon the principles as listed above, the process of withdrawals to the agreed boundaries and the establishment of peaceful relations would be carried out in stages over a period of years, each stage undertaken only when the agreed provisions of the previous stage have been faithfully implemented.

Behind the specific Middle East program a broader foreign policy approach, in method and substance, as related to the Soviet Union, seems to have been shared by Carter and Brzezinski. Brzezinski used to argue that Kissinger did not receive much from the Soviets in exchange for American concessions, hoping for a "spillover" effect to influence Moscow's foreign policy while at the same time alienating the rest of the West with his bilateral deals with the Soviets and alienating the American people and Congress. Accordingly, U.S. political culture was moral, or moralistic. The American people and their representatives thought in moral terms and expected the executive branch at least to try to implement them in its policy. Kissinger did not believe in America's ability to force its values upon others, but instead hoped for a "spillover" effect to develop from structural changes, Soviet domestic necessities, and indirect "step-by-step" development, avoiding crucial moral and "high political" choices (to use Stanley Hoffmann's term). Such a "linkage," or "spillover" effect was not bound to work, because it was methodologically questionable and because the American political system was not made for it. In other words, domestic American linkages to foreign policy making were bound to interfere with the concept since Congress and the public thought in moral terms. An "amoral" foreign policy, based on "spillover" expectations, was bound to run aground on Capitol Hill, and thus become self-defeating, because it could not fulfill Soviet expectations. Yet at the same time, Moscow was left relatively free from American moral pressure both at home and abroad. The United States referred only to Soviet political or military actions and dissociated itself from the moral meaning of Soviet behavior, so that Moscow would not feel itself provoked by a moralistic American approach. Instead, the "spillover" effect should have worked to influence Soviet interests and structures.

Against this strategy, Brzezinski suggested something like a golden mean between America's values and reality. The "nonlinkage" method, openly propagated by the president, was an attempt, in the case of Soviet Russia, to negotiate with Moscow on substantive issues, like SALT 2, demonstrating good will, moral values, and self-restraint while pursuing a specific goal in which American and Soviet interests seem to coincide. At the same time, the "nonlinkage" approach made it possible publicly to demand that the Soviets honor human rights, to put upon them moral and psychological pressure, in this respect, to encourage dissidents, and to satisfy domestic American moral expectations. The Russians, he said, should be granted political, strategic, and perhaps, economic advantages, because of either a common interest or an American interest, which, as in the case of SALT 2, was not divorced from moral considerations. Yet they should forcefully be told, publicly and privately, of their moral obligations as Americans saw them and according to the 1975 Helsinki Agreement, which both superpowers signed and ratified. Moreover, the substantive moralistic approach should also be implemented toward the third world. The Soviet Union should be deprived of its role as caretaker of the emerging nations, which, in turn, should be integrated into the international system because of their legitimate claims and potential power. "Linking" them to the United States would not suffice. Their substantive grievances should be tackled and advanced by American rather than Soviet support. When slowly sensing a major shift in general U.S. foreign policy and in Middle East policy in particular, many Israelis took this approach, especially toward anticipated claims by the Arabs, with apprehension and suspicion.

A comprehensive solution was perceived by conservative Israelis as undesirable because it entailed Arab demands, traditionally backed by U.S. administrations, for Israeli withdrawals to the pre-1967 borders "with minor rectifications." Most conservatives would not trust any arrangement with the Arabs if it entailed almost total withdrawals. Furthermore, most conservatives regarded Israel's fight against the 1969 Rogers Plan, the last American suggestion for a comprehensive solution, as a victory; Kissinger had refrained from suggesting further comprehensive solutions to the Israelis. Thus Carter's plan was a substantive "nonstarter" and a diplomatic defeat for Israel, bound to raise Arab expectations without a quid pro quo. Ideologically inspired conservatives like Mr. Begin would add to their fears Israel's right to the territories, historically perceived and legally based upon the indivisibility of rights to Eretz-Israel as a whole. Moreover, the conservative-hawkish Israelis and the many compromisers, bargainers, and American-oriented "doves" and those who were opposed to Israeli rule over Arabs would not accept a PLO state in the West Bank and the Gaza strip, as endorsed by the Brookings group or as left by the Brookings report for the Palestinians to decide. A PLO state, in common Israel perceptions, equated the establishment of the most radical, least controlled and controllable, irredentistic element in the unstable Arab coalition around Tel Aviv, Jerusalem, and Amman, thus delegitimizing and threatening both Israel and Jordan with Soviet, Libyian, and Iraqi aid.

Carter's repeated public remarks, in the spirit of the Brookings formula, about a "homeland for the Palestinians" and the 1967 borders were perceived in Israel as a return to the Rogers Plan and as showing the acceptance by the administration of the PLO state idea. This was either a rather naive foray by nonexperts like Brzezinski and Quandt into the complexities of the Middle East or a political-economic decision based on Carter's interest in Arab oil and Arab oil money, influenced by "Arabists" like Quandt. If these were the reasons behind the president's plan, Israel should resist them vigorously. Rabin's bargaining methods would not do here any more, and the "step-by-step" approach reached an impass after the Sinai 2.

The same Israelis who had opposed Kissinger's "marginal progress" to the core of the conflict resented it where Kissinger started to hit the core, as they saw it—the issues of the West Bank, Palestinians, and further withdrawals on the Golan Heights. They expected more gains from marginal concessions rather than "spillover" effects, and thus could agree with the Brookings' criticism of the "step-by-step" strategy. But their conclusions would have been diametrically opposed to the Brookings formula: far-reaching Arab concessions, real peace (i.e., Dutch-Belgian type relations), and not just "normalization" in the Brookings and Carter style of formulations for many fewer withdrawals.

Many Israelis resented any withdrawals in the West Bank altogether, preferring Israeli military presence along the river. These Israelis did not only oppose Carter's program, but resented Rabin's maneuvers toward a combined "step-by-step" and comprehensive approach, that might lead to withdrawals on all three fronts.

The Likud Victory and Dayan's Comeback, May–June, 1977

The National Elections

When Mr. Peres took over the alignment's leadership in April, five weeks before the elections, Israel's domestic scene was still dominated by Rabin's resignation and by the impact of the Yadlin affair that had preceded it. The alignment hastily tried to present Peres as a "new," "clean," middle-of-the-road pragmatic leader. He himself, now an all-party candidate, moved clearly from the right, (Rafi's traditional position under Dayan) toward the center (Mapai) and the left (Mapam, which was threatening not to go with Labor and thus to break the alignment). This move satisfied Mapam and the watching Americans, who preferred Rabin, yet it definitely did not satisfy hopes for a "new" leader, since Peres had been a fixture in Israeli politics since the "Lavon Affair;" Peres further angered conservative, hawkish voters, who despised Mapam and resented its influence on the Labor party, and alienated Moshe Dayan, the far right alignment candidate.

The self-styled alternative to the alignment, the Democratic Movement for Change, was caught unprepared when Rabin rescheduled the elections from November to May, 1977. The DMC had just absorbed a former Likud faction, the Free Center, which could not accept Mr. Begin's regiment, and individually joined the DMC. The Free Center, under Mr. Shmuel Tamir, was known as hawkish and individualistic. When several other hawks, tired of existing parties or politicized, joined the DMC, it assumed the image of an unclear mixture: Mr. Yadin and the moderate protest movement, Shinuy, contributed to a reform minded, domestically oriented image of not attaching a supreme value to occupied territories in the traditional Mapai manner, if a solution to the security problem could be found. The hawkish newcomers, even if they stressed a similar set of priorities, modified the DMC's image to portray a rigid approach to withdrawals, mainly from the West Bank. Both elements, Shinuy and Mr. Yadin, and the hawkish newcomers, contained established, Ashkenazi (Israelis of European origin), high-strata officials, professors, managers, and politicians. The DMC had to establish itself in the eyes of the lower strata and the non-Ashkenazi, first or second generation immigrants from Arab countries, a growing element of major importance in Israel's electorate after the fifties. The DMC decided to hold primaries for the party's institutions in order to demonstrate its rules of participation, using the method of "anybody elects everbody," instead of selecting and limiting a number of candidates by their public appeal and political or economic power or potential representation value.[74] The new party hoped to create a framework for participation by the rank and file, including non-Ashkenazi groups who seemed interested. Yet the results were to be expected—the membership preferred to vote for known candidates, like Mr. Yadin himself. Many non-Ashknazi voters preferred well-known Ashkenazi veterans like Mr. Tamir, as no screening process or a consensual agreement about new non-Ashkenazi candidates took place in advance. The new party's image remained, as a result of its own experiments with grass roots democracy and participation, rather "white," professional, and managerial, and its foreign policy remained unclear. As a new party, the DMC was almost barred from T.V. campaigning, reserved by the established parties for themselves. Its declared goal—to become either an alternative to the alignment or a new "blocking minority" in the Knesset, without which no coalition would be possible[75]—seemed to attract more informed, less emotional or less alienated voters (i.e., traditional alignment followers) and smaller liberal parties, like the Independent Liberals and the Civil Right Movement membership.

The Likud campaign, as compared with the 1973 elections, was organized by Mr. Ezer Weizman along simple, seemingly clear-cut and clearly low-level arguments. The Likud simply capitalized on the alignment's corruption cases, associated the late Mr. Offer with Mr. Yadlin, Mr. Rabin, and Mr. Peres, and exploited to the utmost Rabinowitz's bargaining methods—preelection strikes that were mounting as a result of last minute bids by powerful interest groups to force the alignment to buy peace in important public sectors with higher wages and inflation. Likud promised clean management, universal if not egalitarian rules of the game, and an electoral punishment of the corrupt, almost perpetual, alignment regime. Mr. Begin, candidate No. 1 on the Likud list, was slowly recovering from a serious stroke during the campaign; he added his Central European, statesmanlike eloquence, whereas Mr. Peres remained fluent but seemed to lack real substance. The non-Ashkenazi lower strata, which had followed Mr. Begin since the early fifties, was widely enlarged by a non-Ashkenazi and Ashkenazi higher income groups who were disappointed with the alignment's inability to deliver. The youth was outraged by corruption stories and was alienated from a bargaining elite, split and humilitated, or so it seemed, by President Carter.[76] Likud deliberately played down Herut's ideological and legal tradition with regard to the occupied territories and the Arab-Israeli conflict. Mr. Weizman, the campaign manager, stressed rather traditional hawkish, conservation postures common among many Israelis, capitalizing on Carter's remarks and several actions vis-à-vis Israel[77] and the Arabs. An almost humiliating courtesy exercised by the president toward Hafez-el-Assad of Syria, and a constant repetition by the president of a desired "homeland for the Palestinians" were understood in Israel to demonstrate an American decision to bring about Israeli withdrawals to the pre-1967 lines, and to impose, if necessary, a third, PLO state on Israel and Jordan, thus delegitimizing both.

Established alignment followers, who resented Likud populism and foreign policy, tended to vote for the DMC. Other protesters, or alienated lower strata voters, moved from the alignment directly to Likud[78] either because of their desire to punish the alignment, their feelings that at least this corrupt, ideologically hollow, and inefficient elite should be removed, or because they felt that the alignment might be just as opposed to Carter's plans but unable to put up a serious fight against them. Likud jumped from 37 Knesset seats (if Tamir's Free Center defection to the DMC is discounted) to 44 seats. The alignment was severely defeated: it dropped from 51 seats to 32. Mapai's punishment seemed to be the gravest. In the new faction, 18 members belonged to the historical Mapai, 5 to Rafi, 5 to Achdut Ha'Avoda, and 4 to Mapam. The historical elite, which had never managed to acquire an absolute majority in Israel's elections, but without which no coalition was possible, transferred that role now to others—to the 19 Herut seats in a 44-seat, seemingly cohesive Likud block and to a confident NRP, whose aggresive young, Gush Emunim-inspired leadership had purged old, compromising and corrupt leaders, and had suggested the religious party to the nation as a spiritual elite. The NRP was now Likud's natural ally, sharing Mr. Begin's views on Israeli "rights" and settlement rights in the West Bank.

General Sharon, the aggressive war leader, who retained a degree of popularity because of his style and public relations campaign during the war and who changed his mind several times after the war in considering his political future, organized at last a party of his own—Shlomzion. Unable to force himself on the Liberal faction in the Likud, which he had helped to create in 1973, and to become their leader, since Mr. Begin's position in the Herut faction of Likud was uncontested, Sharon first joined Rabin as special adviser, hoping to become chief of staff. When Peres blocked him as Rabin's adviser and future, more independent, chief of staff, Sharon tried his luck with the Liberals, and then created an extreme hawkish, low strata oriented party, which won two seats. It was a natural ally for Likud if they paid the price of an adequate ministerial position for General Sharon. The DMC did relatively well at the alignment's expense, and helped shut out the smaller Liberal parties, yet it did not succeed in becoming a pivotal power. Mr. Begin could master enough seats for a narrow coalition without the DMC because he was ready to make concessions to the ultraorthodox Agudat Yisrael, which had remained in opposition due since 1951 to its religious demands.

Since the alignment appeared to be totally shaken by its defeat, and the DMC was deprived of its anticipated, decisive role, Mr. Begin could assume that his public standing was very strong, for the time being. He opted for a narrow coalition with the NRP, Sharon, and Agudat Yisrael rather than for yielding to DMC demands that he moderate his traditional ideological approach to the conflict and the West Bank. He hoped to acquire an almost automatic Knesset support if Mr. Carter pursued his

Middle East plan, even without incorporating the DMC into his coalition. In foreign affairs, he assumed the nation-wide conservative consensus would give him parliamentary support without yielding in advance to DMC or alignment demands, which might undermine his stance vis-à-vis Mr. Carter. Yet Mr. Begin knew well that his biblical devotion to the West Bank and his legalistic and holocaust-inspired approach to the conflict were not acceptable as such, either to many Israelis or to the U.S. administration. He did not want to fight over American public opinion, his foreign policy target since his resignation from the Meir-Dayan government in 1970, using these arguments only. He was ready, traditionally, to give up most of the Sinai and the Golan Heights in exchange for peace with Egypt and Syria, while retaining the West Bank, and he needed an experienced, healthier, and innovative bargainer to handle a possible Sinai-Golan deal for him. He wanted someone capable of shifting the debate in the United States from the biblical stance (which he, Mr. Begin, retained as one of his basic claims) to strategic and defense political arguments. Ben-Gurion's "disciple" and Begin's rival-friend since 1967 was available. Dayan was offered the foreign ministry in Begin's narrow coalition, an unexpected comeback, in defiance of popular feelings. He readily agreed, and left the shattered alignment to become a one-man, independent faction in the Knesset.

I refuse the temptation, commenting on these events in the summer of 1977, to add something like "thus Mr. Begin demonstrated his firm grip on power," as Ben-Gurion used to do, mobilizing the masses and ignoring their opinion at the same time. Israel is too much of a democracy now to be ruled by Ben-Gurion's methods, as he himself tragically learned. It is too early to predict the viability of a narrowly based coalition led by an ideological legalistic emotional type of a leader like Mr. Begin, who spent most of his political life in opposition, where this mixture in him proved to be highly effective in influencing coalitions after Ben-Gurion's decline. Lacking a cognitive method to agree upon historical-political postulates, thinking in terms of absolute rights and a political-military framework that is logically derived from them (i.e., an indivisible Eretz-Israel) Mr. Begin seems to lack both Ben-Gurion's disguised prudence and the ability to pursue a strategy of active centrism, achieving a compromise between one's rights, goals, and reality and Mr. Eshkol's ability to bargain. Yet as an opposition leader, Mr. Begin was never forced to make compromises, and as a partner to the government of national unity between 1967 and 1970, he did not assume the main responsibility. He preferred to return to his traditional role in the opposition rather than to make compromises over the West Bank negotiations. In 1977, Mr. Begin found himself carrying the main responsibility for a nation whose psyche is a complex mixture of contradictory features. Conservative habits in foreign affairs are blurred with ideological, religious hopes advanced by the retreat of socialist pioneering values. Yet most of the Israelis are not observant, and tend to bargain by nature. Despite their intransigent, "Prussian" image, they are extremely individualistic, cynical, and skeptical, no trigger-happy warriors, but on the contrary very much Jewish—i.e., believers, dreamers, hard-working, almost selfish eccentrics, who are strongly devoted to their community and to Jewish heritage, as many of them interpret it according to their different perceptions. For many, Israel is the embodiment of Jewish survival, but it must be a humane, pragmatic, and civilized Israel to serve that purpose. For the others it must first survive and be accepted as a Jewish state in Israel's historical land, in a cruel and cynical world. Begin and Dayan represent that approach, but I doubt whether they represent the complexity of their nation's history and body politic.

Arab-Israeli Positions and Considerations for Future Scenarios

Arab public demands and strategic considerations in the summer of 1977 with regard to the conflict seemed to be divided along the following lines: Iraq, Libya, South Yemen, and several Palestinian groups in and outside the PLO refuse any recognition of or coexistence with Israel under any circumstances; they are resolved to pursue every possible method to bring about Israel's extinction, and try to influence or isolate Arab regimes that are ready to coexist with the Jewish state. Algeria's standing in this matter has not been clear since its 1976 territorial disputes with Morocco. Iraq and Libya are interested in influencing the Arab coalition as a whole; they are resourceful and their relations with Moscow are good. Both acquire arms in east and west, and are known to have tried to acquire a nuclear capability.[79] They share no borders with Israel, but could either influence Arab regimes with common borders and/or exercise influence on the conflict through interested Palestinians. This element of the Arab coalition is an acknowledged destabilizing factor in inter-Arab relations in general, particularly with regard to the conflict.

Egypt's public demands and positions with regard to the conflict,[80] which seem to be shared by Saudi Arabia, Sudan, Morocco, and North Yemen, are as follows. If Israel is ready, or rather is forced by American pressure, to withdraw to the pre-1967 ADL and to agree to the establishment of a PLO state in former Jordanian-administrated territories in the West Bank and former Egyptian-administrated territories in the Gaza Strip, with some "links" to Jordan, Egypt would be ready to recognize the 1949 ADL as international boundaries. Egypt would then also renounce the state of belligerency with Israel, and would not oppose international, mainly American, guarantees given to Israel, or its final borders.

Egypt is not ready to make "real" peace, i.e., to reconcile itself with the Zionist entity, unless Zionism itself has made far-reaching concessions in its claims and behavior, so that Israel could be "accepted" by the Arab Middle East and integrated into the region. Israel is supposed to abolish "the law of return," which illegally makes Israel a homeland for every Jew in the world and further threatens the Arabs in the whole region, exposing them to a permanent danger of Jewish expansion. Israel is asked, as an alternative, to suspend any further Jewish immigration for the next fifty years. Should Zionism refuse to accept these demands, Egypt is ready for a nonbelligerency arrangement, as described above, if Israel removed the immediate Arab grievances of the occupation of Arab sovereign territory and made it possible for the Palestinians to satisfy their legitimate demands for a sovereign state in a part of their historical homeland. This compromise accepts Israel's 1949 boundaries as internationally recognized and uncontested by the international community, especially by the United States, which, at least for the time being, is politically, morally, and militarily committed to Israel's existence in these borders. Thus the radical, "all-out war" outcry against Israel might be theoretically correct, but unrealistic. The middle-of-the-road, pragmatic solution would be an American-imposed, nonbelligerency arrangement, short of any positive, diplomatic, or trade relations, as long as Zionism did not compromise its own ideology; such an arrangement would formalize the U.S. commitment to Israel, while making it possible for Egypt, Syria, and the Palestinians, who are ready for it, to recover Arab lands and to establish a Palestinian state. This arrangement is not binding on future generations, since it does not end the ideological conflict. It does terminate the territorial and the political conflict, and should be regarded as a reasonable compromise over the Palestinian question, even if their legitimate claims to their homeland as a whole and their grievances as homeless refugees relate directly to the illegality of Zionism, its ideology, and past behavior. Thus the only way to socialize the Palestinians and make them a partner to this far-reaching concession is to let them participate in the diplomatic procedure—an all-out Arab-Israeli conference at Geneva run by the superpowers—intended to bring about Israel's formal acceptance of the same compromise.

Unofficially, the Egyptian press added another consideration to the above-mentioned reasoning: the nuclear factor.[81] In ten years, maintained the Egyptian press since 1975, the Middle East will be nuclearized, and thus future wars will become impossible. I tend to understand this argument as being related to the present rather than the future, saying that Israel's ADL is supported not only by an American commitment but also by a nuclear threat. Egypt is not ready to sacrifice its own survival for the Palestinians, at least as long as the nuclear factor and the American commitment are not neutralized.

Syria's positions are less explicit. President Assad speaks sometimes in terms on renouncing belligerency de facto in exchange for total withdrawal and a Palestinian state, but he remains silent with regard to positive Arab concessions. This sounds like an armistice arrangement of the 1949 model, which left the legitimacy of the borders open.

The PLO's majority position is officially negative toward Israel's very existence, yet Arafat's hints mentioned above lead to the conclusion that they might accept a West Bank-Gaza state, plus former Palestinian territories they claim from Syria and Egypt, after Israel's withdrawal from the Sinai and the Golan.[82] Political concessions vis-à-vis Israel were not mentioned clearly enough, in PLO remarks to Americans or Israelis who met their emissaries, yet the impression was given that they were divided over this in the Fath leadership; nonbelligerency or an armistice, or even a more positive arrangement "for the next twenty years," to quote Arafat's public remarks in May, 1977, are considered.[83] In other words, the PLO is at odds with itself over which political price they should pay for a sovereign, partial Palestinian state, while renouncing claims to the rest of Palestine in Arafat's lifetime, and keeping the ideological conflict open. Both Syria and the PLO, as opposed to Egypt and Saudi Arabia, are more Soviet oriented, and by far more skeptical about American willingness or ability to impose Egypt's compromise upon Israel. Syria is more suspicious of U.S. intentions, having understood Kissinger's "step-by-step" strategy correctly as a measure to gain time, to establish the United States in the region and to divide the Arabs if they could not agree on more pragmatic positions and behavior in the conflict. Syria indeed succeeded in isolating Egypt after Sinai 2 as a result of its separate deal with Israel, and helped bring an end to separate deals between the two. Yet Assad was forced to divert his attention and his army to Lebanon. He fought with the PLO and is now holding them in an uneasy grip. Thus, Syria seems now to agree to an Egyptian comprehensive formula, but could be, together with the PLO, less inclined to make political concessions, more vulnerable to Iraqi criticism, and more ideologically motivated, having in mind the regime's bid for Arab leadership and traditional Syrian claims to Palestine as part of "greater Syria."

Jordan seems to be, since 1967, the only Arab state to express, albeit privately, its readiness to make a formal peace with Israel in exchange for the West Bank. Yet King Hussein had entered an uneasy coalition with Assad's Syria, which might protect them both from isolation in the Arab world, secure Syria's southern flank, and give Hussein, when his Amrican-built and Saudi-financed air defense system is ready in 1978, a better military option if other Arab states resolve to fight Israel or threaten him. Unofficially, Hussein retained his claims on the West Bank, transferred by Arab summits to the PLO, and is ready to absorb it in his Palestinian-American oriented kingdom, with or without PLO consent.

The Americans, until Mr. Begin's victory, seemed to have accepted Sadat's formula as reasonable and to have concentrated on acquiring political concessions from the Arab states, beyond Sadat's nonbelligerency toward real normalization. When the Egyptian president spoke in public on normalization, five years after Israel's withdrawal, during his April, 1977, visit to the United States,[84] this statement was welcomed as a concession, in comparison with his usual remarks about the next generation who are supposed to decide on peace, but as not enough of a concession. The administration hoped that Egypt could be brought to accept some kind of normalization, and seemed to be bound by the Brookings equation that normalization meant almost total withdrawals. Washington tried, at the same time, to extract concessions from the PLO, so that Fath's presence at Geneva would be possible, according to Kissinger's commitments to Israel and Egypt's compromise formula. Assuming a substantive approach to the conflict, the administration accepted the Brookings suppositions with regard to the Palestinians as being one of the cores of the conflict, along with the border and peace questions. Carter's administration began extensively searching for safeguards for Israel.[85] Some of these were: a military treaty with Israel, including a possible U.S. base in Israel; a distinction between legal borders and security zones, to be demilitarized on the Arab side; early warning systems in the security zones; freezing the armed forces on both sides, to prevent a growing conventional gap between Israel and its neighbors and to control the conventional arms race; the retention of a limited number of Israeli settlements in traditional historic Jewish sites, to be returned to Arab sovereignty; freezing the nuclear situation in the area; and possible American support for the retention of a unified Jerusalem honoring Arab religious and political interests in the city at the same time.

All this would be exchanged for Israeli withdrawals to the pre-1967 border with minor rectifications and for Arab commitments not only to end such hostile actions against Israel as armed incursions, blockades, boycotts, and propaganda attacks but also to give evidence of progress in the development of normal international and regional political and economic relations. If the PLO proved unable or unwilling to change its official stance toward Israel, Jerusalem was invited to negotiate with King Hussein. Israel's official and unofficial arguments and actions against this formula would be divided since Begin's ascendancy and Dayan's comeback along the following lines:

a. Zionism is historically legitimate, and derives its legitimacy from the Jewish religion, from Jewish longing for and Jewish continued presence, even if as a minority in the country for two thousand years, and from Jewish existence in the Diaspora, European and Arab alike, which could not guarantee Jewish social, culutral, and political rights, nor Jewish physical survival.[86]

b. Zionism, and hence Israel, does not need any Arab "acceptance," and Zinoists are not interested in being integrated into the Arab Middle East. They claim the whole territory between the Mediterranean and the Jordan River as Israeli national territory, and they are ready to give every Arab there the status of an Israeli citizen, hoping to retain a Jewish majority through immigration from the Soviet Union and the West and a growing birth rate at home.[87]

c. Since Israel is dependent on the United States and since the new government is bound to Security Council Resolution 242, which makes territorial negotiations on the West Bank imperative, Israel is ready officially to negotiate on all territories and will not annex the West Bank. Its strategy in such negotiations would be to prove to American public opinion that the Arabs are not ready for peace, even in exchange for the West Bank. In the meantime, a limited number of settlements will be approved on proper occasions.

d. Israel will be ready to negotiate peace agreements with Egypt, Syria, and Jordan. If both Cairo and Damascus are ready to guarantee peace, or a peacelike agreement, or to withdraw for all practical purposes from the conflict, Egypt might recover most of the Sinai (minus the Gaza Strip and the Israeli wedge between Gaza and Egypt in the Yamit area) and Syria might recover parts of the Golan Heights.[88]

e. Egypt should be confronted with the dilemma of whether or not Sadat was ready to risk a new war, and pay the price of returning to the Soviets for aid and of risking U.S. and Saudi economic aid, while preparing to fight an IDF more balanced and ready than in 1973. Sadat, or his successor, should seriously consider whether Egypt was at all interested in "fighting for the PLO," because Cairo could gain most of the Sinai without firing a shot; Egypt's economic stress might have become a predominant problem, as demonstrated in the January, 1977, riots. Cairo is not to be isolated, this time, but territorial concessions should be made to the Syrians on the Heights.

f. The West Bank would remain in Israeli hands in the foreseeable future, at least until the Arab coalition has finally stabilized, absorbed Israel's rights and territorial claims as a reality, and is ready to normalize its relations with Israel. Even then these rights exclude a total withdrawal to the 1967 lines; such a withdrawal endangers the whole process of stabilization by creating irresistible temptations for the Arabs to harass or to attack Israel. Israel offers to Jordan, in the framework of a proposed peace or nonbelligerency agreement, political standing with regard to West Bank Arabs, and offers West Bank dwellers political representation outside that area through participation in Jordanian elections, the continuation of the "open bridge" policy, and a strict liberal, noninterference occupation regime.[89]

g. A PLO state in the West Bank and Gaza does not only delegitimize Israel and the American-oriented Jordan, but contests Israel's own rights to the West Bank. According to Israel's overwhelming national consensus, such a state—a combination of West Bank dwellers ruled by PLO leaders—will not be able to solve the refugees' problem, as Arab refugees in Syria and Lebanon had been educated to believe in pursuing their return to pre-1967 Israel. If they agree to go to the West Bank, already too small and crowded, and lacking any natural financial resources of its own, they will be regarded by the West Bankers and themselves as foreigners, or alien brethren who should return to their real homes in Jaffa and Haifa. This addition of hundreds of thousands of refugees to the West Bank could create problems of control for any leadership of the strange state, and could be exploited by the "rejectionists"—PLO radicals, and Iraqi and Libyan agents—to the utmost. A permanent state of tension between Israel and its explosive neighbor might be used by PLO leaders unable or unwilling to control their mixed population, half of it acquainted with Israel and having vested interests in law and order and half of it radical by education and expectation, and penniless and educated to hate Israel, to drag the Arab coalition to new escalations. Controlling the immediate vicinity of both Jerusalem and Tel Aviv, the PLO will thus become the trustee of peace in the Middle East.

h. An imposed American solution creates similar temptations in the Arab world, as it would be regarded by many Arabs as a net gain against a net Israeli loss. It would encourage further demands, even if "moderate" Arabs were ready, before having gained these concessions through American pressure, to accept them as final during their lifetime.

i. Arabs are tempted to emotional, less controlled reactions and lack the means to control their vast and contradictory, extremely rich and very poor coalition. Agreements made with Arab dictators like Sadat or Assad might be nullified or transgressed by their successors, whose economic or domestic political situation might drive them to foreign escapades. Israel should therefore lower the profile of its conflict with Egypt and Syria, but refrain from giving away vital territories in the Sinai and the West Bank.

j. Since American soldiers' lives will always be at stake in a hard to control, complex conflict situation, American guarantees might serve the Arabs to undermine Israel's position in the United States or to impose American restrictions on Israel's freedom of action. U.S. ideas on demilitarization, early warning systems, freezing the armies, and the nuclear situation are helpful, but since they limit Arab sovereignty they will be, by definition, limited in time and could not replace territorial changes in Israel's favor.[90]

k. Unforseeable domestic changes in the United States render American commitments questionable. Israel should rely on the United States as long as it possibly can without sacrificing its national interests, claims, and ideology, and should fight for these with Jewish help inside the United States, but mainly it should rely on itself and world Jewry.

l. Israel, under Begin and Dayan, is ready to oppose American plans with regard to the Middle East and risk economic strain, explaining to the nation the reason for it, and mobilizing its fighting spirit and latent ability to sacrifice personal convenience for the sake of higher value. American conventional military aid to Israel could be dispensed with in a political emergency, because Israel has accumulated a reasonable stockpile of hardware since the Yom Kippur War. Likud preferences concerning an Israeli "bomb in the basement" are unknown. After Egypt's departure from Moscow in 1976, Dayan repeated his strong conviction that Israel should adopt an active nuclear policy, together with the above-mentioned offers to withdraw from most of the Sinai and the Golan Heights. Egypt and Syria should be confronted, accordingly, with a nuclear risk "if they go to war over the West Bank," since they can recover other territories without war.[91]

m. The nuclear situation in the Middle East, that is, an Arab nuclear option that might be realized in ten years despite Carter's nonproliferation campaign, dictates the retention of a territorial margin by Israel outside its pre-1967 heartland.[92]

Future scenarios for the Middle East depend on the following factors:

1. The above-mentioned positions and strategic assumptions of the parties themselves (in my opinion, all parties are not interested in arrangements short of their national and coalitionary interests and ideological obligations as they differently confront them with reality. They are not interested in a compromise per se);

2. the parties' ability to neutralize American support for their adversaries or to mobilize American support (working inside the U.S. system, using domestic American bargaining habits, public opinion, interest

groups, and national moods while adopting—or refraining from doing so—more or less acceptable and tangible positions, in American terms, toward each other);

3. the parties' own domestic and coalitionary pressures and political necessities while reflecting on the adversary's positions and strategic assumptions, and on U.S. positions;

4. Arab willingness and ability to mobilize Soviet support, and Soviet willingness and ability to return to an active, military support of Arab states (which also depends on the future of American-Soviet relations and extraregional and domestic Soviet developments);

5. the "capability in place" of both superpowers and their willingness to intervene and neutralize the other superpower in new hostilities in the Middle East;

6. the international oil situation, U.S. perceptions of dependence on Arab oil, and Saudi determination to use the oil weapon (the availability of Alaskan and North Sea oil, the implementations of Carter's energy plan in the early 80's, a possible self-inflicted damage to the Saudis as a result of an economic disarray in the West in a new oil crisis, and whether this might create a lesser degree of economically and psychological dependence on Saudi oil, at least in comparison with the crisis atmosphere of 1973–74 are all factors); and

7. superpower cooperation on Middle East questions: U.S. pressure on Israel and Soviet pressure on Arab clients, such as the PLO and Syria.

Conclusion

The Arab-Israeli conflict has to do, politically, socially, and psychologically, with modern nationalism. Two more or less traditional societies, Jewish and Arab, were involved, internally and with each other, in a process of modernization and nation building. At the same time, they struggled to retain and/or reform their political, cultural, and social traditions. Strong doubts about one's culture, traditional way of life, politics, and even physical survival in the face of challenges by modern threats, contributed to a strong, new national ethos. Thus, Zionism and Arab nationalism share a deep desire to shape reality according to "rights," historically and politically formulated but psychologically motivated. However, different political and sociocultural traditions and different national challenges and options lead the two nationalisms to have many opposing qualities.

Jewish nationalism, it seems to me, might accept, as it did under Ben-Gurion, a large number of ideological, political and substantive (i.e., territorial) concessions to the Arabs because of its social-democratic, "progressive" philosophy and its interest in curing Jewish maladies rather than responding to Arab challenges. In this respect, Jewish nationalism was ready for compromises vis-à-vis the Arabs but was less ready to compromise on Jewish principles; it sought an internal, secular, social, and economic revolution to undo 2000 years of Diaspora life, habits, and culture, and it tried to relink the Jews, as a newborn, changed nation, to the land of the prophets. Practical concessions to Arabs, based on a method of studying history, on understanding the spirit of the time, and on fearing the dangers of a head-on collision with overly powerful external forces and emerging Arab nationalism, were covered by a strong rhetoric and hostile gestures in response to Arab challenges. Being self-centered and interested in the positive development of Jewish sovereignty in partitioned Palestine, this approach was less sensitive to Arab provocations but was not passive toward them. The Israeli reaction to the Arab challenge was constrained by Israel's own priorities, or postulates. These

348

postulates concerned Jews more than Arabs and included a principle derived from Ben-Gurion's cognitive understanding of the spirit of the times (or current historical trends): to refrain at all costs, including territorial concessions, from ruling a large Arab population.

In the late 1950s, social, moral, and cultural aspirations to revolutionize Jewish Diaspora traditions and habits proved to be partially limited in scope and in response. Gaps were opened between Ben-Gurion's postulates and the political, social, and cultural realities in Israel: his foreign and defense concepts were rather defensive, while his style and reputation were offensive and autonomous. His autonomy was limited and self-contrained, yet he helped create behavioral habits that demanded strong reactions against enemy threats and border changes in the event of war, a preemptive strike in the event of a growing Arab challenge, and autonomous action against the enemy, alone if necessary. Ben-Gurion sought to prevent preemptive wars fought alone and resented Israeli rule over the Arab-populated West Bank.

Israel's social, political, and cultural forces, which brought Ben-Gurion down in 1963, made bargaining on domestic and foreign affairs the main approach toward these matters, rather than a cognitive-postulative approach monopolized by a principal leader. Bargaining is a philosophy of life, and takes for granted that politics is a sort of a give-and-take game. If bargaining proves to be impossible and the other side refuses to "play the game," bargainers may feel compelled to use force. Thus, a group of Israeli leaders like Levi Eshkol, Pinhas Sapir, and Moshe Haim Shapira of the old NRP, compromisers and bargainers as they were, were more vulnerable to Arab provocations, threats, and actions when they interpreted those actions as "breaking the rules of the game" and imposing new rules in rejection of a "reasonable" Israeli compromise following the 1967 war, an unnecessary and very poorly handled escalation by both sides. At the same time Eshkol and Sapir bargained with domestic elements, whose legal-ideological and manly-responsive approach to the conflict was different. The outcome, in terms of policy, was a compromise, as usual, that combined all three approaches to Israel's peace with the "defensible borders or nothing" formula of 1967–71 and almost up to 1973. A new war became inevitable as the other side was left to choose between two unacceptable alternatives.

Besides the cognitive-postulative and the bargaining leader, Israel produced two other types of approach to the conflict: the manly-responsive and the legal-ideological. The manly-responsive type of leader, as Dayan used to be and as Meir seems to me to have been at times, is interested in asserting his rights and interests in power relationships. He must guard and enhance his interest in a conflict he perceives as rather "normal," in the sense that he expects the other side to pursue and enhance its own interests and claims just as he knows it is aware of his claims and interests. The manly-responsive type of leader is inclined to react to the other side's challenges almost automatically, as a matter of principle, fearing that the other party will interpret a lack of response as a sign of weakness and will be tempted to escalate its challenges. This approach is sometimes both conservative and fatalistic, in the sense that it expects people to pursue their individual interests, power relationships, different and equal (and thus contradictory) "rights," different traditions, contrasting affiliations, and conflicting obligations. American liberal behavior accordingly originated in circumstances where lucky people could afford it.

The manly-responsive and the bargaining approach are not progressive in thinking about the future and are based on instincts and experience rather than on a broad, cognitive study of history and the spirit of the times. Leaders of these types do not yield bargaining assets or national goals, or both, unless there is no other choice. The business of the statesman is to avoid no-choice situations by using force, threats, and negotiations while remembering that the other side is doing just the same. Reality, in this sense, is not the positive odds against one (manifested in this situation by Israeli rule over a large Arab population and Israel's isolation among the nations) as some "doves" tend to think, but rather the struggle against these odds. One should, therefore, never make substantive concessions in advance; one should sometimes be flexible over details, suggest temporary, interim outlets in order to avoid head-on clashes, and live with unresolved matters (like the Arab populated West Bank). Substantive, (i.e., territorial) concessions in vital areas like the West Bank, small and dominant as the area is in relation to Israel's small and vulnerable pre-1967 heartland, are preceived as a net gain to the Arab side and as a dangerous net loss to Israel. Such a loss, especially if imposed by interested third parties like the United States, is bound to encourage the other side, sooner or later, to respond to ideological, political, and power pressures within the Arab coalition and to demand even more, rather than to accept Israeli concessions as final.

The legal-ideological approach embodied by Mr. Begin works from preconceived "rights" and goals back to reality, trying to transform it accordingly. This approach is based on historical experience and a cultural vision derived from the hazards and the emptiness of Jewish life in the Diaspora and in Israel itself. The "logical" or "legal" method here dictates a fight over principles, which are indivisible. "Rights" are usually not a subject for negotiations and could be pursued by convincing oneself, and third parties about them. Being also self-centered, but not progressive and cognitive, the postulates of this approach ignore the "rights" of the other party to the conflict or offer that party "rights" in the overall framework of its own "rights." The legal-ideological approach in this case is conservative (i.e., pessimistic) about the "real intentions" of the other side and about human nature in general, as is the manly-responsive approach. Bargaining is sometimes thought useless, sometimes self-deceptive and thus self-defeating. Inwardly oriented, its main concern is to educate, convince, and lead the nation to fight for goals for the future as developed from experiences of the past.

Arab nationalism seems to me to share some qualities of Jewish nationalism, but its basic problem is one of reconciling reality with potentials. It works toward "legitimate" goals and "rights" without a modern infrastructure and without a sufficient technical or mental, social, and political base; yet it wants to develop these qualities while preserving the traditions and values of the past. Modern Arab unity and Muslim tradition are probably two sides of the same coin. One cannot, moreover, even if one is obliged to do so, revolutionize Arab society, achieve Arab unity, create a modern Arab world, and eliminate Israel without paying a high price in terms of the sacrifice of traditional values and national, regional, and local frameworks worth preserving or strong enough to demand preservation. Therefore, the Arab compromise, also under Nasser, was to work on several levels: the ideological, proclaimed position was clear and uncompromising, but little was done to implement it. Arab calculations of benefits and loss did not just include their national grievances; the Arabs—like Ben-Gurion—were very sensitive to the international political situation and to international opinion. Egypt calculated actual policy decisions on the basis of a complex compromise between domestic, inter-Arab, and international demands and constraints, obligations to ideology, their actual power, and a projected price.

As long as Israel did not challenge their national sensitivities, self-respect, and ideological obligations too much, many Arabs were ready simply to hate Israel, educate their children to hate it, and let Palestinians, who were directly involved, intimidate Israel. When, after June, 1967, the Israeli challenge became unacceptable, the Arabs combined old and new grievances into one package, making concrete demands without renouncing the right to hate and thus paving the way from their side for the Yom Kippur War. Arabs, like Israelis, are thinking in terms of "rights" and national, natural goals. Some Arabs believe that these rights should be pursued by all means, working back from these goals to reality in order to transform it. Others are more aware of positive facts of life and on the price this transformation—if it is at all possible— might cost; it seems to me that most Arab regimes incline toward the positivist approach. Yet other Arab regimes, "rejectionists" of all colors, and competing pretenders to Arab leadership, might expose the relatively subtle compromise between ideology and reality, between dream and action, and thus enforce new forms of compromise between conflicting pressures and between Arab national aspirations and Arab power. The Arab-Israeli conflict is therefore a group conflict, in which changing coalitions play changing roles.

Historically, it is an asymmetrical conflict in which cognitive-postulative leaders like Ben-Gurion and Sadat act their limited roles in their coalitions, while manly-responsive bargainers, and emotional-postulative or ideological-legalistic leaders, like Nasser, Eshkol, Meir, Dayan, and Begin play their roles in their own and in other camps. The conflict is further asymmetrical because of extraregional interest and input, which can be manipulated by the parties themselves or is conceived of as manipulable by them.

In thinking of the future, the parties sometimes tend to develop a strong sense of imponderability, that is, they would pursue their national aims and yield to domestic pressures while testing reality. The tragic element in the conflict is manifested by the parties' determination to pursue these aims and interests against the concrete facts of life, hoping to impose themselves on reality or at least to demonstrate their wish to do so. Even if the Arabs were defeated in 1967 and were skeptical about a successful Yom Kippur War, their national ethos, vast resources, and sense of humiliation served them well to convert a defeat into an initial victory. The Israelis, on the other hand, went through a very complicated domestic and diplomatic process, after their own humiliation, to demonstrate to the Arabs, to the Americans, and to themselves that grim political realities do not necessarily justify acceptance without a fight. Psychologically and substantively, the conflict is thus composed of the necessity for national groups to assert themselves, which is manifested in general and specific issues: territories; attitudes and claims toward each other; reactions to the other side's attitudes, claims, and actual behavior; interpreting third parties' attitudes and behavior in the context of their own behavior in the conflict; and the inability to synchronize pragmatic retreats from these claims, derived from past lessons and cognitive learning of reality with the other side's pragmatic retreats in a given period.

Attitudes adopted by single parties to the conflict as a result of a complex compromise between domestic coalitionary attitudes and interests are bound to be perceived or presented by the other party as preconceived against it in the framework on the conflict, rather than understood or accepted as a complex compromise, or a verbal concession to ideological and political pressures and not as a working policy decision. Attitudes and ideologies, even if not implemented in practice, seem thus to be binding, or bound to push a possible compromiser to behave accordingly. "Peaceful coexistence" between different national ideologies is, therefore, very difficult in the Middle East. The actual behavior of a party in its coalitionary framework is interpreted in terms of the conflict; economic, political, and personal changes that have nothing to do with the conflict are perceived as actual or potential threats. Actions taken by one party to express a newly won national pride, a newly won sovereignty and independence, might be regarded by the others, or some of the others, as offensive, arrogant, and threatening, or may be consciously presented as such. As a result of these features, parties to the conflict tend to derive "self-fulfilling prophecies" from conflict situations that might have been averted had the parties been able to pursue different strategies with regard to specific grievances or to change their official posture toward each other and toward their own domestic audiences at a given point in time.

According to this perception, had the Arabs attacked Israel on Yom Kippur in the pre-1967 lines, Israel would have been destroyed. Few Israelis are ready to accept an argument that "the Arabs" might not have attacked Israel at all if Israel had not added the events of 1967 to the humiliation and concrete grievances of 1948–49, which alone had never produced an Arab offensive. (For that matter, one must convince most Israelis that the Arabs want peace.) Having lost their foreign political innocence and sense of of dependence upon an international consensus because of their holocaust syndrome, their experience as Jewish minority members abroad and perhaps under Arab majority rule, and "the world's" behavior before the 1967 war many Israelis will not accept peace alone as a guarantee of their survival and self-assertion. Because they fear an escalation process as a result of the gap between Arab ideology and sometimes real behavior, few Israelis would be ready to accept as sufficient my analysis that before 1967 Arab obligations to the refugees and Arab ideological commitments against Israel were not concretized in an operational plan to destroy Israel. Others are not ready to pay for Arab mistakes in 1947, 1949, and 1967 and do not regard it as their business to help "the Arabs" out of their own decisions not to accept partition, not to absorb the refugees, and to continue hostilities and belligerency.

Ben-Gurion's relatively low territorial profile, his willingness to divide western Palestine between Israel and Jordan, his principle not to rule Arabs, and his nuclear deterrence were adequate, at the time, to guarantee Israel's basic security and to lower the profile of the conflict considerably. Israel did not occupy sovereign (Egyptian and Syrian) Arab lands, but a part of Palestine and a part of Jerusalem. The Jordanian West Bank was under Arab rule, slowly integrating into the kingdom's socioeconomic structure. The refugees in Syria, Lebanon, and Gaza were indeed the pariahs of the Middle East, refused integration in these countries while refusing it themselves. Yet a continued low-level conflict might have driven them, slowly, to accept Jordan on both banks as a possible Palestinian homeland or caused them (and Arab governments) to have a growing interest in their respective Arab neighborhoods.

Historical-political, postulative wisdom, a high degree of self-restraint, and a suitable domestic political structure (meaning no pressure from Ben-Gurion's Rafi) could have prevented the 1967 war that destroyed Ben-Gurion's postulates. Israel became an occupant, "expansionist," arrogant foreign element, as the Arabs saw it, helping itself in creating a real Palestinian problem. The world thought Israel responsible both for the plight of the Palestinian refugees and for their Palestinian brethren in the West Bank, who until 1967 had been Jordanians for all practical purposes. Under Israeli occupation the West Bank dwellers were perceived by a growing Arab consensus as Palestinians, because Jordan had lost the territory. Palestinian groups became allies of the Arab regimes in their fight against Israel, and their activities were at first the only manifestation of active Arab resistance to an "arrogant" Israel. Thus Arab demands from Israel were influenced by territorial claims and an obligation toward a Palestinian radical element, which until 1967 could not master a common Arab operational consensus.

In order to prevent the Six-Day War, a similar disguised prudence, a postulative-historical method, self-restraint, and suitable Arab-Egyptian coalitionary structures were needed to stop President Nasser from unifying the Israelis behind the fears and emotions that made it possible for General Dayan and a minority of border revisionists (less emotional, clear-minded advocates of new borders and new relations with the Arabs) to influence a stunned, emotional, and provoked majority.

Nasser's Gestalt-like, noninstrumental Arab rhetoric (i.e., it was not supported by a real modernization process in Egypt although it created the impression that it was); Egypt's domestic regime and Nasser's bid for Arab, Muslim, and African leadership; Arab religious and tribal traditions, some of them unfavorably known to many Israelis living under Arab rule; Arab handling of Jews in Palestine in the past; and Arab hatred campaigns against Israel—all were blurred, at a time when Israel's own positive domestic order and pioneering values were decaying, into an Israeli perception of Arab threats, "real intentions," and potential or terribly imminent danger. Israeli habits of operational instrumentalism played their own role in this sad process. If Arabs bought Soviet weapons, Israelis thought, or indeed bought any other weapons, they would surely use them against Israel or would be tempted to do so. This perception contributed to the Israeli surprise on October, 1973. Yet very few Israelis would accept my version of the Yom Kippur War, especially my analysis of Arab preplanning and Soviet behavior. Israelis, living in isolation and stress conditions in a hostile environment, tend to feel that, had "the Arabs" been given a chance, they would have crushed Israel altogether. Israelis perceived that their nuclear option, if indeed a restraint on Arab preplanning (as I tend to believe), could not be credible in Arab eyes, because many Israelis never thought of nuclear deterrence as a serious matter and because no serious debate took place in Israel about this sensitive issue. Territories, early warnings, and conventional weapons are perceived as the only guarantees of Israel's security.

General Dayan, who might have endorsed a policy of implicit nuclear deterrence, was never able to influence Israel's foreign affairs and defense strategies beyond changing limits. Yet for the Arabs an Israeli nuclear option might not be acceptable even if most of the Israeli cabinet, the decision making framework, never accepted the credibility of a nuclear deterrence. Such an option might be bound to Israel's "expansionist character" and would be incompatible with the Arab self-image, sense of right, and territorial grievances. The Arabs were unable or unwilling to realize that a strong faction in Israel's past coalition, Mapai and Achdut Ha'Avoda, never accepted nuclear deterrence as credible, and that the leftist Mapam deplored it. These factions, not Dayan's Rafi, happened to be in the majority in Israel's coalitions after Ben-Gurion's departure. Yet Dayan's person, style, claims in the conflict, and important marginal influence over the Israeli coalition could be perceived by many Arabs as decisively important in the matters of a nuclear threat, territories, and humiliating Israeli demands that the Arabs change their behavior and claims. As a result of such a reaction, an even greater effort was justified, in Arab eyes, to oppose Israel and teach it a lesson. Many Arabs did not want to, and perhaps could not, understand that Dayan was given a limited free hand by the majority, which checked his positive strategy toward new borders, prevented settlements and limited settlers to a few thousand in the West Bank, having no positive strategy of its own. Indeed, because of this situation, traditional Mapai and Mapam leaders sometimes became even more demanding vis-à-vis Arab official postures than Dayan, who took them for granted and hoped to open a wedge between them and Arab deeds, giving up peace as a target.

Historically, cognitive experience, as manifested in Ben-Gurion's case, based upon ceaseless reading and soul searching and presented in disguised, difficult to read terms and actions, is difficult to transfer to the next generation, which absorbs and distorts the experience according to its own experience and background. Ben-Gurion's constant search for a compact, viable power base to serve his postulates—a sovereign, socially reformed, humanitarian Jewish existence—created a growing rejection of his personal regiment in the same power base and outside it, as the secondary leadership adapted itself to new social realities in a post-pioneering Israel. The image of a socially, culturally, and psychologically reformed sovereign Jewish state, created by Ben-Gurion in order to change the nature of his nation, became divorced from Jewish realities in Israel. A mixture of the fighting Jew, who indeed was raised by the pioneers and who adopted Ben-Gurion's political and military slogans rather than his complicated set of postulates, who rejected ruling Arabs and territorial exaggeration and preferring pragmatic defense postures, was later blurred with traditional Jewish fears, emotionalism, and bargaining habits. Ben-Gurion's latent dependence on foreign powers and "the world," his historically postulated understanding of a compromise between Jewish rights and Arab presence in and around Palestine (which he reluctantly admitted publicly but which set limits on *his* "proud," "sovereign," and autonomous behavior) created a gap between the substance of his policy and its appearance, and was not acceptable to the more optimistic, more autonomous younger generation or to the ideological, self-righteous Jewish right inspired by the unique experience of post World War I anti-Semitism.

Ben-Gurion's Jewish state was an instrument to achieve social, cultural, and moral values. For the Zionist right and members of the younger generation, it was a purpose for itself, the embodiment, in sovereign and religious symbols, of Jewish traditions, experiences, and rights. Since this mixture of right-wing, religious, and state-oriented emotional, responsive, manly, and legalistically bound leaders now took over a vast majority of Jews—those who might not be satisfied with religion, the state, the conflict, and settlements in the West Bank as the sole manifestation of their complex heritage—a trend reverting to social, humane values might be expected if the conflict permitted it. Yet the historical structure and the psychological asymmetry of the conflict are not promising in this respect. A high degree of penetrating other peoples' psyches is needed to synchronize pragmatic retreats from ideological and substantive demands on both sides, and an almost inhumane restraint of built-in constraints in negotiations is needed to control the temptation to view gains by the other side as in a zero sum game.

The ability to control bargaining habits, to rationalize emotions and an almost automatic "manly" response to provocations, and to refrain from consciously or unconsciously raising domestic expectations and thus creating credibility gaps had not been demonstrated by either side in the past. Therefore, one cannot expect a comprehensive, quick resolution of the conflict. Of course, the United States can try to impose a solution and bring about a Brookings compromise with less peace, as peace and total normalization seem to me to be unacceptable to too many Arabs.

The Israelis will resist this as far as they can. They will fight over American public opinion and bargain over marginal issues and Egyptian and Syrian assets; they will try to wait and see how events will settle themselves at the end of a long process in which their rights, power, and interests count. Ruling Arabs might be a lesser evil, as Arabs are generally ruled by unelected, military groups in their own countries. Accordingly, human rights should be granted to Arabs first in Syria, Egypt, Libya, and Lebanon. The PLO wants exclusive Arab, anti-Jewish rights. Anti-Semitism and self-interest, combined with ignorance and naïveté, lay behind European and American demands from Israel. The Jews in Israel (and their Jewish supporters abroad) are fed up with their status as second-class citizens of the world who are not entitled to peace, with border changes as a result of the other party's behavior, and with that party's possible behavior in the future. No other country has been forced to accept refugees or not have at least a territorial compromise after a war it did not lose, and Israel is unlikely, in its present mood and social and political development, to make far-reaching concessions unless it is forced to, and it would not make them without a fight, either political or military.

Peace, simple peace, without prior ideological preconditions, might change the Israeli attitude overnight, even if suspicion might remain, and some occupied territories had to remain with it. Yet peace seems to be as remote as ever, because it means to the Arabs an unacceptable concession on the level most of them tried *not* to follow in practice, the ideological ethos of their nationalism.

Epilogue:
Sadat's Peace and Israel's Response

As I wrote the concluding part of this book in July, 1977, I obviously did not anticipate Sadat's peace initiative; rather, I envisioned some sort of American-sponsored experimentation with a comprehensive peace formula to be negotiated by all parties concerned at Geneva. I did not foresee a breakthrough, either in Israel or in the Arab coalition, over the territorial issue, the Palestinian problem, and the peace issue. Therefore, the conflict appeared to me to be politically deadlocked. President Sadat seems to have combined a similar conclusion, based on his cognitive-postulative approach to politics, with his tendency to break out of impasses, regaining and retaining initiatives while trying to control the complex political processes that otherwise might have controlled him. Hence I believe Sadat's initiative should be analyzed on the basis of the president's overall cognitive-postulative behavior; parallelly, his tactics and other behavioral characteristics should be compared to Israeli substantive preferences and behavioral patterns.

It seems to me that Sadat's initiative was triggered by a sober analysis of two aspects of the Arab-Israeli conflict that he, as President Nasser before him, had never omitted from his past calculations: the aspects of price and of control, as they related to the ideological-political aspect of the conflict. The immediate problems of price and control had been linked to diplomatic and political developments since President Carter's initial adoption of the Brookings formula. That formula demanded peace and normalization from the Arabs in exchange for a phased Israeli withdrawal to the pre–June 1967 lines (with minor rectifications) and a homeland for the Palestinians in the West Bank and Gaza. The whole package was to be negotiated in principle in a comprehensive conference at Geneva. Because of the American commitments to Israel, the procedure at the conference was contingent upon PLO concessions in advance regarding Israel's right to exist at peace with its neighbors. Aiming at a comprehensive solution that must have included the PLO as a representative of the Palestinians, the Carter administration tried to reach a compromise with that organization that would make it possible for the United States to demand the inclusion of the PLO in the Geneva talks. If the PLO were ready to compromise, Israeli arguments about its terroristic character and ultimate goals could have been countered with evidence proving PLO moderation.

Yet both the PLO and Syria were reluctant to recognize Israel at all, let alone in advance, because by so doing they would, by implication, give up Arab rights to the pre-1967 Israel and to the return of the Palestinian refugees. Besides, the U.S. administration was to demand at Geneva not only the recognition of Israel but also peace and cooperation with the Jewish state, controversial issues for the mainstream of the PLO leadership, not to mention its rejectionist elements. Having fought bitterly in Lebanon, the PLO wanted to demonstrate its sovereignty to Syria and its independent stance vis-à-vis the American-oriented Egypt. Syria, on the other hand, pursued a "no formal peace" and "no normalization" policy, while trying to appear as a loyal supporter of the Palestinian cause. Advance demands from the PLO regarding the recognition of Israel, peace, and normalization seemed avoidable if enough pressure could be applied on Washington and/or if the PLO and Syria used their tactics of striving for a Palestinian state in the West Bank and Gaza while hinting at a de facto coexistence with Israel only. The Carter administration seemed to be much more open to PLO arguments than ever before and also to be vulnerable to Saudi pressure. Therefore, the administration's overtures toward the PLO in the winter of 1977 were perceived by the organization's leadership as a step forward, to be accompanied by further American concessions.

The United States tried to accommodate the PLO and Syria in its program, repeating its recognition of Palestinian rights and of the principle of a homeland for the Palestinians (dropping resolution 242, which referred to Palestinians merely as refugees) in a joint communiqué with the Soviet Union, the Palestinians' international patron. The idea was to enlist Soviet support to moderate the official PLO stance, while compensating Moscow for earlier damage done by the American human rights declarations and while negotiating a new SALT 2 agreement.

Israel reacted angrily to the joint communiqué; a conservative-hawkish and pro-Israel coalition emerged in the United States to fight the administration, against unnecessary cooperation with Moscow in the Middle East and against forcing Israel to deal with the terroristic, Soviet-oriented PLO. Yet for Syria and the PLO the communiqué was not enough. Egyptian and Saudi expectations that the PNC would now make a public overture that would justify Washington's support of PLO participation at Geneva went unfulfilled. In the meantime, President Carter and Foreign Minister Dayan worked out an American-Israeli "working paper" in which the Israelis conceded to Washington some Palestinian representation at Geneva (having in mind not PLO, but West Bank emissaries). Israel was cleared in the matter of Palestinian representation, unless the PLO made some overt gesture toward recognition and peace. It did not make that gesture; because of American insistence on peace and recognition at Geneva, Syria seemed to have lost interest. The ball returned to Arab courts and remained there.

President Sadat understood that a low-common-denominator formula acceptable to all Arab parties concerned would not be acceptable either to Washington or to Jerusalem. His own strategy of nonbelligerence in exchange for Israeli withdrawals and a miniature Palestinian state was not enough; Carter naively but decisively wanted peace. Syria and the PLO could hardly agree even to contractual nonbelligerence. If a Soviet-American–sponsored Geneva conference somehow took place, Israel would be able to benefit from radical Arab positions there and so discredit the conference as an unnecessary prestige gain for Moscow. Sadat was not ready to make peace and normalize relations with Israel, yet the Egyptian president wanted to cooperate with the United States and to gain American support in the conflict. He realized that the peace issue was crucial if the strategic diplomatic framework created since 1973, which included a decisive role for the United States, were to be maintained and to lead to Israeli concessions and gains for the Arabs and for Egypt itself. Thus, Sadat feared that because of PLO intransigence before Geneva, and PLO and Syrian positions at Geneva, the conference might not take place at all or might fail, with the blame put squarely on the Arabs. At any rate, Israel would not be the only guilty party; thanks to its allies within the American political system, no pressure would be exercised by Mr. Carter against Israel, a result also of the Soviet context of the Geneva conference and of the Arab failure to make peace. A stalemate could lead to a process of political escalation within the Arab coalition, over which Sadat might lose control. Having renounced his Soviet connection (which Syria and the PLO maintained), Egypt would be accused by radical Arabs of having lost its ability to achieve progress in the Arab-Israeli conflict because of its American connection, while the PLO's and Syria's positions and tactics would indeed render any American support impossible. Egypt's own stance in the peace issue made U.S. support rather questionable. Egypt was thus confronted with the choice of whether to go on cooperating with Washington or to create a viable war option with Soviet aid and Saudi oil squeeze tactics. Soviet aid might cost Egypt a domestic political and economic price unacceptable to Sadat, especially after his break with Moscow in 1976. It might also involve the credibility of a Saudi oil threat in a period of relative supply surplus, Saudi economic incentives to raise the price of crude oil in 1973 (which do not exist in 1977), absolute Saudi control over these issues, and Saudi fears and calculations regarding the Syrian and PLO threats and bids for support that were not necessarily compatible with Egypt's own interests.

The price aspect of the Middle East conflict might further relate here to Sadat's reluctance to risk what came to be accepted in Egypt and in the Arab world as an established victory—that of Yom Kippur—as long as Egypt could enhance its own and Arab interests by other means. Here again, the problems of Soviet aid, which might jeopardize U.S. (and Saudi) economic aid to Egypt, and Russian conditions unaceptable to Sadat are linked to potential further American aid to Israel as a result of an Egyptian rapprochement with Moscow. After all, U.S. commitments to Israel's survival, long acknowledged by Sadat, had rendered inter-Arab debates and positions on Israel's very existence irrelevant. If the Arabs were to cooperate with Washington to recover Arab lands, try to resolve the Palestinian problem on the basis of a viable compromise, and tackle urgent socioeconomic problems, they—or at least some of them—could not avoid the peace issue anymore.

The price aspects of the conflict, I believe, involves a complex set of priorities regarding tradition and change, revolution or reform in Egypt and in the Arab world at large. Sadat discussed this range of problems at length in his debates with Egyptian and Arab social and religious revolutionaries. According to his arguments, a moderate, conservative reform strategy should be adopted to modernize Egypt. A revolutionary approach propagated by the Ba'ath party or by Dr. George Habash calling for unification and modernization of the Arab world or a reactionary, revolutionary departure from the twentieth century back to a pure Islamic past propagated by Colonel Khaddafi are dangerous escapades that might endanger Egypt's traditional values. Instead of reforming Egypt's society while preserving moderate religious habits and social and cultural checks and balances, the revolutionary approach might lead to fanaticism and anarchy, war and destruction. As a Palestinian scholar recently put it, the Arab-Israeli conflict derives its peculiar character from the enormous tension that exists among four different logics in the Arab world: *raison d'état* (of the various Arab states), *raison de la nation* (Pan-Arabism), *raison de la révolution* (unification and modernization achieved by revolutionary methods), and *raison de status quo.*

Egypt's commitments to common Arab causes and to the Palestinians are derived from a modern interpretation of traditional Arab values and Arab history and from Cairo's bid for Arab leadership. Yet if pursued by revolutionary methods or by unrealistic tools, Egypt's own domestic values, Arab interests, and social and cultural assets might be hurt and success would not be guaranteed. Moreover, radicalism was always propagated easily by the Syrians, the Palestinians, the Iraqis, and the Libyans, while Egypt had to pay most of the price of the wars. The radicals pursued their own Syrian, Palestinian, or Libyan interests, though they also sought a pivotal role in Egyptian politics because of Cairo's bid for Arab leadership and its commitments to common Arab causes. Egypt is still committed to these causes, though more realistically, and as the most important Arab country, it assumes leadership in determining what is realistic. In fact, Egypt had tried such a strategy after 1948, but the price control dilemma rendered the policy more and more questionable. It is not only under Sadat that Egypt seems to have considered de facto risks as related to its own capabilities, to different interests of other Arabs, to foreign support of Israel, and to Israel's own power. Data concerning Cairo's *actual* behavior in the conflict since 1948 suggests that Egypt was never ready to pay the full price of its obligation to the common Arab cause in terms of total mobilization and concrete planning toward the destruction of Israel. Since 1949 Cairo, adopting complex and changing compromises, involved itself in political hostilities and ideological commitments toward that goal and in low- and medium-level acts of actual hostility, losing control over them in 1956 and 1967. Between 1967 and 1970 it tried to force a partial military political solution to the 1967 war; Egypt managed to advance its own and other Arab interests by waging a limited war in 1973, having had no other choice. Since then it has continued to advance these interests by a subtle mixture of relative political flexibility and common U.S.-Egyptian-Saudi interests. Political inflexibility could jeopardize the whole process and seriously damage Egypt's domestic, socioeconomic priorities. Therefore, the legacy of new-old nationalism should not be permitted to self-defeat Egypt's own and Arab priorities and realistic goals. Arab rejectionism and Arab peace without peace strategies would mean not just playing into Israel's hand, but assuming a sovereign stance, small and medium powers do not have. Pretending to have this sovereign status is what caused Nasser most of his troubles; he knew well that he had much less power and freedom of action than he pretended to have, yet he was forced to behave as if he had it, involving Egypt in growing trouble and neglecting her socioeconomic misery.

For these reasons, President Sadat decided to adapt Egypt's declared goals to its actual power and connect them to his domestic problems while reassuming a central role in Arab politics. This role had been taken by Saudi Arabia after 1975, and it was shared all too much by marginal powers like the PLO and Syria, who managed to bring the diplomatic process to a standstill. When he went to Jerusalem, Sadat thereby served notice to the other members of the Arab coalition that Egypt, not they, was the pivotal power in that coalition. He had reached the conclusion that ideological commitments denying Israel's very existence and peace were not workable and were diplomatically self-defeating. Sadat did not renounce his obligations to the coalition; he simply adopted Carter's formula: peace, withdrawal to the pre-1967 lines, and self-determination for the Palestinians. The framework of the Jerusalem trip was a Brookings framework; the concession was made basically to the United States, and it, of course, did not entail separate peace or renunciation of occupied territory.

Almost automatically, the bid for sovereignty and Arab leadership by other members of the Arab coalition, such as Syria and the PLO, led them to a violent rejection of Egypt's interpretation of its own sovereignty and the limits of sovereignty of small powers in the modern world. They and the radical Arab regimes joined forces to reject Sadat's initiative, yet since they had no alternative and not enough power of their own to influence events, the initiative remained in Sadat's hands. He left Syria and the PLO aside, yet demanded Israeli withdrawals from all relevant territories and the principle of self-determination for Palestinians in Gaza and the West Bank. He hoped that the strong Begin cabinet would understand and honor his departure from the traditional Arab wish to have a cake and eat it too. It is true that Egypt and the Arabs suffered from the gap between their declared commitments and reality, but Israel suffered enormously too; in the end Israel may find itself confronting such a radicalized Arab world that it will be ready to pay the ultimate price. It is in the interest of Israel to honor Sadat's renunciation of official hatred and rejection and to withdraw, allowing a reasonable compromise on the Palestinian issue; dominating the area on both sides of a tiny Palestinian entity, Israel and Jordan will in fact control its behavior; Egypt's peace is a decisive guarantee against future threats and escalations.

The Israeli response, euphoric as it was, was bound to combine Begin's legalism and ideological commitments and his cabinet's partisan and coalitionary logics with Dayan's instrumental and power approach to the conflict. Sadat's initiative will not altogether change those Israeli convictions aggregated since 1956 that strategic stability is needed to guarantee the desired peace; peace alone, with Egypt pretending to impose it upon unwilling Arabs, is not a guarantee for stability. Even if Sadat's initiative were bound to reduce Begin's and Dayan's traditional responsive rejection of Arab negativism, their combined legal-ideological and strategic-structural approaches to the conflict must have led them to try and honor Egypt's gesture, yet to offer Sadat much less than he demanded. They agreed upon a compromise, which they hoped might be understood and honored by Egypt as a combination of far-reaching concessions regarding Israeli exclusive claims for the West Bank, Egypt's Sinai, and Palestinian self-rule, and legitimate Israeli security demands, ideological and political obligations, and the consequences of Sadat's restrictions as a spokesman for other Arabs who rejected his initiative.

Sadat's initiative is a major breakthrough; Dayan almost gave it up as unrealistic, and thus self-defeating, in light of the events since 1971. Yet its significance might be restrained by the very reasons that triggered it: Sadat's unique personality. His cognitive-postulative approach might be limited to his one-man regime, and Cairo's semiexplosive socioeconomic problems might drive the next regime to a radical foreign policy. No structural guarantees (such a predominant, powerful, conservative middle class or prosperous lower classes) are present to back up Sadat's promises. His impatience and his tendency to force choices upon friend and foe alike are unique, maybe atypical of "Arab behavior," and require an Israeli counterstrategy of patient bargaining. Sadat's charismatic, ideological political gesture should be honored, but charisma is not enough, especially if it is coupled with demands that Israel give up claims to the West Bank and withdraw from it, thus losing control over it, and conceding ideological domestic commitments. To West Bank dwellers, forfeiting Israeli control means Arabs will assume control who are still committed to Israel's destruction, to no reasonable solution to the refugee problem, and to a new sphere of influence for Syria, Iraq, and the Soviet Union. This would be a lost chance to improve Israel's borders so that it would be able to survive in the midst of a turbulent Arab world, including Egypt's explosive home front.

Thus, Israel will insist on formally keeping the West Bank question open for the next five years, while trying to create there a viable alternative to the PLO in the framework of Begin's self-rule program. Yet Israel will refuse to commit itself—even afterward—to Palestinian self-determination and to a complete withdrawal. Begin and Dayan perceive Sadat's initiative as a gesture derived also from Israel's power (as a function of its actual borders, conventional power, and nuclear option), from its standing in America, and from its insistence upon strategic rights and constant repetition of Israeli ideological claims. Hence, Israel will not go beyond returning most of the Sinai to Egyptian sovereignty, keeping some presence in nothern Sinai for a time and controlling Gaza, separating it from Egypt through settlements in the Yamit region. West Bank dwellers will be offered self-rule (elected representation) and an end to the military occupation regime in their densely populated territory. Israel will continue to control the territory as a whole and to allow Jewish settlements in parts of it, yet it will not annex it and it will recognize similar claims by Arabs to sovereignty over the West Bank. After five years, the Israelis will open negotiations with the West Bank Arab government and Jordan on the fate of the territory. The same procedure applies to Gaza. Since Sadat—and Carter—insists upon Israeli recognition of principles, but not upon immediate Israeli withdrawals, Begin's plan should be semantically and diplomatically made acceptable to Egypt by American mediation.

Begin's followers in the militant Herut party, NRP and Gush Emunim activists, and functionaries of the movement for the whole of Eretz Israel regarded Begin's compromise as an outright betrayal by the leader of his avowed ideology, probably a naive response to Sadat's television diplomacy and a temptation to go down in history as a "peacemaker." Their partisan and coalitionary power, when combined with General Sharon's, sufficed to impose new settlements on the cabinet during the most crucial period of the initial negotiations, though the timing was highly embarrassing to the government. After a while, Sadat broke off the direct talks that followed his visit to Jerusalem; he was annoyed by Begin's plan, Arab (including moderate Arab) rejection of or reservations toward his initiative, U.S. initial acceptance of Begin's plan as a step forward, and Israeli settlements, which discredited him even more in the Arab world.

Both parties in the Middle East conflict are looking now toward Washington, and their ability to agree between themselves or to achieve more from each other depends upon their power to mobilize American support for their respective positions, to resist American positions or pressures, and to adopt compromise formulas. For the time being, however, the gap between commitments and realities, between the image of sovereignty and the limits of sovereignty, which contributed so much to the deterioration and the perpetuation of the conflict, are helpful in limiting that conflict as far as Israel and Egypt are concerned.

Appendix A

RESULTS OF ELECTIONS TO THE KNESSET AND KNESSET MEMBERSHIP

	First (1-25-49)		Second (7-30-51)		Third (7-26-55)		Fourth (9-3-59)		Fifth (3-15-61)		Sixth (11-2-65)		Seventh (10-25-69)		Eighth (12-31-73)		Ninth (5-17-77)	
List °	no.	%	no.	%	no.	%	no.	%	no.	%	no.	%	no.	%	no.	%	no.	%
Alignment Labor-Mapam	—	—	—	—	—	—	—	—	—	—	—	—	56	46.2	51	39.6	32	24.6
Alignment Mapai-Achdut Ha'Avoda	—	—	—	—	—	—	—	—	—	—	45	36.7	—	—	—	—	—	—
Rafi-Israel Workers List	—	—	—	—	—	—	—	—	—	—	10	7.9	—	—	—	—	—	—
Mapam-United Workers Party	19†	14.7†	15†	12.5†	9	7.3	9	7.2	9	7.5	8	6.6	—	—	—	—	—	—
Mapai-Israel Workers Party	46	35.7	45	37.3	40	32.2	47	38.2	42	34.7	—	—	—	—	—	—	—	—
Achdut Ha'avoda-Unity of Labor	—†	—†	—†	—†	10	8.2	7	6.0	8	6.6	—	—	—	—	—	—	—	—
Democratic Movement For Change	—	—	—	—	—	—	—	—	—	—	—	—	—	—	—	—	15	11.6
National Religious Party-Mizrahi and Mizrahi Workers	16	12.2	10	8.3	11	9.1	12	9.9	12	9.8	11	8.9	12	9.7	10	8.3	12	9.2
Agudat Yisrael			5	3.6	6	4.7	6	4.7	6	5.6	6	5.1	6	5.0	5	3.8	5	4.8
Agudat Yisrael Workers																		

Party	Seats	%	Seats	%	Seats	%	Seats	%	Seats	%	Seats	%	Seats	%	Seats	%	Seats	%
Likud ‡	—	—	—	—	—	—	—	—	—	—	—	—	—	—	39	30.2	43	33.4
Gahal	—	—	—	—	—	—	—	—	—	—	26	21.3	26	21.7	—	—	—	—
Free Center	—	—	—	—	—	—	—	—	—	—	—	—	2	1.2	—	—	—	—
State	—	—	—	—	—	—	—	—	—	—	—	—	4	3.1	—	—	—	—
Herut	14	11.5	8	6.6	15	12.6	17	13.5	17	13.8	—	—	—	—	—	—	—	—
Liberal Party §	7	5.2	20	16.2	13	10.2	8	6.2	17‖	13.6‖	—	—	—	—	—	—	—	—
Independent Liberals #	5	4.1	4	3.2	5	4.4	6	4.6	—‖	—‖	5	3.8	4	3.2	4	3.6	1	1.2
Citizens Rights Movement	—	—	—	—	—	—	—	—	—	—	—	—	—	—	3	2.2	1	1.2
Moked °°	—	—	—	—	—	—	—	—	—	—	—	—	—	—	1	1.4	2	1.6
Communists	4	—	5	—	6	—	3	—	5	—	1	—	—	—	—	—	—	—
New Communists ††	—	—	—	—	—	—	—	—	—	—	3	2.3	3	2.8	4	3.4	5	4.6
Ha'Olam Ha'Zeh	—	—	—	—	—	—	—	—	—	—	1	1.2	2	1.2	—	—	—	—
Minorities	2	3.0	5	4.7	5	4.9	5	4.7	4	3.9	4	3.8	4	3.6	3	3.3	1	1.4
Shlomzion (Sharon)	—	—	—	—	—	—	—	—	—	—	—	—	—	—	—	—	2	1.9
Others ‡‡	7	10.1	3	3.6	—	—	—	—	—	—	—	—	—	—	—	—	1	2.0
Abstentions and Invalid Votes	0	3.5	0	4.0	0	6.4	0	5.0	0	4.5	0	2.4	0	2.3	0	10.2	0	2.5
Total	120	100	120	100	120	100	120	100	120	100	120	100	120	100	120	100	120	100
Eligible to Vote	506,567		924,885		1,057,795		1,213,483		1,271,285		1,499,709		1,748,710		2,037,478		2,236,293	
Voted	440,095		695,007		876,085		994,306		1,037,030		1,244,706		1,427,981		1,601,098		1,771,726	

Sources: *Statistical Abstracts of Israel*, 1974, Central Bureau of Statistics (Jerusalem: Government Printing Office, 1974); and *Jerusalem Post* (international edition), May 31, 1977.

° In order of Hebrew alphabet and Israeli voting procedures   † Achdut Ha'Avoda included in Mapam   ‡ Likud includes Gahal, Free Center, and State List   § Known as General Zionists until fourth Knesset   ‖ Progressive party (later Independent Liberals) included in Liberal party   # Known as Progressive party until fourth Knesset   °° Moked includes Communists and Thelet Adom Movement (far left Zionists)   †† Known as Rackach (pro-Moscow, non-Zionist Communists) until ninth Knesset   ‡‡ One independent candidate, Mr. Sh. Flatto Sharon, was elected in 1977

Appendix B

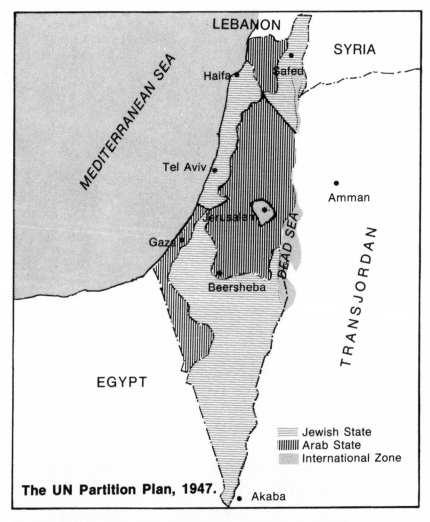

The UN Partition Plan, 1947.

(Reprinted with permission from *Near East Report*, Washington, D.C.)

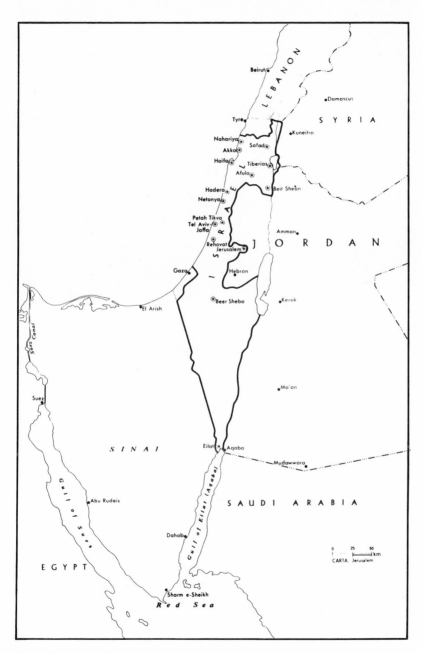

Cease-fire lines of 1967

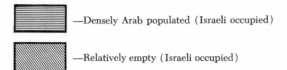

—Densely Arab populated (Israeli occupied)

—Relatively empty (Israeli occupied)

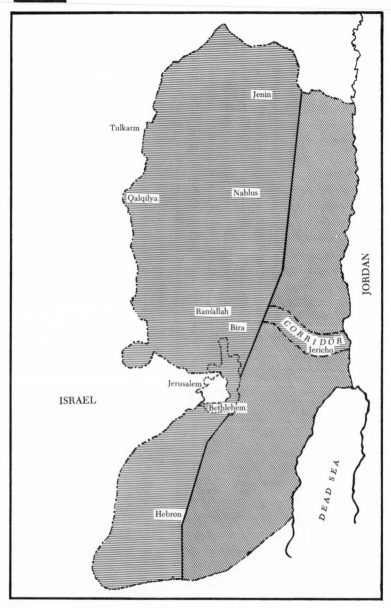

The "Allon Plan" of September, 1967

(Reprinted with permission from *Near East Report*, Washington, D.C.)

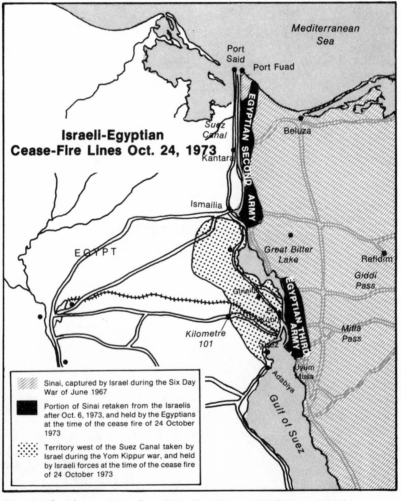

(Reprinted with permission from *Near East Report*, Washington, D.C.)

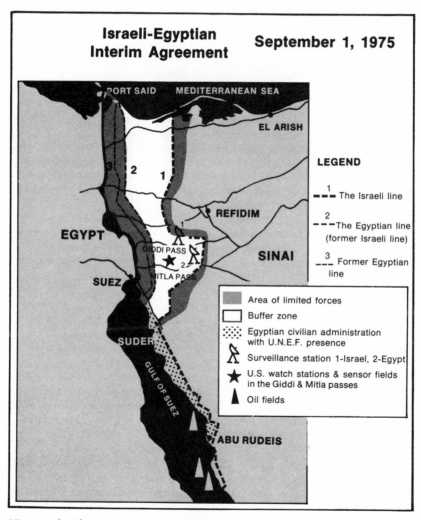

(Reprinted with permission from *Near East Report*, Washington, D.C.)

Abbreviations

ADL	Armistice Demarcation Line
DMC	Democratic Movement for Change
EC or EEC	European Economic Community
GAA	General Armistice Agreement
GHQ	General Headquarters
GOC or OC	General Officer Commanding
IAEA	International Atomic Energy Agency
IAEC	Israeli Air Force
IAF	Israeli Atomic Energy Commission
IDF	Israeli Defense Forces
IRBM	Intermediate Range Ballistic Missle
MBFR	Mutual and Balanced Forces Reduction
NATO	North Atlantic Treaty Organization
NPT	Non-Proliferation Treaty
NRP	National Religious Party
NSC	National Security Council
NWFZ	Nuclear Weapons Free Zone
OAPEC	Organization of Arab Oil Producing Countries
OPEC	Organization of Oil Producing Countries
PFLP	Popular Front for the Liberation of Palestine
PLO	Palestine Liberation Organization
PNC	Palestinian National Council
SALT	Strategic Arms Limitation Talks
SAM	Surface-to-Air Missle
SSN	Surface-to-Surface Naval Missle
UAR	United Arab Republic
UNDOF	United Nations Disengagement Observer Force
UNEF	United Nations Emergency Forces

Notes

Wherever possible, I have used original Hebrew sources. Hebrew words and titles are usually taken verbatim from the original Hebrew publications. English translations appearing here are my own.

Chapter 1

1. For a short, updated bibliography on Zionism and the development of Zionist politics in Palestine, see S. Avineri, "David Ben-Gurion and Some Remarks on his Social Thinking," *Ma'ariv*, September 19, 1975; D. Ben-Gurion, *Rebirth and Destiny of Israel*, ed. and trans. M. Nurock (New York: Philosophical Library, 1954); S. N. Eisenstadt, *Israeli Society* (London: Weidenfeld and Nicolson, 1967); Y. Gorni, *Achdut Ha'Avoda, 1910–1930* (Tel Aviv: Hoza'at Ha'Kibbutz Ha'Meuchad, 1973) (Hebrew); D. Horowitz and M. Lissak, *Mekoroteiha shel Ha'Chevra Ha'Politit Ha'Yisraelit* [The origins of Israel's polity] (tentative) (Tel Aviv: Hoza'at Am Oved, forthcoming) (Hebrew); W. Laqueur, *A History of Zionism* (London: Weidenfeld and Nicolson, 1972); Y. Shapiro, *The Formative Years of the Israeli Labour Party*, Sage Studies in Twentieth-Century History, vol. 4 (London, 1976); and D. Vital, *The Origins of Zionism* (Oxford: Clarendon Press, 1975).
2. On the U.N. Palestine decisions of 1947, see excerpts from the report of the United Nations Special Committee on Palestine, September 3, 1947, and General Assembly Resolution 181 (on the future government of Palestine), November 29, 1947 (J. N. Moore, ed., *The Arab-Israeli Conflict* [Princeton: Princeton University Press, 1974], 3: 259–313, 313–40).
3. There were ups and downs, however, in the American support for an independent Israel in 1948. After having cooperated with the Soviet Union to bring about the General Assembly's partition decision, Washington came under heavy Arab pressure, while the State Department and the Department of Defense regarded a Jewish state as a future source of trouble to American interest. The administration was considering an international regime for Palestine to replace the British, who were withdrawing following the assembly's resolution. Yet, when British troops finally left Palestine on May 14, 1948, and Ben-Gurion proclaimed Israel's independence, President Truman recognized the established fact first. At the same time, the administration proclaimed a total arms embargo on shipments to the Middle East, and Israel was left to fight Western trained and supplied Arab regular armies without American or other Western aid. This traumatic experience led to a vigorous arms supply campaign later.

For newly published sources on the period, see *Foreign Relations of the United States, 1948*, vol. 5, pt. 2 (Washington, D.C.: Government Printing Office, 1976); cf. Clark M. Clifford, "Factors Influencing President Truman's Decision to Support Partition and Recognize the State of Israel" (Paper delivered at the annual conference of the American Historical Association, Washington, D.C., December 23, 1976); and S. L. Spiegel, *The War for Washington: The Other Arab-Israeli Conflict* (New York, forthcoming).

4. For the text of the General Armistice Agreements, see Moore, *Arab-Israeli Conflict*, pp. 380–407: Israel-Egypt armistice agreement, February 24, 1949; Israel-Jordan armistice agreement, April 3, 1949; Israel-Lebanon armistice agreement, March 23, 1949; and Israel-Syria armistice agreement, July 20, 1949.

All GAA prohibited the respective parties from undertaking, planning, or threatening aggressive actions against each other, and accepted the armistice as "an indispensable step toward the liquidation of armed conflict and the restoration of peace in Palestine." It also created a U.N. truce supervision machinery, composed of mixed commissions shared by the parties with a U.N. military observer as chairman. The agreements provided for the demilitarization of specific areas along the Israeli-Egyptian and the Israeli-Syrian ADL and guaranteed the resumption of normal functioning of the Hebrew University's facilities on Mount Scopus, surrendered by Jordanian-held territory, and free access thereto. The same provision dealt with free access to the Jewish holy and cultural institutions on the Jordanian-held territory of Jerusalem. Yet on December 11, 1948, the General Assembly reaffirmed its November, 1947, resolution that Jerusalem as a whole should be internationalized and be placed under "effective U.N. control." The General Assembly resolved (Resolution 194) "that the [Arab] refugees wishing to return to their homes and live at peace with their neighbors should be permitted to do so . . . and that compensation should be paid for the property of those choosing not to return. . . ." (see Moore, *Arab-Israeli Conflict*, pp. 374–76). The assembly also created a Conciliation Commission to implement the resolution. On August 11, 1949, the Security Council endorsed the GAA and instructed the Conciliation Commission "to fulfill the request of the General Assembly in its resolution 194 (III) . . . to extend the scope of the armistice negotiations and to seek agreement . . . on the final settlement." Thus, the parties themselves could adopt conflicting legal attitudes; the Arabs maintained that the repatriation of the refugees conditioned all other aspects of Arab-Israeli negotiations. The Israelis maintained that since the refugees did not wish to live in peace with Israel this provision was not legally binding. They demanded the implementation of the General Assembly and GAA provisions with regard to peace, border agreements, and free access to the holy places. Jordan denied this free access, except to the Israeli-held Mount Scopus, because of an inter-Arab consensus not to cooperate with Israel at all and because of the unclear legal status of the city.

Some Jewish cultural institutions in Jordanian-held Jerusalem were damaged during the hostilities and some were later destroyed. Neither the GAA nor Resolution 194, nor the international community accepted the 1949 ADL as a whole as international boundaries. Israel's standing in West Jerusalem was not recognized, even de facto, by most Western, East Block, and Third World countries (except the Netherlands and several African and South American states). The Middle East status quo was generally based on these territorial, political, and legal arguments and counterarguments until 1967. The U.N. armistice supervision machinery was practically dissolving, when, in 1956, violations of the GAA paved the way to a new war. It is not my intention to return, in this chapter, to Arab arguments against Zionism and Israel's right to exist, which were advanced after the 1948–49 war, since my analysis relates to actual Arab behavior, rather than to Arab ideology. On Arab ideology and behavior in 1950s and 1960s, see note 26, below.

5. West Jerusalem was held by Israel against Jordanian onslaughts during the 1948

war, and expanded in the south; the Jewish quarter in the Old City, including the Wailing Wall area fell into Jordanian hands. Ben-Gurion's orders with regard to a possible recapturing of the Jewish quarter, given just before a cease-fire was to take place, seem to have been derived from a number of calculations on a possible agreement with Jordan on the partition of the city, and a possible Jordanian counterattack against Israel's soft belly in the Tel Aviv area, and from skepticism about the success of the whole endeavor. The Jordanian army, under British command, refrained from advancing beyond the partition borders in most of the country, but concentrated upon wiping out Jewish settlements in territories designated by the partition plan to remain under Arab control and besieged Western Jerusalem. (See also notes 15 and 31.)

6. Israel foreign ministry sources. (The official documents were not released, as a thirty-year limit exists for the publication of secret official documents in Israel. However, a government committee prepared a list of selected documents for publication in 1976). Cf. U.S. Department of State documents on Israeli-Jordanian-American negotiations of 1949, unofficially released in March, 1976, quoted in *Yediot Aharonot Magazine,* March 6, 1976. See also M. Brecher, *Decisions in Israel's Foreign Policy* (London: Oxford University Press, 1974), pp. 26–27.

7. On Arab demands during 1948 with regard to borders and refugees, see *Foreign Relations of the United States, 1948,* pp. 1625–27.

8. See, for example, David-Ben Gurion, "Israel Among the Nations," *State of Israel Government Yearbook, 1952–53* (Jerusalem: Government Printing Office, 1954), pp. 1–14.

9. See Brigadier General Yigal Allon's letter to Ben-Gurion of March 27, 1949, in Y. Cohen, *Tochnit Allon* [The Allon plan] (1971; reprint ed., Tel Aviv: Hoza'at Ha'Kibbutz Ha'Meuchad, 1973), pp. 25–26 (Hebrew). Cf. Y. Allon, *Masach shel Chol* [A curtain of sand] (1959; reprint ed., Tel Aviv: Hoza'at Ha'Kibbutz Ha'Meuchad, 1959), pp. 15, 75, 190 (Hebrew).

Allon argues that Israel is geostrategically encircled by enemies who are actively engaged in concrete and intensive preparations to destroy it. Arab belligerency—in spite of and against the spirit of the 1949 GAA—is manifested not only in concrete military preparations but also in concrete acts of violence. Further, the Arab coalition is a mixture of different nondemocratic regimes; Egypt's political system is based on an act of seizure of power by the military, rather than on a "real," popular revolution. Nasser's regime is an extreme expansionist, fascist system—a combination of Peron's Argentinian fascism domestically, Mussolini's drive for easy gains abroad, a Nazi complex of national superiority, and Spain's social backwardness. Finally, Israel's answer to Arab challenges should be, besides its democratic structure and its social and spiritual advantages, threefold: (1) border settlements and the creation of a defensive system by settlers; (2) a preemptive strike, conditioned by the nature of the enemy's threats and by possible intenvention by foreign powers; and (3) crush the enemy in case of war and impose peace on the Arabs.

See also "Active Defense: A Guarantee of our Existence," *Molad,* July–August, 1967, no. 1/24, 2/212; and Y. Allon, *The Making of Israel's Army* (New York: Universe Books, 1970).

10. For a selected English bibliography of Ben-Gurion's writings, which reflects this complex response to different political, cultural, spiritual, and military challenges before and after 1948, see *Ben-Gurion Looks at the Bible,* trans. J. Kolatch (Middle Village, N.Y.: Jonathan David Publishers, 1972); *Ben-Gurion Looks Back: In Talks with Moshe Perlman* (New York: Simon and Schuster, 1970); *David Ben-Gurion: In His Own Words,* ed. A. Ducovny (New York: Fleet Press, 1968); *Israel, A Personal History,* trans. N. Meyers and U. Nystar (New York: Funk and Wagnalls, 1971); *Israel: Years of Challenge* (New York: Holt, Rinehart and Winston, 1963); *The Jews in Their Land,* trans. M. Nurock and M. Louvish (London: Aldus Books, 1966); *Letters to Paula,* trans. A. Hodes

(London: Valentine Mitchell, 1971); *My Talks with Arab Leaders,* ed. M. Louvish, trans. A. Rubinstein and M. Louvish (New York: Third Press, 1973); *Rebirth and Destiny of Israel* (New York: Philosophical Library, 1954); and *Recollections,* ed. T. Barsten (London: Macdonald, 1970).

The most recent Ben-Gurion biography is Michael Bar-Zohar's *Ben-Gurion* (Tel Aviv: Hoza'at Am Oved, 1977) (Hebrew). Bar-Zohar missed the above-mentioned complexity in Ben-Gurion's foreign and defense thinking, because Ben-Gurion usually did not refer to his postulates and actual choices in analytical terms. Yet Bar-Zohar's book is the first full biography based on Ben-Gurion's diaries and archives and will be quoted as a primary source later in this narrative.

Much more comprehensive and analytical—indeed, revealing young Ben-Gurion's psyche, historical analysis, order of priorities, and iron self-discipline— is Shabtai Teveth's *Kin'at David: Ben-Gurion Hatzair* [David's desire: young Ben-Gurion] (Jerusalem: Hoza'at Schocken; 1977) (Hebrew). Teveth's excellent research is based on primary sources gathered in Israel, the United States, and Turkey (where the young leader spent his formative years as he adopted Zionism and left his native Russian Poland), and on Zionist archives in the West. Even if Teveth does not state them outright, the picture he portrays leads to the following substantive and behavioral conclusions about Ben-Gurion's goals and mehods. First, like other Zionists, Ben-Gurion totally rejected Jewish life in the Diaspora—culturally, socially, and politically. Second, his Zionism was, to a large extent, a personal struggle with hostile (non-Zionist) Jewish, Turkish, and Arab environments, with Zionists who paid lip service to his ideals but did not implement them, and with Zionists who tried to achieve too much too soon. Having developed abroad a negative approach to his nation's "normal" way of life and having watched the few Jews who lived under Turkish rule in Palestine, Ben-Gurion was suspicious about the Jews' ability to transform themselves. Nevertheless, he was determined to transform himself and to create a political instrument that would implement his ideas. Third, he wanted a social-democratic, secular Jewish society based on egalitarian, just, and moral principles, and derived from the Bible rather than from Diaspora traditions, especially from the social and political ethos of the prophets. Finally, he envisioned a piecemeal, personal progress toward such a society, rather than a political miracle, diplomatic or military, that would secure Jewish predominance in Palestine.

This "pessimism" in Ben-Gurion's perception of the traditional Jewish way of life constrained him psychologically, in my opinion, when obstacles were expected to be encountered by the Jews in Palestine. But at the same time, it drove Ben-Gurion to create a fighting nation. He adored fighters and settlers, who symbolized for him the growing success of his main aim—to create a socially balanced, physically working, land-oriented society capable of defending itself. The "defense" itself, the use of military power, the implementation of doctrines of sovereignty—in practice, all the concrete manifestations of principles were hindered, without Ben-Gurion's publicly admitting it, by his fear of the non-Jewish environment, by his "pessimism" with regard to traditional Jewish habits, and by his piecemeal strategy of accumulating power, rather than working back to reality from legal, political and military goals. Ben-Gurion's behavior was determined by cognitive postulates derived from understanding, learning, and analyzing reality while trying to change it.

11. Bar-Zohar, *Ben-Gurion,* pt. 2, pp. 901–20, 970–81; pt. 3, p. 1216.
12. D. Horowitz, "The Israeli Concept of National Security," Levi Eshkol Institute for Economic, Social, and Political Research (Jerusalem: Hebrew University, 1973) (Hebrew).
13. Until the mid-thirties, Ben-Gurion's attitude toward the Arabs was expressed in terms of a common life in Palestine and socialist cooperation against Arab traditional, feudal-capitalist elites. See David Ben-Gurion, *Anachnu, ve'Shcheneinu* (Tel Aviv: Hoza'at Davar, 1934) (Hebrew). Partition became inevitable probably

during the 1930s when violent Arab resistance to Jewish presence and immigration culminated in an open Arab revolt against both British and Jews. (See Ben-Gurion, *My Talks with Arab Leaders*. See also Ben-Gurion, *Israel: A Personal History*, pp. 150–51; and Ben-Gurion's arguments in his letter to the Executive Committee of the Mapai party as early as January, 1937, in which he distinguished between Palestine as a whole and a Jewish state in a part of Palestine, *Shdemot*, 58/75 [1975], pp. 6–13 [Hebrew].)

14. Ben-Gurion's perception of domestic Arab threats and of the vast resources, manpower, and emerging international power of the Arab world strengthened his principle of not ruling Arabs and yet brought him to impose a military regime on Israeli Arabs.

15. Ben-Gurion attached great symbolic and political significance to Jerusalem and its large Jewish population as an asset that should not be cut off from Israel. Yet in January, 1949, Ben-Gurion instructed his military representative in Jerusalem, Lieutenant Colonel Moshe Dayan, to negotiate an agreement with King Abdulla on the division of Jerusalem between Israel and Jordan. He was to use the American and French consuls general, offering to Jordan a concession of parts of Israeli-held and former Arab-populated areas captured by the IDF. Ben-Gurion also offered the internationalization of some parts of western Jerusalem. Abdulla recoiled from concluding political agreements with Israel. Thus, before the General Assembly's next session on Jerusalem in 1949, Ben-Gurion formally annexed the whole Israeli-held part and declared it as the nation's capital. On the annexion, see Brecher, *Decisions*. Cf. Sh. Nakdimon, "Jerusalem: From Internationalization to Israel's Capital," *Yediot Aharonot Magazine*, May 28, 1976.

When Jordan refused, in 1949, to fulfill its GAA commitments with regard to the holy places and Mount Scopus, and to open further the direct road from Tel Aviv to Jerusalem accordingly, Dayan suggested to Ben-Gurion to use force to open the road to all three places. "Not the Arabs," Dayan said, "but we are responsible for the implementation of our rights. If we do not implement them, we thus relinquish them. Ben-Gurion asked me whether these actions would bring about a new war. . . . His basic argument was that we have to concentrate now on the tasks of peace. The absorbtion of the new immigrants was difficult and demanded an enormous investment and attention by the state. . . . Empty spaces must be settled. The whole southern part of the country is unsettled. . . . *We shall not be able to master the country by war and military means only.* In Ben-Gurion's eyes the war was a finished chapter." (Italics mine). See Dayan's memoirs: *Avnei Derech* [Story of my life], Yediot Aharonot edition (Jerusalem: Hoza'at Edanim; Tel Aviv: Hoza'at Dvir, 1976), p. 92 (Hebrew).

At the same time, the prime minister said to his personal aide, "Luckily, we were not able to capture the whole of Jerusalem during the War of Independence. This would have been too much for us, and the world wouldn't allow us to keep it anyhow." (A testimony given to me by Ephraim Evron, now [1977] director general of Israel's foreign ministry.) See also E. H. Bovis, *The Jerusalem Question, 1917–68* (Stanford: Hoover Institution Press, 1971).

16. *Foreign Relations of the United States, 1948*, pp. 1610ff., for British and American reactions to Israel's occupation of the Negev in late 1948 and Israel's further thrust into Egypt.

17. See *Davar*, March 9, April 17, and May 11, 1949.

18. In April, 1954, during his kibbutz movement convention, for example, Allon criticized Mapai in the folowing way: "This regime, which turned us from victors into passive defenders, changed the option of settling the whole country to one of a corridor state" (*Ha'aretz*, April 11, 1954). A year later he said in the same forum, "we should be prepared to negotiate with our neighbors or the country as a whole, but if they threaten the existing borders, we can correct the historical mistake, through the use of force, and rule the whole country" (April 24, 1955).

19. See note 46.
20. See Ben-Gurion's introduction to the semiofficial *Milchemet Ha'Komemyiut* [History of the War of Independence] (Tel Aviv: Hoza'at Ma'arachot, 1949) (Hebrew). Cf. S. Peres, *Kela David* [David's sling] (Jerusalem: Weidenfeld and Nicolson, 1970), p. 134 (Hebrew).
21. Ben-Gurion, *A Personal History*, pp. 314–15, 472–73, 535, 537–40; cf. Ben-Gurion, *Destiny of Israel*, pp. 116–17.
22. Ben-Gurion himself settled in a mid-Negev kibbutz, Sdeh Boker, in the early sixties to set an example. Few followed him.
23. This mixture was falsely described by some followers and observers as Ben-Gurion's "self-reliance doctrine." (See Horowitz, "National Security," p. 6.) In fact, a key to understanding Ben-Gurion's politics was his ability not to tie his own hands with any operational doctrines. Publicly, of course, he emphasized Israel's autonomy of action and deterrence power "until Israel's enemies cease being her enemies." (See Ben-Gurion, *Netzach Yisrael* [Israel's eternity] [Tel Aviv: Hoza'at Mapai, 1964], p. 417 [Hebrew].) Deterrence did not mean action in the path of the proclaimed threat. A political decision had to be made, taking into account the actual strategic and political situation of the course to pursue when deterrence failed. In other words, Ben-Gurion's autonomy was always conditioned by a large number of foreign and domestic political considerations. The autonomous use of force was restricted and controlled by these considerations. Yet, the *official* autonomous stance was loud and clear, and thus misleading. "We are a small nation" Ben-Gurion said in his 1955 Independence Day speech,". . . [but] our future depends not on what the Gentiles *say*, but on what the Jews *do*." (Italics mine). This was one of the most famous and most misleading statements ever made in Israel's history. Whereas Ben-Gurion was very much interested in what the Gentiles *did*, he gave the impression of an autonomous stance, thus creating expectations and credibility gaps. (See quote in Bar-Zohar, *Ben-Gurion*, p. 1143, and his note 82.) In concrete terms, this statement referred to a controversy between Ben-Gurion and his Mapai colleague, Moshe Sharett (see note 27.) Yet it became, taken out of the historical context, one of Israel's national slogans. For a different interpretation of Ben-Gurion's (and other elite members') public language in the period before the 1956 Sinai campaign, as divided into symbols, advocacy, and objectives, see Brecher, *Decisions*, pp. 249–54.
24. Horowitz "National Security," discusses *casus belli*, derived, according to Yigal Allon and Ben-Gurion's deputy, Peres, from their writings and public speeches between 1949 and 1967. *Allon:* (a) an offensive concentration of Arab forces around Israel, which may endanger its security; (b) preparations for an enemy's surprise attack on Israel's air force bases; (c) an enemy attack (even improvised) on nuclear reactors and scientific institutions; (d) Arab guerrilla warfare against Israel, which cannot be contained by passive defense and retaliatory acts; (e) foreign Arab troop concentrations in Jordan, especially in the West Bank; (f) the closure of the Tiran Straits. *Peres:* (a) enemy's concentrations around Israel, causing immediate danger to its existence; (b) the occupation of Jordan by Egypt; (c) the closure of the Tiran Straits.
25. On May, 1950, the United States, Britain, and France published the Tripartite Declaration on security in the Near East, in which they promised to take action immediately, "should they find that [Israel or the Arab states] were preparing to violate frontiers or armistice lines." (See Moore, *Arab-Israeli Conflict*, pp. 575–76.) The declaration was accompanied by the relaxation of arms embargoes to the Middle East and was thus understood in Israel to be an empty political gesture aimed at resupplying the Arabs and mobilizing them against the Soviet Union, whereas the Arabs were aiming against Israel.
26. Since 1954, the United States had developed a Middle East plan based on the following assumptions: (a) the Middle East conflict relates to substantive issues—the border question and the refugee problem—that should be settled; (b) Soviet influence in Egypt is bound to grow if these substantive issues are not resolved

in a compromise; and (c) American arms deliveries to Israel will not be authorized, at least for the time being, to prevent a Soviet-American supply race. (Foreign ministry sources; and Bar-Zohar, *Ben-Gurion,* pp. 1162-63.) This basic framework led to several American mediation efforts in 1954–56, based on Israeli territorial concessions and various solutions to the refugee problems, all in turn based on the General Assembly resolution of December 1949 (Resolution 194) mentioned above.

On the Arab and American positions in the fifties and sixties, see also I. Howe and C. Gershman, *Israel, the Arabs, and the Middle East* (London: Bantam Books, 1972); M. H. Kerr, *The Arab Cold War, 1958–1967* (London: Oxford University Press for the Royal Institute of International Affairs, 1967); M. H. Kerr, *The Arab Cold War, 1958–1970* (London, Oxford University Press, for the Royal Institute of International Affairs, 1970); W. Laqueur, *The Road to War, 1967* (London: Weidenfeld and Nicolson, 1969); B. Lewis, *The Middle East and the West* (London: Weidenfeld and Nicolson, 1968); N. Safran, *From War to War: The Arab-Israeli Confrontation, 1948–1967* (New York: Pegasus, 1969); and S. L. Spiegel, *The War for Washington: The Other Arab-Israeli Conflict* (New York: forthcoming).

On the secret Anderson mission, see Ben-Gurion's diary, quoted by Bar-Zohar, *Ben-Gurion,* pp. 1162–66, n. 48; Ben-Gurion's report on his talks with Anderson, *Ma'ariv,* June 16, 1971; and Brecher, *Decisions,* pp. 259–60, n. 5.

27. Sharett represented a group of Mapai moderates who preferred negotiations with the U.S. and U.N. mediation effort to acquire American and international public support and U.S. arms over Ben-Gurion's mixture of retaliations, and his bids for arms and a NATO-like treaty with the U.S. At the same time, they wanted to test Arab give-and-take capabilities. Sharett's position in Mapai as a former prime minister and acting minister of foreign affairs created a center of resistance to Ben-Gurion's strategy after mid-1956 on both party and coalition levels. For a detailed survey of the party and the coalition situations, public declarations by the elite, and the decision process that led to Sharett's ouster, see Brecher, *Decisions,* pp. 232–61; and cf. Bar-Zohar, *Ben-Gurion,* pp. 1185-93.

28. R. Lapidoth, "Freedom of Navigation with Special Reference to International Waterways in the Middle East," The Leonard Davies Institute (Jerusalem, Hebrew University, 1975), pp. 75–93. Cf. Moore, *Arab-Israeli Conflict,* 3: 595–608. For a survey of the Israeli-Egyptian conflict on the freedom of shipping, see Safran, *From War to War,* pp. 43–44.

29. See Sh. Aronson and D. Horowitz, "The Strategy of Controlled Retaliation: Israel's Reprisal Policy, 1949–1972," *State and Government,* no. 1, (Summer, 1971): 77–100 (Hebrew). Dr. Horowitz enlarged upon our original research in his essay "The Israeli Concept of National Security and the Prospects for Peace in the Middle East," in *Dynamics of a Conflict: A Re-examination of the Middle East Conflict,* ed. G. Sheffer (New York: Humanities Press, 1975), pp. 235–75. On the conscious domestic effect of the retaliations mixed with Ben-Gurion's fears that new immigrants might suffer morally from Arab blows, see Bar-Zohar, *Ben-Gurion,* pt. 3, p. 1138.

30. Sir Anthony Eden, Britain's prime minister, endorsed Nasser's demand for Israeli concessions in the southern Negev in a Guild Hall speech on November 9, 1955, and suggested a general territorial compromise between Israel and its neighbors between the 1947 partition plan and the ADL. Sharett, at the time Israel's prime minister, strongly refused "unilateral territorial concessions." (Bar-Zohar, *Ben-Gurion,* p. 1161.)

31. According to a survey of captured Egyptian intelligence documents published by E. Yaari (*Mitzraim veha' Fedayeen, 1953–56* [Egypt and the fedayeen] [Giv a'at Haviva: Hoza'at Hamerkaz le' Limudim Arviyim ve' Afro-Asiyaniyim, 1975] [Hebrew]), Egypt regarded Israel as a less important military and political challenge until 1954. It assessed the IDF as relatively weak and was occupied with the major problem of removing the British presence in Egypt.

The end of the British presence in Egypt was regarded by several members of the Israeli defense establishment—Chief of Staff Major General Dayan and Military Intelligence Chief Colonel Binyamin Gibli—as a major strategic change. Gibli planned and executed, under obscure circumstances, an Israeli subversive action against British and American installations in Egypt in early 1954 to delay the process of an Egyptian-British understanding on the evacuation of the British bases in Egypt.

This so-called 1954 affair was carried out during Ben-Gurion's retirement at Sdeh Boker, under Defense Minister Pinhas Lavon, who later denied any responsibility for Gibli's action. Dayan's role, if any, has remained unclarified until today. Lavon simultaneously authorized several retaliatory acts against Jordan and Syria, which could have convinced a suspicious Nasser that Israel was working against vital Arab and Egyptian interests. At the least, Egypt's relative lack of interest in Israel changed sharply after the British evacuation and the 1954 affair. Palestinian fedayeen, who until then had operated from Jordan and only sporadically from the Egyptian-held former Palestinian Gaza Strip, were given a free hand in April, 1955. Ben-Gurion returned to the defense ministry following the 1954 affair, because Mapai had made Lavon responsible for it and forced Lavon's resignation. Dayan (and Mr. Peres as director general of the Defense Ministry) was Ben-Gurion's choice for chief of staff before his temporary retirement and retained this position after Ben-Gurion's comeback.

See also Dayan's conversation with Ben-Gurion on July 5, 1956, which clearly reflects Ben-Gurion's skepticism of the IDF's preparedness and fighting qualities, his basic fear of war without foreign aid, his emphasis upon continuous small-scale, retaliatory acts, and Dayan's answer (quoted from the official diary, Office of the Chief of Staff, IDF, and reprinted in Dayan's *Avnei Derech*, pp. 212, 217):

BEN-GURION: During the War of Independence we had no less manpower than the Arabs and we managed with difficulty. . . . [The Arab] advantage in arms now is enormous. Therefore, if we don't improve our army's quality now [and bring it] to its highest point, we could be in very serious trouble. Our basic trouble is that we cannot afford a defeat because this would be the end of it. They can afford a defeat; once, twice, ten times . . . it is nothing. They defeat us once and it's over. We shall not be able to achieve weapon parity with them, . . . we must improve the quality of every soldier. I don't know to what extent our quality really improves. Why do you look at me like that, Moshe?

DAYAN: Is this a problem? . . . We could have taken all these areas that we did not take during the War of Independence. . . . We were not stubborn enough. In armies better than ours, a battalion assaults, and if [repulsed] with 50 percent casualties, another one is sent instead. We didn't do that.

BEN-GURION: . . . I am not talking about Jerusalem. I know why we didn't take [East] Jerusalem, not because we didn't have enough power [to do so . . . but other areas we could not take] and at the time we didn't face such giant [enemy] power. Now we would . . .

DAYAN: The question is, what do you want to achieve?

BEN-GURION: Small but numerous assaults, on a continuous basis . . ."

32. Bar-Zohar, *Ben-Gurion*, p. 1173.
33. Ben-Gurion was primarily interested in some kind of alliance with France and, therefore, encouraged Peres to pursue further cooperation, but he did not agree with French suggestions to embark upon war as soon as possible. (See Ben-Gurion's diaries quoted by Bar-Zohar, *Ben-Gurion*, pp. 1183, 1216–17; cf. Dayan, *Avnei Derech*, pp. 230–31.)
34. Colonel Mordechai Bar-On, head of the Chief of Staff Office, on Ben-Gurion's final decision to go to the 1956 war, in an Israeli Army radio (*Galei Tzahal*) interview on October 27, 1972, as confirmed to me by Ben-Gurion's chief secretary at the time, Mr. Yitzhak Navon, on December 10, 1972.
35. Dayan, *Avnei Derech*, p. 174; See also Ben-Gurion's list of limitations for war a

year later, on September 28, 1956, even if cooperation with France seemed assured (quoted by Dayan, pp. 231–32).

36. On Ben-Gurion's final deliberations before the Suez campaign, see Ben-Gurion's diary (Bar-Zohar, *Ben-Gurion*, pp. 1232–61). See also Dayan's autobiography for his "retaliatory action" idea as agreed upon by Ben-Gurion, and Ben-Gurion's secret agreement with the British and the French on October 24, 1956 (*Avnei Derech*, pp. 262–66).

37. My statement grossly reduced a relatively complex story to its basic elements. This is to say that Ben-Gurion refused to follow Dayan's advice and risk a confrontation with the United States when he realized that France would not support his plan to retain Sharm-el-Sheikh and the Sinai and prevent Arab rule over Gaza. France, who, together with Britain, was forced to abandon the Suez endeavor by American pressure and Soviet threats, secretly agreed with the United States and U.N. Secretary General Dag Hammarskjöld to support a total Israeli withdrawal in exchange for Nasser's commitment "not to trouble the Israelis" in the Gaza area and in the Tiran Straits. (See Bar-Zohar, *Ben-Gurion*, p. 1310).

Ben-Gurion was not ready to launch a campaign against the administration within the United States. Eisenhower had just been reelected, but his strong objections to the Suez campaign were ignored. Ben-Gurion did not really try to bargain for a better public deal, as he was not a bargainer. On the American, Soviet, and Arab positions and decisions with regard to the Suez affair, see Spiegel, *War for Washington*, and Safran, *From War to War*, pp. 100–118, 208, 211–13.

For the U.S. and U.N. assurances received in exchange for the withdrawals and Israel's official stance, see Moore, *Arab-Israeli Conflict*, pp. 609–78, and especially: General Assembly Resolution 998 (ES-I), concerning a plan for an emergency United Nations force, November 4, 1956; exchange of correspondence between Dwight D. Eisenhower, President of the United States, and Israeli Prime Minister David Ben-Gurion, November 7–8, 1956; *aide mémoire* handed to Israeli Ambassador Abba Eban on February 11, 1957, by Secretary of State Dulles; statement by Golda Meir, Israeli Minister of Foreign Affiairs, before the United Nations General Assembly, March 1, 1957; letter from Dwight D. Eisenhower, President of the United States, to Israeli Prime Minister David Ben-Gurion, March 2, 1957; statements of fourteen maritime states concerning freedom of navigation in the Straits of Tiran and the Gulf of Aqaba, March 1, 4, and 8, 1957; and Dag Hammarskjöld's *aide mémoire* on his secret understanding with Nasser, published after the 1967 war (pp. 738–48).

38. Dayan's approach to the Gaza question at the time was based on the assumption that the return of Egyptian control over the strip would guarantee terrorist attacks against Israel from that territory, since no Arab government (nor international control) could prevent Arabs from making these attacks. Only Israeli control would solve the Gaza problem.

Second, Dayan regarded Sharm-el-Sheikh not only as a guarantee of Israeli shipping to and from Eilat but also as an alternative to Nasser's control over the Suez Canal, thus reducing Egypt's strategic control over the flow of oil to Europe through the canal. Speaking of a "basic change in the strategic and political system in the Middle East" through Israeli permanent presence at the Tiran Straits, he might also have had in mind indirect Israeli control over the Suez Canal itself.

Third, Dayan was categorically against any international guarantees made by "anybody in the world," including Nasser himself, of Israel's freedom of passage in the straits, having long ago dismissed them as worthless.

Fourth, Israel should "fight it out" with the United States and the rest of the world and even risk a French arms embargo (France had supplied enough arms before the campaign), rather than give up in advance. (See Dayan, *Avnei Derech*, p. 330). In his official diary, Dayan accused Ben-Gurion of "weakness" for not making decisions on the basis of "a far-sighted policy" (ibid., p. 335). For the decision making process itself, see also Brecher, *Decisions*, pp. 282–315. One of

Dayan's demands was accepted and retained, and the U.N. mixed armistice commissions, chaired by U.N. officers ended. In Dayan's perception, this procedure enhanced alien extraregionally controlled arbitration methods. Arabs and Israelis should, instead, face each other directly, another reason for Dayan to oppose U.N. emergency troops.

39. Bar-Zohar, *Ben-Gurion*, p. 1345, quoting Ben-Gurion's cable to Peres (in Paris) on October 10, 1957, of Ben-Gurion's archive.

40. For the quotations, see Bar-Zohar, *Ben-Gurion*, pp. 1342 (Ben-Gurion's conversation with Professor Yigael Yadin, August 16, 1958, quoted from Ben-Gurion's diaries) and 1343 (Ben-Gurion's briefing to his personal aides, on October 30, 1958, quoted from Ben-Gurion's diaries). It seems that Ben-Gurion was trying to install Yadin as his heir because of his doubts about Dayan. Yadin refused.

41. On the impact of the 1957 withdrawal on future Israeli thinking concerning "political settlements" with Arabs—the forum, locale, and manner of negotiations, territorial conditions, type of concluding document, and the timing of Israel's withdrawal—see Brecher, *Decisions*, p. 315.

42. GHQ sources; cf. E. Weizman, *Lecha Shamaim, Lecha Aretz* [The sky belongs to thee and so does the earth] (Tel Aviv: Hoza'at Ma'ariv, 1975), pp. 210–16 (Hebrew).

43. For a general updated collection in English and Hebrew of sources and analytical essays on the origin and basic features of the Israeli political system, see E. Guttman and Y. Levy, *The Israeli Political System* (Jerusalem: Hoza'at Akademon, 1974); M. Lissak and E. Guttman, *Political Institutions and Processes in Israel* (Jerusalem: Hoza'at Akademon, 1971); Sh. Weiss, *Ha'Knesset* (Tel Aviv: Hoza'at Ahiasaf, 1977) (Hebrew); and A. Rubinstein, *Ha'Mishpat Ha'Konstituzioni Be'Yisrael* [Israel's Constitutional Law] (Jerusalem: Hoza'at Schocken, 1974) (Hebrew). See also E. S. Likhovski, *Israel's Parliament* (London: Oxford University Press, 1971).

44. On the Irgun under Jabotinsky and Menahem Begin, see N. Lucas, *The Modern History of Israel* (London: Weidenfeld and Nicolson, 1974), pp. 117, 211–60. On Jabotinsky, see ibid., 68–69, 73–74, 131–32, 168–71, 213–17. See also ch. 2, note 38 below.

45. P. Medding, *Mapai in Israel: Political Organization and Government in a New Society* (Cambridge: Cambridge University Press, 1972), pp. 6–13; cf. Horowitz and Lissak, *Mekoroteiha*.

46. On the Herut party between 1949 and 1970, see M. Brecher, *The Foreign Policy System of Israel* (London: Oxford University Press, 1972), pp. 118ff., 156, 160, 172–74, 177, 190, 212, 215 n., 304, 417 ff. See also B. Akzin, "On Menachem Begin and the Herut Movement," *Ha'Doar* 46 (August 5, 1965): 7–17 (Hebrew); cf. Lucas, *Modern History of Israel*, pp. 260, 282–83.

47. On Mapai's history, background, and development, especially after 1948, see Brecher, *Foreign Policy System*, pp. 118 ff, 174, 179, 190, 254, 413 ff. On Mapai's differences with Achdut Ha'Avoda and Mapam, see ibid., p. 171. On Mapai's policies, see ibid., pp. 41, 161–64, 245, 248, cf. Lucas, *Modern History of Israel*, pp. 125–26, 130–32, 145, 193.

48. On Mrs. Meir's background, perceptions of the Arabs, and political behavior under Ben-Gurion and Eshkol, see Brecher, *Foreign Policy System*, pp. 219 ff., 247, 291, 302–4, 304–6, 391–94, 403. On Eshkol, see ibid., pp. 44–45; 215–20 ff., 247, 289, 291–302, 316, 395–96.

49. On Hashomer-Hatzair and Mapam, see ibid., pp. 111, 118 ff., 129, 131, 163–66, 171, 174, 176, 181, 190, 415 ff.

50. On Achdut Ha'Avoda, see ibid., pp. 73, 118 ff., 160–62, 169–79, 174, 190, 212 ff., 254, 413 ff., 415 ff., 548.

51. This relates mainly to Mr. Allon's preemptive war ideas (see above, Note 9).

52. See Appendix A.

53. See Bar-Zohar, *Ben-Gurion*, p. 1342.

54. On the Lavon Affair, see for the pro-Lavon version, E. Hassin, and D. Horowitz,

Haparasha [The Affair] (Tel Aviv: Hoza'at Am Hasefer, 1961) (Hebrew); and Ben-Gurion's own version, *Dvarim Kehavaiatam* [Things as they were] (Tel Aviv: Hoza'at Am Hasefer, 1965) (Hebrew).

55. Ben-Gurion used this term while condemning Lavon's behavior before the party's Central Committee on January 20, 1961. See Ben-Gurion, *Dvarim*, p. 114.

56. The moderate left-wing intelligentsia started a publication of its own following the affair. They have since never been able to join a political party and work within its framework, as they used to do before 1960.

57. See Bar-Zohar, *Ben-Gurion*, p. 1365 n.

58. On the Israeli-German arms deal, see I. Deutschkron, *Bonn and Jerusalem* (Philadelphia: Chilton Books, 1970), pp. 270–82. Washington's consent was needed to release American-made Bundeswehr tanks for Israel within the framework of the secret deal.

59. Harel offered to resign when he realized that Ben-Gurion had decided to stop it. (This is based on my own information as a correspondent for the Israeli government radio, *Kol Israel*, in Bonn, 1962–1966. For details, see Bar-Zohar, *Ben-Gurion*, pp. 1523–45.)

60. Ben-Gurion is quoted as having preferred "economic and research cooperation . . . especially with regard to equipment, mainly in [developing] guided missiles" over diplomatic relations with Western Germany (ibid., p. 1357 n.) See also ibid., pp. 1373, 1388–94, about Israeli-French-U.S. relations concerning the nuclear issue. On Israel's early nuclear policy, see Y. Evron, "Israel and the Atom, the Uses and Misuses of Ambiguity, 1957–67," *Orbis* 17 (Winter, 1974): 1306–43; and A. Dowty, "Israel's Nuclear Policy," *State, Government, and International Relations* 7 (Spring, 1975): 5–27. Cf., for an Arab view, F. Jabber, *Israel and Nuclear Weapons, Present Options and Future Strategies* (London: Chatto and Vindus, for the International Institute for Strategic Studies, 1971).

61. Former U.S. Under Secretary of State Joseph Sisco to the author on April 13, 1977. See also Safran, *From War to War*, pp. 132–33; and A. M. Schlesinger, *A Thousand Days* (London: Mayflower-Dell paperback, 1965), pp. 451–52. On Ben-Gurion's personal impression of Kennedy, see Bar-Zohar, *Ben-Gurion*, p. 1394.

62. Ibid., p. 1525 n., and also my taped interview with Sisco, April 13, 1977,

63. Ben-Gurion tried parallelly to negotiate directly with Nasser, probably to prove to himself and to Kennedy that Egypt was not interested in a conflict resolution, and that Kennedy was advancing traditional Arab demands without any Arab concession in exchange for Israeli concessions (Bar-Zohar, *Ben-Gurion*, pp. 1528–29.

64. Statement of President Kennedy at a news conference on May 8, 1963: "We support the *security* of both Israel and her neighbors. . . . We strongly oppose the use of force or the threat of force in the Middle East. . . . In the event of aggression, or preparation for aggression, whether direct or indirect, we would support appropriate measures in the United Nations and adopt other courses of action *on our own* to prevent or put a stop to such aggression" (Richard P. Stebbins, ed., *Documents on American Foreign Relations, 1963* [New York: Simon and Schuster for The Council on Foreign Relations, 1963], doc. 68(b), p. 268). (Italics mine.)

65. The Ben-Gurion-Kennedy exchange of letters was partially published in *Yada'an Ma'riv* (Tel Aviv: Hoza'at Ma'ariv, 1975–76), pp. 38–44 (Hebrew). For the details, see Bar-Zohar, *Ben-Gurion*, pp. 1550–54.

66. Ibid., pp. 1522–23, especially note 27, referring to an entry in Ben-Gurion's diary dated May 27, 1963, in which he reports on his consent to one American inspection visit to Dimona annually.

67. For a Rafi view of the Lavon affair, the shortcomings of Mapai's regime, and its own political priorities, see N. Yanai, *Kera Ba'Zameret* [A breach at the top] (Tel Aviv: Hoza'at Levin-Epstein, 1969) (Hebrew). See also Brecher, *Foreign Policy Systems*, pp. 119, 180–81, 323, 325, 548.

68. See *Department of State Bulletin* (June 22, 1964), pp. 959–60. Cf. Stebbins, *Documents on American Foreign Relations, 1963*, Document 82, p. 326.
69. Foreign ministry sources.
70. One of them, Professor Yuval Neeman, openly published his opinion of the 1963 missle decision on the context of the aftermath of the Sinai 2 agreement in 1975, under the title, "Why I Resigned from the Ministry of Defense," in *Ha'aretz*, February 6, 1976.
71. See Brecher, *Decisions*, p. 322. An executive agreement was an international agreement between the president of the United States and foreign countries, which, unlike a treaty, did not require Senate consent. Such agreements were concluded under the president's constitutional power as commander in chief, although the Constitution makes no explicit provision to this effect. Through executive agreements secrecy could be maintained when debates in the Senate might be dangerous or provocative. Legally, however, an executive agreement was regarded as politically binding. See *The American Political Dictionary*, J. C. Plano and M. Greenberg, eds. (New York: Holt, Rinehart and Winston, 1967). For a critical assessment of the practice under several administrations and a policy statement on the issue, see M. Bundy, "Toward an Open Foreign Policy—the Opportunity and the Problem," in *Has the President Too Much Power?* ed. C. Roberts (New York: Harper's Magazine Press, 1974), pp. 222–33. Cf. E. Hargrove, *The Power of the Modern Presidency* (Philadelphia: Temple University Press, 1974), foreword and pp. 123–74. See A. M. Schlesinger, *The Imperial Presidency* (Boston: Houghton Mifflin, 1973), pp. 85–88, 310–19.
72. See Dayan's article "Germany, Dimona, and the Jordan," *Ha'aretz*, March 26, 1965. Cf. the *New York Times* report on Dayan's articles (March 27, 1965).

    See also the *New York Times* story (November 16, 1963) on Ben-Gurion's hints of possible experiments at Dimona in view of Egyptian threats, and Ben-Gurion's denial in the *New York Times* (November 20, 1963). Cf. also the declaration made by the Scientific Director of Israel's Defense Ministry, Dr. Shimon Yiftah, on December 31, 1963, that Israel had no plans to separate plutonium at Dimona, quoted in Dowty, "Israel's Nuclear Policy," p. 27.

    Agriculture Minister Dayan left Eshkol's government in November 1964. Dayan criticized the government openly—for the first time in the history of Israel—for allowing the American inspection at Dimona, hinting at differences in the cabinet on this issue as early as 1963. On Dayan's relations with Eshkol, which brought about his resignation, see S. Teveth, *Moshe Dayan* (Jerusalem: Hoza'at Schocken, 1971), pp. 544–47 (Hebrew).
73. Allon, in a conversation with the author on March 14, 1977, referring to his basic antinuclear deterrent approach. Cf. Allon, *Masach shel Chol*, pp. 401–2.
74. On Soviet Middle East policy in the early sixties and later, until the Six-Day War, see Y. Ro'i, *From Encroachment to Involvement: A Documentary Study of Soviet Policy in the Middle East, 1954–1973* (New York: Wiley, 1974).
75. See Safran, *From War to War*, pp. 46–47.
76. In his *Ha'aretz* article (Note 72, above).
77. On Syrian-backed Fath, led by Yassir Arafat, and the Egyptian-controlled PLO, chaired by Ahmed Shukeiri, between 1964 and 1967, see Safran, *From War to War*, p. 394; and Kerr, *Arab Cold War*, pp. 151–55.
78. "Operation Rotem" (GHQ sources). Israeli intelligence failure to detect the Egyptians in time led to a personnel shake-up in the Military Intelligence Branch.
79. See Dowty, "Israel's Nuclear Policy," p. 22. See also *New York Times* reports:
    Israeli government, in an effort to reassure the United States of its peaceful intents, permits a second inspection of the Negev reactor. It resists U.S. urging of IAEA control (March 14, 1965);
    The United States and Israel agree on the technical feasibility of an atom desalting and power plan (January 2, 1966);
    The United States believes Israel ordered 30 intermediate-range ballistic missiles from France, a move seen as indicating an intention to develop atomic weapons (January 7, 1966);
    Influential Israeli editors quietly urge the easing of a government and self-

imposed ban on discussion of the spread of nuclear devices (March 7, 1966); Israeli nuclear expert Peres sees Israel undecided on an offer to trade financial aid for an inspection agreement and he foresees great argument if a demand is made. He opposes Israel's being first in the Middle East to build atomic weapons (March 14, 1966);

Premier Eshkol repeats his pledge that Israel will not be the first to introduce nuclear arms into the Middle East (May 19, 1966);

Israel permits a third American inspection at Dimona (June 28, 1966).

For Arab reactions in 1966, see the following *New York Times* reports:

Soviet Deputy Defense Minister Gretchko, in his December visit to Cairo, reportedly refused to send nuclear weapons to Egypt, but pledged protection if Israel developed or obtained such arms (February 4, 1966);

President Nasser says that Egypt would wage a preventive war if Israel manufactures nuclear weapons (February 21, 1966);

In a U.S. television interview, Nasser again threatens preventive war if the U.A.R. finds Israel developing nuclear weapons (April 18, 1966);

On November 23, 1974, Nasser's intimate aid, Mr. Mohammed Heikal, disclosed that the late President Nasser had attempted to get a bomb developing project under way, but failed.

See also G. H. Quester, "Israel and the Nuclear Non-Proliferation Treaty," *Bulletin of the Atomic Scientists*, no. 25 (June, 1969), 7–9, 44–45; and L. Beaton, "Why Israel Does not Need the Bomb," *Middle East*, no. 7 (April, 1969), pp. 7–11.

80. On the Samu' raid, see Aronson and Horowitz, "Strategy of Controlled Retaliation," pp. 90–91. See also Brecher, *Foreign Policy System*, pp. 139, 308, 365; and cf. his general analysis of Eshkol's foreign and defense policies, in particular after 1966, in Brecher, *Decisions*, pp. 327–52. On Ben-Gurion's strong criticism of the Samu' raid, see Bar-Zohar, *Ben-Gurion*, p. 1588.

The Israeli government asked the United States to pass a letter of apology to King Hussein, in which Israel explained the high rate of Jordanian casualties as being a result of a tactical mistake. Washington refused to pass the letter. Shortly afterward, Palestinian uprisings on the West Bank were suppressed by Hussein. He brought to the West Bank American-made tanks that had been supplied to him under the provision not to move them into the area. Israel could hardly protest against this measure, as it followed Israel's raid (foreign ministry sources).

81. For an Israeli analysis of Nasser's Israel policy since 1956, his inter-Arab and domestic considerations, and his holistic position toward Israel (in connection with his verbal commitments toward the "Palestinian Cause," especially after the 1964 Arab Summit), see D. Schueftan, "Nasser's 1967 Policy Reconsidered," *Jerusalem Quarterly* 3 (Spring, 1977): 124–44. Cf. a pro-PLO, yet similar view in D. Pryce-Jones, *The Face of Defeat: Palestinian Refugees and Guerillas* (New York: Holt, Rinehart and Winston, 1972), pp. 51–54.

82. See above, note 79.

83. This first relatively large-scale Israeli aerial attack on Arab territory was recommended by the chief of Israel's army northern command, Brigadier General David Elazar, as the Syrians moved their diversion equipment deeper into Syrian territory to protect it from Israeli tank fire, while work continued on the water diversion project. General Weizman, the chief of operations and former commander of the Air Force, recommended it to Rabin and Eshkol, having in mind a more effective use of the modern IAF, which he had built (GHQ sources. Cf. Weizman, *Shamaim*, pp. 215–16). Eshkol is reported by GHQ sources as having agreed to a military-technical suggestion concerning the Syrian diversion equipment in the broader context of Syrian shellings and Fath raids, which also convinced his moderate NRP ministers to approve the action. General Weizman also initiated the use of an armored brigade in daylight in Samu'. A regular army, according to him, should operate "properly instead of hiding in the night and accepting constraints of traditional retaliatory actions" (GHQ sources; ibid.).

84. Dayan privately said to Weizman, his brother-in-law, following the Mig inci-

dent, "Are you people out of your minds? You are leading the country to war." (See Weizman, *Shamaim*, p. 207.) Dayan understood better a possible Arab reaction to the use of the Air Force, whereas the cabinet regarded it as a limited answer to limited provocations.

According to Mr. Abba Eban, then Israel's foreign minister, the Mig incident was a turning point in the Middle East conflict. The Syrians were expecting the assistance of their planes' suppliers. The Soviet Union had four choices: (*a*) do nothing, and lose its credibility as an Arab ally after having lost two important clients shortly before—Ben Bella of Algeria and Sukarno of Indonesia; (*b*) ask the Syrians to stop their actions against Israel; the Soviet ambassador in Israel however, maintained to the contrary, that the "Fath actions were American provocations"; (*c*) give an open warning to Israel which might tie Soviet hands and force a confrontation with the United States; (*d*) enlist Egypt for Syria's protection, in order to support the Damascus regime and maintain the regional character of the conflict. This was, according to Eban, the final Soviet choice. (See "New Revelations on the Period Prior to the Six-Day War," *Davar*, June 3, 1976.)

85. Rabin, in an interview in the *Bamachaneh-Nahal*, April 11, 1967. Eshkol was reported to have regarded this and two other interviews by his chief of staff as utterly stupid, and to have considered removing him from the job. According to my source, who was personally very close to Eshkol, the Achdut Ha'Avoda ministers Allon and Galili protected former Palmach colonel Rabin, simultaneously trying to prevent a general shake-up at GHQ and a possible succession by the more aggressive and trigger-happy Weizman.

86. See Y. Erez, "A Note from the North," *Ma'ariv*, April 20, 1976. Also GHQ sources. See also Rabin's own postwar version, note 105.

87. See Safran, *From War to War*, pp. 271–302; cf. Sadat's 1977 memoirs, serialized in the Kuwait daily *As-Siyassah*, starting October 31, 1976, especially the November 19, 1976, issue.

88. In Israel's foreign ministry, there is a school of thought that blames U Thant for having begun the inevitable escalation process as he placed Nasser before the dilemma, either to accept humiliation and retain the U.N. forces in their positions or to demand their complete withdrawal. Mr. Ralph Bunche, U Thant's American deputy is regarded as having advised the secretary general to call Nasser's bluff through an either/or dilemma. (Foreign Ministry sources.)

89. On the Israeli government decision making process throughout the entire escalation developments in May and June, 1967, see Brecher, *Decisions*, pp. 361–431. Cf. B. Geist, "The Six-Day War: The Process of Decision Making in Foreign Affairs in a Crisis Situation," *State, Government, and International Relations* 8, (September 1975): 61–85. Geist's article is a condensed version of a Ph.D. dissertation at Hebrew University, Jerusalem. I have added to Brecher and Geist several considerations of the decision makers, which were insufficiently stressed in their excellent research, and have omitted many details that could be read in the original.

90. See Chief of Staff Rabin's introduction to the official army memorial book, *Shisha Yamim* [Six days] (Tel Aviv: Hoza'at Ma'arachot, 1968), p. 3 (Hebrew). Rabin describes the strategic changes that lead to the escalation process of the winter of 1966–1967 and culminated in the general mobilization of May 19, 1967, as follows: (1) The takeover of the Ba'athist radical "Doctor's Regime" in Syria in January, 1966. This is the Israeli nickname for the Ba'athist group that consisted of radical academics who took power from the first Ba'athist government, which established itself in Syria in early 1963. (2) An agreement between Egypt and Saudi Arabia to end Nasser's intervention in Yemen in the winter of 1967. It was regarded by Rabin as a possible reason for Nasser to transfer his force from Yemen to the Sinai. The reasoning is that, having reached no results in the long and weary Yemen campaign, the Egyptian President may have preferred to open a new front with Israel in order to conceal his defeat in Yemen. Another reason

may have been that Nasser preferred to mass his Yemen troops in the Sinai instead of bringing them home. He did not want the domestic difficulties of the Yemenite defeat's becoming publicly felt. (3) The immediate reason given by Rabin for the general mobilization was the withdrawal of the UNEF from the ADL on May 19, which triggered an "almost total mobilization" of the IDF. The central, Jordanian command did not mobilize, because GHQ regarded the Jordanian border as safe, since the conservative King Hussein was not expected to join the radical Egyptian-Syrian front against Israel. In the same article, Rabin says in retrospect that the Israeli actions against Syria in the winter of 1966–1967, and the preventive army concentrations along the Syrian border that followed them, could have been interpreted as an Israeli provocation against the Ba'athist regime.

91. See Eban interview in *Davar*, Note 84.
92. See Weizman *Shamaim*, p. 210.
93. Gen-Gurion to Israeli military correspondents on May 24, 1967, at the hotel Neveh-Midbar, near Beer Sheba (as recorded by the writer); cf. his position at Rafi meetings after the mobilization (May 21, 1967). See Bar-Zohar, *Ben-Gurion*, pp. 1588–91. Cf. also Eban and former Transport Minister Moshe Carmel's testimonies to *Davar*, June 3, 1976, according to which he asked both Eshkol's ministers the following question: "What's going on? Are we going to war—in the wrong time, wrong place, and with the wrong enemy? Are you willing to endanger Israel's cities? In 1956 I did not start any action before having secured Tel Aviv and the other cities with a French Air Force umbrella, and you are ready to get involved in a war just like that?" On May 21, Ben-Gurion met Chief of Staff Rabin, and according to a version quoted by Bar-Zohar (*Ben-Gurion*, p. 1589), he blamed both Eshkol and Rabin for the Samu' action and the operations against Syria, and made them responsible for a possible "end of the Third temple." The argument was, as one could expect, that Eshkol and Rabin helped provoke a general turmoil because of their lack of postulative thinking or leadership qualities. Instead of preserving the status quo, they provoked the enemy first and lead Egypt into an impasse that would lead to war, where the chances were uncertain without foreign aid. According to Weizman, Rabin suffered a nervous breakdown after his talk with Ben-Gurion and declared himself ready to transfer his job to Weizman. Rabin had adopted Ben-Gurion's criticism that he was, partially at least, to blame for a possible war. According to my inquiry, Rabin indeed did not resume his normal functions as chief of staff until several weeks later, even though he returned to office 24 hours after the Weizman incident.
94. See Dayan, *Avnei Derech*, p. 402: "What [Nasser] did is serious, . . . by setting a supposition that Israel is not capable of fighting the Arabs. If this supposition of Nasser's is not to be changed, our future is gloomy. That's why we should fight him . . . a big clash, in which his main force would be destroyed or hurt." Rabin's GHQ, according to my sources and Dayan (ibid., pp. 399–403), was thinking in terms of an overall air attack against Egypt's air force, but also in terms of a *limited* land war to occupy Gaza and fight Egyptian reinforcements on their way to the strip, in order to create a bargaining asset to be returned later to Egyptian control in exchange for Egyptian concessions.
95. Rabin's estimation of Israeli casualties was reported to the divisional commanders at the southern front as 50,000. Action was taken in several cities for a mass burial (according to my own information as a war correspondent at the time, on assignment in General Sharon's divisional headquarters). Rabin is reported by Weizman as having been skeptical about the planned air action against the Arab air forces, which was executed on June 4. This plan was regarded as the official Israeli army war plan, and one can imagine Weizman's disappointment in his chief of staff, who, in the moment of truth, failed to back the official plan.
96. The Israeli government sent an unofficial warning to Egypt not to close the Straits (U.S. State Department sources).
97. See Geist, *Six-Day War*, p. 63.

98. See Brecher, *Decisions*, p. 402.
99. See Brecher, *Decisions*, p. 410 ff. Foreign ministry and GHQ sources; cf. Dayan, *Avnei Derech*, pp. 412–32, which includes a great deal of the secret American-Israeli correspondence and exchange of views during the crisis. For the U.S. position, see Spiegel, *War for Washington*, and Eugene V. Rostow, "Israel in the Evolution of American Foreign Policy" (Paper delivered at the annual meeting of the American Historical Association, Washington, D.C., December 28, 1976, pp. 34 ff.
100. See Polés [pseud. for Dr. Sh. Gross], "Our Foreign Policy Options," *Ha'aretz,* February 27, 1976, in which General de Gaulle's arguments with Israel on the eve of the Six-Day War are published for the first time at great length. (Also foreign ministry sources.)
101. Dayan in a *Ma'ariv* interview, February 20, 1976.
102. See Eban in the *Davar* interview, June 3, 1976. The then foreign minister reports that Secretary of State Dean Rusk told him that the Egyptian forces in the Sinai were deployed in defense positions. Secretary of Defense McNamara is quoted as having told Eban that, according to American assessments, Egypt was awaiting an Israeli attack. The Pentagon concluded that if Israel struck first, it would win in four days. If Egypt struck first, Israel would win in ten days. At any rate, the Pentagon estimated that in pure military terms, Israel was stronger than Egypt.
103. See Moshe Dayan, *Mapa Hadasha, Yechasim Acherim* [A new map—different relations; a collection of Dayan's speeches and writings, 1967–69] (Haifa: Hoza'at Shikmona, 1969) (Hebrew); and notes 14, 31, and 38 in this chapter. See also Brecher, *Foreign Policy System*, p. 318 ff. For Dayan's military-political basic principles before the Six-Day War, see also his article, "Israel's Border and Security Problems," *Foreign Affairs* 33, no. 3 (January, 1955): 110–18; cf. Brecher, *Foreign Policy System*, pp. 335–39.
104. See Dayan, *Mapa Hadasha*, pp. 56–57: "I would like to stress that we are heading for trouble, because we are not ready to return to the former borders and the former relations, in contrast to so many other countries that did return after a war to the old boundaries and former relations. But we should know that the Arabs—and mainly the Palestinian Arabs—not only remember such changes, they were raised upon changes. . . . I simply wanted to say that our claims should not be understood as if they were entirely destroying an existing order. It is not true that the Palestinian Arabs have been living for 2,000 years in fixed . . . frameworks, which we are trying to destroy. We are talking about changes in a changing reality, in a region in which every ten years a far-reaching change occurs. In spite of this, there is one point that differentiates us in our bid for change. All former changes took place among the Arabs themselves—between Syria and Palestine, between the Hashemite Kingdom and the Arabs of the "West Bank"—whereas we are trying to bring about changes in the relations between we Jews (the "outside element" in this area) and the Arabs: the Jews want to widen their share in an Arab area. This is the difference—quite a difference—and this is why [they] scream."
105. Dayan was nominated as Israel's fourth chief of staff in 1953. Under his predecessors, Major Generals Dori and Yadin, the IDF was created, had won the 1948-49 war, and had adopted its typical army reserve structure. Yet, after the war the regular army assumed the character of a European (largely British) standing force and lost more of its former characteristics of enthusiasm, unorthodox thinking, and operational elasticity. This development could be understood in political terms since Ben-Gurion decided to disband special units that were politically oriented toward Achdut Ha'Avoda and Herut and to dismiss commanders who were associated mostly with Achdut Ha'Avoda and other political parties. The disbanded units and the dismissed commanders, however, were regarded as the less orthodox and more imaginative ones. See E. N. Luttwak and D. Horowitz, *The Israeli Army* (London: Allan Lane, Penguin Books, 1975), p. 88.

Dayan, when appointed chief of staff, brought back enthusiasm and unorthodox strategic thinking. He quickly instilled a new and aggressive spirit throughout the regular army, thanks to his leadership, his reprisals policy, and his emphasis upon special units that carried out the retaliatory acts. This brought about a race in the rest of the land forces to prove their respective abilities in battle. (See Luttwak and Horowitz, *Israeli Army*, pp. 160–61.)

Yet, as both a tactician and a strategist, Dayan remained controversial, at least for a professional and critical observer of his public image. His role as a medium-rank field commander and later as the commander of the Jerusalem area in the 1948–49 war was regarded in several GHQ circles as more spectacular than militarily effective. His 1956 campaign was criticized—from a purely operational point of view—as based upon a misunderstanding of modern tank warfare (see Major General Ch. Laskow, and Brigadier General M. Zorea's review of Dayan's Sinai dairy in *Ma'ariv*, October 10, 1965; and cf. Luttwak and Horowitz, *Israeli Army*, p. 113). A brilliant but unbalanced critique of Dayan's roles in the 1956 and 1967 wars is contained in B. Amidror's series of articles on the Israeli army's performance after 1955 until after the October, 1973 war, in *Ha'Olam Ha'Zeh* (1974, 1975, and 1976) (Hebrew).

106. See Dayan's speech at Roi Rotberg's funeral on May 1, 1965 in *Davar*, May 2, 1965; cf. Teveth, *Moshe Dayan*, p. 240. See also Dayan, *Mapa Hadasha*, pp. 19–29.
107. Thus Dayan gave up the night retaliations in 1956 as noneffective, dismissing "this status of no war, no peace. We have to force our neighbors to choose between stopping terrorism and going to war against us." See Dayan, *Avnei Derech*, p. 250.
108. See above, Note 38.
109. See Dayan, *Mapa Hadasha*, p. 48:

> There is something deplorable and there is something positive in this so-called Arab mentality. The negative aspect is the inclination of the Arabs to cheat and to deceive themselves and others consciously. This starts with a false or incorrect report given by a field commander either to explain a failure or to make a hero of himself, by exaggerating his situation and the number of Jews killed. It ends with the president of Egypt or the king of Jordan, who know that the information was falsified, but still accept it. Again [they do this] either to explain their failure or to make heroes of themselves. Consciously, they live in a world that is false and the reason for that is almost similar to drug addiction. Sometimes I think that all the Arabs in every field act as if they were under the influence of drugs. But the illusion is worse than lying. Lying is conscious and you master it. Illusion would master you.
>
> The positive other side of Arab mentality is expressed in their attachment to the glory of the great Arab nation. This patriotism is not always expressed in deeds, but is reflected in a spiritual identification of the past—with the glorious days of Salah-a-Din. When the Arabs use the term the noble Arab nation, we used to smile because we see them only in their present situation, but they really believe in this.
>
> Arab mentality does not interest me as a psychological issue. It explains to me why the Arabs do not want peace . . . not because reality makes it difficult for them, but because their mentality shields reality from them.

110. See Dayan, *Mapa Hadasha*, p. 15.
111. See Dayan, *Mapa Hadasha*, p. 18: "In six days we have achieved the war aims, which were the outcome of the causes of the war that was enforced upon us by the Arabs. Today, we are facing no war aims, but the goals of peace. We want a state of Israel that will retain its uncompromising Jewish character, demographically and structurally. We want borders that will ensure Israel's security. We want to have equal international rights, including the freedom of shipping. We want borders that will reflect the connection between the Jewish people and their

historical land. We want a state that will be recognized by its neighbors. We want peace treaties that will also solve the Palestine refugee problem."

This set of contradictory goals is typical of Dayan's approach to the conflict and to politics in general. Politics in the pursuance of one's own contradictory aims against the adversaries' contradictory goals and behavior.

112. Basically, this decision—as far as Dayan was concerned—might be connected with his recommendation to Ben-Gurion in 1949 "to implement our rights" in Jerusalem (see above, Note 14), which had been ignored since then by Jordan, and also with Dayan's perception of Jordan's basic dependence on inter-Arab consensus vis-à-vis Israel, which would not permit Amman to fulfill obligations to Israel if territory were to be returned to Jordanian control (see Dayan, *Avnei Derech*, pp. 542–43). The moderates—Eshkol, Sapir, and the NRP—could not prevent the annexation of the holy city once it fell into Israeli hands, backed by Dayan, Begin, and Achdut Ha'Avoda ministers (ibid., p. 494; and mainly prime minister's office sources).

113. GHQ sources; cf. ibid., pp. 429–30.

114. See Teveth, *Moshe Dayan*, p. 593; and Dayan, *Avnei Derech*, pp. 502–3.

115. The concept of "secure borders," mainly Israeli's presence on the Jordan river and Sharm-el-Sheikh and a possible cordon sanitaire in the Sinai and on the Golan Heights, was developed shortly after the Six-Day War simultaneously by three ministers and former generals—Dayan, Transport Minister Carmel, and his Achdut Ha'Avoda colleague and personal rival, Allon. (See interview in *Ha'aretz*, September 5, 1967.) Allon reached the conclusion that security requirements should be disconnected, when politically possible, from an Israeli-ruled Arab population.

The "Allon Plan" of September, 1967, suggested an Israeli presence in strategic areas of the West Bank and Sharm-el-Sheikh. The Golan was excluded, due to the official Syrian totally uncompromising position. The Arab-populated areas in the West Bank should have been returned to Arab rule, most probably to Jordan, when King Hussein would be ready for peace. Allon conceived this plan, as he reported later in a closed meeting, after "three long days of thinking, which led me to revise my historical-ideological approach to the West Bank and to adopt Ben-Gurion's basic law not to rule too many Arabs." (Achdut Ha'Avoda sources; cf. Cohen, *Tochnit Allon*.) Allon's plan was neither rejected nor approved by the cabinet, but the operative parts of the plan, saying that Jewish settlements in these strategic areas would remain in Israeli hands, gained the majority's consent. On the concept as a whole, see D. Dishon, ed., *The Middle East Record, 1967*, The Shiloah Center for Middle Eastern and African Studies (Jerusalem: Israel Universities Press, 1971), p. 250.

116. In an interview with the American correspondent, John McCowen Roths, of the *Saturday Review*, Ben-Gurion said: "Peace, genuine peace, is our most vital need, and to achieve it every sacrifice would be worthwhile, including withdrawal to the pre-1967 borders. If I were now prime minister, I would initiate this principle." Referring to specific conquered territories, Ben-Gurion told the American correspondent: "Sinai? Sharm-el-Sheikh? Gaza? The West Bank? Let them all go. Peace is more important than real estate. We do not need territories. With adequate irrigation, the Negev can support all the Jews in the world who desire to come." Quoted by D. Bar-Nir, "Ben-Gurion: Peace, Not Real Estate," *New Outlook* 14 (June–July 1971): 63; cf. Bar-Zohar, *Ben-Gurion* 1579–80 n.

Chapter 2

1. See, for example, General Sharon's interview on the Israeli radio (July 9, 1967). When I interviewed Sharon for this broadcast, having served under him as a war correspondent during the successful campaign in the central Sinai sector in which he commanded a division, Sharon expressed his colleagues' and his own

belief that the Arabs would need about fifteen years to recover and that he was confident that his generation would no longer fight.

2. See N. Kiss, "The Influence of Public Policy on Israel's Public Opinion, 1967–74," *State, Government, and International Relations* (September 8, 1975), pp. 36–60 (Hebrew). A primary source for Israeli public opinion trends is the *Current Survey* of Israel's public opinion, since 1967 regularly conducted at the Institute of Communication at the Hebrew University in Jerusalem, upon which Miss Kiss's research was based. See also Z. Sternhell, "The trend to the right in Israel, 1967–72," Levi Eshkol Institute for Economic, Social, and Political Research (Jerusalem: Hebrew University, 1972) (Hebrew); and R. Isaac, *Israel Divided: Ideological Politics in the Jewish State* (Baltimore: The Johns Hopkins University Press, 1976). See also Lissak and Guttman, *Political Institutions.*

3. Prime minister's office sources. Cf. note 6 below for details.

4. Prime minister's office sources.

5. Foreign ministry sources. Cf. *New York Times* report, July 16, 1967: "U.S. officials see capability of Israel's producing nuclear weapons in three or four years." This assessment followed the speculation that Israel might choose to develop nuclear weapons if the Soviet Union reequipped the Arab military forces.

6. On American policy in the Middle East in 1967–68 following the Six-Day War, see Rostow, "Israel in American Foreign Policy," and Spiegel, *War for Washington.* My statement is also based on my interviews with Sisco on March 31 and April 13, 1977.

U.S. Policy Statements after the June war of 1967:

a. On 13 June, 1967, in his statement before the Security Council, Ambassador Arthur J. Goldberg pointed out that the demand by the Soviet Union for an immediate Israeli withdrawal to the June 4 borders would mean the renewal of hostilities. Goldberg's argument rested on the demand for a real peace, which would remove the reasons that led to the war in the borders. (See Stebbins, *Documents on American Foreign Relations, 1967,* doc. 40, pp. 131–39 [especially p. 135.])

b. President Lyndon B. Johnson reaffirmed the new U.S. policy in his address "Principles for Peace in the Middle East," delivered before the State Department Foreign Policy Conference for Educators on June 19, 1967 (See *Department of State Bulletin* 57, no. 1463 [July 10, 1967]: 31–34: "An immediate return to the situation as it was on June 4 is not a prescription for peace, but for renewed hostilities. . . . Certainly, troops must be withdrawn, but there must also be recognized rights of national life, progress in solving the refugee problem, freedom of innocent maritime passage, limitation of the arms race, and respect for political independence and territorial integrity." These were the "Five Principles" put forward by Johnson as a precondition for any Israeli withdrawal.

c. On the basis of the "Five Principles," Ambassador Goldberg offered a "U.S. Plan for Permanent Peace" in his statement before the Fifth Emergency Session of the U.N. General Assembly, June 20, 1967. (See Stebbins, ed., *Documents,* doc. 42, p. 146.)

d. At the Glassboro meeting between President Johnson and Soviet Premier Alexey Kosygin on June 23 and 25, 1967 (where three-quarters of the talks dealt with the Middle East), President Johnson presented to his Soviet counterpart a detailed "11-point package plan for settling Middle East problems." The plan embodied the "Five Principles" of June 19 and had been drawn up by a committee under Mr. McGeorge Bundy: (1) withdrawal of Israeli troops from conquered lands; (2) acceptance of Israel as a state by its Arab neighbors; (3) elimination of the state of war between Israel and its neighbors; (4) settlement of the rights of the belligerents (prisoners' exchanges); (5) a reaffirmation of the non-use of force or threat of force in the area; (6) right of passage through international waterways (Suez Canal, Tiran Straits); (7) slowdown or restriction of the arms race in the Middle East (the U.N. should maintain a record of the selling of arms to the Middle East countries); (8) permanent solution of the Arab refugee problem (Johnson suggested in principle the right of choice between return and integration into the Arab countries, but he believed, however, that a vast majority would not opt for returning); (9) study of the question of how to obtain an effective U.N. presence in the Middle East; (10) establishment of mediation procedures for the area; and (11) organization of a social and economic development program.

Kosygin's reaction to the plan was that he "would be willing to discuss it after the Israeli troops withdrew." "He and Johnson differed over the question of time and the extent of the withdrawal of troops and the future size of the Israeli state" (*The Middle East Record, 1967*, D. Dishon, ed., The Shiloah Center for Middle Eastern and African Studies [Jerusalem: Israel Universities Press, 1971] 3: 40).

e. The demand for a full and real peace after the June war by both Israel and the United States has been criticized as somewhat unrealistic by Secretary of State Dean Rusk, in a speech on July 19, 1967: "One can understand why Israel believed the time had come to sit down and make final peace settlements with its neighbors . . . and there is some question as to whether any of the governments in that area can, in fact, do that and survive. . . ." Rusk stressed the importance of the role of the U.N. and, in general, the quiet and diplomatic work behind the scenes (*Department of State Bulletin* 57, no. 1467 [August 7, 1967]: p. 165.

7. Dayan disclosed this cabinet decision for the first time publicly after the Yom Kippur War in a *Ma'ariv* interview on September 20, 1974. His statement has been confirmed by prime minister's office sources. See also Dayan's *Avnei Derech*, pp. 490–92.

8. Egyptian policy statements after June, 1967:

President Nasser, in his speech of June 9, said that the first task facing the Arabs was "to remove the traces of this aggression." In terms of actual power, he held that "despite the setback, the Arab nation, with all its potential and resources, is in a position to insist on the removal of the traces of the aggression" (Dishon, *Middle East Record, 1967*, p. 256).

Although diplomatic relations with the United States had been severed by the U.A.R., the Egyptian presidential adviser on foreign affairs, Mr. Mahmud Fawzi, met twice with Secretary of State Rusk during the General Assembly Emergency Session of the end of June. Rusk informed Fawzi of U.S. plans for the solution of the Middle East crisis. Fawzi replied that Egypt would not negotiate as long as one Israeli soldier remained on Arab territory (see *Ruz-al-Yussuf*, August 7, quoted in Dishon, *Middle East Record, 1967*, p. 256). Syria refrained from assuming any active role in the inter-Arab and Arab-American discussions, adopting a totally negative approach to any deliberations vis-à-vis Israel short of complete withdrawals and satisfying the uncompromising Fath demands. Under General Jadid, a Baath'ist doctrinaire, Damascus later isolated itself until 1970 from the rest of the Arab coalition also in connection with its rival Baath'ist regime in Iraq, with the pro-Western Jordan, and with Egypt, as a result of Nasser's adoption of Resolution 242.

9. Immediate post-war Israeli public positions:

Prime Minister Eshkol told the Knesset on June 12 that "Israel is not prepared to return to the situation that prevailed up to a week ago" (he did not refer to new borders) and that "a new situation has been created that can serve as a starting point in direct negotiations for a peace settlement with the Arab countries." Eshkol did not point out any concrete proposals for such a settlement (Dishon, *Middle East Record, 1967*, p. 274).

In a unanimously adopted government resolution of July 30, 1967, it was formally declared that "Israeli forces would not withdraw from the cease-fire lines except as a result of direct negotiations with the Arab countries concerned" (see *Ha'aretz*, July 31, 1967).

On August 14, shortly before the Khartoum conference, Foreign Minister Abba Eban recapitulated Israel's position before foreign correspondents. He said that now was the moment "to replace the 1949 armistice agreements with stable arrangement that would create normal and peaceful relations between Israel and its neighbors." Eban saw such an arrangement in terms of a "directly negotiated peace settlement," but he refused to spell out in public "Israel's conditions for a peace treaty; . . . wisdom dictated that the views on the territorial problems involved should not be made public" (see *Middle East Record, 1967*, p. 274).

10. According to Premier Eshkol in a press interview with *Ma'ariv* on October 4, 1967, King Hussein tried to establish contact with Israel in secret. Israel answered the attempts by mediators who were acting with Hussein's knowledge (before the Khartoum conference) in trying to find out Israel's position: "Israel was ready to state its position only in direct negotiations." (*Middle East Record, 1967*, p. 259.)

On the slow emergence of the Allon Plan as a framework for an operational consensus in the Israeli cabinet with regard to the West Bank, see Cohen, *Tochnit Allon*, esp. pp. 120–23. Accordingly, many cabinet ministers practically endorsed the territorial aspects of Allon's Plan in 1968 as a blue print for future Israeli presence in the area. They did not, however, endorse Allon's idea—to try and encourage an autonomous Palestinian region in the West Bank, separated from the Palestinian organizations abroad—as long as King Hussein was regarded as unreliable and as long as he was not ready to negotiate on the Plan (see Cohen, *Tochnit Allon*, pp. 66–70). The cabinet majority did not want to alienate Hussein as a future partner or to create a Palestinian entity that might be hostile to Israel despite Israel's wish to cooperate with it. (Prime Minister's Office sources).

11. The Khartoum Resolutions of the Arab summit conference of September 1, 1967, are printed in Moore, *Arab-Israeli Conflict*, vol. 3, p. 788.

For the "three no's," see the following citation. "Third, the Arab Heads of State agreed on unifying their efforts in joint political and diplomatic action at the international level to ensure the withdrawal of Israeli forces from the occupied Arab territory. This is within the framework of the basic Arab commitment, which entails no recognition of Israel, no conciliation or negotiation with her, and the upholding of the rights of the Palestinian people to their land."

In a speech on September 8, 1967, Secretary Rusk emphasized that "those who live in the Middle East have the primary responsibility for finding answers and some basis on which coexistence is tolerable and that applied to both sides." There was a certain sign of resignation in his remarks, and it seems that from this moment on, the United States attempted to reach, through Resolution 242, a minimum of agreement and retreated from direct participation in negotiations with the parties (see *Department of State Bulletin* 57, no. 1474 [September 25, 1967], p. 387).

Eshkol was reported to have asked the United States, which had pressed Israel in August, 1967, to modify its initial position (since "the Arabs were modifying theirs"), to wait until after the Khartoum summit. Immediately following the summit, Washington and Jerusalem differed in their assesments of the operational meaning of the Khartoum decisions. Israel supplied the United States with internal evidence of Nasser's uncompromising stance in the closed meetings, in direct contrast to his less radical behavior in talks with Western intermediates (U.S. intelligence sources). This information may explain Secretary Rusk's above statement.

12. See Draft Resolution of the Union of Soviet Socialist Republics to the Security Council S/8252 (November 20, 1967), *Israel's Foreign Relations*, M. Medzini, ed. (Jerusalem: Ministry of Foreign Affairs, 1972), pp. 473–74. In this draft, Moscow suggested a complete Israeli withdrawal from the occupied territories and also several other principles that were rejected by the Arabs, such as the right of all states in the Middle East to exist, their territorial integrity, and innocent passage through international waterways.

13. Security Council Resolution S/242 (November 22, 1967) in *Israel's Foreign Re-*

lations, p. 474. The resolution was adopted unanimously. It speaks of "withdrawal of Israeli armed forces from territories occupied in the recent conflict." The French version speaks of "des térritories," which means "[from] the territories," and was interpreted by the Arabs and their supporters as meaning from *all the* territories.

14. Interview, March 31, 1977.
15. See M. Heikal, *The Road to Ramadan* (London: William Collins Sons and Co., 1975), p. 54. Heikal cites Nasser's argument with senior army commanders concerning Resolution 242 on November 25, 1967: "Everything you hear us say about the U.N. Resolution is not meant for you.... The Israelis ... are never going to evacuate [the occupied] areas unless they are made to do so.... What has been taken by force can only be recovered by force.... If I were Levi Eshkol or Moshe Dayan I would do the same as they, ... I don't see that even if they wanted to they could withdraw.... What they are saying now will inevitably harden into official policy and they will become bound by it. So you don't need to pay any attention to anything I may say in public about a peaceful solution." Heikal's quote should not be taken literally, as many parts of his book reveal retroactive wisdom. Yet if nothing else, it reflects certain moods and general tendencies in contemporary Arab behavior.
16. In fact, the ambassador's acceptance of Resolution 242 was decided upon between Prime Minister Eshkol and Foreign Minister Eban. Minister Begin immediately protested, and Dayan backed him, because Resolution 242 implied withdrawal from the West Bank. The cabinet could not reach a decision; it neither endorsed nor rejected the ambassador's statement. Begin's strategy at the time was to influence the cabinet to tie its own hands with regard to withdrawals short of a peace treaty in general, and especially any withdrawals from the West Bank. The split in the cabinet made it possible for Begin and Dayan to maintain that Israel, in fact, *did not* accept Resolution 242. Mr. Sapir, Mr. Eban, and Mapam ministers maintained Israel did, because the government did not repudiate the ambassador. (Prime minister's office sources.)
17. See Brecher, *Decisions*, pp. 480–81.
18. Opinions in the Israeli foreign affairs establishment differed on Ambassador Jarring's personal abilities as a mediator in the Middle East conflict. Due to its relatively less important meaning, I have omitted most of the details concerning his efforts, until late 1970, when they assumed a short-lived significance.
19. See Heikal, *Road to Ramadan*, pp. 88–89.
20. The Fath group under Yassir Arafat was established in Syria in 1964, following some earlier experiments with other Arab regimes. However, it was not allowed to operate from within Syria itself "in a manner calculated to bypass the consequences," see Pryce-Jones, *Face of Defeat*, p. 52. Fath was regarded by Nasser as too autonomous and not as ready to accept Egyptian influence as the PLO, which was established in the same year under Ahmed Shukeiry. In 1968, Nasser was ready to accept Arafat's leadership. He needed an aggressive Palestinian partner operating in Israel's rear, mainly from Jordan. Nasser allowed Arafat to take over the PLO leadership and to operate radio stations and political activities on Egyptian soil, but no direct attacks against Israel were allowed, in order not to lose control and trigger an Israeli counteraction. See "The Palestinian Question and its Political Ramifications," *Ma'arachot*, vol. 238–39, (August–September, 1974): pp. 16–19. Arafat became formally PLO chairman in 1969, after much maneuvering between Fath, now acceptable to Egypt, and other Palestinian groupings (like the PFLP under George Habash). These groups accepted an overall PLO superstructure without renouncing their own organizations. Several other organizations, including the Syrian-dominated Saika, joined under similar conditions. According to Heikal, Nasser assured Arafat that Resolution 242 was "not designed for you," *Road to Ramadan*, p. 64.
21. For a version of the Israeli-Egyptian limited war along the Suez canal from 1968–71, see L. Whetten, *The Canal War* (Cambridge, Mass.: MIT Press, 1974). For

military details, see Luttwak and Horowitz, *Israeli Army*, pp. 319–20; cf. Y. Arad, *Elef Yamim* [A thousand days] (Tel Aviv: Hoza'at Ma'arachot, 1971) (Hebrew), for the official Israeli version. Brigadier General Arad was at the time the chief Israeli army education officer.

22. Sisco interview, March 31, 1977.
23. There has been no serious research done on "Jewish money" and American politics. On the general attitude of the U.S. Congress, mainly the House of Representatives, toward Israel from the late sixties until 1976, see M. C. Feuerwerger, "Congress, Foreign Aid, and American Policy toward Israel" (Ph.D. diss., Harvard University, 1977); see also Feuerwerger's introduction to his article "Ford and Israel," *Midstream* 21, no. 8 (October, 1975): 30–36.

    On Zionist influence on Jewish voting behavior and support for Israel, see R. Silverberg, *If I Forget Thee, O Jerusalem: American Jews and the State of Israel*, (New York: William Morrow, 1970); and D. Huff, "A Study of a Successful Interest Group: The American Zionist Movement," *Western Political Quarterly* 25, no. 1 (March, 1972): 109–24.
24. See S. D. Isaacs, *Jews and American Politics*, (New York: Doubleday, 1974); and Gabriel Almond, *The American People and Foreign Policy* (New York: Praeger, 1965), p. 186.
25. See *American Jewish Yearbook*, 1968 and 1969 (Philadelphia: The Jewish Publication Society of America), and the "Jewish Agency Annual Budget," for 1967, 1968, 1969 (Jerusalem: mimeograph).
26. This was done mainly in Congress, owing to the importance of the Jewish voters to senators and representatives, to Jewish influence in the social and political environments of Congress members, and to the basic "pro-Israel" stance of both houses. For the perceptions of House members of their reasons for supporting Israel, see Feuerwerger, *American Policy toward Israel*, ch. 3.
27. Kissinger met a group of Israeli scholars in Jerusalem in February, 1968, at Major General Elad Peled's home, the writer among them. The security adviser to Governor Rockefeller was on his way home from Moscow and, probably, Paris and North Vietnam. Peled was at the time the director of Israel's Defense College, before which Professor Kissinger had lectured on U.S. and Israeli security dilemmas. In a closed lecture in 1966, Kissinger is quoted as having said, "ultimately, Israel has no choice but to rely on nuclear deterrence."
28. See Quester, "Nuclear Non-Proliferation Treaty," pp. 7–9, 44. On the advantages of an ambiguous official Israeli stance on the nuclear issue, see A. Dowty, "Israeli Perspectives on Nuclear Proliferation," in *Security, Order, and the Bomb*, ed. J. J. Holst (Oslo: Universitets Forlaget, 1972), pp. 142–51.
29. For a discussion of Israel's nuclear capability as a deterrent to Soviet involvement in the Middle East, see J. B. Bell, "Israel's Nuclear Option," *Middle East Journal* 26 (Autumn, 1972): 378–88; and A. Haselkorn, "Israel: From an Option to a 'Bomb in the Basement'?" in *Nuclear Proliferation: Phase 2*, ed. R. M. Lawrence and J. Larus (Lawrence, Kansas: University of Kansas Press, for the National Security Education Program, 1975), pp. 149–82.
30. See Rusk's official statement on the Middle East, "The Rights of the Nations," at the U.N. Assembly of October 2, 1968 (*Department of State Bulletin* 59, no. 1530 [October 21, 1968]: 408).
31. Foreign Ministry Sources. Curiously enough, the *New York Times* reported on November 21, 1968, that Israel had realized its nuclear option with a bomb.
32. According to U.S. State Department sources, the "Rusk Plan" was never approved by President Johnson, but rather was a declaration of intent, conceived by the secretary himself during the last days of the outgoing administration.
33. See Sapir's biography by A. Avneri, *Sapir* (Givatayim: Hoza'at Peleg, 1976) (Hebrew).
34. See Golda Meir's autobiography, *Hayay* [My life] (Jerusalem: Weidenfeld and Nicolson, 1975) (Hebrew). This book reveals Meir's general style and approach to politics, but her attitude toward the conflict and her behavior during her period

of office as prime minister (1969–74) are better reflected in her Hebrew press interviews and public speeches at the time.

35. See Meir's interviews and speeches. March 18, 1969: "Our fate will not be decided by foreigners," *Yediot Aharonot;* April 22, 1969: "I think that right now the defense minister is more important than the prime minister," *Yediot Aharanot;* April 16, 1969: "The world must permit Israel to seek peace in its own fashion," *Yediot Aharanot;* March 18, 1969: "Peace will come only after direct negotiations," *Yediot Aharonot.*

36. See Appendix A.

37. See Uriel Tal's in-depth analysis, "The Land and the State of Israel in Israeli Religious Life" *Rabbinical Assembly Proceedings* 38 (1976): 1–40; and Tal's "Jewish Self-Understanding and the Land and State of Israel," *Union Seminary Quarterly* 26, no. 4 (Summer, 1971): 376–81. See also chapter 3, note 3.

38. See Begin's *The Revolt* (Los Angeles: Nash Publications, 1972); cf. A. Hertzberg, *The Zionist Idea,* The Jewish Publication Society of America (New York: Meridian Books, 1960), pp. 557–70. For a recent analysis of Begin's Irgun and its ideological background, see J. Bowyer Bell, *Terror out of Zion: Irgun Zvai Leumi, Lehi, and the Palestinian Underground, 1929–49* (New York: St. Martin's Press, 1977). On Herut's slow emergence from political isolation in the early sixties, see D. Nachmias, "The Right-Wing Opposition in Israel," *Political Studies* 24, no. 3 (September, 1976), and his very useful references.

39. For the details see Brecher, *Decisions,* pp. 460–63.

40. See, for example, *Ha'aretz* (March 15, 1973), "Golda Meir Denies Palestinian Identity: Until 1967 We Didn't Hear Anything about Them."

41. Foreign office and prime minister's office sources. See also Golda Meir, "Not So Long Ago I Met with a Very Important Arab Leader Abroad," *Ma'ariv,* September 2, 1973, and Minister Galili's statement in *Ma'ariv,* July 23, 1976, "We have repeatedly made generous offers to Hussein, but he has declined."

42. See the following Israeli press reports and interviews of early 1969: Brigadier General (res.) E. Peled, "Israel Two Years after the War," *Yediot Aharonot,* April 22, 1969; Minister Begin: "The main thing is to avoid domestic weakness," *Yediot Aharonot,* April 21, 1969; The chief of staff surveyed the security horizon at the "Journalist Journal:" "Most Egyptian Officers Would Fail the Israel Defense Forces Entrance Exam," *Yediot Aharonot,* April 20, 1969; and Allon: "Military Technology is Developing More Quickly Than Arab Sociology," *Yediot Aharonot,* April 7, 1969.

43. See H. Brandon, *The Retreat of American Power* (New York: Doubleday, 1973); cf. W. L. Kohl, "The Nixon-Kissinger Foreign Policy System and U.S.-European Relations: Patterns of Policy Making," *World Politics* 28, no. 1 (October, 1975): 1–43. See also *Retreat from Empire?,* R. E. Osgood, ed. (Baltimore: The Johns Hopkins University Press, 1973); J. G. Stoessinger, *Henry Kissinger: The Anguish of Power* (New York: W. W. Norton, 1976), esp. p. 84. See also my Sisco interviews on March 31 and April 13, 1977, and my interviews with Kissinger's aides, Winston Lord (Chief, Planning Office, Department of State) and Helmut Sonnenfeldt (Councillor, Department of State), on December 12 and December 17, 1976.

44. For Kissinger's background briefings at the time, see D. Landon, *Kissinger: The Uses of Power* (London: Robson Books, 1974); cf. "United States Foreign Policy of the 1970s: Building for Peace," *Weekly Compilation of Presidential Documents* (March 1, 1971), p. 311. For a critical summary, see A. Hartley, "American Foreign Policy in the Nixon Era," *Adelphi Paper* 110, (Winter, 1974–75). For Nixon's Middle East speeches in 1969, see Medzini, *Israel's Foreign Relations,* pp. 662–63.

45. See E. O'Ballance, *Arab Guerrilla Power, 1967–72* (London: Faber, 1974); cf. Pryce-Jones, *Face of Defeat,* pp. 158–66. For the Israeli official treatment of the Jordanian-PLO complex at the time, see, for example, "Golda Meir: Order in

Jordan—Not at Our Expense," and Chief of Staff Bar-Lev: "We Shall Intervene in Certain Circumstances," *Ma'ariv*, September 27, 1970. See also Dayan's interview in *Ma'ariv*, October 4, 1970: "We are Now Stronger than the Other Side."

46. For a published analysis of the Middle East talks between Sisco and Dobrynin in Washington, and the Four-Power talks, which were conducted parallelly between their U.N. representatives in New York, see M. Brecher, "Israel and the Rogers Peace Initiative," *Orbis* 18, no. 2 (Summer, 1974): 402–26; cf. his *Decisions* pp. 454–517. See also "Negotiations among the Major Powers, April–December, 1969," in Stebbins, *Documents on American Foreign Relations, 1968–69*, p. 202, Doc 59. Cf. R. J. Pranger, "American Policy for Peace in the Middle East, 1969–1971: Problems of Principle, Maneuver, and Time," *Foreign Affairs Studies, American Enterprise Institute* (1971), pp. 9–13. The Sisco quotation is from my interview of March 31, 1977.

47. For the Israeli official reaction to the four- and two-power talks see, for example: "Dayan: The Big Four Are Indeed Big and We Are Small, But We Must Stand Firm," *Yediot Aharonot*, April 17, 1968; "Dayan: The Egyptians Don't Have the Capability to Defeat Us in the Autumn, the Spring or the Summer; If the Four-Powers Proposals Mean Suicide We Shall Have the Strength to Say No," *Yediot Aharonot* April 7, 1969; and "Begin: Sharp Differences with the United States on the Way to Peace," *Yediot Aharonot* May 7, 1969. See also "Eban: My Three Requests from the United States—to Help Maintain the Balance of Power, Deter Great Power Intervention, Remain Faithful to the Formula that Our Forces Will Not Move from Their Positions without an Agreement on Peace and Borders," *Yediot Aharonot*, January 3, 1969.

48. See Brecher, "Rogers Peace Initiative," p. 403; confirmed by Foreign Office sources.

49. For the text of Secretary Rogers' December 9th speech, see *United States Foreign Policy—Middle East, Basic Documents, 1950–1973* (Washington, D.C.: United States Government Printing Office, 1974), pp. 37–44.

50. For the official government statement, see *Jerusalem Post*, December 11, 1969; cf. D. Margalit, *Sheder min Ha'Bayit Ha'Lavan* [White House dispatch] (Tel Aviv: Hoza'at Otpaz, 1971) (Hebrew). Margalit's book is based upon primary sources (secret cabinet protocols) and extensive interviewing. His information was rechecked by me in every specific case. Information omitted by Margalit at the time, because of the censorship of state secrets on official documents, but released later, mainly by some of the principle actors (Dayan, Allon, and Eban), was reintroduced by me and will be substantiated in separate notes. The Rogers proposal had an interesting impact upon the coalition discussions between Mrs. Meir and her potential partners in the grand coalition. Mr. Begin's Gahal block, which bargained hard with the alignment after the general elections of October 28, 1969, joined the coalition without further negotiations when the proposals became known, in order to help fighting them off.

51. For an authoritative version, see *New York Times*, December 22, 1969.

52. See *Ha'aretz*, December 21, 1969.

53. "Summing up with Sisco," *Jerusalem Post Magazine*, March 26, 1976. The later quotation was taken from the March 31, 1977, interview.

54. Speaking to the Egyptian National Assembly in Cairo on November 6, 1969, Nasser rejected "political half-solutions to resolve the Middle East crisis" and declared that the Arab states had "no other alternative but to go along a road covered with blood" to recover the Arab territories occupied by Israel. He said: "The liberation should be for all Arab lands. Foremost among these are Jerusalem, the West Bank, the Gaza Strip, and the Golan Heights." Nasser charged that the United States "actually has assumed the position of our enemy," while "our friend is the Soviet Union." He claimed that the United States was arming Israel and that Americans were fighting in the ranks of the IDF. See H. H. Schulte, Jr., ed., *Facts on File* 29, no. 1515 (1969): 721.

55. GHQ sources. Cf. Margalit, *Sheder*, pp. 36–50.

56. Prime minister's office sources, and also Ambassador Rabin in briefings to the Israeli press in 1970 and later in talks with Israeli professors in March, 1974.
57. U.S. Department of Defense and White House sources.
58. For an Israeli analysis of the Soviet assistance to Egypt at the time, see I. Diamant-Kass, "The Soviet Military Policy in the Middle East, 1970–1973," *Soviet Studies* 26(4) (October, 1974): 502–21; Y. Ro'i and I. Diamant-Kass, "The Soviet Military Involvement in Egypt, January, 1970–July, 1972," The Leonard Davies Institute for International Relations (Jerusalem: Hebrew University, 1974), Research paper no. 6; "Superpower Rivalry in the Arab-Israeli Dispute: Involvement or Commitment of the USSR in the Middle East, 1973," M. Confino and Sh. Shamir, eds. (New York: John Wiley and Sons, 1973), p. 160. Accordingly, the Soviets informed the United States of their intention to deploy their air defense system in Egypt. This information is confirmed by a Rand Corporation paper, "Changing Military Perspectives in the Middle East," Rand paper RM–6355–FP, September, 1970. The problem for Washington was, of course, whether or not the Russians went beyond a "reasonable" measure of involvement in Egypt, when Soviet pilots started flying air defense missions for Egypt in forward areas.
59. See above, Note 29.
60. White House sources.
61. See Brecher, "Rogers Peace Initiatives," p. 407.
62. See Margalit, *Sheder*, pp. 78–79, confirmed by foreign ministry sources.
63. Ibid., p. 98.
64. Foreign ministry sources.
65. Mrs. Meir meant the futile Jarring mission, which practically died out in 1969 due to both sides' unchanged position. For her Knesset speech, see *Divrei Ha' Knesset* (Jerusalem: Government Printing Office, 1970), p. 1864. Begin's Gahal realized, after some angry deliberations, that Meir's tactic was meant to place the burden of intransigence on the Arabs (who would not agree to negotiate seriously, even under the terms of Resolution 242), rather than to lead to Israeli withdrawals. Gahal thus abstained, with the prime minister's consent, from the vote in parliament on Mrs. Meir's statement.
66. Prime minister's office sources. For the published documents, see Secretary Rogers' news conference on June 25, 1970, *Department of State Bulletin* 63, no. 1620 (July 13, 1970): 25 ff.
67. See Security Council Document S/9902, an American "Note to the Secretary General on the Jarring Mission, for the Information of the Security Council," of August 7, 1970, *Foreign Policy—Middle East, Basic Documents, 1950–1973*, pp. 45–46.
68. The Security Council cease-fire resolution of June 6, 1967, called for an immediate cease-fire without mentioning a return to June 5 borders. (See U.N. Document S/Res/233 [June 7, 1967], in Moore, *Arab-Israeli Conflict*, pp. 732–34.) The resolution was adopted unanimously, then was accepted by Jordan on June 7, by Egypt on June 8, and by Syria on June 9–10, 1967. The Egyptian-Israeli cease-fire had gone into effect on June 8, 1967, after Israel's occupation of the Sinai. On July 1, 1967, Israel reported that an Egyptian force of about 120 men had crossed the Suez Canal. Fighting broke out, and Egyptian and Israeli forces fought several sharp ground and air fights from July 1–9, 1967. The U.N. Security Council met in an emergency session on July 8 and approved on July 10 a proposal by Secretary General U Thant to station U.N. observers on the Suez cease-fire lines to supervise the cease-fire. In March, 1969, Nasser declared the cease-fire null and void, but the U.N. observers remained along the cease-fire lines between Egypt, Syria, and Israel.
69. For the prevailing public positions of the Israeli leadership at the time, see, for example, "Golda Meir—Not Only Have We to Keep the Cease-fire," *Davar*, September 1, 1970. "Golda Meir—Never Did I Accept a Cease-fire That Was One-sided Only," *Davar*, September 7, 1970. "Mrs. Meir—Israel Has No Intentions Whatsoever to Return to the Jarring Talks as Long as the Situation along the

Suez Canal is not Repaired," *Ma'ariv*, September 20, 1970. "Golda: I Have no Mandate to Make Concessions," *Ma'ariv*, July 2, 1970.

On the cabinet decision itself, see Minister Begin's interview, "The Right to a Homeland, and the Right to Security," *Yediot Aharonot*, August 7, 1970.

70. Prime minister's office sources, confirming Margalit, *Sheder*, pp. 132–34.

71. Ibid., p. 135.

72. Prime minister's office sources, confirming Margalit, *Sheder*, p. 136.

78. Heikal, *Road to Ramadan*, p. 94. The Soviets agreed to send SA-3 missles and are trying to *expel* the Soviet military presence, not so much of advisers, but the combat pilots and the combat personnel, before they become so firmly established."

74. See *Presidential Documents*, Foreign Policy Report 7, no. 9 (Washington, D.C.: Government Printing Office, March, 1971): 344–48.

75. See above, note 69; prime minister's office sources.

76. See *Soviet Weekly*, July 11, 1970.

77. On the Soviet-Egyptian military and political relations in 1970, see Heikal, *Road to Ramadan*, pp. 83–90, 93–95. Cf. Sadat's *Memoirs*, serialized in Kuwait newspaper, *As-Siyassah*, between October 31, 1976 and June 16, 1977, esp. November 17 and 26, 1976.

78. Heikal, *Road to Ramadan*, p. 94. The Soviets agreed to send SA-3 missiles and pilots.

79. Ibid., pp. 94–95.

80. Foreign ministry sources, confirming Brecher, "Rogers Peace Initiatives," p. 414, and his sources (*Davar*, August 2, 1970, and *Ma'ariv*, November 26, 1970). Dayan confirmed the Nixon letter for the first time in a public lecture in the Technion of Haifa in 1976, later published in *Ma'ariv* under the headline "You Can Make the Arabs Sign an Agreement in Writing Only When a Sharp Sword is at their Throats" (May 4, 1976).

81. For the most detailed story of the incident, see *Heil Ha'Avir* May/June 1976, pp. 7–11 (Hebrew).

82. Dayan to Tel Aviv high school students, in *Yediot Aharonot*, July 29, 1970.

83. See above, note 69, on Begin's published position. For the internal cabinet debates I have used prime minister's office sources. For a detailed content analysis of data and advocacy statements relating to the Rogers proposals (Meir, Dayan, Galili, Allon, and Eban), see Brecher, *Decisions*, ch. 8, and tables 24–28.

84. Foreign ministry sources.

85. Foreign ministry sources.

86. See *Jerusalem Post*, August 2, 1970; cf. Brecher, *Decisions*, p. 496 ff.

87. See *Divrei Ha'Knesset, 1970*, August 4, 1970, pp. 2755–56.

88. Foreign ministry sources.

89. GHQ sources, describing Dayan's calculations.

90. Foreign ministry sources.

91. Kalb and Kalb, *Kissinger, p.* 195.

92. See Sadat's *Memoirs*, December 16, 1976.

93. Kalb and Kalb, *Kissinger*, p. 192, cf. W. B. Quandt, "Lebanon, 1958, and Jordan, 1970," ed. B. Blechman and S. Kaplan, a research paper on the use of armed forces as a political instrument after World War II, prepared for the Foreign Policy Program, the Brookings Institution, 1977.

94. Kalb and Kalb, *Kissinger*, p. 200, as confirmed by foreign ministry sources.

95. Ibid., pp. 200–203, confirmed by White House sources.

96. In an interview with the author in Arlington, Virginia, on October 10, 1975.

97. Kalb and Kalb, *Kissinger,* p. 200, confirmed by White House sources.

98. Ibid., p. 206.

99. Washington embassy sources.

100. Kalb and Kalb, *Kissinger,* p. 209.

101. See above, note 96. Cf. Zumwalt's interview after the crisis itself in *U.S. News and World Report* (September 13, 1971), pp. 72–77, in which the admiral relates

American relative naval flexibility in 1970, which had been limited very much since the U.S. intervention in Lebanon in 1958, to Nixon's decision to *reinforce* the Sixth Fleet beyond its normal establishment during the crisis.

102. See interview with Chief of Staff Bar-Lev, in *Bamahaneh*, the Israeli army weekly (June 19, 1971) (Hebrew); cf. an interview with Major General Mordechai Hod, the IAF commander, in *Ma'ariv* (June 11, 1973). Both declared the war of attrition was won by Israel because of Egypt's military losses.

Chapter 3

1. See D. Patinkin, *The Israeli Economy: The First Decade* (Jerusalem: Falk Project for Economic Research in Israel, 1960), and D. Horowitz, *The Economics of Israel* (Oxford and New York: Pergamon Press, 1967); cf. Bank of Israel *Annual Reports*, 1968 (Jerusalem: Government Printing Office) (Hebrew and English). See also M. Michaeli, *Israel* (New York: National Bureau of Economic Research, 1975).

2. See Weizman, *Shamaim*, pp. 180–81; quotation from H.D.S. Greenwood, "An Israeli Hardliner on Threshold of Power," *Washington Post*, May 5, 1977.

3. See Uriel Tal's "Land and State of Israel," p. 13, on Rabbi Zvi Yehuda Kook, the spiritual and political leader of Gush Emunim. The "Gush" as a spiritual and political movement could, accordingly, be traced back to the immediate post-1967 period; its unique character relates to a Kook rejection of the NRP as a spiritual-religious guide. It was a political party instead, which traditionally had bargained with Mapai on the religious status quo in Israel and had adopted, under Moshe Haim Shapira, a minimalist approach to the territorial question. Rabbi Zvi Yehuda (see also one of his few public interviews, *Ha'aretz*, July 29, 1977) inherited from his late father, Rabbi Avraham Yitzhak Kook, an "organic conception" of religion, Jewish history, and territory, which he "transformed," according to Tal, "into an uncompromising political platform." Accordingly, "current reality in Israel [is seen] as the beginning of redemption . . . [or] as a more advanced stage, a real eschatological stage that possesses a mystical rythm. One of the formulations is given and promulgated by Rabbi Zvi Yehuda Kook: . . . , [people] speak of the begining of the redemption. In my opinion, this is already the *middle* of the redemption. . . . According to Rabbi Zvi Yehuda, the return to Zion, its settlement and conquest and the Kingdom of Israel being rebuilt anew. . . . This is the revelation of the Kingdom of Heaven. . . . The Israel Defense Forces are total sanctity; it represents the rule of the people of the Lord on His land. . . . We must know that the Kingdom of Heaven is being revealed in this Kingdom, even in the Kingdom of Ben-Gurion" (p. 9).

Kook's firm, seemingly clear message happened to coincide with the decline of political, socialist Labor Zionism as a solution to Jewish existential problems and as an identity factor, giving the younger generation a sense of historicity. Since Socialist Zionism rebelled against tradition, including religion, but yet was very much attached to the religious tradition and Jewish cultural-historical longing for the Land of Israel, members of the younger generation exposed to the ahistoricity and spiritual emptiness of the post-pioneering era could indeed develop an inclination toward a neoreligious approach to reality and to their claim on Eretz-Israel. See *Shana Acharei Ha'Milchama: Siach Lochamin* [A year after the war: young people talk], mimeographed (Ein Shemer, 1968) (Hebrew); see also the traditional religious-scholarly rejection of Kook's eschatology by E. E. Urbach, *On Judaism and Education* (Jerusalem: The School of Education of Hebrew University, 1967). Religious folklores and a religious way of life typical of Ashkenazi and non-Ashkenazi Jews first abandoned by the largely secular Jewish Socialist state could be revived by younger, Ashkenazi and non-Ashkenazi members of the NRP's youth movement, Bnei Akiva, which was much more open to Rabbi Kook's influence than the party's bargaining functionaries.

4. An example of this process, and of a strong rejection of Meir's and Dayan's foreign policy (especially the prolonged Israeli rule over a large Arab population), was the case of Mr. Arie Liova Eliav, Secretary General of the alignment after Mrs. Meir. In the early 1970s he voluntarily resigned and became an outspoken opponent of Meir's foreign and Sapir's domestic policies. See Eliav's book *Eretz Ha'Zvi* [Land of Heart] (Tel Aviv: Hoza'at Am Oved, 1972). Eliav resigned from the alignment after the Yom Kippur War and joined several left-wing combinations. See also J. L. Talmon, *Israel among the Nations* (London: Weidenfeld and Nicholson, 1970); Talmon offers a liberal humanistic analysis of Israel's cultural and historical dilemmas.

5. This process relates first, among other phenomena, to the unique role played by the two mass-circulated afternoon papers, *Yediot Aharonot* and *Ma'ariv*, in shaping Israel's public opinion after the "Lavon Affair." *Ma'ariv* was influenced by a group of former Jabotinsky followers, Polish-born Zionists who later generally backed Ben-Gurion's style and bold gestures until the withdrawal from the Sinai in 1957. Even afterwards, until the "Affair," the paper used to refrain from criticizing Ben-Gurion and his regime. Later it started to play a growing role as a conservative-hawkish, sometimes histerical, but at the same time well-informed opinion maker. After 1967 *Ma'ariv* supported more and more a strong, anticoncession, pro-settlement, autonomous line, disclosing real American pressures or warning against imposed solutions. It started publishing right-wing columns (by Moshe Shamir and Eliezer Livne, who had moved to the right from former Socialist and even far left positions) together with left wing ones. The same process was followed by *Ma'ariv*'s main commercial rival, *Yediot Aharonot*, which opened its pages to the columns of the Stern gang ideologist, Dr. Israel Sheib, and extreme conservative-hawkish writers of a less spectacular past and polemic style, and to far left critics of Meir and Dayan's regiment, like Amos Keynan. A very interesting role has been played in both papers after 1967 by conservative-hawkish women columnists.

6. See Brigadier General J. Raviv, "Early Experiments toward an Interim Agreement between Israel and Egypt," *Ma'arachot* 243–44, April–May, 1975, pp. 2–17. Raviv was at the time (1971–72) Dayan's adjutant general.

7. Ministry of Defense sources.

8. See a report by John Kimche, a reliable Dayan "spokesman" abroad, in the London *Evening Standard*, November 3, 1970; cf. *Davar*, November 4, 1970.

9. Foreign ministry instructions to Israel's foreign missions abroad, and November 6, 1970, quoted by Raviv, *Interim Agreement*, p. 6.

10. Ibid., p. 7.

11. Sadat's speeches (a Hebrew translation of the Egyptian President's major public speeches), on file at The Shiloah Center of Middle Eastern and African Studies, Tel Aviv University.

12. *Newsweek*, February 15, 1971.

13. For the complete text of Dr. Jarring's letters and the replies of Israel and Egypt (Israel's position as conveyed to Dr. Jarring on February 26, 1971), see Medzini, *Israel's Foreign Relations*, pp. 498–535.

14. Prime minister's office sources.

15. Cf. Sadat, *Memoirs*, December 16, 1976: "when I asked for 'a peace agreement,' I did not mean a 'peace treaty.' The difference between the two is very large. What I meant was a 'test of intentions' . . . whether they [Israel] were sincere about what they offered us. . . . Furthermore, . . . it is the United States which is . . . behind Israel. . . . Nasser realized this fact very belatedly."

16. File, The Shiloah Center.

17. See "Sadat on the Russians: 'They didn't Want to Help,'" *Newsweek*, August 7, 1972. Cf. Sadat, *Memoirs*, December 16, 1976: "Here . . . the Soviets said, 'We will give you the offensive weapon . . . provided it is operated by orders from the Soviet Union.' I said . . . 'Nasser had offered to accept Soviet missile crews and that the commander of the [Egyptian] air force would be a Soviet officer. He also

offered to enter into a treaty and you said no. He told you, "Let us make the treaty an alliance," that is ... Nasser had offered to join the Warsaw Pact.' They said, "This is very true.' I said, 'I reject this offensive aircraft.' "

18. See Y. Nimrod, "Israel and Nuclear Weapons," *Davar*, April 13, 1976. Mr. Nimrod is an Arab expert for the Mapam party.

19. Sadat's difficulties with the Russians may have been further connected with the coup attempt against President Nimeiry of Sudan in July, 1971. The coup was supported, if not inspired, by Sudanese communists, and thus was regarded by Sadat as a Soviet-backed attempt against a "legitimate" sister Arab regime. See Heikal, *Road to Ramadan*, pp. 122–143.

20. UPI dispatch from Cairo on April 8, 1971. Quoted in Raviv, *Interim Agreement*, p. 7.

21. For a summary of the Egyptian press on April 2, 1971, see ibid., p. 8.

22. Israeli intelligence sources.

23. Prime minister's office sources.

24. Hebrew translation quoted in Raviv, *Interim Agreement*. For the English version, see *New York Times*, May 26, 1971.

25. See Sadat's two speeches before the Arab Socialist Union conference on July 18, 1972, and July 24, 1972 (File, Shiloah Center).

26. The 1971 war between India and Pakistan, in which the Soviet Union was involved as the main source of India's military effort, was described by Sadat in a speech in early 1972 as the reason behind Soviet reluctance to supply Egypt during the "year of decision." (File, Shiloah Center).

27. See Sadat, *Memoirs*, December 23, 1976.

28. See Sadat's speech of September 16, 1971 (File, Shiloah Center).

29. Dinitz interview, Washington, D.C., June 10, 1977.

30. See details of Meir's *aide mémoire* to the U.S. Ambassador Barbour of April 10, 1971, in Raviv, *Interim Agreement*. Cf. Dayan's Israeli T.V. interview on May 14, 1971, printed in *Ha'aretz*, May 16, 1971.

31. Foreign ministry sources.

32. See Sadat's speeches (File, Shiloah Center).

33. For Sadat's initial contacts with Arab leaders after his inauguration, see Heikal, *Road to Ramadan*, pp. 114–47, which contains also a description of the Ali Sabri affair; cf. *Memoirs*, December 23, 1976.

34. In 1971 the English version, *Israel and Nuclear Weapons: Present Options and Future Strategies*, was published in London for the International Institute for Strategic Studies. According to Mr. Jabber, now (1977) assistant professor of political science at UCLA, the Arabic version was published later.

35. *New York Times*, July 22, 1970.

36. In November, 1973, Heikal, who lost his ministerial position under Sadat but retained his position as editor of the semiofficial newspaper, *Al-Ahram*, and maintained a critical approach toward Sadat's foreign policy, was much more explicit on the nuclear issue. According to a *New York Times* report on November 24, Heikal expressed his conviction that Israel had nuclear weapons and might use them as a "psychological blackmail" against the Arabs. He was quoted as having written, in *Al-Ahram* on November 23, that the Arab world needed "to build, buy, or borrow nuclear weapons to deter Israel."

37. Heikal, *Road to Ramadan*, pp. 155–56.

38. Ibid., pp. 76–77.

39. Ibid., pp. 167-68.

40. *Memoirs*, December 16, 1976.

41. See "Golda Meir: It Is Absurd to Demand That Israel Pay for the Opening of the Suez Canal," *Ha'aretz*, April 5, 1971; "Mrs. Meir: The Next Step by Egypt," *Ha'aretz*, April 28, 1971.

42. See Secretary of State Rogers' address before the 26th session of the United Nations General Assembly, October 4, 1971, *United States Foreign Policy, Middle East: Basic Documents*, pp. 51–54.

43. Raviv, *Interim Agreement*, p. 10.
44. See Heikal, *Road to Ramadan*, p. 156. During the October visit Egypt received some items, probably subsonic Kelt missiles carried by TU-16 bombers, which had been refused by the Soviets earlier. According to Sadat's memoirs, his diplomatic overtures toward the United States were synchronized with Soviet supplies: he accelerated his diplomatic efforts before actually receiving missiles or other items (rather than promises) and calmed down while absorbing them, then renewed his diplomatic efforts in anticipation of new shipments (*Memoirs,* December 16, 1976).
45. Hebrew translation in Raviv, *Interim Agreement,* p. 10.
46. Kalb and Kalb, *Kissinger,* p. 208.
47. Prime minister's office sources.
48. Prime minister's office sources.
49. Raviv, *Interim Agreement,* p. 11.
50. Heikal, *Road to Ramadan,* pp. 157–59. This time, Heikal reports, Egypt was given the TU-22 bomber to replace the obsolete TU-16 and the T-62 tank.
51. Cf. *Memoirs,* January 7, 1977, according to which this meeting with the Soviets was, in fact, "the turning point in [Soviet-Egyptian] relations," because Sadat received only "a promise for certain old missiles" (probably short-range Frog ballistic missiles), when he wanted the longer range surface-to-surface Scud missile.
52. See Hartley, *Nixon Era,* pp. 5, 18–19. For a critical review, see G. Liska, *Beyond Kissinger: Ways of Conservative Statecraft* (Baltimore and London: The Johns Hopkins University Press, 1975), pp. 89–104.
53. On Nixon's Moscow visit, and especially on SALT 1, see J. Newhouse, *Cold Down* (New York: Holt, Rinehart and Winston, 1973). See also E. A. Kolodziej, "Foreign Policy and the Politics of Interdependence: The Nixon Presidency," *Polity* 9, no. 2 (Winter, 1976): 121–58 and his detailed bibliography.
54. My interviews with Lord and Sonnenfeldt, December, 1976, and a conversation with Kissinger's personal aide, Peter Rodman, in Washington, D.C. on April 29, 1977.
55. This refers to Kissinger's well-known notion that "Power no longer translates automatically into influence" (*American Foreign Policy: Three Essays* [New York: Norton, 1969], p. 60).
56. Ibid., p. 93.
57. See "Agreements signed during General Secretary Brezhnev's visit to the United States," June 18-22, *Department of State Bulletin* 69, no. 1778, pp. 158–75; see also ibid., pp. 114–29; cf. *Current History* 65 (October, 1973), pp. 173–77.
58. See "Presidential Assistant Kissinger discusses agreements signed, transcripts of news conferences," June 21–22, 25, *Department of State Bulletin,* pp. 134–57; cf. Kalb and Kalb, *Kissinger,* pp. 438–42.
59. See *Presidential Documents* 9, July 2, 1973, and the *New York Times* news analysis for the first week in July.
60. According to Sisco (March 31, 1977, interview), Kissinger agreed first to a more far-reaching Palestinian clause in Moscow related to a possible Russian effort to restrain Hanoi subordinating this clause to his desired "global package" with the Soviets. Sisco realized that the national security adviser was not acquainted with the details and the code language of the Middle East conflict, and brought about a milder formulation than the original, which Kissinger and the president were ready to accept.
61. Transcript of the Nixon-Frost interview of May 12, 1977, *New York Times,* May 13, 1977.
62. An interesting example is a lecture delivered by Professor Herbert Spiro, at the time a State Department official, at the International Political Science Association congress at Montreal, Canada, in August, 1973. Spiro referred to the U.S.-Soviet relations as consolidated and further based upon a tacit agreement to refrain from involvement in regional conflicts, which would endanger the rela-

tions between them. Professor Carl Deutsch commented, saying that the super-powers may have won time, "say, 20–30 years. But what would happen later, when the poor, and those who have nothing to lose, would have access to power and means of destruction?"

63. The Jackson amendment was passed by the House of Representatives on September 25, by a vote of 306 to 4.

64. Kohl, "Nixon-Kissinger Foreign Policy System," pp. 33–34.

65. In a letter to the author, September 1974.

66. See Sadat's *Memoirs,* January 7, 1977: "All of a sudden a magician emerged on the international political stage.... He beat the hat with the stick and a rabbit came out. This rabbit was called détente between Russia and the United States. ... This was a surprise." See also the January 19, 1977, section of the memoirs, relating to the Moscow détente agreement: "I was not optimistic. What could the Soviets possibly say after the 'détente' statement ... about a new thing called 'military relaxation' ... [regarding] all that was said or asked? [to the Arabs and by the Arabs]"

67. From 1948 through 1969, approximately 7,600 Soviet Jews emigrated to Israel. After 1970, emigration to Israel increased dramatically. Since 1973, however, that emigration has fallen off. The approximate figures shown below indicate the numbers of Soviet exit visas for Israel issued to Soviet citizens: 1,000 in 1970; 14,000 in 1971; 31,500 in 1972; 33,500 in 1973; 20,000 in 1974; 13,000 in 1975; and 14,000 in 1976 (Source: "Soviet Jewish Emigration," *GIST,* Bureau of Public Affairs, Department of State, Washington, D.C., July, 1977).

According to Heikal, Sadat first mentioned Jewish emigration from the Soviet Union to Israel in a letter to Brezhnev on April 12, 1970. In this letter Sadat wrote explicitly that, "any new [Soviet-] American policy would be against our interests" (*Road to Ramadan,* p. 169). Heikal later quotes the following short conversation he had with Sadat on détente: "One day I said to [the president], 'I'm afraid it looks as though détente is going to become a reality and impose itself on us before we can impose ourselves on it. The détente will set conditions for the Middle East problem instead of the Middle East problem setting conditions for the détente.' [Sadat answered], 'Maybe we will just be able to catch the last part of the tail of the détente'" (pp. 205–6). Between April and June, Sadat and Brezhnev continued an exchange of positions, in which the Egyptian president complained that arms deliveries were delayed and that the United States was more firmly behind Israel than the Soviet Union was behind the Arabs (pp. 169–70). On the expulsion of the Soviet personnel itself, see below.

68. See Liska, *Beyond Kissinger,* pp. 69–70.

69. Kissinger, *American Foreign Policy,* p. 88.

70. A summary of Sadat's two speeches of July 18 and July 24, 1972 (in the Shiloah Center File), follows:

Sadat reported on his other trips to Moscow. All of them dealt with arms supplies. He revealed in detail the contents of his Moscow talks in April, 1972, his fourth visit to the Soviet Union, when his aim was to define a common position with the Soviet leaders before the Nixon visit to Moscow. He emphasized three issues: (a) the rejection of the limitation of arms supplies to the Middle East at this stage, "because it served Israel, which possessed stocks of weapons and continued to occupy our territory;" (b) the rejection of any agreement for the continuation of the no peace, no war situation, "because this means that Israel would gain in the long run;" (c) the rejection of relinquishing any Arab territory.

Sadat then said: "After we received the Soviet explanation of Nixon's talks with the Soviet leaders, I felt, in the light of this, the need for a pause (*waqfah* in Arabic) with the friend." Sadat said that this "pause" was taking place in the framework of the Egyptian-Soviet friendship, and that there was no need for "hysteria." Sadat's decision was composed of three elements: (a) the termination of the mission of the Soviet military experts and advisers as of July 17 (already implemented at the time of the speech); (b) transfer of all military equipment and installations to the Egyptian army (already implemented, but in another part of his speech Sadat mentions only the first decision as "already implemented"); (c) the calling for an Egyptian-Soviet meeting in the framework of the Friendship Treaty.

In the second part of his speech Sadat reviewed at length the international political situation, giving more time to an analysis of U.S. policy than in all the previous speeches. He accused the United States of maintaining, together with Israel, the following three principles: (a) preventing the implementation of Resolution 242 compelling Israel to retreat to the June 4 borders; (b) preventing the imposition of any settlement of the crisis that was not the result of direct negotiations between Israel and the Arabs; (c) maintaining Israel's military supremacy in all circumstances. These were according to "pledges" the United States had made, which directed U.S. policy in the Middle East. Sadat analyzed the political and diplomatic moves since 1967, and came to the conclusion that "the U.S. attitude is the serious attitude in the crisis, and not the Soviet attitude. The serious attitude is the U.S. attitude, and it will remain the U.S. attitude."

Turning back to the Soviet Union, Sadat said that Moscow had supported Egypt politically, economically, and militarily, but that their assessments of attitudes differed.

> They are undoubtedly a big power with commitments, conditions, responsibilities, and so on. They also have their own way of calculating situations and their strategy, and we have our own problems, strategies, and calculations. . . . Perhaps to them the Middle East problem is not the most important problem. It certainly is not the most important problem. But to me, the problem of the occupation of the territory and the Middle East problem is not only the most important problem, but it is also sleep, life, food, waking hours, and water. It is my problem. It is the problem of my occupied territory. That is why I said there would be differences.

Sadat especially criticized the fact that when he proposed to the Soviet Union a common strategy, they did not reject it, but gave him reassurances. "The Soviet Union reassures me. It does not say no. It reassures, reassures, and reassures, but in the end I look around at what is being implemented and find myself in a whirlpool and unable to control events." Sadat repeated that the Soviet position was that of a friend who was trying to exploit it, "but I will not respond to this exploitation at all, in any form." The United States, however, helped Sadat's enemy with everything it possessed, so that, according to Sadat the "most essential duty" was to confront the United States. Elaborating on this last idea, how the United States could be confronted by the Arab world on a national level, he stated that because of the fact that the United States possessed the means to put pressure on Israel, and because of the fact that the Arabs possessed the means to put pressure on the United States, he would not keep silent, but would try to coordinate the Arab "values" economically, strategically, and politically." See also G. Golan, *Yom Kippur and After: The Soviet Union and the Middle East Crisis*, (Cambridge: Cambridge University Press, 1977), pp. 21–28.

71. See Heikal's report on the three secret meetings held on February 24–25, 1973, between Kissinger and the Egyptian president's national security adviser, General Hafez Ismail, in Connecticut (*Road to Ramadan*), p. 202.

72. Dinitz interview, June 10, 1977.

73. Ministry of Defense sources.

74. These "on-going supplies" were promised to Mrs. Meir again, in her February–March visit to the United States (embassy sources in Washington). Mrs. Meir followed Hafez Ismail to the United States and the news about the new American-Israeli arms deal brought about a "great disillusionment on the Egyptian side" (Heikal, *Road to Ramadan*, p. 203). In fact, her visit had been preplanned, and Ismail was probably sent in advance to circumvent an American-Israeli arms agreement.

75. Embassy sources in Washington, confirmed by Pentagon sources.
76. GHQ sources; cf. Major General Shumuel Gonen's Israeli T.V. interview on June 17, 1976, with details in *Ma'ariv* June 18. Gonen was the G.O.C. southern front between July and mid-October, 1973.
77. Interview on June 17, 1977 with Major General Avraham Adan, at the time G.O.C. armored corps (at the time of the interview Israeli military attaché, Washington, D.C.)
78. Interview with Lieutenant General David Elazar, Chief of the General Staff between December, 1972, and February, 1974 (Tel Aviv, October 11, 1974).
79. Ibid.
80. See "Report of the Commission of Inquiry: the Yom Kippur War," The Agranat Commission (Tel Aviv: Hoza'at Am Oved, 1974), pp. 4, 196–200. The commission was named after its chairman, Justice Shimon Agranat.
81. Military intelligence sources.
82. See, for example, Sadat's speech to naval officers in Alexandria on July 29, 1972; cf. his speech of October 15, 1972, before the people's assembly (File, Shiloah Center).
83. For a survey of Dayan's statements, see Z. Klein, "The War: a Surprise or a Trap?," *State, Government, and International Relations* 6 (Fall, 1974): 127–42; cf. Z. Schiff, "Could a Surprise War be Repeated?," *Ha'aretz*, September 8–9, 1977.
84. The "Skyhawk Case," i.e., the Israeli decision to buy a large number of aircraft (which proved to be incapable of supporting ground forces in missile areas already in the end phase of the "War of Attrition") instead of investing in a modern artillery force, is regarded by military experts such as Edward N. Luttwak as one of the reasons for Israel's setbacks in October, 1973 (Luttwak interview, Washington, D.C., February, 1977).
85. Dayan repeated such statements several times after the Russians left Egypt. A public declaration to this effect was made before cadets of the National Defense College on September 11, 1972 (see Schiff, "Surprise War," and *Ha'aretz*, July 24, 1973).
86. The platform, drafted by Galili, was interpreted as a major victory for Dayan, who made it clear that the new settlements provided for in the document must all be inside Israel when the final borders were decided upon. The major provisions of the document include the following:
    a.   The development of new Israeli settlements in the occupied territories (Israel Radio reported 35 additional settlements);
    b.   The authorization of the Israel Lands Authority to acquire real estate in the occupied territories by "every effective means, including through companies and individuals who will buy land in coordination with the Authority;"
    c.   The creation of a special cabinet committee to approve the purchase of land in the territories by individuals and private companies for "constructive and not speculative purposes;"
    d.   The acquisition of additional land by the government to the south and east of Jerusalem for the continued development of the capital;
    e.   The development of a regional center—Yamit, the nucleus of a future city—at the southern end of the Gaza Strip (800 housing units by 1977–78);
    f.   Development of a major industrial zone near Kalkilyah and Tulkarem, in the West Bank;
    g.   Further projects, like an industrial center on the Golan Heights, a regional center in the Jordan Valley, and improvements on the northeastern shore of the Lake Tiberias, as well as on the northwestern shore of the Dead Sea;
    h.   A major program to improve and develop the roads, services, hospitals, and schools of the West Bank and Gaza. (The program was presented without stating any details of its financing. Finance Minister Sapir, who did not belong to the supporters of the document, announced, however, that he was willing to grant 300 million Israeli pounds to finance the program.)

Two days later Foreign Minister Eban, another leading Israeli dove, stated that the Galili document on the territories "changed nothing" (Eban had been abroad when it was accepted). He dismissed the document, saying "It does not bind anyone as it stands . . . and it certainly does not contain anything that justifies all these meetings." (He referred to the great number of inner party meetings that preceded the adoption and in which he was not present or consulted sufficiently). According to Eban, the Galili document added nothing to the "oral law" of 1969. Dayan immediately rejected Eban's interpretation of the document, claiming that it represented a major turning point in the party's stand on the policy in the occupied territories. (For the document, see *Ha'aretz* and *Ma'ariv*, August 23, 1973; for Eban's and Dayan's statements, see *Jerusalem Post*, August 23, 1973. See also "Dayan: In the years to come we shall build a new Israel and expand Jerusalem in every direction," *Yediot Aharonot*, October 3, 1973). After the Yom Kippur War, Finance Minister Sapir said that Dayan won the party battle using "blackmail methods."

87. Israel repeated to the presidents its formula—direct negotiations and no return to the June 4, 1967, borders—whereas the presidents recommended a complete withdrawal as a precondition for a political settlement (Foreign ministry sources. This is also the source for the above description of the Algiers Conference).
88. Foreign ministry sources, and Dinitz interview, June, 1977.
89. Kissinger, *American Foreign Policy*, p. 69. About Kissinger's early attitude toward Israel, see Kalb and Kalb, *Kissinger*, p. 525: "In 1947, as a Harvard freshman, he had shared the Establishment view that the creation of a separate Jewish state in the Middle East would be, as he later put it, a potential historic disaster. He believed, at the time, that the Zionists would have been 'better off forming a federal state with Jordan.' Once he visited Israel and stayed for a couple of days in a Jordan Valley kibbutz, near the Syrian border, he changed his mind. The Jews had established a state, against all probability. They had performed a miracle. Privately and professionally, he was determined to help it survive."
90. Ibid., p. 191. Cf. E. R. F. Sheehan, "Step by Step in the Middle East," *Foreign Policy* (Spring, 1976), pp. 3–70, especially p. 9. Sheehan's article was released with official State Department support just before Matti Golan's much publicized anti-Kissinger version (see note 93). Sheehan's article is also available as a book: *The Arabs, Israelis, and Kissinger: A Secret History of American Diplomacy in the Middle East* (New York: Readers Digest Press, 1976).
91. Kalb and Kalb, *Kissinger*, p. 463: "Overnight, this . . . Arab assault . . . shook Kissinger's assumption that the spirit of détente would encourage the Soviet Union to use its influence . . . to head off war." See also p. 525.
92. Ibid.
93. GHQ and foreign ministry sources. On the Meir-Kissinger exchange of cables on the eve of the war, see also M. Golan, *Ha'Sichot Ha'Sodiot shel Henry Kissinger* [Kissinger's secret conversations] (Jerusalem: Hoza'at Schocken, 1976), pp. 40–44. Golan's book is also available in English: *The Secret Conversations of Henry Kissinger: Step by Step Diplomacy in the Middle East* (New York: Quadrangle/New York Times Book Co., 1976).
94. Elazar, in an interview with the writer on October 11, 1974; cf. the Agranat Commission report, p. 5.
95. Foreign ministry and prime minister's office sources.
96. See the Agranat Commission report, pp. 4–10; see also Elazar interview, October 1974.
97. Elazar to the author; cf. U. Milstein, "Talks with Lieut. General (res.) David Elazar," *Davar Hashavua*, May 7, 1976: "Dayan was not sure whether a war would indeed break out, and he resented a dramatic mobilization on Yom Kippur. He feared that our mobilization would become known in the world and we would be blamed for having started the war. He believed that our regular forces, deployed along the borders, plus the air force, would be able to curb any attack."

98. A member of the cabinet to the author, on February 20, 1974.
99. General Shumuel Gonen to the author, on March 2, 1974. This refers to the first discussion on October 3, 1973, between the members of a small circle of senior ministers—Dayan, Allon, Galili, and Meir—on a possible Arab attack. Most of this meeting was devoted to an intelligence report made by Brigidier General Arie Shalev, who conveyed to the senior ministers his superiors' assessment that Egypt and Syria were conducting maneuvers. The superior, Major General Eliahu Zeira, was sick and did not attend the last meeting.

   The government's attention was very much diverted at the time by an Arab terrorist attack on a train that carried Soviet Jews to Austria. The attack brought about a decision by Chancellor Bruno Kreisky of Austria to change arrangements for Jewish transit passengers from the Soviet Union. Mrs. Meir went to Vienna to protest to Kreisky over that; her arguments failed and she returned on October 2, to Israel, to start campaigning for the October 31 elections. Her party's most important election slogan was about the "continued calm along the borders."
100. Elazar, on October 3 (Paratrooper Day): "The enemy should know that the IDF has long arms. When they reach him, they turn to fists" (Ha'aretz, October 4, 1973).
101. See, for example, H. Herzog, Milchemet Yom Ha'Din [The war of atonement] (Jerusalem: Hoza'at Edanim, 1975), available in English as The War of Atonement (London: Weidenfeld and Nicolson, 1975); and Z. Schiff, Reidat Adama Be'October [Earthquake in October] (Tel Aviv: Hoza'at Bittan Medan, 1974). The primary sources for a detailed history of the war, the unpublished parts of the Agranat Commission report and the inquiries made by, or gathered by, the Historical Branch, GHQ, IDF are classified as state secrets for the next thirty years.
102. General Adan interview, July, 1977. The Egyptians were expected to have serious difficulties in overcoming the sand rampart erected along the canal by IDF engineers during the war of attrition. Tank fire along the canal should have seriously interfered with Egyptian efforts to build bridges and to move troops along the canal.
103. IAF sources.
104. Major General Israel Tal, Chief of Operations under Elazar, and Major General Ariel Sharon, O. C. southern command between 1972 and July, 1973, emphasized the role of the armor placed between the strongholds rather than the strongholds themselves. Sharon closed some of them and removed the paratroopers, replacing them with second class reservists. Major General Shumuel Gonen, who took office as Sharon's successor three months before the war, also tended to accept this. Elazar preferred a relatively small Israeli presence along the canal and a concentrated armored force behind the strongholds, which would seek the main thrust of the enemy invading force and destroy it (Elazar to the author, October, 1974).
105. Gonen to the author, March, 1974. The Egyptians were very quick to cross the canal and could move large bodies of troops because of their success in also breaking down the sand ramparts with powerful water cannons. Instead of concentrating its attack on the large Egyptian concentrations around the bridges, the IAF wasted its effort on the bridges themselves, which were quickly repaired (IAF sources).
106. GHQ sources: Gonen's staff interviewing, April–May 1974; Sharon's and Adan's staff interviewing, June–July, 1974, and June, 1977.
107. Gonen to the author, March 1974: cf. Dayan, Avnei Derech, pp. 596–98.
108. See Herzog, Yom Ha'Din, p. 113; cf. Dayan's cabinet speech on October 6, at 10 p.m.: "I did not share [Gonen and Elazar's] optimism. The Egyptians had achieved by now an enormous success, and we were badly molested. They bridged and crossed, and we not only did not prevent them from doing so, but we almost did not punish them. . . . I was tortured by the question, 'What happened?' Was our concept wrong, or its implementation? What happened to the three main ele-

ments—the armor, the air force, and the strongholds—that should have interfered with the crossing and severely punished the invading enemy? . . . In the
meantime, the crossing became a fact. . . . I was tired and tense. I realized that
a gap had opened between the cabinet and me. My words about the successful
crossing, my emphasis upon our ability to hold a second, rather than the first, canal
line, were disliked by those present. . . . I said that I distinguished between Israel
and the Sinai. . . . The advantage is that the battle with Egypt takes place in the
desert, not in the real Eretz-Israel, with its civilian population" (*Avnei Derech*,
p. 581).

109. See Ch. Wakebridge, "The Syrian Side of the Hill," *Military Review* (February,
1976), pp. 20–30.

> "At dawn on the 7th . . . the Syrians moved forward again, having by this time
> some 900 tanks and 840 guns [against roughly 100 Israeli tanks and a dozen
> artillery pieces], on the plateau . . . until they were ordered to halt at 1700 that
> evening. By then [most of the southern and central sectors of the Golan Heights]
> had been taken, and one unit of some 30 tanks had reached the customs
> house . . . only four miles short of the Benot Ya'akov bridge over the Jordan
> River. . . . When ordered to halt the Syrian units were just fanning out [in the
> broader, southern and central sectors] toward the Jordan River. . . . Since the
> edge of the rim overlooking the upper Jordan Valley was within reach of some
> Syrian units, this decision to halt is one of the most inexplicable and intriguing
> one of the war. . . . The [Syrian] plan called for the bombing of the Benot
> Ya'akov bridge at H-hour, to be immediately followed by insertion of com-
> mandos by helicopter to deny [this main supply and reinforcement line] from
> the Israelis. General Tlass [the Syrian chief of staff, in an interview with Wake-
> bridge] admitted this omission, but would not discuss it except to say that he
> considered the Jordan River to be the natural Syrian boundary. An initial seiz-
> ure of the bridge would have severely hampered Israeli reinforcement tanks,
> vehicles, and guns. . . . one of the main unanswered questions of the war was
> why the Syrians halted at 1700 on the 7th, when some of their thrusts might
> well have succeeded in reaching the Jordan River. There was little in the way
> of Israeli defense to stop them. . . . Tlass . . . admitted such an order, . . . hesi-
> tated, and said that the time had not yet come to discuss the reasons for it."

110. GHQ sources.

111. Dinitz interview, June, 1977.

112. For the Egyptian-Libyan futile merger plan, which preceded the Egyptian-Saudi
entente, see Heikal, *Road to Ramadan*, pp. 184–98. It seems that one of the reasons
for the failure of the merger plan was Khaddafi's bid for a general war, backed by
nuclear weapons, to destroy Israel. This meant a relatively long period of no
Arab military activity (except for the Palestinian organizations) until they acquired the bomb. Sadat did not have that time, and after the summer of 1971, he
developed the notion of a "limited war" which could be fought relatively soon if
the Russians (at the time Khaddafi's traditional enemies) would supply the necessary conventional weapons.

113. See "President Sadat interviewed on May 15 Anniversary," Middle East News
Agency, Cairo, May 16, 1977 (U.S. State Department translation). The whole
OPEC cartel, and mainly Iran, was eager to obtain higher oil prices, and would
exploit any Arab political move for its members' economic benefit. On the background of the oil embargo and the price increase afterwards, see, for example, S.
Krasner, "The Great Oil Sheikdown," *Foreign Policy* 13 (Winter, 1973–74):
123–38; W. J. Lewy, "An Atlantic-Japanese Energy Policy," *Foreign Policy* 11
(1973); cf. Ch. Issawi, "Oil, the Middle East, and the World," *The Washington
Papers* (Washington, D.C.: Sage Publications, 1972).

114. See Heikal, *Road to Ramadan*, p. 204, and Sadat's *Memoirs*, January 26, 1977.

115. See Kissinger, *American Foreign Policy*, p. 93, cf. pp. 79–80, 206–7, 209.

116. See Heikal, *Road to Ramadan*, pp. 204–5: "Since 1967 the credibility of the

whole regime had been at stake. . . . After the anti-climatic year of decision, the youth exploded. . . . The army had been in state of almost complete mobilization. . . . By 1973, Egypt had almost become the laughing stock of the Arab world. We claimed to be the leader and protector of the Arabs, but gave no lead to our own people and showed ourselves unable to protect our own territory. We asked others to use their oil weapons. Each day that passed was a day of humiliation for Egypt."

117. Ibid., p. 199.
118. The hurried evacuation became known to the Israelis, but no consequences were drawn, since an Arab war without Russian advisers seemed to be even more unlikely (GHQ sources).
119. GHQ sources; see Golan, Yom Kippur, pp. 85–86; according to her analysis, "Moscow decided to send arms . . . in response to the first signs of [Arab] retreat . . . to prevent a serious Arab defeat and obtain credit in the eyes of the Arabs."
120. Sadat's speech before the Arab Socialist Union conference, April 4, 1974 (File, Shiloah Center); cf. the detailed section in the Memoirs, February 3, 1977.
121. The IAF launched several aerial attacks against Damascus and other Syrian cities, mainly against industrial and oil targets there, following a Syrian missile attack against an IAF base. The short-range Russian-made Frog missiles landed first on two Israeli towns, and caused civilian casualties. Thus, the IAF was ordered to attack military targets in a civilian area, like the Damascus International Airport, which served incoming Russian transport planes, and the Syrian general staff and air force staff buildings in Damascus (IAF sources). Golan (Yom Kippur, p. 86) links the bombing with the Soviet air lift, as an immediate sign of Arab needs for which Brezhnev was waiting, in order to give the green light for an operation already prepared.
122. Tass dispatch from Moscow, October 13, 1973. The Israeli navy was able to contain the Syrian and Egyptian navies to their ports, and constantly attacked them there, simultaneously bombarding off-shore targets. The Soviet ship was hit during an attack on Tartus harbor on October 11 (GHQ sources; cf. Golan, Yom Kippur, pp. 94–95).
123. Israel indeed refrained from attacking Egyptian cities, except Port Said, which had been practically deserted since the 1969 war of attrition. After the Israeli crossing, on October 15, the Egyptians launched two Scuds into the Israeli bridgehead on the west side of the canal; their AA missile system was partially destroyed by the Israeli ground forces and the IAF controlled the air around the area. The Scuds did not cause any harm (IAF sources).
124. U.S. Department of Defense sources, and Mr. Joseph Alsop in a letter to the author on January 11, 1976.
125. On Kissinger's notes to Brezhnev on October 7, reminding him of the two détente communiqués pledging "the two superpowers . . . to do everything in their power so that conflicts or situations will not arise which would serve to increase international tensions," see Kalb and Kalb, Kissinger, p. 463. For the Secretary's public speech of October 8, 1973, before the Center for Democratic Organization Research, see New York Times, October 9, 1973.
126. Sisco Interview, March, 1977, and Rodman conversation, April 29, 1977.
127. Prime minister's office and embassy sources in Washington.
128. Ibid.
129. E. Luttwak and W. Laqueur, "Kissinger and the Yom Kippur War," Commentary, 58, no. 3 (1974): 33–40; cf. Golan, Hasichot, pp. 47–63.
130. Sisco and Dinitz interviews, and Rodman conversation. Cf. W. B. Quandt, "Kissinger and the Arab-Israeli Disengagement Negotiations," Journal of International Affairs 9, no. 1 (1975): 37. According to Quandt, Israel's request for a "cease-fire in place" on October 12 delayed the airlifting. My impression is that it enhanced it.
131. Initially, the crossing operation ran into the most serious technical difficulties, and at first the bridging equipment could not reach the canal because of a fierce re-

sistance in the rear of the Second Egyptian Army. See Herzog, *Yom Ha'Din,* p. 212; cf. Dayan, *Avnei Derech,* pp. 642–46.

132. Heikal, *Road to Ramadan,* p. 232; cf. Sadat's *Memoirs,* February 3, 1977: "Kosygin must have been angry. . . . I did not expect much from him. [The Soviets] did not believe in our ability to fight and feared that we would involve them if we were to enter into a war and also involve them with the United States. Particularly because the Soviet Union and the United States were experiencing détente. . . . They did not want us to undermine détente and force them into a military confrontation with the United States. . . . Very frankly, without regret, I must say there is no friendship between big and small states. Only interests. There is no permanent friendship, but permanent interests."

133. Kalb and Kalb, *Kissinger,* pp. 482–83.

134. Heikal, *Road to Ramadan,* p. 234.

135. Dinitz interview, which fully corresponds with the Kalbs' story (*Kissinger,* p. 482).

136. President Nixon sent to the U.S. Congress on October 19 an emergency request for 2,200 million U.S. dollars in immediate military aid to Israel, saying that this was needed to prevent a "substantial imbalance" of military power in the Middle East. The president made his request to Congress a day after 67 senators had introduced a resolution calling for unlimited aid for Israel to offset Soviet supplies to the Arab states, and after a similar resolution by 220 Congressmen had been presented in the House of Representatives.

For the official documents see: (*a*) U.S., Congress, House, *Requesting Emergency Security Assistance for Israel and Cambodia, Message from the President of the United States* (transmitting a request for emergency security assistance for Israel and Cambodia, together with a draft of proposed legislation for those purposes), 93rd Cong., 1st sess. October 23, 1973, H. Doc. 93–170. (*b*) U.S., Congress, House, Committee on Foreign Affairs, *Emergency Security Assistance Act of 1973: Report Together with Minority and Supplemental Views,* prepared by Mr. Morgan, 93rd Cong., 1st sess., December 6, 1973, 93–702. See also M. C. Feuerwerger, "The Emergency Security Assistance Act of 1973 and American-Israeli Relations," *Midstream* (August/September, 1974), pp. 20–38.

137. Kalb and Kalb, *Kissinger,* p. 484.

138. Elazar, Gonen, and Adan interviews.

139. Dinitz interview.

140. See draft Resolution S/11036 adopted by the Security Council at the 1747th session as Resolution S/338, on October 22, 1973, Moore, *Arab Israeli Conflict,* vol. 3, p. 1138.

141. Foreign ministry and prime minister's office sources, confirming Golan, *Hasichot,* p. 81, which is based on the official Israeli protocols of Kissinger's talks in Israel.

142. Ibid., and foreign ministry sources.

143. See Golan, *Hasichot,* p. 82.

144. GHQ sources.

145. Golan, *Hasichot,* as confirmed by GHQ sources.

146. GHQ sources.

147. Dinitz interview, June, 1977.

148. Gonen interview; cf. Dayan, *Avnei Derech,* pp. 663–64.

149. Adan interview.

150. As a war correspondent attached to the IAF, the author had the opportunity to watch Egyptian actions on October 22 when the cease-fire went into effect, and was violated locally by Egyptian forces first.

151. See Draft Resolution S/11039, adopted at the 1948 meeting of the Security Council as Resolution 339. See also Moore, *Arab-Israeli Conflict,* p. 1139.

152. White House sources, confirming Golan, *Hasichot,* p. 84.

153. U.S. Department of Defense sources. According to the Kalbs (*Kissinger,* p. 470), three Soviet airborne divisions had been put on alert already on October 10. See also Golan, *Yom Kippur,* pp. 122–23.

154. See the *Ma'ariv* transcript, published on May 4, 1976, of a lecture by Dayan before students at the Technion in Haifa: "Israel gave up the surrender of the Third Egyptian Army because the United States told [it] that if Israel would not allow food and water to reach the Egyptians and made them prisoners, 'we shall disassociate ourselves from you.' The Israeli government had to decide which it was ready to give up—the Third Army or the United States! This was not done by any tricks; the demand was made in the name of the president of the United States, and was done openly [though not publicly]. I think that the reason for that move was their willingness to open the way for friendship between Egypt and the United States. Their official arguments were that if we didn't do that, then the Soviet Union would intervene in the war and send Soviet soldiers to help the besieged Egyptians. I think that if the Americans had not pressed us, both Suez City and the Third Army would have fallen, and our bargaining position would have been far better."
155. U.S. Intelligence sources; cf. the *Washington Post* story (May 18, 1977) on "Task Force 157," which had picked up the Soviet nuclear cargo back in 1973 and was disbanded by President Carter in the spring of 1977.
156. *Time*, April 12, 1976.
157. See R. C. Weinland, "Superpower Naval Diplomacy in the October, 1973, Arab-Israeli War," a Brookings Institution research paper prepared as a supplementary to a Brookings study, "The Requirements for U.S. Military Involvement in the Mediterranean, Middle East, and Indian Ocean," especially the plottings of U.S. and Soviet ship locations in the Mediterranean between October 1 and November 17, 1973 (prepared at the Center of Naval Analysis, Office of the Chief of Naval Operations, Mem. Ser. 96/1976, September 26, 1974).
158. U.S. intelligence sources.
159. See *New York Times* transcript of May 13, 1977.
160. Zumwalt interview, October, 1975.
161. Ibid.
162. In a conversation with the author in New York, October 30, 1975.
163. Rear Admiral Rectanus, U.S.N., to the Israeli military attaché, Major General Mordechai Gur. Rectanus also warned that the U.S. Navy was "globally overstretched." Weinland, in his above-mentioned plots, maintains that, when the crisis mounted, the Sixth Fleet was deployed in such a way that the Soviets would have to shoot their way through it in order to get their forces to Egypt. Weinland does not accept Zumwalt's arguments about Soviet advantages in the Mediterranean, and maintains that the Red Fleet could have interfered with American freedom of action, as compared with the 1958 Lebanese landing. Yet if the United States was ready to take heavy casualties, it would have prevented a Soviet landing in Egypt. Weinland's plots, however, do not include Soviet submarines, and his analysis is based upon U.S. relative immunity from Soviet naval missiles; both the red submarines and Soviet SSNs seemed to have worried Zumwalt and Rectanus a great deal more.
164. Kissinger's T.V. interview on October 25, 1973; see *New York Times* transcript, October 26, 1973.
165. Rodman conversation.
166. See Draft Resolution S/11046, adopted unanimously by the Security Council in its 1750th meeting on October 25, 1973. See also Moore, *Arab-Israeli Conflict*, p. 1139.
167. Prime minister's office sources. See also Golan, *Hasichot*, pp. 88–89.
168. Prime minister's office sources, confirming Golan, *Hasichot*, pp. 90–98.
169. Embassy sources in Washington. The author was sent there for a public relations mission on behalf of the foreign ministry on October 27 and usually accompanied the Israeli military attaché, Major General Mordechai Gur, to his briefings at the Pentagon. Gur, who was not yet acquainted with the details of the war, needed an eye-witness for his briefings.
170. Still in active reserve service as a division commander, Sharon gave interviews to

the foreign press (see *New York Times* of November 14, 1973), in which he criticized his superiors for their strategic and tactical decisions. Sharon, who had retired from the army three months before, refrained from criticizing Dayan, in hopes of a possible reactivation as chief of staff. He resigned in July, 1973, since this position was regarded by the majority of cabinet as reserved for more politically moderate generals than the aggressive (and original) Sharon. He then entered politics as a candidate for the Gahal right-wing parliamentary list, and brought about an alignment between all right-wing parties in the framework of the newly created Likud.

171. Prime minister's office sources.

172. Kalb and Kalb, *Kissinger,* p. 510; cf. Sheehan, "Step by Step," pp. 16–17.

173. Prime minister's office and foreign ministry sources.

174. See R. Cox, "On Thinking about Future World Order," *World Politics* 28, no. 2 (January, 1976): 175–96. Cox makes a distinction between the "natural-rational approach," the "historical-dialectical approach," and the "positivist-evolutionary approach."

175. Achieving and maintaining equilibrium in the international system has been, of course, a central subject in Kissinger's writings since *A World Restored* (Boston: Houghton Mifflin Co., 1957). For the latest published version, see *American Foreign Policy,* pp. 53–65.

176. For Ernst Haas's relevant writings, see *The Uniting of Europe: Political, Social, and Economic Forces, 1949–57* (Stanford: Stanford University Press, 1958), especially p. 16; "Technocracy, Pluralism, and the New Europe," in *A New Europe?,* ed. S. Graubard (Boston: Houghton Mifflin, 1964), p. 71; and "The Uniting of Europe and the Uniting of Latin America," *Journal of Common Market Studies* 5 (June, 1967), especially p. 327.

177. See Sheehan, "Step by Step," p. 17.

178. Ibid., pp. 18–23.

179. See S. Hoffmann, *Obstinate or Obsolete? The Fate of the Nation State: Functionalism and International Organization* (Stanford: Stanford University Press, 1969). We shall see later that Hoffmann criticized Kissinger's step-by-step policy on the same high political grounds that brought him to suspect Haas's empirical theory of European integration.

180. See Dayan on the Kilometer 101 talks (*Avnei Derech,* pp. 676, 693).

181. GHQ sources.

182. See Golan, *Hasichot,* pp. 108–12; cf. Sheehan, "Step by Step," p. 17, confirmed by foreign ministry sources.

183. Foreign ministry sources.

184. For the official text, see *Ha'aretz,* November 12, 1973 and Golan, *Hasichot,* pp. 110–11.

185. See Sheehan, "Step by Step," p. 22.

186. Foreign ministry sources.

187. See Golan, *Hasichot,* pp. 116–17.

188. The whole Israeli press of October 24 to December, 1973, should be read for that matter, and no specific quotations were or are necessary. Yet a book entitled *The Blunder (Hamechdal)* in Hebrew, which was hastily prepared for publication in November, 1973, vividly reflects the impact of the war upon opinion makers and public opinion (published by the authors, Y. Ben-Porath, U. Dan, Y. Geffen, et. al., Tel Aviv).

189. Gershom Shocken, the *Ha'aretz* editor, coined this term after the failure of the counteroffensive on October 8. Many experienced journalists in all papers, who until then had supported Dayan and reflected his views, sensed that the public was turning against him. Thus, they turned their fire in his direction fairly early—some during the war itself—and helped create an anti-Dayan atmosphere, which soon engulfed Mrs. Meir and Mr. Sapir. See the perspective analysis by T. Smith, "The First Israeli Revolution," *New York Times Magazine,* December 30, 1973.

190. Foreign ministry sources; cf. Golan, *Hasichot,* p. 117 and Sheehan, "Step by Step," pp. 24–25.

191. On November 28, an Arab summit meeting at Algiers agreed to negotiations with Israel, says Sheehan (ibid., p. 25), and designated the PLO as the "sole representative" of the Palestinians at Geneva. Syria refused to attend the conference, and Jordan did not agree to the PLO "sole representation." The secret Algiers resolution spoke of "the commitment to the restoration of the national rights of the Palestinian people in the manner decided by the PLO in its capacity as the sole representative of the Palestinian people."

192. Sadat's interview with the Kuwait newspaper, As-Siyassah; complete transcript in Al-Hamishmar, September 17, 1975 (Hebrew).

Chapter 4

1. American supply depots in West Germany were used during the fighting for Israeli necessities, with or without Bonn's knowledge at the beginning. The federal government permitted the supplying effort until the first cease-fire, on October 22, 1973, when it leaked some details to the press and thus was "forced" to stop. The presence of an Israeli ship in Bremerhaven was discovered by a German journalist at the same time. (The sources are interviews conducted by the author in Bonn and Frankfurt am Main, early in 1974.)

2. For the attitude of the EEC countries toward the Middle East crisis, in the general framework of U.S.-European relations after the dollar crisis of 1971, see F. Mellah, "L'attitude de l'Europe face à la crise pétrolière," Chronique de Politique Estrangère 27, no. 3 (May, 1974): 357–90; H. Schmidt, "The Struggle for the World Product," Foreign Affairs 52, no. 3 (April, 1974): 437–51; and W. Ungerer, "Auswirkungen der Ölkrise," Aussenpolitik 25, no. 2 (1974): 214–28.

3. On the November 6, 1973, declaration of the foreign ministers of the European Economic Community (calling on Israel and Egypt to return to the cease-fire lines of October 22 before the encirclement of the Egyptian 3rd Army by Israeli troops and calling on Israel "to end the territorial occupation that it has maintained since the conflict of 1967"), see the New York Times, November 7, 1973. Copenhagen reaffirmed the EC foreign ministers' November 6 Middle East declaration (see the New York Times, December 16, 1973).

4. This refers to the so-called d'Avignon Committee, which held closed meetings under the chairmanship of the director general of the Belgian Foreign Ministry on the Middle East issue after 1972. The participant EEC members had divided the issues of the conflict among themselves and submitted recommendations to the committee, yet the Council of Ministers did not officially endorse them (Foreign ministry and EEC sources).

5. Sisco interview (March, 1977); cf. Stoessinger, Anguish of Power, pp. 190–91.

6. Daily summary of the U.S. news media, compiled by the Israeli Embassy in Washington, November–December, 1973, and January–February, 1974.

7. The writer had a first-hand opportunity to talk to Washington newsmen in the framework of his mission there in October–November, 1973. Some (Jewish) staff members of the Washington Post, for example, were outspoken in criticizing Israel in these terms.

8. During Mrs. Meir's November visit to Washington, Mr. Joseph Alsop visited the Israeli military attaché, General Gur, at the embassy. Alsop painted a very gloomy picture indeed, of both Soviet intentions and capabilities to intervene, should Israel refuse to lift its siege on the Third Egyptian Army. Gur reminded his guest of the difficulties involved for the Soviets if they risked intervention. Alsop's published version, several days later in the New York Times, was somewhat less alarming (Embassy sources in Washington).

9. This is based on my talks and interviews with senatorial aides in Washington during the October–November, 1973, period. Most of them expected a growing voters' pressure to end the oil crisis on Israel's account.

10. See J. W. Fulbright, The Crippled Giant: American Foreign Policy and its Domestic Consequences (New York: Vintage Books, 1972), pp. 107–49. Fulbright

had been advocating a new American Middle East policy since 1968. In 1971 he suggested American guarantees to Israel in exchange for a complete Israeli withdrawal from the occupied territories, stressing the necessity for U.S.-Arab cooperation, to promote American economic and geopolitical interests.

11. See, for example, Z. Brzezinski, "The Deceptive Structure of Peace," *Foreign Policy,* no. 14 (Spring, 1974), pp. 35–36; R. A. Falk, "What's Wrong with Henry Kissinger's Foreign Policy," *Alternatives,* no. 1 (1975), pp. 79–100; J. L. S. Girling, " 'Kissingerism,' The Enduring Problems," *International Affairs* 51, no. 3 (July, 1975), 323–43; T. Szulc, "Is He Indispensable? Answers to the Kissinger Riddle," *New York,* July 1, 1974; and A. Wildavsky, "The Decline of American Foreign Policy" (Paper, Graduate School of Public Policy, University of California, Berkeley, April, 1974).

This selection combines both moderate-conservative and liberal-pragmatic and moralistic criticism of Kissinger, which effectively neutralized him in the election summer of 1976. Israeli hawks like Dayan were already hoping for such a process in early 1974, as they started to regard Kissinger's tactics as no less dangerous to Israeli interests than a clear-cut traditional American foreign policy. They were also influenced by such specific American criticism of Kissinger's Middle East policy as the above-mentioned *Commentary* essay by Luttwak and Laqueur, and by Hans Morgenthau's repeated argument that Kissinger was forcing Israel into far-reaching concessions without a substantial Arab quid pro quo (see "Professor Morgenthau: 'Far-Reaching Concessions to Arabs will Prevent War in the Short Run, but Mean Suicide for Israel,' " *Yediot Aharonot,* November 5, 1974).

12. See Golan on the U.S.-Israeli negotiations on the eve of the December, 1973, Geneva Conference, (*Hasichot,* pp. 117, 128); confirmed by foreign ministry sources.

13. This relates mainly to Kalb and Kalb's version of the Defense Department's attitude to the American resupply effort to Israel during the war (*Kissinger,* pp. 464–74), as partially confirmed by Sisco (March, 1977, interview). Accordingly, both Secretary Schlesinger and his deputy, Clements, were not supportive toward Israel during the supply crisis beyond the positions of the president and Kissinger.

14. According to Dinitz (June, 1977, interview), Mrs. Meir was influenced during her November, 1973, visit to the United States by former Governor Nelson Rockefeller, more than by other American interlocutors, to try the Kissinger method.

15. See, for example, "Winter Fuel Shortage, How Bad?," in *U.S. News and World Report,* December 12, 1973.

16. See J. E. Akins, "The Oil Crisis: This Time the Wolf is Here," *Foreign Affairs* (April, 1973), pp. 464–90; and the statements of Secretary Kissinger and federal energy administrator William Simon at a joint news conference held on January 10, 1974 (U.S. Department of State, *Department of State Bulletin* 70, no. 1806 [February 4, 1974]: 109–22). See also the two *Congressional Quarterly* books, *Energy Crisis in America* (March, 1974) and *Continuing Energy Crisis in America* (January, 1975), and *The Project Independence Report* by the Federal Energy Administration (November, 1974), all published by the Government Printing Office, Washington, D.C. Cf. *Energy and the U.S. Foreign Policy,* J. A. Yager and E. B. Steinberg, eds. (1974; reprint ed., Cambridge, Mass.; Ballinger Publishing Co., for the Ford Foundation, 1975).

17. See J. Amuzegar, "The Oil Story: Facts, Fiction, and Fair Play," *Foreign Affairs* 51, no. 4 (July, 1973): 657–75, and also *The Economist,* January 5, 1974.

18. See W. E. Griffith, "The Fourth Middle East War, The Energy Crisis, and U.S. Policy," *Orbis* 27, no. 4 (Winter, 1974): 1168, 1174–78.

19. This was, of course, my superficial impression upon arrival there on a public relations mission for the Israeli Foreign Ministry. At the time I did not realize that the conference, which was presented by both the Israeli and American governments as a "peace conference," was in fact a temporary show. (See Kissinger's arrival statement, U.S. Mission Geneva press release, December 20, 1973).

20. For the official Soviet view, see *World Marxist Review* (December, 1973), pp.

52–59. Cf. "Soviet Objectives in the Middle East," a report by a study group of the Institute of Conflict, London (January, 1974); and Golan, *Yom Kippur,* pp. 153–60.

21. See U.N. press release, Geneva, GSC/60, December 15, 1973.

22. Foreign ministry sources, confirming "A Long Way to Geneva," *Ha'aretz,* September 29, 1974; cf. U. Milstein, "Talks after the War: Interviews with Abba Eban," *Davar,* October 7, 1974; and Golan, *Hasichot,* pp. 120–24.

23. Prime minister's office sources, and Golan, *Hasichot,* pp. 125–26.

24. For Gromyko's Geneva speech see Golan, *Yom Kippur,* pp. 160–68.

25. See U.S. Department of State, *Department of State Bulletin* 72, no. 1855 (January 14, 1975), quoted in *Statements on the Middle East, November 29, 1973–June 24, 1974,* U.S. Information Service (Washington, D.C.: Government Printing Office 1974).

26. See U.N. press releases 469 and 470, Geneva, December 22, 1973.

27. Foreign ministry sources; see also Golan, *Hasichot,* pp. 140–41.

28. On December 5–6, 1973, the Labor party adopted a revised election platform after 12 hours of intense debate in which most party leaders favored an open renunciation of the original Galili document (see chapter 3, note 86). Finance Minister Sapir stated that the Galili document had been adopted "under the threat of a party split" and that it was "in shreds." Golda Meir said that the Galili document was not a political program, but an operative working program for the territories. She said she was aware that the money needed to implement it was not available now. She rejected Sadat's statement that the Galili document had caused the war and said that "the path to Geneva is not paved with its shreds." The discussion of whether the new platform substituted or merely supplemented the Galili document, and of what would be the relation between the two, was not settled by a vote, in order not to threaten party unity. A summary of the new program follows:

1. The strengthening of the Israel Defense Forces would be the primary condition for the safeguarding of Israel's security and the maintenance of peace.

2. Israel's central goal was the attainment of peace and cooperation with the peoples of the area.

3. The peace conference due to open in December would be a major event in the history of the Middle East.

4. Israel would strive for a peace agreement to be obtained through peace negotiations without prior conditions. Negotiations should be conducted without pressures or attempts at coercion from any side.

The peace agreement should ensure:

5. Elimination of all kinds of hostile actions, blockades, and boycotts;

6. Defensible borders, based on a territorial compromise, which would enable Israel to defend itself effectively against any military attack or blockade (Israel would not return to the lines of June 4, 1967, which were a temptation to aggression);

7. The preservation of the Jewish character of the state of Israel; and

8. The inception of an era of normal relations between Israel and its neighbors in the political, economic, social, and cultural spheres.

9. The peace agreement with Jordan would be based on the existence of two independent states: Israel, with united Jerusalem as its capital, and an Arab state to the east.

10. In the neighboring Jordanian-Palestinian state, expression could be given to the identity of the Palestinian and Jordanian Arabs, in peace and good neighborly relations with Israel.

11. Israel was against the establishment of an additional, separate Palestinian Arab state west of the Jordan.

12. Until the conclusion of a peace agreement, Israel would observe the cease-fire and any interim agreements between Israel and its neighbors as temporary arrangements on the road to peace.

13. In the absence of peace treaties or interim agreements, Israel would continue

to maintain the situation as determined at the time of the cease-fire.

14. An effort would be made to continue and strengthen settlement, in accordance with decisions made by the government of Israel from time to time, with priority for security considerations. (See *Jerusalem Post,* December 6 and December 28–29, 1973).

29. See Dayan's Knesset speech on December 26, 1973 (*Divrei Ha'Knesset,* January 29, 1974, p. 281).

30. The Knesset convened on October 23, 1973, to discuss the government's decision to accept an American-sponsored cease-fire. In this session the Likud opposition launched its first bitter attack against the coalition, blaming it for the "blunder" of not having declared general mobilization in time, and for not having advanced the armored regulars into the canal line. On October 25, Justice Minister Shapira, one of the traditional, moderate Mapai leaders, threatened to resign unless Dayan drew conclusions.

On October 26, Mrs. Meir declared her confidence in the defense minister. As a result Shapira resigned; both the press and the opposition demanded an inquiry into the following problems: (*a*) according to which assumption did the political level decide not to call up the reserves? (*b*) what was the intelligence gathered before October 6, and why was this intelligence interpreted wrongly? (*c*) what were the orders given to the regular forces on Yom Kippur? (*d*) why was the misleading information given to the public when the war broke out? (*e*) what went wrong with Israel's security concept, which had guided it until the war?

This last problem was of paramount importance to some members of the coalition, like Shapira, who resigned as a protest against Dayan's (and Meir's) policy as a whole. Allon expressed criticism, but did not resign. Publicists like former General Matti Peled (see *Ma'ariv,* October 26, 1973) and Uri Avneri (see *Ha'Olam Ha'Zeh,* November 1, 1973) followed a similar approach, blaming Dayan's and Meir's basic foreign political concepts, and linking Dayan and Meir's approach to the Arabs, and their notion of "secure borders" to their inability to foresee a full-scale war and prepare the army for it. Yet the main opposition leader, Mr. Begin, restricted his criticism to the "lack of minimal precautionary measures" to avoid surprise despite enough intelligence warnings (see *Ma'ariv,* November 4, 1973, and November 9, 1973).

31. For the internal regiment in the Herut party and Gahal, see Y. Lichtenstein's M.A. thesis and H. Kristal's Ph.D. thesis (Hebrew University, Jerusalem, 1975 and 1977, respectively), the first research done on the basis of primary sources. Both describe Herut as an organization run from the top by Mr. Begin personally and as a group of personal, absolutely loyal, friends, mostly former Irgun colleagues. Newcomers, like General Weizman, who joined the party in 1968 and tried to transform it to a modern, more open, two-way political system, were rejected by Mr. Begin. They played an important role in the 1970 vote on whether to leave Meir's coalition, in accordance with Begin's demand, and refuse the "Rogers Initiative." Having almost failed Begin in that vote, Weizman's influence was later systematically reduced by party loyalists. Accepting Begin's supreme authority, Weizman returned to play an important role in Herut and the Likud after the Yom Kippur War.

32. The movement was relatively small but yet it was influential; some of its members were public figures, like former General Avraham Yoffe, and former Mapai and Mapam followers and publicists, like Eliezer Livne and Moshe Shamir.

33. See Appendix A.

34. Foreign ministry sources; cf. Dayan, *Avnei Derech,* pp. 692–96.

35. Prime minister's office sources, Defense ministry sources, and Golan, *Hasichot,* pp. 154–70.

36. See Sheehan, "Step by Step," pp. 32–34, and Golan, *Hasichot,* pp. 160–76.

37. Foreign ministry sources.

38. See *Ha'aretz* and *Jerusalem Post,* January 19, 1974; "U.S. Announces Egypt-Israeli Agreement on Forces Separation," and Secretary Kissinger's news conference of

January 22, 1974, *Department of State Bulletin* 70, no. 1807 (February 11, 1974).

39. For the agreement map, see Appendix B.

40. Israel was approached again and again about this matter in February, 1974, yet it still regarded the matter as an internal Jewish-American humanitarian affair (prime minister's office sources).

41. See Secretary Kissinger's news conference of December 27, 1973, *Department of State Bulletin* 70, no. 1804 (January 21, 1974).

42. See W. Gumpel, "UdSSR: Energiekrise und Nahostkrise," *Aussenpolitik* 1/74 (January 25, 1974): 32–41.

43. See Golan, *Yom Kippur*, pp. 213–26.

44. See "Knesset Approves Separation Agreement amid Heckling and Angry Exchanges," *Ma'ariv*, January 23, 1974.

45. For Dayan's version of the domestic and partisan events that led to his final resignation, see *Avnei Derech*, pp. 729–36.

46. The Agranat Commission, nominated by the cabinet on November 18, 1973, was asked to inquire into the following subjects: "(*a*) the information available on the days before the Yom Kippur War about the steps undertaken by the enemy and his intentions to start a war; the evaluations and decisions relating to this information, which were made by the military and civilian authorities; (*b*) the readiness of the Israel Defense Forces generally, its preparedness in the days before the Yom Kippur War," and its actions before October 8, 1973 (See "The Agranat Commission Report" p. 10).

47. Most of them were led by a reserve army captain, Motti Ashkenazi, who commanded the only Israeli position in the Bar-Lev line, which remained in Israeli hands. See "4,000 Support Ashkenazi at Anti-Dayan Protest," *Jerusalem Post Weekly*, March 5, 1974, and "Ashkenazi Joining Other Protest Groups and Reservists Protest," *Jerusalem Post Weekly*, March 26, 1974.

48. See Sheehan, "Step by Step," pp. 34–36. According to this source, the Syrian shuttle was the price Kissinger paid to end the Arab oil embargo. By February the Arab oil princes already "were alarmed by Europe's penury and plagued with doubts. Syria urged a prolongation but the oil princes sent [Saudi Foreign Minister] Saqqaf and [Egypt's Foreign Minister] Fahmy to Washington to strike a bargain: Do something for Syria . . . and the embargo will stop. Kissinger promised to try— in March the embargo was suspended" (p. 36). Indeed, on March 18 1974, a communiqué was issued in Vienna announcing that Abu Dhabi, Algeria, Bahrain, Egypt, Kuwait, Qatar, and Saudi Arabia had agreed to lift the oil embargo on the United States and at the same time to treat Italy and West Germany as "friendly countries" with respect to oil deliveries. On the other hand, Libya and Syria declined to lift the U.S. embargo and Libya also refused to give its assent to any increase in production.

49. Foreign ministry sources.

50. The relatives of the POWs held in Egypt and Syria organized quickly and were engaged in public activities and indoor meetings with cabinet and Knesset members to advance their cause. The sensitivity of the issue, in the press and the cabinet, was extremely high; no minister dared publicly to subordinate it to the larger political developments. IDF tradition was taken as an obligation that no Israeli soldiers should be left to be taken prisoners, and the government had to demonstrate to the public that once Israeli POWs were taken, it would do its utmost to release them. This was always connected with the very harsh treatment for Israeli POWs in Arab (except Jordanian and Lebanese) camps.

51. Foreign ministry sources, confirming Golan, *Hasichot*, pp. 186–188

52. Ibid., p. 188.

53. Since the Yom Kippur War a new General Staff branch, the planning branch, was created under Major General Avraham Tamir, in addition to the five "classical" branches (operations, intelligence, personnel, quartermaster general, and training).

General Tamir and his staff, together with Dayan's personal staff, were actively preparing contingency plans before the shuttle and during the talks concerning the town of Kuneitra and the line in general.

54. There were altogether 19 settlements on the Golan Heights by the end of 1975, of which 8 were kibbutzim, 4 moshavim, 5 other collective smallholders' settlements, and 2 rural centers, according to Jewish Agency Settlement Department sources. The erection of the Golan settlements, between 1967 and 1975, was due to a curious combination of the initiatives of the settlers themselves and the support of Achdut Ha'Avoda, the NRP, Rafi, and Gahal. The settlers were mostly members of Achdut Ha'Avoda and other kibbutz movements, the NRP, and small-holder cooperative movements. The Mapai majority was reluctant to accept the settlements, but given the coalitionary situation in the face of Syrian hostility, the fact that the Syrian inhabitants had evacuated the area in 1967, and the general support for Golan settlements, Mapai had to accede.

55. See Sheehan, "Step by Step," p. 39. The secretary is reported to have used the antiretreat mood in Israel in his talks with Assad to convince the Syrian leader that the Israelis made considerable concessions. The antiwithdrawal atmosphere was created by the press and opposition circles, and was backed by Rafi and NRP circles, *inter alia*, specifically to reach these results.

56. See Golan, *Hasichot,* p. 197.

57. GHQ sources.

58. On the United Nations Disengagement Observers Force (UNDOF), see U.N. document S/RES/350 (1974), adopted by the Security Council on May 31, 1974; see also Moore, *Arab-Israeli Conflict*, pp. 1193–97.

59. On the different aspects of the oil crisis and oil policies of the OPEC members and Iran in 1974–75, see A. Alkazaz, "Oil Problems Seen from the Arab Point of View," *Inter Economics* (July 7, 1975), pp. 206 ff.; J. Perry, C. Carey, and A. G. Carey, "Industrial Growth and Development Planning in Iran," *Middle East Journal* 29, no. 1 (Winter, 1975): 1–15; D. A. Rustow, "Who Won the Yom Kippur War and Oil Wars?," *Foreign Policy* 17 (Winter, 1974–75): 166–75; and D. Schliepke, "Regional Development and Oil Strategy: The Case of Algeria," *Inter Economics* (July 7, 1975), pp. 202–6.

60. On the NATO meetings in Ottawa and Brussels, see *Department of State Bulletin* 71, no. 1828 (July 8, 1974), and press release 255, June 19, 1974.

61. The Cairo-Riadh-Teheran axis was widely discussed at the time in semiofficial American circles in Washington and in the Middle East capitals. Professor William Griffith of M.I.T. presented it openly to Israeli colleagues in a lecture in Jerusalem in late winter of 1974. Griffith was regarded in Israel as closely associated with the U.S. Department of State and with Arab oil interests.

62. On David Rockefeller's 14-day tour of the Middle East and his announcement of the establishment of a Chase Manhattan Bank representative office in Cairo, marking the first American banking representation in Cairo since 1966, see *New York Times,* February 8, 1974.

63. Sadat's statements on the Palestine question:

Before the Yom Kippur War, Sadat never made his position on the Palestinian problem explicit. He supported the PLO, but did not clearly expose his ideas; whether he supported the "Democratic, secular state idea" or whether he preferred a separate Palestinian state cannot be answered with the material made public.

Immediately after the war, however, in an article in the Cairo *Al-Ahram* of November 12, 1973, Lutfi-Al Khouli (the paper's Palestinian expert, who usually stated Sadat's policies) urged the Palestinians to take part in a peace conference if asked to do so: "The Palestinians should attend this meeting at the insistence of their two allies, the Arabs and the Soviet Union. The Palestinian revolution, if it takes part in that conference, will lay down the principle of a democratic Palestinian state." Khouli said that the Palestinians should consider the following points: the value of recognition by international circles and even by Israel, the maintenance of their unity, the need to assure a land for the Palestinian people, and keeping the support and cooperation of their allies" (See *Arab Report and Record*, [1973], p. 527).

This position was maintained until July 18, 1974, when a joint communiqué was issued after Sadat and Hussein held talks in Alexandria. In it, Sadat and Hussein declared "the Palestine Liberation Movement to be the legitimate representative of the Palestinians, except the Palestinians residing in the Hashemite Kingdom of Jordan." They agreed also on the need for the PLO to take part independently in the Geneva peace conference "at the appropriate stage, in support of the Palestinian people for self-determination." This statement was attacked heavily by the PLO, which had been recognized at the Algiers summit conference of November 27, 1973, as the "*sole* representative of *all* Palestinians." It was not clear whether "Palestinians residing in the kingdom of Jordan" included those living in the West Bank (*Arab Report and Record* [1974], p. 314). The Palestinians living in the East Bank could also have been regarded by the PLO as represented by that organization. Five days later, in a speech commemorating the anniversary of the 1952 revolution, Sadat merely said that "the international recognition of the PLO as the legitimate representative of the Palestinian people" was among the most important results of the October War (speech on July 23, 1974, ibid., p. 295).

With the pressure on Sadat growing, he was forced to clarify his position on the Palestinian problem. In an interview with the London *Observer* on October 6, 1974, he was asked whether he had changed his mind after the Algiers summit meeting and again after the July 18 communiqué with King Hussein. Sadat repiled: "There was no contradiction. I support the Algiers summit declaration, but my interpretation is this: The PLO is the sole and legitimate representative of all the Palestinians in the West Bank, in the Gaza Strip, Lebanon, Syria, Kuwait, and so on. But I can't understand how they can represent those who are in the Jordanian army or the Jordanian government." Sadat added that this meant that the PLO should not represent Palestinians in the east bank of the Jordan. He was in favor of a separate Palestinian state in the West Bank and the Gaza Strip, where the Palestinians would have "the right to achieve whatever relations they like with King Hussein" (ibid., p. 439).

At a press conference on October 30, 1974, after the Rabat summit, where Hussein had officially and publicly "lost" the West Bank to the PLO, Sadat said that the new interpretation of the Rabat resolution on the Palestinians was that a new state, Palestine, had emerged and that there were now five confrontation states—Egypt, Syria, Palestine, Jordan, and Lebanon. (ibid., p. 467).

64. For the official documents on Nixon's visit, see *Weekly Compilation of Presidential Documents* 10, no. 25 (June 17, 1974): 611–53; and *Department of State Bulletin* 71, no. 1829 (July 15, 1974). Nixon remained in the Middle East until June 18, 1974.

65. Israeli intelligence sources.

66. See also Sheehan, "Step by Step," p. 44.

67. When asked, in an ABC interview of April 15, 1975, whether Israel had tactical nuclear weapons, Mr. Rabin answered, "No," adding, "No doubt Israel is ready to do the ultimate for its defense, but we believe that we live in an era in which we can do it with conventional weapons" (prime minister's office transcript). See also Chapter 6, notes 31 and 66.

See also General Gur, in a *Davar* interview, "We Should Not Count on Nuclear Deterrence," June 19, 1975: "I think that in any foreseeable future [we] should base [our national defense] on conventional power, and we can make it. If nuclear weapons are introduced, we shall have to find an answer to nuclear weapons. But relying on it as a deterrent, this may seriously impair our security." Gur thus reversed a statement he made in January, 1975 (see *Ha'aretz*, January 19, 1975), to the contrary. The chief of staff had been quoted as having said that a balance of terror would determine the Middle East borders (i.e., freeze them) in ten years, and this would prevent large-scale hostilities. The reason for this reversal of Gur's published opinion is unclear, and might have reflected a cabinet consensus with regard to nuclear deterrence. When Gur first spoke, in January, he might have reflected his own or Dayan's or Peres's approach to nuclear deterrence.

68. Mr. Abba Eban, the former Mapai foreign minister, had no power base of his own in the alignment, and his personal relations with the former ambassador in Washington, Rabin, who had usually reported directly to Mrs. Meir, were strained. Allon, a defense expert and Achdut Ha'Avoda representative, had to be compensated for the defense post, which went to Rafi again, and thus became foreign minister. Allon had served until then as minister of education and minister of labor.

69. For the details of Dayan's actual policy in the West Bank, see S. Teveth, *The Cursed Blessing, the Story of the Occupation of the West Bank* (London: Weidenfeld and Nicolson, 1970), pp. 7–20.

70. Hammer and the American-born Ben-Meir represented a younger NRP generation, which, although a minority in the party, could greatly influence majority decisions on religious and foreign policy matters. Operating along Rafi's line in the alignment, the NRP minority could force the majority in its direction while threatening a party split, or it could advance accusations by Hammer and Ben-Meir that the NRP compromised upon ideological issues. Traditionally, the party always did compromise on the issue of occupying the whole country, but had never been forced to admit it. It was ready to compromise on some religious matters, when modern reality forced it to do so, but was never condemned for it by its young leadership. Thus, when the NRP minority threatened party unity on the territorial and religious issues, the majority preferred to stay out of the narrow coalition that was regarded by Hammer and Ben-Meir as too "dovish."

71. See Golan, *Hasichot*, p. 221. According to this source, Kissinger suggested the Jericho plan to Allon during his visit to the United States on July 28, 1974. Yet on July 21 the cabinet decided to refrain from any interim agreements with Jordan. Thus, Kissinger is reported to have suggested an "interim interim" agreement—to transfer Jericho to U.N. supervision (i.e., not to return it to Hussein's rule) in the meantime, but yet to demonstrate a "move" in the West Bank. Answering my question in a faculty meeting at the Hebrew University, Rabin later said that Jordan insisted upon a complete Israeli withdrawal as one alternative, or else on a partial withdrawal along the *whole Jordan line*. The Jordanians, who had direct channels to the Israelis, were thus reported as having no interest in the Jericho plan.

72. See Chapter 1, note 110.

73. See Golan, *Hasichot*, p. 222; cf. the American-Jordanian communiqué of August 18, 1974, which did mention a Jordanian-Israeli interim agreement as a subject of "consultations" between Washington and Amman (*Department of State Bulletin* 71, no. 1837 [September 9, 1974]). According to Sheehan, Ford and Kissinger indeed promised Hussein that an Israeli withdrawal in the Jordan valley shared equal priority with another withdrawal in the Sinai ("Step by Step," p. 46). Yet Hussein apparently demanded a withdrawal along the whole valley, rather than a limited withdrawal around Jericho.

74. Foreign ministry sources, and Golan, *Hasichot*, p. 222.

75. Foreign ministry sources.

76. See M. Golan and D. Margalit, "The Interim Agreement; A Post Mortem," *Ha'aretz*, September 5, 1975, as confirmed by foreign ministry sources.

77. Prime minister's office sources.

78. See Sheehan, "Step by Step." According to this source, Jordan had to compete with Egypt, which pressed Kissinger for another Israeli withdrawal as soon as possible.

79. Text of resolution adopted on October 29, 1974, at Arab summit meeting held in Rabat, Morocco on October 27–30, 1974 (*New York Times*, October 30, 1974), concerning the Palestinian issue.

"The seventh Arab summit has decided:

1. To affirm the rights of the Palestinian people to return to their homeland and to self-determination;
2. To affirm the rights of the Palestinian people to establish an independent national authority, under PLO leadership as the sole legitimate representative of the Palestinian people on any liberated Palestinian territory (The Arab states must support this authority when set up in all fields and at all levels);
3. To support the PLO in the exercise of its responsibilities in the national and international fields in the framework of Arab commitments;
4. To invite Jordan, Egypt, Syria, and the PLO to work out a formula governing their relations in the light of these decisions and in order to implement them; and
5. To affirm the undertaking of all the Arab states to safeguard Palestinian national unity and not to interfere in internal affairs regarding Palestinian action."

80. A group of American scholars (including Michael Walzer of Harvard, who, together with other Jewish intellectuals, met Kissinger in December, 1974, and Richard Ullman of Princeton) reported to a selected group of Israelis on their impression of U.S. policy after Rabat in a meeting in Jerusalem in January, 1975, at which the author was present. (See R. Ullman, "After Rabat: Middle East Risks and American Roles," *Foreign Affairs* 53, no. 2 [January, 1975]: 284–96.)
81. This refers to the 1974 Congressional elections, which returned a larger democratic majority, with many new—and younger—House members, and to the general atmosphere following Watergate. For Kissinger's arguments against Congress in that period, see "Kissinger Speaks out on Foreign Policy," *Time* (European edition), October 27, 1975, pp. 13–15.
82. See above, note 80. Stanley Hoffmann developed this argument very strongly during the meeting. Cf. his article, "A New Policy for Israel," *Foreign Affairs* 53, no. 3 (April, 1975): 405–31.

Chapter 5

1. This relates mainly to the activities of Gush Emunim, which joined forces for this purpose with young NRP and Herut activists during Kissinger's March shuttle. A representative source of the anti-Kissinger campaign and the general attitude of the extreme ideological and political right is the periodical *Zot Ha'aretz* of the Movement for the Whole of Eretz-Israel.
2. For a theoretical discussion, see A. Tversky and W. Edward, eds., *Decision Making: Selected Readings* (Harmondsworth, Middlesex: Penguin Books, 1967), pp. 27–44.
3. For a theoretical discussion, see J. A. Rosenau, ed., *Domestic Sources of Foreign Policy* (New York: Free Press, 1967), pp. 148–55.
4. See also Rosenau's *The Scientific Study of Foreign Policy* (New York: Free Press, 1971).
5. This refers mainly to *Ma'ariv* and *Yediot Aharonot*. See also Peres' interview in *Ma'ariv*, March 26, 1976.
6. The former minister of defense chose first, after his resignation, to refrain from public activities. By January, 1975, he reappeared, and delivered several lectures at the Bar-Illan Orthodox University in Tel Aviv, amid protests of members of the families of the war casualties. Slowly, Dayan regained a public position as a speaker in similar meetings, but could not recover his former political standing. His "draw theory" became widespread through his speaking meetings and the rightist press (mainly *Ma'ariv* and *Yediot Aharonot*) after January.
7. "In background briefings, in public appearances, and by circulating rumors, Peres succeeded in creating for himself the image of a cabinet member who defended Israel's interests to the utmost. [Israel] should not concede the [Sinai] passes but for nonbelligerency—this was his message to the nation. But Peres . . . never made

the mistake that Rabin did. . . . he never said it in public. He succeeded in creating a tough image, without nailing himself down to any formula" (Golan, *Hasichot*, pp. 232–33). According to this source, Peres spread rumors in December, 1974, that if the cabinet endorsed a decision to concede the passes for less than nonbelligerency, he would resign, and thus he threatened (indirectly again) a party split. Columnist Hagai Eshed of *Davar* usually presented Peres' positions to the broader public.

8. A typical argument in this direction was given to the Israelis by Professor Griffith in his repeated appearances in Israel (see Chapter 4, note 61) and by Dr. Edith Trunzo of the (American) Atlantic Institute in Paris in an interview with the author during her research mission in the Middle East in the winter of 1974, quoting American Embassy in Cairo estimates, and hinting at the growing American-Egyptian economic cooperation. See also "U.S.-Egyptian Joint Cooperation Commission Meets at Washington," *Department of State Bulletin* 71, no. 1838 (September 16, 1974) (Press Release no. 334, dated August 19, 1974), pp. 380–83.

9. One of these promises was the American bid to offer Egypt (and Israel) atomic reactors for peaceful use, given to Sadat during President Nixon's 1974 visit to the Middle East. Israel was at first very reluctant to accept the deal, which would allow Egypt to develop a nuclear infrastructure, if not to use the reactor for military purposes. The Israelis were also sensitive to the inspection procedure in both reactors, to avoid a general inspection arrangement that might include the Dimona reactor and an Egyptian demand that Israel sign the NPT. Israeli hesitations, combined with new Congressional approval, appropriation and inspection procedures, delayed a final decision on the reactor supplies to both Egypt and Israel until late 1977.

10. See the following Sadat interviews: ORTF (France), January 12, 1974; ABC (United States), February 7, 1974; Hearst Newspapers (United States), July 10, 1975.

The last interview, which was given by Sadat to Kingsbury Smith, the chief foreign correspondent for Hearst, may be representative.

> Question: When a final peace agreement is attained, would you agree to Israel's joining a common market with its Arab neighbors?
> Answer: Could you imagine that after 27 years of hatred, bitterness, suspicion, and wars, in one moment, just like that, you can agree upon a common market and normal relations? A cooling period must first elapse. It is a very complicated and difficult problem, which can not be solved in one step. Some time must elapse first. (*Ma'ariv*, July 10, 1975)

11. See Kissinger's *Time* interview (Chapter 4, note 81); cf. *Department of State Bulletin* 72, nos. 1854, 1855 (January 6 and January 13, 1975), concerning his actual steps (Brussels NATO meeting, Presidents Ford and Giscard d'Estaing meeting in Martinique on December 13 and December 23, 1974, and "Department Reviews Main Elements of the Strategy to Resolve the Oil Crisis"). These activities were preceded by the Vladivostok meeting between President Ford and Secretary General Brezhnev, on November 24, 1974, in which the momentum of the SALT negotiations was maintained. See *Department of State Bulletin* 71, no. 1852 (December 23, 1974).

12. Foreign ministry sources.

13. Foreign ministry sources, quoting reports on Kissinger's closed briefings and private talks with newsmen and journalists in Washington after the breakdown of the negotiations; see also notes 14, 49, and 51 below and chapter 6, note 1.

14. Kissinger carefully avoided blaming either Egypt or Israel publicly, so that it was impossible to get public statements by him after the breakdown of his March, 1975, shuttle. The *New York Times* reported on March 24, however, that "In private, Mr. Kissinger seemed upset by what he regarded as a short-sighted attitude in Israel in not taking a more flexible approach. Israel's interests would have been better served, he believed, by making a compromise rather than in facing the Arabs as a group in Geneva." On March 26 the *New York Times* quoted Kissinger

as saying that he "foresaw mounting trouble in the Middle East, especially for Israel," and the same day James Reston wrote, in an article entitled, "Kissinger's Latest Dilemma," "Washington is pretending publicly to be even-handed, but in private is blaming Israel."

15. Since the January, 1974, Israeli-Egyptian agreement, relations between Cairo and Moscow obviously deteriorated, and arms shipments to the Egyptian air force had been reduced. At the same time, the U.S.S.R. enhanced its military aid to Syria, delivering new weapons systems that had not been introduced to the Middle East at all until then, and were not given to Egypt (Israeli intelligence sources).

16. Even afterward, Egypt was still able to purchase Soviet spare parts for its land forces from the Soviet Union. Plane parts were probably prohibited, or their supply seriously reduced. Egypt tried to buy jet engines in 1975–76 in China and India, and considered replacing MIG engines with American- or European-made ones, besides commencing a plan for production itself (Israeli intelligence sources).

17. Sharon was the generating power behind the creation of the Likud, the alignment of Gahal, and two other small center-right parties, but he did not emerge as the recognized leader of the new conglomerate. He then refrained from inner-party activities, without a power base of his own to challenge Mr. Begin's predominant role in the new block. He concentrated upon antiwithdrawal campaigns, for example, in two Israel T.V. interviews on March 19 and March 30, 1975.

18. GHQ sources.

19. Besides Gush Emunim, NRP youth groups, and Herut youngsters, several other exparliamentary *ad hoc* groupings became active in March against withdrawal in the Sinai, mainly through rallies and newspaper advertising. The proagreement majority in the alignment (Mapan and many former Mapai activists) was not engaged in a public effort to gain support for a questionable agreement, from the split leaderships' point of view, which in any case might not have been concluded. The public arena was thus occupied almost solely by the opposition and exparliamentary groupings.

20. Prime minister's office sources.

21. Foreign ministry sources.

22. See, for example, Kissinger's news conference of November 21, 1973 in *Department of State Bulletin* 69, no. 1798 (December 10, 1973), p. 708 and especially p. 720.

23. For the official suggestion, see "The United States and a Unifying Europe: The Necessity for Partnership," address by Secretary Kissinger before the Pilgrims of Great Britain in London on December 12, 1973 (*Department of State Bulletin* 69, no. 1801 [December 31]: 777–81).

24. Wilson formed a minority government on March 4, 1974.

25. The American policy toward France in the winter of 1974 was a conscious attempt to isolate it in the EEC and mainly to separate it from West Germany and Britain, if Paris would confine its opposition to a common western oil and Middle East policy under U.S. leadership (American Embassy sources in Brussels).

26. A careful examination of Kissinger's press conferences since the Arab oil boycott began yields, however, a clear-cut American tendency toward a unified consumers' front, and later toward some kind of cooperation between consumers and producers. See Kissinger's press conference of January 3, 1974, for example, *Department of State Bulletin* 70, no. 1805 (January 28, 1974): 78–79. See also Kissinger's speech at the University of Chicago, November 14, 1974; cf. his *Business Week* interview on December 23, 1974, in *Department of State Bulletin* 72, no. 1857 (January 27, 1975): 97–106.

27. See, for example, W. Tapley Bennett, Jr., "United States Discusses Role of Industrialization in the Developing Countries" (Statement made before the Second General Conference of the United Nations Industrial Development Organization, Lima, Peru, March 12–26, 1975). Mr. Bennett was Deputy U.S. Representative to the U.N. (U.S.-U.N. Mission Press Release 26, March 28, 1975). See also Kissinger's TV interview with Bill Moyers in January 1975, in *Dialogue* 8, no. 2 (1975), esp. pp. 6–10.

28. See Kissinger's *L'Express* interview on April 12, 1975, in *Department of State Bulletin* 72, no. 1872 (May 12, 1975), especially p. 612.
29. Foreign ministry sources.
30. This relates to the deteriorating conditions in South Vietnam and Cambodia. Kissinger was accused both of having brought about a "paper peace" and of intending to give aid to the two regimes in southeast Asia. The "paper peace" argument would be heard again as an argument of principle against Kissinger's diplomacy in the context of the Middle East: Israeli (and liberal American) circles would join forces with American Liberals against his "half solutions" from opposite directions. See, for example, "Kissinger's Paper Peace," by former under secretary of state, George Ball, *Atlantic* (February, 1976), pp. 41–49.
31. Testimony to the author by former Harvard (and Columbia University) colleagues.
32. Embassy sources in Washington, confirmed by Israeli journalists based in Washington at the time. At the same time, Rabin backed the administration on Vietnam in Jewish circles, in the context of a common Israeli-American anticommunist denominator, and sometimes ran into severe difficulties with Jewish Liberal elements.
33. See Rabin's Israeli T.V. interview on January 23, 1970.
34. Mapam Central Committee sources on a closed meeting with Rabin in February, 1975.
35. Rabin's ABC interview of February 7, 1975; cf. his *Ha'aretz* interview of December 3, 1974.
36. Foreign ministry sources, and Golan, *Hasichot*, pp. 233–39.
37. Prime minister's office and defense ministry sources.
38. See *New York Times*, March 24, 1974, substantiated and detailed by Foreign Ministry sources.
39. Defense ministry sources.
40. Ford Motor Company announced during the negotiations its intentions to invest in Egypt and build a truck factory there.
41. For the Egyptian response, cf. besides my foreign ministry and defense ministry sources—also following published sources: Peres' *Ma'ariv* interview of March 26, 1976, and Rabin's *Yediot Aharonot* interview of the same date.
42. Foreign ministry sources.
43. Foreign ministry sources.
44. Defense ministry sources.
45. See Hagai Eshed's *Davar* articles of March 30 and April 11, 1975, "Towards the Geneva Conference" and "Allon to Washington;" cf. Peres' above-mentioned *Ma'ariv* interview.
46. Defense ministry sources. Some indiscretions were included in Matti Golan's original manuscript, which was banned and confiscated by the Israeli censorship and later released in a milder version.
47. On the Ford message, see Y. Harif, "The Known and Unknown," *Ma'ariv*, March 28, 1975, and H. Eshed, "Kissinger Made It Clear to Rabin that There Was No Threat in Ford's Message" (content: "U.S. will not finance a standstill against her political interest") *Davar*, March 28, 1975.
48. In a closed meeting on August 24, 1975.
49. Foreign ministry sources.
50. William Safire, in an article called "Henry's Two Faces" in the *New York Times*, March 27, 1977, accused Kissinger of playing a double game, publicly trying to appear as even-handed, but in fact putting all the blame for the breakdown of the negotiations on Israel. He describes one of his tactical moves: when he reported to a Congressional committee on his negotiations, Kissinger afterward told the reporters that the senators had been "violently anti-Israel," when in fact none of the participants of the meeting confirmed this interpretation by Kissinger to Safire.
51. See Chapter 4, note 82.
52. See *Yediot Aharonot*, March 28, 1975: "Kissinger: You Should Be Longing for the Interim Agreement" ("Do the Israeli people at least know the bitter reality in which they live?") and "Kissinger: I Felt as a Witness to a Greek Tragedy;" cf. Joseph Alsop: "Kissinger's Pessimism" (Hebrew translation), *Davar*, February 4,

1975. Mr. Alsop later repeatedly blamed Israel for the March, 1975, failure.
53. Foreign ministry sources.

Chapter 6

1. The term "reassessment" (of U.S. policy toward Israel and/or the Middle East situation in general) was used by previous American administrations in their diplomatic correspondence with Israel, and even publicly. In the summer of 1970, President Nixon ordered a "reassessment" of the Middle East problem that preceded the Rogers' initiative. For the Israelis in 1975, the term meant a possible change in the American strategy—the abandonment of the step-by-step approach in favor of an attempt at a general settlement in which the American position would necessarily be different from Israel's.

See Kissinger's news conference on March 26, 1975, in which, for the first time in public, he outlined the basics of the step-by-step strategy:

> The step-by-step approach . . . attempted to separate the Middle East problem into individual and, therefore, manageable segments. . . . Our policy had been designed . . . to segment the issues into individual elements, to negotiate each element separately and therefore to permit each party to adjust itself domestically and internationally to a process of gradual approach toward peace. Now that this approach has to be abandoned, we face an entirely new situation in which, in all probability, all problems will have to be negotiated simultaneously, and in which, instead of a forum in which Israel deals with one Arab country through the mediation of the United States, the strong probability is that Israel will have to deal with all Arab countries in a unilateral forum.

(*Department of State Bulletin* 72, no. 1868 [April 14, 1975]: 461–65). See also Sheehan, "Step by Step," p. 54: "he took the [Israeli] refusal very personally—as directed not only against the United States, but, above all, at himself. For weeks after his return to Washington, Kissinger sulked and raged, castigating Israeli blindness to aides and visitors alike compulsively telephoning distinguished Jews all over the country to complain of Israel's intransigence. His much trumpeted 'reassessment' . . . was his revenge on Israeli behavior."

According to Sheehan, three options were considered during the reassessment period (April–June, 1975): (1) a final settlement (1967 borders, American guarantees, and Soviet participation); (2) a quasifinal settlement between Israel and Egypt (most of the Sinai for political nonbelligerency); and (3) failing the first and second option, a return to the step-by-step diplomacy. These options involved, as Sheehan reports President Ford to have discussed with former Senator Fulbright, an open appeal over the heads of the Jewish lobby and Congress direct to the American people. Ford hesitatd, whereas Kissinger was not really interested in a comprehensive approach that would include the PLO and the Soviets. A semifinal agreement with Egypt would have brought similar demands from other Arab states. Thus, the step-by-step approach emerged again as the only viable strategy.

2. For Ford's reaction, see *New York Times*, March 28 and April 21, 1975, and White House press release, April 21.

3. Defense ministry sources; see also "Is a Confrontation with the U.S. Expected?," *Ha'aretz*, March 28, 1975; and "An Analysis of the Beginning of the Confrontation with the Administration," *Davar*, April 7, 1975.

4. During April, the administration delayed Israel's request for 2.5 billion dollars in military and economic assistance until the end of the so-called "reassessment." On May 21, 1975, 76 senators sent a letter to President Ford saying that they expected the administration to submit a foreign aid request to Congress "that will be responsive to Israel's urgent military and economic needs." The letter was drafted by 19 senators, among whom the Republican Jewish senator from New York, Jacob Javits, played the major role. The letter said that the senators continued to support

Israel's insistence on "secure and recognized boundaries that are defensible" and that "any Israeli withdrawal must be accompanied by meaningful steps toward my Arab neighbors." The letter stressed also the heavy flow of Soviet arms to the Arab states and the need to "keep the military balance from turning against Israel" (*New York Times*, May 22, 1975).

5. Embassy sources in Washington, and interview with Mr. Mel Elfin, Washington Bureau Chief, *Newsweek*, October 21, 1975.

6. Prime minister's office sources, and Rabin in a meeting with Hebrew University professors, April 19, 1975, in Jerusalem.

7. Defense ministry sources.

8. For the published documents concerning the Salzburg meeting on June 1–2, 1975, see *Weekly Compilation of Presidential Documents*, June 9, 1975.

   Concerning American financial and economic aid to Egypt and other aid measures, see "U.S. Economic and Business Relations with the Middle East and North Africa," address by Deputy Assistant Secretary Sober, *Department of State Bulletin* 74, no. 1929 (June 14, 1976): 760–63. According to Sheehan, "Step by Step," p. 59, "Ford repulsed Sadat's pleas for a public commitment to the 1967 borders and soothed him instead with a restatement of Nixon's secret promise [to this effect]."

9. Foreign ministry sources; cf. the Cairo weekly, *Achbar al Yaum*, interview with the Egyptian economics minister, quoted in *Ha'aretz*, July 14, 1976, "Egypt Needs 12 Billion Dollars." See also A. L. Gray, "Egypt's Ten-Year Economic Plan," *Middle East Journal* 30, no. 1 (1976): 36–48. See also note 43.

10. Prime minister's office sources; see also D. R. Tahtinen, *The Arab-Israeli Military Balance Since October, 1973* (Washington , D.C.: The American Enterprise Institute for Public Policy Research, 1974); H. Rattinger, "From War to War to War: Arms Races in the Middle East," *International Studies Quarterly* 20, no. 4 (December, 1976): 501–31.

11. Foreign ministry sources.

12. Defense ministry sources (confirming Golan, *Hasichot*, p. 243).

13. Prime minister's office sources, confirming Sheehan, "Step by Step," p. 59. Ford and Kissinger endorsed Sadat's demands for the passes and the Suez oil, stressing that Israel could not count on substantial American aid until it negotiated a new interim settlement, and warning Rabin that otherwise the United States would endorse the immediate comprehensive approach to the conflict.

14. Foreign ministry sources, confirming Golan, *Hasichot*, pp. 247–48. Sheehan does not to mention the Virgin Islands talks, and moves most of the substance of the negotiating process to the shuttle period itself.

15. Kissinger and Rabin met in Bonn on July 10, 1975 (details from prime minister's office sources). Kissinger enlisted Chancellor Schmidt to persuade Israel to behave "reasonably."

16. This may be explained by Sharon's failure to establish himself in the Likud party (at least) as one of the recognized leaders of the Likud liberal faction, to which he had originally belonged when he entered politics in 1973. His unorthodox manners and hard-line foreign and security policy isolated him in the liberal party higher leadership, which derived its power from middle-class Landsmannschaften of formerly central European Jewish voters, and resented the populist tendency in Sharon's behavior upon entering politics. The general himself resumed his bid for the command of the IDF as Rabin's "general consultant," and hoped to exert influence on the defense establishment from the prime minister's office.

17. Prime minister's office sources.

18. See Kissinger's news conference at Minneapolis, July 15, 1975 (*Department of State Bulletin* 73, no. 1884 [August 4, 1975]: 72); and his September 22 speech before the General Assembly (*Department of State Bulletin* 73, no. 1897 [October 13, 1975]: 548).

19. Foreign ministry sources privately to the press (and the author) in July, 1975; see also *Davar*, July 29, 1975: "Everyone is Suspicious of Everyone Else."

20. To this, another global consideration should be added. By the end of July, 1975, the conference on security and cooperation in Europe was due to be held in Helsinki, Finland. (For the published conference material, see *Department of State Bulletin* 73, no. 1888 [September, 1975].) The conference satisfied Soviet demands in Europe (in exchange for some Western claims concerning human rights and cultural exchange between the two blocks) in the spirit of the concept of limited détente after 1973. Western concessions at Helsinki helped generate a growing criticism of Kissinger on Capitol Hill and an even greater desire to look into his agreements with foreign countries. This must have combined with criticism in Congress of Kissinger's handling of the Turkish-Greek dispute over Cyprus in the winter of 1974–75.

21. This relates first to the Muslim summit meeting at Jidda (Saudi Arabia), in the summer of 1975, which endorsed a Syrian-PLO proposal to exclude Israel from the General Assembly, and also to further Syrian initiatives in this connection, which should have been discussed by the nonaligned nations later in the summer of 1975. Egypt could have (and did) helped to fend off a decision to this effect by its nonaligned allies if a new Sinai agreement could have been reached beforehand. Kissinger promised in public, at the same time, that Washington would resist such a measure, yet the United States could not possibly block a General Assembly majority. It could, using its veto right in the Security Council, prevent Israel's expulsion from the U.N. altogether.

22. Egypt had another obvious trump card at its disposal: in mid-July Cairo threatened not to prolong the UNEF mandate, which was due to expire by the end of July. The threat was aimed more at the Americans, who feared an escalatory process as a result of it, than at the Israelis, who assessed Egypt's readiness for war as relatively low. Cairo moved parts of its forces inside Egypt into the canal zone, and a partial Israeli mobilization countered this move. Obviously Israel abandoned its intelligence assessment doctrine in favor of partial mobilizations in case of Arab troop movements, to avoid surprise attacks.

23. For the published texts of the agreement, annex, and U.S. proposals, statements, and interviews (Rabin, Kissinger, and Sadat), see *Department of State Bulletin* 73, no. 1892 (September 29, 1975): 457–480.

24. U.S., Congress, House, Committee on International Relations, *Middle East Agreements and the Early Warning System in Sinai*, 94th Cong., 1st sess., September 8–25, 1975.

25. U.S., Congress, House, Committee on International Relations, *To Implement the United States Proposal for the Early Warning System in Sinai: Report, Together with Supplemental and Additional Views, to Accompany H. J. Res. 683*, 94th Cong., 1st sess., 1975, H. Rept. 94–532.

26. Senator Case Act of August 22, 1972, set limits upon presidential power to conclude executive agreements with foreign countries without Congressional knowledge, if not Congress' approval (cf. Chapter 1, note 67). Theoretically, a president who was ready to take the risk could conclude secret executive agreements with foreign countries, provided that they remained secret indeed. The Case Act and the growing influence of the Senate and House on presidential freedom of action in foreign affairs might lead to the conclusion that the chief executive lost much of his power in this domain to Congress. For an updated description of executive-Congressional relations, see J. L. Sundquist, "Congress and the President: Enemies or Partners," in *Setting National Priorities: The Next Ten Years*, ed. H. Owen and Ch. L. Schulze (Washington, D.C.: The Brookings Institution, 1976).

27. U.S. Congress, Senate, Commitee on Foreign Relations, *Early Warning System in Sinai: Hearing on S. Memoranda of Agreements between the Governments of Israel and the United States*, 94th Cong., 1st sess., October 6–7, 1975, pp. 1–253, especially p. 209.

28. This relates mainly to the Nixon-Thieu understanding before the 1972 Paris agreements, which became known to the American public in the winter of 1975. Kis-

singer told Israeli newspaper editors in a closed meeting on August 24, 1975, that Nixon intended to fulfill his promises and send the big bombers against North Vietnam in the event of a new attack by the South, as it happened in the winter of 1975. Yet Congress tied his hands, in the meantime, with specific Vietnam legislation. No wonder that the Israelis (and Congress) may have been interested in and open and formal Sinai agreement. This may explain Representative Hamilton's move to attach the leaked *New York Times* documents to the House report on the technicians.

29. See, for example, *New York Times,* October 22, 1975.
30. Prof. Yuval Neeman, Mr. Peres's adviser, hints in a *Ha'aretz* article (see Chapter 1, note 66) at such demands, later refused by the United States, as one of the reasons for his resignation from the defense ministry.
31. Embassy sources in Washington. Even before the Sinai agreement, the CIA leaked assessments pointing to Israel's conventional and nuclear advantage. See, for example, *New York Times,* July 31, 1975; see also R. J. Pranger and D. R. Tahtinen, *Nuclear Threat in the Middle East,* Foreign Affairs Study no. 23 (Washington: The American Enterprise Institute for Public Policy Research, 1975). Following these reports, and his traditional convictions, and considering possible diplomatic benefits, Mr. Allon proposed, on September 30, 1975, in a speech to the General Assembly (*Jerusalem Post,* October 1, 1975), consultations with all states concerned to create a Nuclear Weapons Free Zone (NWFZ) in the Middle East. In January, 1976 (*Ma'ariv,* January 28, 1976), while discussing the government's anxiety over Arab nuclear programs, Allon reiterated Israel's readiness "to open direct negotiations" on a NWFZ even before a general peace agreement was at hand. Allon's proposals seem to have been based on two considerations: first, a directly negotiated NWFZ had obvious political advantages to Israel and was safer (because of safeguard and inspection clauses negotiated between the parties) than the more general NPT; second, an Arab refusal to negotiate directly with Israel might help relieve the pressure on Israel with regard to the nuclear issue, following the above-mentioned U.S. reports.
32. On the Saudi sales since late 1974, see *Near East Report* 19, no. 3 (January 15, 1975): p. 9; and the legislative calendar of the House of Representatives, No. 6, January 17, 1976, committee on International Relations, September 23, October 21, and December 17, 1975. See also "Department Discusses U.S.-Saudi Arabia Defense Relationship," statement by Assistant Secretary Atherton, *Department of State Bulletin* 74, no. 1917 (March 22, 1976): pp. 377–81. Israel knew, as Mr. Sisco testified before the House committee, that there was no "absolute guarantee" to prevent the transfer of American-made Saudi weapons to Arab "confrontation states," such as Egypt and Jordan. Moreover, in the spring of 1975, the administration started negotiations with Amman on a ground-to-air missile deal. Jordan would, thus, become more protected against Israeli air raids, and might risk open hostilities, which it had not done in October, 1973. The Saudis were expected to finance the deal. On U.S.-Egyptian arms deals and their possible ramifications, see A. H. Cahn and Y. Evron, "The Politics of Arms Transfers: U.S. Arms Sales to Egypt" (paper, Program for Science and International Affairs, Harvard University, 1976).
33. "How Israel got the Bomb," *Time* (April 12, 1976), pp. 39–40; see above, note 31.
34. U.S. State Department sources.
35. Foreign ministry sources, confirming D. Margalit, "New Relations with the United States," *Ha'aretz,* May 10, 1976.
36. Dayan, in a press conference in Paris on March 19, 1976, and in a lecture in Tel Aviv on March 29, 1976. See S. Aronson, "Nuclearization of the Middle East: A Dovish View," *Jerusalem Quarterly* 2 (Winter, 1977): 25–44. For a detailed discussion of the official government stance on the nuclear issue and public reactions to Dayan's suggestions, see note 66.
37. See Chapter 3, note 67.
38. This relates mainly to some Jewish leaders and community activities, and less to

the organized Zionist and pro-Israel rank and file. See, for example, "U.S. Jews are ready to cash Israeli checks, but demand consultations before signing," Rabbi Arthur Herzberg, president of The American Jewish Congress in a *Ma'ariv* interview on July 2, 1976; cf. Daniel Elazar's conclusion in *The Yom Kippur War: Israel and the Jewish People* (New York: Arno Press, 1974), p. 31, that the chief consequence of the war has been "the increasing centralization of power and authority," particularly in the hands of the fund-raising local Jewish federations.

39. See Resolution A/Res/3379, adopted by the assembly on November 10, 1975, by a roll call vote of 72 to 35, with 32 abstentions. The Assembly resolution preceded a similar text, adopted at the conference of Ministers for Foreign Affairs of the nonaligned countries in Lima, Peru, August 25–30, 1975. The United States denounced the Zionism is Racism equation (see *Department of State Bulletin* 73, no. 1901 [December 1, 1975]: 788–94).

40. For Egypt's U.N. efforts on behalf of the PLO, see below, note 49. For Sadat's visit, see *Department of State Bulletin* 73, no. 1900 (November 24, 1975): 721–36, esp. p. 730 (Sadat's address to the Congress on November 5, 1975). During this visit the United States and Egypt initialed a statement on cooperation in peaceful uses of atomic energy.

41. The U.N. Assembly adopted, on November 10, 1975, by a roll call vote of 101 to 8, with 25 abstentions, resolution A/Res/3375, calling for the invitation of the PLO to participate "in all efforts, deliberations, and conferences on the Middle East that are held under the auspices of the United Nations," and requesting the Secretary General to "secure the invitation" of the PLO to the Geneva Conference, although the U.N. role at Geneva was restricted to a cooperation with the two chairman—the U.S.S.R. and the United States. On the same date, the Assembly passed with the same margin of votes, resolution A/Res/3376, establishing a "committee on the Exercise of Inalienable Rights of the Palestinian People." The U.S. representative at the U.N., Daniel P. Moynihan, opposed both resolutions (see *Department of State Bulletin* 73, no. 1901 [December 1, 1975]: 795–96).

42. This refers to the statement made by Harold H. Saunders, Deputy Assistant Secretary of State for Near Eastern Affairs, before the Special Subcommittee on Investigations of the House Committee on International Relations, on November 12, 1975. See partial transcript in *Department of State Bulletin* 73, no. 1901 (December 1, 1975): 797–800. Cf. Kissinger's statement before the Senate Foreign Relations Committee on October 7, 1975, quoted by Saunders, "We are prepared with *all* the parties toward a solution of *all* the issues yet remaining—including the issue of the Palestinians;" see Saunders's own remarks, "In many ways, the Palestinian dimension of the Arab-Israeli conflict is the heart of that conflict." This was Sadat's formulation in his senate address and before, whereas the Israeli official stance since 1949 has been that Arab hostility (i.e., inter-Arab ideology and politics), specifically the Arab *states'* opposition to Israel, was the reason for the conflict. Saunders thus seemed to have accepted a basic Arab argument, which might legitimize not only the PLO but also its initial claims for a separate Palestinian entity in the West Bank and Gaza.

43. In addition to this, the United States became the most important food supplier to Egypt between 1974 and 1976. See U. S. Department of Agriculture press release of October 28, 1975, on long-term credit arrangements for wheat supplies to Egypt: see also Ch. W. Holster, "The Contribution of the U.S. to Egyptian Development," *Middle East Journal* 30, no. 4 (Autumn, 1976): 539–44.

44. Israeli intelligence estimates, January, 1976. See also R. E. Mallakh and M. Kadhim, "Arab Institutionalized Aid: An Evaluation," *Middle East Journal* 30, no. 1 (1976): 471–85 and its sources.

45. Egypt renounced the treaty in mid-March, 1976. According to R. G. Weinland, "Egypt and Support for the Soviet Mediterranean Squadron, 1967–1976" (Paper, The Brookings Institution, 1977), the Soviets did not only lose a major maintenance base for their surface fleet, but also a support base for their submarines. The Soviet squadron's ability to maintain a combatant deployment in the Mediterranean with-

out escalating the number of the ships required to retain that deployment and the support given to them without Alexandria considerably declined.

46. According to Israeli Defense Ministry sources, the Khurds appealed for American political support mainly for Washington's intervention on their behalf in Teheran. Kissinger is reported to have refused to exercise American influence on the shah, hoping at the same time to demonstrate to the Iraqis that their problems might be solved by American, not Russian, moves in coordination with the American-Iranian ally. If so, this American tactic may have helped widen the gap between Syria and Baghdad. Syria, with Russian aid, diverted the Euphrates waters for domestic use, thus causing damage to Iraqi interests, because the river was flowing to Iraq through Syrian territory. The two Ba'athist regimes in Syria and Iraq were traditionally hostile to each other and the Euphrates question added to their mutual hostility. See M. Ma'oz, "Syria under Hafiz-al Assad: New Domestic and Foreign Policies," The Leonard Davies Institute for International Relations (Paper, Hebrew University, Jerusalem, 1975).

47. Israeli intelligence sources. Besides a possible French-Iraqi cooperation, Iraq and Italy signed, on January 19, 1976, an agreement on the peaceful use of atomic energy. See also "Israeli General Sees Iraq near Nuclear Capacity," Washington Post, July 30, 1977. Accordingly, General Gur, the IDF chief of staff, said that Iraq might be able to develop a nuclear capacity within five to seven years with France's help.

48. This may be connected to a larger flexibility, and greater pragmatism by the Syrian Ba'ath regime under President Assad, who realized that Syria (and Libya) remained the only exclusive Soviet partner in the Arab coalition, as Egypt and Saudi Arabia, even Iraq, and later the Sudan (in cooperation with Egypt against Libya), moved away from Soviet influence and yet were able to extract for themselves several national benefits. A greater flexibility, if not an outright change of orientations, was now needed, from the Syrian standpoint. And Assad was able to convince the party or force it, when his personal grip on power consolidated after the Yom Kippur War, to accept pragmatic cooperation with the pro-Western Jordan without renouncing Soviet aid. Syria always retained its national stance toward the Soviet Union, and refused to sign a treaty of cooperation that Sadat first accepted and then renounced. See M. H. Kerr, "Hafiz Assad and the Changing Patterns of Syrian Politics," International Journal 28, no. 4 (1975): 689–706. See also D. Dishon, "The Web of Inter-Arab Relations, 1973–1976," Jerusalem Quarterly, no. 2 (Winter, 1977), pp. 45–59.

49. On December 4, 1975, the Security Council was convened to discuss an Egyptian-Lebanese request for a meeting to discuss "Israeli aggression against the Palestinian Refugee Camps in Lebanon" and the participation of the PLO in the debate. This move preceded an Israeli aerial attack on PLO bases in Lebanon, in the framework of the constant small war between the Palestinian organizations based in Lebanon and Israel after 1969. The council adopted a procedural proposal for the participation of the PLO in the debate. Under article 27 of the U.N. charter, decisions of the council on procedural matters shall be made by an affirmative member of nine members. Sweden provided the ninth vote. After the debate, in which a PLO representative participated and which obviously turned out to be a general discussion on the Palestinian problem, the United States vetoed the draft resolution, as it failed to mention the reasons for Israel's aerial attack and condemned Israel alone, threatening sanctions against it.

The Egyptian move followed Security Council resolution S/Res/381 1975 of December 1 to extend the UNDOF mandate through May, 1976, and to reconvene on January 12, 1976, to continue the debate on the Middle East problem, including the Palestinian question. On Syrian insistence, the president of the Council (Yakov Malik of the USSR) read a statement after the vote to the effect that when the Council reconvened on January 12, the PLO would be invited to participate in the debate. The United States could not veto this arrangement, which was endorsed by the majority of the council, and probably preferred it over a possible cancellation of the U.N. mandate by Syria. Since then, the PLO has been represented in the Middle East Security Council debates, along with Israel, which once boycotted the discussion but later resumed participation. On January 26, 1976, the United States vetoed a draft resolution to include the PLO into the framework of the Geneva Conference. See *Department of State Bulletin* 74, no. 1912 (February 16, 1976): 189–97.

50. See I. Rabinovich, "The Lebanese Crisis: An Interim Assessment of its Significance and Prospects," The Shiloah Center for Middle Eastern and African Studies (Tel Aviv: Tel Aviv University, 1976); see also D. Robinson Divine, "The Meaning of War: Lebanon, 1975–1976" (Paper, Smith College, 1976).

51. Assad first sent one reinforced division, and later another. Following Iraqi threats along his eastern border, he sent another division to the Iraqi border, and was left with minimal forces on the Golan (Israeli intelligence sources). The Lebanese civil war and a possible Syrian intervention brought about a smooth renewal of the UNDOF mandate in May, 1976, through the Security Council, without any attempt on Damascus' part to try and enhance the PLO's position, or its own, in exchange for the renewed mandate.

52. Embassy sources in Washington.

53. See M. Y. Muslib, "Moderates and Rejectionists within the Palestinian Liberation Organization," *Middle East Journal* 30, no. 2 (Spring, 1976): 127–40; see also W. B. Quandt, F. Jabber, and A. M. Lesch, *The Politics of Palestinian Nationalism* (Berkeley: University of California Press, 1973).

54. Middle East News Agency dispatch from Cairo, March 20, 1977.

55. State Department sources. This was the official Soviet position after the Geneva Conference that brought about Soviet reservations toward the most radical PLO groupings and the "Rejection Front." See Golan, *Yom Kippur*, pp. 249–50; and A. Yodfat, "The U.S.S.R. and the Palestinian Organizations," *Hamizrah Hehadash* 25, no. 4 (1975): pp. 273–92.

56. See, for example, G. A. Geyer, "Arafat in a State of Optimism: How Long Will It Last?," *Washington Post*, May 28, 1977.

57. "Sadat Sets New Conditions for Peace," *Washington Post*, December 12, 1976; cf. "Sadat Says his Goal is Normalization of Ties with Israel," *New York Times*, April 7, 1977. Normalization, in Sadat's terms, was an agreement on nonbelligerency guaranteed by the superpowers.

58. Assad's interview with French television, May 1976, published in *Middle East Journal* 31, no. 1 (Winter, 1977): 59 (bibliography section.)

59. *Washington Post* from Cairo, December 29, 1976.

60. See, for example, R. Bilski, "Welfare in a State of Siege," *Jerusalem Quarterly*, no. 2 (Winter, 1977), pp. 73–93; and H. Pack, "Israel's Economy and the Role of External Funds" (Paper, Swarthmore College, 1977).

61. See E. Torgovnik, "The Election Campaign: Party Needs and Voter Concerns," in *The Elections in Israel, 1973*, ed. A. Arian (Jerusalem: Jerusalem Academic Press, 1973).

62. See T. Peled and I. Kahneman, "Events and Public Opinion: The Case of the Israeli-Egyptian Interim Agreement" (Paper presented at the International Political Science Association Congress, Edinburgh, 1976); and A. Arian, "Peacemaking and Israeli Politics" (Paper, Tel Aviv University, 1976).

63. On the controversy over Gush Emunim, see Sh. Hareven, "Sociological Model and Reality," N. Rotenstreich, "Religious Conviction and Political Behavior," E. Goldman, "Messianic Interpretation of Current Events;" and J. O'Dea, "The Religious Aspect," *Forum* no. 1, 26 (1977): 27–40.

64. Defense ministry (Military Occupation Coordination) sources.

65. Yadin's meetings with Hebrew University colleagues in May and June, 1976 (I was present), and the DMC party platform, published in *Ha'aretz*, April 17, 1977. See also Y. Marcus, "Israel's Self-Inflicted Wounds," *New York Times Magazine*, April 24, 1977.

66. Rabin expressed himself publicly on the nuclear and conventional deterrence again

in April, 1976, following Dayan's advocacy of a nuclear deterrence (mentioned above, note 36). In a Mapam club meeting in Tel Aviv he reiterated that the official nuclear policy had not changed, and said further, "Conventional power suffices to guarantee Israel's security in the near future. Attempts to rely on mystical weapons are negative" (see transcript in *Ma'ariv*, April 8, 1976). In a NBC interview on April 5, 1975, Rabin said: "while we have the present lines there is no need for a preemptive strike, and as long as we will have the means to defend ourselves, that is to say, to get arms from our own sources and from the U.S." Following Mapam's public criticism of Dayan's nuclear deterrence stance (see M. Bentov, a leading Mapam veteran: "not a nuclear option, but a peace option," *Al Hamishmar*, April 14, 1976), Defense Minister Peres seemed to have joined the official, territorial-conventional stance, rejecting Dayan's arguments that Israel could not support a prolonged conventional arms race. In a *Davar* interview (April 30, 1976) Mr. Peres said that Israel could support, "even though not without difficulty," such a race during the next ten years. He added that the nuclear option "served us well until now," so that Israel should not relieve the Arabs of their doubts about it. Mr. Allon criticized Dayan openly because of his "pessimism" with regard to the conventional race (see "Yigal Allon on the Balance of Terror and the Nuclear Options," *Ha'aretz*, September 9, 1976).

67. Foreign ministry sources; see Y. Harif, "The Controversy between Allon, Rabin, and Galili on the Settlement in Judea and Samaria," *Ma'ariv*, January 1, 1977.

68. See *Ha'aretz*, January 25, 1977.

69. See the following Israeli press reports on Rabin's visit and the Brookings Institution's Middle East program: "Brookings Report was the Blueprint," *Jerusalem Post*, March 15, 1977; "Rabin Forecasts Tough Clash with U.S. over Final Borders," *Jerusalem Post*, March 15, 1977; "Senior Sources in Jerusalem Respond: Carter's Speech at News Conference Means the Revival of Rogers' Plan; A Disappointing End to Rabin's Talks in Washington," *Ha'aretz*, March 10, 1977; M. Golan, "Comparative Exercise: The New Administration Adopted the Brookings Method," *Ha'aretz*, March 18, 1977; M. Golan, "Toward an Imposed Settlement: The Brookings Document . . . Recommends . . . Worsening Pressures by the U.S. . . . ," *Ha'aretz*, March 25, 1977; and D. Margalit, "The Folly and the System," *Ha'aretz Magazine*, April 1, 1977.

On Carter's Middle East remarks during Rabin's visit until the May, 1977, elections, see also note 72.

70. See *Toward Peace in the Middle East* (Washington, D.C.: The Brookings Institution, 1975).

71. The Brookings study group, none of whom were fellows of the institution itself, (except for Henry Owen, the institution's director of foreign policy program and a former chief of planning at the State Department), was composed of 11 professors or higher education professionals, five of them Middle East experts (and especially experts on Arab affairs), one expert on both Arab and Israeli foreign and domestic politics, one expert on U.S. decision making on the conflict after 1948, one Soviet and general international politics expert, and one who almost did not attend. The group also included one official of the Council on Foreign Relations, two Jewish American public and business figures, and two Arab Americans of similar affiliations (ibid., and study group sources).

72. Carter's three main comments on the Middle East were made in Washington on March 9, 1977 (during Rabin's visit), on March 16, 1977, at Clinton, Mass., and in Washington on May 12, 1977. In the March 9 news conference (see *Weekly Compilation of Presidential Documents*, March 14, 1977, p. 328), Carter emphasized, among other things, the notion of mutually recognized borders, while making a distinction between "recognized borders" and "defense lines" that "may or may not conform in the foreseeable future to those legal boundaries." Second, he spoke on an "interim state, maybe of two years, four years, eight years, or more" in which "there would be a mutual demonstration of friendship and an end to the declaration of state of war." Third, Carter spoke of "stabilization of the situation

in the Middle East" in terms of an end to belligerence, a recognition of Israel's right to exist in peace, the opening up of borders with free trade, tourist travel, and cultural exchange between Israel and its neighbors. Fourth, Carter added that "this would involve substantial withdrawal of Israel's present control over territories [and] some minor adjustments to the 1967 borders."

In the Clinton news conference the president repeated his remarks about the border and peace issues and added a third "ultimate requirement for peace." "There has to be a homeland for the Palestinian refugees.... The exact way to solve the Palestinian problem is one that first of all addresses itself right now to the Arab countries and then ... to the Arab countries negotiating with Israel" (*Weekly Compilation of Presidential Documents*, March 21, 1977, p. 358).

In the May 12 news conference (transcript in the *Washington Post*, May 13, 1977) Carter repeated that "there cannot be ... any reasonable hope for a settlement ... without a homeland for the Palestinians. The exact definition of what that homeland might be, the degree of independence of the Palestinian entity, its relationship with Jordan, perhaps Syria and others, the geographical boundaries of it, all have to be worked out between the parties involved." This remark, five days before the elections, clashed directly with Israeli traditional claims that the core of the conflict had nothing to do with the Palestinian refugees, but the refugee question embodied the Arab states' unwillingness to control and absorb them. Carter's general and rather careless use of words like "homeland," whose character might be determined by the PLO in some kind of connection with Jordan and even Syria, seemed to be an American acceptance of Sadat's formula for a Palestinian state, or else a naive handling of complex matters by a president influenced by Brzezinski, who in turn was influenced by Quandt (embassy sources in Washington).

73. Brookings study group sources; cf. *Toward Peace in the Middle East*. See also Brzezinski's "Deceptive Structure of Peace" and *Between Two Ages: America's Role in the Technetronic Era* (New York: Viking Press, 1970); cf. Carter's Notre Dame address on foreign policy (transcript in the *New York Times*, May 23, 1977).

74. The DMC introduced a single transferable vote system, which could be used by every eligible party member to vote for every candidate who offered himself for the Knesset list. See the Democratic Movement for Change newsletter, no. 2, Tel Aviv, March 24, 1977 (English).

75. The Democratic Movement for Change newsletter, no. 3, Tel Aviv (English).

76. On the potential role of the non-Ashkenazi, low-income strata as Likud voters if the Labor party were not able to meet their economic expectations in times of economic crisis (when the impact would be divided unevenly between them and other social groups), and whose standard of living might sink even lower because of an unequal distribution of economic and social power and the states' economic and military needs, see M. Lissak and E. Guttman, eds., *Political Institutions*. See also "The Labor Party: The Curtain Falls," *Ha'aretz Magazine*, June 10, 1977; S. Weiss, "The Turn of the Non-Ashkenazi," *Ha'aretz*, May 25, 1977; and H. Smith, "The Likud: The Younger Generation List, the Alignment, the Seniors List," *Ma'ariv*, April 29, 1977.

77. This relates to several executive decisions by the Carter administration since February, 1977, concerning past promises to Israel or Israeli requests. The administration refused to honor a Ford promise made to Rabin during the election campaign to supply Israel with a modern type of concussion bomb because of its "inhumane" nature (which made these bombs well suited to knock out Arab planes hidden in concrete, heavily reinforced shelters that proved to be highly effective during the October War). The executive branch refused, further, to grant Israel permission to export Kfir jets to Ecuador (as the engine is U.S.-made) and explained this by its policy of supplying no modern weapon systems to parts of Latin America.

78. See the following statistical data, compiled by Dr. Avraham Diskin, Department of Political Science, Hebrew University, Jerusalem, on the differences between the 1973 and the 1977 elections.

	Jerusalem Neighborhoods		Tel Aviv Neighborhoods		Haifa Neighborhoods	
	Higher-Income	Lower-Income	Higher-Income	Lower-Income	Higher-Income	Lower-Income
Alignment	− 13%	− 12%	− 14%	− 11%	− 16%	− 13%
DMC	+ 22	+ 9	+ 21	+ 3	+ 26	+ 2
Likud	− 6	+ 4	− 5	+ 6	− 7	+ 6

In clear-cut Ashkenazi and non-Ashkenazi urban neighborhoods in other cities, the distribution of the votes was as follows:

	Ashkenazi Neighborhoods	Non-Ashkenazi Neighborhoods
Alignment	− 17%	− 16%
DMC	+ 26	+ 3
Likud	− 1	+ 10

79. According to Israeli intelligence sources, Libya has been actively pursuing a policy of recruiting Arab and non-Arab nuclear experts since early 1973. Experts are directly approached by Libyan agents in international conferences.
80. The latest, and seemingly most explicit, statement on writing this note was made by Mr. Asmat Abdel Meguid, Egypt's U.N. ambassador, in his op-ed article, "Egypt's Approach to Peace," in the *New York Times,* July 1, 1977. The information is also based on State Department sources.
81. See, for example, *Al-Ahram,* March 18, 1976. Very little is known about a possible Egyptian military nuclear effort. Two countries could cooperate with Egypt in secret on that matter: India, who had cooperated with Egypt on mutual defense projects in the past, and Pakistan, who was supposed to acquire a French nuclear reactor with military potential in 1977.
82. PLO sources, U.N. observation mission, New York.
83. See above, note 56. The information about PLO internal debates is also derived from conversations in Washington, D.C., in January, 1977, with Dr. Matti Peled, a member of an Israeli minority group that favored a PLO state, and that negotiated with self-styled PLO moderates in Paris in the summer and autumn of 1976.
84. See "The Sadat Formula," *Washington Post,* April 8, 1977.
85. White House and embassy sources in Washington.
86. See "Menahem Begin, on Extremism and Terrorism," excerpts from a dialogue between Mr. Begin and Dr. William Berkowitz, *New York Times,* May 27, 1977. This is also based upon Mr. Begin's *The Revolt* (New York, 1953), and an analysis of Begin's almost weekly contributions to *Ma'ariv* since 1971.
87. Ibid.; see also Begin's ABC interview on May 22, 1977. This is also based on the briefings of Mr. Shumuel Katz (Begin's personal friend and political follower since the mid-1940s) in Washington following the Likud victory in late May and early June, 1977. The Likud did not address itself in final terms to the substance of Israeli-Arab rights when they chose Israeli citizenship. Nor is it clear, yet, upon writing this note, whether the Likud had its own plan for Israeli-Arab citizens, who were granted formal civil rights under Eshkol but did not integrate fully to Israeli society. See J. Landau, *The Arabs in Israel: A Political Study* (London: Oxford University Press, 1969); for further information and a recent case study (the case of Bir'im and Ikrit), see B. Kimmerling, "Sovereignty, Ownership, and 'Presence' in the Jewish Arab Territorial Conflict," *Comparative Political Studies* 10, no. 2 (July, 1977): 155–76.
88. Katz briefings; cf. Y. Harif, "Begin Agreed in Advance to Dayan's Knesset Remarks," *Ma'ariv,* June 24, 1977; see also Harif's "Moshe Dayan: What I am Doing is Good for the Jews," *Ma'ariv,* May 27, 1977. The Sinai and Golan withdrawals were already common to Begin and Dayan in the early days of the grand coalition under Mr. Eshkol.

89. This is called, in Dayan's jargon, "the functional approach" to the West Bank question; see Harif, "Moshe Dayan."
90. Katz briefings.
91. See above, note 36, with regard to Dayan's nuclear stance. The above-mentioned strategic political considerations with regard to the instability of the Arab world, future relations with the United States, and the willingness to accept a showdown with the U.S. administration (if it could not be averted without sacrificing vital Israeli interests) and to fight over American public opinion are common to Dayan (since 1957) and a number of leading Herut members. Most outspoken on these issues is the highly influential Knesset member, Professor Moshe Arens, who has been, since the last elections, chairman of the Knesset committee on foreign affairs and defense.
92. This view was publicly underlined by several Likud experts such as Prof. Yosef Rom (Ma'ariv, July 22, 1976) and Mr. Arens (Ma'ariv, April 8, 1977). Both Arens and Rom are engineers, an interesting case of technician expertise with aspirations in strategic political matters, relatively new in Israel.

Selected Bibliography

PRIMARY SOURCES: DOCUMENTS

State of Israel Government Yearbooks (1950–76). Jerusalem: Government Printing Office.

Israel Ministry of Foreign Affairs. "Israel's Foreign Relations, Basic Documents." Edited by Meron Medzini. Mimeographed. Jerusalem, 1972.

Divrei Ha'Knesset [Official record of the Knesset] (1950–76). Jerusalem: Government Printing Office.

Bank of Israel Annual Report (1950–76). Jerusalem: Government Printing Office.

"Jewish Agency Budget" (1967–69). Mimeographed. Jerusalem: Jewish Agency Publications.

Doch Va'adat Agranat [The Agranat Commission report]. Tel Aviv: Hoza'at Am Oved, 1974.

The Shiloah Center for Middle Eastern and African Studies. *Middle East Record, 1967.* Jerusalem: Israel Universities Press, 1971.

Arab Report and Record (ARR). London: Arab Report and Record.

Sadat, Anwar. Speeches (May 16, 1977). Cairo: The Middle East News Agency. (U.S. Department of State translation also available.)

Sadat, Anwar. Speeches (Hebrew translations of the Egyptian president's major public speeches). On file at The Shiloah Center for Middle Eastern and African Studies, Tel Aviv University.

U.S. Congress. House of Representatives. *Executive Documents* (1973–76).

U.S. Department of State. *Department of State Bulletin* (1967-77). Washington, D.C.: Government Printing Office.

U.S. Department of State. *United States Foreign Policy: Middle-East, Basic Documents, 1950–1973.* Washington, D.C.: Government Printing Office.

U.S. Department of State. *Foreign Relations of the United States, 1948.* Vol. 5, pt. 2, Washington, D.C.: Government Printing Office, 1976.

Weekly Compilation of Presidential Documents (1973–77). Washington, D.C.: Government Printing Office.

Moore, John Norton, ed. *The Arab-Israeli Conflict.* Princeton: Princeton University Press, 1974. Vol. 3, "Documents."

Stebbins, Richard P., ed. *Documents on American Foreign Relations.* New York:

Simon and Schuster for The Council on Foreign Relations, 1963.

PRIMARY SOURCES: MEMORABILIA AND OTHER WRITTEN SOURCES
Memorabilia and Books by Principal Actors and Official or Public Records and Reports

Allon, Yigal. *Masach shel Chol* [A curtain of sand]. 1959. Reprint. Tel. Aviv: Hoza'at Ha'Kibbutz Ha'Meuchad, 1968.

Arad, Yitzhak. *Elef Yamim* [A thousand days]. Tel Aviv: Hoza'at Ma'arachot, 1971.

Begin, Menachem. *The Revolt*. Los Angeles: Nash Publications, 1972.

Ben-Gurion, David. *Anachnu ve'Shcheneinu* [Our Neighbors and we]. Tel Aviv. Hoza'at Davar, 1934.

————. *Ben-Gurion Looks Back: In Talks with Moshe Perlman*. New York: Simon and Schuster, 1970.

————. *David Ben-Gurion: In His Own Words*. Edited by A. Ducovny. New York: Fleet Press, 1968.

————. *Israel, A. Personal History*. Translated by N. Meyers and U. Nystar. New York: Funk and Wagnalls, 1971.

————. *Israel, Years of Challenge*. New York: Holt, Rinehart and Winston, 1963.

————. *Iyunim Ba'Tanach* [Bible studies]. Tel Aviv: Hoza'at Am Oved, 1969. Available in English as *Ben-Gurion Looks at the Bible*. Translated by J. Kolatch. Middle Village, N.Y.: Jonathan David Publishers, 1972.

————, ed. *The Jews in Their Land*. Translated by M. Nurock and M. Louvish. London: Aldus Books, 1966.

————. *Letters to Paula*. Translated by A. Hodes. Valentine Mitchell, 1971.

————. *My Talks with Arab Leaders*. Edited by M. Louvish. Translated by A. Rubinstein and M. Louvish. New York: Third Press, 1973.

————. *Netzach Yisrael* [Israel's eternity]. Tel Aviv: Hoza'at Mapai, 1964.

————. *Rebirth and Destiny of Israel*. Edited and translated by M. Nurock. New York: Philosophical Library, 1954.

————. *Recollections*. Edited by T. R. Barnsten. London: MacDonald, 1970.

Brzezinski, Zbigniev. *Between Two Ages: America's Role in the Technetronic Era*. New York: Viking Press, 1970.

————. "The Deceptive Structure of a Peace." *Foreign Policy*, no. 14 (Spring, 1974), pp. 35–36.

Clifford, Clark M. "Factors Influencing President Truman's Decision to Support Partition and Recognize the State of Israel." Paper presented at the annual conference of the American Historical Association, Washington, D.C., December 23, 1976.

Cohen, Yeruham. *Tochnit Allon* [The Allon plan]. Tel Aviv: Hoza'at Ha'Kibbutz Ha'Meuchad, 1973.

Dayan, Moshe. *Avnei Derech* [Milestones]. Yediot Aharonot edition. Jerusalem: Hoza'at Edanim; Tel Aviv: Hoza'at Dvir, 1976. Available in English as *Story of My Life*. London: Weidenfeld and Nicolson, 1976.

————. "Israel's Border and Security Problem." *Foreign Affairs* 33, no. 3 (January, 1955): 110–18.

————. *Mapa Hadasha, Yechasim Acherim* [A new map, different relations: a collection of Dayan's speeches and writings, 1967–69]. Haifa: Hoza'at Shikmona, 1969.

Golan, Matti. *Ha'Sichot Ha'Sodiot shel Henry Kissinger* [Kissinger's secret conversations]. Jerusalem: Hoza'at Schocken, 1976. Available in English as *The Secret Conversations of Henry Kissinger: Step by Step Diplomacy in the Middle East*. New York: Quadrangle/New York Times Book Co., 1976.

Heikal, Mohammed. *The Road to Ramadan*. London: William Collins Sons and Co., 1975.

Kissinger, Henry A. *American Foreign Policy: Three Essays*. New York: Norton, 1969.

————. *A World Restored*. Boston: Houghton Mifflin Co., 1957.

Margalit, Dan. *Sheder min Ha'Bayit Ha'Lavan* [White House dispatch]. Tel Aviv: Hoza'at Otpaz, 1971.

Meir, Golda. *Hayay* [My life]. Tel Aviv: Hoza'at Ma'ariv, 1975. Available in English as *My Life*. London: Weidenfeld and Nicolson, 1975.

Peres, Shimon. *Kela David* [David's sling]. Jerusalem: Weidenfeld and Nicolson, 1970. Available in English as *David's Sling*. London: Weidenfeld and Nicolson, 1970.

Sadat, Anwar. Memoirs, serialized in the Kuwait newspaper, *As-Siyassah*, in Arabic, between October 31, 1976, and June 16, 1977. (Official U.S. English translation, mimeographed, Washington, D.C., 1976–77.)

Schulte, H. H., Jr., ed. *Facts on File* (1970–74). New York: Facts on File, Inc.

Sheehan, Edward R. F. "Step by Step in the Middle East." *Foreign Policy* (Spring, 1976), pp. 3–70. Available as *The Arabs, Israelis, and Kissinger: A Secret History of American Diplomacy in the Middle East*. New York: Readers Digest Press, 1976.

Weizman, Ezer. *Lecha Shamaim, Lecha Aretz* [The sky belongs to thee and so does the earth]. Tel Aviv: Hoza'at Ma'ariv, 1975. Available in English as *On Eagles' Wings: The Personal Story of the Leading Commander of the Israeli Air Force, Ezer Weizman*. New York: Macmillan Co., 1977.

"Toward Peace in the Middle East." Report of a study group at the Brookings Institution, Washington, D.C., 1975.

Current History: The Monthly Magazine of World Affairs. Philadelphia.

GIST. Washington, D.C.: U.S. Department of State, Bureau of Public Affairs.

World Marxist Review. Moscow.

Shisha Yamim [Six days] Tel Aviv: Hoza'at Ma'arachot, 1968.

Toldot Milchemet Ha'Komeniyut [History of the War of Independence]. Tel Aviv: Hoza'at Ma'arachot, 1959.

Biographies

Avneri, Arie. *Sapir*. Givatayim: Hoza'at Peleg, 1976.

Bar-Zohar, Michael. *Ben-Gurion*. Tel Aviv: Hoza'at Am Oved, 1977.

Teveth, Shabtai. *The Cursed Blessing: The Story of the Occupation of the West Bank*. London: Weidenfeld and Nicolson, 1970.

————. *Kin'at David: Ben-Gurion Hatzair* [David's desire: young Ben-Gurion]. Jerusalem: Hoza'at Schocken, 1977.

————. *Moshe Dayan: Biographia* [A biography of Moshe Dayan]. Jerusalem:

Hoza'at Schocken, 1971. Available in English as *Moshe Dayan*. Translated by Leah Zinder and David Zinder. Boston: Houghton Mifflin Co., 1973.

Israeli, Zionist, and Arab Newspapers and Periodicals Used as Primary Sources

Al-Ahram. Arabic, daily newspaper, Cairo.
Al-Hamishmar. Hebrew, daily newspaper, Tel Aviv.
As-Siyassah. Arabic, daily newspaper, Kuwait.
Bamahaneh. Hebrew, Israeli Defense Forces weekly, Tel Aviv.
Bamahaneh-Nahal. Hebrew, official Israeli Defense Forces monthly magazine, Tel Aviv.
Davar. Hebrew, daily newspaper, Tel Aviv.
Davar Hashavua. Hebrew, weekly magazine, Tel Aviv.
Ha'aretz. Hebrew, daily newspaper, Tel Aviv.
Ha'Doar. English, Zionist weekly, New York.
Ha'Olam Ha'Zeh. Hebrew, weekly magazine, Tel Aviv.
Heil Ha'Avir. Hebrew, Israel Air Force magazine, Tel Aviv.
Jerusalem Post. English, daily newspaper, Jerusalem.
Ma'arachot. Hebrew, Israeli Defense Forces quarterly, Tel Aviv.
Ma'ariv. Hebrew, daily newspaper, Tel Aviv.
Molad. Hebrew, quarterly, Tel Aviv.
New Outlook. English, quarterly, Tel Aviv.
Shdemot. Hebrew, The Kibbutz Movement quarterly, Tel Aviv.

OTHER HEBREW SOURCES

(Papers by) Hamerkaz le'limudim Arviyim ve'Afro-Assiyaniyim, Giva'at Ha-viva [Center for Arab and Afro-Asian Studies, affiliated with the Mapam party].
(Papers by the) Leonard Davies Institute for International Relations. Hebrew University, Jerusalem.
(Papers by the) Levi Eshkol Institute for Economic, Social, and Political Re-search. Hebrew University, Jerusalem.
Forum: A Quarterly on the Jewish People, Zionism, and Israel. Jerusalem: World Zionist Organization, Organization and Information Department.
Porath, Y., ed. *Hamizrah Hehadash* [New east]. Israel Oriental Society. Hebrew University, Jerusalem.
Jerusalem Quarterly. Jerusalem: The Middle East Institute.
Medina, Mimshal ve'Yechasim bein Leumiyim [State, government, and inter-national relations] (1971–76). Jerusalem: Hebrew university, Department of Political Science and Department of International Relations. First published by the Political Science Department only, as *Medina u'Mimshal* [State and government].

Index

Abdulla, King of Jordan, 3–5, 8
Adan, A., 176
Adenauer, K., 40
Agranat, S., 209
—Agranat Commission, 234–36, 408 n. 80
Allon, Y.: and Allon Plan, 79–80, 87, 103, 251, 392 n. 115, 395 n. 10; and Ben-Gurion, 8–9, 377 n. 9; on cease-fire of 1970, 126–27; "conventional" territorial defense concepts of, 53, 96, 193, 321, 392 n. 115; and Dayan, 49, 53, 69, 73, 99; on deep penetration bombing of Egypt, 117; and Eshkol's government, 46, 48; as foreign minister, 249, 321, 329; on Jordan, 79, 87, 103, 251; nuclear policies of, 45, 52–53, 329, 431 n. 31, 435 n. 66; peace concepts of, 377 n. 9, 379 n. 18; on preemption, 53, 377 n. 9; on Sinai straits question, 57, 67, 268, 399 n. 50
—Allon Plan, 53, 79, 87, 103, 107, 251, 329, 392 n. 115
Aloni, S., 236, 250
Amit, M., 74
Anderson, R., 12
Arafat, Y.: as Fath leader, 396 n. 20; as PLO chairman, 119, 246, 317–19, 320, 396 n. 20
Aran, Z., 31–32, 45
Aref, A. S., 60
Arens, M., 310, 438 n. 92
Assad, H.: agreement of, with Saudi Arabia, 317–18; alliance of, with Jordan, 314; attitude of, toward Israel, 318; characterization of, 166; and Lebanon, 315–17, 342, 434 n. 51; negotiates with Iraq, 314–16; and PLO, 315–18, 342, 359–60; relations of, with Egypt, 166, 210, 313, 317–18, 342, 363; role of, in Golan negotiations, 239–43; strategy of, in October War, 178–79, 185, 314; and

United States, 337; and U.S.S.R., 433 n. 48

Bar-Lev, H., 95, 174
Bar-Zohar, M., 41
Begin, M.: attitude of, toward Sadat's peace initiative, 363–65; background of, 21, 104; and Ben-Gurion, 23, 69; characterization of, 21–22, 104–5, 337; Dayan as ally of, 75, 79, 122, 339; as Gahal leader, 105–6, 127, 399 n. 50; and grand coalition, 75, 80, 103, 127–28; as Herut leader, 104, 419 n. 31; as Irgun leader, 21–22, 105; "legal-ideological" behavior of, 79, 84, 104–5, 127–28, 137, 325, 334, 344, 350, 351, 363, 396 n. 16, 437 n. 86; as Likud leader, 336, 365, 419 n. 30; non-Ashkenazi support for, 105, 337, 436–37 nn. 76–78; as prime minister, 320–21, 338–39, 344–46; and Six-Day War, 75, 79
Ben-Aharon, Y., 103–4
Ben-Barka, M., 52
Ben-Gurion, D.: and Achdut Ha'Avoda, 24, 26, 30, 39, 45–46; on Arab behavior in conflict, 6, 13, 41, 44, 76; armistice agreements of, 9; and armistice lines (ADL), 14; background of, 20, 378 n. 10; and ballot law, 24, 27, 30; and Begin, 23; and bid for autonomy, 7, 19, 80, 356, 380 n. 23; and Britain, 6, 12, 16, 23; and *casus belli,* 17, 26; in controversy with Sharett, 380 n. 23; and Dayan, 13, 15, 17, 18–19, 32, 56, 64, 74, 77, 80–81, 96; and defensive strategy, 10, 18, 42, 52, 54, 77, 84; on deterrence, 10, 41, 380 n. 23; and domestic priorities, 6, 10–11, 77, 137–38, 356; and Egypt, 6, 7, 12–19, 28–29, 64, 69; and France, 12, 15, 41–42, 52, 68; and Gaza

443

The Johns Hopkins University Press

This book was composed in Caledonia linotype with Bodoni Modern display type by Keith Press, Inc., from a design by Alan Carter. It was printed on 50-lb. Publishers Eggshell Wove and bound in a pyroxylin-impregnated cloth by The Maple Press Company.

Library of Congress Cataloging in Publication Data

Aronson, Shlomo, 1936–
    Conflict and Bargaining in the Middle East.
    Includes bibliographical references.
    1. Jewish-Arab relations—1949–
2. Israel—Foreign relations.   I. Title.
DS119.7.A684   327.5694'017'4927   77–10967
ISBN   0–8018–2046–4